Government Spending Percent of Nominal, GDP

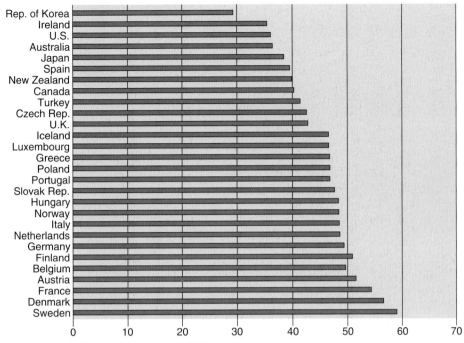

Rep. of Korea
Ireland
U.S.
Australia
Japan
Spain
New Zealand
Canada
Turkey
Czech Rep.
U.K.
Iceland
Luxembourg
Greece
Poland
Portugal
Slovak Rep.
Hungary
Norway
Italy
Netherlands
Germany
Finland
Belgium
Austria
France
Denmark
Sweden

(axis: 0 10 20 30 40 50 60 70)

Source: World Bank, World Development Indicators (2003).

Highest Inflation (%)
Annual Average, 1990–2003

Congo, Dem. Rep.	2478.7
Georgia	1655.8
Armenia	837.8
Nicaragua	788.3
Angola	770.8
Turkmenistan	748.5
Ukraine	615.7
Brazil	613.2
Peru	569.6
Belarus	489.5
Kazakhstan	445.0
Tajikistan	415.6
Azerbaijan	345.1
Uzbekistan	283.2
Russia	280.6
Moldova	213.4
Croatia	192.9
Kyrgyz Republic	191.4
Argentina	183.4
Macedonia	178.3

Source: IMF, World Economic Outlook Database (June, 2004).

Stock Markets' Capitalizations ($mn 2003)

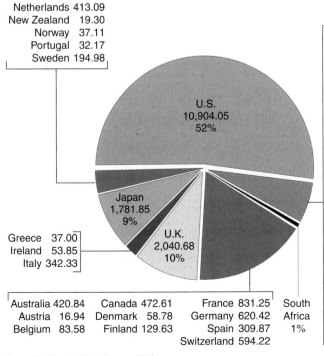

Netherlands 413.09
New Zealand 19.30
Norway 37.11
Portugal 32.17
Sweden 194.98

U.S. 10,904.05 52%

Japan 1,781.85 9%

U.K. 2,040.68 10%

Greece 37.00
Ireland 53.85
Italy 342.33

Australia 420.84	Canada 472.61	France 831.25	South
Austria 16.94	Denmark 58.78	Germany 620.42	Africa
Belgium 83.58	Finland 129.63	Spain 309.87	1%
		Switzerland 594.22	

Emerging Markets 1,284.99 6%

Argentina	2.40
Brazil	90.35
Chile	20.87
China	51.40
Colombia	1.02
Czech Rep	4.02
Egypt	2.78
Hong Kong	236.31
Hungary	9.90
Indonesia	13.78
India	47.42
Israel	30.35
South Korea	207.42
Malaysia	52.04
Morocco	1.30
Mexico	82.60
Pakistan	2.45
Peru	3.23
Philippines	4.30
Poland	10.22
Russia	46.59
Singapore	72.21
Thailand	21.81
Turkey	13.53
Taiwan	256.69

Source: The Financial Times (January, 2004).

Lowest Inflation (%)
Annual Average, 1990–2003

Belize	−1.03
Saudi Arabia	0.55
Japan	0.65
Bahrain	0.68
Oman	0.93
Panama	1.12
Bosnia and Herzegovina	1.2
Brunei Dar	1.56
Singapore	1.56
Dominica	1.86
France	1.91
Switzerland	1.93
Austria	2.03
Belgium	2.07
Germany	2.12
Taiwan	2.14
Finland	2.2
Denmark	2.22
ʰ⸱⸳⸳	2.31
	2.32

MACROECONOMICS
UNDERSTANDING
THE WEALTH
OF NATIONS

SECOND EDITION

MACROECONOMICS

UNDERSTANDING THE WEALTH OF NATIONS

David Miles

Professor of Finance

The Tanaka Business School

Imperial College

London

Andrew Scott

Professor of Economics

London Business School

London

WILEY   John Wiley & Sons, Inc.

PUBLISHER Steve Hardman
ASSOCIATE PUBLISHER Judith R. Joseph
PROJECT EDITOR Cindy Rhoads
SENIOR EDITORIAL ASSISTANT Jessica Bartelt
SENIOR PRODUCTION EDITOR Valerie A. Vargas
MARKETING MANAGER David Woodbury
NEW MEDIA EDITOR Allison Morris
TEXT and COVER DESIGNER Madelyn Lesure
COVER CREDIT Chapter openers and back cover (abacus): © Masataka
                         Yamakita/Photonica
                         Front Cover (bridge): © David Noble/Taxi/Getty Images
PRODUCTION SERVICES mb editorial services

Copyright © 2005   John Wiley & Sons, Ltd, The Atrium, Southern Gate
                     Chichester, West Sussex, PO19 8SQ, England

                     Telephone: (+44) 1243 779777

Email (for orders and customer service enquires): cs-books@wiley.co.uk
Visit our Home Page on www.wileyeurope.com or www.wiley.com

ISBN 0-470-86892-9

Typeset in 9.5/12 pt Times Ten Roman by GGS Book services, Atlantic Highlands, USA.
Printed and bound in Great Britain by Martins the Printers, Berwick-upon-Tweed,
Northumberland.
This book is printed on acid-free paper responsibly manufactured from sustainable forestry
in which at least two trees are planted for each one used for paper production.

10 9 8 7 6 5 4 3 2 1

BRIEF CONTENTS

CONTENTS

We wrote the first edition of this textbook in the firm belief that there was scope for a different approach to teaching students macroeconomics. This approach is one that pays great attention to real-world data and actual events and also reflects a belief that both economic models and current research could be made accessible to introductory students and would help explain how the global economy works.

However convinced we may have been that such an approach was possible, writing the first edition was still something of an experiment. As economists, we never forget that the market is the ultimate arbiter of success. We have therefore been enormously reassured both by the sales and feedback that the first edition received. The global focus of the book was rewarded with a wide geographical distribution of sales; our blending of data, textbook models, and summaries of recent research meant the book has been adopted at the undergraduate level and even for Master's and Ph.D. programs in economics as well as the MBA market for which it was originally designed. The use of contemporary data has also led to the book being adopted for economics courses in various government departments.

Most reassuring of all has been the feedback from students—they seem to have enjoyed reading the book and feel they understand the economy, as well as economics, better as a result. This positive feedback helped motivate us to work on this second edition, and convinced us to preserve the same key ingredients:

- A focus on making the reader a "sophisticated" consumer of economics. We do so by stressing the logic and intuition of economics rather than resorting immediately to technical model building and curve shifting.
- A global outlook using historical and contemporary data from around the world.
- Introducing substantive real-world issues first to motivate students and then introducing concepts and frameworks to explain them. Rather than illustrate models with insert boxes, we integrate the facts and the analysis.
- Utilizing textbook models as well as summaries of recent and advanced research.

But experience and feedback have also led us to make a number of improvements:

- *Increased global focus* We have added more examples from a broader range of countries. We have supplemented the chapter on global trade and the three chapters on global financial markets by adding a completely new chapter on globalization and global institutions.
- *Updated charts and issues* A feature of the textbook commented on by students and instructors alike is the wealth of data from a range of countries. All of this has been extended, where possible, to the end of 2003. We have also added analysis of recent economic developments including the "post-2000" U.S. slowdown, the breakdown of WTO talks, the Argentinean currency crises, and so forth.
- *Pedagogic changes* The book covers a huge range of countries and issues. In order to streamline the presentation and make students aware of the key issues

and concepts, we have added Key Concepts and Key Points to each chapter. We have shortened each chapter and also dropped the separate chapters on the banking sector and real estate, though much of that material reappears elsewhere.

- *IS-LM* The success of the book in undergraduate courses led to a strong demand for the development of a consistent analytical framework that built on each chapter. We have therefore integrated at the end of several chapters a development of the workhorse IS-LM model. However, we have done so in a self-contained way that enables business school students to avoid this material without any loss in understanding or continuity.

TEACHING FROM THIS BOOK

Different business schools and undergraduate colleges tend to teach different types of macroeconomics courses and the comprehensiveness of the book easily enables this. Obviously, instructors can choose whatever sequence of topics they prefer, but below we outline 3 different 10-topic courses that could be taught.

MACROECONOMICS—UNDERSTANDING THE GLOBAL ECONOMY A comprehensive course covering growth, business cycles, exchange rates, stabilization policy, and trade (as taught at the London Business School).

Lecture 1—Data and Definitions, Chapters 1–2
Lecture 2—Capital Accumulation and Endogenous Growth, Chapters 3, 4, and 6
Lecture 3—Technological Progress, Chapter 5
Lecture 4—Labor Markets, Chapter 7
Lecture 5—Trade, Chapters 8–9
Lecture 6—Fiscal Policy, Chapter 10
Lecture 7—Money and Inflation, Chapter 11
Lecture 8—Exchange Rates, Chapters 19–21
Lecture 9—Business Cycles, Chapter 14
Lecture 10—Stabilization Policy, Chapter 16

MACROECONOMICS: BUSINESS CYCLES AND INTERNATIONAL MACROECONOMICS A course focusing on business cycles and the international economy but excluding the supply side issues of growth, labor markets, and trade.

Lecture 1—Data and Definitions, Chapters 1–2
Lecture 2—Fiscal Policy, Chapter 10
Lecture 3—Money and Inflation, Chapter 11
Lecture 4—Consumption and Investment, Chapters 12–13
Lecture 5—Business Cycles, Chapter 14
Lecture 6—Stabilization Policy, Chapter 16
Lecture 7—Monetary Policy, Chapter 15
Lecture 8—Exchange Rates: PPP, Chapter 19
Lecture 9—Exchange Rates: Exchange Rate Regimes and Crises, Chapter 21
Lecture 10—Global Capital Markets, Chapter 20

MACROECONOMICS: GLOBAL BUSINESS AND FINANCIAL MARKETS   A course focusing on the drivers of demand in world markets and the interaction between financial markets and the wider economy (as taught in several MBA programs).

Lecture 1—Data and Definitions, Chapters 1–2
Lecture 2—Trade and Globalization, Chapters 8–9
Lecture 3—Fiscal Policy, Chapter 10
Lecture 4—Money and Inflation, Chapter 11
Lecture 5—Consumption and Investment, Chapters 12–13
Lecture 6—Business Cycles, Chapter 14
Lecture 7—Stabilization Policy, Chapters 15–16
Lecture 8—The Equity Market, Chapter 17
Lecture 9—The Bond Market, Chapter 18
Lecture 10—Exchange Rates and Global Capital Markets, Chapters 19–21

SUPPLEMENTARY MATERIAL

WEB SITE (http://www.wiley.com/college/miles)   A robust Web site provides support to both students and instructors. Students are able to take practice quizzes on-line so as to help assess their understanding of core concepts within the text. All of the instructor's teaching aids are also provided by chapter electronically within a password-protected environment.

INSTRUCTOR'S MANUAL   Provides guidance to instructors on how best to use the textbook, through its chapter summaries, learning objectives, teaching suggestions, additional examples, answers to end-of-chapter exercises, and additional problems and solutions. This on-line resource also includes case studies with discussion questions to drive classroom discussion or to help facilitate homework assignments.

TESTBANK   Offers an extensive set of multiple-choice questions relating to the concepts and topics within the text via the companion Web site. A customizable version is available on the companion Web site.

POWERPOINT PRESENTATIONS   A set of over 1,000 PowerPoint slides is available to instructors within the companion Web site located at www.wiley.com/college/miles. These slides contain all the charts, figures, and tables in the textbook as well as some additional material, such as key topics and concepts within each chapter.

BUSINESS EXTRA SELECT (www.wiley.com/college/bxs)   Business Extra Select enables you to add copyright-cleared articles, cases, and readings from such leading business resources as INSEAD, Ivey, Harvard Business School Cases, *Fortune*, *The Economist*, *The Wall Street Journal*, and more. You can create your own custom CoursePack, combining these resources with content from Wiley's business textbooks, your own content (such as lecture notes), and any other third-party content. Or you can use a ready-made CoursePack for Miles and Scott, *Macroeconomics, Second Edition*.

ACKNOWLEDGEMENTS

When we discovered how much work it was to write the first edition, we consoled ourselves with the fact that producing a second edition would be much quicker. We were wrong—it wasn't. Our task was, however, once more helped enormously by the skill and efforts of John Wiley's U.S. and European offices. We remain enormously indebted to Steve Hardman who originated the project many years ago and has remained supportive ever since. We suspect he has found participating in the subsequent birth of his children a far easier experience as a result of his efforts with this gestation. Steve has also been assisted by the excellent and enthusiastic efforts of Anna Rowe who has been instrumental in generating what we believe are significant improvements to the first edition. Being a global textbook means we have been helped not just by John Wiley, Europe but also John Wiley, U.S. where Leslie Kraham and especially Cindy Rhoads have once more managed the difficult task of politely, but menacingly, pointing out that timetables are not works of fiction. We are also indebted to their lengthy efforts at getting U.S. based faculty to help make this a truly globalized product. If the book succeeds, it will also be in no short measure to the efforts of Sheralee Connors who did fantastic service in editing the text and simplifying its flow. The manuscript was further improved by the copyediting of Martha Beyerlein.

Further debts have been incurred by students and fellow faculty at Imperial College and London Business School. We deeply thank Francis Breedon, Fabio Canova, Antonio Ciccone, Francesco Giavazzi, Wouter den Haan, Jean Imbs, Richard Portes, Morten Ravn, and James Sefton—not just for their suggestions as to how to teach macroeconomics, and in some cases even supplying material, but above all for agreeing to use the textbook in their courses. The final substantive contribution came from our administrative support team—Bernadette Courtney and Roma van Dam. Continual assistance and unvoiced complaints are a wonderful combination for which we are deeply grateful. We have also benefited from extensive comments on successive drafts of both the first and second editions from several instructors who teach macroeconomics. In addition, we've enlisted a Review Board to participate in an in-depth analysis of the second edition by means of an online assessment portal. We can only hope that the time all of these instructors kindly spent away from their own research and teaching in aiding us to improve our book's content is well rewarded by the end product.

REVIEWERS

Krishna Akkina, *Kansas State University*
Samuel Andoh, *Southern Connecticut University*
Ivo Arnold, *Nijenrode University*
Charles Bean, *London School of Economics*
Raford Boddy, *San Diego University*
Phil Bowers, *University of Edinburgh*
Michael W. Brandl, *The University of Texas at Austin*
Thomas Cate, *Northern Kentucky University*
Grabriele Camera, *Purdue University*
Steven Cunningham, *University of Connecticut*
David N. DeJong, *University of Pittsburgh*
Raphael DiTella, *Harvard Business School*
Joseph Eisenhauer, *Canisius College-Buffalo*
Can Erbil, *Brandeis University*
Lynne Evans, *University of Durham*
Jean Fan, *Xavier University, Cincinnati*
Antonio Fatas, *INSEAD*

Adrien Fleiddig, *California State University-Fullerton*
Jim Fralick, *Syracuse University*
Lynn Geiger, *Eastern College*
Satyajit Ghosh, *University of Scranton*
Fred R. Glahe, *University of Colorado*
John Glen, *Cranfield School of Management*
Gregory Hess, *Oberlin College*
Beth Ingram, *University of Iowa*
Owen Irvine, *Michigan State University*
Sherry L. Jarrell, *Wake Forest University, Babcock Graduate School of Management*
Peter Jonsson, *Fayetteville State University*
Judith Jordan, *University of the West of England*
Veronica Z. Kalich, *Baldwin-Wallace College*
Tim D. Kane, *University of Texas-Tyler*
Cem Karayalcin, *Florida International University*
Yoobai Kim, *University of Kentucky*

Ben Knight, *University of Warwick*
Jim Knudsen, *Creighton University*
William E. Laird, *Florida State University*
Stefanie Lenway, *University of Minnesota, Carlson School of Management*
Thomas Lubik, *The Johns Hopkins University*
Chris Martin, *Brunel University*
Kent Matthews, *University of Wales, Cardiff*
Stuart McDougall, *University of Otago*
B. Starr McMullen, *Oregon State University*
Patrick McMurry, *Missouri Western State College*
Mico Mrkaic, *Duke University*
John Nader, *Grand Valley State University*
Akorlie Nyetepe-Coo, *University of Wisconsin-La Crosse*
Nilss Olekalns, *University of Melbourne*
Allen Parkman, *University of New Mexico*
Daniel Pavsek, *Shenandoah University*
Chung Pham, *Professor Emeritus of Economics at University of New Mexico*

Mark Pingle, *University of Nevada*
Stephen Regan, *Cranfield School of Management*
Mary S. Schranz, *University of Wisconsin-Madison*
Carole Scott, *State University of West Georgia*
Harry Singh, *Grand Valley State University*
Case Sprenkle, *University of Illinois-Champaign-Urbana*
Raymond Strangways, *Old Dominion University*
Mark Strazicich, *University of Central Florida*
Oren Sussman, *University of Oxford*
Dominic Swords, *Henley Management College*
Randolph Tan, *Nanyang Technological University*
Peter Taylor, *University of the West of England*
Paul Wachtel, *New York University, Stern School of Business*
William Weirick, *University of Louisiana*
Mike Wickens, *University of York*
Chunchi Wu, *Syracuse University*
Chi-Wa Yuen, *University of Hong Kong*
Eric Zivot, *University of Washington*

REVIEW BOARD

Johnson Samuel Adari, *Texas Tech University*
Francis Ahking, *University of Connecticut-Storrs*
Krishna Akkina, *Kansas State University*
Leon Battista, *City University of New York*
Edward Bierhanzl, *Florida A & M University*
Doug Bunn, *Brigham Young University-Idaho*
James Butkiewicz, *University of Delaware*
Dale DeBoer, *University of Colorado-Colorado Springs*
Erick Elder, *University of Arkansas Little Rock*
Yee-Tien Fu, *Stanford University*
Marvin Gordon, *University of Illinois at Chicago*
Satyajit Ghosh, *University of Scranton*
Brian Jacobsen, *Wisconsin Lutheran College*
Manfred Keil, *Claremont McKenna College*
Jongsung Kim, *Bryant College*
Richard Mark, *Dowling College*
Benjamin Matta, *New Mexico State University*

Ida Mirzaie, *John Carrol University*
Phil Murray, *Webber International University*
John Nader, *Grand Valley State University*
Jamal Nahavandi, *University of New Hampshire*
Luis Rivera, *Dowling College*
Malcolm Robinson, *Thomas More College*
William Seyfried, *Winthrop University*
Mohamad Shaaf, *University of Central Oklahoma*
Tayyeb Shabbir, *University of Pennsylvania*
Dorothy Siden, *Salem State College*
Robert Sonora, *University of Texas Arlington*
Jack Strauss, *Saint Louis University*
Osman Suliman, *Millersville University*
Willem Thorbecke, *George Mason University*
Charles Waldauer, *Widener University*
Chris Weber, *Seattle University*
Ky Yuhn, *Florida Atlantic University*

Finally we thank our families—Faye, Georgia, Oscar, and Harriet and Lorraine, Helena, Louis, and Kit. Perhaps the book would have been written in half the time without them but life would have been less than one-tenth as interesting.

What Is Macroeconomics?

Overview

In this chapter we show you what macroeconomics is about by looking at some of the big questions that macro-economists ask: Why do some countries enjoy a standard of living many times greater than others? How does growth in productivity evolve over time? Why does the economy fluctuate between expansions and contractions? What impact do changes in interest rates or in oil prices have upon the economy? We draw out what is distinctive about macroeconomics and contrast it with microeconomics, and illustrate this distinction by focusing on the types of risk that affect individuals and companies.

Key Concepts

Aggregation	Idiosyncratic Risk	Microeconomics
Economics	Macroeconomics	Technical Progress

1.1 What Is Macroeconomics About?

Most books begin by defining their subject. But definitions are tricky and often are not the best way to introduce a subject. Imagine trying to interest people in tennis by defining what tennis is and how it is played. Far better to let them watch a match or try to play themselves. This approach also applies to macroeconomics. Understanding how the economy works helps us interpret the past; it makes our world more comprehensible; and it helps us to think intelligently about the future. Such skills help us make better decisions. However, we think offering a sophisticated definition of macroeconomics is a poor way to convince you of these things. To demonstrate its relevance, we prefer to illustrate the types of issues macroeconomics deals with.

Consider the economic situation in June 2003. The world's financial markets were anxiously examining every comment that Alan Greenspan, the chairman of the U.S. Federal Reserve Board, uttered in public, unsure of whether interest rates were likely to be cut yet further to fend off the risk of deflation or be increased as the economy

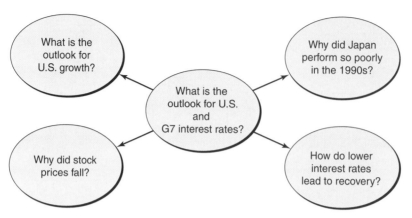

FIGURE 1.1   Macroeconomic questions.

recovered and the threat of inflation reappeared. These issues raise a number of macro-economic questions, some of which are illustrated in Figure 1.1.

These are all questions that macroeconomics tries to answer, and this textbook should give you the intellectual apparatus to participate in the debate. After reading it, you will be able to offer your own informed opinion about whether Greenspan did the right thing in 2003. More important, you will be able to judge whether Greenspan's successors do the right thing in 2013.

But macroeconomics is far more than just an intellectual toolkit for understanding current events. It is also about understanding the long-term forces that drive the economy and shape the business environment. Between 1870 and 2003, for example, the real value of the output of goods and services produced *per person* in the United States increased more than ninefold. Over this same period, the U.S. population increased more than six-fold, and the total amount of goods and services produced in the United States increased by nearly 6000%. Not all countries have grown so swiftly. Over the same period, output per person in the Australian economy increased only slightly more than fourfold. Had Australia grown at the same rate as the United States over this period, it would have produced enough extra output to roughly double the standard of living for *every* man, woman, and child in the country. Politicians out for votes can only dream of that kind of largesse.

Compared to many other countries, Australia's performance was good. In 1913 the output produced per person in Bangladesh was worth roughly $617 and by 2002 this total had risen to only $775.[1] By contrast, over this period the value of the output produced per person in Japan had increased from $1,334 (around three times the Bangladeshi level) to around $19,000 (almost 30 times Bangladeshi output) (see Figure 1.2). These calculations show why a leading macroeconomist and Nobel prizewinner says that, "Once one starts to think [about questions of economic growth] it is hard to think about anything else."[2]

---

[1] These figures are quoted in terms of what are called "constant prices." We shall go into more detail about this in the next chapter, but essentially it means that everything is measured in terms of what a dollar could buy in the United States in 1985. We should also stress that cross-country comparisons of historical data are not among the most reliable aspects of economic measurement.

[2] Lucas, "On the Mechanics of Economic Development," *Journal of Monetary Economics* (1988).

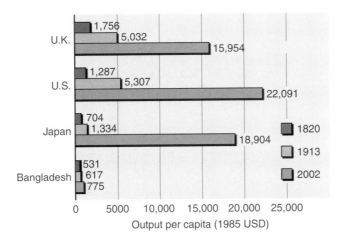

F I G U R E 1 . 2 Output differences over the long term. The average level of output per person differs dramatically across countries. *Source:* International Financial Statistics (2003).

Why have some countries grown so fast while others have stagnated? Can government policy boost a country's growth rate? These questions force us to examine key economic issues—the role in fostering growth of investment in machines and infrastructure, such as roads; the importance of education and skills; and the critical role of technological progress, such as new inventions. These are important issues, both for individual firms and for society. These issues are as relevant to households and businesses as the short-term considerations about what the U.S. Federal Reserve Board will do with interest rates; in fact, they are probably much more important.

Understanding these issues is important because it is crucial to an assessment of which economic actions will bring prosperity and which are more likely to fail. Understanding the mechanisms at work in generating economic outcomes is also intellectually challenging and interesting. Some people come to economics thinking it is all about trying to forecast what might happen in the economy next year. But in fact, understanding the underlying forces at work and the links between different parts of the economy is far more interesting, valuable, and challenging than trying to guess what will happen to house prices or output based on recent trends. And, while forecasting is only a small part of what economics is about, it is also something much better done when one has an understanding of the mechanisms generating economic outcomes.

The above examples (the conduct of monetary policy and the sources of overall economic growth) suggest that macroeconomics is about the economy as a whole. In part this is correct: macroeconomics does focus on how the whole economy evolves over time rather than on any one sector, region, or firm. Yet macroeconomics also considers the important issues from the perspective of the firm and/or the individual consumer. It is the overall, or *aggregate*, implications of tens of thousands of *individual* decisions that companies and households make that generates the macroeconomic outcomes.

Throughout this book we shall consider many such macroeconomic issues from the perspective of firms, governments, and society. We will approach issues by analyzing the aggregate implications of the decisions many firms and consumers make, decisions that are generally interdependent.

1.2   But What about That Definition?

These examples have given you some ideas about the issues macroeconomics addresses, and they may even have aroused your interest in the subject. We hope so, because at this point we need to give you a more detailed insight into macroeconomics and its relationship with its sister discipline, microeconomics. In other words, it is time to turn to definitions.

DEFINITION

Economics is the study of the allocation of scarce resources.

The basic idea is simple: each of us has an almost inexhaustible list of desires, but most of us have a finite amount of money (or, more generally, resources) with which to satisfy these desires. The British economist Adam Smith, whose book *Wealth of Nations* (published in 1776) was arguably the first seminal treatise on economics, famously phrased this discussion in terms of whether a country should produce guns or butter. Today the choice is between more esoteric items—we all might like to buy a new top of the line cell phone *and* regularly eat steak or lobster for lunch, but household finances dictate one or the other (and you had better get used to the crummy sandwich from the snack bar if you go for the new cell phone). Economics studies the best way to allocate the resources that are available across these competing needs. Not all these needs can be satisfied, but economics should be able to help you (and society) meet as many of them as possible.

Market economies allocate resources through prices. Prices tell producers what the demand for a particular product is—if prices are high, then producers know the good is in demand, and they can increase production. If prices are low, producers know that demand for the product is weak, and they should cut back production. Thus the market ensures that society produces more of the goods that people want and less of those that they do not. By studying prices, consumers decide which goods to purchase and which to avoid; by examining prices and chasing profits, producers determine which goods to provide.

But what is *macro*economics? Broadly speaking, economics has two components: **microeconomics** and **macroeconomics**. As shown by the examples in Figure 1.3, microeconomics essentially examines how individual units, whether they be consumers or firms, decide how to allocate resources and whether those decisions are desirable. Macroeconomics studies the economy as a whole; it looks at the *aggregate* outcomes of all the decisions that consumers, firms, and the government make in an economy. Macroeconomics is about aggregate variables such as the overall levels of output, consumption, employment, and prices—and how they move over time and between countries.

In terms of prices, microeconomics focuses on, for instance, the price of a particular firm's product, whereas macroeconomics focuses on the exchange rate (the price of one country's money in terms of that of another country) or the interest rate (the price of spending today rather than tomorrow).

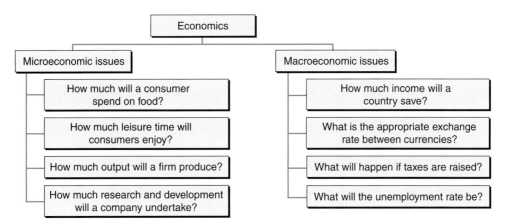

FIGURE 1.3 **Macroeconomic and microeconomic issues.** Macroeconomics focuses on aggregate outcome; microeconomics looks at individual markets, firms, or households.

1.3 The Difference between Macro and Microeconomics

These distinctions show that a gray area exists between micro and macroeconomics that relates to **aggregation**—at what point do the actions of a number of firms cease to be a microeconomic issue and become a macroeconomic issue? To answer that question, let's think of another way of outlining the differences between microeconomics and macroeconomics. In microeconomics the focus is on a small group of agents, say a group of consumers or two firms battling over a particular market. In this case economists pay a great deal of attention to the behavior of the agents the model is focusing on. They make assumptions about what consumers want or how much they have to spend, or about whether the two firms are competing over prices or market share, and whether one firm is playing an aggressive strategy, and so on. The result is a detailed analysis of the way particular firms or consumers should behave in a given situation.

However, this microeconomic analysis does *not* explain what is happening in the wider economic environment. Think about consumers' choice of what goods to consume. In addition to consumers' own income and the price of the goods they wish to purchase, their decisions depend on an enormous amount of other information. How high is unemployment? Is the government going to increase taxes? Is the exchange rate about to collapse, requiring a sharp increase in interest rates? Or consider our two firms competing over a market. If one firm is highly leveraged (i.e., has a lot of debt), it may not be able to adopt an aggressive price stance if it fears that interest rates are about to rise sharply because then the losses from a price war might bankrupt it. Similarly, if imported materials are important for the firm's production process, then a depreciating currency will lead to higher import costs, reducing profit margins even before the firm engages in a price war. While none of these background influences—shifts in interest rates or movements in the exchange rate—are under the control of the firm or consumer, they still influence their decisions.

The economy, as a whole, represents the outcome of decisions that millions of individual firms and consumers make. While each particular firm does not significantly affect inflation or the growth of output in the whole economy, the economic performance of an economy does reflect the combination of all these millions of decisions. For instance, the U.S. Federal Reserve will be concerned about the overall change in the level of prices in the United States, monitoring the economy for signs of inflation. The inflation rate reflects the number of firms that are increasing prices and the amount by which each firm is raising prices. In other words, all of the individual pricing decisions that millions of firms make determine the macroeconomic environment.

While microeconomics is mainly concerned with studying in detail the decisions of a few agents, taking as given the basic economic backdrop, macroeconomics is about studying how the decisions of all the agents who make up the economy create this backdrop. Consider, for instance, the issue of whether a firm should adopt the latest developments in information technology (IT), which promise to increase labor productivity by, say, 20%. A microeconomic analysis of this topic would focus mainly on the costs the firm faces in adopting this technology and the likely productivity and profit gains that it would create. Macroeconomics would consider this IT innovation in the context of the whole economy. In particular, it would examine how, if *many* firms were to adopt this technology, costs in the whole economy would fall and the demand for skilled labor would rise. Combined with the resulting increase in labor productivity, this would lead to an increase in wages and the firm's payroll costs. It might also shift demand away from unskilled towards skilled workers, causing the composition of unemployment and relative wages to change.

This example reveals the differences between the two approaches. The microeconomic analysis is one where the firm *alone* is contemplating adopting a new technology, and the emphasis is on the firm's pricing and employment decisions, probably holding wages fixed. In other words, the analysis assumes the firm's decisions do not influence the background economic environment. In contrast, the macroeconomic analysis examines the consequences when *many* firms implement the new technology and investigates how this affects economy-wide output, wages, and unemployment. Both forms of analysis have a role to play, and which is more appropriate depends on the issue to be analyzed and the question that needs to be answered.

1.4 Why Should People Be Interested in Studying Macroeconomics?

When one of the authors first agreed to teach at a business school, an eminent microeconomic theorist told him that macroeconomics should not be taught to MBA students. Of course, the theorist argued that microeconomics, with its detailed focus on the behavior of individual firms, should be compulsory for students. But the only macroeconomic issue business people needed to know, he argued, was what the economy would be doing over the next few years. They could best find this out by buying a macroeconomic forecast. Taking a course in macroeconomics was a waste of time.

This is a rather dispiriting argument. If the microeconomist's contention is right, then very few people are likely to find studying macroeconomics worthwhile. Not surprisingly, we think it is wrong, and that there are several benefits for those who study macroeconomics.

UNDERSTANDING ECONOMIC POLICY ISSUES BETTER

The one argument the critical microeconomist would accept for teaching macroeconomics to people who were not going to become professional economists was that it enabled them to sound knowledgeable about current affairs at social events, or to avoid sounding dumb when being interviewed on CNN. We believe the benefits of studying macroeconomics are far more substantial in areas of more importance than keeping up appearances.

Managers at any international company, for example, need to understand the institutional structure of the global economy. Any firm that wants to succeed must understand the behavior of other organizations that affect its market. Viewed in this light, firms are involved in a game in which the prizes are profits. The other players in the game include governments (whether it be a national government or an international organization like the International Monetary Fund or the World Trade Organization) and other firms. Government policy and the structure of government provide the framework of rules within which firms operate.

In Chapter 8 we will discuss free trade and the battle between Airbus of Europe and Boeing of the United States. For each firm, success in the marketplace requires understanding not just the products and strategy of the opposition but also the policy stance of European and American governments as well as the attitude of international organizations like the World Trade Organization. Understanding the interests and behavior of the government and its policies is therefore an important part of corporate strategy, and this requires a good understanding of macroeconomics. Any firm considering investing in Argentina would need to consider the potential for another currency crisis—which is a macroeconomic question.

THE RELATIVE SIGNIFICANCE OF AGGREGATE AND FIRM-SPECIFIC UNCERTAINTY

Understanding macroeconomics is not simply a useful aspect of the public relations role of the business person; nor is it solely related to better understanding government policy. The health of a company or of an individual's job prospects and portfolio depends on the macroeconomy. Macroeconomic events like changes in interest rates, fluctuations in exchange rates, and shifts in the overall level of stock market prices affect individuals and companies. More local events—like a rise in the wages of the company's workforce or the bankruptcy of a competitor—are also important. Both types of factors—the localized and the general—are uncertain. Economists distinguish between two types of uncertainty: aggregate and idiosyncratic. Aggregate uncertainty affects all firms and sectors in the economy; idiosyncratic uncertainty affects only a few individuals, firms, or industries. Macroeconomics is essentially about the aggregate sources of uncertainty that affect firms, workers, and consumers.

But which source of uncertainty is more important for individual health—idiosyncratic or aggregate? Evidence (covering firms and consumers) shows that the biggest source of uncertainty in the short term for most firms is the idiosyncratic component. All firms should worry about loss through illness of key personnel, major clients canceling contracts, litigation, fire and theft, and so forth. For households, or individuals, idiosyncratic risk is also generally more important than systematic (or aggregate) uncertainty. Whether you pass an exam; how well you get along with your first boss; whether you avoid serious illness in your forties and fifties—for most people these things are likely to be more important for their standard of living over their lifetime than fluctuations in aggregate output or in inflation.

Consider the case of unemployment. In recessions unemployment rises, but not everyone becomes unemployed. Most people carry on with their regular job even through the worst recessions. Many people even find new jobs because many firms are hiring. Figure 1.4 shows employment trends in U.S. manufacturing over a volatile 20-year period (1973–1993). It shows that every year U.S. manufacturing had large inflows into work (job creation) and into unemployment (job destruction). For instance, 1975 was a recession year in the United States and around 320,000 manufacturing jobs were lost. However, even during these enormous layoffs, around 110,000 more new jobs were being created. Exactly what happens to unemployment depends on whether the flow of people into work is larger than the flow of people moving out of work. For instance, in 1975 unemployment increased sharply because the job destruction rate was more than twice the job creation rate.

Therefore, the aggregate measure of unemployment, while important, gives an incomplete picture of what is happening to individuals in the labor market. Idiosyncratic factors are significant—even during the worst recession some firms (bankruptcy administrators?) will be doing well and hiring workers; it is just that more firms are doing badly. Business cycle peaks and troughs represent what is happening to most firms, and

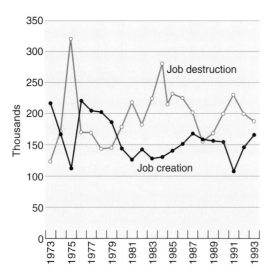

FIGURE 1.4 **Job creation and job destruction in U.S. manufacturing.** In any one year many new jobs are created and many existing jobs are lost. *Source:* John Haltiwanger's homepage, www.bsos.umd.edu/econ/haltiwanger

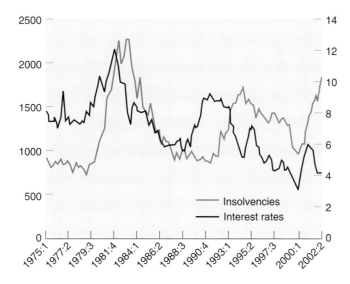

FIGURE 1.5 **Interest rates and bankruptcies in the Netherlands.** Interest rates have a major impact on the number of bankruptcies. *Source:* Statistics Netherlands.

it is much harder for a firm to succeed in a recession when the overall business climate is poor, but because idiosyncratic factors are important, even in the worse recessions, many firms will be thriving.

This does not mean macroeconomics is unimportant to business. For instance, in the early 1980s, and again in the early 1990s, the Netherlands experienced a recession where high interest rates combined with extensive corporate debts led (with a lag of a few years) to many corporate bankruptcies. As Figure 1.5 illustrates, these insolvencies can largely be accounted for by aggregate factors.

Aggregate uncertainty is also important because it generates a type of risk that, by definition, all firms and consumers share. Most people today are unlikely to spend their entire career within one firm, or even in one industry; the only source of uncertainty that is fully portable between jobs in different industries is aggregate uncertainty. Understanding macroeconomic uncertainty will therefore prove useful to all future employees and in all future occupations. We think that the knowledge obtained in this book will be relevant throughout your life.

LONG-RUN FACTORS

The most important reason for studying macroeconomics is its long-run significance. In the previous section, we suggested that only a small part of corporate uncertainty in any one year is due to aggregate or macroeconomic uncertainty. However, the further ahead one looks, the more important aggregate uncertainty becomes. As we stressed earlier, macroeconomics reflects the decisions and actions of all agents in the economy. For instance, if one firm or sector makes a significant technological innovation, then eventually this will spread to the rest of the economy. Thus macroeconomics is about dynamics that eventually change the nature of a firm's markets, its competitors, and the demands the firm places on its own managers and workforce.

Consider, for instance, the case of two U.S. car manufacturers—General Motors (GM) and Ford. Thirty years ago they were among the very largest U.S. companies.

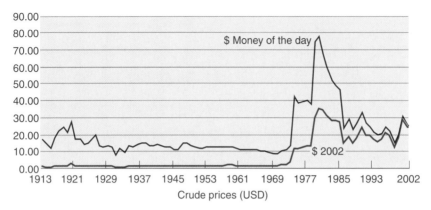

FIGURE 1.6 **Real oil prices 1913–2002.** Oil prices have shown huge volatility over the twentieth century. *Source:* BP Statistical Review of World Energy (June 2003).

During this 30-year period, the managements of GM and Ford have had to cope with many changes in how the economy operates. One of the major technical innovations of the last decade has been the IT revolution. This has led to substantial changes in how cars are manufactured and marketed and also increased the importance of a skilled workforce. The world economy has also become more internationalized, and competition between car producers in different countries has become intense. Oil prices have moved dramatically over the past 30 years as shown in Figure 1.6. This has had an enormous impact on the overall demand for cars and on the *types* of cars that are demanded. Governments across the world have responded to a growing realization of the damaging environmental impact of burning fossil fuel by raising gasoline taxes and requiring stricter emissions controls, affecting the design of cars. These global economic trends have dramatically changed the business environment for car producers.

Coping with technical change and with shifting patterns of demand for new types of cars, ensuring a sufficient number of suitably trained workers, and battling against foreign competitors have been an important part of how GM and Ford have tried to remain profitable. The longer-term factors that GM and Ford have had to cope with (international competition, technological progress, training the workforce, changing governmental regulations and taxes, and responding to shifts in the world price of oil) are all macroeconomic, compared to more short-term issues, such as whether to drop prices, what the appropriate level of output is, and whether the firm should focus on niche sectors of the market.

Economy-wide trends mean that corporate success today cannot guarantee success in the future, no matter how well a firm operates; new technology, new products, and new opportunities all threaten an established firm. As of February 2004, the market capitalization of Ford and General Motors was a little under $30bn each, compared to $286bn for Microsoft and $195bn for Intel—it would have been impossible to have foreseen this 30 years ago. Understanding these long-run forces and responding appropriately to them are crucial for the health of both you and any company you might work for; it is the subject of much of this textbook.

SUMMARY

Economics is the study of the allocation of scarce resources. Macroeconomics studies how the economy as a whole allocates resources, for instance, how the overall level of saving in an economy is determined; how the total level of investment is generated; how the level of unemployment evolves; the pattern of overall imports and exports; what determines the level of training of the workforce. Macroeconomics is therefore essentially about the backdrop of economic activity against which firms, governments, and consumers make their decisions. However, this backdrop of economic activity represents nothing other than the overall effect of the thousands of decisions made by millions of different consumers and firms.

Because macroeconomic factors have a huge impact on financial markets and on the demand for goods and services produced by companies, they are an important determinant of corporate performance. Businesspeople are increasingly expected to contribute to the policy debate, and because the long-run trends in the business world are driven by macroeconomic factors, a crucial part of a business education must be the study of macroeconomics.

CONCEPTUAL QUESTIONS

1. (Section 1.1) What factors do you think explain why the United States is so rich and Bangladesh is so poor? What do you think accounts for the growth that most economies have shown?

2. (1.3) Figure 1.5 shows the pattern of bankruptcies and interest rates in the Netherlands. What do you think might account for this pattern? What can firms do to try to minimize this cyclical risk of bankruptcy?

3. (1.3) Figure 1.6 shows the real price of oil since 1913. What other industries besides automobile manufacturers are affected by fluctuations in oil prices, and how are they affected? What are the effects on individual consumers? How do you suppose that national economies of oil-producing nations are affected by changes in oil prices? What about the economies of countries that use a lot of imported oil?

4. (1.4) Consider the differing impact of microeconomic and macroeconomic factors in the near term prospects of

    (a) a graduating student

    (b) a restaurant in a village

    (c) a restaurant in an airport

    (d) a manufacturer of low-price cars

    (e) a manufacturer of luxury sports cars

ANALYTICAL QUESTIONS

1. (Section 1.1) Consider the data in Figure 1.2. What growth rate will Bangladesh have to show to catch up with the 2002 U.K. and U.S. per capita income level within 10 years? 20 years? 30 years? How would population growth affect your calculations?

2. (1.3) Consider an economy made up of 5 equal sized firms (labeled A to E). Under one scenario the output of each firm alternates between

Firm	A	B	C	D	E
Output	1	2	3	4	5

And

Firm	A	B	C	D	E
Output	5	4	3	2	1

What is the balance between idiosyncratic and aggregate risk in this economy?

How does your answer change if each firm oscillates between

Firm	A	B	C	D	E
Output	3	3	3	3	3

And

Firm	A	B	C	D	E
Output	4	4	4	4	4

The Language of Macroeconomics:

The National Income Accounts

Overview

Macroeconomics has a strong empirical bias that is reflected in a near obsession, at least in the media, with data and statistics. But knowing how to interpret data depends on understanding what the statistics are trying to measure, and this requires a conceptual framework. In this chapter we explain the concepts behind key macroeconomic variables and how measures of them are constructed. Our focus is on explaining the concepts of GDP and the National Income Accounts.

Key Concepts

Chain Weighting

Gross Domestic Product (GDP)

Gross National Income (GNI)

Human Development Index (HDI)

National Acounts—Expenditure, Income, and Output Measures of GDP

Real vs. Nominal Variables

Value Added

2.1 What Do Macroeconomists Measure?

At the foundation of macroeconomics is a concern with human welfare. But human welfare is notoriously hard to calculate, particularly in macroeconomics where the relevant measure is the welfare of society as a whole. Even if we could accurately measure individual welfare, how can we compare levels of happiness across individuals and construct an aggregate measure?

Rather than try and directly measure welfare, macroeconomists take a short cut. They focus on the amount of goods and services—the "output"—produced within an economy. The justification for this is simple—if an economy produces more output, then it can meet more of the demands of society. Using output as a measure of welfare obviously begs many questions. Does output reflect social value? What about cultural and political freedoms and problems of inequality and health? These questions suggest that output will only be an approximation to wider concepts of welfare—an issue we investigate later in this chapter. But producing more output should enable a society to increase its standard of living.

2.2   How Do Macroeconomists Measure Output?

Imagine that a country produces only one good—onions. To measure output in this economy you only have to count the number of bags of onions that are harvested. But what if the country also starts growing garlic? The first, and obvious, response is to count both the number of bags of onions and of garlic. But this raises difficult issues. What if one year there is a harvest of four bags of onions and two of garlic, and the next year there are two bags of onions and four of garlic? Has output increased, decreased, or remained the same? While this example might seem trivial, the question it raises is not. Before World War II there was no clear answer and rather than have a single measure of overall output in the economy, there existed a collection of disparate production numbers concerning pig iron production, railway freight tonnage, and so forth. Today the most commonly used measure of the output of an economy is Gross Domestic Product, or GDP—a concept we examine in detail below.

The main problem in our example is knowing how to add onions and garlic together. In the real economy, the problem is even more complicated—how to add together Big Macs, computers, cars, haircuts, university courses, and so forth. The economist's solution to this problem is a simple one: *multiply each good by its price and then add them all together*. For instance, if onions sell at $1 and garlic at $2, then in Year 0 we have:

Output Year 0

2 garlic @ $2 (= $4) + 4 onions @ $1 (= $4) = Total Output of $8

If prices are unchanged in Year 1 we have:

Output Year 1

4 garlic @ $2 (= $8) + 2 onions @ $1 (= $2) = Total Output of $10

Therefore, we could say that output has increased by $2, or 25%, between Year 0 and Year 1. Because garlic has a higher price it achieves a higher weight so that the doubling of garlic production more than offsets the halving of onion output leading to an increase in aggregate output. While we have formulated this calculation in terms of garlic and onions, output in an economy also includes the services that lawyers, accountants, dentists, and so forth, provide as well as physical goods such as onions. In order for this method to arrive at a measure of output that connects with welfare, it is critical that prices are not simply random numbers but reflect social values. At the heart of economics is the notion of an "invisible hand" which implies that prices reflect the value society places on different goods, so that by multiplying each unit of output by its price, we can measure how society values total output.

REAL VERSUS NOMINAL OUTPUT

Crucial to measuring output is the multiplication of the quantity produced of each good by its market price (excluding any consumer or producer taxes). However, the introduction of prices adds a potential distortion—what happens if prices rise over time? For instance, assume in Year 2 the quantity of goods provided in our onion/garlic economy does not change but that all prices double so that a bag of onions now costs $2 and a bag of garlic $4. Using the same methodology as before, we arrive at the following measure of output:

Output Year 2

4 garlic @ $4 (= $16) + 2 onions @ $2 (= $4) = Total Output of $20

This suggests a problem—even though the amount of onions and garlic harvested has remained the same, our calculation suggests aggregate output has doubled. To overcome this problem we need to distinguish between *real* and *nominal* output or between output in *constant* and *current* prices respectively. The basic problem is that in economics we use money as a measure of value, just as scientists use grams and ounces and meters and miles. However, money does not keep a constant value over time because of inflation—after a period of 10% inflation, a $10 bill buys 10% less.

The calculations of output we have performed so far have been for *nominal output*—that is, we multiply the output of each good by its *current* price in each year. Economists calculate *real output* by using for every year the same *constant prices* as weights. For instance, let us choose prices in Year 0 (onions cost $1 and garlic $2) as our base year. Then we would calculate real output (in Year 0 $) as shown in Table 2.1. Real output increases only because the quantity of goods being produced has increased and not because prices have changed.

Nominal output changes every year because of output changes and because the weights (prices) attached to each output have altered. By using real output, we abstract from the latter and focus purely on changes in output across different industries. Because economists are ultimately interested in welfare, they want to measure the *production* of output and thus prefer to focus on real output or real GDP.

This method of calculating GDP requires selecting a base year. The choice of a base year implies fixing the relative value that society places on onions and garlic, but this may alter over time. In response to this, governments periodically change the base year and the constant prices used in calculating GDP. If relative prices alter significantly, this rebasing leads to substantial revisions in historical GDP growth figures (see Analytical Question 2 for an example). In particular there exists a "substitution" problem. As the price of commodities falls, consumers tend to respond by buying more of them. For instance, the price of personal computers falls by around 20% per annum, and in response purchases rise strongly (see Chapter 5). As a result, the output of goods

TABLE 2.1 Calculating Real GDP

	Onions	Garlic	Output
Year 0	4	2	8
Year 1	2	4	10
Year 2	2	4	10

whose relative price is falling (such as computers) tends to increase faster than average, and commodities whose relative price is rising grow more slowly. However, in using constant prices we do not revise the weight attached to these industries—the old comparatively high price of computers will be used as a weight for the rapidly increasing computer output *even though relative prices have since fallen*. The use of constant prices therefore exaggerates growth after the base year because of this substitution bias. To overcome this, governments are moving away from using constant prices when calculating real GDP and instead using chain weights. Chain weights were first introduced in the United States in 1996 and are being adopted in many countries.

The key to chain weights is that rather than using constant prices, they allow prices to gradually evolve over time. Because the price weights change slowly over time this reduces the substitution problem. To see how chain weights work in practice see Table 2.2, which extends our onion and garlic economy for two more years. Chain weights calculate the growth in GDP between Year 4 and 3 by using BOTH Year 3 prices and Year 4 prices. Using Year 3 prices the growth is 44/31 = 1.419 (e.g 41.9%) and using Year 4 prices it is 54/38 = 1.421. Taking a (geometric) average of these two gives growth of 42%. The growth between Years 3 and 2 is then calculated using Year 3 as base prices and then also using Year 2 prices. The average of these is 19.6%. Notice how this method uses "chain weights"—Year 4 growth uses Year 4 and Year 3 prices, Year 3 real GDP growth uses Year 3 and Year 2 prices, and so forth. In this way, two successive years share some common prices, but prices are allowed to evolve over time. Having worked out growth rates using this method, we then need to choose a base year, say Year 2, and set this as our value of real GDP—in our example, 20. With growth of 19.6% between Year 3 and 4, according to the chain weights, this means output rises to 20 × 1.196 in Year 3 = 23.92 and then growth in Year 4 is 42% so real GDP increases to 33.97. Comparing these results with those obtained using constant price GDP shows how chain weighting reduces GDP growth through reduction of the substitution problem. In 2003 when the U.K. introduced chain weights, the Office of National Statistics estimated that real GDP growth was revised downwards by 0.2% in 2001 through the shift from constant prices to chain weights.

Because changes in nominal GDP reflect *both* increases in output and changes in prices, while changes in real GDP only reflect output changes, we can use the gap between the two to measure prices. In our example the nominal, or current price, level of output in Year 2 is 20. The real value of output (using Year 0 prices) is 10. So a measure of how prices, on average, have moved between Year 0 and Year 2 is determined by how much current price GDP differs from real GDP. We call the resultant index of overall prices the GDP deflator, which is defined as:

Nominal GDP/Real GDP

TABLE 2.2   Calculating Chain Weighted GDP

	Onions—Output	Onions—Prices	Garlic—Output	Garlic—Prices
Year 2	2	2	4	4
Year 3	2	3	5	5
Year 4	3	4	7	6

The percentage change in this price index from year to year is a measure of overall inflation. In our example, the price index rises from 1 to 2 in Year 2—inflation is 100%.

> **KEY POINT**
>
> Real GDP focuses on how production in the economy changes by using constant prices. Nominal GDP changes because of changes in production and changes in prices.

2.3 Output as Value Added

While our simple story of onion and garlic enabled us to focus on the critical role of relative prices in estimating output, it also simplified our story in a misleading way. When economists focus on GDP what they want to measure is *value added*, but multiplying the quantity sold of each commodity by its price measures revenue generated. This is not the same as value added. Consider the case of a table that a retailer sells for $400. If the retailer sells 10 tables, this amounts to $4000 of output. However, before the retailer can sell the table, other steps in the chain must occur. First, the retailer must purchase the tables from a manufacturer for, say, $200 per table. Second, the manufacturer has to purchase wood from a lumberyard at a cost, say, of $100 per table. If we were to count every stage of the production process, then output might seem to be $7000. That is:

$1000 (output from lumberyard = $100 × 10) + $2000 (manufacturing output = $200 × 10) + $4000 (output from retailing = $400 × 10) = $7000

But this would be incorrect—the $4000 gives the value to society of the tables; that is how much consumers are prepared to pay for them. The $7000 figure is misleading because it *double* (actually triple) *counts*. It includes the value of the wood three times—in the wood the lumberyard sells, in the table the manufacturer sells to the retailer, and then again when the retailer sells the table to the consumer. To avoid this we need to *either* ignore all the intermediate steps and the intermediate industries (the lumberyard and the manufacturer) and just focus on final sales *or* calculate the *value added* of each industry and then calculate output as the sum of each industry's value added.

> **DEFINITION**
>
> **Value added** is the difference between the value of the output sold and the cost of purchasing raw materials and intermediate goods needed to produce output.

Thus, in our example, the value added of the lumberyard industry is $1000. Value added in the manufacturing industry is also $1000 (10 tables sold at $2000 *minus* the input cost of wood of $1000). Finally, the value added of the retail outlet is $2000 (10 tables sold at $400 but purchased at $200). Combining all these, we arrive at a measure of output or valued added of $4000—exactly equal to the final sale value of all the tables. Focusing on value added makes it clear that the contribution of each sector depends on the *additional* value it creates. In our example, the retailer adds more value than any other sector (presumably through point of sale information, delivery, warranties, and so forth). However, the key point is that consumers and producers, not economists, decide the relative importance of each sector by the prices they set and are prepared to pay. If prices reflect social value, then this will produce a direct link between measures of output and welfare. Not all commentators, however, agree that such a link exists. For instance, Naomi Klein in her best-selling book *No Logo*, comments on the "absurdity" that a $1 white T-shirt becomes a $100 fashion item when a leading designer name is printed on it. From a value added perspective there is no absurdity—consumers place little value on the physical manufacturing of white T-shirts, hence the $1 price tag. But consumers do place an enormous value added on marketing, advertising, and design.

> **KEY POINT**
>
> GDP measures the value added produced in an economy—the difference between the value of output sold and the cost of intermediate inputs and raw materials.

 ## 2.4   National Income Accounts

THREE MEASURES OF OUTPUT—OUTPUT, INCOME, AND EXPENDITURE

Table 2.3 shows our table example in more detail, and we can see how value added is spread across the different sectors of the economy. This is called the *output* measure of GDP—the sum of the value added created in each sector. Figure 2.1 shows a similar breakdown of value added for the U.S. economy in 2002. The most striking feature of Figure 2.1 is how small a role the traditional sectors of the economy play—agriculture only accounts for 1% of value added output, mining 1%, construction 5%, and manufacturing 14%. In total, the industrial sector produces only 20% of GDP compared with 80% for the service sector, including government, telecoms, transport, finance, and so forth. The reasons for this dominance of the service sector are twofold. Firstly, manufacturing experiences rapid productivity growth compared to services and this tends to push down relative manufacturing prices. Secondly, as income rises people tend to re-

TABLE 2.3   **GDP as Value Added**

Sector	Product	Price	Profits	Salaries
Retailer	10 tables	@$400 each	750	1250
Manufacturer	10 tables	@$200 each	300	700
Lumberyard	Wood	$1000	150	850

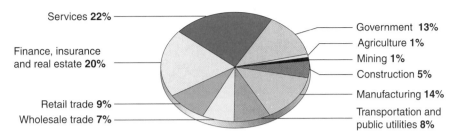

Services **22%**

Finance, insurance and real estate **20%**

Retail trade **9%**

Wholesale trade **7%**

Government **13%**

Agriculture **1%**

Mining **1%**

Construction **5%**

Manufacturing **14%**

Transportation and public utilities **8%**

FIGURE 2.1   **Output measure of U.S. GDP, 2002.** Manufacturing and agriculture account for a small proportion of modern economies. *Source:* Bureau of Economic Analysis.

spond by demanding more services, which again pushes up the relative price of services. Both these factors tend to boost the size of the nonindustrial sector in the economy. Figure 2.2 shows that as a country gets richer first its share of manufacturing and then its share of services increase with agriculture declining. In other words, as countries get wealthier they switch towards more higher value added outputs.

So far we have concentrated on the *output* measure of GDP. But we can show that this is identical to two more concepts—the income and the expenditure measure. To create value added, factors of production—labor and capital (buildings and machines)—have to be used and of course paid. Labor will be paid wages and salaries and overtime. The owners of capital are paid in various ways—rents, dividend payments, interest payments, and through retained profits (if the owners of the capital are also the owners of the firm). Table 2.3 shows that *all* the value added created has to be paid out as income to either labor or capital (the sum of profits + salaries in Table 2.3 equals the output measure of GDP). Using the income of labor and capital to calculate output is called the *income* approach to measuring GDP. We have just shown that

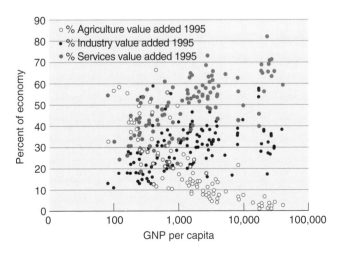

FIGURE 2.2   **Sectoral composition of output and GNP per capita, 1995.** As countries become richer, the share of agriculture declines and at first manufacturing increases and then services increase. *Source:* World Bank.

TABLE 2.4   U.S. National Income 2002
Labor receives the larges proportion of GDP as income.
Figures US$bn (percentages of total in brackets).

Compensation of employees	6,017	[71.5%]
Corporate profits	796	[9.5%]
Rental income	130	[2%]
Proprietors income[1]	771	[9%]
Net interest	698	[8%]
Total national income	8,413.9	[100%]

Source: Bureau of Economic Analysis.

[1]Income from noncorporate business activity, e.g.,
profits of family run businesses.

the *income* and *output* approach both arrive at the same measure of GDP. Table 2.4 shows the income measure of U.S. GDP in 2002 and reveals that 71.5% of GDP was paid out to labor and 28.5% in various forms to owners of capital. Figure 2.3 shows the income share of labor for a wide range of economies, which suggests that this 70–30 split of value added between labor and capital is a useful rule of thumb for most countries.

There is one further way of calculating GDP: the *expenditure* method. Returning to Table 2.3 we can measure output by ignoring all the intermediate stages of production (the lumberyard and the manufacturer) and simply value the expenditure on the final good (the tables sold by the retailer). This is the expenditure measure of output and, if measured properly, this will arrive at the same answer as the income and output measure. In our example only one commodity is produced—tables—and these are bought by the consumer. But in practice, a range of commodities and services are produced and used for different purposes. The expenditure measure of output shows the breakdown across these categories.

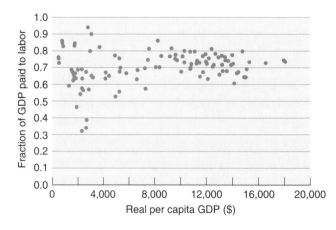

FIGURE 2.3   **Labor income share across countries.** Labor gets paid around 70% of GDP. *Source:* Figure 5—Gollin, "Getting Income Shares Right," *Journal of Political Economy* (April 2002) 110, 2, 458–474.

The goods and services produced within an economy have four basic uses:

- consumption by individuals (C)
- consumption and investment by government (G)
- investment by the private sector (I)
- exports (X)

The government expenditure here is on actual purchases of goods and services (either for consumption or investment) and excludes what are called *transfer payments*, such as pensions and social security payments. Although transfer payments involve the government spending money, they do not involve the government directly purchasing the output produced by the economy and so should be excluded from our analysis here. Government consumption will include a range of activities but a significant component will be the wages and salaries paid to civil servants in return for the services they provide. Government investment will include the building of roads, schools, tanks, and so forth. In Chapter 13 we will focus in detail on investment but note here that investment refers not to placing money in a bank account or stock market fund (these are examples of savings) but instead to firms increasing their capital stock, e.g. buying new machines, building new factories, and so forth.

Demand in the economy arises from these four categories:

Aggregate Demand = Consumption + Investment + Government Expenditure + Exports

or

$$AD = C + I + G + X$$

This demand must either be met from domestically produced output (Y) or from imports (M). Because expenditure on goods must equal sales of goods (demand must equal supply), we therefore have

Output + Imports = Consumption + Investment + Government Expenditure + Exports

or

$$Y + M = C + I + G + X$$

From this equation we arrive at the expenditure measure of output:

Output = Consumption + Investment + Government Expenditure + Net Exports

or

$$Y = C + I + G + (X - M)$$

Crucial to arriving at this expenditure measure of output was the assumption that supply equals demand. To ensure this is the case, it is important to include in investment the *unsold* output that firms produce—their increase in inventories or stock building. This ensures that supply equals demand but makes it necessary to break investment down into *gross fixed capital formation* (the new capital stock installed) and *change in inventories* (unsold output).

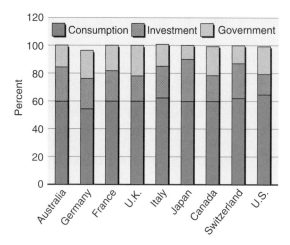

FIGURE 2.4 **Expenditure components as percentage of GDP, 1970–2002.** Investment has been slightly larger than government spending in most developed countries in recent decades, but consumption is far larger than either. *Source:* IMF, *International Financial Statistics* (2003).

Figure 2.4 shows the expenditure breakdown of GDP for a number of countries between 1970 and 2002 (net exports is the missing component that makes everything add to 100%). In all cases consumption accounts for most of the output produced in an economy—ranging from 55% in Germany to 66% in the United States. There is a wider range of variation in investment and government expenditure, and as we shall see in Chapter 4, differences in investment rates are crucial to understanding differences in the standard of living across countries.

KEY POINT

GDP can be measured either as value of output produced, the income earned in the economy by capital and labor, or the expenditure on final products.

GDP OR GNI?

In measuring the output of an economy we need to define what we mean, for instance, by the Italian economy. Is this the output produced by all Italians (both individuals and firms) or the output produced by everyone living in Italy? In other words, how do we deal with the output created by German firms based in Italy or the earnings of Italians living abroad? In broad terms, GDP, or *Gross Domestic Product*, is the measure of output based on Italy as a geographic concept whereas GNI, or *Gross National Income*,[1] focuses on the income of a country by adding and subtracting from GDP various flows of income between countries.

To move from Italian GDP to Italian GNI we need to make several additions to GDP—all the profits Italian firms earn overseas that they *remit* (e.g., send back to Italy); all the wages and salaries earned by Italians overseas that are remitted; any other overseas investment income earned by Italian firms/households that are also remitted; and aid *received* by Italy. Several deductions also need to be made—the profits made in

---

[1] Until recently GNI was often referred to as GNP or Gross National Product. As will become clear, the concept is much more about income than production.

Italy by non-Italian firms that are repatriated; the wages and salaries earned by non-Italians based in Italy that they remit; any investment income earned by foreign investors in Italy that are remitted abroad; and any overseas aid payments made by Italy.

Thus, Italian GDP would include the output produced within Italy by Italians and anyone else, such as Germans or Albanians, who are working in Italy. However, if Albanians send some of the income they earn in Italy back to Albania, then these remittances would *not* be included in Italian GNI (only in Italian GDP) but would be included in Albanian GNI (but not in Albanian GDP). We need to draw a similar distinction for corporate profits. Consider the case of a German bank based in Rome. The value added the bank creates will be paid out in wages to its workforce and profits to its owners. The part of the profits that the bank remits to the head office of the bank in Germany will be included in German but not Italian GNI. However, these profits will be included in the measurement of Italian, not German, GDP.

For some economies the distinction between GDP and GNI is trivial, but for others (see Figure 2.5) the difference can be huge. In Ireland, GDP has been substantially in excess of GNI because so many overseas firms moved there in the 1980s and 1990s. These firms pay wages and make profits that boost both Irish GDP and GNI. But profits repatriated out of Ireland are excluded from Irish GNI. This means that Irish GNI is 23% less than Irish GDP. A similar, but less pronounced, phenomenon occurs in Mexico and Poland where, because of NAFTA and EU enlargement, these countries have received much U.S. and German Foreign Direct Investment (FDI—for example, building of foreign owned factories) causing GDP to grow faster than GNI. In contrast, Japan has many multinational enterprises (MNEs) that operate overseas so that their GNI exceeds GDP. The same holds for Namibia and Bangladesh but the explanation is not remittances received from firms working overseas but from workers' remittances. Each of these countries has a large number of nationals working overseas who remit some of their income—for that reason GNI exceeds GDP in these economies.

Is it best to use GDP or GNI as a measure of the standard of living? The answer is—it depends! By focusing on income, GNI tells us which countries are currently rich. Instead GDP tells us which countries produce the most. In the long run, it is countries

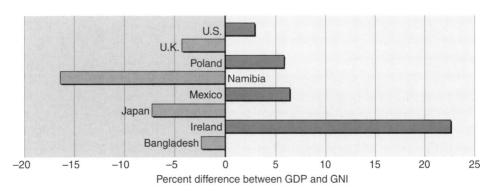

FIGURE 2.5 **GDP compared to GNI, 2002.** Countries that receive high levels of FDI have GDP greater than GNI. Dividend payments and workers' remittances make GNI greater than GDP. *Source:* World Bank.

with high GDP that are wealthiest. If a country has high GNI and low GDP and experiences a shock that wipes out its foreign assets, then GNI will fall to the level of GDP and the country will become poor. However, if a country that has high GDP but higher GNI experiences a similar shock, it will still be rich and because of its high productivity will be able to continue to attact inward investment, produce high output and income, and so be able to rebuild its foreign assets.

KEY POINT

GDP measures the value of output produced in an economy but GNI shows the income earned, taking into account net worker, investor, corporate, and government remittances.

2.5 How Large Are Modern Economies?

Figures 2.6 and 2.7 give some idea about the overall size of modern economies and which are the largest. Figure 2.6 shows a snapshot of the global economy taken in 2002. It reveals that the United States is a little larger than the European Union (EU—the 15 countries prior to EU enlargement) and together they account for 60% of world GDP. The largest EU economy, Germany, had a total GDP of $1990bn (see Figure 2.7), less than a quarter of U.S. GDP of $10380bn. The Japanese economy, the second largest, is around a quarter of the size of the U.S. and EU economies. The economies of the rest of the world added together generate about 30% of world output. Given that the population of China alone is greater than those of the United States, the EU, and Japan combined, world output is clearly unevenly distributed

In making international comparisons it is necessary to convert all measures of GDP into a common currency. For instance, the Japanese economy is measured in yen and the United States economy in dollars. To compare their relative size, we need to convert these measures into common units, say, by multiplying the Japanese GDP statistic by the current dollar–yen exchange rate. This is the method used in Figures 2.6 and 2.7. This can lead to significant variation over time in the estimated size of different economies. For instance, if the U.S. and Japanese economies each grow at 2% in national currency terms but the dollar appreciates by 10%, then the U.S. economy grows 10% more than

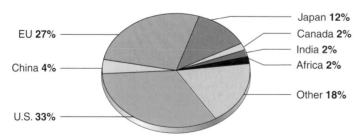

FIGURE 2.6 **World GDP 2002 ($32trn).** World economy is dominated by rich advanced nations. *Source:* IMF, *World Economic Outlook* (2003).

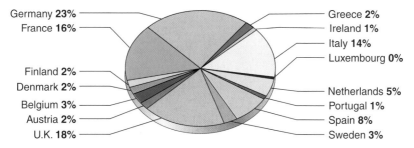

FIGURE 2.7 **EU GDP, 2002.** Germany is the largest European nation. *Source:* IMF, *World Economic Outlook* (April 2003).

the Japanese economy when both are expressed in dollar terms. A further problem with using these market exchange rates to convert different countries' GDP into a common currency is that they make no allowance for the fact that prices differ across countries. A dollar can buy a lot more in India when converted into rupees than it can in the U.S., which should be taken into account when arriving at standard of living measures.

To overcome these problems, we can use purchasing power parity (PPP) rather than market exchange rates when converting GDP into a common currency. A full analysis of PPP is provided in Chapter 19, but for now we simply note that when calculating Indian real GDP using PPP exchange rates it is as if we used the dollar prices charged in the United States as weights in our GDP calculation for India and the United States. If Indian prices are cheaper than U.S. prices at current market exchange rates (i.e., if a U.S. tourist in India finds prices cheap), then using PPP exchange rates will boost the size of the Indian economy relative to the market exchange rate method. By contrast, if a country has high prices, e.g., Japan, using PPP exchange rates reduces the size of the economy. Figure 2.8 shows IMF estimates of world GDP using PPP rates. As we might expect, the relative size of the Japanese economy shrinks substantially, as do the European and U.S. economies. China and India become much larger—using these PPP estimates China becomes the second largest economy in the world.

If we are to use our estimates of GDP as a measure of the standard of living, then we should focus not on GDP but GDP per head of the population or *GDP per capita*. For instance, the Greek economy in 2002 was worth $133bn compared to only $21bn

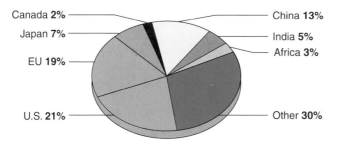

FIGURE 2.8 **World GDP, 2002 ($bn PPP adjusted).** Using PPP exchange rates, China becomes the second largest economy. *Source:* IMF, *World Economic Outlook* (April 2003).

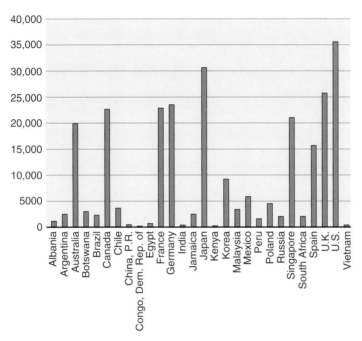

FIGURE 2.9 **GDP per capita, 2002 ($)**. There are large differences in GDP per capita across countries. *Source:* WEO Database (April 2003) www.imf.org

for Luxembourg. However, because the population in Greece is nearly 30 times that in Luxembourg, Luxembourg has a per capita GDP over four times larger than Greece. Figure 2.9 shows estimates of GDP per capita (calculated using market exchange rates) for 28 economies. This measure reveals enormous differences in the standard of living—from about $35,000 in the United States to about $100 in the Democratic Republic of Congo, $475 in India and $960 in China.[2]

KEY POINT

Using market exchange rates, the world economy is dominated by rich advanced nations. Using PPP exchange rates to account for differences in prices reveals a more substantial size for emerging markets.

2.6   Total Output and Total Happiness

There are two interpretations of our measures of output. The most straightforward is that GDP is a measure of the scale of economic activity. But we have also referred to it as a measure of the standard of living. Is this defensible or is GDP simply too narrow a concept? In the words of Bhutan's King Jigme Singye Wangchuk, it may be that *"Gross National Happiness is more important than Gross National Product."*

[2] Using PPP exchange rates would reduce these discrepancies.

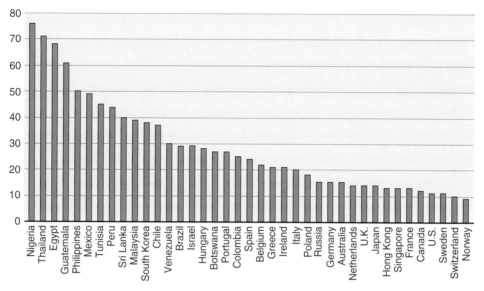

FIGURE 2.10   **Estimates of underground economy (% of GDP).** Some economies are characterized by large underground markets. *Source:* Erste and Schneider (1998) "Increasing shadow economies all over the world?—Fiction or reality?" 12A Discussion Paper 26.

There are two separate issues lurking here. The first is a measurement one—is GDP correctly measured and, if not, does this reduce its ability to approximate the standard of living? The second is a conceptual one—even if it is properly measured, does GDP really capture our concepts of welfare?

Focusing on the first issue—is GDP correctly measured—the answer is undoubtedly "No." One problem is that a large amount of economic activity is not declared to governments—perhaps it is illegal activity, involved with tax evasion or simply not declared to the statisticians. This underground economy is often quite substantial—Figure 2.10 shows estimates of the size of this underground activity relative to GDP. In some cases it amounts to more than 70%, and everywhere it is substantial.

Another problem is that GDP tends to focus on economic activity that takes place in a market transaction (whether official or underground). For instance, at any one time many families in an economy have one adult who earns an income in the marketplace, which the family uses to buy goods and services from the market, and another adult who remains outside the market but nevertheless provides goods and services—child care, cooking meals, household administration. All these activities, whether market- or nonmarket-based, produce output, and if we were to include these nonmarket-based activities, GDP would be substantially larger.[3] The size of this household production is

[3] Consider the case in which you take your parents out to a restaurant for a meal. GDP includes the entire value added of this transaction. If by contrast, you buy the ingredients and cook the meal yourself, then GDP includes only the value added of the ingredients. However, the economic activity is still the same—someone is still cooking the meal. GDP includes a chef getting paid for cooking but not you cooking at home. Of course, if you are a lousy cook then perhaps your value added is zero or negative.

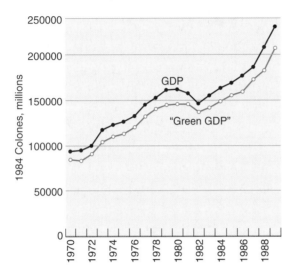

FIGURE 2.11 **Costa Rican GDP and Green GDP.** GDP can be adjusted to allow for environmental damage. *Source:* Hamilton and Lutz, *Green National Accounts*, World Bank Environment Department Papers 39 (July 1996).

substantial. For 2000, the U.K. Office of National Statistics estimates that compared with GDP of £892bn, household production provided services that would have been worth £693bn if purchased through the market with childcare accounting for £220.5bn.

Another measurement problem for GDP is environmental pollution and the destruction of natural resources. When a factory produces chemicals but also puts pollutants into the air, it is producing both a good and a bad. But if only the chemical output is traded in the market place and no one pays for the pollution, then when using prices to measure GDP we will overstate the value of this output—the price should be lower reflecting the "bads" that come with production. This problem is worsened if the government spends money "cleaning up" the environment. In this case, the chemical production and environmental cleanup are included in GDP but the environmental damage is not. Notice that this is a measurement rather than a conceptual issue. If we could measure the value of the pollution created, we could deduct this from our measure of output and arrive at what is sometimes called "Green GDP." Figure 2.11 shows such a calculation for Costa Rica where forest and fish stock depreciation and soil erosion is deducted from standard GDP calculations to arrive at a measure of Green GDP.

OUTPUT AS WELFARE?

The second issue with GDP is whether, even if correctly measured, it reflects welfare. The nineteenth century historian Thomas Carlyle referred to economics as "a dreary, desolate and indeed quite abject and disturbing [subject]; what we might call . . . the dismal science" because in his opinion what is inspiring and motivating in humanity cannot be captured by supply and demand diagrams. Tables 2.5 and 2.6 show measures based on survey questions asking U.S. and European citizens over nearly 20 years about their level of happiness. During this period output has increased substantially in all of these countries, and in most of them the proportion of citizens who are "very happy" or "very satisfied" has also risen (although not for the citizens of Belgium, Ireland, and the United Kingdom). These tables therefore support the view that increases

TABLE 2.5   Happiness in the United States: 1972–1990

	1972	1980	1990
Very happy %	30.3	33.9	33.4
Pretty happy %	53.2	52.7	57.6
Not too happy %	16.5	13.3	9.0
Number in sample	1606	1462	1361

Source: Blanchflower, Oswald, and Warr, "Well being over time in Britain and the USA," London School of Economics mimeo (1999).

in aggregate output lead to higher levels of welfare in general, although the link is clearly not perfect.

For economists, measures of aggregate output are still the dominant indicators of the standard of living, but alternative measures have been suggested. Prominent among these is the United Nations Human Development Index (HDI). This index rests on the notion that the amount of goods a country can potentially consume is not the sole measure of the standard of living. Instead, what matters is whether individuals have the resources (or capabilities) to participate in society and fulfill their potential. Many factors will contribute to an individual's capacities but the HDI focuses on education, health, and income. A sub-index between 0 and 1 (1 being the highest score possible) is recorded for each of these three components, and then an average score is taken as the HDI for that country. For instance, in the 2003 report New Zealand had a score for life expectancy of 0.88, for education 0.99, and GDP 0.88 for an overall HDI of 0.917.

TABLE 2.6   Life Satisfaction in European Countries
Proportion of samples who report themselves as "very satisfied."

Country	Average 1973–81	Average 1982–90	Well-being increased?
Belgium	39.5	24.7	No
Denmark	51.7	62.8	Yes
France	12.4	13.7	Yes
W. Germany	18.8	23.4	Yes
Ireland	38.8	31.1	No
Italy	9.0	13.2	Yes
Luxembourg	34.6	39.1	Yes
Netherlands	41.3	41.8	Yes
U.K.	31.7	30.9	No

Source: Oswald, "Happiness and Economic Performance," *Economic Journal* (1997).

The interesting feature of the HDI is that not only does it blend together information on GDP *and* health and education but that it also assumes that as countries get richer, increases in income per capita become less important. To see this, consider how the subindices for the HDI are calculated. The subindex for life expectancy is given by

HDI Life Expectancy Index = (Life Expectancy − 25)/(85−25)

so that a country with life expectancy of 85 has a score of 1 and another with life expectancy of 55 a score of 0.5. Notice that regardless of the initial level of life expectancy, a ten year increase in life span always increases this subindex by 10/60. The education subindex is calculated as

HDI Education Index = $\frac{2}{3}$ × Adult literacy rate   and $\frac{1}{3}$ × Gross enrollment rate (% of school age children enrolled in education)

Again, a feature of this subindex is that a 10% increase in both literacy and enrollment rates (e.g., a rise of 0.1) will always feed into an increase in the education subindex of 0.1. The calculation of the subindex for income is more complex and is given by

HDI Income Index = [log(GDP per capita PPP$) − log(100)]/[log(40,000) − log(100)]

The use of logarithmns has several implications (see Analytical Question 6). The first is that the impact of extra income on the HDI depends on the initial level of income—as a country gets richer, more income leads to ever smaller increases in the HDI. For instance, a country with $100 of income per head has an income subindex of 0, but a country with income per capita of $1100 has a subindex of 0.40. By contrast, a country with income per head of $39,000 has an HDI income index of 0.995 whereas an extra $1000 would only boost the index by 0.005 to 1. This nonlinear treatment of income in the HDI also leads to different conclusions about changes in prosperity across countries over the last 130 years. For instance, output per head in India in 2002 was around 60% of Belgian per capita GDP in 1870. In other words, contemporary India apparently has a lower average standard of living than nineteenth-century Belgium. However, using the HDI index, India today has roughly the same level of welfare as Belgium in 1870. The major factor in explaining this equality is life expectancy in the two countries. Life expectancy was around 40 years in Belgium in 1870 and is over 50 in contemporary India. In other words, the higher life expectancy in India today offsets the lower GDP per head compared with Belgium in 1870.

The aim of the HDI is to provide a broader view of welfare than just income. Figure 2.12 plots the rank of a country according to its GDP per capita (e.g., 1 means the country has the highest GDP per capita, 2 the second highest, and so forth) against the rank of a country based on the HDI index. As the figure shows, the correlation is very strong—94%. Countries that have high education and high life expectancy also tend to have high GDP per capita. There are, of course, exceptions. Many either current or previously communist economies have very low levels of GDP per capita but good health and education. For instance, Cuba, Ukraine, and Georgia rank 52nd, 75th, and 88th respectively in terms of their HDI, but using GDP per capita their rank is 90th, 98th, and 121st. By contrast, many of the Middle Eastern oil exporting countries have high GDP but low HDI (Qatar, Kuwait, UAE, and Saudi Arabia rank 44th,

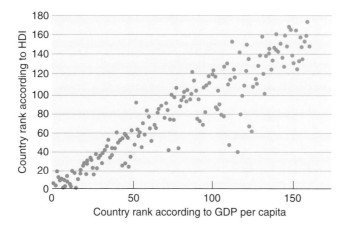

FIGURE 2.12 **Comparing welfare ranking by HDI and GDP.** Countries that perform well at producing GDP also do well in delivering high levels of life expectancy and education. *Source:* United Nations Human Development Index (2003).

46th, 48th, and 73rd in terms of HDI but 25th, 29th, 23rd, and 40th in terms of GDP). Further, some of the more successful African economies are pulled down in their HDI scores due to the AIDS epidemic and poor life expectancy (South Africa, Namibia, and Bostwana rank 111th, 124th, and 125th in terms of HDI but 47th, 65th, and 60th in terms of GDP). However, although there are these patterns of outliers, the overall correlation remains strong—GDP seems a useful approximation for even broader measures of welfare.

KEY POINT

GDP suffers from several measurement and conceptual limitations but seems to correlate reasonably well with broader welfare measures.

SUMMARY

Section 2.1 suggested that central to macroeconomics is the provision of a consistent set of data on key variables. Ultimately economists are interested in welfare, but in practice they focus on output in the belief that increases in output increase a country's welfare.

In Section 2.2 we showed how macroeconomists measure output by summing the output of all the goods and services an economy produces. They distinguish between real and nominal GDP. Nominal GDP captures how both changes in prices and shifts in production affect value. By contrast, movements in real GDP reflect changes due to different levels of output and is the better measure of the health of an economy.

Section 2.3 showed how GDP is a measure of value added—the difference between the value of output sold and the cost of purchased raw materials and intermediate inputs.

Section 2.4 considered the National Accounts and how the output of value added in an economy equals the income earned as well as total expenditure. Gross Domestic Product measures the output produced within an economy and Gross National Income adds and substracts the various income flows that occur between countries. The most common measure of the standard of living in an economy is real GDP *per capita*.

Section 2.5 showed the world economy is dominated by the large industrialized economies, with the U.S., EU, and Japan accounting for 33%, 27%, and 12% of world GDP respectively. However, when we take account of differences in prices across countries using PPP exchange rates, the relative size of these economies falls.

Section 2.6 compared GDP with the United Nations Human Development Index and suggested that, while it was a narrower concept, it did approximate well to broader measures of welfare.

CONCEPTUAL QUESTIONS

1. (Section 2.2) "[An economist] is someone who knows the price of everything and the value of nothing." (Adapted from George Bernard Shaw.) Discuss.

2. (2.3) Coffee beans cost only a few cents when imported. But to buy a coffee at a coffee bar costs far more. What does this tell you about value added?

3. (2.3/2.4) Try to explain to someone who had never thought about measuring the value of economic activity why the output, income, and expenditure ways of measuring national production should give the same answer. It helps to think of a simple economy producing only two or three different things.

4. (2.5) Would you expect that a country where the share of wages and salaries in GDP was falling, and the share of profits and interest was rising, to be one where consumption as a percent of national income was also shifting? Why? Would you expect the distribution of income to become more unequal? Suppose the trends were due to demographic shifts, more specifically to a rapidly aging population. Would this change your answers?

5. (2.5) Do you think it is easier to evaluate the relative welfare of different generations of people in one country (by comparing per capita GDP over time), or to compare the relative standards of living in different countries at a point in time (by converting current per capita GDPs into a common currency)?

6. (2.5) How would you treat the activities of criminals in GDP accounting? What about the activities of the police force?

7. (2.6) The Beatles claimed that "I don't care too much for money, money can't buy me love." (Shortly after first making this claim they joined the ranks of the richest people in the world.) Does their claim undermine the use of GDP to measure welfare?

ANALYTICAL QUESTIONS

1. (Section 2.2) The price of the four sorts of goods produced in an economy in 2000 are:

Good	A	B	C	D
Price	8	9	4	2
Quantity	1000	400	600	1000

The prices of the goods in 2001 are:

Good	A	B	C	D
Price	9	6	8	3

What is the overall rate of inflation between 2000 and 2001? Would it help to know the levels of output of goods in 2001? How might that information be used to construct an alternative measure of inflation?

2. (2.2) Use Table 2.2 to calculate real GDP using constant prices for years 2, 3, and 6. How do your estimates of GDP growth compare with those achieved via chain weighting? What is the direction of the substitution bias?

3. (2.3) Consider an economy with three productive sectors: mining and farming; manufacturing; and retailing. Manufacturers produce goods each year with a sale value of 500. They sell 400 to retailers and 100 direct to the private sector and to government for consumption. Retailers buy goods for 400 from manufacturers and buy 50 from the agricultural sector. Retailers sell goods for consumption for 500. Manufacturers buy goods worth 200 from mining and agricultural firms. Farmers also sell 100 direct to the private sector for consumption. Mining companies sell nothing directly to government or households for consumption.

    What is value added in each sector and what is total output for the economy?

4. (2.4) A country has overseas assets worth 12% of GDP. Overseas assets earn a return of 7%, which is distributed back to the home country. Other countries own assets in the domestic economy worth 8% of GDP and these assets earn a return of 11%. What is the difference between GDP and GNI?

5. (2.4) The national accounts of Australia for 2002 show (in A$bn):

Total consumption	$418 billion
Investment	$158 billion
Government spending	$125 billion
Total exports	$151 billion
Total imports	$156 billion

What is GDP? Suppose consumption increases by 10% but output only rises by 5%. Investment and government spending both increase by 3%. What happens to the gap between exports and imports?

6. (2.6) Use a calculator or, even better, a spreadsheet to plot the relationship between GDP per capita and the HDI index for GDP. What assumptions is this formula making? Do you think these are plausible?

The Wealth of Nations—The Supply Side

Overview

This chapter focuses on why GDP varies so much across countries and over time. It begins by documenting the huge increase in output the world has experienced over the last 100 years and the benefits of this long-run growth—supporting a larger population, greater life expectancy, increasing income per head and reductions in poverty. We then analyse why GDP per capita varies so much across countries, focusing on differences in productivity and labor utilization. We argue that for sustained increases in GDP per capita, improvements in labor productivity are critical. We introduce the production function to explain how output increases over time through increases in the capital stock, labor, and total factor productivity. We examine the magnitude of these factor inputs and how they boost output and offer a numerical framework with which to explain observed GDP growth. We analyze the historical drivers of economic growth and establish stylized facts that we will seek to explain in later chapters.

Key Concepts

Capital Stock	Marginal Product of Capital	Pro-poor Growth
Employment Rate	Participation Rate	Total Factor Productivity (TFP)
Growth Accounting	Production Function	Trend growth
Labor Force	Productivity	

3.1 The Importance of Economic Growth

Figure 3.1 shows GDP per worker across the world since 1870. Two facts stand out: the enormous increase in output over time, even though growth started at different dates and has occurred at different rates; and the significant differences across countries in their level of output. In this chapter we begin to offer a framework within which to understand this long-run growth and cross-country variation. In this section we show how important economic growth is and how substantial the gains are from helping

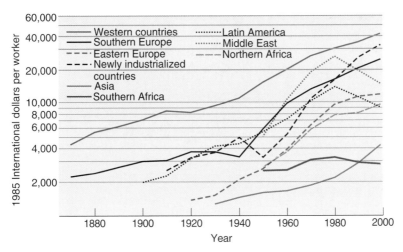

FIGURE 3.1 **Output per worker, 1870–2000.** The twentieth century saw dramatic increases in productivity around the world. *Source:* Baier, Dwyer, and Tamura, *How important are capital and total factor productivity for economic growth?* Clemson University mimeo, 2004.

poorer countries become rich. Our aim is to show that long-run growth is the most important subject in macroeconomics.

Since 1870 the U.S. economy has grown at an annual rate of 1.75% (in per capita terms), and the United States is now one of the richest countries in the world. If instead the U.S. economy had grown at only 1% per annum over this period, then U.S. per capita output would now be roughly the same level as in contemporary Mexico and Hungary and *lower* than in Greece or Portugal. Conversely, if the United States had grown at an annual rate of 2.75% (as Taiwan and Japan did), then current per capita output in the United States would be more than three times its current level. As a leading macroeconomist has written:

> *Is there some action a government of India could take that would lead the Indian economy to grow like Indonesia's or Egypt's? If so, what exactly? If not, what is it about the "nature of India" that makes it so? The consequences for human welfare involved in questions like these are simply staggering: once one starts to think about them, it is hard to think about anything else.*[1]

Table 3.1 shows estimates of the trend rate of growth for a range of economies over time. If we can understand the policy levers that explain these variations in trend growth, then governments have the potential to affect one of the most fundamental variables that influence welfare.

To see how important long-run growth is, consider the following calculations of Nobel Laureate Robert Lucas. Lucas seeks to answer two questions: How much of cur-

---

[1] Lucas "On the Mechanics of Economic Development" *Journal of Monetary Economics*, (1988, vol 22, pp. 3–42). Note that in recent years, India's economy has indeed been growing very fast.

TABLE 3.1   Estimated Trend Rates of Growth in Output per Capita
Industralized nations have seen trend growth slow over time to around 1–2½%.

	1860–1914	1920–39	1951–73	1974–89	1990–98
Belgium	0.90	1.01	3.90	2.09	1.7
Denmark	1.77	1.58	3.46	1.59	2.1
France	0.96	0.78	4.92	1.42	1.2
Germany	1.47	2.91	5.11	1.26	0.9
Italy	1.47	0.21	5.31	2.05	1.3
Sweden	1.52	3.03	3.42	1.62	0.9
U.K.	1.04	1.56	2.24	1.83	1.8
U.S.	1.70	0.86	1.54	1.89	2.2

Source: Crafts and Toniolo, *Economic Growth in Europe Since 1945* (Cambridge: Cambridge University Press, 1996) and Bassanini, Scarpetta, and Visco, "Knowledge, Technology and Economic Growth: Recent Evidence from OECD Countries." National Bank of Belgium Working Paper No. 6, (May 2000).

rent consumption should an economy be prepared to give up to increase its growth rate by a specified amount? How much current consumption should an economy be prepared to give up to remove business cycle fluctuations?[2] Lucas calculates that a permanent increase in trend growth from 2% to 3% is worth 20% of current consumption for the U.S. economy, while raising trend growth from 3% to 6% is worth 42% of current consumption, more than $2.6 *trillion*. By contrast, to remove all business cycle fluctuations, the United States should give up only 0.1% of its current consumption. In other words, economic growth is a hugely important topic.

For the intuition behind this result, consider Figure 3.2, which shows GDP for an imaginary economy growing at an underlying trend rate of 2.5% per year. The business

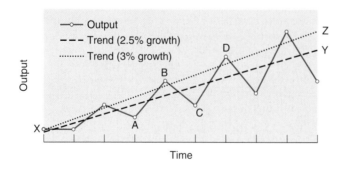

FIGURE 3.2   **Relative importance of trend growth and business cycles.** Trend growth exerts a bigger influence on welfare than business cycle fluctuations.

[2] This is only a thought experiment—Lucas is not saying that spending this money will produce these results.

cycle is defined (see Chapter 14) as fluctuations around a trend, in other words, the movement from A to B and then on to C and D. These business cycles contribute substantially to the volatility in GDP but do not influence trend growth. Therefore we can link the value people place on avoiding business cycles to how much they dislike short-run uncertainty, e.g., not knowing whether next year they will be at C or D. By contrast, how much they should pay to increase the growth rate depends on how they value higher output. If the economy could somehow shift the long-term growth rate from 2.5% to 3%, then instead of ending up at a point like Y, it would be at Z where output is much higher. Removing business cycles is about reducing uncertainty; boosting long-run growth is about giving people more output/income. How important business cycles are depends on how much volatility they produce and how much society dislikes uncertainty. Given the relatively small size of U.S. business cycles (consumption growth varies between −2% and 5%), Lucas concluded that the main benefits flowed from higher growth—issues of growth are much bigger and more important than the volatility of short-term fluctuations. Of course, none of this means that business cycles are unimportant, only that the cost of business cycle uncertainty is relatively small compared to the benefits of higher long-run growth.

KEY POINT

The gains from boosting the long-run rate of growth in an economy are enormous and much larger than the gains from stabilizing business cycles. Even small differences in growth rates have a substantial impact over long periods of time.

What form do these welfare gains of economic growth take?

GROWING POPULATION

A huge increase in world population has been both produced by, and in turn supported, economic growth. Thomas Malthus (1766–1834), an English clergyman, wrote his *Essay on the Principle of Population* in 1798 in which he prophesied that limited natural resources constrained population size.[3] With the stock of natural resources fixed, he reasoned the only way of producing more output was to use more labor. However, with a finite amount of natural resources, there was a limit to the size of the population and thus also a limit to the amount of output the population could produce. But over the last 200 years, the interaction between increases in the capital stock and increasing technological knowledge has meant that Malthusian fears of a limit on world population have not been realized. Since Malthus wrote, world population has risen more than sixfold—see Figure 3.3.

---

[3] The following gives a good taste of Malthus' work:

The power of population is so superior to the power in the earth to produce subsistence for man, that premature death must in some shape or other visit the human race. The vices of mankind are active and able ministers of depopulation. They are the precursors in the great army of destruction; and often finish the dreadful work themselves. But should they fail in this war of extermination, sickly seasons, epidemics, pestilence, and plague advance in terrific array and sweep off their thousands and ten thousands.

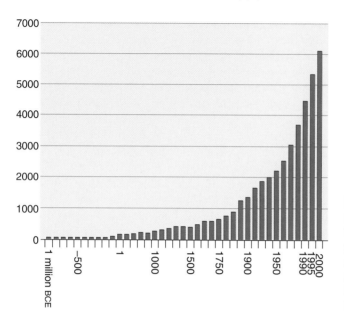

FIGURE 3.3   **World population (in millions) from 1 million BCE.** World population continues to rise sharply. *Source:* Kremer, *Quarterly Journal of Economics* (1993), updated United Nations.

LIFE EXPECTANCY

Table 3.2 shows the proportion of a group of newborn babies in England in 1662, and in the United States in 1993, who could be expected to survive to different ages. In 1662 a newborn baby in England had a 64% chance of surviving to age 6 compared to a 99% chance in modern America. Life expectancy depends on many things, not the least of which are medical knowledge and diet. Higher income helps by enabling better nutrition and financing the production of medicines and medical research.

IMPROVEMENTS IN THE STANDARD OF LIVING

It is not just that there are more people living today, and that people are living for longer, but also that average income per head has increased. Table 3.3 shows how real

TABLE 3.2   **Survival Rates in England, 1662, and the United States, 1993**
Economic growth occurred at the same time as dramatic improvement in life expectancy.

Age	0	6	16	26	36	46	56	66	76
England 1662	100	64	40	25	16	10	6	3	1
U.S. 1993	100	99	99	98	97	95	92	84	70

Source: Peter Bernstein, *Against the Gods* (New York: John Wiley, 1995). © 1995 John Wiley. Reprinted by permission of John Wiley and Sons, Inc.

TABLE 3.3 **Growth in Real GDP per Capita, 1900–2000**

The twentieth century saw huge increases in GDP per capita around the world.

Country	1900 Real GDP per capita	2000 Real GDP per capita	Growth Multiple (2000 GDP/1900 GDP)
Australia	4,299	25,534	5.9
Austria	2,901	23,681	8.2
Belgium	3,652	23,784	6.5
Canada	2,758	26,922	9.8
Denmark	2,902	26,627	9.1
Finland	1,620	23,798	14.7
Italy	1,746	21,794	12.5
Netherlands	3,533	23,664	6.7
New Zealand	4,320	18,824	4.4
Norway	1,762	27,043	15.3
Sweden	2,561	23,661	9.2
Switzerland	3,531	20,830	5.9
Czechoslovakia	1,729	14,844	8.6
Hungary	1,682	10,443	6.2
U.S.S.R.	1,218	8,012	6.6
Chile	1,949	9,919	5.1
Colombia	973	5,380	5.5
Mexico	1,157	8,766	7.6
Peru	817	4,583	5.6
Venezuela	821	6,420	7.8
Bangladesh	581	1,684	2.9
China	652	3,746	5.7
Indonesia	745	3,637	4.9
Pakistan	687	2,006	2.9
Philippines	1,033	3,423	3.3
Taiwan	759	17,056	22.5
Thailand	812	6,856	8.4
Egypt	509	4,184	8.2
Ghana	462	1,349	2.9

Source: Maddison, *Monitoring the World Economy 1820–1992* (OECD Table D-1, 1995) and Heston, Summers, and Aten, *Penn World Table Version 6.1* (Center for International Comparisons at the University of Pennsylvania (CICUP), October 2002).

GDP per capita has increased between 1900 and 2000. The increases in average standard of living are substantial in many cases—Taiwan has seen a more than twenty-twofold increase in income per head and even the worst performer in the table, Ghana, has seen average income nearly triple.

POVERTY REDUCTION

The World Bank measures poverty as the number of people living on less than $1 a day (using PPP exchange rates) and an alternative measure of less than $2 a day. By any standards, these are extremely low levels of income (not enough to provide clean water, sanitation, and adequate food, let alone health and education). Yet according to the World Bank, in 1998 more than 2.8 billion people were living on less than $2 a day and nearly 1.2 billion on less than $1 a day—see Table 3.4. Even worse, the number of people living in poverty has increased over time. Reducing world poverty is a major policy aim, summarized in the United Nation's Millenium Development Goals, which aim to reduce by half the proportion of people living on less than $1 a day. This involves reducing poverty from 29% to 14.5% of world population and reducing the number of poor people from 1.2 billion to 890 million by 2015.

The number of people living in poverty depends on the level of average GDP per capita and the degree of inequality in society. Even countries with high levels of average income will have poverty if they are characterized by extreme inequality. Reducing poverty therefore requires either boosting GDP per capita or reducing inequality by redistributing resources towards the poor. In recent years the emphasis

TABLE 3.4 **World Poverty**
World poverty is substantial and remains a key challenge for development economies.

	Number of People Living on Less than $1 a day (PPP) (millions)		Number of People Living on Less than $2 a day (PPP) (millions)	
	1987	1998	1987	1998
East Asia and Pacific	417.5	278.3	1052.3	892.2
(excl. China)	114.1	65.1	299.9	260.1
Eastern Europe and Central Asia	1.1	24	16.3	92.9
Latin America and Caribbean	63.7	78.2	147.6	182.9
Middle East and North Africa	9.3	5.5	65.1	62.4
South Asia	474.4	522	911	1095.9
Sub-Saharan Africa	217.2	290.9	356.6	474.8
Total	1183.2	1198.9	2549	2801

Source: World Bank, *Poverty Trends and Voices of the Poor,*
www.worldbank.org

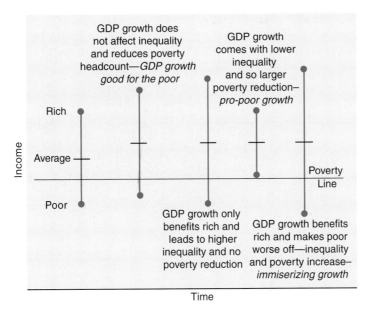

F I G U R E 3 . 4   **Growth and poverty linkages.** GDP growth can theoretically have varied effects on poverty.

in reducing poverty has switched away from redistribution and towards GDP growth. The World Bank and IMF have begun to stress that a central way of reducing poverty is to boost GDP growth and, in particular, they strive to achieve "pro-poor" GDP growth.

Whether GDP growth will automatically reduce poverty depends on its relationship with inequality—Figure 3.4 considers the various alternatives. If the benefits of GDP growth accrue only to the rich, then GDP growth will boost inequality but leave poverty unaffected. It may even be possible that GDP growth in a modern sector of the economy leads to declines in traditional sectors where the poor are mainly based. In this case, GDP growth produces widening inequality and higher levels of poverty— immiserizing growth. Alternatively, if GDP growth does not affect inequality, then everyone enjoys the same proportional increase in income and poverty falls (GDP growth good for the poor). The most efficient way to reduce poverty is through pro-poor growth—this is GDP growth that reduces inequality so that more of the benefits accrue to the poor leading to a faster reduction in headcount poverty.

The relationship between growth and inequality is highly contentious, but a consensus is beginning to emerge. Figure 3.5 shows there is enormous diversity in country experience so that sometimes GDP growth leads to higher inequality but in other cases lower inequality. Amongst this diversity no general relationship between inequality and growth can be discerned. But if GDP growth does not on average affect inequality, then it must be the case that GDP growth reduces poverty (in Figure 3.4 this is shown as

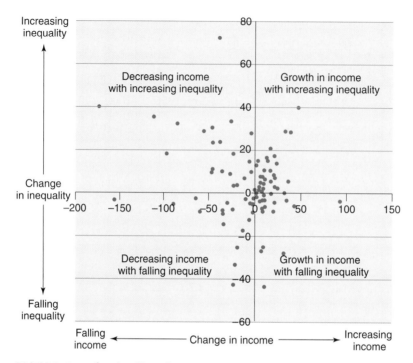

F I G U R E 3 . 5 **Growth and inequality.** There is no systematic relationship between GDP growth and changes in inequality. *Source:* Adams, *Economic Growth, Inequality and Poverty*, World Bank Discussion Paper (2003).

GDP growth good for the poor)—as shown in Figure 3.6. Therefore, because GDP growth does not systematically affect inequality, *on average* it is good for the poor. Whether the focus is on broad geographic regions or small areas, there is a strong negative relationship between GDP growth and poverty. Not all countries benefit equally from this relationship—South Asia has seen fast GDP growth but a disappointing reduction in poverty while the Middle East and North Africa saw very little GDP growth but a sharp fall in poverty. In other words, the Middle East experienced more pro-poor growth. It is a subject of active research as to which policies produce pro-poor growth. Given that much poverty is found in the rural sector and amongst females, policies aimed at these groups can be expected to have pro-poor effects, e.g., land reform improving the incentives and assets of the poor, education policies aimed at females.

KEY POINT

GDP growth on average does not affect inequality and so helps reduce poverty. Pro-poor GDP growth increases average GDP per capita, reduces inequality, and leads to the most rapid reductions in poverty.

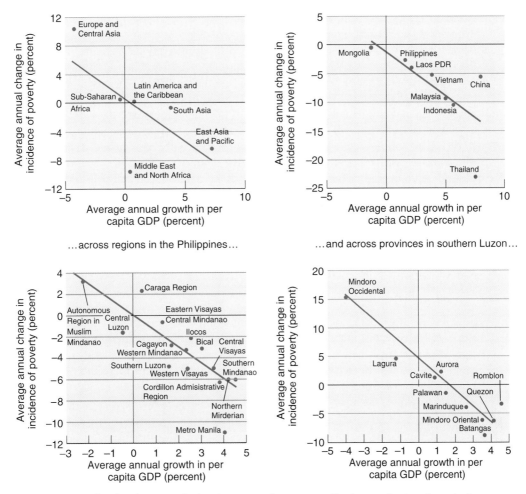

FIGURE 3.6 **Growth and poverty reduction.** GDP growth seems an effective mechanism for reducing poverty. *Source:* World Bank.

3.2 Explaining Cross-Country Income Differences

To understand why some countries produce high levels of GDP per capita compared to others, consider the following identity:

$$\text{GDP/Population} = (\text{GDP/Hours Worked}) \times (\text{Hours Worked/Employment})$$
$$\times (\text{Employment/Labor Force}) \times (\text{Labor Force/Population})$$

This equation enables us to perform a simple decomposition of GDP per capita. The first term on the right-hand side (GDP/Hours Worked) is called hourly productivity—it records how much GDP is produced for every hour worked in an economy. The other three terms on the right-hand side reflect the labor market. The term (Hours worked/Employment) is the average hours worked per person employed. But not everyone in society is employed—some individuals do not want to participate in the labor market, e.g., children, retired individuals, parents staying at home raising children, while others do want to participate but are unable to find a job. These individuals are captured in the last two terms on the right-hand side. The term (Employment/Labor Force) is called the employment rate—it is the proportion of individuals who want a job and who have one. This is equal to one minus the unemployment rate—the proportion of individuals who are willing to work but do not have a job. The final term—(Labor force/Population)—is called the participation rate. It is the percentage of the population who wish to have a job and be part of the labor force. The participation rate will depend on demographic factors (number of school-age children and pensioners, and so forth), cultural factors (attitudes towards childcare, female participation in the labor force) and economic factors (how generous are pensions, how easy it is for firms to hire part time workers, and so forth).

Table 3.5 shows for a sample of OECD (Organisation for Economic Cooperation and Development—see Chapter 9) countries the breakdown of GDP per capita across these four components. The United States has the highest level of GDP per capita—around $33869 per person. However, although the United States has the highest output per head, it does not have the highest hourly productivity. The reason why the United States scores so well on GDP per capita is that average hours worked is high and the United States performs well in achieving low unemployment and a high participation rate. It is interesting to compare France and the United Kingdom—both countries have roughly similar GDP per capita even though French hourly productivity is around a third more than the United Kingdom's. The reason is that U.K. employees work around 14% longer hours on average, experience a lower unemployment rate, and a higher participation rate.

TABLE 3.5 Decomposition of GDP per Capita 2001, US$ PPP

GDP per capita varies across countries due to differences in productivity, hours worked, unemployment, and population structure.

	GDP per Capita ($PPP)	Hourly Productivity ($PPP)	Average Annual Hours Worked	Employment Rate	Participation Rate
U.S.	33869	38.28	1821	0.952	0.51
Japan	25480	27.96	1821	0.949	0.53
Korea	15226	13.66	2447	0.961	0.47
Denmark	28360	37.28	1482	0.957	0.54
France	24230	39.27	1532	0.915	0.44
Germany	25427	36.67	1467	0.920	0.51
Italy	25055	38.29	1606	0.904	0.45
Netherlands	27337	40.08	1346	0.976	0.52
Norway	30691	43.86	1364	0.964	0.53
Sweden	25580	32.65	1603	0.950	0.51
U.K.	24819	30.92	1711	0.949	0.49

Source: Authors' Calculations, OECD and BLS, www.bls.gov/fls/flsgdp/pdf

From Table 3.5 it can be seen that there are two broad sets of policies required to raise GDP per capita. The first are those that focus on boosting hourly productivity; the second are labor market policies aimed at lowering unemployment and raising the participation rate. Although both channels are important, only the first—raising hourly productivity—can produce sustained faster growth. There is a limit to how low unemployment can fall and how many people are prepared to work but no such limits constrain hourly productivity.

KEY POINT

GDP per capita is the product of hourly productivity and the number of hours worked. Hours worked can be affected by labor market policies such as lowering unemployment and raising participation rates, but this cannot occur indefinitely. Boosting hourly productivity is the only means to achieve sustained long-run growth.

3.3 The Production Function and Factor Inputs

The productivity of each hour worked will depend on many things—the capital stock the worker has to interact with, the education and skills of the employee, the level of technology in the firm, the efficiency with which a firm combines capital and labor and incentivizes good working practices, and so forth. This suggests that we can ultimately think of GDP as being produced by three factors: capital, labor, and Total Factor Productivity (or TFP)—a catchall term that reflects any factor which influences the efficiency with which capital and labor are combined to produce output. The relationship between these three inputs and GDP is called the production function and is shown in Figure 3.7.

CAPITAL STOCK

The capital stock of a country is the collection of durable assets that help generate output of goods and services. The capital stock is normally divided into three components: residential buildings, nonresidential buildings, and equipment (e.g., machines). As Table 3.6 shows, physical capital, especially buildings, lasts for years. A firm invests in capital to produce more output in the future, not just today. By contrast, when a firm hires a worker or uses raw materials in the production process, the service provided is instantaneous. Table 3.6 indicates how long equipment and buildings last in five industrialized nations. For instance, in the United States a new machine can be expected to boost

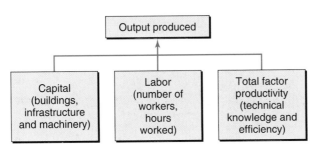

FIGURE 3.7 **The production function.** Output is produced by combining capital, labor, and total factor productivity.

TABLE 3.6   **Average Length of Life of Physical Capital (in Years)**

The capital stock provides economic services over prolonged periods.

	U.S.	U.K.	Germany	France	Japan
Equipment	12	13	15	11	6
Structures	40	66	57	34	42

Source: O'Mahoney, "Measures of Fixed Capital Stocks in the Post-War Period: A Five Country Study," in van Ark and Crafts (eds.), *Quantitative Aspects of Post-War European Economic Growth* (Cambridge University Press, 1996), pp. 165–214.

production for 12 years, while a building provides 40 years of productive services. Because capital is a stock that accumulates over time, it is much larger than the flow of GDP produced within a year. This can be seen in Table 3.7, which shows that the ratio of capital to GDP in OECD countries ranges mostly between 2 and 3.

Our interest is in the ability of the capital stock to boost output, and so we *exclude* residential structures from our measure of the capital stock. We also exclude most of the capital stock of the household sector, which consists of a vast array of consumer durables such as refrigerators, microwaves, and televisions. These commodities should last (hopefully!) for years and provide a flow of services, but these are not recorded in GDP. We therefore define the capital stock as the machines and buildings used in the production of GDP. Figure 3.8 shows that for industrialized nations, buildings account for around 60% of the capital stock.

Figure 3.9 shows that over the same time as GDP increased so strongly there was a substantial increase in the capital stock per worker through sustained investment. Understanding the role of capital accumulation will therefore be a key component of our model of economic growth.

LABOR

We have already examined in some detail the structure of the labor force. As shown in Figure 3.10, for the United States in 2002 the population consists of four categories—the employed and the unemployed (which together make up the labor force) and then

TABLE 3.7   **Capital Stock Divided by GDP, 1992**

The capital stock is large relative to the flow of output (GDP) it produces.

	U.S.	France	Germany	Netherlands	U.K.	Japan
Machinery and Equipment	0.86	0.74	0.70	0.78	0.65	1.07
Nonresidential Structures	1.57	1.52	1.63	1.53	1.17	1.95
Total	2.43	2.26	2.33	2.31	1.82	3.02

Source: Table 2.1 Maddison, *Monitoring the World Economy: 1820–1992* (Paris: OECD, 1995). Copyright OECD.

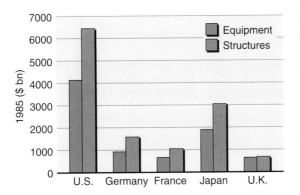

FIGURE 3.8 **Relative importance of structures and equipment in capital stock.** Structures are a larger part of capital stock than equipment. *Source:* O'Mahoney, "Measures of Fixed Capital Stocks in the Post-War Period: A Five Country Study" in van Ark and Crafts (eds.), *Quantiative Aspects of Post-War European Economic Growth* (Cambridge: Cambridge University Press, 1996), pp. 165–214.

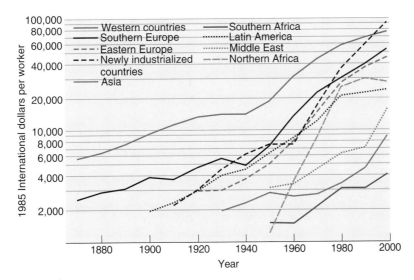

FIGURE 3.9 **Capital stock per worker, 1870–2000.** Increases in capital through investment is a key factor behind GDP growth. *Source:* Baier, Dwyer, and Tamura, *How important are capital and total factor productivity for economic growth?* Clemson University mimeo, 2004.

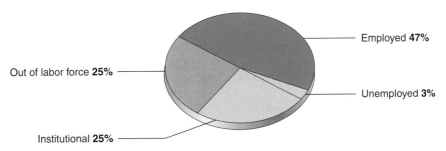

FIGURE 3.10 **U.S. population by labor market status, 2002.** Around one-half of the U.S. population participates in the labor force (excluding the military). *Source:* Bureau of Labor Statistics.

TABLE 3.8 **Total Employment, 1870–1992 (000s)**
Rising populations have led to big increases in employment.

	1870	1913	1929	1938	1950	1973	1992
Austria	2077	3122	3282	3113	3215	3160	3546
Belgium	2141	3376	3636	3316	3341	3748	3802
France	17800	19373	20170	18769	19663	21434	22557
Germany	9511	16039	17647	19656	21164	27160	29141
Italy	13770	17644	19016	19287	18875	22708	25652
Norway	706	984	1132	1267	1428	1676	2004
U.K.	12285	18566	18936	20818	22400	25076	25465
Australia	630	1943	2355	2592	3459	5838	7736
Canada	1266	3014	3960	4183	5030	8843	12316
U.S.	12285	18566	18936	20818	22400	25076	25465
Japan	18684	25751	29332	32290	35683	52590	64360
Greece		2018			2600	3232	3634
Spain		7613			11662	13031	12642
Argentina					6821	9402	11603
Chile					2256	2896	4588
Mexico					8563	15044	26412
Venezuela					1571	3331	6055
South Korea					6377	11140	18376
Taiwan					2872	5327	8632

Source: Maddison, *Monitoring the World Economy: 1820–1992* (Table J.4), OECD
and Economic Outlook 2003, Statistical Annex, Table 16, www.oecd.org

those out of the labor force (those who do not want a job) and those who are institutional (the part of the population for whom jobs are not viable—the military forces, prison population, school-age children, and so forth).

While countries' capital stocks have increased substantially over time, statistics on labor input are more ambiguous. Table 3.8 lists employment (in thousands) for a range of countries. In every case employment has risen substantially[4] but this increase has been offset by a fall in annual hours worked per person employed. Table 3.9 shows that for most economies (South Korea and Taiwan excepted), employees were working fewer hours in 2002 compared with the past. As a result, in many economies, especially in the more mature OECD economies, total hours worked declined during the second half of the twentieth century. The situation is different in Japan, Canada, and Australia and in the emerging market nations listed in Table 3.10.

[4] A rising population means that increased employment does not necessarily equate with less unemployment.

TABLE 3.9   **Annual Hours Worked per Person Employed, 1870–1992**
As countries get richer, they tend to work fewer hours per person.

	1870	1913	1929	1938	1950	1973	1992
Austria	2935	2580	2281	2312	1976	1778	1576
Belgium	2964	2605	2272	2267	2283	1872	1581
France	2945	2588	2297	1848	1926	1771	1542
Germany	2941	2584	2284	2316	2316	1804	1563
Italy	2886	2536	2228	1927	1997	1612	1490
Norway	2945	2588	2283	2128	2101	1721	1465
U.K.	2984	2624	2286	2267	1958	1688	1491
Australia	2945	2588	2139	2110	1838	1708	1631
Canada	2964	2605	2399	2240	1967	1788	1656
U.S.	2964	2605	2342	2062	1867	1717	1589
Japan	2945	2588	2364	2391	2166	2042	1876
Greece					2200	2000	1720
Spain					2200	2150	1911
Argentina					2034	1996	1826
Chile					2212	1955	2005
Mexico					2154	2061	2062
Venezuela					2179	1965	1868
South Korea					2200	2683	2800
Taiwan					2200	2570	2500

Source: Maddison, *Monitoring the World Economy: 1820–1992*, (Table J.2),
OECD Labor Force Statistics, www.oecd.org

TOTAL FACTOR PRODUCTIVITY

TFP captures the impact of *all* the factors that affect output but are not explicitly mentioned as a factor of production—it is a measure of the efficiency with which productive inputs are combined to produce output. As we have only specified the capital stock and hours worked as inputs into the production function, our version of TFP includes the level of education/skills in the work force, technology, geography, institutions and government policies, amongst many other factors that we will consider in detail in Chapter 5. Figure 3.11 shows an estimate of TFP for broad geographic regions—increases in TFP have been a source of long-run growth but also account for substantial cross-country variations in GDP.

Increases in any of these three factors—capital, labor, or TFP—will boost GDP. However, given our focus in the previous section on productivity, it should be obvious that increases in output produced by working more hours are not as beneficial as increased GDP from higher hourly productivity. From the production function this suggests that we should focus on capital and TFP as the sources of long-run

TABLE 3.10   Total Hours Worked (millions), 1870–1992

Rising employment but falling average hours worked means that total hours worked have not increased everywhere.

	1870	1913	1929	1938	1950	1973	1992
Austria	6096	8055	7486	7197	6353	5618	5588
Belgium	6346	8794	8261	7517	7628	7016	6011
France	52421	50137	46330	34685	37871	37960	34783
Germany	27972	41445	40306	45523	49016	48997	45547
Italy	39740	44745	42368	37166	37693	36605	38221
Norway	2079	2547	2584	2696	3000	2884	2936
U.K.	36658	48717	43288	47194	43859	42328	37968
Australia	1855	5028	5037	5469	6358	9971	12617
Canada	3752	7851	9500	9370	9894	15811	20395
U.S.	36413	48364	44348	42927	41821	43055	40464
Japan	55024	66644	69341	77205	77289	107389	120739
Greece					5720	6464	6250
Spain					25656	28017	24159
Argentina					13874	18766	21187
Chile					4990	5662	9199
Mexico					18445	31006	54462
Venezuela					3423	6545	11311
South Korea					14029	29889	51453
Taiwan					6318	13690	21580

Source: Maddison, *Monitoring the World Economy: 1820–1992*, (Table J.4), OECD and OECD Labor Force Statistics, www.oecd.org

growth—only by providing workers with more machines and better technology is it possible to continually raise productivity. Table 3.11 shows how hourly productivity has increased over time for a range of countries. Between 1870 and 1992 the hourly productivity of a German worker has increased from $1.58 per hour to $27.55—enabling Germans to combine higher income with fewer hours worked. In 1870 the average German employee worked more than 56 hours per week but by 2002 this had fallen to 28 hours, but the massive increase in productivity means that output per worker has risen by 850%.

KEY POINT

The long-run sources of growth in GDP per capita and productivity must be capital accumulation and improvements in Total Factor Productivity.

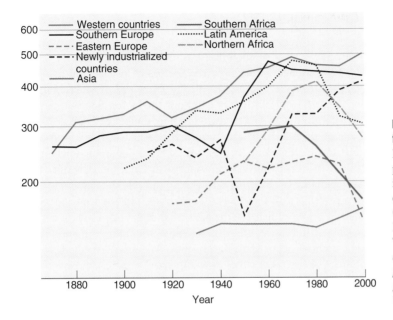

FIGURE 3.11 **Total factor productivity, 1870–2000.** Differences in total factor productivity are an important source of cross-country differences in GDP per capita. *Source:* Baier, Dwyer, and Tamura, *How important are capital and total factor productivity for economic growth?* Clemson University mimeo, 2004.

TABLE 3.11   **Labor Productivity (GDP per Hour Worked), 1870–1992 (1990$)**
Increases in hourly productivity produce sustainable growth in GDP per capita.

	1870	1913	1929	1938	1950	1973	1992
Austria	1.39	2.93	3.31	3.36	4.07	15.27	24.21
Belgium	2.12	3.60	4.81	5.27	6.06	16.53	28.55
Denmark	1.51	3.40	5.11	5.31	5.85	15.94	21.81
Finland	0.84	1.81	2.57	3.07	4.00	13.42	20.45
France	1.36	2.85	4.15	5.35	5.65	17.77	29.62
Germany	1.58	3.50	4.37	4.84	4.37	16.64	27.55
Italy	1.03	2.09	2.89	3.79	4.28	15.58	24.59
Netherlands	2.33	4.01	6.32	6.26	6.50	19.02	28.80
Norway	1.09	2.19	3.42	4.30	5.41	14.05	25.61
Sweden	1.22	2.58	3.29	4.27	7.08	18.02	23.11
Switzerland	1.75	3.25	5.38	5.90	8.75	18.28	25.37
U.K.	2.61	4.40	5.54	5.98	7.86	15.92	23.98
Japan	0.46	1.03	1.78	2.19	2.03	11.15	20.02
Australia	3.32	5.28	6.47	7.16	8.68	16.87	22.56
Canada	1.61	4.21	5.21	5.26	9.78	19.09	25.32
U.S.	2.26	5.12	7.52	8.64	12.66	23.45	29.10

Source: Maddison, *Monitoring the World Economy: 1820–1992* (OECD 1995)

3.4   Growth Accounting

In order to assess the relative role of capital, labor, and TFP in producing GDP growth, we need to know how changes in each of the factors of production leads to changes in output. The ***marginal product of capital*** or the ***marginal product of labor*** captures this information. The marginal product of capital is the increase in output that adding one further piece of machinery generates—keeping unchanged the level of hours worked and total factor productivity. The marginal product of labor is the increase in output that results from adding one further unit of labor—keeping unchanged the capital stock and TFP. It is crucial to the definition of the marginal product that only one factor input is being changed—the idea is to isolate the role of each input.

Consider the case of a printing firm that has 20 employees and has to decide how many machines to purchase. Table 3.12 lists the output and marginal product of capital that the firm can produce using different numbers of machines when the firm has 20 employees and each machine embodies the same technology. We have assumed in this case that the marginal product of capital declines as the firm buys more machines. This is an assumption about how technology works in practice, and we will show in Chapters 4 and 6 that different assumptions about the behaviour of the marginal product of capital have enormous implications for our theories of growth.

THE COBB-DOUGLAS PRODUCTION FUNCTION

So far we have simply said that increases in capital, employment, and TFP lead to increases in output. But if we can be more precise about the relationship between outputs and inputs, then we can create a much more detailed model of growth. To do this economists often assume that a *Cobb-Douglas* function characterizes the production function. With a Cobb-Douglas function[5]

$$\text{Output} = \text{TFP} \times \text{Capital Stock}^a \times \text{Hours Worked}^{1-a}$$

Where a is a number between 0 and 1 so that GDP is increasing in TFP, capital, and labor. It can be shown that for this production function[6]

$$\text{Marginal Product of Capital} = a \times \text{TFP} \times (\text{Hours Worked/Capital Stock})^{1-a}$$

TABLE 3.12   **Output and the Marginal Product of Capital**

Number of Machines	1	2	3	4	5
Output produced	10	19	26	31	34
Marginal product of capital	10	9	7	5	3

[5] The following section requires some mathematical knowledge to fully understand the derivations, but the general inutition of the approach should be accessible for the reader who does not have this knowledge.

[6] It requires only straightforward differentiation of the production function since the marginal product of capital equals $\partial y/\partial K$. Write the Cobb-Douglas production function $y = \text{TFP } K^a L^{1-a}$ where y is output, K is capital, and L is hours worked. $\partial y/\partial K = a \text{ TFP } (L/K)^{1-a}$ and $\partial y/\partial L = (1-a) \text{ TFP } (K/L)^a$. If capital earns its marginal product, then the total payments to those who supply capital is $K \, \partial y/\partial K = ay$, and if the hourly wage is the marginal product of labor, the total wage bill is $L\partial y/\partial L = (1-a)y$. Thus a is the share of profit (the returns to capital) in total value added (y) while $1-a$ is labor's share.

and

Marginal Product of Labor = $(1 - a) \times$ TFP $\times$ (Capital Stock/Hours Worked)^a

Assuming $0 < a < 1$, the Cobb-Douglas production function has a marginal product of capital and labor that are both decreasing—the more machines (workers) a firm has, the lower the marginal product of capital (labor).

We can use the production function and data on inputs and output to estimate the role of each factor of production in producing long-run increases in GDP—an exercise known as growth accounting. Taking logarithms of the production function gives

Logarithm (Output) = Logarithm (TFP) + $a \times$ Logarithm (Capital)
$+ (1-a) \times$ Logarithm (Hours Worked)

So that

Change in Logarithm (Output) = Change in Logarithm (TFP) + $a \times$
Change in Logarithm (Capital) + $(1-a) \times$ Change in Logarithm (Hours Worked)

Because the change in the logarithm of a variable is approximately equal to the percentage change in a variable we therefore have

% Change in Ouput = % Change in TFP + $a \times$ % Change in Capital + $(1-a)$
$\times$ % Change in Hours Worked

Therefore we can calculate the amount of output growth that results from capital accumulation ($a \times$ % change in Capital Stock) and similarly for the contribution of hours worked [$(1 - a) \times$ % change in Hours Worked]. We attribute whatever output growth is left unexplained by changes in capital and hours worked to TFP, the unobserved factor input. All that we need to undertake growth accounting (aside from data on output, capital, and employment) is to find out the appropriate value of a. We can do this if we assume that capital and labor get paid their own marginal product—that is, workers' wages reflect the value of the extra output they produce, and the return earned by the owners of capital reflects the extra output that capital generates. Assuming that factors get paid what they produce, as measured by their marginal product, amounts to assuming competitive markets. In this case, capital income is MPK $\times$ K and labor income is MPL $\times$ L. Assuming a Cobb-Douglas production function, capital income is $(a \times y/K) \times K = ay$ and labor income is $[(1 - a) \times y/L] \times L = (1 - a)y$. Therefore we can measure a by calculating the share of GDP paid out to capital. In most OECD economies (as we saw in Chapter 2), around 30% of GDP is paid out to owners of capital, and the remaining 70% is paid out as income to labor, so that a is approximately 0.3.

As this outline of growth accounting shows, TFP is calculated as a residual—it is the output growth that is left unexplained by recorded increases in factor inputs. As a consequence, any errors in measuring output, capital, or labor will affect our estimates of the importance of TFP. Further, we have assumed a production function with only two factors of production—capital and labor—so that TFP captures all other influences. But we could extend our production function by incorporating additional variables. For instance, in Chapter 6 we will introduce human capital, a measure of the skills and education of the workforce, into the production function. As we include additional variables in the production function, the role of TFP in accounting for growth should shrink.

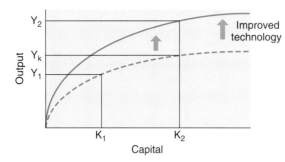

FIGURE 3.12 **Growth accounting.**
Technological improvements and
capital deepening drive growth.

KEY POINT

Growth accounting uses the production function to calculate the importance of capital, labor, and other factors of production in producing GDP growth. TFP is defined as a residual—whatever is left unexplained by other variables.

For an intuition as to exactly what growth accounting does, consider Figure 3.12. Between Year 1 and Year 2 the capital stock of the country has increased (from K_1 to K_2) and the technology available has improved, so the production function also shifts up as well. As a result, output increases from Y_1 to Y_2. Growth accounting calculates how much of this extra output has arisen from capital accumulation and how much from technological progress. Y_1 to Y_K gives the contribution from capital accumulation alone—that is, the output increase that comes from keeping the technology fixed but increasing just the capital stock, which means, staying on the old production function. Y_K to Y_2 gives the growth that results from technological progress—this shows the extra output that technological progress produces *keeping fixed the capital stock*. Note that growth accounting distinguishes between investment in additional machines (moving along a given production function) and changes in technology (upward shifts in the production function), whereas in reality new technology comes embodied in the machines purchased this year. However, in growth accounting we are performing a *logical* analysis—how much output growth would have occurred *if* new technology were not available this year? For this logical exercise, it does not matter if capital and technology increases are always implemented simultaneously. In principle, we can disentangle the two influences.

3.5 Growth Accounting—An Application

Figure 3.13a–c shows the results of a growth accounting exercise for Japan, the United Kingdom, the United States, and Germany for the period 1913–1992. Figure 3.13*a* shows the results for 1913–1950. During this period in Japan, capital accumulation could account for 1.2% annual growth in output, increased labor input for 0.3% growth per year, and TFP 0.7%. Therefore annual growth in GDP was 2.2% per year over this period (1.2 + 0.3 + 0.7). Close examination of Figure 3.13 shows

1. 1950–1973 (the so-called "Golden Age") was a period of rapid output growth.
2. For the United Kingdom and Germany, increases in labor input do not contribute much to recent output growth.

3. In 6 out of the 12 cases, capital accumulation was the most important factor in explaining growth. TFP was the most important component on five occasions. Only once—in the United States between 1973 and 1992—was labor input the most important.

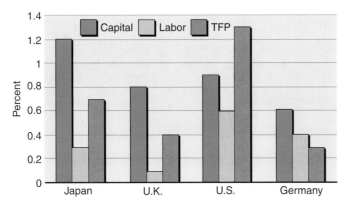

(a) 1913–1950

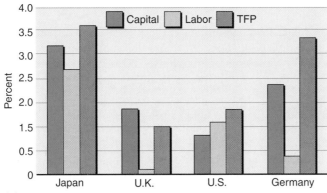

(b) 1950–1973

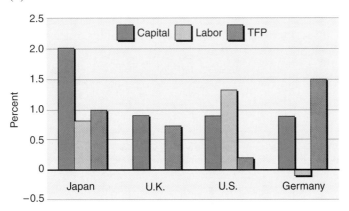

(c) 1973–1992

FIGURE 3.13 **Growth accounting for Japan, Germany, the United Kingdom, and the United States.** TFP and capital growth have accounted for the largest parts of growth in developed economies. *Source:* Crafts, *Globalization and Growth in the Twentieth Century*, IMF Working Paper 11/44 (2002).

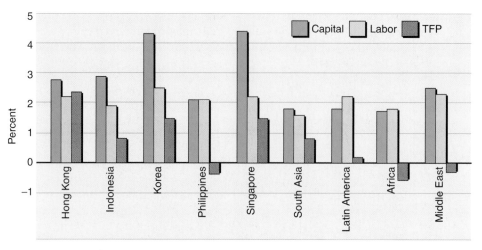

F I G U R E   3 . 1 4   **Growth accounting emerging markets, 1960–94.** In emerging economies, labor force growth has been more important than in developed economies and greater reliance on factor inputs rather than TFP. *Source:* Crafts, *Globalization and Growth in the Twentieth Century*, IMF Working Paper 00/44 (2000).

Figure 3.14 shows the results of a similar growth accounting exercise for economies that started their growth processes later. As in Figure 3.13, the most important component of growth was capital accumulation. However, unlike the more mature industrialized countries in Figure 3.13, for these emerging nations, TFP played a surprisingly small role in accounting for growth. Instead, increases in labor input were the second-most important component.

Over the next few chapters, we will look at each of these factors of production in turn and examine more closely how they produce output growth. We will also combine all the factors of production to offer a theory of growth that helps account for the cross-country differences outlined above. In Chapter 4 we focus first on the most important component of growth: capital accumulation. Chapter 5 then incorporates into the analysis technological progress—a key component of TFP, the second-most important factor of production for advanced nations. Chapter 6 examines two different models of economic growth and assesses which one best accounts for the facts shown in Figures 3.13 and 3.14. Chapter 7 then examines the role of the labor market in explaining cross-country differences in output.

SUMMARY

In Section 3.1 we showed that since the mid-nineteenth century world output has increased by an unprecedented extent. While initially focused in a small group of countries, this growth has spread to most of the world's economies. This increase in output has vastly increased output per head, supported a rising world population, boosted life expectancy and reduced poverty. The welfare implications of economic growth are enormous. If governments could raise trend growth rates, the benefits would substantially outweigh those of removing business cycle fluctuations. Even small changes in growth rates have large long-run effects.

Section 3.2 showed that GDP per capita is driven by hourly productivity and the number of hours worked. The number of hours worked is determined by labor market variables reflecting average hours worked, the employment rate and the participation rate. In the long run continual growth in GDP per capita is driven by improvements in productivity.

Section 3.3 introduced the production function that summarizes the relationship between factor inputs and GDP. Capital and labor are the two basic factor inputs. Total factor productivity measures the efficiency with which inputs are combined to produce output and reflects a broad range of influences. Increases in productivity depend on capital accumulation and higher TFP.

Section 3.4 used the production function to attribute growth in GDP across various factor inputs and TFP. Relying on assumptions about the marginal product of capital and labor and measuring TFP as a residual, this growth accounting offers a numerical decomposition of GDP growth.

Section 3.5 applied growth accounting to a range of countries. According to this approach, the most important variable explaining increased output across countries over the last 100 years has been capital accumulation. The next most important factor varies. For the mature industrialized nations, TFP has been important. For emerging markets, it has been increases in labor input.

CONCEPTUAL QUESTIONS

1. (Section 3.1) Examining Figure 3.1, what factors do you think explain why growth occurs earlier in some regions than others?

2. (3.1) Consider three economies, each of whom has GDP per capita of $100. Trend growth in these economies is 2%, 2.5%, and 5%. Calculate GDP per capita for each economy after 5, 10, 20, 50, and 100 years.

3. (3.1) If a 1% increase in GDP per head reduces poverty by 2%, then the elasticity of poverty with respect to GDP growth is 2. If population growth in this country is 2%, then in order to achieve a 2% reduction in poverty it requires a 3% increase in GDP and a 1% increase in GDP per capita. To meet the Millenium Development targets, countries need to achieve an approximate 5% reduction in poverty per annum. Calculate the required growth in GDP for the following countries (all numbers from the African Development Bank Annual Report 2002).

	Elasticity of Poverty with Respect to GDP	Population Growth
Ethiopia	0.43	2.5
Ghana	2.2	2.2
Sub-Saharan Africa	1.03	2.3
Algeria	1.87	1.9
Egypt	3.3	1.8
N. Africa	2.30	2.3

4. (3.2) Use Table 3.5 to calculate how much of the variation across countries in GDP per capita is due to differences in hourly productivity, average hours worked, employment, and the participation rate.

5. (3.3) Figure 3.9 shows that capital stock per worker varies enormously across countries and over time. What factors do you think contribute to these differences?

6. (3.3) The United States is one of the richest nations in the world and benefits from high levels of TFP. What features of U.S. society do you think can explain this?

7. (3.4) The Republic of Arden has experienced a 5% increase in output this year, a 2% rise in its capital stock, and a 3% increase in hours worked. Assuming a Cobb-Douglas production function where capital income accounts for 30% of GDP, calculate how much output growth is explained by capital accumulation, labor, and TFP.

ANALYTICAL QUESTIONS

1. (Section 3.4) You will need a spreadsheet for this exercise. Assume TFP = 1 and set initial capital stock and employment to 1. Let output be given by $TFP \times K^{0.3}L^{0.7}$. Calculate output, the marginal product of capital, and the share of output paid to capital when labor is fixed at 1 and capital varies between 1 and 10. Repeat for the marginal product of labor when capital is set to 1 and labor varies between 1 and 10.

2. (3.4) GDP in an economy is growing at 3% a year in real terms. Population is constant. The government decides to allow a significant increase in immigration so that the population (and the workforce) start to grow by 1% a year. Output is produced in the economy according to a Cobb-Douglas production function. The share of labor income in GDP is 70%. How much higher will GDP be as a result of the new immigration policy after 20 years? How much higher will per capita GDP be?

4. (3.4) Output in an economy is produced when labor hours (H) are combined with capital (K) in a way which reflects TFP to produce output (y). The relation is: $y = TFP. K^{0.27} H^{1-0.27}$. What is the share of labor income in output? What happens to the share of profits (i.e., capital's share in output) when there is a change in TFP? (Comment on your answer.)

5. (3.4) Use the production function of Question 4 to calculate
   (a) What happens to the marginal product of labor if H rises 10% with no change in other inputs?
   (b) What happens to the marginal product of capital if K increases by 15% with no change in other inputs?
   (c) What happens to the marginal product of labor and to output per person employed if labor and capital both rise by 7%?

Capital Accumulation and Economic Growth

Overview

In this chapter we examine the relationship between increases in the capital stock and economic growth. We first discuss whether an economy can always grow if it increases only its capital stock. Under certain plausible assumptions, we show this is not possible, and that poorer countries should therefore grow faster than wealthy ones, whose economies will depend more on technological progress than capital accumulation. We then discuss why countries with high investment rates also have high standards of living and we consider the optimal investment rate for countries. Finally we analyze the rapid growth of the Southeast Asian economies, the extent to which they have relied on capital accumulation, and the implications of this pattern for China.

Key Concepts

Convergence	Golden Rule	Southeast Asian Growth Miracle
Depreciation	Investment	Steady State

4.1 Capital Accumulation and Output Growth

Figure 4.1*a* plots per capita real gross domestic product (GDP) and the per capita capital stock for a group of countries. Figure 4.1*b* focuses on the growth in GDP and capital between 1965 and 1990 for the same group of countries. Countries that have had large increases in their capital stock have also seen large increases in their GDP. For instance, Botswana during this period has seen a near twenty-fold increase in its capital stock, and largely as a consequence, its GDP per capita has more than quadrupled. This is both the largest increase in capital and the largest increase in output. Evidently capital accumulation matters greatly for both a country's standard of living and its rate of growth.

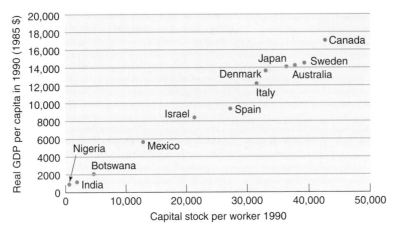

FIGURE 4.1a   **GDP per capita versus capital stock per worker in 1990.** *Source:* Summers and Heston dataset, Penn World Tables 5.5, http://pwt.econ.upenn.edu

HOW MUCH EXTRA OUTPUT DOES A NEW MACHINE PRODUCE?

If capital helps produce more output, a key question in economic growth is whether this link can be maintained indefinitely. Imagine that an economy experiences no improvement in total factor productivity (TFP, which is introduced in Chapter 3) or increase in hours worked but only adds to its capital stock. Will this capital accumulation produce economic growth forever or will capital accumulation eventually prove ineffective? The answer to this question depends on the behaviour of the marginal product of capital (MPK). In Chapter 3 we defined the MPK as the increase in output that occurs when the capital stock increases but TFP and labor input remain unchanged. Consider the case of a firm that publishes textbooks and has four printing presses. The introduction of the fourth printing press enabled the firm to increase its production by 500 books per week. Will a fifth machine increase production by more than 500 books, by less than 500 books, or by exactly 500 more books? If the fifth machine leads to an increase in

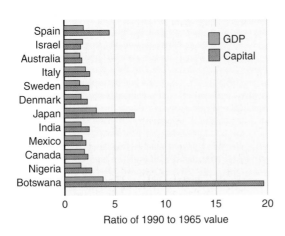

FIGURE 4.1b   **Capital growth and GDP growth 1965–1990.** Countries that have accumulated substantial stocks of productive capital have reached higher standards of living. *Source:* Summers and Heston, Penn World Table 5.5, http://pwt.econ.upenn.edu

production of more than 500 books (that is, if it causes a larger increase than the fourth machine generated), we have *increasing marginal product of capital*. If the increased production is less than 500 books, then we have *decreasing marginal product*, and if the increase equals 500, we have a *constant marginal product of capital*.

Why might the marginal product of capital be decreasing? Consider again the publishing company and assume it has 10 employees, each working a fixed shift. With four machines, there are two and a half employees per machine. If we hold fixed the technology and hours worked as we increase the number of machines, we are going to encounter problems. There will be fewer and fewer operator hours to monitor the machines, so each machine will probably be less productive. Even if each new machine produces extra output, the boost in output will probably not be as high as from the previous machine. Note the importance of assuming that labor input and technology remain unchanged.

Of course not all firms or industries will be characterised by decreasing marginal product of capital. Consider the case of a telephone. When a country has only one telephone, the marginal product of that initial investment is zero—there is no one to call! Investment in a second telephone has a positive boost to output; there is now one channel of communication. Investment in a third telephone substantially increases communications—there are now three communication links, and so the investment increases the marginal product of capital. Adding more and more telephones increases even further the number of potential communication links. Telephones are an example of a technology that benefits from network effects, which are often characterised by increasing marginal product of capital.

The behaviour of the MPK is a question about technology, not economics. Even so, we will show that different assumptions about the MPK have enormous implications for our models of long-run growth. If the MPK is diminishing, then it is not possible to grow forever from capital accumulation—the output boost from investment declines with additional capital until growth does not occur. If, instead, the MPK is constant or even increasing, then capital accumulation can produce growth forever even in the absence of labor or TFP increases.

DECREASING MARGINAL PRODUCT, OR IT DOESN'T GET ANY EASIER

In this chapter we shall assume that the marginal product of capital is decreasing for the aggregate economy and discuss what this implies for economic growth. In Chapter 6 we consider alternative assumptions and examine the empirical evidence for each case.

Figure 4.2 shows the case of diminishing marginal product of capital. At point A the country has little capital, so new investment leads to a big boost in output. At point B the capital stock is so large that each new machine generates little extra output. Figure 4.2*a* shows how the capital stock is related to *increases* in output (the marginal product of capital), but we can also use this relationship to draw a production function summarizing how the stock of capital is linked to the *level* of output. This is shown in Figure 4.2*b*. At low levels of capital, the marginal product is high, so that small increases in the capital stock lead to a big jump in output, and the production function is steeply sloped. Thus point A in Figure 4.2*b* corresponds to the same level of capital in Figure 4.2*a*. However, at high levels of capital (such as point B), each new machine generates only a small increase in output, so that the production function starts to flatten

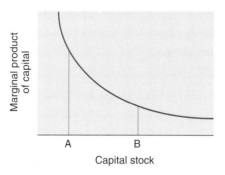

FIGURE 4.2a   **Marginal product of capital.**   FIGURE 4.2b   **The production function.**
A concave production function implies a declining marginal product of capital.

out—output changes little in this range even for large changes in the capital stock. The slope of the production function in Figure 4.2*b* is actually the MPK—hence at low capital the MPK is high and with high capital it is low.

KEY POINT

With decreasing marginal product of capital, output growth from capital accumulation eventually slows to a halt.

4.2   Savings, Investment, and Interest Rates

CHOOSING THE CAPITAL STOCK

The extra revenue a new machine contributes is the price at which output is sold (p) multiplied by the MPK. If this amount is greater than the cost of a new machine (which we denote r^0) then it is profitable for a firm to install the machinery. So if MPK $> r^0/p$, it is profitable to add to the capital stock. In Figure 4.3, the cost of an additional machine is shown by the horizontal line r^0/p. At point A, the marginal product of capital is higher than the cost of an additional machine, so the firm increases its capital stock. This continues until it reaches B, where the last machine contributes just as much to revenues as it does to costs. By contrast, at C each new machine loses money, so the capital stock should be reduced. Crucial to this analysis is the cost of capital, which will be examined in detail in Chapter 13, but for now we focus on just one element: the interest rate.[1] We can think of the cost of the machine as the interest rate (r) that would need to be paid on a loan used to buy it. If we assume that it costs $1 to buy a unit of capital (so we measure everything in terms of the price of a machine), then the interest cost is just r. Therefore to be profitable, the investment project must produce at least the rate of interest. As the interest rate changes, so does the desired level of capital—if

[1] The cost of capital also includes depreciation, taxes, and changes in the price of capital goods.

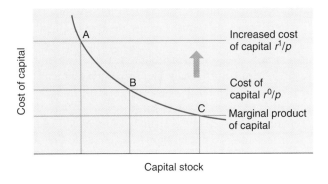

FIGURE 4.3 **Investment and the cost of capital.** Increases in the cost of capital reduce the optimal capital stock.

the interest rate increases, then the cost of capital shifts to r^1/p (as in Figure 4.3) and the firm desires less capital. If the interest rate falls, investment demands will be high. Therefore the relationship between investment and the interest rate is negative.

DETERMINING INTEREST RATES

When a firm wishes to increase its capital stock, it has to finance this increase at the current level of interest rates. The firm has to either use its own savings or borrow those of other economic agents. Let us assume that as interest rates increase, so does the level of savings. In other words, as banks or financial markets offer higher rates of return on savings, individuals and firms respond by spending less and saving more. Therefore the relationship between savings and the interest rate is positive (see Figure 4.4).

Consider the case where the interest rate is R_A. At this level, interest rates are so low that savers are not prepared to save much, and savings are at S_A. However, low interest rates make capital investment attractive as the marginal product of capital is higher than the interest rate. As a result, firms are keen to borrow and desire investment I_A. There are not enough savings to finance this desired level of investment, which frustrates firms' investment plans. Because of the gap between the marginal product of capital and the interest rate, firms are prepared to pay a higher interest rate to raise funds for investment. This puts upward pressure on interest rates, which in turn leads to

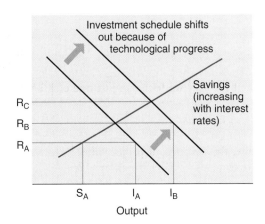

FIGURE 4.4 **Investment, savings, and interest rates.** Technical progress increases investment and may also drive rates of return (interest rates) up.

increases in savings, which can be used to finance the desired investment. This process will continue—with interest rates increasing—until savings equal investment at the interest rate R_B.

We can use Figure 4.4 to analyze what happens to interest rates when investment or savings shift. Consider the case of an improvement in technology that leads to an improvement in the marginal product of capital. For a given level of interest rates this means an increase in investment, and so the investment schedule shifts to the right in Figure 4.4. If interest rates remain unchanged at R_B, then investment will be too high at I_B relative to savings. This will see firms competing for funds and bidding up interest rates. This increase in interest rates will persuade some firms not to invest and will also induce more savings until eventually the market returns to equilibrium at R_C.

Figure 4.4 is just a supply and demand diagram, and interest rates are determined where the supply of loans (savings) equals the demand for loans (investment). Equilibrium in the loan market means that savings equals investment, and we will often use these terms interchangeably in this chapter. At a global level it is true that savings equals investment; in the absence of intergalactic capital markets, world investment has to be funded by world savings. At a national level, however, savings do not have to equal investment. Countries can either borrow or lend money overseas using global capital markets (see Chapter 20 for a fuller discussion). Even so, we can still expect any given country's savings and investment to be closely correlated over the long run. Countries that borrow money today (e.g., have investment greater than savings) will eventually have to repay these loans and this means that in the future savings will exceed investment. Therefore, in the *long run*, savings and investment will be similar. If there are persistent differences between savings and investment rates for a country, then this will show up in the long run as different growth in GDP and GNI.

KEY POINT

In the world capital markets, long-run real interest rates vary to ensure that savings equals investment.

4.3   Why Poor Countries Catch Up with the Rich

We return now to our discussion of decreasing marginal product of capital. Consider two economies that have similar levels of employment and TFP. This means that we can think of both economies as sharing the same marginal product curve of Figure 4.2a or equivalently the same production function as in Figure 4.2b. However, one economy has a much higher capital stock. Figure 4.5 shows these two economies as being at K_A and K_B. Diminishing marginal product implies that the economy at K_A will find it easier to grow through investment than the economy at K_B. Assume both countries increase their capital stock by the same amount. The low capital stock country increases capital from K_A to K_B while the wealthier economy moves from K_B to K_C. The result is that output in the low capital country rises from Y_A to Y_B and in the richer economy from Y_B to Y_C. Therefore, the *same* investment will bring forth a *bigger* increase in output in the poorer economy than the richer one. In other words, because of

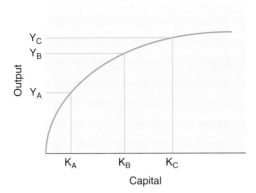

FIGURE 4.5 **Poor countries grow faster than wealthier countries.** A given increase in the capital stock generates more extra output for a country with relatively low capital.

decreasing marginal product, growth from capital accumulation becomes more and more difficult the higher the capital stock of a country becomes. This "catch-up" result implies a process of convergence among countries and regions—for the same investment poorer countries grow faster than wealthier ones and inequalities across regions should decrease over time.

Figure 4.6, which displays the dispersion (as measured by the standard deviation) of income per head across U.S. states, shows some evidence for this. Since 1900 the inequalities of income across states have been dramatically reduced as poorer states, such as Maine and Arkansas, have grown faster than wealthier ones, such as Massachusetts and New York. This is consistent with the assumption of decreasing marginal product and its implication of catch-up.

Comparing income across U.S. states is a good test of the theoretical predictions of catch-up because our analysis depends on countries or regions sharing the same production function. This is likely to be the case across U.S. states. But finding other examples of countries that satisfy these conditions is not easy—low capital countries like India or Botswana also tend to have access to lower levels of technology than countries such as Japan or Australia. However, the circumstances of war and subsequent economic recovery offer some further support for assuming decreasing marginal product. Figure 4.7 shows that between 1945 and 1946, just after World War II, West German capital stock and output both fell. According to decreasing marginal product of capital,

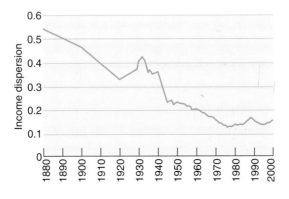

FIGURE 4.6 **Income dispersion across U.S. states.** Income inequality between states in the United States has declined greatly since the end of the nineteenth century. *Source:* Barro and Sala-I-Martin, *Economic Growth* (New York: McGraw Hill, 2003).

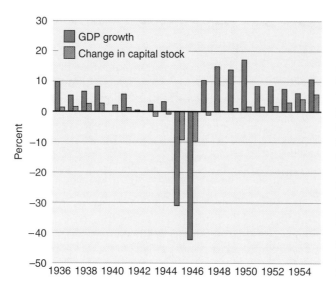

FIGURE 4.7 **West German GDP and capital growth 1936–55.** West German GDP grew rapidly in the 1950s as the capital stock was rebuilt after the war. *Source:* Capital stock data from Maddison, "Macroeconomics Accounts for European Countries," in van Ark and Crafts (eds.), *Quantitative Aspects of Post-War European Economic Growth* (Cambridge: Cambridge University Press: 1996).

this suggests that after the war the ratio of output growth to capital growth (a measure of the MPK if employment and TFP don't change) should increase compared with pre-war. Relatively small amounts of investment should produce high GDP growth after 1946, exactly what Figure 4.7 shows happened between 1947 and 1952. Table 4.1 shows a similarly sharp bounce back in output after WWII for other European nations. As a consequence of the war, European output and capital declined sharply to levels seen several decades earlier. However, within only a few years these countries had regained the lost output as the depressed level of capital meant investment benefited from high marginal product of capital.

TABLE 4.1   **Post-War Reconstruction in Europe**

	Pre-War Year GDP Same as 1945	Year Reached Pre-War High
Austria	1886	1951
Belgium	1924	1948
Denmark	1936	1946
Finland	1938	1945
France	1891	1949
Germany	1908	1951
Italy	1909	1950
Netherlands	1912	1947
Norway	1937	1946

Source: Crafts and Toniolo, "Postwar Growth: An Overview," in Crafts and Toniolo (eds.), *Economic Growth in Europe Since 1945*, (Cambridge University Press, 1996).

4.4 Growing Importance of Total Factor Productivity

In this section we show a further implication of diminishing marginal product—total factor productivity (TFP) is more important for wealthier economies than for poorer ones. To see the intuition behind this result, imagine two publishing firms each with 10 employees. One firm has 3 printing presses, while the other has 10. Consider the impact one more machine will have for each firm compared to the introduction of new software that improves the productivity of all machines. For the firm with only three machines, the technological progress (the new software) will have only a limited effect—with only three machines, the software will not improve productivity a lot. However, this firm gains significantly from the introduction of a new machine because its capital stock is so low that its marginal product of capital is high. By contrast, the other firm already has as many machines as employees, so it will benefit very little from an additional printing press. However, with 10 machines to operate, the technological progress will have a more substantial impact. If we apply this example to countries, we can expect capital accumulation to be more important to growth relative to TFP for poorer nations and the opposite for capital-rich countries. This is exactly what we saw in Figure 3.14 in Chapter 3 for the more mature industrialized nations and emerging markets.

To show this argument graphically, consider the production function in Figure 4.8. In Year 0 the production function is the solid line, but because of technological progress, the production function shifts up—for a given level of capital, the improved technology increases output. Now consider two economies—A and B—both of which

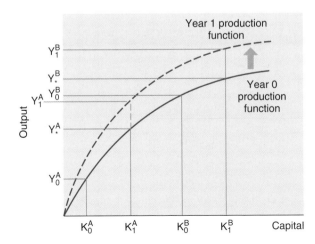

FIGURE 4.8 **The impact of technological progress and economic maturity.** The greater the capital stock, the more valuable is technological progress.

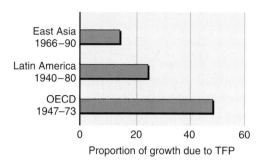

FIGURE 4.9 **Importance of TFP in growth.** Richer countries get more growth from TFP. *Source:* Crafts, "Productivity Growth Reconsidered" *Economic Policy* (1992) vol. 15, pp. 388–426.

increase their capital stock by the same amount. For country A, the capital stock has risen from K_0^A to K_1^A. Without technological progress, the increase in output would have been Y_0^A to Y_*^A. However, because of technological developments, more output can be produced for any given level of capital, so that with a capital stock K_1^A country A can produce Y_1^A in Year 1.

In Figure 4.8 we see that output has increased by a total of $Y_1^A - Y_0^A$, of which $(Y_*^A - Y_0^A)$ is due to the addition of extra capital and $(Y_1^A - Y_*^A)$ is due to technological progress. We can use the same argument for country B and show that capital accumulation (without technological progress) leads to an increase in output of $(Y_*^B - Y_0^B)$, whereas at this new higher level of capital (K_1^B), the improved technology increases output by $(Y_1^B - Y_*^B)$. As the diagram shows, the proportion of growth that TFP explains is higher in country B than country A—technological progress has a bigger impact for capital-rich countries. This implies that wealthier economies, such as those belonging to the OECD, will have a much greater dependence on TFP for producing economic growth than less developed nations. By contrast, emerging economies will be more reliant on capital accumulation than they will on TFP, a conjecture that Figure 4.9 supports. For the periods shown, we suggest that the OECD countries were high capital stock countries, the Asian economies low capital stock countries, and Latin American economies in the middle. Clearly TFP has been much more important for growth among the more developed nations.

> **KEY POINT**
>
> As countries get richer, the source of their economic growth shifts from capital accumulation towards improvements in total factor productivity.

 4.5 The End of Growth through Capital Accumulation

THE STEADY STATE—A POINT OF REST

We have just shown that with a declining marginal product of capital, the relative importance of capital accumulation declines as the capital stock increases. In this section we go further and show how countries *always* reach a point where they cannot grow any more from capital accumulation alone. This point is called a steady state and should be considered as an equilibrium for the model with decreasing MPK. The steady state is a point of rest for the capital stock—efforts to raise or lower the capital stock are futile, and it will always return to this equilibrium level.

INVESTMENT AND DEPRECIATION

Two factors cause the capital stock to change over time. The first is that firms invest in new machinery and structures, so that the capital stock is increasing. But another factor, "depreciation," reduces the capital stock. Whenever they are used, machines are subject to wear and tear and breakdown. Economists call this process of deterioration *depreciation*—the reduction over time in the productive capabilities of capital. Note that economists use the term "depreciation" in a different sense than accountants do. In accounting, "depreciation" refers to reductions in the book value of an asset, which may bear little relation to the physical ability of a machine to produce output. Because of depreciation, we need to distinguish between different measures of investment. Gross investment is the amount of new capital being added to an economy. It includes both the repair and replacement of the existing capital stock as well as new additions. Net investment equals gross investment less depreciation and represents the increase in the capital stock from one year to another. Figure 4.10 shows, for a sample of developed economies, gross investment and depreciation as a percentage of GDP. This figure suggests that net investment is typically about 5–10% of GDP.

Allowing for gross investment and depreciation, the capital stock evolves over time as

$$K(t) = K(t-1) + I(t) - D(t)$$

where $K(t)$ is the capital stock at time t, $I(t)$ is gross investment, and $D(t)$ is depreciation: $I(t) - D(t)$ is net investment. The steady state is the point where the capital stock does not change, so that $K(t) = K(t-1)$, which can only occur when $I(t) = D(t)$ so that gross investment equals depreciation. The country purchases just enough machinery each period to make up for depreciation.

CONVERGENCE

So far our analysis has been based only on a technological assumption about the marginal product of capital. To complete our model of growth we need to make some economic assumptions. The first concerns gross investment, which for simplicity we assume

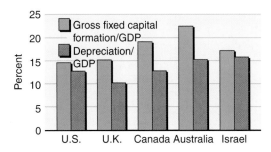

FIGURE 4.10 **Investment and depreciation in selected OECD countries in 2002.** Gross investment exceeds net investment substantially due to depreciation on large capital stock of OECD countries. *Source:* IMF IFS Database (2003).

equals a fixed proportion of output: for example, $I(t) = bY(t)$, where $Y(t)$ is GDP. How much of GDP is invested varies across countries, but let us assume that 20% of output is invested, that is, $b = 0.2$. In Figure 4.11 we show the production function of the economy and the investment function this implies. Because investment equals 20% of output, the investment line is just a scaled-down version of the production function. The other assumption we make concerns depreciation. We assume this occurs at 5% per annum—in other words, around 5% of the capital stock is retired or needs to be repaired each year. Therefore $D(t) = dK(t)$, where $d = 0.05$. Note that investment is a proportion of output and thus is related to the production function, while depreciation is linked to the capital stock. Figure 4.11 shows depreciation as a straight line—if you double the capital stock, you double depreciation.

Consider point A in Figure 4.11. At this level of capital stock, I_A (20% of the output produced) gives the amount of investment. At this level of capital, depreciation is only D_A so that gross investment exceeds depreciation, net investment is positive, and the capital stock is increasing. As the capital stock increases, the gap between investment and depreciation narrows. Decreasing marginal product implies that each new machine leads to a smaller boost in output than the previous one. Because investment is a constant proportion of output, this means each new machine produces ever smaller amounts of new investment. However, depreciation is at a constant rate—each new machine adds 5% of its own value to the depreciation bill. At point B, the depreciation and investment lines intersect. This defines the steady state capital stock where gross investment equals depreciation. At this point the last machine adds just enough extra output to provide enough investment to offset the extra depreciation it brings. At this point the capital stock is neither rising nor falling but stays constant.

Imagine instead that the economy starts with a capital stock of C. At this point depreciation is above investment, net investment is negative, and the capital stock is declining. The country has so much capital that the marginal product of capital is low. As a consequence, each machine cannot produce enough investment to cover its own depreciation; firms are not providing enough investment to cover maintenance and repairs and so the capital stock moves back to the steady state at B. Therefore when the capital stock is below its steady state level, it is increasing, and if it is above the steady state

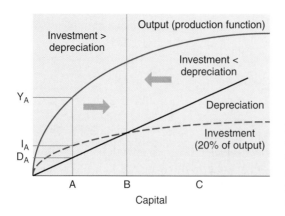

FIGURE 4.11 **The steady state.**
If the stock of capital is below B, net investment is positive and the capital stock is growing. If the capital stock is above B, depreciation exceeds gross investment and the capital stock declines.

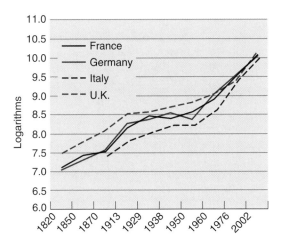

FIGURE 4.12 **Convergence in real GDP per capita in Europe, 1820–2002.** Levels of output in the major four European industrial countries have converged since the end of the nineteenth century. *Source:* Maddison based on data from Table D1.a, pp. 194–95 (1995), *Monitoring the World Economy 1820–1992*, Paris: OECD. Updated to 2002 by author using IMF data.

level, then capital declines. Regardless of where the economy starts from it will end up at the steady state—the steady state is the equilibrium for the model with decreasing MPK. Without diminishing MPK, the production function would not flatten out, a steady state would not exist, and capital accumulation could produce output growth forever.

Assuming countries share their steady state, then eventually they will all converge on approximately the same output per capita. (Diminishing MPK predicts catch-up across similar countries.) Supporting evidence for this is offered in Figure 4.12, which shows real GDP per capita between 1820 and 2002 for four major European countries. In 1870 the United Kingdom was substantially wealthier than other European nations. However, by 2002 these large gaps in the standard of living had been substantially reduced: the gap between the richest and poorest countries was only 12%, relatively small by historical comparison.

KEY POINT

Decreasing marginal product of capital implies the existence of a steady state to which the economy eventually converges. At the steady state, the economy does not grow through capital accumulation and investment equals depreciation.

4.6 Why Bother Saving?

INVESTMENT AND THE STANDARD OF LIVING

Because the steady state is the point at which there is no growth in output through capital accumulation, growth at the steady state must be due either to increases in labor input or to improvements in TFP. Assuming that countries cannot continually reduce their unemployment rate, and that all countries eventually have access to the same

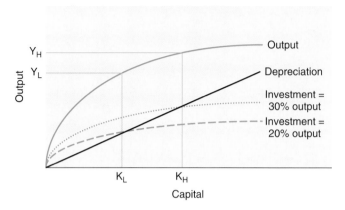

FIGURE 4.13   **Steady state depends on investment rate.** The higher the rate of investment, the greater the steady state capital stock.

technology, this implies that at the steady state countries will all grow at the same rate—the rate of technological progress. Whether one country is investing more than another does not matter—*at the steady state, capital accumulation does not influence the growth rate*. Why then should countries encourage high levels of investment if such investment makes no difference to the long-run growth rate?

The answer to this question is simple. While the investment rate makes no difference to the trend growth of the economy, it does influence the *level* of the steady state capital stock. The more investment a country does, the higher its steady state standard of living.

To see this, imagine two countries, one of which invests 20% of its output and the other 30%, as in Figure 4.13. Otherwise both countries are identical—they have access to the same production function, have the same population, and the same depreciation rate. For both countries their steady state occurs at the point at which investment equals depreciation—K_L for the low investment rate country and K_H for the high investment country. Therefore the level of output in the low investment country is Y_L, substantially below Y_H. Countries with low investment rates will therefore have a lower standard of living (measured by GDP per capita) than countries with high investment rates. Low investment rates can only fund a low level of maintenance, so the steady state occurs at a low capital stock and, via the production function, at a low output level. However, at the steady state, both countries will be growing at the same rate—the rate at which technological improvements lead to improvements in the production function. Therefore, while long-term growth rates are independent of the investment rate, the *level* of GDP per capita is definitely related to the amount of investment. As Figure 4.14 shows, the implication that high investment countries are wealthier than low investment countries is supported across a wide range of economies.

KEY POINT

The higher the investment rate of a country, the greater its steady state capital stock and its output level.

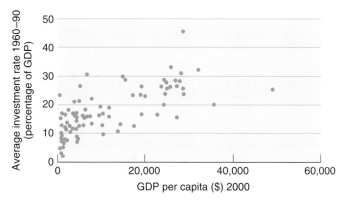

FIGURE 4.14   **Output and investment in the world economy.** Higher investment countries tend to have higher incomes—each point represents the income level in 2000 of a country mapped against its average investment rate from the previous 40 years. *Source:* Summers, Heston, and Aten, Penn World Table 6.1, http://www.nput.econ.nperr.edu

THE LONG RUN IS A LONG TIME COMING

Decreasing marginal product of capital and the concept of a steady state suggest that in the long run a country's growth rate is independent of its investment. But the experience of Asia over the last few decades (see Figure 4.15) is hard to square with this—countries with the highest investment rates have had the fastest GDP growth.

To reconcile Figure 4.15 with the implications of decreasing marginal product of capital, we must stress that only in the steady state is growth independent of the investment rate. Consider the high and low investment countries of Figure 4.13. At K_L, the low investment country has no more scope for growth through capital accumulation—it is already at its steady state. However, also at K_L, the high investment country still has gross investment in excess of depreciation, so its capital stock will continue to rise until it reaches its steady state at K_H. Therefore, while the low investment rate country shows zero growth, the high investment rate country shows continual growth *while it is moving*

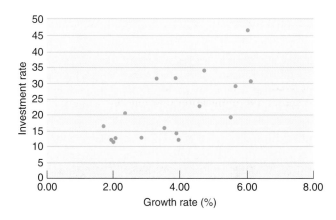

FIGURE 4.15   **Growth and investment in 17 Asian countries 1960–2000.** In developing Asian countries there has been a positive link between investment and growth. *Source:* Author's own calculations based on Summers and Heston, Penn World Table 6.1 and *World Economic Outlook* (April 2003) www.imf.org

toward its steady state. If the transition from K_L to K_H takes a long time (more than 25 years), then our model can still explain why investment and growth are strongly correlated.

Examining our model and using plausible numbers for investment rates and other key economic parameters shows that the movement from K_L to K_H does indeed take a long time. For instance, after 10 years only 40% of the distance between K_L and K_H has been traveled; after 20 years just under two-thirds of the gap has been reduced. Therefore decreasing marginal product of capital can explain correlations between investment and economic growth over long periods, as economies move to their steady state. This result also implies that if a country can raise its investment rate substantially it will benefit from higher GDP growth for several decades.

KEY POINT

In the steady state, long-run growth is independent of the investment rate. The transition to a steady state can take several decades and, during this period, higher investment countries will experience higher growth.

4.7   How Much Should a Country Invest?

The previous section showed that countries with high levels of investment will also have high levels of GDP per capita. Does this mean that countries should seek to maximize their investment rate?

THE GOLDEN RULE AND OPTIMAL LEVEL OF INVESTMENT

The answer to this question is no. Output per head is an imperfect measure of the standard of living. The trouble with investment is that for a given level of output, the more a country invests the less it can consume. For instance, an economy with an investment rate of 100% would have an enormous level of GDP per capita, but it would only produce investment goods. However, at the opposite extreme, an economy with an investment rate of zero would have high consumption today but low consumption in the future because depreciation would cause its capital stock to continually decline, leading to lower levels of future output. The situation is like that in the fishing industry. Overfishing reduces the stock of fish and diminishes the ability of the fish to breed, making future catches and thus also future consumption low. However, catching no fish at all would lead to a rapid increase in fish stocks but we would have none to eat. Ideally we want to catch enough fish every day to both sustain a constant stock and also provide enough for our consumption.

Economists have a similar concept in mind when they consider the ideal rate of investment. This ideal rate is called the "Golden Rule" rate of investment. We have shown that countries with different levels of investment have different steady states and so different levels of consumption. The Golden Rule compares all of these different steady states (i.e., examines different investment rates) and chooses the investment rate that delivers the highest consumption in the steady state.

If for simplicity we ignore the government sector and assume no trade, then from Chapter 2 we know that consumption must equal output less investment ($C = Y - I$). In the steady state, investment also equals depreciation ($I = dK$), so steady state consumption, C^{ss}, must equal output less depreciation ($C^{ss} = Y - dK$). According to the Golden Rule, the capital stock should be increased so long as steady state consumption also rises. Using our expression for steady state consumption, we can see that increases in capital boost consumption as they lead to higher output. Each extra unit of capital boosts output by the marginal product, so that steady state consumption—other things being equal—is increased by MPK. But other things are not equal because the addition of an extra unit of capital also increases depreciation by d, which tends to lower steady state consumption. Therefore the overall effect on steady state consumption from an increase in capital is

Change in steady state consumption from increase in capital

= Marginal Product of Capital − Depreciation Rate = MPK − d

For low levels of capital, MPK exceeds d and steady state consumption increases with the capital stock and higher investment. But as the capital stock increases, the marginal product of capital declines until eventually MPK = d. At this point, steady state consumption cannot be raised through higher investment. Further increases in the capital stock would decrease MPK to less than d—steady state consumption would be declining. Therefore the Golden Rule says that to maximize steady state consumption, the marginal product of capital should equal the depreciation rate.

What level of investment does the Golden Rule suggest is optimal? To answer this question, we need to make an assumption about the production function. We shall assume, as previously, that output is related to inputs via a Cobb-Douglas production function where $Y = TFP \times K^a L^{1-a}$. In Chapter 3, we stated this leads to:

MPK = aY/K

so that the Golden Rule implies that steady state consumption is maximized when

MPK = aY/K = d

However we also know that in the steady state, investment equals depreciation, or using our earlier assumptions

$I = bY = dK$ = depreciation

or

bY/K = d

Comparing the Golden Rule condition and this steady state definition, we can see they can only both be true when $a = b$. That is, when the term that influences the productivity of capital in the production function (a) equals the investment rate (b). When we discussed the Cobb-Douglas production function in Chapter 3, we showed how a was equal to the share of capital income in GDP, which empirically was around 30–35%. Therefore the Golden Rule suggests that the optimal investment rate is approximately 30–35% of GDP—investment at this rate leads to the steady state with the highest level of consumption.

TABLE 4.2   Investment as Percentage of GDP, 1965–2000

Country	Investment Rate	Country	Investment Rate	Country	Investment Rate
Algeria	22.8	Chile	16.1	Germany	26.1
Cameroon	8.2	Venezuela	23.1	Italy	26.6
Egypt	7.2	India	12.6	Netherlands	26.2
South Africa	14.2	Israel	31.4	Norway	32.8
Canada	24.8	Japan	33.9	Spain	26.4
Mexico	19.9	Singapore	46.6	Sweden	23.8
U.S.	21.0	Austria	28.5	U.K.	20.3
Argentina	19.2	Denmark	26.0	Australia	26.8
Brazil	22.5	France	27.2	New Zealand	23.6

Source: Author's calculation based on Summers and Heston, Penn World Table 6.1.

Table 4.2 shows average investment rates for a wide range of countries. Singapore, Norway, and Japan stand out as having high investment rates, and France, Germany, and Italy fare reasonably well, but the United States and the United Kingdom score poorly according to this test. The United States and the United Kingdom are underinvesting relative to the Golden Rule, and if this continues, they will eventually have a much lower future level of consumption than if they invested more (all other things being equal). We should stress that at this point we are assuming countries *only* differ in their level of investment, but in Chapter 5 we will consider many other ways in which they vary. One of these is in the quality of financial systems. Higher investment is only good for an economy if the financial system efficiently allocates investment to projects with a high rate of return.

KEY POINT

An investment rate of around 30–35% of GDP leads to steady states with high levels of consumption. Investment rates above or below this range lead to lower levels of steady state consumption—either because the capital stock is too low, which leads to low output, or capital stocks are so high that investment crowds out consumption.

ARE ECONOMIES EFFICIENT?

The Golden Rule suggests that an economy can have too much capital—the investment rate can be so high that maintaining the capital stock becomes a drain on consumption. A simple test determines whether economies are efficient, that is, whether they have too much capital.[2] If an economy is capital efficient, the operating profits of the corporate sector should be large enough to cover investment. If they are, then the corporate sector has been a provider of funds for consumption. But if investment exceeds profits,

[2] This test is explained in detail in "Assessing Dynamic Efficiency" by Abel, Mankiw, Summers, and Zeckhauser, *Review of Economic Studies* (1989), vol. 56, pp. 1–20.

TABLE 4.3 **Contribution of Capital Sector to Consumption**
(Cashflow less investment [less depreciation less residential investment] expressed as a percentage of GDP).

Year	U.S.	U.K.	South Korea	Germany	France
1984	8.8	5.3	14.6		5.3
1985	7.6	6	15.2		5.6
1986	7.1	5.4	16		8.1
1987	8.3	5.8	13.8		7.9
1988	8.6	5.5	12.9		7.8
1989	9	3.9	9.3		8.1
1990	8.3	2.5	3.6		7.5
1991	8.3	2.9	2.9	4.1	6.6
1992	8.3	6	2.8	3.2	6.8
1993	8.8	9	3.2	4.1	6.6
1994	10	10.7	4	6.9	9.2
1995	9.7	10.2	2.5	8.3	9.4
1996	9.9	10.3	0.6	9.6	9

Source: OECD *National Accounts Volume II 1998.* Copyright OECD.

then the capital stock has been financed at the expense of consumption. Table 4.3 shows, for a sample of OECD countries, the value of profits less investment relative to GDP. In every case the number is positive, suggesting that these countries' stock of capital is not too high. However, the South Korean numbers are particularly interesting. By the end of the sample period, the South Korean capital stock was close to becoming a drain on the personal sector—a point we shall return to when we consider the Asian crisis in Chapter 21.

 4.8 The Asian Miracle—A Case Study in Capital Accumulation?

RAPID SOUTHEAST ASIAN GROWTH

This chapter has focused only on the contribution capital accumulation makes to economic growth. It is useful to see how far this framework helps explain the dramatic economic growth in Southeast Asia.[3] Table 4.4 lists real GDP per capita for a variety of OECD and Asian economies. In 1950, the wealthiest Asian country was Singapore,

[3] In 1997 this region suffered a major financial and currency crisis (described in Chapter 21) that seriously disrupted GDP growth, so we exclude this period from our assessment of the Asian growth miracle.

TABLE 4.4 **Real GDP Per Person in 1950, 1973, and 2002 (Constant Prices, 1990 $)**

Country	1950	1973	2002
U.S.	9573	17593	26781
Switzerland	8939	16607	23913
U.K.	6847	13494	24198
Sweden	6738	13416	24782
Denmark	6683	13152	22786
Netherlands	5850	12940	22586
Norway	5403	12763	22029
Belgium	5346	11992	22216
France	5221	11905	21064
West Germany	4281	11308	19761
Finland	4131	11017	22043
Austria	3731	10768	20077
Italy	3425	10409	19329
Ireland	3325	10229	26830
Spain	2397	8739	20243
Portugal	2132	7779	18476
Singapore	2038	7568	17164
Hong Kong	1962	7023	15795
Greece	1951	6768	15702
Japan	1873	5412	13264
Malaysia	1696	3669	12410
Philippines	1293	3167	11867
Taiwan	922	2840	9297
Korea	876	1956	7524
Indonesia	874	1750	4277
Thailand	848	1538	3377
China	614	1186	3549

Source: Crafts, *East Asian Growth Before and After the Crisis*, IMF Working Paper 98/137 and IMF WEO Database 2003.

which was ranked seventeenth in our sample—slightly richer than the poorest European nation, Greece. Between 1950 and 1976, the European nations approximately doubled their level of GDP per capita, but the Asian economies performed substantially better and this fast growth continued for the remainder of the twentieth century, although punctuated by a severe crisis in 1997. The most impressive growth occurred from 1973 to 2000 when the level of GDP per capita rose almost fourfold in Singapore; in less than one generation its standard of living quadrupled. Most of the Southeast Asian economies experienced similar large increases in the standard of living. By con-

TABLE 4.5 Asian Investment Rates, 1960–2000 (% GDP)

Hong Kong	Japan	Korea	Malaysia	Philippines	Singapore	Thailand	Taiwan
28.9	33.9	30.5	22.7	16.3	46.7	31.5	19.2

Source: Summers, Heston, and Aten, Penn World Table 6.1,
http://www.nput.econ.nperr.edu

trast, OECD nations saw relatively little growth—although Ireland and Norway both doubled their standard of living, most other European countries had only a 20–40% improvement.

The dramatic growth experienced in this region is the major success amongst emerging economies since 1950, and attempting to repeat it elsewhere remains the ultimate aim of development economics. In 1960 South Korea and Taiwan had a similar standard of living to Senegal, Ghana, and Mozambique. Between 1960 and 1990, these African countries had static or declining standards of living, whereas the Asian standards of living increased six- or seven-fold. What made these Asian Tigers grow so fast?

A GROWTH ACCOUNTING APPROACH—WHERE'S THE MIRACLE?

The production function implies that to increase output it is necessary to increase either labor, capital, or TFP. The Southeast Asian nations are certainly characterized by high rates of increases in factor inputs. Table 4.5 shows investment rates for the region, all of which are extremely high compared with the OECD rates listed in Table 4.2. Table 4.6 shows employment growth for a variety of countries and illustrates a rapid increase in this variable for Southeast Asia as well. While OECD countries were experiencing a

TABLE 4.6 Employment Growth
(Percentage change in hours worked per person between 1973 and 1996)

Country	Average Growth	Country	Average Growth
Austria	−2.1	Switzerland	−11.0
Belgium	−17.4	U.K.	−11.3
Denmark	−5.3	West Germany	−19.1
Finland	−18.7	Hong Kong	11.8
France	−23.4	Indonesia	19.8
Greece	−11.5	Japan	−8.3
Ireland	−18.5	Korea	37.7
Italy	−17.9	Philippines	−12.5
Netherlands	−14.4	Singapore	36.8
Norway	−5.8	Taiwan	6.2
Portugal	11.1	Thailand	13.1
Spain	−31.7	U.S.	19.0
Sweden	−7.5		

Source: Crafts, "East Asian Growth Before and After the Crisis," IMF Working Paper 98/137, 1996.

declining birth rate and sometimes falling populations, the proportion of the Southeast Asian population aged between 15 and 64 years—the crucial working age population—was increasing rapidly.

In a controversial study, Alwyn Young claimed that a growth accounting exercise for these fast-growing Southeast Asian economies suggests that growth was almost entirely due to this increase in capital and labor (see Figure 4.16). We can think of this region as a case study in capital accumulation—for each country, the most important factor behind economic growth has been capital. Only in Hong Kong did TFP contribute a substantial amount to economic growth. In Singapore, Young calculates that TFP growth has actually been negative. In other words, Singapore should have witnessed an even larger increase in GDP given the extraordinary increase in capital and labor that occurred. Young suggests this negative TFP growth is a result of Singapore's ambitious development plans. The government intervened in many facets of the economy—from the provision of compulsory savings via the pension scheme to choosing which industries to develop. As a result, the industrial structure has frequently changed, with the economy moving from textiles to electrical goods to financial services and currently to the IT and communications industry. Young argues that this frequent reorientation of the economy has been a source of inefficiency. Rather than learn how to optimally exploit the technology of the existing industrial structure, Singapore has grown through massive investment in new industries. As a result, it has had minimal TFP growth.

Young's findings have generated much debate. Subsequent studies argued that Young's calculations were incorrect and that TFP growth had actually been far more substantial for Singapore.[4] If true, Young's result puts the Asian growth "miracle" in a different perspective. For mature industrialized economies at their steady state, the im-

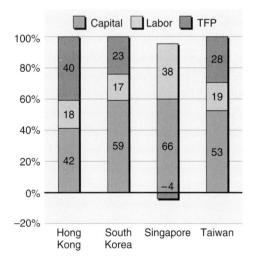

FIGURE 4.16 **Growth accounting for Asian Tigers, 1966–90.** Increases in inputs of labor and capital accounted for most of the growth of the Asian Tigers over the period when they increased output most rapidly. *Source:* Young, "Tyranny of Numbers: Confronting the Statistical Realities of the East Asian Growth Experience," *Quarterly Journal of Economics* (1985) vol. 110, pp. 641–680.

[4] Collins and Bosworth, "Economic Growth in East Asia: Accumulation versus Assimilation," Brookings Papers in Economic Activity (1996) vol. 2, pp. 135–91; and Sarel "Growth and Productivity in ASEAN Countries," IMF Working Papers 97/97, 1997.

portant source of growth is TFP—these nations have already achieved their growth through capital accumulation. If anything is mysterious about economic growth, it surely relates to this TFP category. Increasing output by increasing factor inputs via capital accumulation or increases in employment is not a miraculous process. However, growth through TFP means that economies can produce more output even without using extra factor inputs. Young's calculations suggest that as far as TFP growth is concerned, the advanced nations may not have much to learn from the Asian Tigers. There may, however, be more pertinent lessons for emerging countries in this growth miracle. The experience of the Asian countries shows that through increasing investment rates and rapid employment growth it is possible to experience extremely rapid rates of growth of around 7% per decade. Through these high investment rates, these countries managed to telescope into 30 years the growth that took established industrial countries around 100 years to achieve. They therefore set a guide as to the fastest possible growth for developing economies.

KEY POINT

Southeast Asia achieved rapid economic growth over a 30 year period mainly as a result of substantial increases in capital and, to a lesser extent, employment. Total factor productivity contributed relatively little. It can be thought of as a case study of capital accumulation.

DOES IT MATTER?

Does it matter if increases in factor inputs drove Southeast Asian economic growth? At one level, the answer is no—the huge increases in the standard of living these economies attained cannot be denied. That Singapore now has one of the highest standards of living in the world is not a statistical mirage. On the other hand, it does matter, for two reasons. The first is to emphasize that this growth has not been miraculous but has required sacrifices. Singapore has such high levels of capital today because it had high investment rates in previous decades. Lower consumption in previous decades paid for current prosperity. The current generation of Singaporeans are benefiting from these sacrifices, but their high standard of living has come at a cost.

The second reason for concern is the implications that decreasing marginal product of capital have for future economic growth in the region. If technology is characterized by decreasing marginal product of capital, then the Asian Tigers will eventually reach their steady state if they are not already there. Figure 4.17 shows Young's calculations of the marginal product of capital and suggests that by the end of the 1980s, decreasing marginal product had already set in. Because of their high investment rates, this steady state will be at high levels of output per head. However, once at this steady state, the economy will cease to grow very fast through capital accumulation, and instead these countries will have to pay attention to the factors that drive TFP. This is clearly recognized by governments in the region, as revealed by the following quote from the Singaporean government website: *Singapore has recognised the need to deregulate closed sectors and shift into a knowledge-based economy*. In other words, Singapore is aiming to place a greater emphasis on technology and efficiency gains. Just because Singapore, according to Young's calculations, has no history of strong TFP growth does not mean it cannot produce strong TFP growth in the future.

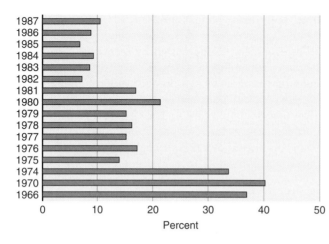

FIGURE 4.17 **Real return on capital in Singapore.** As the capital stock grew, the rate of return on capital in Singapore trended down. *Source:* Young, "Tyranny of Numbers: Confronting the Statistical Realities of the East Asian Growth Experience," *Quarterly Journal of Economics* (1985) vol. 110, pp. 641–680.

4.9 China—A Big Tiger

The previous section suggested that Southeast Asia grew rapidly because of a substantial increase in factor inputs based around high investment rates and a fast-growing population. The result has been a huge increase in the standard of living of these countries. However, while these economies have grown substantially, they remain small-to-medium-sized economies due to the size of their population. For instance, South Korea has a population of 47.3 million, while Hong Kong and Singapore have only 6.7 million and 4.1 million, respectively. Therefore the rapid growth in these countries has not substantially affected the world's economy. However, the same cannot be said of China with its enormous population of 1.3 billion. China seems to be embarking on the same growth pattern as Southeast Asia 30 years ago, with a huge increase in population and employment (see Table 4.7), high levels of investment (see Figure 4.18), and a substantial shift of resources from agriculture into industry. The result has been rapid rates of growth (see Figure 4.19) suggesting that China may be able to repeat a similarly rapid economic transformation as the other East Asian economies. Table 4.8 shows a growth

TABLE 4.7 **Chinese Employment Growth**

Years	Percentage Growth
1980–85	17.7
1986–90	28.1
1990–95	6.3
1996–97	2.4

Source: International Financial Statistics, IMF.

TABLE 4.8 **Growth Accounting for China**

	1953–77	1978–99
Physical capital	3.66	4.69
Labor quantity	1.05	1.36
Human capital	2.12	1.34
TFP	−0.37	2.31
Total GDP	6.46	9.72

Source: Wang and Yao, "Sources of Chinese Economic Growth 1952–99," World Bank Discussion Paper (July 2001).

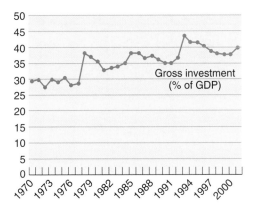

FIGURE 4.18 **Chinese investment rate.** Chinese growth is supported by extremely high investment rates. *Source:* IMF International Financial Statistics.

accounting analysis for China and reveals a similar pattern to the other fast growing Asian economies. The vast majority of growth arises from increases in factor inputs rather than TFP, although the switch from socialist economic policies to market based ones that began in 1978 has seen a growing role for TFP.

Naturally a proper analysis of future growth prospects in China requires a much deeper examination than just focusing on investment rates. China faces many difficulties if it is to continue growing at this rate—in particular the need to shift an enormous part of the economy from state-controlled means of production and distribution to more market-oriented systems. Moreover, tensions over the weakness of China's financial system, in particular its banks, and the conflict between economic reform and the political status quo are growing. Pollution is also a major problem. All this means that Chinese economic growth is not guaranteed and that future economic growth may be volatile. However, China is pursuing a development path similar to that of the Asian Tigers of 30 years ago—large capital accumulation and increases in employment. Our analysis suggests that China can produce decades of fast growth based solely on high capital accumulation rather than reliance on technological progress. China will not need to focus on improving TFP to improve its standard of living for many years.

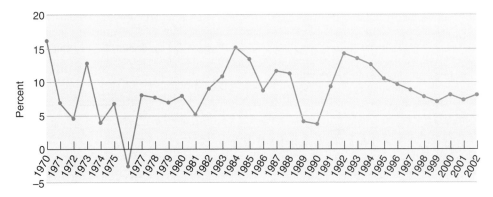

FIGURE 4.19 **Chinese GDP growth.** Chinese GDP is growing at a sustained rate of 7–10% per annum and displaying rapid convergence with OECD nations. *Source:* IMF International Financial Statistics.

> **K E Y   P O I N T**
>
> Although China faces many difficult issues before its development process is complete, it would appear to be showing a magnified version of the growth seen earlier in Southeast Asia—rapid GDP growth rates produced by high levels of investment and high employment growth.

SUMMARY

This chapter has examined the link between the capital stock and the standard of living and economic growth. In Section 4.1 we reviewed a concept central to our discussion: the marginal product of capital—the additional output that investment in a new machine brings. The marginal product of capital can be either increasing, constant, or decreasing. We discussed the consequences of assuming decreasing marginal product of capital whereby each new machine leads to a smaller increase in output than the last machine.

In Section 4.2, the assumption of decreasing marginal product of capital was used to show how interest rates keep savings and investment balanced over the long run.

In Section 4.3, we showed how the assumption of decreasing marginal product implies that capital-poor countries will grow faster than capital-rich ones, so that countries or regions will show convergence.

In Section 4.4, we saw that decreasing marginal product also implies that wealthier countries will depend more on TFP improvements than on capital accumulation.

In Section 4.5, we explained the reasons why, eventually, under decreasing marginal product, countries will arrive at a steady state where investment equals depreciation—where for a given investment rate, a country cannot grow any further through capital accumulation, and growth is due either to improvements in TFP or increases in employment.

In Section 4.6, we saw that the steady state level of capital depends crucially on the investment rate—the higher the investment rate is, the larger the steady state capital stock and the higher the level of output.

Section 4.7 introduced the Golden Rule of investment. Using the Golden Rule, we can show that an investment rate between 30–35% of GDP leads to steady states with high levels of consumption.

In section 4.8, we considered the dramatic growth of Southeast Asia between 1960 and 1995 and argued that this was mostly due to factor accumulation, in particular, high investment rates. If true, this implies that growth in this region will slow down in coming years.

Finally, in section 4.9 we considered a much larger economy, China, which appears to be repeating the same general growth pattern—high investment and employment growth leading to rapid output growth.

CONCEPTUAL QUESTIONS

1. (Section 4.1) Consider separately the case of decreasing, constant, and increasing marginal product of capital and where investors can either invest in a bank account and earn interest rate R or invest in the capital stock of a country. Using a diagramatic analysis, examine in each case where investors will place their funds and the implications for convergence.

2. (4.1) What technologies might experience increasing marginal product of capital? Do they experience increasing marginal product over all ranges?

3. (4.2) Using Figure 4.4 show what happens to interest rates, investment, and savings when (a) there is a downward reassessment to the productivity of capital and (b) a demographic shift whereby the proportion of 45–64 year olds increases (an age group with high savings).

4. (4.3) After World War II, Germany experienced rapid growth in output from relatively little investment. But between 1913 and 1929 its GDP growth was on average 0.1% and showed no such sharp recovery from World War I. What might explain these differences?

5. (4.8) What can mature industrialized nations learn from the rapid growth of Southeast Asian nations?

6. (4.9) In 2002 the U.S. economy measured $10.4 trillion, Japan $4.2 trn, Germany $1.9 trn, and China $1.22 trn. Assuming trend growth of 2.5% in the three OECD nations, how long until China overtakes them if it grows at 5% per annum? 7%? 9%?

ANALYTICAL QUESTIONS

1. (Section 4.1) Use a spreadsheet to consider the following Cobb-Douglas production function where $Y = TFP \times L^{0.7} K^a$. The marginal product of capital is given by $a \times Y/K$. Setting TFP and $L = 1$, examine the behaviour of the MPK as it varies between 0.3 and 1.

2. (4.5) The steady state level of consumption in an economy (C^{ss}) is equal to steady state output (Y^{ss}) minus steady state depreciation. The latter is the depreciation rate (d) times the steady state capital stock (K^{ss}). We assume here that there is no technological progress. Thus

$$C^{ss} = Y^{ss} - d\,K^{ss}$$

What is the impact on steady state consumption of a small increase in the steady state capital stock? What level of investment maximizes the steady state rate of consumption?

3. (4.6) Use the Cobb-Douglas production function of question 1 where a = 0.3 and a depreciation rate of 0.1. Examine the steady state outcomes of an economy that invests 20% and 30% of GDP. How many periods would it take for an economy with a 20% investment rate to reach its new steady state if it increases its investment rate to 30%?

4. (4.7) Consider the economy of question 3 and compare the steady state level of consumption as you change the investment rate. Show that the Golden Rule result of setting the investment rate equal to a in the production function optimises consumption in the steady state.

5. (4.7) The simple Golden Rule says that the optimal level of capital is one where the marginal product of capital equals the depreciation rate. If people attach less weight to the enjoyment they get from consumption in the future than consumption today, then does it make sense to abide by the Golden Rule? Is there a better rule? If such an economy ever found itself with the Golden Rule level of capital, should it preserve the capital stock by setting gross investment equal to depreciation?

Total Factor Productivity, Human Capital, and Technology

Overview

In order to account for the magnitude of cross-country differences in income and to better explain the evolution of GDP per capita over time, we extend our model of capital accumulation to include changes in Total Factor Productivity (TFP). We focus in particular on the role of human capital and institutions in influencing the wealth of nations. We show how countries with high TFP not only produce more output from a given capital stock but will also choose a higher level of steady state capital. We then introduce technological progress into our analysis and show how this leads to the continual evolution of the steady state so that even rich nations experience persistent growth. We examine the role of Foreign Direct Investment in transferring technology and assess the claims of the New Economy to be a third Industrial Revolution.

Key Concepts

Corruption	Institutions	Social Capital
Foreign Direct Investment (FDI)	New Economy	Technological Progress
Human Capital	Rent Seeking	Total Factor Productivity (TFP)
Information and Communications Technology		

5.1 The Role of Total Factor Productivity

So far, **Total Factor Productivity** has reflected the influence of *any* factor that affects output other than capital accumulation or labor input. In this chapter we examine the role of TFP and explicitly identify some of its influences. Allowing for variations in TFP enables us to better explain the wide variations in GDP per capita rather than having to rely solely upon capital accumulation.

Consider an economy that increases its efficiency in producing output from a given level of capital: it increases its TFP. This increase might arise from an improvement in education or as a result of an improvement in technology, which is the example shown in Figure 5.1. As shown in Figure 5.1, this leads to the production function shifting upwards—for a given level of capital, the higher level of TFP enables more output to be produced (B instead of A). Therefore one reason why GDP per capita varies so much across countries is differences in TFP. Countries that use effectively the latest technology and possess the most efficient social organizations will produce the highest level of output from a given level of capital—they will be on the TFP frontier. But only a few countries will be on this frontier—for other countries, geography may have an adverse effect on the economy, corruption may be rampant, or vested interests in society may prevent the adoption of new technologies.

Returning to Figure 5.1, we can see another implication for countries with higher TFP. The upward shift in the production function that comes from higher TFP means that even if a country does not change its investment rate, it can reach a higher steady state. Recall from Chapter 4 that the steady state capital stock is the point where investment equals depreciation. Higher TFP means more output and so, for the same percentage investment rate, the country can provide more investment and can thus cover a larger amount of depreciation. Therefore, a higher level of TFP enables a higher steady state level of capital to be supported. Thus countries with high TFP will have higher levels of output not only from the upward shift in the production function but also because of the increase in the steady state of capital stock.

KEY POINT

Increases in TFP boost GDP through two channels: (1) the direct effect of the upward shift in the production function so that, for given capital, firms can produce more output, and (2) an indirect effect whereby, for the same investment rate, an increase in TFP leads to an increase in steady state capital and output.

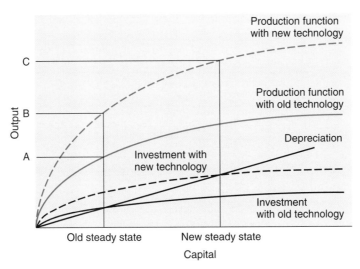

FIGURE 5.1 **The impact of TFP on output.** Technical progress increases output directly (A→B) and has a further effect (B→C) through its impact upon the steady state capital stock.

5.2   Human Capital

HUMAN CAPITAL AND ECONOMIC GROWTH

So far, our production function has only allowed a role for labor in terms of hours worked. There is another way that labor can contribute, though, and that is through **human capital**. Human capital refers to the skills and knowledge that accumulate over time in individuals, the labor force, and society. Many different skills make up human capital—learning acquired at school, on the job training, learning by doing, and shared social knowledge and conventions. Like physical capital and unlike hours worked, human capital is durable—it can provide benefits over several periods. Being durable, it can be increased by investment, such as in education or training. Sadly, human capital can also be decreased through depreciation: How much of this chapter will you remember tomorrow? Next year?

By introducing human capital into our model, we now have three factors of production—physical capital, human capital, and hours worked. In addition, we still have a TFP term reflecting all other influences. This TFP term is different from that in Chapter 4, as we have now explicitly included human capital as a factor of production, leaving a diminished role for TFP. Allowing for education extends our growth model in three main ways.

1. Using Figure 5.1, the effect of boosting human capital is to shift the production function so that more output can be produced for a given level of physical capital. We should expect countries with high human capital to produce higher levels of GDP per capita, exactly what is shown in Figure 5.2.
2. From Figure 5.1 we can see that countries that boost their human capital will see an improvement in their steady state. This means that mature industrialized economies, such as the OECD nations, that have reached their steady state can still produce growth if they can improve their human capital and so boost the

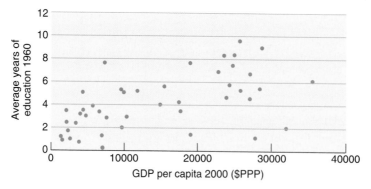

FIGURE 5.2   **Education and the standard of living.** There is a strong correlation between the amount of education and the standard of living. *Source:* Barro and Lee, International Data on Educational Attainment, Harvard University CID Working Paper 42 (2002) and Penn World Tables 6.1.

TABLE 5.1 Contribution of Education to Annual Output Growth 1950–90
Human capital helps explain long-run trend growth.

	France	Germany	Japan	U.K.	U.S.
Annual Growth (%)	5.04	5.92	9.27	3.03	3.65
Capital	2.40	3.19	4.33	2.40	1.62
Labor—Hours	−0.09	0.01	0.89	−0.09	0.58
Labor—Skills	0.39	0.19	0.52	0.20	0.48
Total Factor Productivity	2.34	2.53	3.53	0.52	0.97

Source: Crafts, "Productivity Growth Reconsidered," *Economic Politics* (1991) vol. 15, pp. 387–426.

steady state. Table 5.1 shows an extended growth accounting exercise for OECD countries that allows for human capital. While the contributions to growth of capital accumulation and TFP dominate, differences in human capital (here denoted "Labor—Skills") do play an important role in explaining growth rates.

3. Adding human capital to our model helps provide a richer story about investment flows between countries. If countries differ only in their capital stocks and have identical TFP, then diminishing marginal product of capital implies that investment should flow to predominantly poor countries. For instance, if the only difference between countries was in their capital stock, then the MPK in India would be 58 times higher than in the United States.[1] In response to such enormous differences, we would expect huge investment flows from the United States to India. However, these simply do not occur. This suggests that there are other influences on the U.S. MPK that offset the influence of diminishing returns. Examining Figure 5.3, we can see that higher human capital in the United States could fulfill this role. Differences in the level of human capital between the United States and India (see Table 5.2) mean that the United States is characterized by the higher MPK schedule so that, for any given level of capital, investment earns a higher return in the United States than India. Because of the

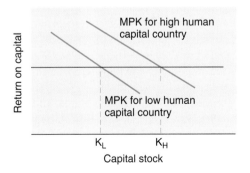

FIGURE 5.3 **Effect of education on the marginal product of capital.** Differences in education can explain why investment still flows to rich countries.

[1] R. E. Lucas, "Why doesn't capital flow from rich to poor countries?" *American Economic Review* (1990) pp. 92–96.

TABLE 5.2   **Average Years of Schooling in 2000 (Population Aged over 15)**
There exist substantial differences in education across countries.

U.S.	12.1	Japan	9.5	Italy	7.2	Nicaragua	4.6
New Zealand	11.7	Ireland	9.4	Mexico	7.2	Kenya	4.2
Canada	11.6	Netherlands	9.4	Malaysia	6.8	Ghana	3.9
Australia	10.9	U.K.	9.4	China	9.8	Pakistan	3.9
South Korea	10.9	Hungary	9.1	Botswana	6.3	Vietnam	3.8
Germany	10.2	Argentina	8.8	South Africa	6.1	Uganda	3.5
Poland	9.8	France	7.9	Egypt	5.1	Tanzania	2.7
Denmark	9.7	Chile	7.6	India	5.1	Singapore	7.0
Israel	9.6	Spain	7.3	Brazil	4.9		

Source: Barro and Lee, *International Data on Educational Attainment*, Harvard University
CID Working Paper 42 (2002).

differences in human capital, both countries face the same return on investment
when India has capital stock K_L and the United States has K_H. Human capital
offsets the effects of diminishing marginal product of capital and helps explain
why investment doesn't flow heavily to only low capital stock countries.

KEY POINT

Differences in human capital help explain output differences across countries—high human capital
produces more output and increases the steady state. Continual improvements in education can help
achieve long-run growth even in the capital rich OECD nations. High levels of human capital can offset the
impact of diminishing marginal product of capital and help explain why investment still flows into capital-
rich countries.

INCREASING HUMAN CAPITAL

Figure 5.4 shows total government expenditure on education for a range of countries. It is
noticeable that richer countries spend a greater proportion of their GDP on education
compared to poorer nations. Because their GDP is also larger, these richer countries
clearly spend much greater amounts per person on education—for instance, in 2001 the
Netherlands spent $6192 per student, compared to $228 in Peru and $592 in South Africa.

While this section has shown that increasing human capital is important for growth,
it is perhaps too easy to say that education matters for growth—it also matters what education is provided, how governments allocate their expenditure funds, and how that
education is used. For instance, between 1960 and 1985, sub-Saharan Africa increased
its human capital at an annual rate of 4.25%, much faster than East Asia whose human
capital grew at 2.8%. However, this faster growth in human capital did not translate
into more rapid growth—Africa saw annual growth of 0.6% compared to 4.1% in East
Asia.

Figure 5.5 shows one reason why developing countries have seen disappointing returns from their educational expenditure—their efficiency in education expenditure is

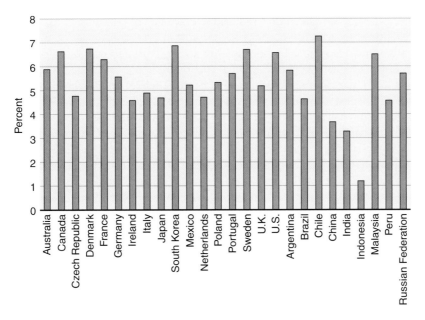

FIGURE 5.4 **Government expenditure on education (% GDP, 2000).** Richer countries spend a greater proportion of GDP on education. *Source:* OECD.

low. The efficiency index is 100 if no students drop out of school during the year or if no students are repeating a year of schooling for which they have previously enrolled. Dropouts and repetitions in part reflect the quality of schooling being offered. They also reflect the cost to students and their families, not only in terms of fees but, more importantly, in terms of foregone income that can be earned outside of school, for instance, through helping to harvest crops.

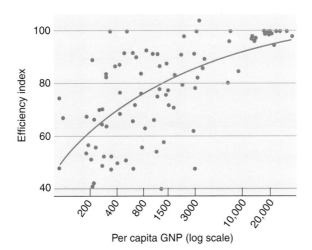

FIGURE 5.5 **Relationship between GNP per capita and schooling efficiency.** (Efficiency Index = 100 if no dropout or repetitions) Low income countries experience high dropout rates from school and inefficient education expenditure. *Source:* Mingat and Tan, *The Mechanics of Progress in Education,* World Bank Discussion Paper 2015 (November 1998).

Other problems also exist that reduce the efficiency of educational expenditure in poorer countries. In rich OECD countries, the cost of providing a year of education for a university student is around 18 times that for a year of primary school. In poor nations the ratio is much higher—around 89. On average most countries spend around 15–20% of average GDP per capita on each child at primary school, although this tends to be higher for the richest economies. The situation for tertiary education is very different, with poorer countries spending around 1000% of average GDP per capita on each college student, compared to around 100% for richer nations. From the national perspective, this suggests poorer nations should focus more on primary education and that money spend on tertiary education may produce a lower return. The inefficiencies from this allocation of educational expenditure are further worsened if rich countries accept these college educated individuals as immigrants, leading to a "brain drain" from the poorer countries.

So what forms of educational expenditure are most effective at increasing human capital? This is the critical question in how government educational policies can help boost long-run growth. Table 5.3 shows a survey of several studies of developing

TABLE 5.3   **Determinants of Efficient Education Expenditure**
Teacher salaries and pupil–teacher ratios do not seem to be strongly correlated with educational performance. First column shows number of studies considered, second column shows number of studies where variable listed is important, third column expresses this as a percentage.

	Number of Studies	Positive and Significant Relation	Confirmation Percentage
Primary Schools			
Teacher's salary level	11	4	36.4
School–teacher pupil ratio	26	9	34.6
Teacher's years of schooling	18	9	50.0
Teacher's experience	23	13	56.5
Class instructional time	17	15	88.2
Class frequency of homework	11	9	81.8
School library	18	16	88.9
School textbooks	26	19	73.1
Secondary schools			
Teacher's salary level	11	2	18.2
School–teacher pupil ratio	22	2	9.1
Teacher's experience	12	1	8.3
Class instructional time	16	12	75.0
School textbooks	13	7	53.8

Source: Fuller and Clarke, *How to Raise the Effectiveness of Secondary Schools? Universal and Locally Tailored Investment Strategies.* Educational and Social Policy Discussion Paper Series No. 28 (Washington, DC: The World Bank, 1994).

economies. The survey examined in what percentage of research studies particular features have been shown to have improved human capital. While this is a contentious area, it is interesting to note that raising teacher salaries and reducing class sizes are not guaranteed to be effective means of improving educational performance. Instead, instructional time in class seems to be the factor that contributes most, at both the elementary and secondary levels.

 ## Total Factor Productivity

EMPIRICAL IMPORTANCE OF TFP

Our model can now account for differences in GDP per capita through variations across countries in physical and human capital. However, Figure 5.6 shows there still remains a substantial role for TFP in explaining the wealth of nations. Figure 5.6 suggests that if a country has high TFP, it is highly likely that it also has high productivity and GDP *even without knowing the country's physical and human capital.* Table 5.4 develops this theme by examining how much of productivity differences can be accounted for through variations in physical and human capital and TFP. Output per worker in India is 9% of the level of the United States. If India had the same level of TFP and educational achievement as the United States but differed only in capital stock, then its output per worker would be 71% of that of the United States. If the only difference between the countries was educational achievement, then Indian output would be 45% of the U.S. level. However, the most important factor explaining differences in output per worker in the United States and India is total factor productivity. Even if India had the same capital stock and educational achievements as the United States, its output would only be 27% of the U.S. level. Therefore, low output in India is due not only to low factor inputs but also to the relative inefficiency with which India uses these factor inputs. As Figure 5.6 shows, this finding is not restricted to India—differences in total factor productivity can account for much of the differences in output per worker across countries.

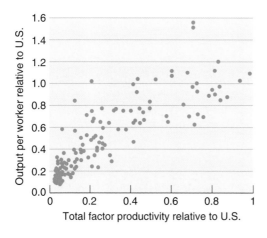

FIGURE 5.6 **Output and TFP across countries.** Differences in TFP account for major differences in GDP. *Source:* Hall and Jones, *Why do Some Countries Produce So Much More Output Per Worker Than Others?* NBER Working Paper 6564. *The Quarterly Journal of Economics* (1999) Vol. 114. No. 1, pp. 83–116. © by the President and Fellows of Harvard College and the Massachusetts Institute of Technology.

TABLE 5.4   **Explaining Differences in Output per Head**
Variations in capital and education can account for only some of the cross-country variations in GDP per capita. Each column shows productivity in a country relative to the U.S. if the only difference from the U.S. was the factor input listed at the top.

	Capital	Education	TFP	Output per Worker
Canada	1.00	0.90	1.03	0.93
Italy	1.06	0.65	1.21	0.83
France	1.09	0.67	1.13	0.82
U.K.	0.89	0.81	1.01	0.73
Spain	1.02	0.61	1.11	0.68
Japan	1.12	0.80	0.66	0.59
Mexico	0.87	0.54	0.93	0.43
Korea	0.86	0.76	0.58	0.38
Iran	0.98	0.47	0.64	0.30
Chile	0.99	0.66	0.40	0.26
Peru	0.94	0.62	0.41	0.24
Egypt	0.45	0.58	0.72	0.19
Pakistan	0.58	0.39	0.57	0.13
India	0.71	0.45	0.27	0.09
Sudan	0.84	0.34	0.23	0.07
Lesotho	0.68	0.48	0.19	0.06
Kenya	0.75	0.46	0.17	0.06
Rwanda	0.44	0.34	0.29	0.04
Uganda	0.36	0.39	0.22	0.03

Source: Hall and Jones, "Why Do Some Countries Produce So Much More Output Per Worker Than Others?" *The Quarterly Journal of Economics* (1999) Vol. 114, No. 1, pp. 83–116. © by the President and Fellows of Harvard College and the Massachusetts Institute of Technology.

KEY POINT

Even after removing human capital from TFP, differences in TFP still account for substantial variation in GDP across countries.

THE IMPORTANCE OF INSTITUTIONS

Why do some countries use factor inputs more efficiently than others? The scope of factors that might influence TFP is huge—ranging from technology, government policy and legal institutions to sociocultural norms, religious beliefs, geography, and climate. The breadth of this list reveals that economic growth is not the sole province of economics.

One element of TFP that many economists, inspired by the work of Nobel Laureate Douglass North, feel is of critical importance is **institutions**. The definition of "institutions" is a broad one reflecting the "rules of the game" in society—that is the explicit and implicit behavioral norms that provide economic incentives to society. These institutions are not limited to government organizations existing in a building, but extend to a wide range of social behavior and influences.

Whilst this broad definition of institutions is important for understanding the mechanisms of economic growth, it makes it extremely difficult to find a reliable way of measuring the quality of institutions. For this reason, many researchers focus on a narrower concept relating to the role of government institutions concerning:

- *Property Rights*—Is there an independent legal system which upholds the rights of owners of private property?
- *Regulatory Institutions*—Do governments act to curb monopoly powers and abuse of workers and consumers?
- *Macroeconomic Stabilization*—Are there institutions, such as independent central banks and fiscal rules, that help achieve low and stable inflation, sustainable public finances, and low levels of unemployment?
- *Social Insurance*—Does the government provide for groups disadvantaged by geography, disease, famine, or other external circumstances? Does the government help achieve equal opportunities for broad segments of the population?
- *Conflict Management*—Do there exist political institutions that can legitimately arbitrate between inconsistent demands of different political or ethnic groups without producing conflict or rebellion?
- *Political Rights*—Are there sufficient constraints on the actions of powerful interest groups or political parties to stop them exploiting their power in ways harmful to the economy?

Because of the importance of institutions and governance, the World Bank has developed a range of indicators to measure their quality across countries. These measures of institutions reflect six themes:

1. *Voice and accountability*—a measure of civil liberties and political rights
2. *Political Stability and Lack of Violence*—a measure of the likelihood that the government will be overthrown by unconstitutional means
3. *Government Effectiveness*—a measure of the quality of public services and bureaucracy and the independence of the civil service
4. *Regulation Quality*—measured by the status of effective curbs on excessive bureaucracy, price distortions, and other market unfriendly policies
5. *Rule of Law*—measured by perceptions of incidence of crime, the predictability of the judiciary, and enforcement of contracts
6. *Corruption*—indicated by measures of bribe-taking and other corrupt behavior

The economic importance of these measures of institutional quality can be readily seen in Figure 5.7. High quality institutions, as measured by an average of these six indicators, produce higher levels of GDP per capita, faster growth rates, and less volatility in output.

While these results show the importance of institutions, they also raise two key issues relevant for emerging markets. The first is that, although institutions are widely

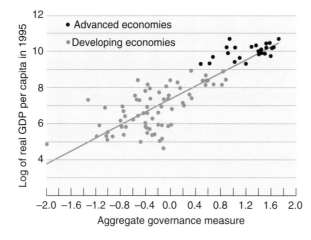

FIGURE 5.7 **Institutions matter.** Variations in institutions are strongly correlated with differences in GDP per capita. *Source:* IMF World Economic Outlook April 2003

recognized as being important, this does not mean there is widespread agreement as to what these institutions should look like. The type of institutions that succeed in a country may depend on the culture and history of the nation and be difficult to duplicate in another society. The institutions that successfully generate GDP growth in India and China, for example, may need to be different from those of the United States and Europe. The other implication is that, if economic growth depends upon adopting the "correct" institutional structure, then achieving economic success in emerging markets may be extremely difficult. It is relatively straightforward for a country to change its economic policies by, for example, increasing its education, privatizing its utilities, or reducing its trade barriers. Changing the underlying sociocultural norms that make up its institutional structure is much more difficult.

KEY POINT

A key determinant of TFP is institutions. The quality of governance, related to the rule of law and the absence of corruption, is a critical component of institutions.

RENT SEEKING AND CORRUPTION

Why are institutions so important? In Chapter 2 we showed how GDP is a measure of the value added that a society produces. We also saw how total income in society is equal to the value added produced. However, while society can only earn income by producing value added, the same is not true at the individual level. An individual can either earn income by making value added (what we will call being an entrepreneur) or through taking the value added someone else has produced, in which case they are a **rent seeker**. A classic example here might be the difference between a merchant (entrepreneur) and a pirate (rent seeker).

The ultimate sources of economic growth lie in innovation and in creating output. For the good of society as a whole, as few people as possible should engage in rent-seeking activity. Rent seeking lowers growth in three ways:

1. The rent-seeking sector absorbs labor that would otherwise go into entrepreneurial activities.
2. By earning income from the value added that entrepreneurs create, rent seekers act as a tax and decrease the supply of entrepreneurs.
3. If the rewards to rent seeking are high, the most talented people become rent seekers and the quality of entrepreneurs suffers.

The costs of rent seeking can be enormous. For instance, in 1980, rent seeking cost the Indian economy the equivalent of an estimated 30–45% of GDP and lowered Indian TFP growth by 2% per year between 1950 and 1980.[2]

As a leading social historian has commented, "It is often assumed that an economy of private enterprise has an automatic bias towards innovation, but this is not so. It has a bias only towards profit."[3] Institutions are needed to ensure that individuals do not engage in rent-seeking behavior, but rather they make profits in ways that increase the value added of their societies. The role of institutions in achieving this is profound and may, for instance, help explain why the Industrial Revolution happened in Western Europe in the eighteenth century rather than 400 years earlier in China. In 1400, China had a higher level of *per capita* output than Western Europe ($450 in 1985 prices compared to $400) and had introduced many innovations. Yet, by 1820, Chinese output was unchanged, while that of Europe had risen to $1050 and continued to rise throughout the Industrial Revolution.

One possible explanation for this poor performance is the allocation of talent in China and the weak social incentives to take part in entrepreneurial activity. As one author notes:

> *What was chiefly lacking in China for the further development of capitalism was not mechanical skill or scientific aptitude, nor a sufficient accumulation of wealth, but scope for individual enterprise. There was no individual freedom and no security for private enterprise, no legal foundation for rights other than those of the state, no alternative investment other than landed property, no guarantee against being penalized by arbitrary exactions from officials or against intervention by the state. But perhaps the supreme inhibiting factor was the overwhelming prestige of the state bureaucracy, which maimed from the start any attempt of the bourgeoisie to be different, to become aware of themselves as a class and fight for an autonomous position in society. Free enterprise, ready and proud to take risks, is therefore quite exceptional and abnormal in Chinese economic history.[4]*

Many economic historians believe that the Renaissance period in Western Europe—with its emphasis on rationality, individuality, and the introduction of a legal system recognizing individual property rights—provided exactly this scope for industrial enterprise and triggered the Industrial Revolution. The result was a social system

---

[2] Mohammed and Whalley, "Rent seeking in India: Its Costs and Policy Significance," *Kyklos* (1984) vol. 37, and Hamilton, Mohammed, and Whalley, "Applied General Equilibrium Analysis and Perspectives on Growth Performance," *Journal of Policy Modeling*, (1988) vol. 11.

[3] Hobsbawm, *Industry and Empire from 1750 to the Present Day* (Penguin: Harmondsworth 1969).

[4] Balazs, *Chinese Civilization and Bureaucracy* (New Haven: Yale University Press 1964).

that not only encouraged individuals to take up commercial activity to earn profit, but also encouraged higher output and greater productivity.

The above analysis assumes that it is fairly easy to identify a rent seeker and an entrepreneur, but this is not necessarily so. For instance, is a lawyer engaged in an expensive lawsuit concerning intellectual property rights a rent seeker or an entrepreneur? We shall, for fear of an expensive lawsuit, leave you to decide for yourself. Another question is whether or not rent seeking is a problem for modern industrialized economies. Researchers Murphy, Shleifer, and Vishny (to widespread amusement in the economics profession) actually do identify lawyers as rent seekers. They also identify engineers as entrepreneurs, and suggest the number of students enrolled in engineering courses as a measure of how much talent a society allocates towards value-added endeavors. Using these definitions, they studied the growth performance between 1960 and 1985 of 91 countries to determine the influence of student enrollments in engineering and law on economic growth. The results suggest that every 10% increase in engineering enrollments boosts growth by 0.5% and that every 10% increase in legal enrollments *lowers* growth by 0.3%. It would probably be unfair to change educational policy on the basis of these results (and one wonders what the analysis would be if either engineers or lawyers were replaced by MBA enrollments or economists with Ph.D.s), but it does suggest that rent seeking can become a problem for modern economies. What matters for growth is not just education, but the use that society makes of that education.

The presence of substantial raw materials in a country can lead to poor quality institutions. The advantage of natural resources is that they can be sold and the money raised used to increase the physical and human capital stock and so boost value added. The disadvantages are twofold. First, the revenues raised from raw materials open up plenty of opportunity for rent seeking and corruption to flourish. A society can expend more effort controlling its raw materials than creating value added, which can lead to conflicts. Second, governments are protected from the need to implement reforms to boost economic growth through their ability to use revenues raised from raw materials to subsidize inefficient low-income sectors of the economy. Some commentators even go so far as to discuss the "natural resource curse." This is shown dramatically in the case of Nigeria in Figure 5.8. In 1965 Nigerian GDP per capita was $245 and oil revenues were equivalent to $33 per person. By 2000, oil revenues had risen to $325 per person, and a total of $350bn had been earned in oil revenues over this time period, but GDP per capita remained at $245. Figure 5.8 shows why—the substantial oil revenues helped finance a dramatic increase in investment and education but led to a substantial worsening of TFP. Although GDP itself increased (as shown in Figure 5.8), it only grew in line with population so GDP per capita remained essentially unchanged. The net result was stagnant GDP per capita and rising inequality and poverty.

Corruption is a form of rent seeking that is present in many countries. It is not necessarily bad for an economy; it may even boost growth if it helps "oil the wheels of trade." However, empirical research suggests that, in general, corruption does adversely affect TFP and the level of output in an economy. Table 5.5 shows the most and least corrupt countries (as surveyed annually by Transparency International—www.transparency.org) and confirms that the least corrupt economies (10 is no corruption, 0 is complete corruption) are richer than the most corrupt. However, with international investment flows growing in importance, it should be remembered that it

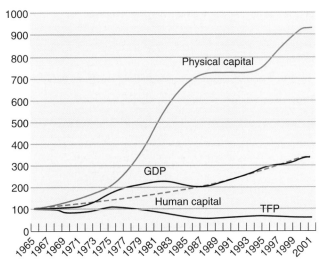

FIGURE 5.8 **Declining Nigerian TFP.** Declines in TFP offset the increases in investment and education so that Nigerian GDP shows only small increase. *Source:* Sala-I-Martin and Subramanian, *Addressing the Natural Resource Curse: An Illustration From Nigeria*, Working Paper 9804, http://www.nber.org/papers/w9804

TABLE 5.5 **Corruption Perceptions Index 2002**
(Rank of 1 means least corrupt, and 102 is the most corrupt in the survey.)

Rank	Amongst Countries		Rank	Amongst Countries	
1	Finland	9.7	81	Albania	2.5
2	Denmark	9.5		Guatemala	2.5
	New Zealand	9.5		Nicaragua	2.5
4	Iceland	9.4		Venezuela	2.5
5	Singapore	9.3	85	Georgia	2.4
	Sweden	9.3		Ukraine	2.4
7	Canada	9.0		Vietnam	2.4
	Luxembourg	9.0	88	Kazakhstan	2.3
	Netherlands	9.0	89	Bolivia	2.2
10	U.K.	8.7		Cameroon	2.2
11	Australia	8.6		Ecuador	2.2
12	Norway	8.5		Haiti	2.2
	Switzerland	8.5	93	Moldova	2.1
14	Hong Kong	8.2		Uganda	2.1
15	Austria	7.8	95	Azerbaijan	2.0
16	U.S.	7.7	96	Indonesia	1.9
17	Chile	7.5		Kenya	1.9
18	Germany	7.3	98	Angola	1.7
	Israel	7.3		Madagascar	1.7
20	Belgium	7.1		Paraguay	1.7
	Japan	7.1	101	Nigeria	1.6
	Spain	7.1	102	Bangladesh	1.2

Source: Transparency International.

TABLE 5.6   **Corruption Perceptions Index 2002**
Low index relflects greater likelihood of paying a bribe.

Rank	Amongst Countries		Rank	Amongst Countries	
1	Australia	8.5	11	Spain	5.8
2	Sweden	8.4	12	France	5.5
			13	U.S.	5.3
	Switzerland	8.4			
4	Austria	8.2		Japan	5.3
5	Canada	8.1	15	Malaysia	4.3
6	Netherlands	7.8			
				Hong Kong	4.3
	Belgium	7.8	17	Italy	4.1
8	U.K.	6.9	18	South Korea	3.9
9	Singapore	6.3	19	Taiwan	3.8
			20	China (People's Republic)	3.5
	Germany	6.3	21	Russia	3.2

Source: Transparency International.

is not just the nationality receiving the bribe that matters but also who pays the bribe. Table 5.6 shows, for a sample of countries, which nations have companies most likely to pay a bribe (10 being companies who do not pay bribes).

A final influence for TFP we shall consider is trust. While it is important to have a good rule of law, not every transaction can be enforced through legal means. For this reason, an indispensable part of a successful economy is trust between contractual partners. This aspect of institutions is captured in the concept of **social capital**—a cultural phenomenon denoting the extent of civic mindedness of members of a society and the degree of trust in public institutions. Societies marked by high social capital will also be marked by cooperation, and this is more likely to lead to higher value added activities rather than to rent seeking, corruption, and crime. The role of social capital has been invoked as one (amongst several) reason why the former Communist economies performed so poorly when they began the transition to capitalism. The transitions of these nations have often been characterized by disappointing GDP performance, although they had high levels of physical and human capital. However, they also scored poorly on institutional quality, especially corruption and financial systems. Figure 5.9 also shows that these economies were marked by relatively low rates of social capital compared to other nations—membership of civic societies and degree of trust are much lower in these nations than elsewhere.

KEY POINT

Successful economies need institutions that encourage individuals to earn their income through engaging in value added activities rather than rent seeking.

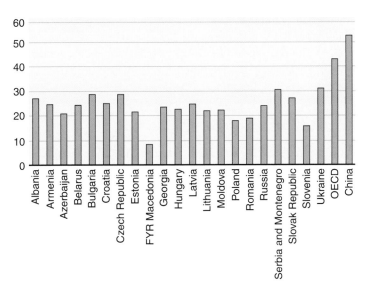

<small>FIGURE 5.9</small> **Social capital in transition economies, 1995.** Formerly socialist economies in transition often have poor social capital. *Source:* Raiser, Haerpfer, Nowotry, and Wallace, "Social Capital in Transition: A First Look at the Evidence," European Bank for Reconstruction and Development Working Paper No. 61.

FINANCIAL INSTITUTIONS

We have so far focused on broad social and cultural factors that influence TFP but there are also many more directly economic related factors. One of the most important of these is the quality of a country's financial institutions. In Chapter 4 we stressed the importance of a high investment rate. But equally as important is the existence of a financial system that is able to raise sufficient funds from savers and allocate them to the investment projects that offer the highest rates of return. Investing heavily in ill-advised projects will be of no long-term benefit to a country. Figure 5.10 examines the

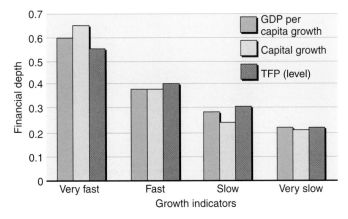

<small>FIGURE 5.10</small> **Size of financial sector boosts GDP and TFP.** Better quality financial institutions help produce faster economic growth. *Source:* King and Levine, *Quarterly Journal of Economics,* (1993).

performance of developing countries between 1960 and 1989 to show how a well-functioning financial system helps boost growth. Those with well-developed financial systems (as measured by the ratio of M3 to GDP—see Chapter 11) saw faster growth in GDP per capita and capital and also saw higher levels of TFP.

5.4 The Importance of Technological Progress

Our focus on institutions and TFP was needed to explain the variation in GDP per capita across countries. However, we now need to use TFP to account for another deficiency in our model based just on physical and human capital. For a given level of TFP, diminishing MPK means that countries eventually reach a steady state, and at this point there is no further growth in the economy. But Table 3.1 shows that, although growth has slowed down, the rich OECD nations continue to show positive trend growth. More than 150 years after the Industrial Revolution, it is implausible that they have not yet reached their steady state. To explain this continual growth in rich nations, we need to examine the role of **technological progress**.

An improvement in technology acts as an increase in TFP—similar to that in Figures 5.1 and 5.3—which leads to higher output and further growth. Because technological progress occurs continuously, this suggests that the steady state of the economy is forever shifting. When technological progress occurs at a modest pace, the shift in the steady state is small and the GDP growth created is moderate. But during periods of major technological developments, the shift in the steady state might be substantial and produce fast growth for many years until the new steady state is reached.

Because technological progress increases the steady state, a growth accounting analysis will show output growth from both TFP and capital accumulation. This can be seen in Figure 5.11, where the increase in TFP and the resulting change in the steady state capital stock leads to an increase in output of $Y_B - Y_A$. $Y_B - Y_C$ gives the direct increase in output from technical progress, but the additional capital accumulation resulting from technical progress leads to a further rise in output of $Y_C - Y_A$. Technological progress ensures that capital accumulation continues indefinitely as the steady state continuously changes. Without technological change, the economy settles down to a static steady state and shows no growth.

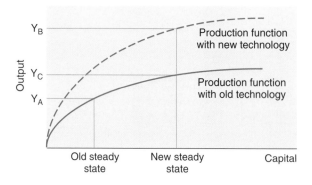

FIGURE 5.11 **Technological progress and growth accounting.** Technical progress increases output directly and has a further effect though its impact upon the equilibrium capital stock.

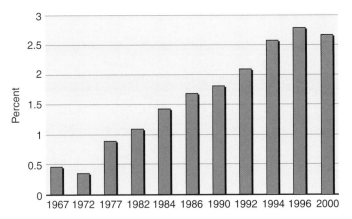

FIGURE 5.12   **South Korean R&D as percentage of GDP.** As countries approach their steady state, R&D becomes more important. *Source:* OECD, *Main Science and Technology Indicators: 2003 edition.*

KEY POINT

Because of technological progress the steady state continues to evolve. This leads to higher output because: (1) capital becomes more productive, and (2) the steady state capital stock increases.

This analysis suggests that the incentives for firms to engage in research and development increase as countries approach their steady state. We would therefore expect mature economies to focus more on R&D than emerging markets, which will focus more on capital accumulation. Figure 5.12 supports this hypothesis by showing the substantive increase in R&D expenditure experienced by South Korea. Rapid growth in South Korea was initially based around high rates of capital accumulation, but as diminishing MPK began to set in, increasing emphasis was placed on R&D. As shown in Figure 5.13, spending on R&D is highest among the richest countries, who rely upon it as their source of growth.

If technological progress is the main source of growth for the richest nations, then we can expect them to grow more slowly than countries who are not yet at their steady

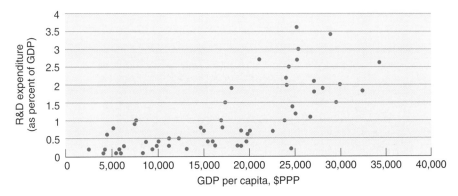

FIGURE 5.13   **Rich Countries do more R&D.** *Source:* UN Human Development Report (2003).

state and who can still grow through capital accumulation alone. Richer countries will experience slower growth due to diminishing MPK and the trials and tribulations that accompany R&D.

KEY POINT

As economies approach their steady state, they will focus increasingly on R&D. In the long run, technological progress is the sole source of growth for wealthy nations.

5.5   Foreign Direct Investment and Technology Transfer

In order for emerging markets to catch up with more advanced nations, they need to increase their capital stock, adopt more sophisticated technology, and move towards the TFP frontier by utilizing more economically efficient means of production and organization. An important vehicle through which this can occur is **Foreign Direct Investment** (FDI)—that is, overseas firms either building production plants in a country or taking a significant stake in a domestic firm, as when Ford or GM constructs a factory in Thailand or Phillips builds an assembly plant in Malaysia. FDI provides both additional capital, improved technology and better TFP to the country receiving the investment. As Figure 5.14 shows, FDI grew substantially during the 1990s, although not all regions benefited equally from it. One reason for increasing FDI is the growing importance of multinational enterprises (MNEs). As we shall show in Chapter 8, falling impediments to trade and declining transportation and communication costs have substantially in-

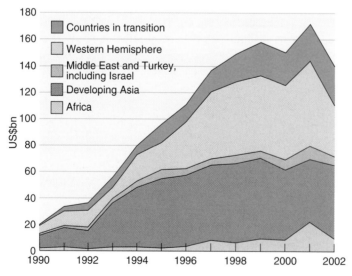

FIGURE 5.14   **FDI inflows into emerging markets.** FDI flows increased sharply during 1990s. *Source: IMF World Economic Outlook Database (April 2003).*

TABLE 5.7   FDI Flows to Selected Emerging Markets

	FDI Value Added (% GDP)	FDI Employment (% Total)	FDI as % of Total Investment	Productivity in Firms Receiving FDI ($)	Productivity in Domestic Firms ($)
China	4.3	9.5	12.1	7199	2633
Hong Kong	98.5	2.5	36.7	35881	26259
Malaysia	26.8	16.6	17.1	22940	13923
Taiwan	15	4.1	2.7	97193	20533

Source: UNCTAD World Investment Report 2002.

creased world trade. Much of this trade is internal between different parts of the same parent MNE, as global companies have taken advantage of lower trading costs by slicing production up across different countries. As components are then shipped across countries to complete assembly, world trade rises.

KEY POINT

Foreign Direct Investment encourages convergence between emerging markets and OECD nations through providing capital accumulation, technology, and TFP transfer.

Studies of firms support the TFP-enhancing role of FDI. For instance, a study of Venezuelan firms between 1976 and 1989 found that, across all sectors, firms that received FDI tended to have 70% higher productivity, 60% higher wages, and more than eight times higher exports than domestic firms. Table 5.7 shows the relative importance of FDI for investment, GDP, and employment; it also shows that foreign firms have higher productivity than domestic based firms.

5.6   The Impact of ICT

During the 1990s, OECD countries invested substantially in **Information and Communications Technology** (ICT) so that by 2000 it accounted for between 20% and 45% of all investment. This investment in ICT was particularly marked in the United States, the main focus of this section. This substantial investment encouraged much talk about a **New Economy** and was accompanied by rapid growth in GDP and surging stock markets. Particularly noteworthy was the increase in TFP growth. From 1913 to 1972 U.S. TFP grew at 1.6% per annum and then slowed to 0.6% between 1972 and 1995. But as ICT investment increased, TFP growth for the period 1995–99 rose to 1.8%. In this section we review two questions: (1) How important was ICT to the fast growth in the United States during the 1990s? (2) Is the New Economy as significant as the second Industrial Revolution at the end of the nineteenth century, when electrical power and the combustion engine were developed?

NEW ECONOMY—A GROWTH ACCOUNTING APPROACH

Until the mid 1990s, the debate over ICT focused around the Solow paradox, a statement by Nobel Laureate Robert Solow that, "You can see the computer age everywhere but in the productivity statistics." However, by the second half of the decade Solow's paradox began to disappear—the impact of ICT *could* be seen in the productivity numbers. Table 5.8 shows a growth accounting approach to U.S. labor productivity growth that increased by nearly 1% during the period 1996–2001 over the level during 1991–95.

However, a closer examination of the productivity numbers reveals a complex picture. There are three ways in which investment in ICT can boost GDP.

1. through capital accumulation as ICT investment boosts the capital stock (capital deepening)
2. TFP gains in sectors that *produce* ICT (e.g., productivity gains in making semiconductors and computers)
3. TFP gains in sectors that *use* ICT (e.g., productivity gains in retail and finance as a result of their ICT investment)

From Table 5.8 we see that of the 0.89% increase in productivity growth between 1995 and 2001, 0.67% was due to capital accumulation, 0.4% from TFP increases and a loss of 0.2% from labor/human capital. However, of the capital accumulation effect, 0.56%

TABLE 5.8   Growth Accounting and the New Economy

	1974–90	1991–95	1996–2001
Growth of labor productivity	1.36	1.54	2.43
Contributions from			
Capital deepening	.77	.52	1.19
Information technology capital	.41	.46	1.02
Computer hardware	.23	.19	.54
Software	.09	.21	.35
Communication equipment	.09	.05	.13
Other capital	.37	.06	.17
Labor quality	.22	.45	.25
Total productivity growth	.37	.58	.99
Semiconductors	.08	.13	.42
Computer hardware	.11	.13	.19
Software	.04	.09	.11
Communication equipment	.04	.06	.05
Other sectors	.11	.17	.23
Total IT contribution	.68	.87	1.79

Source: Information Technology & Productivity: Where are we now and where are we going? Federal Reserve Bank of Atlanta Economic Review (2002 Q3).

was produced through ICT investment, with only 0.11% from non-ICT investment. Further, of the 0.4% TFP increase, 0.36% was achieved in sectors *making* ICT rather than *using* ICT.

Industries involved in manufacturing ICT have achieved substantial productivity growth. Between 1995 and 1999, productivity in U.S. office equipment manufacturing increased by more than 250%, and telecommunications manufacturing productivity increased by 80%, compared to 26% in the whole of U.S. manufacturing. As a result of this soaring productivity in producing computers, their prices have fallen dramatically—in 1961 the price index for computer hardware and peripherals was 61640, but by 1999 it had declined to 36—an annual fall in prices of 19.4%. In response to these sharp price declines produced by rapid productivity growth, U.S. industry invested heavily in ICT equipment as firms substituted this newer technology for existing technology. For example, employees in most industries are now more likely to send e-mails rather than faxes, use PCs rather than typewriters, and surf the Web rather than scour libraries. But does this represent merely substitution between techniques or a substantial shift in the productive capacity of the economy? Is perhaps the main motivation behind adopting ICT equipment its falling price rather than because it is a compelling means of boosting productivity?

This suggests a mixed record for ICT. On the one hand, the huge investment in ICT capital and productivity gains in the ICT producing sector boosted labor productivity growth by 1.79% per annum. On the other hand, despite this huge investment, the evidence of increasing TFP in the ICT using sectors is modest. This mixed performance has led to a substantial debate about the merits of ICT. Skeptics argue that the impact of ICT cannot be compared with that of previous major inventions such as electricity, the combustion engine, or even indoor plumbing! Even the telegraph caused communication costs to fall more dramatically than the Internet. Moreover, much ICT-based activity involves duplicating existing activities rather than generating extra value added—firms now have to duplicate sales efforts by both mailing catalogs and maintaining Web sites. Further, much of this commercial activity on the Web is not creating value added but redistributing sales among existing firms—it is competition for market share rather than new markets. Skeptics of the New Economy also point out that ICT is about information, which is an intermediate good and not value added. Finally, computing developments may not automatically improve productivity—employees may use the Web to pursue their private hobbies rather than boost firm productivity. Figure 5.15 may not be as compelling as some of our previous empirical evidence, but it may nonetheless convince some readers!

KEY POINT

Substantial productivity gains in making ICT equipment has driven down prices and encouraged firms to undertake major ICT investment. Productivity gains in making ICT and the substantial capital accumulation of ICT have both boosted GDP significantly.

WHY HASN'T THE IMPACT OF ICT BEEN GREATER?

Given the enormous impact that ICT has had on the business world, it may seem strange to suggest that it has not dramatically increased productivity. However, it is worth returning to our concept of GDP as value added to think through how ICT may

FIGURE 5.15   **Economists Wonder . . .**
Source: Boston Globe

have affected output. In Table 5.9 we return to our example from Chapter 2 of a value added chain including a lumberyard, manufacturer, and retailer. Consider what happens when, as a result of ICT and B2B (business to business) technologies, the manufacturer can now reduce its costs and purchase lumber at a cost of $750, compared to $1000. Although the manufacturing firm has reduced its costs, it has not increased total value added in the whole economy. All that has occurred is that the value added that used to be produced by the lumberyard is now captured by the manufacturer. Total GDP remains unaltered. In order for ICT to raise GDP, it needs to boost value added/productivity. For instance, if as a result of ICT the manufacturer can now produce 12 rather than 10 tables out of a given quantity of wood, then value added has increased—from given inputs, including raw materials, the company can produce more output. For ICT to really make an impact on the economy, it has to raise value added rather than merely reduce costs.

Proponents of the New Economy argue that the impact of ICT is already substantive and will increase over time. For instance, Paul David[5] suggests that it took 40 years before electricity substantially affected output. When electricity was first introduced,

TABLE 5.9   **Technology and Redistributing the Value Chain**

Sector	Product	Price	Profits	Salaries
Retailer	10 tables	@$400 each	750	1250
Manufacturer	10 tables	@$200 each	475	775
Lumberyard	Wood	$750	100	650

[5] David, "The Dynamo and the Computer: An Historical Perspective on the Modern Productivity Paradox," *American Economic Review Papers and Proceedings* (1990) vol. 80, no. 2, pp. 355–61.

many factories were located near a water source to make the most cost efficient use of steam power. Electricity introduced some immediate benefits, for instance, a reliable source of lighting and energy for 24 hours a day, but its full impact was not felt for decades. To use electricity most efficiently, new machines had to be developed, the factory floor reconfigured, and production relocated. For example, electricity made elevators reliable, which in turn enabled skyscrapers to be built. Obviously this new type of building could not be developed immediately. It may also take decades to realize the full benefits of ICT. According to this argument, it is too early for the ICT revolution to generate a large increase in output, but it will eventually materialize.

Another reason why TFP gains from ICT use are only beginning to emerge is shown in Figure 5.16. Across a wide range of manufacturing firms, the worst productivity growth is achieved in firms that spend a lot on ICT adoption but do not alter their working practices in response to this new investment. As an example, consider the banking industry, a major investor in ICT, which at first simply purchased PCs for employees and effectively asked them to perform the same tasks as before but using PCs. Not surprisingly, this did little to boost productivity or earn a good return on investment. But firms that have spent on ICT and at the same time reformed their operating methods have experienced rapid productivity growth (the U.S. retailer Wal-Mart is most cited in this respect). This suggests that, over time, as firms discover how best to exploit this technology and make the necessary workplace practice reform, the ICT-using sectors will benefit from increased TFP growth. Note, however, that this suggests that the productivity benefits from ICT will not be the same across all countries—countries that produce ICT equipment will benefit from high GDP growth, as will those with industries capable of flexible responses.

The above argument suggests that ICT did play a substantial role in boosting U.S. GDP growth during the late 1990s even if TFP gains have not yet been substantial outside of the ICT manufacturing sector. But what of our second question: Is it a third

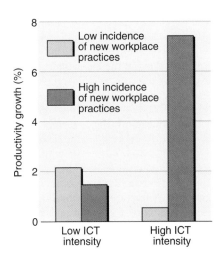

FIGURE 5.16 **IT, productivity growth, and workplace practices.** Without changes in workplace practices, high levels of ICT investment yield poor productivity growth. *Source:* Arnal, Ok, and Torres, *Knowledge, Work Organisation and Economic Growth,* OECD Labor Market and Social Policy Working Paper 50 (2001).

TABLE 5.10   ICT as Third Industrial Revolution?

	U.S. ICT		U.S. Electricity	U.K. Steam
	1974–95	1996–2001	1899–1929	1800–50
Capital	0.5	1.0	0.2	0.08
TFP	0.2	0.8	0.1	0.02
TFP Spillovers	?	?+	0.2	0
Total	0.7	1.8+	0.5	0.10

Source: Crafts, "Quantifying the Contribution of Technological Change to Economic Growth in Different Eras: A Review of the Evidence," LSE Department of Economic History, Discussion Paper 79/03.

Industrial Revolution? The fact that TFP growth has not spread across the whole economy suggests this is not the case. Yet the comparison with steam and electricity shown in Table 5.10 suggests that the magnitude of the ICT impact has been much greater, albeit so far for a shorter time period, than anything witnessed before.

KEY POINT

Evidence of more widespread TFP gains from using ICT is slowly emerging and appears linked with the ability of firms and industries to respond flexibly.

SUMMARY

In order to account for wide variation in GDP per capita across countries we have to introduce variations in Total Factor Productivity to supplement the effect of capital accumulation. In section 5.1, we showed that higher levels of TFP not only enable greater output to be produced from a given capital stock, but also lead to a larger steady state capital stock. The richest nations define the TFP frontier, although many countries will find themselves unable to reach this level.

In section 5.2, we talked about human capital. Reflecting the skills and knowledge of the work force, human capital contributes to explaining differences in income unrelated to physical capital. Increases in human capital offset the effects of diminishing marginal product of capital and help explain why not all investment flows to the poorest countries. For wealthy nations at their steady state, increases in human capital trigger further increases in output and investment.

In section 5.3, we saw that, even allowing for differences in human capital, there remains a substantive role for TFP in accounting for income differences. TFP reflects myriad influences but one of the more important is the role of institutions, broadly conceived, in providing incentives for individuals to make profit in ways that are advantageous for society. Good governance, lack of corruption, an optimal allocation of talent, and high social capital are all important in boosting TFP. There is some evidence that ownership of substantial raw materials may harm GDP through adverse effects on institutional quality.

In order to explain continual growth in rich nations, we introduced technological progress in section 5.4. Technological progress increases over time, boosting output and the capital stock. With no technological progress, the capital stock reaches its steady state level and the economy ceases to grow. Technological progress provides two additional channels for growth: it produces more output from a given level of factor inputs, and it boosts the desired level of capital. For countries at their steady state, technological progress is the long-run source of growth, so the importance of R&D to a country increases with its income.

In section 5.5, we saw that Foreign Direct Investment is increasing in importance and encourages convergence among countries. FDI leads both to an increase in the capital stock and a transfer of technology to the recipient country and so contributes to growth in developing nations.

In section 5.6, we discussed the importance of information and computer technology to TFP. The data suggest that the durable manufacturing sector, and in particular the computer-related industries, generated most of the TFP gains in the U.S. economy in the late 1990s. The substantial gains in these industries have led to dramatic declines in ICT equipment prices, which have encouraged large increases in the ICT capital stock and substitution away from older forms of technology. This ICT capital accumulation has increased output and was a factor in the late 1990s U.S. economic boom. The magnitude of this ICT impact is substantial compared to previous Industrial Revolutions. However, the impact on the productivity of ICT users has remained modest and appears linked with the flexibility of firms in adjusting their working practices.

CONCEPTUAL QUESTIONS

1. (Section 5.1) Consider an economy well known to you and assess which factors of its TFP are relatively strong compared to other countries and which ones are relatively poor. What steps could be taken to improve TFP?

2. (5.2) Do you think that the marginal product of human capital is decreasing or increasing? Why?

3. (5.2) Should developing countries spend money on establishing universities in their own countries?

4. (5.3) What steps could a government take to remove corruption?

5. (5.3) Considering the importance of institutions, what advantages and disadvantages are there to joining the EU for the various ex-Communist economies such as Poland and the Czech Republic?

6. (5.4) In this chapter we have assumed that the level of technology can be adjusted independently of the capital stock. However, in practice, investing in new technology means investing in new machines. Use Figure 5.11 to analyze the implications of this.

7. (5.4) How would a technological development that boosted output but produced a higher depreciation rate affect output and capital?

8. (5.5) Is it better to develop your own technological champions or to rely on foreign direct investment?

9. (5.6) How have IT developments affected your productivity?

10. (5.6) Consider some of the items you regularly purchase and how they have been affected by ICT. Which sectors/firms have increased their value added share and which have lost out?

11. (5.6) Do developments in biotechnology have a better claim than ICT to be a third Industrial Revolution?

ANALYTICAL QUESTIONS

1. (Section 5.1) Consider an economy in which output in period t is produced by the Cobb-Douglas production function:

$$Y_t = A_t K_t^b L_t^{1-b}$$

Y_t is output at time t; K_t is capital at time t; L_t is labor employed at time t; A_t is TFP at time t. (You can review the Cobb-Douglas function in Chapter 3)

Saving, which equals gross investment, is 25% of output. The depreciation rate of capital is 5% a period. Initially, TFP is constant at 1, labor input is constant at 100, and b is 0.3.

   (a) Calculate the initial steady state level of output.
   (b) What happens in the short run if TFP suddenly rises from 1 to 1.2?
   (c) What is the new long-run level of steady state output, assuming TFP stays at 1.2?
   (d) What is the growth in the capital stock between the old steady state and the new one?

2. (5.2) Consider an economy in which output in period t is produced by the Cobb-Douglas production function:

$$Y_t = A_t HK_t^a K_t^b L_t^{1-b}$$

Y_t is output at time t; K_t is capital at time t; L_t is labor employed at time t; A_t is TFP at time t; HK_t is human capital; and a and b are both greater than 0.

   (a) What happens to GDP when human capital is increased?
   (b) Assuming $0 < a < 1$, what shape is the marginal product of human capital?
   (c) As K is increased, what happens to the marginal product of human capital?

3. (5.2) What do you think accounts for the results of Table 5.3?

4. (5.3) On the Web, visit http://info.worldbank.org/governance/ and compare the institutional quality of two countries of your choice.

5. (5.3) The quality of financial institutions is important for the level of TFP. Consider the merits and demerits of bank-based systems compared to those relying upon equity markets. Should governments privatize the financial system or leave it under state control?

6. (5.3) Consider Table 5.4 and assess the relative importance of investment, education, and TFP in explaining cross-country income differences.

7. (5.4) What difference is there between invention and innovation? How do these affect the marginal product of capital over time?

8. (5.4) What explanations can you suggest to explain Figure 5.13? Why do some countries do more R&D than others? Does this matter?

9. (5.6) Use Table 5.9. How is the economy likely to respond if, as a result of B2B innovations, the cost of lumber falls from $1000 to $750 and this is passed down the value chain in terms of lower prices? What will happen to GDP/value added?

Endogenous Growth and Convergence

Overview

In this chapter we develop endogenous growth models. These models drop the assumption of decreasing marginal product of capital (MPK), denying the existence of a steady state so that instead capital accumulation can produce growth forever. Interactions between physical and human capital are suggested as one reason why the MPK may not be diminishing. If these spillover effects are pronounced, poverty traps may exist, condemning poor regions not only to grow more slowly than wealthier regions, but also to remain poor in absolute terms.

We examine historical growth patterns and find that, across a wide sample of countries, no pattern of convergence exists; on average, poor countries do not grow faster than wealthy ones. However, when we consider similar countries, we find strong evidence in favor of convergence. We reconcile this evidence by introducing the idea of conditional convergence—among countries that share a similar steady state, poorer countries will grow faster than wealthier ones—but comparing across countries with different steady states, we should find no clear patterns of convergence. We then consider what determines a country's steady state and how policy measures might affect it. We review the poor economic growth performance of Africa, focusing on policies, geography, colonialism, and institutions, and conclude by examining the historical record and principles underlying development aid.

Key Concepts

Colonialism	Endogenous Growth	Poverty Traps
Conditional Convergence	Geography	Steady State Determinants
Constant and Increasing MPK	Overseas Development Assistance	

6.1 Endogenous Growth

The Solow neoclassical model that we have developed so far offers a rich framework for analysis, especially when we allow for differences in total factor productivity. However, it is not a very satisfactory model for explaining long-run growth. Once countries reach their long-run steady state, continual growth only occurs through changes in technological progress. However, the model is focused on capital accumulation and provides no explanation for what drives technological progress. In other words, it offers an *exogenous* theory of long-run economic growth. By contrast, **endogenous growth** theories try to outline in detail the mechanisms that cause long-run economic growth. There are many ways of explaining economic growth, and endogenous growth theory refers to a wide range of models, but in essence they are of two types. One type produces continual growth by avoiding the notion of a steady state so that capital accumulation can produce growth without limit. The other type focuses on endogenous explanations of how total factor productivity changes over time.

GROWTH WITHOUT END

To remove the steady state from our analysis, we need to drop the assumption of decreasing MPK. If instead we assume that there exists **constant MPK**, then the production function becomes a straight line—as shown in Figure 6.1. Every new machine installed leads to an increase in output identical to the increase from the previous machine. If investment is a constant proportion of output (as we previously assumed), the investment schedule is also a straight line and no longer flattens out. In this situation, as shown in Figure 6.1, the investment and depreciation lines do not intersect, and no steady state exists. Investment always exceeds depreciation and so the capital stock is always growing and GDP growth does not slow down. With constant MPK, long-run growth becomes endogenous and is explained by investment.

The absence of a steady state rules out the convergence result we stressed in Chapter 4—poor countries need no longer grow faster than wealthier nations. This model also suggests that if government policy can boost investment, it not only increases the capital stock but *permanently* affects the growth rate. To see this, consider the following. The change in the capital stock equals investment less depreciation. If investment equals a proportion (*s*) of output, and depreciation is a proportion (d) of the capital stock then

$$\text{change in capital stock} = \text{investment} - \text{depreciation} = s\text{Y} - \text{d K}$$

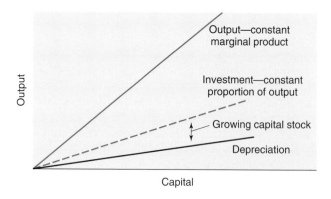

FIGURE 6.1 **Constant marginal product and endogenous growth.** With a constant marginal product of capital, there is no steady state level of the capital stock.

A constant MPK implies that doubling the number of machines doubles output. Therefore output is simply a multiple of the capital stock or Y = AK, where A reflects total factor productivity. Therefore

change in capital stock = sY − dK = sAK − dK

The percentage growth in the capital stock is equal to the change in the capital stock divided by capital (K), so we have

% growth in capital stock = change in capital stock/capital stock

$$= sY/K − dK/K = sA − d$$

so that the increase in the capital stock depends positively on the investment rate, s. Therefore, if the government can change the investment rate, it leads not just to a one-time increase in the *levels* of capital and output (as in Chapter 4) but to a *permanent* increase in the *growth rates* of capital and output.

KEY POINT

Endogenous growth models explain long-run growth by avoiding the assumption of diminishing MPK and so avoid the existence of a steady state. Assuming constant MPK means that investment affects both the level of GDP and its long-run growth rate.

WHY CONSTANT MARGINAL PRODUCT?

The previous subsection has shown that dropping the assumption of declining MPK leads to very different growth implications. But is a constant MPK justifiable? Assuming a Cobb-Douglas production function where Y = AK^aL^b, then the MPK = $a\,AK^{a-1}L^b$. If $a < 1$, then $a − 1$ is less than zero and an increase in the capital stock reduces the MPK (e.g., there is decreasing MPK). If instead, $a = 1$ then $a − 1 = 0$ and the MPK = $AK^0L^b = AL^b$ so that increasing the capital stock has *no* effect on the MPK (e.g., there is constant MPK). Therefore, endogenous growth would seem to hinge on $a = 1$. As discussed in Chapter 4, however, we know that capital income is around 30% of GDP so a = 0.3. Surely this rules out a constant MPK and endogenous growth?

A BROADER CONCEPT OF CAPITAL

One way to generate a constant MPK is to focus on the positive interaction between physical and human capital that we outlined in Chapter 5. The more human capital there is in a country, the higher the marginal product of physical capital. That is, the more skilled the workforce, the higher the productivity of machines. However, the higher the level of physical capital in an economy, the greater the marginal product of human capital. That is, the more machines in an economy, the greater the return from investing in skills and education. By focusing on a broad measure of capital (both physical and human), this interaction may sustain constant MPK.

Figure 6.2 shows how these forces interact. Each panel shows the marginal product of human or physical capital, and each marginal product curve is drawn for a fixed level

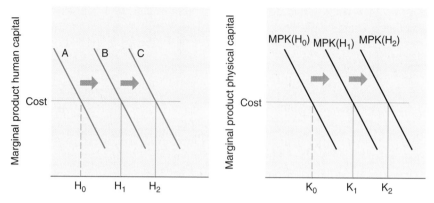

FIGURE 6.2   **Interaction between human and physical capital.** Increases in human capital generate more investment in physical capital and vice versa. As the productivity of human capital rises from A to B, the stock of human capital increases from H_0 to H_1 and this raises the productivity of physical schedule from $MPK(H_0)$ to $MPK(H_1)$. The resulting increase in physical capital ($K_0 \rightarrow K_1$) further boosts the productivity of human capital (B→C).

of the other form of capital. *Therefore, holding fixed the other form of capital, both display decreasing marginal product.* Let us assume that an increase in technological knowledge boosts the marginal product of human capital—skilled labor is now more productive. This shifts the marginal product of human capital curve out from A to B in the left panel of Figure 6.2. Assuming no change in the cost of education, this encourages the economy to increase its stock of human capital to H_1. This increase in human capital boosts the productivity of physical capital—the marginal product curve shifts out to $MPK(H_1)$ in the right-hand panel. Given the cost of capital, this means the economy increases its capital stock to K_1. However, this new higher level of physical capital means that the marginal product of human capital improves, and the marginal product curve for human capital shifts out to C. As a result, more human capital is accumulated to reach the level H_2. This increase in human capital in turn shifts the marginal product of physical capital out [to $MPK(H_2)$], and the virtuous circle continues. Therefore, although each category of capital on its own has decreasing marginal product, if we think of capital as including both human and physical capital, then we have constant marginal product of capital.

By using a Cobb-Douglas production function extended to allow for human capital, we can show this effect more easily. In this case the production function becomes

$$\text{output} = A \times (\text{human capital})^b \times (\text{physical capital})^a \times (\text{hours worked})^c$$

The marginal product of human capital is $b \times$ output/(human capital), and for physical capital it is $a \times$ output/(physical capital). Both marginal products are declining, keeping fixed the other factors of production. However, if human capital is increasing with physical capital, e.g., human capital = $D \times$ physical capital, then we can substitute out human capital from the production function and arrive at

$$\text{output} = (A \times D^b) \times (\text{physical capital})^{b+a} \times (\text{hours worked})^c$$

If $b + a = 1$, then this becomes

output $= A^* \times$ physical capital $\times$ (hours worked)^c

where $A^* = \mathbf{A} \times \mathbf{D}^b$

This is the same AK production function (e.g., $Y = AK$) that we outlined when we discussed the straight line production function in Figure 6.1. The closer $b + a$ is to 1, the more the production function becomes a straight line and the slower the MPK diminishes. Therefore even if $a = 0.3$, as previously suggested, so long as $b = 0.7$ then we may have constant marginal product of capital. The more important human capital is in producing GDP growth, the more chance we have of endogenous growth being important.

ENDOGENOUS GROWTH AND GOVERNMENT POLICY

The key to producing a constant MPK was a spillover between human and physical capital—when education improves, benefits spill over to firms' investments. This is important because spillovers are a form of market imperfection—left to its own devices, the market will not arrive at the best outcome, and this suggests a potentially useful role for government intervention. When each firm assesses whether to undertake investment, it compares the benefits and costs of the project. But each firm considers only the private benefits for itself—it does not factor in the additional benefits in the form of higher education and increased marginal product of human capital. As Figure 6.3 shows, the result is that the social return exceeds the private return, due to the gains of workers when firms invest. Because of the low private return, the firm does not do enough investment. The firm chooses the capital stock A where the private return equals the cost rather than capital stock B in which the social return equals cost. The government can, however, rectify the situation by offering a subsidy, so that the cost to the firm falls. Thus, while the firm still chooses investment by equating private return to cost, it now chooses the socially optimal investment level B. Therefore endogenous growth theory can provide a rationale for the government to boost long-run economic growth.

KEY POINT

Interactions between physical and human capital can postpone diminishing MPK and even lead to an endogenous growth model with constant MPK. Because of the existence of these spillovers, government policy can be used to improve the economy.

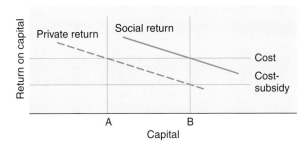

FIGURE 6.3 **Spillovers and subsidies.** A subsidy to bring down the cost of capital can induce firms to undertake the right level of investment (level B) even though they take account only of private returns.

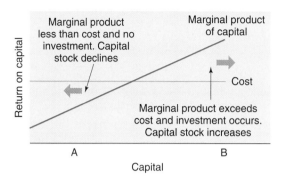

FIGURE 6.4 **Increasing marginal product and poverty traps.** If the marginal product of capital increases as capital employed rises, then poverty traps are possible.

6.2 Poverty Traps

There exists a third possibility about the MPK—the case of **increasing marginal product**. If the marginal product is increasing, this yields even richer growth implications. In particular, we can explain the existence of **poverty traps** that keep poor regions or countries poor. Figure 6.4 shows two regions in an economy—one with a low capital stock (A) and another with a high capital stock (B). For region A, the MPK is less than the cost of investment, so it does not invest. However, because we are now assuming that the MPK is increasing with the capital stock, the capital rich region (B) will make the investment because, for it, the MPK exceeds the cost of investment. Depreciation and no investment will lead to region A seeing its capital decline and becoming poorer, while continued investment and increasing marginal product will lead to high output and accelerating growth in region B.

Increasing marginal product means countries and regions don't show signs of catch-up, or convergence, but instead *diverge*—the rich get richer while the poor remain poor. Under this assumption, one would expect to find economic activity heavily concentrated in a few successful areas that showed continual high growth rather than spread equally across regions. Given that 54% of global GDP is produced from an area that accounts for only 10% of global land, and that the United States produces 50% of its GDP from only 2% of its land mass while the least productive 50% of U.S. land accounts for only 2% of its GDP, there is some support for this view. Figure 6.5 shows the

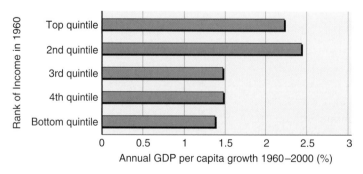

FIGURE 6.5 **Economic growth ranked by initial income.** The very poorest countries have not grown faster than the average—quite the reverse. *Source:* Penn World Table 6.1.

average growth in per capita output between 1960 and 2000 for over 100 countries. There are five groups of countries. The bottom quintile was the poorest 20% of countries in 1960, the top quintile was the richest 20% of the countries, and the other quintiles reflect intermediate ranks. Overall, the gap between rich and poor countries has widened between 1960 and 2000, with the poorest countries having the lowest growth.

The assumption of increasing marginal product also helps to explain why, in global capital markets, investment flows mostly to wealthy nations. Between 1970 and 1994, the poorest 20% of countries received only 1% of total gross global capital flows, or the equivalent of 6 cents per person. By contrast, the richest 20% of the countries received 88% of total capital flows, or $189 per person. If the marginal product of capital is increasing, then the return to investment will be highest in the richest nations, and investors will rationally avoid portfolio investment in poor, undeveloped nations.

What justification can we give for increasing MPK? Observing many industries, professions, and even neighborhoods, we can see that individuals tend to associate with individuals of similar levels of human capital. For instance, the quality of economists within an academic department (or students within a university) tends to be similar, although quality will vary widely across different universities and business schools. This may have to do with interdependencies in the production function—it is important to avoid "weak links in the chain." For instance, the space shuttle *Challenger* exploded because one of its many thousands of components malfunctioned. That small imperfection destroyed a complex scientific project. Companies can fail because of bad marketing even if the rest of the firm functions well. With such strong interdependencies (spillovers), we would expect to find highly skilled individuals working with each other, while less skilled individuals also group together. As Michael Kremer[1] notes—Charlie Parker worked with Dizzy Gillespie and Donny Osmond worked with his sister Marie.

These interdependencies typify poverty traps. In a poverty trap, the individual's incentive to avoid poverty is weak. If you are surrounded by high-quality human capital, then you have a large incentive to increase your human capital. However, if you are surrounded by low-quality human capital, your incentives are poor—with many weak links in the chain, your gains from increased education are going to be much smaller. This is why individuals and nations can get stuck in a poverty trap.

KEY POINT

If the MPK is increasing, then poverty traps exist whereby poor nations receive no investment and remain poor while rich countries continue to invest and grow, leading to divergence in incomes across countries.

6.3 Convergence or Divergence?

In previous sections we have shown how different assumptions regarding the MPK produce fundamentally different implications for growth. In outlining each of these alternative assumptions on the MPK, we have shown evidence that is consistent with each theory, but which theory best explains the facts?

[1] Kremer, "The O-ring Theory of Economic Development," *Quarterly Journal of Economics* (1993) August pp. 551–576.

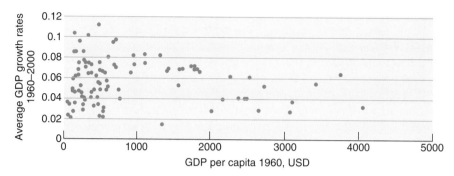

FIGURE 6.6 **Convergence—all countries.** There is no tendency for convergence across all countries. *Source:* Penn World Table 6.1.

The key distinction between the Solow or neoclassical growth model, based on the assumption of decreasing marginal product, and the endogenous growth theories of this chapter is convergence. With decreasing marginal product, we expect to find convergence—poorer countries should grow faster than rich ones. According to endogenous growth theories, there should be no such simple negative correlation between initial income and subsequent growth. Therefore, to test the competing theories we should simply examine historical evidence. If there is a negative correlation, we have convergence, and the neoclassical model based on decreasing marginal product is the more appropriate framework.

Figure 6.6 shows the level of GDP per capita in 1960 and the average growth rate between 1960 and 2000 for a wide range of countries. Considering all countries together, there is no evidence of convergence; there is no negative correlation between initial income and subsequent growth. While some poor countries grow very fast, there is a range of growth experiences—some grow quickly, while in others, standards of living fall further.

Figure 6.6 considers a broad range of different economies including developed (OECD) countries, African countries, emerging markets in Southeast Asia, and some formerly communist economies. If, however, we consider groupings of economies based on similar characteristics, then different results appear. Figure 6.7 shows the

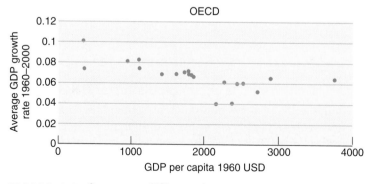

FIGURE 6.7 **Convergence—OECD economies.** Within OECD countries, convergence seems to exist. *Source:* Penn World Table 6.1.

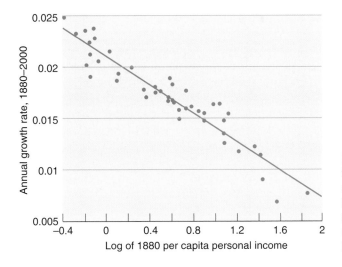

FIGURE 6.8 **Convergence—the U.S. states.** Output converges within the United States. *Source:* Barro and Sala-i-Martin, Economic Growth (New York: McGraw Hill, 2003).

same data, but focuses on just the OECD economies—there is now substantial evidence of convergence. The fastest growing OECD nations were those that were poorest in 1960. Spain, Portugal, and Mexico, for example, have grown faster than Germany, France, and the United Kingdom. Figures 6.8 and 6.9 show similarly strong evidence in favor of convergence when we examine U.S. states and regions in Western Europe.

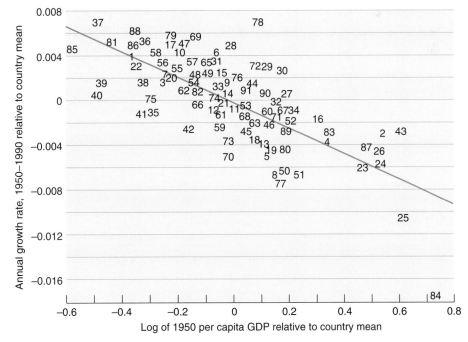

FIGURE 6.9 **Convergence—European regions.** Output seems to converge within Europe also. *Source:* Barro and Sala-i-Martin, Economic Growth (New York: McGraw Hill, 2003).

Convergence is also found when similar charts are drawn for Canadian provinces and Japanese prefectures.

These figures show that when we consider regions or economies that display similar characteristics, we find strong evidence of convergence, so that within similar groups, relatively poor countries grow faster than the relatively rich. We can think of groups of countries as being like different species. Elephants are one species—if you find a small elephant, it is probably still growing and is on its way to becoming the size of an average elephant. But now look at squirrels. Small squirrels will grow to catch up with average squirrels, but they will not catch up to average elephants; all squirrels are small relative to elephants.

Proponents of the neoclassical model refer to the "iron law of convergence"—when they look at similar groupings of regions, they find that, on average, about 2% of the discrepancy between rich and poor regions is removed each year. This convergence occurs slowly—it takes 35 years to reduce the discrepancy by half. However, the evidence suggests that, although it may be slow, some form of convergence is occurring whereby poorer regions (such as the south of Italy or Maine and Arkansas in the United States) do grow faster than wealthier regions (such as the north of Italy or Massachusetts).

RECONCILING THE EVIDENCE

When we consider all countries simultaneously, we find no evidence in favor of convergence (Figure 6.6), but when we consider similar groupings of economies, we find strong evidence (Figures 6.7–6.9). How can we explain this?

The explanation is based on the idea of **conditional convergence**. The neoclassical model does *not* imply that capital poor countries grow faster than capital rich countries. Instead it implies that, among countries sharing the *same* steady state, we will find convergence. To see this, consider Figure 6.10 where we show four economies (A, B, C, and D) that differ only in their steady state capital stock. Countries A and B tend toward steady state 1, while C and D tend toward steady state 2. Note that we have assumed that all four economies share the same production function (they have access to the same technology, the same human capital, and so forth), so we are also assuming that their steady states differ only because of differences in investment rates. If we ignored their different steady states and examined all four countries simultaneously for convergence, we would find none. Countries B and D are near their steady state and will grow more slowly than A and C. Overall, we will find no clear negative correlation between initial income and subsequent growth. However, when we compare similar groupings that

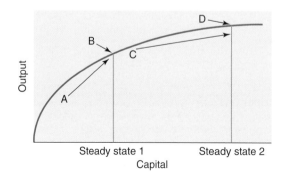

FIGURE 6.10 **Conditional convergence.** Countries that start out with capital stocks A and B converge on a lower steady state than countries that start out with capital at C or D.

share a steady state (A and B; C and D), then we will find convergence. Conditional convergence helps explain the mixed evidence in support of convergence in Figures 6.7–6.9 but it also raises the question of why the steady state differs across countries.

KEY POINT

There is no evidence that income levels across all countries are converging, but when similar countries are examined, then the evidence for convergence is strong. This is consistent with the Solow model of decreasing MPK but where countries have different steady states.

6.4 Determinants of the Steady State

We have already discussed a wide range of factors that should influence the steady state of the economy—investment, human capital, allocation of talent, corruption, and governance, to name a few. But can we use data to assess which of these factors is most important in influencing the steady state?

According to the Solow model, fast-growing economies are those that are far from their steady state. Therefore we have that

$$\text{Growth in GDP per capita} = b \times [\text{Steady State GDP} - \text{GDP}(0)]$$

Where GDP(0) denotes initial income and b is a positive coefficient that determines how rapidly a country converges to its steady state. But our previous reasoning tells us that steady state GDP is influenced by numerous factors such that

$$\text{Steady State GDP} = a1 \times \text{Education} + a2 \times \text{Investment} + a3 \times X$$

where X reflects the influence of any other variables that influence steady state GDP and a1 and a2 are coefficients that reflect the impact of Education and Investment on steady state GDP respectively. We can combine these two equations to get

$$\text{Growth in GDP per capita} = b \times a1 \times \text{Education} + b \times a2 \times \text{Investment}$$
$$+ b \times a3 \times X - b \times \text{GDP}(0)$$

or

$$\text{Growth in GDP per capita} = c1 \times \text{Education} + c2 \times \text{Investment}$$
$$+ c3 \times X - b \times \text{GDP}(0)$$

It is possible to use econometrics, the application of statistical methods to economic data, with published data on GDP, investment, education, and different choices for X (e.g., openness, corruption, and so forth) and estimate this equation to answer the following questions:

1. *Do countries show convergence?* If GDP growth is *negatively* related to initial income (b > 0), then we have convergence.
2. *Which variables influence the steady state?* Any variable for which c1, c2, or c3 is statistically significant can be said to affect the steady state.
3. *What impact does a variable have on steady state GDP?* The coefficients c1, c2, and c3 can be used to calculate the long-run impact of different variables on GDP.

Not surprisingly for such an important topic, there is much argument over the appropriate econometric techniques that should be used to estimate this equation and to identify robustly the factors that determine growth. Even so, a number of general points related to the questions above can still be made about this empirical literature.

1. The data seem to support the notion of conditional convergence (b > 0), not surprisingly given Figures 6.7–6.11. This finding in favor of convergence suggests that the marginal product of capital is decreasing and not constant or increasing as in the endogenous growth models. In Section 6.1, we argued that interactions between physical and human capital could lead to a constant MPK if b = 0.7, but estimates from these growth equations suggest that b = 0.3.[2] In other words, interactions with human capital slow down the rate at which the MPK declines, but they are not strong enough to lead to a constant MPK.

2. Most studies find a robust positive effect on the steady state from investment, health, and education.

3. The effect of other variables is more controversial and often harder to robustly detect. With relatively few countries to examine and with so many variables being highly correlated (such as health, education, and openness), it is difficult

TABLE 6.1 **Determinants of Steady State**
Many variables are found to impact on steady state, but the most robust are investment, education, and health.

Always Significant	Frequently Significant	Often Significant	Sometimes Significant
Education—primary school enrollment	Regional dummies (Latin America, Sub-Saharan Africa—negative)	Real exchange rate overvaluation (negative)	Government consumption (negative)
Investment	Rule of law	Black market premiums (negative)	Financial sophistication
Health—life expectancy	Political rights	Primary products (% exports—negative)	Inflation (negative)
	Religious dummies (Confucian, Muslim, Protestant)		Ethnic diversity (negative)
	Openness		Civil liberties
	Degree of capitalism		Revolutions, coups, wars (negative)
			Religious dummies (Buddhism, Catholic)
			Public investment

(Sala-i-Martin, "I Just Ran Four Million Regressions," *American Economic Review* (May 1997) 87 (2) 178–183.

[2] Mankiw, Romer, and Weil, "A Contribution to the Empirics of Economic Growth," *Quarterly Journal of Economics* (1992) vol. 107, pp. 407–437.

to reliably identify the main determinants of the steady state. Some variables, such as openness, are frequently found to be significant, but they sometimes appear to lose their importance when other variables are introduced. Table 6.1 summarizes which economic variables are found to robustly influence the steady state, which ones frequently are found to influence long-run GDP, and which variables have been found important by some researchers, but are not always prevalent.

GOOD AND BAD STEADY STATES

Table 6.2 shows for a selection of countries some of the key variables that influence the steady state. Given our steady state analysis and the concept of conditional convergence, the table makes for sobering reading. Conditional convergence says that countries that are furthest away from their steady state grow fastest. This is hardly reassuring for Sierra Leone, for example, which has the worst measures for four out of the six criteria shown and second worst for the remaining two categories. This suggests that Sierra Leone has a poor steady state and will not grow much—even though it is currently poor, it has poor steady state determinants and so weak growth prospects. By contrast, India would appear

TABLE 6.2   **Determinants of Steady State for Selected Countries, 2001**

Steady state determinants vary widely across countries. Civil Liberty is an index reflecting democratic and political freedoms (1 being highest level of freedom). Fertility is average births per female. Government Consumption and Investment are expressed as a percentage of GDP, and Education and Life Expectancy are recorded in years.

Country	Civil Liberties	Fertility (Births per female)	Government consumption (% GDP)	Education—average years of schooling*	Investment (% GDP)	Life Expectancy (Years)
Egypt	4.8	5.0	10.1	5.1	16.4	68.3
S. Africa	5.2	4.6	18.9	7.9	14.7	50.9
Nigeria	6.2	6.6	4.8	–	8.8	51.8
Sierra Leone	5.2	6.5	29.7	2.0	34.5	34.5
U.S.	1	1.8	18.2	12.3	24.1	76.9
South Korea	3.2	2.3	10.4	10.5	27.0	75.2
Italy	1	1.4	18.2	7.0	26.4	78.6
France	1	1.8	23.3	8.4	27.5	78.7
Japan	1	1.7	17.5	9.7	25.8	81.3
Australia	1	2.0	17.9	10.6	29.7	79.0
Brazil	2.2	3.6	19.2	4.6	19.4	67.8
Sweden	1	1.7	27.2	11.4	17.8	79.9
Mexico	3.8	3.8	11.2	6.7	19.6	73.1
India	2	4.5	12.8	4.8	21.7	63.3

*2000

Source: Barro and Lee, *International Data on Educational Attainment: Updates and Implications*, CID Working Paper no. 42 (IMF IFS April 2003) http://www2.cid.harvard.edu/ciddata/barrolee/Appendix.xls

to have better fundamentals and should benefit from higher growth. These numbers show that being poor does not guarantee growth. But if these poor nations could shift their steady states (and Table 6.1 suggests that government policy can have both positive and negative influences on the steady state), then their growth prospects would improve.

KEY POINT

Econometric studies find that investment, health, education, initial income, and openness to trade are important determinants of a country's steady state.

6.5   Why Is Africa So Poor?

Economic growth in Africa (particularly sub-Saharan Africa) has been continually disappointing. Figure 6.11 shows growth in real GDP per capita for a range of countries since 1820. For the entire period, Africa has been both the poorest and often the slowest growing region so that, as a result, 15 out of the 20 poorest nations in the world are in Africa. Although there have been some success stories, most noticeably Botswana, the region has remained a challenge to policymakers.

Our steady state analysis helps to explain why Africa has seen such poor growth. Africa scores poorly on many of the key determinants of the steady state—low investment, low educational achievement, and low scores on measures of social infrastructure. Moreover, Africa's strong protectionist policies have limited its ability to show convergence. But why has Africa had such low investment and consistently inappropriate government policies?

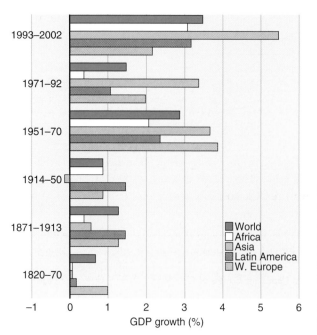

FIGURE 6.11 **Performance of major regions 1820–2002 (1990 $ GDP per capita).** Africa's poor economic performance has been a persistent feature of the world economy. *Source:* Maddison, Monitoring the World Economy 1820–1992; OECD and IMF WEO Database (2003).

ETHNO-LINGUISTIC DIVERSITY

One explanation for Africa's poor growth performance that has been the subject of much research is its ethno-linguistic diversity. Many African countries are composed of several large cultural groups, each with its own language and practices. In part this is the legacy of European colonialism, which at the end of the nineteenth century created national boundaries that served European needs rather than boundaries that created ethnic homogeneity.

Ethno-linguistically diverse nations tend to have poor government policy. Such polarized societies may be more prone to competitive rent seeking—each group tries to extract resources from other ethnic groups—and will find it more difficult to reach agreement over public goods (for instance, the location of roads and transport routes). This in turn leads to bad social infrastructure because it produces a gap between the return to individuals and that to society. As one Nigerian academic commented, "the struggle for power [after independence] was so absorbing that everything else, including development, was marginalized."[3] Easterly and Levine[4] found that high levels of ethno-linguistic diversity are associated with the existence of substantial informal markets, lower financial development, low provision of infrastructure, and low education.

Ethno-linguistic diversity may also lead to civil war. Civil wars tend to damage an economy more than conflicts between different nations. Civil wars are fought entirely on a country's own territory and so destroy much of its capital. They tend to leave a legacy of distrust that reduces social capital and hinders economic growth even after the conflicts are over. One study finds, however, that if a society is ethnically either homogenous or very diverse then the risk of a civil war is not high. Only societies with a few large and competing ethnic groups have a high risk of civil war.[5]

Table 6.3 shows the 10 most and least fractionalized economies, according to one measure of ethnic diversity. The strong presence of African economies among the most fractionalized suggests that ethno-linguistic diversity may explain some of Africa's poor economic performance.

EFFECTS OF GEOGRAPHY

An alternative explanation of Africa's poor growth focuses on its **geography** and the related issues of climate and disease. Bloom and Sachs[6] suggest that Africa's growth is restricted because it is poorly placed to benefit from trade. As Table 6.4 shows, Africa has the highest proportion of its population living in landlocked regions. As a result, trading costs for African economies are much higher than for economies closer to ocean coasts. One way to measure transportation costs is to examine the gap between the cost of imports inclusive of freight and insurance costs, and the cost of exports measured as freight on board. In other words, the cost of a commodity before it is exported and the

[3] Ake, *Democracy and Development in Africa* (Washington DC: The Brookings Institution, 1996).

[4] Easterly and Levine, "Africa's Growth Tragedy," *Quarterly Journal of Economics* (1997) vol. 112, pp. 1203–1250.

[5] Collier and Hoeffler, "On Economic Causes of Civil War," *Oxford Economic Papers* (1998) vol. 50, pp. 563–573.

[6] Bloom and Sachs, *Geography, Demography and Economic Growth in Africa*, Brookings Papers on Economic Activity (1999).

TABLE 6.3 **Ethnic Diversity**
Africa is characterized by relatively high levels of ethnic fractionalization. Table shows the probability of two individuals drawn at random being members of different ethnic groups in a country.

Most Fractionalized		Least Fractionalized	
Uganda	0.930	Korea, South	0.002
Nigeria	0.850	Japan	0.012
Madagascar	0.879	Korea, North	0.039
Liberia	0.908	Tunisia	0.039
Kenya	0.859	Vanuatu	0.041
Congo, Dem. Rep. (Zaire)	0.875	Malta	0.041
Congo	0.875	Bangladesh	0.045
Chad	0.862	Portugal	0.047
Cameroon	0.863	Kiribati	0.051
Central African Republic	0.829	Swaziland	0.058

Source: Alesnia, Devleeschauwer, Easterly, Kurlat, and Wacziarg, "Fractionalisation," *Journal of Economic Growth* (2003) 8, pp. 155–194.

cost when it arrives. The gap between these prices is 3.6% in the United States, 4.9% in Western Europe, 9.8% in East Asia, 10.6% in Latin America, and an extraordinary 19.5% in sub-Saharan Africa. While part of these costs are undoubtedly due to poor transport infrastructure, they also reflect geographical location. If trade is important for growth, geography will act as a handicap for Africa.

TABLE 6.4 **Geographical Characteristics of Selected Regions**
Relative to other regions, sub-Saharan Africa suffers from a large amount of tropical land and land-locked geography.

	GDP Per capita ($)	Population (millions)	Land Area (mill km²)	Land in Tropics (%)	Population w/100km Coast (%)	Population w/100km Coast/ River (%)	Landlocked Population (%)	Distance to Core market (km)	Coastal Density (pers/km²)
Sub-Saharan Africa	1865	580	24	91	19	21	28	6237	40
Western Europe	19230	383	3	0	53	89	4	922	109
East Asia	10655	1819	14	30	43	60	0	3396	381
South Asia	1471	1219	4	40	23	41	2	5744	387
Transition Economies	3902	400	24	0	9	55	21	2439	32
Latin America	5163	472	20	73	42	45	3	4651	52

Source: Bloom and Sachs, *Geography, Demography and Economic Growth in Africa*, Brookings Papers on Economic Activity (1999).

Ninety-three percent of sub-Saharan Africa has a tropical climate. Throughout the world, tropical regions are poorer than nontropical areas. The only successful countries with a mostly tropical climate are Hong Kong and Singapore. In both Australia and Brazil, the tropical regions are substantially poorer than the nontropical regions. The most successful economic areas in Africa are in the north and the south, which are the only nontropical areas of the continent. The five North African nations have a GDP per capita (1995) of $4371, nontropical South Africa's 1995 GDP per capita was $7348, while tropical sub-Saharan Africa's was only $1732. In terms of climate, soil, disease, and ecology, tropical regions suffer many handicaps. Agriculture is less productive in tropical areas, and agricultural (and nonagricultural) innovations tend to be designed for the temperate regions, making their adoption problematic in the tropics. These factors place a major restraint on sub-Saharan Africa's standard of living.

Linked to the tropical climate are the acute problems Africa faces from malaria. Every year an estimated 2 million Africans die from malaria (over 20% of total African deaths). Although modern medicine has dramatically reduced the threat of malaria in southern Europe, the Caribbean, and parts of North and South Africa, eradicating malaria from tropical regions still remains a huge task. Historically, malarial countries have grown more slowly than others. Between 1965 and 1990, real output per capita in African countries with severe incidence of malaria grew only 0.4% per year, while in other African countries it grew by 2.3%.

Africa also faces serious problems from the spread of AIDS. Between 1985 and 1995, more than 4 million Africans died from AIDS-related conditions; by 2005 another 10 million may be dead. Of the 30 million people with the HIV virus, 22 million are in sub-Saharan Africa. This represents 60% of the men, 80% of the women, and 90% of the children in the world who have the virus. With per capita medical expenditure in Africa of around $10–15 per year, even the cost of screening for AIDS is prohibitive, let alone the $16,000 annual cost of drug treatment. Because the incidence of AIDS is highest in the age group that is most economically active, this represents a heavy burden in lost output as well as lost lives.

But how much of Africa's weak growth is due to geography and how much to bad policy? In Table 6.5 we show the conclusions of one study trying to explain why African growth has been so weak. From 1960 to 1990, growth in sub-Saharan Africa was, on average, 4.2% below that in Southeast Asia. Convergence factors (a low initial capital stock in Africa) are estimated to have boosted growth in Africa by 1.4%. However, adverse geographic considerations and public policy both reduced growth. Geography was the larger of these two influences, reducing growth by 3%, compared to Southeast Asia. Much of this growth shortfall was due to malaria and poor life expectancy. Additional effects came from Africa's largely landlocked nature. Bad public policy reduced African output growth by 2.1%. The most unfortunate policy was to restrict international trade, but the poor quality of public institutions and education also weakened growth.

COLONIAL INFLUENCES

If geography is a determining influence on economic performance, then Africa has a difficult future ahead because its geography cannot be altered. The existence of these natural handicaps can be used to justify special efforts on the part of rich countries to help fund R&D and treatment of diseases such as AIDS, malaria, TB, and others that afflict Africa.

TABLE 6.5   Explaining Growth Differences by Geography
This table gives a breakdown of overall growth into elements due to various factors. For example, for Sub-Saharan Africa, Bloom and Sachs estimate that geography would have the effect equivalent to losing 3% from productivity growth. Convergence forces (starting with a relatively low capital stock) is worth +1.4%. The overall impact of government policy was to knock about 2.1% off productivity growth.

	Sub-Saharan Africa	South Asia	Latin America
Total growth	−4.2	−2.8	−3.6
Convergence	1.4	1	−1.1
Total geography	−3	−0.8	−0.2
Coastal density	−0.7	0	−0.5
Interior density	0	−0.3	0.1
Tropics	−0.1	0.1	−0.1
Malaria	−1	−0.1	0.3
Life expectancy	−1.2	−0.5	0
Total policy	−2.1	−2.1	−1.8
Openness	−1.2	−1.2	−1
Public institutions	−0.7	−0.9	−0.7
Secondary education	−0.2	−0.1	0
Unexplained	−0.5	−0.8	−0.6

Source: Bloom and Sachs, *Geography, Demography and Economic Growth in Africa*, Brookings Papers on Economic Activity (1998).

However, an alternative view argues that geography is not the final determinate of economic success. Instead, it is the quality of institutions that explains low GDP in Africa, and these are in turn explained by the interaction between geography and **colonialism**. This alternative argument has two stages. The first is to show that geography is not destiny. Proponents of this position do this by pointing out that Africa's geography has not always hampered its development. In 1500, there were many examples of flourishing African cities which were at least on a par with those of Western Europe.

The second stage of the argument is to offer an alternative explanation for Africa's poor performance; this is shown in Figure 6.12. Figure 6.12 shows that ex-colonies where early colonists experienced high rates of settler mortality have low GDP and weak institutions today. Theorists reason that, where European settlers faced adverse geography leading to high mortality rates, they did not establish large colonial populations. Instead, the colonizers developed institutions that focused on extracting rents from a country, and exporting it to the colonial power—Belgian's King Leopold and his control over the Congo is a famed example of such activity. By contrast, where geography produced lower mortality rates, settlers designed institutions aimed at generating value added, rather than extractive institutions. After various colonies became independent nations, these institutional forms

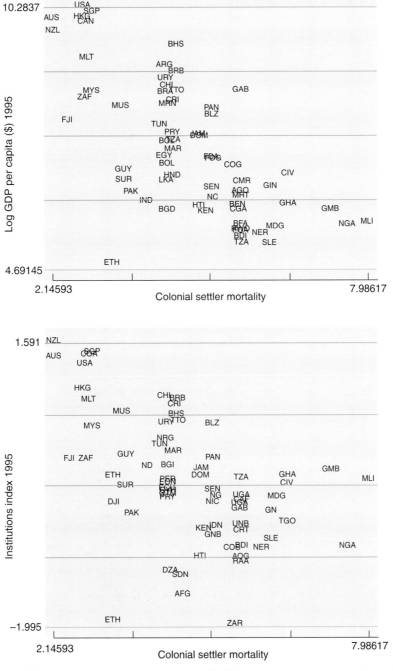

FIGURE 6.12 **Geography, institutions, and GDP.** Where colonial settlers experienced high mortality rates, exploitative institutions developed and have exerted a long-run negative impact on GDP. *Source:* Acemoglu, Robinson, and Johnson, "The Colonial Origins of Comparative Development: An Empirical Investigation" *American Economic Review* (Dec. 2001) vol. 91, pp. 1369–1401.

TABLE 6.6   **Institutional Quality in Africa, 2002**
Africa is characterized by poor governance and institutional quality, although there are some exceptions. Countries are ranked by percentile (0 is the worst and 100 is the best).

Country	Voice and Accountability	Political Stability	Government Effectiveness	Regulatory Quality	Rule of Law	Control of Corruption
Botswana	71.2	71.4	79.9	74.7	72.7	75.3
Democratic Republic of Congo	2	0	1.5	3.1	0.5	1.5
Kenya	28.3	21.6	18.6	35.1	13.9	11.3
Mozambique	43.4	63.8	42.8	26.8	29.9	14.9
Nigeria	26.3	10.3	10.8	11.3	5.2	3.1
South Africa	70.7	42.7	69.1	69.1	59.8	67.5
Tanzania	37.9	35.7	36.1	33.5	38.7	15.5
Uganda	24.2	11.4	43.8	54.1	21.1	19.1
Zimbabwe	7.1	8.6	22.2	4.1	5.7	6.2

Source: Aggregate Governance Indicators 2002, World Bank, http://www.worldbank.org/wbi/governance/pdf/2000kkzcharts_ppp.xls

persisted. In former colonies where settler mortality rates were low, high-quality value adding institutions were established and used and these boosted GDP growth. By contrast, in those with bad geography and high settler mortality rates, rent seeking institutions were established. Politics became a battle for control of the state, and society became focused on rent seeking and not entrepreneurship. According to this argument, geography has no direct impact on GDP—its influence works entirely through its impact on the quality of a country's institutions and not all ex-colonies fare badly (e.g., United States and Australia) depending on interaction of geography and institutions.

Table 6.6 shows the relative standing of institutions in a sample of southern and eastern African countries. It shows that, as regions, they do have relatively poor quality institutions and that, within regions, the richer nations (Botswana and South Africa) have better institutions.

KEY POINT

For nearly two centuries, Africa has remained poor and suffered from low growth. This disappointing performance is in part due to poor policies, but the region has also suffered from further problems due to ethnic conflicts and adverse geography. Geography has had a lasting influence by affecting the type of institutions colonial powers established and bequeathed to countries post-independence.

6.6   Does Aid Work?

Overseas development assistance (aid given by rich countries to poor nations) is around 0.25% of GDP for most OECD nations. Unfortunately, the evidence that aid reliably boosts GDP or investment is weak (William Easterly[7] refers to the idea that aid

---

[7] Easterly, *The Elusive Quest for Growth* (Boston: MIT Press, 2002).

boosts GDP as the myth of benevolent aid—one of the five myths of development). We can use our growth models to explain the disappointing results of development aid. According to the previous section, Africa suffers from a number of factors that lead it to have a poor steady state, a low MPK, and a low investment rate. Our analysis in Chapter 4 says that countries with high investment rates have high GDP. Based on this kind of thinking, aid policy in the 1950s and 1960s was to provide funds to boost investment. But if a country has a low MPK, any funds it receives will not be invested but used for other purposes. As the then deputy director of the World Bank's Economic Development team said in 1947, "When the World Bank thinks it is financing an electrical power station it is in reality financing a brothel." Only if aid changes investment incentives or if a country has a high MPK but is short of funds will aid boost investment. Easterly refers to this as the myth of the benevolent intervention—the idea that by focusing on one policy aim (such as investment, education, or family planning), aid can boost income in poor countries.

This suggests that aid will work if it is given to countries with good steady states but low capital stocks, in other words, poor countries with good policies. This intuition is supported by empirical evidence.[8] Studies suggest that, for every 1% of GDP received in aid, the economies of countries with good policies grow by 0.5%, whereas aid given to countries with poor policies doesn't raise output. This suggests that aid agencies should make aid conditional on the policies that countries implement. However, there is little evidence that aid can be used to successfully persuade a country to adopt better policies (Easterly calls this the myth of the benevolent condition). Hence aid agencies are increasingly focusing on the issue of the "ownership" of reform—if countries can be persuaded that policy reforms are in their interest, then reform is much more likely to be successful.

This discussion has so far focused on the failures of aid due to poor policies in recipient economies, but a further reason why aid has not always been successful in raising GDP is the motivation of donor countries in giving aid (what Easterly refers to as the myth of the benevolent government). Many countries focus on providing aid to former colonies, and during the cold war the United States and the Soviet Union often used aid as a political rather than economic instrument. Table 6.7 shows the results of a

TABLE 6.7   **Determinants of Aid Flows**

Countries do tend to receive more aid the poorer they are, but other political factors also influence aid flows. Table quotes elasticity of aid with respect to each variable, e.g., for every 1% lower GDP, the United States increases aid by 1.29%.

	Income	Openness	Democracy	UN Friend	Own Colony	Other Colony	Egypt	Israel
U.S.	−1.29	0.91	0.43	0.05	0.4	0.04	4.21	4.11
U.K.	−0.73	0.87	0.16	0.06	0.69	−0.04	0.14	−2.32
France	−0.28	0.59	0.05	0.06	1	0.13	2.58	0.29
Japan	−0.17	1.09	0.13	0.11	1.65	0.1	1.07	−0.15
Germany	−0.49	0.17	0.1	0.1	0.18	0.13	1.51	3.4

Source: Alesina and Dollar, "Who gives foreign aid to whom and why? *Journal of Economic Growth* (2000) vol. 5, pp. 33–64.

[8] Burnside and Dollar, "Aid, Policies and Growth," *American Economic Review* (2000) vol. 90 (4) pp. 847–868.

study on what determines how much aid OECD nations give to countries. The poorer the recipient country is, the more aid it receives, with the United States and United Kingdom making aid particularly sensitive to income. Further, the more open to trade and the more democratic a country is, the more aid it receives. Political factors also matter—if the country votes alongside the donor nation in the UN, if it is a former colony or involved in the Middle East, then it also tends to receive more aid.

The notion of giving aid to countries with good policies is entirely consistent with our analysis of the steady state. However, if the institutional analysis of the previous section is correct, then this focus on good policies may be inappropriate. If it is good institutions that matter, then persuading governments to adopt good policies may be ineffective. A good example here is privatization—without appropriate regulation and control, privatizing a monopoly will do little to improve the health of the economy (the last of Easterly's myths—the myth of the benevolent market). One recent study[9] suggests that this is this case. Whether a country has good or bad policies does not matter for growth; it is only institutions that are important. If true, this suggests that the successful use of development aid will be even more difficult than getting recipient countries to adopt growth-orientated policies.

KEY POINT

Aid does not systematically boost GDP growth, but it does if the recipient country has good policies. For this reason, aid policies are increasingly focused on providing development assistance to countries that adopt growth-orientated economic policies.

SUMMARY

In section 6.1, we showed that assuming that the MPK is constant rather than decreasing leads to dramatically different predictions from the growth model we developed in Chapters 4 and 5. With constant marginal product, a steady state level of output does not exist, and we should not expect to find convergence across countries. Interactions between physical and human capital may postpone diminishing MPK and even lead to a constant MPK.

In section 6.2, we saw that, if spillovers and interactions are particularly marked, it may even be that the MPK is increasing, in which case poverty traps may exist. In a poverty trap, individuals have poor incentives to invest in either human or physical capital. As a result, wealthy nations get wealthier while the poorer nations stay poor.

In section 6.3, we considered the evidence for different assumptions about the MPK. When we examined growth since 1950 among a wide range of countries, we found no evidence of convergence; poor countries do not grow faster than rich countries. This suggests that the assumption of diminishing MPK is inappropriate. However, when we considered similar groupings of countries, like the OECD nations, we found strong evidence of conver-

---

[9] Easterly and Levine, "Tropics, Germs and Crops," *Journal of Monetary Economics,* 50: 1 (January 2003).

gence. We introduced the notion of conditional convergence, which is the idea that countries grow fastest when they are furthest away from their steady state, but that different countries will have different steady states. As a result, only similar nations will show any evidence of convergence.

In section 6.4, we examined what determines the steady state of a nation and found that investment, health, education, and an open economy are important.

In section 6.5, we reviewed the disappointing growth performance of Africa. For over two centuries, Africa has been both the poorest and slowest growing region in the world economy. In part this can be attributed to Africa's poor steady state due to low levels of investment, education, the closed nature of African economies, and poor social infrastructure. However, ethnic diversity, the landlocked nature of much of Africa, and its tropical climate and diseases are also important. Africa also suffers negatively from poor quality institutions which may be a legacy of the interaction between geography and colonialism.

In section 6.6, we considered the role of developmental aid for poor countries such as those in much of Africa. Every year rich nations spend around 0.25% of their GDP on overseas development assistance. Aid only boosts GDP when given to countries with good policies; more general aid has no impact. One reason why aid has not always been effective in boosting GDP is that it has often been used by donor countries to achieve political rather than economic aims. Aid policy is now increasingly focused on providing assistance to countries with good policies.

CONCEPTUAL QUESTIONS

1. (Section 6.1) Do models that assume decreasing MPK offer a theory of economic growth?

2. (6.1) Can human knowledge and ingenuity support a constant MPK?

3. (6.2) If individuals live in an area characterized by a poverty trap, will they not just move to a prosperous region? Should policymakers therefore worry about poverty traps?

4. (6.3) Can conditional convergence explain *any* pattern of cross-country differences in standards of living?

5. (6.4) Do empirical studies of the determinants of the steady state tell us anything more than that the richest economies are OECD economies? Are OECD economies a successful blueprint for emerging nations, and can their key factors be easily transplanted? Why?

6. (6.4) What role can governments play in improving the steady state? What does this imply about the relationship between the size of government and GDP per capita?

7. (6.5) What steps can a country take to change its institutions? What difficulties might it experience?

8. (6.5) What incentives do pharmaceutical companies have to undertake R&D in medicines for treating AIDS? Malaria? Erectile dysfunction? What can policymakers do about this?

9. (6.6) Does it matter if development aid just boosts government consumption in poor African economies? Why or why not?

10. (6.6) If it is good institutions rather than good policies that matter, what implications does this have for aid agencies?

ANALYTICAL QUESTIONS

1. (Section 6.1) Assume that there are no diminishing returns to capital and that, as shown in Figure 6.1, output is simply a constant proportion (*a*) of the capital stock. Investment is also a constant fraction (*b*) of output, and depreciation is a proportion (d) of the capital stock. The change in the capital stock is total investment minus depreciation. Show how the proportionate rate of change of the capital stock depends upon the relative magnitudes of *a*, *b*, and d. What happens to the growth of capital if *b* doubles from 0.1 to 0.2?

2. (6.3) Suppose that two economies share a common steady state so that there is convergence between them. The poorer country closes 2% of the income gap between them each year. What proportion of the initial gap in income between the two countries is closed after 20 years? After 40 years how much of the initial gap remains?

3. (6.3) Repeat the analysis of Figure 6.10 when the high investment rate economy also has access to more productive technology. What does this imply about the scale of inequality we should expect to find across countries?

4. (6.3) Draw the MPK schedule so that, over a certain initial range of capital, there is increasing MPK and then this is followed by diminishing MPK until the MPK declines to a level higher than that achieved in poor countries. What pattern of cross-country growth will this produce? How does this compare with the data described in this and earlier chapters?

Unemployment and the Labor Market

Overview

In this chapter we consider the final determinant of how much output a country can produce—the number of people employed. We begin by reviewing the key data definitions for the labor force and examine how these variables differ across countries and demographic groups. We then complete our analysis of long-run growth by examining the impact of capital accumulation and technological progress on the labor market and show how higher productivity generates higher wages but may not change the unemployment rate. This leads to the notion of a country's natural rate of unemployment—a long-run equilibrium concept that determines what fraction of the workforce is economically active. We show how this natural rate depends on the structure of product and labor markets and review empirically its key determinants. We examine how the natural rate is related to flows into and out of unemployment and employment protection legislation and how it is influenced by labor market reform. We conclude by reviewing recent developments in equality and the impact of immigration.

Key Concepts

Active Labor Market Spending
Employment Protection Legislation (EPL)
Employment Rate

Labor Force
Marginal Product of Labor
Natural Rate of Unemployment
Participation Rate

Real Wage
Unemployment Rate
Wage Bargaining

7.1 Labor Market Data

Not everyone in the population is involved in the labor market—as shown in Figure 7.1. The first important distinction is between the working-age population (normally defined as those aged between 15 and 64) and the rest of the population. However, not even all the working-age population is in the labor market. Many will be

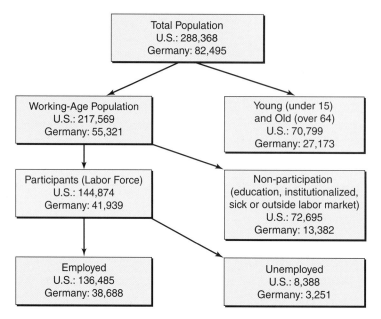

FIGURE 7.1 **Labor market status of population (thousands).** *Source:* OECD.

taking full-time educational courses, some will be institutionalized (for instance, in jail), others sick or simply not wanting a job (for instance, those who remain at home raising children or caring for relatives). The remainder—all those of working age who are willing and able to work—make up the **labor force**. The proportion of the civilian noninstitutional population who are in the labor force is called the **participation rate**. The labor force in turn is made up of those who have a job—the employed—and those who are willing to work but do not have a job—the unemployed. The proportion of the labor force employed defines the **employment rate** and the proportion of the labor force unemployed defines the **unemployment rate**.

One complication in measuring unemployment is who counts as being unemployed. The best measure is one based on survey data that counts respondents as being unemployed if they do not have a job but are actively seeking work. However, some countries calculate unemployment numbers on the basis of whether individuals are entitled to receive unemployment benefits. Because not everyone without a job receives unemployment benefits, and because not everyone receiving benefits is looking for a job, this is not a reliable indicator of unemployment. When examining cross-country evidence on unemployment, consistent definitions based on survey data are important.

Table 7.1 shows variations across OECD countries for a range of labor market variables. For every variable there are major cross-country differences and these will make a significant difference to GDP per capita. For instance, in Italy only around 56% of the population is employed, compared to 72% in the United States. The average of hours worked is also larger in the United States.

TABLE 7.1 Cross-Country Variation in Labor Market Statistics 2002
Early retirement index is 100-participation rate of 55–64 years.

Country	% of 15–24-Year-Olds Employment	Early Retirement	Female Employment Rate	% Part-time Employment	% Part-time Jobs Held by Females	Average Weekly Hours Worked	Employment Rate	Unemployment Rate
Australia	60.6	49.9	68.5	27.4	68.6	35.08	69.4	6.4
Czech Republic	33.7	57.5	74.6	2.9	73.4	38.08	65.7	7.3
France	23.3	62.8	71.6	13.7	79.3	29.71	61.1	9.1
Germany	45.4	57.0	71.9	18.8	84.1	27.77	65.3	8.7
Italy	26.7	69.9	54.0	11.9	74.4	31.13	55.6	9.0
Japan	41.0	34.6	63.9	25.1	67.5	34.79	73.2	9
Netherlands	66.9	57.3	72.5	33.9	75.4	25.77	73.2	2.4
New Zealand	56.8	34.5	71.8	22.6	74.3	34.92	72.4	2.8
Norway	56.9	30.3	80.6	20.6	79.1	25.81	77.1	5.2
Spain	36.6	57.3	54.2	7.6	75.9	34.75	59.5	11.9
Sweden	46.5	28.3	82.4	13.8	71.8	30.40	74.9	11.4
Switzerland	65.3	33.9	78.1	24.7	83.4	29.63	78.9	4.9
U.K.	61.0	44.8	73.8	23.0	80.4	32.83	72.7	2.5
U.S.	55.7	38.1	72.3	13.4	68.0	34.90	71.9	5.1

Source: OECD, *Economic Outlook* (2003), Statistical Annex Table 21, www.oecd.org and Labor Force Statistics, www.oecd.org

---

KEY POINT

The participation rate is the proportion of the population who make up the labor force, which in turn consists of the employed and the unemployed. The unemployment rate is the percentage of the labor force without a job. Variations in employment and unemployment are a major influence of GDP per capita.

7.2 A Long-Run Model of the Labor Market

Chapters 3 through 6 focused on long-run developments in GDP per capita and on how capital accumulation and technological progress affect output. We now complete this analysis by considering how these factors affect the labor market.

LABOR DEMAND AND THE PRODUCTION FUNCTION

The key concept of the production function for the labor market is the **marginal product of labor** (**MPL**)—the amount of extra output that one more worker can produce *keeping fixed the stock of capital and the level of technology.* The MPL is assumed to be decreasing with the level of employment: "too many cooks spoil the broth," as shown in Figure 7.2.

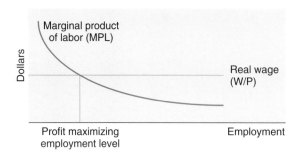

FIGURE 7.2 **Diminishing marginal product of labor (MPL).** As more hours are worked, with a fixed stock of machines and a given technology, the marginal product of labor falls.

When a firm considers how many workers to employ, the MPL plays a key role. Each additional worker produces extra output equal to the MPL. If the firm can sell this output for a price P, then hiring one more worker yields additional revenue of P × MPL. However, every additional worker increases a firm's costs—the firm has to pay wages, employment taxes, recruitment and training costs, and so forth. We summarize these costs in a wage term, W. If P × MPL exceeds W, then hiring an extra worker leads to an increase in profits, while if P × MPL is less than W, profits fall. Alternatively, we can say if MPL > W/P, the firm should hire workers, and if MPL < W/P, the firm should reduce its workforce. The term W/P is the **real wage** and reflects how much the firm has to pay its workforce relative to the price of its output. The firm is at its profit maximizing employment level when the real wage just equals the MPL.

We can use the MPL to arrive at a labor demand curve—a relationship between the firm's real wage and the level of employment demanded by firms. As we change the level of the real wage, as in Figure 7.3, we alter the desired level of employment. Therefore the MPL traces out a negative relationship between real wages and labor demand—in other words, *the MPL curve is the labor demand curve.*

We now use this result to show what happens to labor demand when there is capital accumulation and technological progress. An increase in either the stock of capital or the level of technology means that each worker becomes more productive—for a given level of employment, the marginal product of labor increases, and the MPL curve shifts out—as in Figure 7.4. Because the MPL and labor demand curves are the same, investment and technological progress shifts out the labor demand curve to the right.

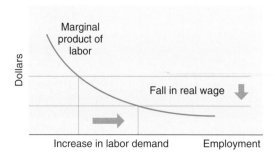

FIGURE 7.3 **Declining real wage leads to higher labor demand.** A fall in real wages will raise the firm's profit maximizing level of labor demand.

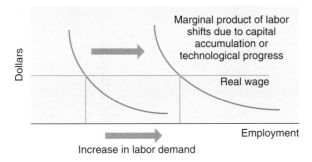

FIGURE 7.4 **Effect of capital accumulation and technological progress on labor demand.** More capital and better technology increases the marginal product of labor and raises the demand for labor at a given real wage.

LABOR SUPPLY

To complete our analysis, we must also consider labor supply. When the real wage increases, it affects the supply of labor in two ways. First, it becomes more expensive *not* to work. The cost of enjoying another hour of leisure is the wage you would have earned if, instead, you worked. An increase in real wages makes leisure more expensive and, in itself, leads to an increase in the supply of labor. This is called the *substitution effect*—as the price of a good increases (in this case leisure), people substitute something for it (in this case work).

However, there is a second, offsetting effect when the real wage rises. People become wealthier and want to consume more of most goods, including leisure. This *income effect* leads people to consume more leisure and supply less labor as real wages rise. What happens to the supply of labor when wages increase depends on whether the income effect or substitution effect dominates. In Figure 7.5a we show the case in which the substitution effect dominates and labor supply is increasing with the real wage. In Figure 7.5b, the income effect dominates, and finally, in Figure 7.5c, we show what happens if the income and substitution effect exactly offset each other.

The case shown in Figure 7.5c offers the best explanation of the long-run facts of the labor market—no trend increase in unemployment, but substantial increases in

FIGURE 7.5a
Substitution effect dominates.

FIGURE 7.5b **Income effect dominates.**

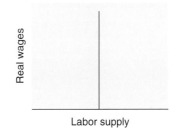

FIGURE 7.5c **Income and substitution effect cancel out.** How labor supply responds to a wage depends on the relative size of the income and substitution effects.

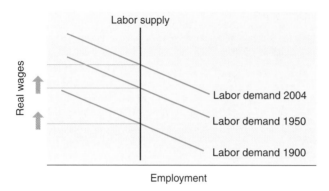

FIGURE 7.6 **Long-run model of labor market.** If the long-run supply curve of labor is vertical, rightward shifts in the demand for labor generate higher real wages at a constant level of employment.

both labor productivity and real wages. To see why, consider Figure 7.6. As capital accumulation and technological progress grew between 1900 and 1950, the MPL increased, causing an outward shift of the labor demand curve. But the labor supply curve is vertical—no additional hours are supplied. As a result, firms compete among themselves for workers and bid wages up. Firms are prepared to pay these higher wages because productivity has increased. But because of the vertical supply curve, the higher wages do not lead to extra hours worked. Competition between firms continues until the real wage has been bid up to offset the productivity improvements, and firms no longer wish to hire more worker hours. At this point, labor demand is once more equal to labor supply. Further increases in labor demand bring forth additional increases in wages. The long-run impact of capital accumulation and technological progress is therefore an increase in average wages and no change in employment. Further long-run productivity improvements, whether from capital accumulation or technological progress, feed through one for one into real wages.

Figure 7.6 suggests that over time the employment rate remains approximately constant. Over the business cycle, employment/unemployment will show short-term fluctuations around this level, but eventually it will return to this *equilibrium* level. Economists refer to this equilibrium as **the natural rate of unemployment**. The natural rate is a long-run concept that characterizes the average unemployment rate over, say, a decade.

KEY POINT

Over the long run, increases in the capital stock and technological progress shift the labor demand curve but, because of a limited labor supply response, they produce equal increases in productivity and wages and no change in the employment rate.

7.3 The Natural Rate of Unemployment

Table 7.2 shows OECD estimates of the natural rate of unemployment in 2001 for several countries. These marked variations in the natural rate of unemployment reflect differences in the underlying structure and policies of countries, as we outline in this section.

TABLE 7.2   **OECD Estimates of Natural Rate of Unemployment**

	1991	2001
Falling natural rate, average 1991 = 8.4		
Ireland	14.3	6.4
Netherlands	7.1	4.0
U.K.	8.2	5.5
Denmark	7.3	4.9
Spain	13.4	11.5
Canada	8.8	6.9
Belgium	8.8	7.2
New Zealand	7.0	5.4
Norway	4.9	3.6
Portugal	4.7	3.8
Australia	6.8	6.2
France	9.7	9.3
Stable natural rate, average 1991 = 5.3		
U.S.	5.4	5.1
Italy	9.3	9.2
Switzerland	1.7	1.8
Austria	4.8	4.9
Rising natural rate, average 1991 = 5.1		
Germany	6.7	7.3
Greece	8.3	9.8
Japan	2.4	3.9
Finland	6.8	8.6
Iceland	1.5	3.5
Euro zone	8.6	8.3
OECD	6.3	6.1

Source: OECD, *Employment Outlook*
(September 2003).

INTUITION BEHIND THE MODEL—COMPETING MONOPOLY POWERS

In outlining our model of unemployment, we move away from the assumption that the labor and product markets are competitive. Instead, we examine a model where both firms and workers seek monopoly power—they can influence the prices or wages that they charge and do not have to accept the going market rate.

When firms have monopoly power, they set price above cost. This means they try and set prices at a certain level above wages (an important component of costs) and thus put downward pressure on the real wage (the wage relative to prices). Monopoly power in the labor force reflects workers' ability to influence their own wage rather than have to accept the established market rate. The most obvious form of such monopoly power is labor unions, and this is how we will think of monopoly power in the model. However, you do not need to belong to a labor union to be able to influence your wage. Many workers have some form of monopoly power simply because of the hassle to the firm of hiring a replacement, including having the position vacant for a time and advertising and hiring costs. For all these reasons, the firm has an incentive to keep people in employment, which gives employees some ability to influence their wage relative to the market average. We assume that workers seek as high a real wage as possible, but the higher unemployment is, the more cautious they are in their wage demands.

This model suggests that unemployment is the mechanism that reconciles the monopoly demands of firms and workers. Market equilibrium requires that the demands of firms and workers be in agreement. This can only occur when unemployment is at a level that leads unions to seek real wages consistent with the profit margins firms seek. The more monopoly power either firms or workers have, the higher the natural rate of unemployment will be.

> **KEY POINT**
>
> To explain unemployment, we need to introduce monopoly power in the product and labor markets.

7.4   A Diagrammatic Analysis

Figure 7.7 shows the model diagrammatically. The horizontal line is the firm's price-setting curve—it shows the real wage consistent with the firm's desired profit margin. For simplicity, we assume that the only costs a firm faces are its wages, and that the firm wants a profit margin of $x\%$. The price (P) of the firm's output therefore equals $W(1 + x/100)$, where W is the wage rate (or unit labor cost). This pricing rule sets $P/W = 1 + x/100$ or alternatively $W/P = 1/(1 + x/100)$. Again for simplicity, we also assume in Figure 7.7 that the firm's desired profit margin (x) is always the same, regardless of the rate of unemployment—the price setting curve, therefore, is a flat line.

The other part of Figure 7.7 is the wage setting curve. This downward sloping line shows the real wage that labor unions seek for a given unemployment rate. The higher the level of unemployment, the more restrained unions' wage demands are. The intersection of the price and wage setting curves is an equilibrium point where the real wage that firms are prepared to pay equals the real wage that the unions demand. This is the natural rate of unemployment. *Only at this level of unemployment are the wage demands of workers consistent with the profit margins firms seek.*

Consider the case where unemployment is at the low rate of U_L. With unemployment so low, the real wage demands of workers are too high for firms. Unemployment will start to rise above U_L toward the natural rate as firms reduce employment. Rising unemployment leads unions to moderate their wage demands. Eventually, the increase in unemployment produces enough wage restraint that the demands of firms and workers are consistent, and unemployment stabilizes at its natural rate.

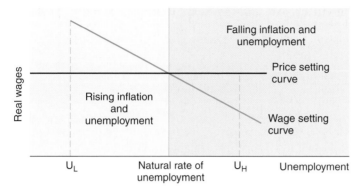

FIGURE 7.7 **Determinants of the natural rate of unemployment.** When unemployment is above the natural rate, the wage that firms are prepared to pay exceeds the wage that labor is able to negotiate; the opposite is true when unemployment is below the natural rate.

If instead, the unemployment rate is above the natural rate, for instance at U_H, the process works in reverse. At this level of unemployment, union wage demands are modest, and firms can achieve a high profit margin. In response they start to hire more workers, so that unemployment falls toward the natural rate.

KEY POINT

Unemployment is the mechanism that reconciles the wage demands of workers with the profit margins sought by firms. The greater the monopoly power of either firms or workers, the higher the unemployment rate.

 ## Determinants of the Natural Rate

We have characterized the behavior of firms by the price setting rule

$$W/P = 1/(1 + x/100)$$

where x is the firm's desired markup. We can also characterize the behavior of unions by

$$W/P = A - bu$$

where u denotes the unemployment rate, so that union wage demands are lower when unemployment is high. The constant A reflects the factors that influence the wages labor unions demand, and the coefficient b determines the sensitivity of wage demands to unemployment.

In equilibrium, the wage demands of workers must be consistent with the price setting decisions of firms, so that

$$1/(1 + x/100) = A - bu$$

We can rearrange this to arrive at an expression for the natural rate of unemployment ($u*$):

$$u* = (1/b)(A - 1/(1 + x/100))$$

Therefore, we can think of three separate influences on the natural rate:

1. Product market power (x). The greater is monopoly power in the product market, the higher is unemployment.
2. The sensitivity of wage demands to unemployment (b). Unemployment is the means of reconciling the competing demands of firms and workers. The less responsive wage demands are, the higher unemployment must be.
3. The monopoly power of labor unions (A). The greater the strength of unions, the higher their wage demands will be. This leads to higher unemployment.

We now proceed to examine the institutional factors that affect each of these three influences.

PRODUCT MARKET COMPETITION AND THE NATURAL RATE

As we change the monopoly power of firms and the size of their profit margin, we shift the position of the price setting curve and change the natural rate of unemployment. In a country with more powerful monopolies, firms set prices that are high relative to wages, which implies a low real wage. The price setting curve shifts down, leading to a higher natural rate of unemployment. The intuition is straightforward—monopolists charge a higher price and produce less output and thus set a lower level of employment. In order for unions to accept these low real wages, unemployment has to be high. Therefore less competitive product markets lead to higher unemployment. Figure 7.8 shows that, across OECD countries, economies with less competitive product markets do have lower employment rates, as our model predicts.

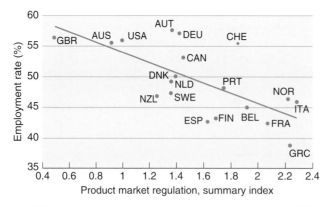

FIGURE 7.8 **Employment and product market competitiveness in OECD countries.** More regulated and less competitive product markets lead to lower levels of employment. *Source:* Nicolleti, Bassanini, Ernst, Jean, Santiago and Swaim, *Product and Labor Markets Interactions in OECD Countries*, Economic Department Working Papers 312.

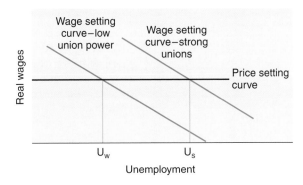

FIGURE 7.9 **Stronger unions lead to higher unemployment.** If labor power increases, it may cause higher unemployment with little gain in terms of higher real wages. Here, because the price setting curve is flat, more labor union power simply increases unemployment from U_W to U_S

THE INFLUENCE OF LABOR MARKET STRUCTURE

Figure 7.9 shows two economies that differ only in their labor market structure. The economy in which workers have more monopoly power has a wage setting curve further to the right and has a higher natural rate of unemployment. The labor force may be able to exercise more monopoly power for five reasons: (1) strong labor union membership and union rights, (2) generous unemployment benefits, (3) large numbers of long-term unemployed, (4) regional and skill mismatch, and (5) high levels of taxes on labor. We now consider each of these factors and how they vary across countries.

UNION MEMBERSHIP   The more members a union has, or the more people its negotiations cover, the more monopoly power the union can exploit. Figure 7.10 shows measures of labor union strength across OECD economies. When considering union influence, we need to distinguish between membership and coverage. Coverage (or collective bargaining) refers to the proportion of the workforce whose pay is determined by union negotiations—within a firm or industry, wage negotiations by unions are often extended to nonunion members. Empirical studies suggest that coverage influences unemployment more than union membership does.

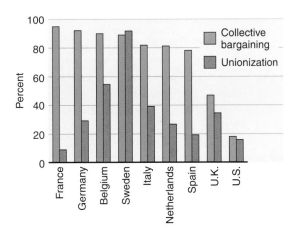

FIGURE 7.10 **Union membership and coverage amongst OECD economies, 1994.** The significance of labor unions differs substantially across countries. *Source:* OECD, *Jobs Study* (1994).

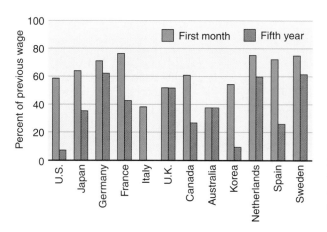

FIGURE 7.11 **Unemployment benefit replacement ratios, 1997.** In most countries, the level of benefits to the unemployed falls after a period out of work; in some cases, most notably in the United States, the decline in benefits to those who stay out of work is very large. *Source: Assessing Performance and Policy* (1999). Copyright OECD.

UNEMPLOYMENT BENEFITS   If unemployment benefits are high and last for a long time, they increase the monopoly power of those employed in two ways. First, generous benefits cushion the effects of being unemployed and lessen the motivation to look for new work. This reduces competition for jobs. Second, generous unemployment benefits also reduce the cost of becoming unemployed and these make the employed more aggressive in their wage demands.

Figure 7.11 shows the **replacement rate** for a variety of OECD economies. The replacement ratio is unemployment benefits expressed as a percentage of previous earnings. Most countries have reasonably generous replacement rates for the first year, but after this benefits fall substantially. This is intended to give people protection against the initial shock of unemployment while minimizing their negative impact (the rightward shift in the wage setting curve due to the reduced threat of unemployment). The positive effects of unemployment benefits arise from two sources: first, as an insurance policy to workers, and second, because governments are effectively subsidizing job searches. Benefits encourage the unemployed worker to spend more time searching for a job that is more suitable to him or her rather than having to accept a first job offer. The better the match between job and worker, the higher the productivity in a country, so subsidizing job searches has social benefits.

PROPORTION OF LONG-TERM UNEMPLOYED   The monopoly power of those in employment is lessened if the unemployed compete effectively with the employed for jobs. However, the greater the proportion of long-term unemployed, the less intense this competition is. The longer people are unemployed, the more work-relevant skills they lose, and the lower their chance of becoming employed. As a result, the greater the proportion of long-term unemployed, the more monopoly power the employed possess. This leads to a rightward shift in the wage setting curve and upward pressure on unemployment.

Figure 7.12 shows, for a variety of economies, the proportion of unemployed who have been unemployed for six months or more and for a year or more. Those countries in the figure with high levels of unemployment (e.g., France, Germany, and Italy) also have high levels of long-term unemployed. Note the low levels of long-term unemployed in the United States. As we shall see, the American labor market is particularly effective at finding jobs for the unemployed quickly.

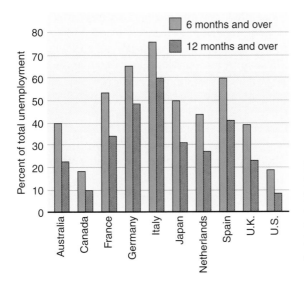

FIGURE 7.12 **Proportion of long-term unemployed amongst OECD economies, 2002.** In Europe the proportion of those unemployed who have been without work for many months is higher than in North America and Japan. *Source:* OECD, *Employment Outlook* (2003).

REGIONAL AND SKILL-BASED MISMATCH   If one area of the economy is booming but is in a different part of the country from an area that is doing badly, then the employed will face weaker competition from the unemployed if there is little mobility across regions (see Figure 7.13). Similarly, if the unemployed are mostly unskilled, but the employed have high levels of skill, then unemployment will not effectively restrain the wage demands of the employed. Therefore, for a given level of unemployment, the greater the regional or skill mismatch, the higher the natural rate of unemployment.

LABOR AND CONSUMPTION TAXES   Because of taxes, it is important to distinguish between the *consumer* and the *producer* real wage—a distinction we have ignored so far. The real wage is the nominal wage divided by the price, but the relevant wages and prices differ for the producer and the consumer. For consumers, the wage is what they receive after the deduction of taxes relative to prices, which include all retail taxes such

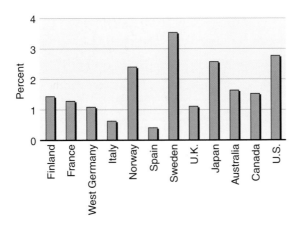

FIGURE 7.13 **Percent of population who change regions per year, 1980–1987.** Labor mobility is higher in the United States than in most other developed economies. *Source:* OECD, *Employment Outlook* (1999).

as general sales tax (GST) or value-added tax (VAT). The producer wage is the gross wage that firms pay out plus any additional employer taxes or social security contributions. Three tax rates influence the gap between the producer and consumer real wage: payroll taxes (taxes that either the employer or employee pay and that are normally related to social security contributions); income taxes; and consumer price taxes. Because the last two affect both the employed and the unemployed, economists think that payroll taxes influence the natural rate the most. These tax wedges shift the wage setting curve further to the right and thus increase the natural rate. The wage curve shifts out because the higher taxes are, the greater the wage unions seek to provide a given real standard of living for their members. As Table 7.3 shows, these tax wedges are large in most developed countries.

TABLE 7.3   **Tax Wedges in OECD Countries**

Tax wedges drive a gap between the real wages workers take home and the cost of labor to employers. In many developed economies these tax wedges are very large.

	Total Taxes on Labor (%) = Payroll Tax Rate plus Income Tax Rate plus Consumption Tax Rate					
	1960–64	1965–72	1973–79	1980–87	1988–95	1996–2000
Australia	28	31	36	39	—	—
Austria	47	52	55	58	59	66
Belgium	38	43	44	46	49	51
Canada	31	39	41	42	50	53
Denmark	32	46	53	59	60	61
Finland	38	46	55	58	64	62
France	55	57	60	65	67	68
West Germany	43	44	48	50	52	50
Ireland	23	30	30	37	41	33
Italy	57	56	54	56	67	64
Japan	25	25	26	33	33	37
Netherlands	45	54	57	55	47	43
Norway	—	52	61	65	61	60
New Zealand	—	—	29	30	—	—
Portugal	20	25	26	33	41	39
Spain	19	23	29	40	46	45
Sweden	41	54	68	77	78	77
Switzerland	30	31	35	36	36	36
U.K.	34	43	45	51	47	44
U.S.	34	37	42	44	45	45

Note: These data are based on the London School of Economics, Centre for Economic Performance OECD dataset.

Source: Nickell, "Labor Market Institutions and Unemployment in OECD Countries," CESIfo DICE Report, 2/2003.

KEY POINT

Competition between the employed and the unemployed is critical in maintaining a low natural rate of unemployment. Strong trade unions, high benefits, a large proportion of long-term unemployed, regional and skill mismatches, and high taxes all reduce competition between unemployed and employed and lead to higher unemployment.

7.6 What Lowers Unemployment?

The previous section focused on factors that increase the natural rate of unemployment. Here we discuss influences that *lower* unemployment. We focus on two such beneficial factors: active labor market spending and coordinated wage bargaining. In each case, the effect is to shift the wage setting curve leftward and to lower the national rate of unemployment.

ACTIVE LABOR MARKET SPENDING

Active labor market spending refers to a range of policies that governments use to boost employment and reduce unemployment (see Table 7.4). One policy is to assist the unemployed's job search—improving information flows about job availabilities, helping individuals with application forms and interview techniques, and offering re-training. Other active labor market policies subsidize the creation of jobs for the unemployed, offer loans to individuals who want to start their own businesses, subsidize firms that hire those who have been unemployed for a long time, and so on.

TABLE 7.4 **Active Labor Market Spending (% GDP), 2000–2001**
In continental Europe, governments have devoted substantial resources to trying to make labor markets work better.

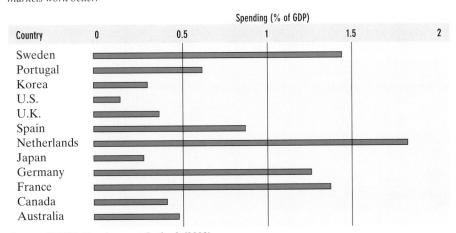

Source: OECD, *Employment Outlook* (2003).

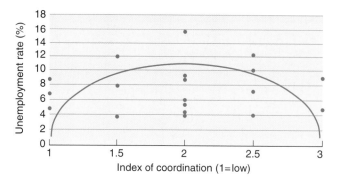

FIGURE 7.14
Coordination of wage bargaining and unemployment across OECD countries. *Source:* Nickell, *Labour Market Institutions and Unemployment in OECD Economies*, DICE Report, Summer 2003 CES-Ifo

COORDINATED WAGE BARGAINING

In a previous section, we argued that the stronger the monopoly power of unions, the higher the natural rate of unemployment. Yet some countries with the most extensive union coverage (in particular Scandinavia) also have low unemployment rates. To explain this, we need to recognize that whether or not unions are bad for unemployment depends *both* on the degree of monopoly power the workforce possesses *and* how it exercises this power. In particular, if wage bargaining occurs at a highly centralized level between unions and firms, then the adverse unemployment effects may be small.

Consider the case of numerous strong unions that each negotiate separately with their employers and try to achieve as high a wage as possible compared with other unions. Of course, not all unions can do this—they cannot all outperform each other. Their uncoordinated attempts at boosting wages only generate higher unemployment to restrain their wage demands. If instead, the unions coordinate their bargaining, they will realize that additional wage demands will only boost unemployment (especially if employer organizations are also coordinating their negotiations). As a result, their wage demands will be more modest and unemployment will reconcile the competing demands of firms and the workforce at a lower equilibrium level.

Figure 7.14 shows estimates of how centralized wage bargaining was in different countries between 1995 and 1999 and compares *the level of centralization with unemployment rates*. This figure offers some support for the notion that both coordinated wage bargaining and decentralized labor markets produce lower unemployment.

KEY POINT

Unemployment is caused by the interaction of the monopoly power of firms and workers. Active labor market policies reduce the monopoly power of workers and coordinated wage bargaining restrains the use of monopoly power.

7.7   A Flow Approach to the Natural Rate of Unemployment

To enhance our understanding of the labor market, we now focus on a different perspective that focuses on flows into and out of unemployment. This enables us to review the effectiveness of **employment protection legislation** (**EPL**), which aims to reduce unemployment by restricting the ability of firms to fire workers.

Every period, some of those who are employed lose their jobs. This may be for voluntary reasons (they did not like their job and quit) or involuntary ones (their firm is downsizing and they are fired). These inflows increase unemployment. However, in every period other people cease to be unemployed. They either withdraw from the labor force or find work. The natural rate of unemployment is an equilibrium at which there is no tendency for unemployment to change. But for unemployment not to be changing, the inflow into unemployment must equal the outflow. We can use this fact to derive an expression for the natural rate of unemployment.

The inflow *into* unemployment equals the number of people employed (L) multiplied by the probability that a person loses his or her job (p). The outflow *from* unemployment equals the number of people who are unemployed (U) multiplied by the probability of an unemployed person finding a job (s).

The natural rate of unemployment occurs when inflows and outflows equal each other, that is when

unemployment inflows = pL = sU = unemployment outflows

We know, by definition, that employment plus unemployment equals the labor force (LF), so that LF = L + U or L = LF − U. We can therefore write our equilibrium condition as

$$p(\text{LF} - \text{U}) = s\text{U}$$

As the unemployment rate (u) equals the unemployed divided by the labor force (U/LF), we can write this expression as

$$p(\text{LF/LF} - \text{U/LF}) = s\text{U/LF}$$

or

$$p(1 - u) = su$$

where u is the unemployment rate (U/LF). Rearranging this gives us an expression for the natural rate of unemployment

$$u^* = p/(p + s)$$

In other words, the natural rate of unemployment depends positively on p, the probability that an employed person becomes unemployed, and negatively on s, the probability an unemployed person finds a job.

THE IMPACT OF EMPLOYMENT PROTECTION LEGISLATION (EPL)

EPL is a label for a variety of measures that governments take to protect those in employment from dismissal. These include laws about formal dismissal practices, severance pay, notice periods, the number of warnings firms have to give a worker before he or she can be fired, whether government has to approve a corporate downsizing, and so forth.

Table 7.5 shows considerable variation in the scale of EPL among OECD economies. For instance, according to the OECD, U.S. employers face no meaningful administrative processes before they can dismiss workers and legally have to offer no notice or severance pay, even after 20 years of service. By contrast, in Belgium, firms have to give 9 months notice to workers with more than 20 years of tenure. Most countries require no severance

TABLE 7.5   Indicators of Strictness of Employment Protection in OECD, Late 1990s

Procedure column shows OECD ranking of administrative restrictions on dismissal process where 0 is free from restrictions and 3 where restrictions are most severe.

Country	Procedures	Notice Period (for Length of Employment)			Severance Pay (for Length of Employment)			EPL Rank (1 Least Protected)
		9 months	4 years	20 years	9 months	4 years	20 years	
Austria	2.0	1.0	1.2	2.5	0.0	2.0	9.0	12
Belgium	0.5	2.0	2.8	9.0	0.0	0.0	0.0	13
France	1.8	1.0	2.0	2.0	0.0	0.4	2.7	17
Germany	2.5	1.0	1.0	7.0	0.0	0.0	0.0	16
Ireland	1.5	0.3	0.5	2.0	0.0	0.2	2.2	5
Netherlands	3.0	1.0	1.0	3.0	0.0	0.0	0.0	10
Switzerland	0.5	1.0	2.0	3.0	0.0	0.0	2.0	7
U.K.	1.0	0.2	0.9	2.8	0.0	0.5	2.4	2
Italy	1.5	0.3	1.1	2.2	0.7	3.5	18.0	19
Portugal	2.0	2.0	2.0	2.0	3.0	4.0	20.0	20
Spain	2.0	1.0	1.0	1.0	0.5	2.6	12.0	18
Canada	0.0	0.5	0.5	0.5	0.0	0.2	1.3	4
U.S.	0.0	0.0	0.0	0.0	0.0	0.0	0.0	1
Australia	0.5	0.2	0.7	1.2	0.0	1.0	1.0	6
Japan	1.5	1.0	1.0	1.0	0.0	1.5	4.0	11
Korea	1.8	1.0	1.0	1.0	0.0	2.0	6.0	
New Zealand	0.8	0.5	0.5	0.5	0.0	1.5	5.0	3

Source: OECD, *Employment Outlook* (June 1999) p. 55.

pay within the first year of employment, but Portugal and Turkey require 20 months of severance pay after 20 years of work. Such large institutional differences in EPL significantly affect the operation of labor markets. The final column of Table 7.5 shows the OECD's overall assessment of the severity of employment legislation. Southern European countries tend to have the highest level of EPL, while the English-speaking countries have the lowest levels.

EPL seeks to make it costly for firms to fire people and so tries to produce a lower value of p (probability of becoming unemployed) and a reduction in the natural rate of unemployment. However, EPL also adversely affects s—the probability of the unemployed finding a job. When hiring employees, firms have to remember that at some future date they may wish to terminate the employment. The more costly it is to fire people, the more expensive it is to hire them. Therefore we can expect EPL to have offsetting effects on unemployment—it lowers job destruction rates but reduces job creation. Its overall impact on unemployment is an empirical question.

Figures 7.15a through 7.15f (and associated econometric work) show that for OECD economies:

(a) Countries with strong EPL have low employment rates—increased hiring costs reduces the demand for labor.

(b) EPL is not correlated with unemployment. This suggests that the reduction in employment is matched by a similar fall in the participation rate and in the size of the labor force. A key reason for the drop in participation is that EPL makes part-time jobs less attractive for employers and the absence of such jobs reduces female participation in the labor force.

(c) Countries with strong EPL have lower levels of outflows *and* inflows into unemployment (both p and s decline). This explains why unemployment does not vary with EPL—the declines in inflows and outflows offset each other.

(d) Countries with strong EPL have greater job security and longer job tenure, but unemployment also lasts longer. EPL, therefore, benefits workers who are employed at the cost of those without jobs.

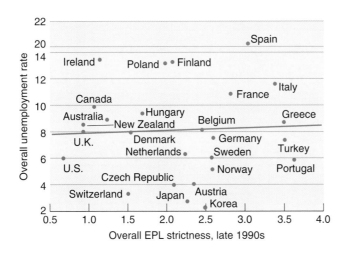

FIGURE 7.15a **EPL and unemployment.** No strong relationship between EPL and unemployment.

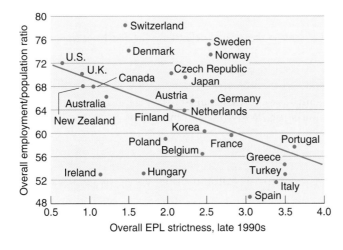

FIGURE 7.15b **EPL and employment rates.** Strong EPL typically means a lower employment rate.

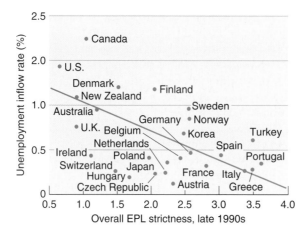

FIGURE 7.15c **EPL and unemployment inflows.** Stronger EPL reduces job losses.

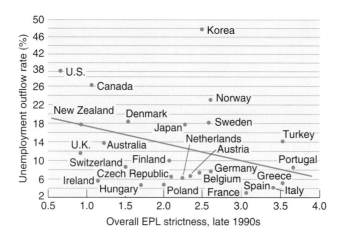

FIGURE 7.15d
EPL and unemployment outflows. Strong EPL lowers job creation rate.

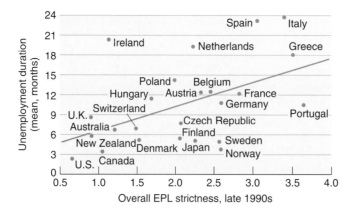

FIGURE 7.15e
EPL and unemployment duration. Stronger EPL increases length of employment.

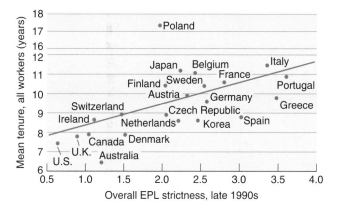

FIGURE 7.15f

EPL and duration of employment.
EPL improves job tenure.
Source: All diagrams OECD,
Employment Outlook (June
1999).

The benefits of EPL tend to accrue to those already in work, while the disadvantages hurt the unemployed. Why would a country adopt legislation that benefits the employed at the expense of the unemployed? Political considerations help answer this question. In most economies, around 90–95% of the labor force is employed. Further, in countries with strong labor unions, the demands of the employed can be easily coordinated and voiced, whereas the unemployed have no such organization. As a result, governments come under political pressure to adopt EPL.

KEY POINT

Unemployment depends on both the probability of the employed being fired and the probability of the unemployed being hired. EPL tries to lower unemployment by reducing the firing rate. It also tends to lower the hiring rate, however, so that, overall, it does not reduce unemployment. Instead, it increases job tenure and the length of unemployment spells.

7.8   Labor Market Reform

There is currently growing support for continental Europe to enact labor market reform, which would remove government restrictions, reduce the power of unions, and increase the role of market forces. The motivation for this is based on our theoretical framework, which suggests that lower benefits, weaker unions, and less EPL will stimulate labor market turnover and reduce unemployment. Further motivation comes from the currently low rate of unemployment in the United States, which according to most of the statistics we have examined in this chapter, has a low level of government intervention in the labor market. Final evidence comes from countries such as Chile and the United Kingdom that enacted labor market reform and then saw unemployment decline.

There are, however, also arguments against market-oriented reform. One maintains that, while such reforms lower unemployment, they bring other concerns. Deregulated labor markets have experienced dramatic increases in income inequality, which offsets the advantages of low unemployment. The other criticism is that because more flexible labor markets lower wages and produce greater inequality, they also lead to higher levels of crime. Crime is expensive for society (just think how much richer you would be if there was no need to pay insurance premiums against theft or taxes to finance the police force and prisons). For instance, in 1993, when U.S. unemployment was at 6.6%, the U.S. prison population amounted to 1.9% of the workforce, and a further 4.3% were on parole, giving a total of those outside of work but physically able to work of 12.8%, which was close to continental European unemployment rates. If this criminal population is linked to the greater flexibility of U.S. labor markets (and this is by no means an accepted proposition), then labor market reform becomes less attractive. It can cost over $30,000 a year to keep a person in prison—considerably more than paying for continental European levels of social security. Of course, the key issue here is whether inequality, rather than other features of a society, produces the crime.

Finally, it is argued that market-oriented reform may not be the only way to reduce unemployment. It is useful here to examine why unemployment declined in the 1990s in the United Kingdom and the Netherlands. Table 7.6 shows estimates about why unemployment fell in each country. The differences are clear. The United Kingdom has focused on a market-oriented approach by weakening union strength and lowering replacement rates and tax wedges. By contrast, the Netherlands reduced unemployment though increased active labor market spending and coordination measures.

The results suggest that governments may have other options besides just market-oriented reform packages—particularly if they start from a position of strong but unco-ordinated unions and low levels of active labor market expenditure. Of course, some countries may have little choice. For instance, in the United Kingdom the labor unions were so strong and numerous that coordinating their actions may have been impossible,

TABLE 7.6 **Explaining Netherlands and United Kingdom Unemployment Declines**

The decline in unemployment rates in the United Kingdom and in the Netherlands in the 1990s was substantial, but the factors explaining the fall in joblessness are very different.

Changes in:	Netherlands	U.K.
Union density	−0.83	−1.47
Union coverage	0.58	−1.25
Active labor market spending	−1.09	0.16
Union + employer coordination	−2.53	0
Benefit replacement rate	−0.41	−0.48
Tax wedge	−0.24	−0.72
Total	**−4.52**	**−3.76**

Source: Nickell and Van Ours, "The Netherlands and the UK: A European Unemployment Miracle," *Economic Policy* (Blackwell Publishers, 2000) vol. 30, pp. 135–180.

and so only weakening their rights, powers, and immunities would have worked. But the experience of the Netherlands suggests this may not be the only way to proceed.

KEY POINT

Government intervention in the labor market can either worsen monopoly power and so increase unemployment or make competition operate more effectively and so lower unemployment. This opens up two potential routes of labor market reform—the more market orientated approach of the United Kingdom or the coordinated actions of the Netherlands.

7.9 Widening Inequality

Figure 7.16 shows that during the 1980s and 1990s income inequality increased in several countries. Given that inequality had narrowed for most of the twentieth century, these trends generated much comment and analysis. This rising inequality manifested itself most obviously in a growing gap between the wages of skilled and unskilled workers—in the United States between 1980 and 1995 the ratio of wages for college-educated employees to those with only high-school education rose from 1.42 to 1.62. This substantial rise in the wages of skilled workers is all the more dramatic because the

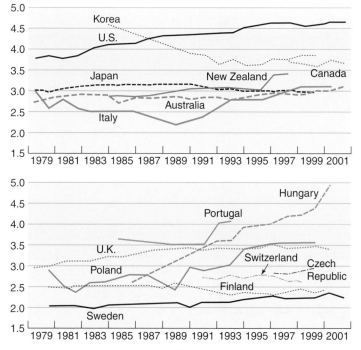

FIGURE 7.16   **Rising inequality in OECD income.** *Source:* OECD, *Employment Outlook* (September 2003).

supply of skilled workers increased during this time. For the wages of skilled workers to rise, it must therefore be that this increase in supply was offset by an even bigger increase in demand.

What underlies this surge in demand for skilled workers and the associated decline in the demand for the unskilled? The two most popular hypotheses are the increase in global trade and the spread of new technologies associated with computers and information technology. As we shall see in Chapter 8, trade implies that the demand for factors of production that countries have in abundance should increase. Therefore, increasing trade predicts rising demand for skilled workers in the OECD. Although this issue is hotly contested, the current consensus from economists is that trade can only explain around 20% of the increased inequality; trade between OECD and emerging markets is not large enough to have substantially affected inequality. Moreover, increases in inequality have occurred across all industries by roughly the same amount; they have *not* been more acute in industries more exposed to trade.

A more popular explanation for this increase in demand for skilled workers is general technological change associated with computers and information technology. The evidence suggests that computers, capital equipment, and skilled labor are seen as complements in production—computers are used more intensively in industries with skilled labor and high levels of capital intensity. Table 7.7 shows that the near doubling in the diffusion of computers across the U.S. workforce between 1984 and 1993 is heavily concentrated among the more highly educated. Rising inequality between skilled and unskilled workers would appear to be mainly a result of the complementarity between computers and skilled workers.

KEY POINT

Technological progress has boosted the demand for skilled labor, but reduced that for unskilled. As a result, even though there has been a large increase in the supply of skilled labor, skilled wages have risen relative to unskilled. Increased trade has also contributed more modestly towards this increase in skilled wages.

TABLE 7.7 **Percentage Diffusion of Computers Amongst U.S. Workforce**

	1984	1989	1993
All workers	25.1	37.4	46.6
High school dropout	5.2	7.7	10.4
High school	19.2	28.4	34.6
Some college	30.6	45.0	53.1
College graduates	42.1	58.6	70.2

Source: Autor, Katz, and Krueger, "Computing Inequality: Have Computers Changed the Labor Market?" *Quarterly Journal of Economics* (November 1998).

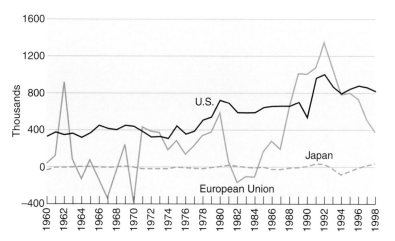

FIGURE 7.17   **Immigration trends.** *Source:* Coppel, Dumont, and Visco, *Trends in Immigration and Economic Consequences*, OECD Economics Department Working Papers No. 284

7.10 Immigration

Figure 7.17 shows that immigration into OECD economies has risen in recent years and is increasingly becoming a policy issue. A common fear of immigration is that it will lead to an increase in unemployment for native workers. Figure 7.18 suggests that this fear is unfounded—countries that experience high levels of immigration do not suffer from higher levels of unemployment. However, although native workers do not suffer from high unemployment, it appears that this is because their wages fall—for every 10% increase in foreign workers, the wages of native workers falls by around 3–4%.[1]

We can use the marginal product of labor to understand the impact of immigration on the economy. Figure 7.19 shows that, before immigration occurs and at the prevailing wage, employment is A and wages are C. Total labor income is given by the rectangle

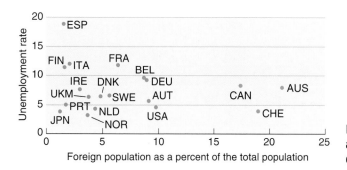

FIGURE 7.18   **Immigration and unemployment rates in OECD countries, 1998.**

[1] Borjas, *The Labor Demand Curve Is Downward Sloping: Reexamining the Impact of Immigration on the Labor Market*, NBER Working Paper 9755 (2003).

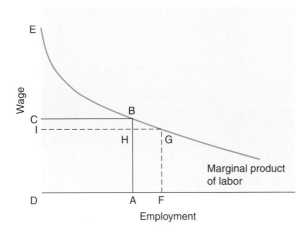

FIGURE 7.19   **Effect of immigration on labor and capital income.**

ABCD and the remaining output (BCE) is paid out as capital income, so that total output equals capital plus labor income—as in Chapter 2. With an influx of immigration, employment rises by AF, which as discussed above, lowers wages to the new level I. Labor income is now given by FGID with AFGH being the earnings of immigrant workers and AHID the earnings of native workers. The fall in wages has reduced the earnings of native workers by HBCI—the bigger the fall in wages caused by immigration, the bigger this negative impact on native workers. While native workers lose (depending on the magnitude of the wage fall), the owners of capital gain—capital income is now GEI. The increase in capital income is made up of HBCI (the gain from native workers) and the area GBH. The area GBH is known as the migration surplus—it is the gain to society from the increase in labor supply that immigration brings about. The extra output that immigrants produce is not all paid out as wages, and hence society gains by the excess—GBH. While this is the net gain from immigration (ignoring any fiscal calculations), there is also the distribution effect that reallocates HBCI from native workers to owners of capital.

KEY POINT

Immigration does not seem to have increased unemployment for native workers, but instead causes wages to fall. Not all the extra output that immigrants produce is paid out in wages, so that overall the receiving country gains—even though native workers lose while owners of capital gain.

SUMMARY

We have completed our long-run analysis of the economy by providing a model of the labor market in which capital accumulation and technological progress increase the demand for labor and produce rising productivity and real wages and a higher standard of living.

In section 7.2, we explained the concept of a natural rate of unemployment—a long-run equilibrium to which the economy tends to return.

In sections 7.3 and 7.4, we outlined a model of the natural rate based on the interaction between producers and the labor force where both possess a degree of monopoly power. Unemployment reconciles the conflicting profit demands of firms with the real wage aspirations of workers.

In section 7.5, we saw that stronger labor unions, high levels of unemployment benefits, a large proportion of long-term unemployed, substantial regional variations in unemployment, high labor taxes, and greater monopoly power among firms lead to higher unemployment.

In section 7.6, we also examined two factors, active labor market spending and coordinated wage bargaining, that lower unemployment.

In section 7.7, we outlined a model of the natural unemployment rate based on inflows and outflows into unemployment. We showed that EPL varies across countries. The greater the degree of EPL, the lower are inflows into unemployment. But this is offset by the fact that employment protection also reduces outflows from unemployment. As a result, the data suggest that employment protection does not influence the aggregate unemployment rate, but instead increases job tenure and the duration of unemployment.

In section 7.8, we discussed the advantages of current proposals to decrease the strength of EPL in continental Europe. One of the potential disadvantages was the possibility of greater income inequality.

In section 7.9, we saw that inequality has widened in many OECD labor markets over the last two decades. This is the result of a sharp decline in the demand for unskilled workers and a large increase in the demand for skilled workers. The most plausible explanation for this trend is technological developments connected to information technology with a lesser role played by increasing international trade.

Finally, in section 7.10, we saw that rising immigration is increasingly becoming a policy issue in OECD economies. Our analysis (ignoring fiscal issues of taxation and benefits) suggests that, overall, a country benefits from immigration; although wages of native workers fall, this is offset by rising capital income.

CONCEPTUAL QUESTIONS

1. (Section 7.1) A country has a working age population of 70 million, a total population of 100 million, unemployment of 5 million, and employment of 45 million.

   (a) What is its labor force?

   (b) What is its participation rate?

   (c) What is the participation rate as a proportion of the working-age population?

   (d) What is its unemployment rate?

2. (7.1) In Greece, the participation rate (as percentage of working-age population) in 1998 for men aged 15–24 was 44.3%; aged 24–54, 94.2%; and aged 55–64, 57%. For the United States, these numbers were 68.4%, 91.8%, and 68.1%. In Greece, the corresponding figures for women were 37.3%, 59.4%, 24.4%, and for women in the United States, 63.3%, 76.5%, and 51.2%. What do you think explains these cross-country differences?

3. (7.2) If the population was prepared to work substantially longer hours for higher wages, what would be the long-run impact of capital accumulation and technological progress on the labor market?

4. (7.3) What influences the wage demands you make of your employer?

5. (7.5) How do the following affect the natural rate of unemployment: (a) an increase in tariffs on imported goods, (b) making unemployment benefits taxable, (c) more expenditure on retraining programs for the unemployed, (d) increases in indirect taxes on product prices, and (e) increases in income tax on labor income?

6. (7.7) If generous welfare payments support the long-term unemployed, is employment protection legislation a good thing?

7. (7.8) Is there a link between the flexibility of U.S. labor markets and its large prison population?

8. (7.9) What type of workers have computers displaced and why have they increased the demand for skilled labor? Will skilled labor and computers always be complements in production?

9. (7.9) The United Kingdom and the United States have highly deregulated labor markets and have also seen much larger increases in inequality than has continental Europe, due to declining demand for unskilled workers. What might explain this difference?

10. (7.10) How might consideration of the tax and benefit system alter the finding of a migration surplus for countries?

11. (7.10) How might government policy respond to the redistributive impacts that immigration brings about? Why do governments often restrict immigration to areas where there is a shortage of skilled workers?

ANALYTICAL QUESTIONS

1. (Section 7.2) A family has a target of $1500 for the income that it needs to earn each week. Both adults in the family work at flexible jobs where they have a choice over how many hours to work. They decide that the relative number of hours they should work should be equal to the ratio of their hourly wage rates. The female earns $20 an hour and the male $15. How many hours does each of them work? What happens when the female gets a 20% wage rise to $24 an hour? What happens if both adults get a 20% pay rise? What does this imply about their income and substitution effects?

2. (7.2) Using a spreadsheet, consider the Cobb-Douglas production function:

$$Y_t = A_t K_t^b L_t^{1-b}$$

where Y_t is output at time t; K_t is capital; L_t is labor hours worked; A_t is total factor productivity at time t; and b is 0.3. Analyze how the marginal productivity of labor changes when:

(a) A increases by 10%
(b) K increases by 10%
(c) L increases by 10%
(d) b falls from 0.4 to 0.3

3. (7.4) In an economy, firms set prices at a markup of 20% over costs. Costs are all in the form of wages, so that P = (1.2) W. Labor unions enter into bargains with firms on wages. The higher is unemployment, the less powerful are unions and the lower is the real wage they can achieve in negotiations. The real wage that gets negotiated is:

$$W/P = 1 - 2u$$

where u is the fraction of the workforce unemployed. What is the equilibrium fraction of the labor force unemployed?

4. (7.4) Consider the economy described in Question 3. The government now decides to charge income tax on wages at a rate of 15%. Companies have to pay tax on their profits of 20%; profits per unit produced are simply price minus cost, and the cost is the wage. Assume that firms continue to want to get a net of tax profit margin of 20% of costs. Labor unions bargain so that real wages *after income tax* are still given by the expression: $1 - 2u$. What happens to the equilibrium unemployment rate?

5. (7.7) Suppose the probability of a worker losing his or her job in a year is 2%. The probability of someone unemployed finding a job within a year is 40%. What is the equilibrium unemployment rate? What happens if the government takes measures to free up the labor market that will double the chances the unemployed have of finding a job and also double the chances of those with jobs becoming unemployed?

International Trade

Overview

The global economy is becoming more interconnected. In recent decades, world trade has increased faster than world Gross Domestic Product (GDP), with the majority of this trade in manufactured goods. We consider the advantages of free trade by outlining the theory of comparative advantage, which shows that all countries—even those that are less efficient at production—can benefit from free trade. The Heckscher-Ohlin model tells us in which industries a country has a comparative advantage—those which require the intensive use in production of factors that a country possesses in abundance. We examine the evidence for this model, and we consider other factors that help explain the observed pattern of trade. How much a country gains from trade depends on the terms of trade—the price of exports relative to imports—and we examine how this has varied for a range of countries.

We then consider why protectionism enjoys political support. We outline the Stolper-Samuelson Theorem, which states that some groups in society lose because of free trade while others gain, and we consider to what extent increasing levels of trade can explain widening income inequality. We consider the debate in favor of subsidizing key industries to boost a nation's competitiveness and argue that such a debate confuses trade with economic growth. Finally, we consider the ideas and applicability of "New Trade Theory," which maintains that, for some industries, protectionism or export subsidies can benefit an economy.

Key Concepts

Comparative Advantage	Hecksher-Ohlin Model (H-O)	Stolper-Samuelson Theorem
Competitiveness	New Trade Theory	Strategic Trade Policy
Factor Endowments	Opportunity Cost	Terms of Trade
Factor Price Equalization	Prebisch-Singer Hypothesis	Vested Interest

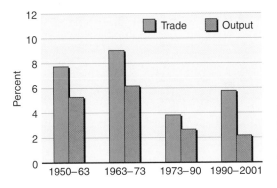

FIGURE 8.1 **Growth in world merchandise trade and output.** World trade grows faster than GDP as the world becomes more open. *Source:* WTO, Annual Statistical Report (2002).

8.1   Patterns of World Trade

Figure 8.1 shows that world trade has been consistently growing faster than world output, so that the world economy is becoming increasingly interconnected. Table 8.1 shows that in 2002 total world trade was $7.9 trillion, with merchandise trade accounting for 80.1% of this total. The largest component of this merchandise trade is manufacturing, which makes up around 60% of *total* world trade. Given that Chapter 2 showed manufacturing to account for 20–35% of most countries' GDP, this implies that manufacturing is heavily exposed to fluctuations in the world economy.

Table 8.2 shows which countries are most involved in international trade. Note that the European Union (EU), the United States, and Japan together account for about 41% of merchandise exports. However, as we saw in Chapter 2, these regions combined amount to around 70% of world GDP. Therefore, relative to their size, these regions are underrepresented in world trade. This is, in fact, a general rule—large economies tend to be more closed, that is, exports are a smaller proportion of their GDP than they are in smaller economies. The most obvious example of this is Hong Kong, which accounts for 4.1% of world trade even though its population is only 7.5 million—around 2% of the population of the pre-enlargement EU and 2.6% of the United States. However, Table

TABLE 8.1   **Composition of World Trade 2002 ($bn)**

Merchandise	6270
Manufacturing	4708
Agriculture	582
Mining	788
Services	1570
Transportation	350
Travel	480
Other commercial services	740
Total	7840

Source: WTO, International Trade Statistics (2003)

TABLE 8.2   **Top 20 Exporters of Merchandise Goods and Services, 2002 ($bn and %)**

Large economies account for a smaller proportion of trade than world GDP.

Rank	Exporters	Value	Share of World Trade
1	EU trade with rest of world	939.8	19.0
2	U.S.	693.9	14.0
3	Japan	416.7	8.4
4	China	325.6	6.6
5	Canada	252.4	5.1
6	Hong Kong, China	201.2	4.1
	domestic exports	18.3	0.4
	re-exports	182.9	3.7
7	Korea, Republic of	162.5	3.3
8	Mexico	160.7	3.2
9	Taipei, Chinese	135.1	2.7
10	Singapore	125.2	2.5
	domestic exports	66.8	1.4
	re-exports	58.3	1.2
11	Russian Federation	106.9	2.2
12	Malaysia	93.3	1.9
13	Switzerland	87.9	1.8
14	Saudi Arabia[1]	73.9	1.5
15	Thailand	68.9	1.4
16	Australia	65.0	1.3
17	Norway	61.0	1.2
18	Brazil	60.4	1.2
19	Indonesia[1]	57.1	1.2
20	India	49.3	1.0

[1] WTO estimate.

Source: WTO, Annual Report (2003).

8.2 also shows that the richer OECD nations account for a much larger proportion of services than manufacturing trade. Table 8.3 summarizes the geographical flow of world trade. The major trade flows are within the EU, within North America (NAFTA), and exports from Asia to the United States.

KEY POINT

Trade is increasing at a faster rate than output, leading to increased global interactions. Manufacturing trade accounts for around two-thirds of total trade, with OECD countries being more dominant in services than manufacturing trade.

TABLE 8.3   Regional Trade Flows, 2002 ($bn)
Internal trade within North America, Europe, and Asia are largest trade blocs, followed by Asia's exports to United States.

Origin	Destination							
	North America	Latin America	Western Europe	C/E. Europe/ Baltic States/CIS	Africa	Middle East	Asia	World
North America	382	152	170	7	12	20	204	946
Latin America	215	54	44	3	4	5	23	350
Western Europe	270	55	1787	168	66	68	208	2657
C/E. Europe/Baltic States/CIS	14	6	176	80	4	7	24	314
Africa	24	5	71	1	11	3	24	140
Middle East	38	3	40	2	9	17	116	244
Asia	394	39	260	21	26	48	792	1620
World	1336	315	2549	282	133	169	1391	6272

Source: WTO, Annual Statistical Report (2003).

8.2   Comparative Advantage—How Countries Benefit from Trade

The Nobel Prize winning economist Paul Samuelson was once challenged by the mathematician Stanislaw Ulam to name one proposition in the social sciences that was both true and nontrivial, and in response he named the Theory of Comparative Advantage. This theory says that *all* countries can benefit from trade, even if they are less productive in *every* industry than other nations. What matters is *not* whether a country is the most productive in the world at producing a commodity. Instead, countries gain from trade by exporting commodities in which their productivity disadvantage is least pronounced, that is, by specializing in what they are least bad at—or *comparatively* good at.

The theory of comparative advantage is essentially an invisible hand/free market argument. It says that free trade best promotes the welfare of countries. Comparative advantage says that nations should specialize in their productive activities and should focus on those activities in which their advantage is greatest or their disadvantage least. It implies that all countries benefit from trade *even if they have low productivity*. This is exactly what happens in everyday economic life. Consider the case of a highly qualified lawyer who can earn $1000 an hour. Let us assume that this lawyer has high productivity in whatever she does. For example, she can type twice as fast as her personal assistant, can make a better meal in less time than the chef in her firm's cafeteria, and can drive across New York more directly and quickly than a taxi driver. She is also, of course, more productive as a lawyer than her assistant, the chef, or the taxi driver. In other words, the lawyer has an absolute advantage in all these activities. However, the optimal strategy for her is not to do everything herself. Every hour she spends typing up case notes, making meals, or driving herself around town costs her $1000. Far better to use this time on legal work and then purchase the other services at a cheaper rate.

Therefore, the lawyer will focus on the activity that is most productive for her. A similar argument applies to the other characters. The chef would earn little as a lawyer, is a hopeless typist, and cannot drive. His comparative advantage is to cook. Therefore, his best strategy is to specialize as a chef and then purchase whatever legal or transport services he needs. In everyday life we all specialize in activities that we are *relatively* good at—this is the theory of comparative advantage.

To demonstrate in detail the theory of comparative advantage, we consider Eurasia and Oceania, two economies that each produce two commodities: onions and garlic.[1] Comparative advantage relies on many assumptions, but the two key ones for our purposes are that trade between countries is competitive—countries cannot exploit a monopoly position—and that, within a country, factors of production (i.e., capital and labor) are mobile, and the economy has a constant natural rate of unemployment (see Chapter 7).

We assume that Eurasia's population is 10 and Oceania's is 40. The key to our analysis is productivity levels in each country. We assume that in Eurasia it takes 2 people to produce a bag of onions and 5 to produce a bag of garlic. By contrast, in Oceania it takes 8 people to produce a bag of onions and 10 for a bag of garlic. Table 8.4 shows the state of production technology. These assumptions imply that Eurasia is more efficient than Oceania in producing both commodities. Oceania therefore has an absolute advantage in neither industry. However, because of comparative advantage, both countries can gain from free trade. The key concept is **opportunity cost**.

In economics, every activity has an opportunity cost. Opportunity cost is what you could have done had you not pursued your current activity—it is the opportunity you forgo when you make a choice. For instance, the opportunity cost of us writing this textbook is the research papers we could have written instead or the consulting income we might have earned. The opportunity cost of reading this book for you might be meeting a friend, going to a film, reading a novel, or reading a management textbook. In our example, the opportunity cost of producing more garlic is producing fewer onions. This happens because if unemployment remains constant, Eurasia can only increase garlic production by moving labor from onions into the garlic fields. Because every bag of gar-

T A B L E 8 . 4 Production Technology for Eurasia and Oceania
Table shows the number of individuals in each country required to produce one bag of commodity listed in first column.

	Eurasia	Oceania
Onions	2	8
Garlic	5	10

[1] We discuss a world of two commodities and two economies, but the analysis also holds for any circumstance where the number of countries does not exceed the number of commodities.

lic requires 5 people to produce it, while a bag of onions needs 2 people, the opportunity cost of producing one bag of garlic for Eurasia is 2.5 (=5/2) bags of onions. However, in Oceania it takes 8 people to produce a bag of onions and 10 to produce a bag of garlic. For Oceania the opportunity cost of producing one bag of garlic is therefore 1.25 (=10/8). In other words, it is cheaper in an opportunity cost sense for Oceania to produce garlic than it is for Eurasia. *Oceania is said to have a* **comparative advantage** *in producing garlic.*

We now show diagrammatically how both countries benefit from free trade. We assume that on world markets two bags of onions can be exchanged for one bag of garlic. We shall show that, at this world price, free trade benefits both Eurasia and Oceania. Note that this is *not* the only price at which trade benefits both countries, but neither is it the case that at *all* prices trade benefits both countries.

The solid triangular area in Figure 8.2 shows Eurasia's production possibility set—all the combinations of onions and garlic that Eurasia can produce given its workforce and technology. Eurasia has a workforce of 10 people and requires 2 people to produce one bag of onions. Therefore if everyone specializes in onion production, the country can produce at most five bags of onions and zero bags of garlic. This gives us the top point in the production possibility set. If instead, Eurasia devotes all its resources to garlic production (which requires five people per bag), it can produce two bags of garlic and zero bags of onions. This gives us the other extreme point on the production possibility frontier. However, there are also many intermediate positions where Eurasia does not specialize, but allocates some labor to onion production and some to garlic. Eurasia can reach any point on the line drawn between these two extreme points of specialization and the slope of the line reflects the opportunity cost—how much of one commodity is forgone by producing more of the other. All points on this line represent where Eurasia is producing the maximum amount of onions and garlic it can produce given the allocation of labor between the two industries. However, Eurasia can also produce output inefficiently, so that the shaded triangular area gives the full set of production possibilities.

The production possibility set shows the consumption possibilities for Eurasia if it does not trade—in this case Eurasia can only consume what it produces. However, if

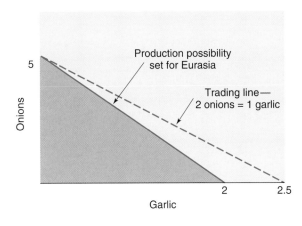

FIGURE 8.2 **Production and trading sets for Eurasia.** Trade allows Eurasia to achieve higher levels of consumption than when relying on domestic production.

Eurasia starts to trade, it can sell two bags of onions for one bag of garlic—as shown by the trading line in Figure 8.2. If Eurasia concentrates on onion production, it has five bags of onions that it can swap on international markets for 2.5 bags of garlic.[2] Therefore, allowing for trade, Eurasia can consume five bags of onions and zero bags of garlic, or it can consume zero bags of onions and 2.5 bags of garlic. It can also consume any combination between these two extreme points if it decides to sell some, but not all, of its onion production. Because the trading line lies everywhere above the production possibility set, Eurasia can do better for itself through international trade than if it tries to be self sufficient. The optimal strategy for Eurasia is to specialize entirely in onion production and then sell onions to acquire the amount of garlic it wants to consume. After all, even though we are producing an economics textbook, we have no desire to purchase one! This separation of production and consumption enables the economy to operate efficiently.

But Table 8.4 shows us that Eurasia is more efficient at producing both onions and garlic. Therefore it is hardly surprising that the country benefits from free trade. Can we show that Oceania, which is relatively inefficient, also benefits? Figure 8.3 shows the production and trading possibilities for Oceania. Oceania has 40 people, and it takes 8 to produce a bag of onions and 10 to produce a bag of garlic. Therefore at most Oceania can produce five bags of onions and no garlic or four bags of garlic and no onions. Again, the shaded area shows the production possibility set. The same international prices apply to Oceania, so it can swap two bags of onions for one of garlic. Therefore, if Oceania focuses on garlic production and produces four bags, it can trade and obtain up to eight bags of onions—compared to only five if it is self-sufficient. Thus *both* Eurasia and Oceania can benefit from trade even though Oceania has no absolute advantage in either industry. It is comparative advantage that matters and, as a result, both countries gain.

However, as we noted earlier, not all possible prices make trade beneficial. For instance, if international prices are 2.5 bags of onions for one bag of garlic, Eurasia is no better off with trade—it can do just as well being self-sufficient. But if Eurasia does not trade, Oceania loses the benefits of free trade. Rather than do that, Oceania can suggest

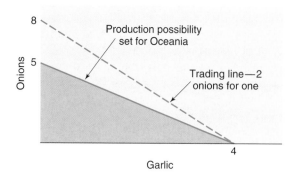

FIGURE 8.3 **Production and trading sets for Oceania.** Oceania, too, can enjoy the scope to consume more of both goods once it trades and specializes in producing the good where its comparative advantage lies.

[2] Eurasia will not focus on garlic production because, at most, it can produce two bags of garlic which, given international prices, can be swapped for four bags of onions, less than it can produce itself.

alternative prices (for instance, two bags of onions for one of garlic) until both countries benefit. Therefore, unless prices are restricted—through tariffs or other forms of protectionism—they will eventually move to a range that promotes trade.

> **KEY POINT**
>
> Comparative advantage means that all countries can benefit from free trade even if they are characterized by low levels of productivity. Underlying this result is the concept of opportunity cost, which means that countries have a comparative advantage in industries that they are relatively or comparatively best at.

The theory of comparative advantage says that all countries can benefit from trade. However, there are some things comparative advantage does *not* imply:

(a) Comparative advantage says all countries gain from trade, but not that all countries become wealthy. As we saw in Chapters 3 though 6, the standard of living in a country depends on its *absolute* productivity. In our example, Eurasia is more productive than Oceania and so has a better standard of living (compare the level of onions per capita in each country). However, both Eurasia and Oceania will have higher standards of living under trade, *compared to* self-sufficiency.

(b) While both Eurasia and Oceania benefit from trade, they do not benefit equally. The greater the price of garlic in world trade, the greater the gains for Oceania and the less the gains for Eurasia. The key concept here is the *terms of trade*—the ratio of the price of a country's exports to its imports. The higher the terms of trade, the more the country benefits from trade.

(c) Comparative advantage only says that a country gains from trade in the aggregate. It does not say that *every* citizen benefits. For example, garlic producers in Eurasia will not benefit from trade with Oceania. We will examine the distributional implications of free trade in detail later.

Figure 8.4, taken from a seminal study, shows empirical support for comparative advantage. The figure shows, for a variety of industries, the relative productivity of the United States (compared to the United Kingdom) and the relative amount of exports from the United States in each industry. The scale shows that for every industry, productivity in the United States was greater than in the United Kingdom. In other words, the United States had an absolute productivity advantage in all industries. Yet the United Kingdom still managed to export more than the United States in several industries (where the ratio of U.S. to U.K. exports is less than 1). Figure 8.4 shows that the United Kingdom out-exported the United States in those industries in which the U.S. productivity advantage was least pronounced. In other words, the United States focused its export performance on those industries in which its productivity advantage was greatest compared to the United Kingdom (pig iron and motor cars). This left the United Kingdom to specialize in those industries in which its productivity deficit was *smallest* (beer and textiles)—exactly what comparative advantage implies. One implication of comparative advantage is that industries in a country are not just in competition with the same industry overseas, but also with other industries in their own country.

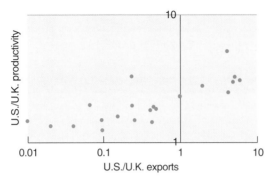

FIGURE 8.4 **Comparative advantage in the United States and the United Kingdom, 1937.** Just before World War II, the United States and United Kingdom appeared to specialize in production and export of goods where they had comparative advantages—although the United States had an absolute advantage in production of nearly all goods. *Source:* G. D. A. MacDougall, "British and American Exports," *The Economic Journal* (1951) vol. 61, pp. 703–707.

Figure 8.4 suggests that, even if the United States steel industry can match the Korean steel industry in terms of productivity, U.S. steel producers still may not succeed internationally if they have below average productivity in the whole economy.

KEY POINT

Comparative advantage implies that all countries gain from trade, but not that all countries gain equally from trade or that all countries will have the same income level.

8.3 The Terms of Trade

The **terms of trade** is the ratio of the price of a country's exports to the price of its imports. The higher the terms of trade, the more benefits a nation captures from trade. Figure 8.5 shows variations in the terms of trade between 1970 and 2002 for Australia, Japan, the United Kingdom and the United States. For all countries there has been a decline in the terms of trade over this time period, although for the United Kingdom the decline is small. A major impact on the terms of trade for rich countries has been the fluctuations experienced in the price of oil. In 1973 and 1979 there were huge increases in oil prices (from around $3 to $10 in 1973 and from around $10 to $30 in 1979). With the exception of the United Kingdom from 1979 onwards, all these countries are net importers of oil, so they see sharp declines in the terms of trade during these years. Changes in the terms of trade affect the magnitude of the gains countries reap from free trade. Between 1970 and 2002 the terms of trade for the United States fell by 22.5%. Over this period U.S. imports were on average 10% of GDP (beginning at around 5% and ending at 14%). Therefore, a 22.5% increase in the price of imports relative to exports means that the U.S. gains from trade *fell* by around 2.25% of GDP (22.5% of 10%). This does not mean the United States did not gain from

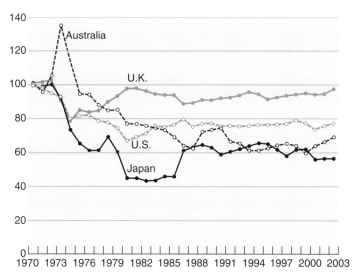

FIGURE 8.5 **Terms of trade for Australia, Japan, the United Kingdom and United States.** Terms of trade display substantial variation over time. *Source:* IMF, *International Financial Statistics* (2003).

trade—comparative advantage tells us otherwise. But adverse shifts in the terms of trade meant that the United States gained *less* than it otherwise would have done.

Adverse shifts in the terms of trade have been a particular problem for countries that export mainly agricultural products—as shown in Figure 8.6. Agriculture over this period has experienced substantial increases in both production and productivity but is characterized by low price and low income elasticity of demand. As a consequence, rising income and falling prices have not stimulated demand by as much as output has increased—this has produced a dramatic fall in agricultural prices relative to prices in general. The prediction that commodity prices fall in value over time is known as the **Prebisch-Singer hypothesis**. It was used as a justification for governments in developing countries to promote the growth of nonagricultural industries, in order to avoid this term of trade deterioration. The Prebisch-Singer hypothesis has not gone uncontested,

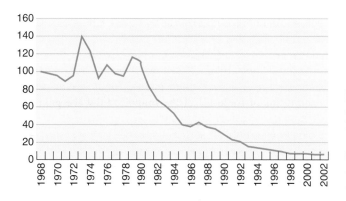

FIGURE 8.6 **Real agricultural raw material prices.** Basic indicators show an adverse term of trade shift for agricultural exporters. *Source:* IMF, *International Financial Statistics* (2003).

however. The main criticism is that the increased prices of manufactured and service goods reflects improvements in their quality. When these prices are quality-adjusted, the fall in relative agricultural prices is greatly diminished.

8.4   What Goods Will Countries Trade In?

Comparative advantage says all countries benefit from trade and have a comparative advantage in some industries. But what can we say about the type of industry in which a country has a comparative advantage?

The **Heckscher-Ohlin (H-O) model** (named after two Swedish economists) answers this question. Based on certain key assumptions, the H-O model predicts that:

China, for example, with its 1.2 billion population, should have a comparative advantage in labor-intensive commodities; Saudi Arabia has a comparative advantage in exporting oil-based products; and Canada has a comparative advantage in commodities that require the extensive use of land.

How well does H-O account for the actual pattern of trade? Table 8.5 shows the composition of trade between China and the United States and demonstrates that H-O can explain some trading patterns. In commodities that require more skilled labor, R&D, and high quality capital (chemicals and other transport, i.e., aircraft), the United States exports substantial amounts to China. However, in commodities that require more intensive use of labor and less sophisticated capital and technology (clothing and other consumer goods such as DVD players, and so forth), then China exports these to the United States.

However, although H-O scores some successes, many features of international trade conflict with its simple predictions. Figure 8.7 shows the composition of U.S. merchandise imports in 2002 and reveals that the United States, despite having a high capital stock, imports mainly capital-intensive goods. How can we explain this?

DIFFERENCES IN TASTES

The H-O model assumes that all countries have the same preferences, so that trade patterns reflect only supply considerations. However, variations in demand also explain trade patterns. For instance, the U.S. state of Virginia exports 30 tons of poultry feet to

TABLE 8.5   **Chinese–U.S. Merchandise Trade, 2002**
China–U.S. trade pattern offers support for Hecksher-Ohlin model.

	China Exports to U.S. (% of total)	U.S. Exports to China (% of total)
Iron and steel	0.7	0.4
Chemicals	3.3	19.5
Other semimanufactures	9.8	5.5
Power generating machinery	0.6	1.7
Other nonelectrical machinery	4.4	14.8
Office and telecommunication equipment	26.3	26.9
Electrical machinery and apparatus	7.8	6.2
Automotive products	1.4	1.1
Other transport equipment	2.0	11.3
Textiles	2.6	0.9
Clothing	7.9	0.0
Other consumer	33.4	11.7

Source: WTO, Annual Statistical Report (2003).

Southeast Asia every month.[3] The H-O model cannot account for this trade because the United States does not have a comparative advantage compared to Asia in poultry production. This trade literally results from different tastes—Southeast Asian cuisine, but not American, uses chicken feet. Therefore, the United States may import capital-intensive goods because the U.S. demand for such goods may be so overwhelming that it has to import them even though it has a comparative advantage in producing those commodities itself.

However, differences in tastes are unlikely to explain the pattern of trade shown in Figure 8.7. First, U.S. capital-intensive imports are surely too big to be explained by taste differences. Second, if the United States has a bias for any particular commodity, it is for luxury goods that require substantial amounts of skilled labor as input. Differences in tastes are not, therefore, enough to completely rectify the H-O model.

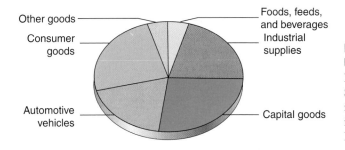

FIGURE 8.7   **Composition U.S. merchandise imports, 2002.** Even though the United States is a capital rich country, its imports tend to be capital intensive. *Source:* U.S. Census Bureau.

[3] This and many other fascinating trade facts are discussed in detail in Yarbrough and Yarbrough, *International Economics* (Fort Worth: Dryden Press, 2002).

TRADE RESTRICTIONS

The H-O model assumes the existence of free trade. Even though trade restrictions have been reduced over time, they still distort trade patterns. As we shall see in the next chapter, there exist substantial tariffs and quotas that prevent the operation of free trade and interfere with the predictions of the H-O model.

IS THE UNITED STATES CAPITAL INTENSIVE?

We have assumed that only two factors of production exist—capital and labor—but this is simplistic. In reality, output is produced using many different inputs—raw materials, skilled and unskilled labor, land, machinery, and so forth. More detailed modeling of these factor inputs, in particular human capital, may explain why U.S. imports are so capital intensive.

While the United States has high levels of physical capital, its labor force also has high levels of schooling. This suggests that its comparative advantage lies in the export of goods that require the intensive use of human capital. The data support this theory. One study finds that U.S. exporting industries use a higher proportion of workers with 13 or more years of schooling, whereas import-competing industries use a higher proportion of workers with 8 or fewer years of schooling.[4]

Table 8.6 breaks down the types of goods that some countries exported or imported in the mid-1960s. If a country exports a good that involves the intensive use of a

TABLE 8.6   **Factor Intensity of Trade for Selected Countries, 1967**
M means the country imports goods that use the factor in the relevant row relatively intensively. X means that the country exports these kinds of goods.

	U.S.	Canada	Germany	Japan	Mexico	Philippines
Capital stock	X	X	M	M	M	M
Labor force	M	M	M	X	X	M
Professional/technical workers	X	M	X	X	X	M
Management workers	M	M	X	X	X	M
Clerical workers	M	M	X	X	X	M
Sales workers	M	M	M	M	X	X
Service workers	M	M	M	M	X	X
Agricultural workers	X	X	M	M	X	X
Production workers	M	M	X	X	M	M
Arable land	X	X	M	M	X	X
Forest land	M	X	M	M	X	M
Pasture land	M	X	M	M	X	M

Source: Bowen, Leamer, Svelkauskas, "Multicountry, Multifactor Tests of the Factor Abundance Theory," *American Economic Review* (1987) vol. 77, pp. 791–809.

[4] Baldwin, "Determinants of the Commodity Structure of U.S Trade" *American Economic Review* (1971) vol. 61, pp. 126–146.

factor, it is marked with an X. If it imports such a commodity, it is marked with a M. The table reveals some plausible results—the United States exports goods that require the intensive use in production of human and physical capital; Canada exports land-intensive commodities; Germany and Japan have a comparative advantage in goods that require skilled labor; Mexico imports capital-intensive goods; and the Philippines exports commodities that require unskilled labor. Thus, a more detailed breakdown of factors of production shows more support for the H-O model. However, the H-O model is still not entirely vindicated. The authors of this study examined whether the export–import patterns in Table 8.6 were consistent with independent measures of factor abundance in each country. While there were some successes, there were also many failures.

DIFFERENCES IN TECHNOLOGY

As well as assuming that countries are identical in their tastes, the H-O model also assumes that they all have access to the same technology. Therefore the only explanation for trade is supply side differences in factor abundance. However, at any given time, countries will be using different technologies. This is another reason why trade may not agree with the predictions of H-O. British wine is to be appreciated more for the effort taken in producing it rather than its taste—the lack of sunshine means that, regardless of cost structure, the United Kingdom will always import wine. The lack of suitable weather means that TFP for British wine making is low compared to other countries.

INTRA-INDUSTRY TRADE AND IMPERFECT COMPETITION

One particular problem for the H-O model is that, especially amongst OECD countries, much trade is intra-industry. An example is France selling Peugeot cars to Italy and Italy exporting Fiats to France.

Consider the following measure of intra-industry trade for a particular sector:

1 − absolute value (exports − imports)/(exports + imports)

The term absolute value (exports − imports) is the value of net exports, ignoring whether they are positive or negative. This measure ranges from 0 to 1. Imagine a country that specializes in car production and exports many cars but imports none. In this case, our measure of intra-industry trade (given that imports of cars are zero) would be 1 − exports/exports = 1 − 1 = 0. If instead the country has no car industry, so that car exports are zero, but imports are large, the measure would be 1 − imports/imports = 1 − 1 = 0. Therefore, if trade in an industry is in only one direction (exports or imports), this measure is 0. When a country both imports and exports cars, so that net exports are zero, the measure is 1 − 0/(exports + imports) = 1. Therefore, the closer this measure is to 1, the greater the extent to which trade is intra-industry.

Figure 8.8 shows measures of intra-industry trade for 11 countries and reveals considerable intra-industry trade among the most developed nations. The H-O model cannot explain this—what type of factor endowment can explain why Italy produces Fiats while the French produce Peugeots? We therefore need a different model.

To develop this model, we make two assumptions. The first is that consumers like variety. On entering a car showroom, they wish to select from a range of colors, models, and manufacturers rather than be faced with no choice. Because consumers

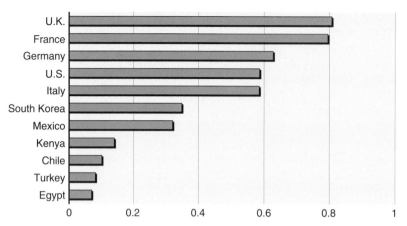

FIGURE 8.8 **Extent of intra-industry trade.** A very high proportion of trade for developed countries represents exports of types of goods or services that the country also imports. *Source:* Grimwade, *International Trade: New Patterns of Trade, Production, and Investment* (London: Routledge, 1989). Reprinted with permission of Routledge.

value variety, the producer of each different type of car has some monopoly power—consumers do not treat Fiats and Peugeots as identical. The second assumption is that car production is characterized by increasing returns to scale—the more cars that are produced, the lower the unit cost. Therefore, if restricted to a small output, the costs—and therefore the price—of the car will be high.

Now consider what happens when the economy is closed to trade. Consumers want a wide range of models to choose from, but this means that production runs have to be inefficiently small and car prices will be high. Although consumers value product variety, there is a limit to what they are prepared to pay for it. As a result, the country will produce a limited range of products to benefit from the increasing returns to scale, e.g., Italian consumers would buy Fiats; the French, Citroens; and the Germans, Volkswagens. Now consider what free trade between countries does. Because car producers can now sell to export markets, they can achieve large production runs with no increase in the level of demand in their domestic economy. Therefore they can keep costs and prices low. Meanwhile, consumers can now choose among different car models at reasonable prices because producers are still benefiting from increasing returns. German consumers can now choose to buy Volkswagens, Fiats, or Citroens. Trade in this case is still beneficial—production is efficient, and consumers benefit from greater product variety—but the pattern of intra-industry trade looks different from what H-O predicted.

KEY POINT

The Hecksher-Ohlin model explains trade through differences in factor endowments—a country has a comparative advantage in producing goods that require as an input a factor the country possesses in abundance. While this helps explain substantial amounts of trade, we also have to allow for differences in tastes, trade restrictions, and high levels of intra-industry trade.

8.5 Distributional Impacts of Trade

The theory of comparative advantage is unambiguous—free trade is good for a country. Why then do countries clash so often over trade and why are trade restrictions so common? Table 8.7 shows that, although many people in different countries do have positive attitudes towards trade, there is also substantial opposition. To try to explain these conflicts, we focus on four issues: the effect of trade on the distribution of income; concern over a nation's competitiveness; alternative theories of trade (so called "New Trade Theory") that argue that countries can benefit from trade restrictions; and political economy arguments that see trade barriers as the result of the interaction of different interest groups. In the next chapter, we extend this argument to consider the pros and cons of globalization and especially the role of trade liberalization for developing economies.

TRADE AND INCREASING INCOME INEQUALITY

Comparative advantage shows that a country *as a whole* can benefit from free trade—it does not show that *everyone* within a country benefits. Some groups within society are better off as a result of trade, but the standard of living of others declines. The country as a whole benefits from trade, suggesting that the gains outweigh the losses. Therefore, the gainers *could* compensate the losers and still benefit from trade. Without some redistribution of this sort, however, trade will generate losers.

The **factor price equalization theorem** says that as trade occurs, relative factor prices in each country eventually converge. In other words, wages and the cost of capital adjust until they are in the same ratio across countries. Consider a country that has an abundance of capital (say, the United States) and another country whose comparative advantage lies with labor-intensive commodities (e.g., Mexico). H-O says the United States will export capital-intensive commodities to Mexico and import labor-intensive goods. As a result, the demand for capital will increase in the United States but the demand for labor will fall, and the demand for labor will rise in Mexico but the demand for capital will decline. This will put downward pressure on both U.S. wages and the Mexican rental price of capital. *As a result of trade, wages should fall in the United States and rise in Mexico, and the rental price of capital should increase in the United States and fall in Mexico.* In fact, we can go further and say that factor prices should be equalized across countries—Mexican and U.S. wage costs should become the same.

Figure 8.9 shows hourly manufacturing wages for a selection of countries. There is huge variability. Given the factor price equalization theorem, it is understandable that free trade troubles many people. If U.S. wages fall to Mexican levels, then free trade will lead to serious social problems in the United States. However, the situation is not as dramatic as Figure 8.9 suggests. Factor price equalization implies that *identical factors of production should be paid the same even if they are in different countries.* But unskilled labor in the United States is not the same as unskilled labor in Mexico. In a U.S. factory, unskilled workers have access to much higher levels of capital and probably to higher levels of technology. Therefore, U.S. unskilled workers will have a higher level of productivity than Mexican workers and U.S. firms can pay a higher wage. If the productivity of U.S. workers is twice that of Mexican workers, then their wage can be twice

TABLE 8.7 Opposition to Free Trade, 1995

Percentage response to following survey question

Now we would like to ask a few questions about relations between (respondent's country) and other countries. How much do you agree or disagree with the following statement: (Respondent's country) should limit the import of foreign products in order to protect its national economy.

1. Agree strongly
2. Agree
3. Neither agree nor disagree
4. Disagree
5. Disagree strongly

Country	Agree Strongly (%) (1)	Agree (%) (2)	Neither Agree Nor Disagree (%) (3)	Disagree (%) (4)	Disagree Strongly (%) (5)	Missing Values(%)
Germany, West	15.13	23.71	18.49	26.83	9.52	6.32
Germany, East	25.98	30.39	16.99	17.32	4.74	4.58
U.K.	23.16	40.17	18.53	12.38	1.42	4.35
U.S.	21.29	43.09	16.02	10.39	2.93	6.29
Austria	37.84	31.98	10.92	12.61	3.87	2.78
Hungary	45.40	25.80	15.80	6.90	2.60	3.5
Italy	25.78	34.73	14.53	16.09	6.58	2.29
Ireland	24.25	41.35	10.87	19.62	2.72	1.21
Netherlands	5.12	23.93	28.24	31.93	5.51	5.27
Norway	9.10	28.49	27.37	22.79	4.91	7.33
Sweden	12.42	28.09	29.24	17.52	6.40	6.33
Czech Republic	25.56	26.55	17.73	17.19	9.54	3.42
Slovenia	24.03	26.83	17.95	20.46	3.96	6.76
Poland	30.04	34.86	12.70	11.76	2.63	8.01
Bulgaria	53.57	23.80	4.98	3.26	4.52	9.86
Russia	35.58	24.48	11.74	15.02	6.81	6.37
New Zealand	17.64	34.23	19.37	19.85	4.99	3.93
Canada	14.13	31.69	21.58	21.84	6.03	4.73
Philippines	12.75	53.75	16.33	15.17	0.83	1.17
Japan	14.09	16.80	29.54	14.97	19.03	5.57
Spain	21.21	50.12	10.97	9.25	0.98	7.45
Latvia	50.19	20.79	9.87	9.00	4.12	6.03
Slovak Republic	26.66	28.75	15.99	16.14	8.57	3.89
Mean	23.57	31.22	17.80	16.66	5.48	5.26

Source: Mayda and Rodrik,"Why are some people (and countries) more protectionist than others?" Harvard University Kennedy School, mimeo 2002.

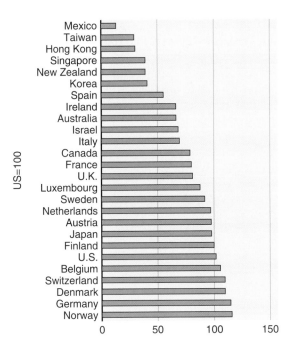

FIGURE 8.9 **Hourly manufacturing wages, 2001.** Wage rates differ spectacularly across countries that trade with each other. *Source:* U.S. Bureau of Labor Statistics

as high. Therefore factor price equalization refers to productivity-adjusted wages (unit labor costs), rather than to the hourly wage rate. In Figure 8.10 we plot wages and productivity relative to the United States for a wide variety of countries. The data support the theory: countries with high productivity can pay high wages without violating factor price equalization. As a consequence of trade, wage differentials reflect productivity differences rather than any scarcity value.

However, even though U.S. and Mexican unskilled wages do not have to be equal, the factor price equalization result still implies that unskilled wages fall in the United States as a result of trade with Mexico. The benefits of free trade in the form of lower

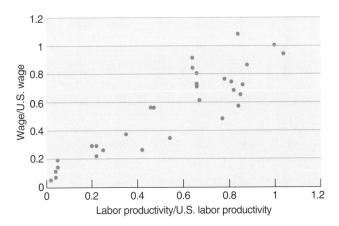

FIGURE 8.10 **Relative wages and productivity.** Wage differences across countries largely reflect differences in labor productivity. *Source:* Trefler, "International Factor Price Differences: Leontief was Right!" *Journal of Political Economy* (1993) vol. 101, pp. 961–987.

import prices partly offset this fall. However, we have one more important trade result to outline—the **Stolper-Samuelson Theorem**. This says that trade increases the real income of owners of the abundant factor of production and decreases the real income of owners of the scarce factor. In our U.S.–Mexico example, this means that the real income of U.S. skilled labor increases, while that of unskilled workers declines.

It is estimated (see Chapter 7) that increases in trade account for 5–20% of the increase in inequality that the United States experienced in the 1980s and 1990s. The reason for this relatively modest impact is that, although imports increased sharply during this period, they still remained a minor part of the economy, and imports from low-wage economies were an even smaller component.

KEY POINT

Trade has substantial distributional implications so that, although the country as a whole benefits, some sectors gain and others lose. As a consequence of trade, wage differentials reflect productivity differences across countries.

8.6 Competitiveness

One reason why governments often engage in restrictive trade policies is the issue of **competitiveness**—the ability to outperform rival nations in certain key high-value-added activities. Paul Krugman attacked this notion of competitiveness, and the following section is a summary of his critique. In essence, Krugman's critique of "competitiveness" tries to spell out what comparative advantage actually implies. Krugman's main criticism is that comparative advantage says that *all* countries can benefit from trade, whereas the competitiveness argument implies that trade is a zero-sum game—if one side wins, then the other side loses.

Competitiveness makes sense in a business setting. Consider the constant battle for market share between Coca Cola and Pepsi. Coke can only gain market share at the expense of Pepsi, so the rationale for competition here is clear. But comparative advantage says this analogy cannot be carried over to countries. What is good advice to CEOs may not be sensible for heads of state.

COUNTRIES DO NOT GO BANKRUPT

If Coca Cola gains 100% market share, then Pepsi goes bankrupt, and this would be disastrous for Pepsi's management, workforce, and shareholders. What happens to the United States if the Koreans dominate the semiconductor industry? The United States does not go bankrupt—companies and governments go bankrupt, but not countries. If the United States loses out to Korea in the semiconductor industry, it retains a stock of physical capital, human capital, and labor and can still produce output. Further, comparative advantage tells us that a country always has a relative advantage in some industry. If the semiconductor industry in the United States starts to decline, then other industries will be expanding—biotechnology, software, or the film industry. Instead of bankruptcy, a country undergoes an industrial restructuring. For instance, the set of industries in the United Kingdom with comparative advantage has continually evolved—from textiles to coal to steel and, more recently, to financial services, fashion, and music.

All these changes have distributional implications, but overall the United Kingdom still benefits from trade. Naturally, the textile industry will campaign vigorously against cheap foreign imports because that industry may face ruin. But the country itself does not face ruin—a declining textile industry frees resources for another industry to expand.

IS TRADE BETWEEN COUNTRIES ADVERSARIAL?

Imagine that Pepsi introduces a new wonder drink that tastes fantastic and sells for half the price of other soft drinks. This would be unmitigated bad news for Pepsi's rivals. The marketing manager for Coca Cola will not enthuse to its board that employment and wages in Pepsi factories are booming, increasing the potential market for Coca Cola. Neither will the manager stress the benefits to Coke's own workforce of the availability of a cheaper and better-tasting product. Pepsi and Coca Cola are adversaries.

But what if Korea announces a new smaller and cheaper computer chip that increases processing speed twentyfold? Is this bad for the United States? It is almost certainly bad news for computer chip manufacturers in the United States, but not for the rest of the U.S. economy. Two things have happened:

- First, U.S. firms can now get access to cheaper and better products that will improve productivity in a range of industries and therefore increase the U.S. standard of living. An example of this effect is that when the United States in 2002 increased tariffs on steel imports to help protect the U.S. steel industry, other firms that required steel as an input formed the 49-to-1 group. The name signified that, for every employee in the steel industry, there were 49 employees in U.S. industries that would now have to pay more for their steel.
- Second, the Korean economy will be performing strongly on the strength of the additional profits, investment, and employment that this innovation generates. This, in turn, will increase the demand for U.S. goods in Korea.

Of course, trade restrictions could prevent the importation of the new technology or prevent U.S. firms from exporting to Korea. Then these benefits will not materialize. But if there is free trade, the innovation will benefit the United States. This example shows clearly the difference in perspective between being the CEO of a company and the leader of a country.

Competitiveness confuses two distinct notions: economic growth and comparative advantage, or absolute and relative productivities. Advocates of competitiveness want their country to focus on high-productivity industries. Capital accumulation, education, and technological progress are means of increasing productivity. Therefore, government policies that encourage the development of capital- and skill-intensive industries are to be welcomed. However, all of this is about the *absolute* level of productivity. By contrast, comparative advantage tells us that trade is about *relative* productivity. A country always has a comparative advantage in some industries and so will always benefit from trade. However, we also stressed that trade does not make all countries equally wealthy. Countries with high levels of productivity will always have a higher standard of living than countries with low levels of productivity. It is, of course, better for a country to have high productivity, but whether it does or not, free trade policies improve welfare. In other words, a country should invest in education, encourage investment, and try to stimulate technological progress, but these policies should not interfere with free trade between countries.

The danger with a single-minded obsession with competitiveness is that it leads one to think of success as doing better than other countries. But Chapters 3 though 6 suggested that a country should try and maximize its own productivity growth rather than outperform rivals. Consider the imaginary case in which the French and German economies are both experiencing long-run productivity growth of 2% per year, but the Germans suddenly achieve an increase of 4%. In some sense, the French have lost their competitiveness, but what does this mean? France will experience some disutility from this faster German growth rate (individual happiness does depend in part on comparisons with your neighbors, and a much larger German economy would probably affect the role of France in international politics). But, in essence, nothing has happened to the French standard of living—it is still growing at 2% per year.

Failure to recognize this distinction between absolute and relative productivities can lead to trade restrictions. Comparative advantage shows that all countries gain from trade, which therefore implies that all countries lose from trade barriers. This reasoning underpins Krugman's statement that competitiveness is a dangerous obsession.

KEY POINT

Comparative advantage implies that trade between countries is not a zero-sum game, so trade should not be viewed as a competition in which a country has to outperform its rivals.

8.7   Strategic Trade Theory

We have so far taken a passive view of comparative advantage—according to H-O, the resource endowments of a country determine competitive advantage. However, alternative models, known as **new trade theory**, imply that simply accepting a country's current comparative advantage is not optimal and that anti-free trade policies can be used to transform comparative advantage. For instance, Switzerland has a comparative advantage in the production of precision engineered luxury watches—an advantage that partly reflects historical accident. At some point in the past, Switzerland had many craftsmen who could produce high-quality watches, so the industry was established in Switzerland. A range of industries then developed nearby to supply components, and an expanding workforce acquired the skills to make watches. Thus Switzerland established a reputation for producing fine watches. The status of the Swiss watch industry reflects a comparative advantage accumulated over many years, an advantage that reputation and know-how have strengthened. This suggests that countries do not need to accept as inevitable their current comparative advantage. Perhaps government policies (such as import protection or export subsidies) can develop an industry that will eventually become the country's comparative advantage.

Consider the aircraft industry, which is characterized by extreme increasing returns to scale—because of huge development costs, average unit production costs decrease sharply as output increases. Consider the interaction between two firms: the U.S. firm Boeing and the European conglomerate Airbus. This example combines many features. The industry is a large and important one—Boeing is the United States' largest exporter. The industry is high tech/high value added and of strategic importance to the United States and Europe. Europe and the United States have continually clashed over whether government support of Boeing and Airbus violates free trade principles.

TABLE 8.8   Airbus–Boeing Payoff Matrix—No Government Intervention

First figure in each cell represents the payoff to Boeing, the second figure is the payoff to Airbus.

		Airbus	
		Enter	Don't Enter
Boeing	Enter	−$100mn, −$100mn	$500mn,0
	Don't Enter	0,$500mn	0,0

To develop our model, we utilize Table 8.8, which is a payoff matrix showing the profits Boeing and Airbus earn in response to different actions by each firm. To keep the analysis simple, we focus on the case in which each firm simply decides whether to enter the market or not. The first number in each cell gives the profits Boeing earns, and the second those Airbus earns.

We treat Boeing and Airbus symmetrically—each gets the same profits if they find themselves in the same circumstances. Table 8.8 shows that if both Boeing and Airbus produce planes, then they each lose $100 million. The reason is that if they share the market, then neither benefits from increasing returns to scale, so costs are high; competition also keeps prices low, and both lose money. However, if Boeing enters but Airbus does not, then Airbus makes zero profits, and Boeing earns $500 million. Boeing captures the whole market, with benefits from increasing returns to scale and a monopoly position. If only Airbus enters the market, it makes $500 million, and Boeing earns zero. Obviously if neither enters the market, they each make zero profit.

The best strategy for each firm depends on what it thinks the other firm will do. If Boeing knows that Airbus is going to enter the market, its best strategy is to withdraw—in this case, it makes zero profit rather than losing $100 million. If, however, it knows that Airbus has no intention of entering the market, then Boeing's best strategy is to enter. The same considerations hold for Airbus. If Boeing is already in the market and is committed to maintaining a presence, Table 8.8 says that Airbus should choose not to enter. In that case, Europe would not have an airplane manufacturing industry and would have to buy planes from an American monopoly provider.

We now show how this model provides different policy implications from those of comparative advantage. Imagine that Europe decides it needs an airplane manufacturing industry and offers a subsidy to Airbus of $200 million if it produces planes. Table 8.9 gives the new payoffs to Boeing and Airbus.

TABLE 8.9   Airbus–Boeing Payoff Matrix—European Subsidy $200mn

		Airbus	
		Enter	Don't Enter
Boeing	Enter	−$100mn,$100mn	$500mn,0
	Don't Enter	0,$700mn	0,0

Airbus profits remain unchanged if it does not enter—the subsidy is only paid if Airbus produces. However, if Airbus enters, profits increase by $200 million, the amount of the subsidy. Thus if Boeing enters the market, the subsidy converts the operating loss of $100 million for Airbus into a total profit of $100 million, while if Boeing withdraws from the market, Airbus profits are now $700 million. The European subsidy—the instrument of **strategic trade policy**—changes the industry; regardless of what Boeing does, Airbus' optimal strategy is to produce planes. Therefore Boeing has to select a strategy by comparing outcomes along the top row of Table 8.9. Given that the subsidy means that Airbus is definitely going to enter the market, Boeing either loses $100 million by producing, or earns zero profits by withdrawing. The best strategy for Boeing is therefore to cease production and leave the market to Airbus. The European subsidy has worked spectacularly. In return for a subsidy of $200 million, Europe gains monopoly profits of $500 million and Europe gains a comparative advantage in an industry perceived as being of strategic economic importance.

This example (based on imperfect competition and increasing returns) makes a focus on competitiveness seem more sensible than a search for comparative advantage. In this model, trade is a zero-sum game—what Airbus captures, Boeing loses. Further, trade protection measures (subsidizing Airbus) increase welfare for Europe—contrary to what the static theory of comparative advantage implies. If this model captures important aspects of reality, then free trade policy may not be best, and government interventions in key industries can bring benefits.

However, we should not end our account of the model here. By paying a subsidy to Airbus, Europe has captured the market, but the U.S. government is unlikely to remain inactive while its largest exporter ceases production. Table 8.10 shows the payoffs if the United States also pays a $200 million subsidy to Boeing.

The best course of action for Boeing now is to produce no matter what Airbus does. The EU subsidy also means that Airbus' optimal strategy is to produce no matter what Boeing does. Therefore both firms enter the market and the relevant cell is the top left corner of Table 8.10—both firms make profits of $100 million. However, this profit includes the subsidy—each firm has an operating loss of $100 million because prices are set too low and costs are high. The U.S. retaliatory action makes the EU intervention no longer advisable. Europe is now paying a subsidy of $200 million so that Airbus can make an operating loss of $100 million. Only air travelers in other countries gain from the subsidies. Competition between Airbus and Boeing leads to cheaper airplanes, which in turn leads to cheaper travel. European and American taxpayers overpay for this benefit, but citizens of other countries benefit without having to finance the subsidy.

TABLE 8.10   Airbus–Boeing Payoff Matrix—U.S. and EU pay $200mn subsidy

		Airbus	
		Enter	Don't Enter
Boeing	Enter	$100mn,$100mn	$700mn,0
	Don't Enter	0,$700mn	0,0

Given that both firms are losing money without the subsidies, this situation is unlikely to continue. Three possible outcomes suggest themselves:

- Boeing and Airbus come together and agree to coordinate their price setting and both raise prices in order to restore profitability.
- Subsidies continue, but each firm tries to produce products that do not compete so fiercely against the other, enabling prices to rise. For instance, Boeing has been researching the development of extremely fast planes whilst Airbus has developed a large capacity plane.
- The EU and United States effectively engage in a poker game whereby they raise the subsidies they provide in the hope that the other country pulls out from the competition. This would likely trigger complaints by the losing country to the World Trade Organization regarding unfair subsidies.

So does new trade theory support strategic trade policy? We have shown that *under some circumstances* trade can be a zero-sum game and that suitable policy can lead a country to gain a comparative advantage in a key industry. However, the model also suggests many caveats. First, strategic trade policy works only under specific conditions—substantial increasing returns and imperfect competition. Such industries account for only a small part of the economy, and therefore the potential gains from strategic trade policy, even if successfully implemented, are small. Second, the benefits of strategic trade policy depend on how other countries react. Retaliatory responses or trade wars produce losses that outweigh any gains from import restrictions or subsidies. Therefore, new trade theory offers not general prescriptions for trade policy, but insights for specific circumstances.

KEY POINT

Some industries characterized by increasing returns and imperfect competition may benefit from trade restrictions or subsidies—in contradiction to the implications of comparative advantage. Such policies may, however, trigger a trade war between nations and are probably applicable to only a narrow set of industries.

8.8 Political Economy and Vested Interest

A major reason why governments implement trade restrictions stems from political lobbying. The Stolper-Samuelson Theorem says that with free trade some groups in society lose, and others gain. The groups that lose may lobby the government for protection from foreign competition. Whether they succeed depends on how strategically important they are to the government, how forcefully they make their argument, and how strong the arguments of the groups who stand to gain are. Often the group who stands to lose from free trade is a readily identifiable industry that is concentrated in a particular region. Further, although the region may be small relative to the economy, each individual in it stands to lose substantial amounts, e.g., their jobs. By contrast, those who gain may be a large but diverse group, each of whose members only benefit slightly from free trade. Such diffuse groups will also find it expensive to coordinate their efforts in lobbying for reductions in trade protectionism.

Consider U.S. tomato producers concerned about cheaper Mexican imports. Millions of U.S. consumers will benefit from cheaper imported tomatoes—but by only a few cents per purchase. By contrast, if millions of consumers buy Mexican tomatoes, thousands of workers on U.S. tomato farms will become unemployed and lose their income as will the farm owners. Comparative advantage tells us that the combined gains of consumers are greater than the tomato industry's losses. But the large number of consumers, their widespread locations, and their small individual gains mean that they will not combine to lobby the government in support of cheap Mexican tomatoes. The tomato industry, however, will lobby vociferously against them. The government will therefore face pressure from an antitrade lobby, but no corresponding support for free trade policies. If the tomato-growing industry is concentrated in a particular region, then the political representatives for that area will be sensitive to the lobbying, as will the government, if it is worried about an election. As a result of these factors the United States tomato industry was given exemptions when the United States and Mexico ratified NAFTA. This political economy argument helps explain why governments adopt economic policies that are not economically efficient. It is often easier for a government to provide protection to a sector rather than to allow that sector to undergo a potentially painful process of relocation and restructuring.

Empirical analysis of industries that are most likely to receive protection from trade pressures in OECD countries shows that they tend to have high levels of employment, high employment/output ratios, a high proportion of unskilled workers, and monopoly power. The adverse distributional implications of free trade, which lead governments to try to protect high-employment, unskilled industries, explain the first three findings. Coordination effects explain the final factor—it is much easier for an industry concentrated around a few firms to finance and coordinate a lobbying effort than for an industry that has many small firms.

SUMMARY

In section 8.1, we reviewed evidence that world trade has been increasing at a faster rate than world GDP so that the world is becoming increasingly interconnected. The majority of trade is in manufactured goods.

In section 8.2, we saw that economists' support for free trade is based on the concept of comparative advantage, which says that all countries can benefit from trade if they specialize in goods in which their productive advantage is greatest or their productive inefficiencies are least. A country's gains from free trade depend on the terms of trade. In section 8.3, we saw that, over the past few decades, terms of trade have shifted to benefit oil-exporting nations and reduce the gains of countries that export agricultural products.

In section 8.4, we examined evidence for the Heckscher-Ohlin model, which says that countries have a comparative advantage in goods whose production involves the intensive use of a factor that the country possesses in abundance. This prediction accounts for some of the observed patterns of trade, but tariffs and differences in tastes and technology lead to anomalies. The H-O model also fails to account for the substantial amount of intra-industry trade, which requires a model that combines increasing returns with consumers' desire for variety.

In section 8.6, we saw that, even though economic theory clearly shows the advantages of free trade, trade restrictions remain popular because countries try to maintain their "competitiveness" in certain industries. The distributional implications of free trade, discussed in section 8.5, help explain this support for trade restrictions.

In section 8.7, we examined new trade theories, combining increasing returns and imperfect competition, which suggest that under certain circumstances restrictive trade policies can be beneficial. But, in section 8.8, we saw that restrictive trade practices are largely the rational response of governments to lobbying pressures, and they usually come at the cost of economic inefficiency.

CONCEPTUAL QUESTIONS

1. (Section 8.1) Why is world trade rising faster than world output? Why is so much trade in manufactured goods?

2. (8.2) Review your transactions in the marketplace over the last week. What is your comparative advantage?

3. (8.2) Very few individuals are self-sufficient and most engage in the marketplace. Why then do so many people not accept the theory of comparative advantage?

4. (8.2, 8.7) The automobile manufacturer VBW is threatening to remove production from your country because productivity in its plants is too low. However, if the government pays a large enough subsidy, the firm will stay. Examine the merits and demerits of such a policy for the firm, government, and consumers.

5. (8.3) In some OECD countries, agriculture is heavily protected, and governments provide public support at least in part to preserve traditional life styles. What are the merits and demerits of using trade restrictions to achieve this aim?

6. (8.4) What is the comparative advantage of your country? Can the Heckscher-Ohlin model explain it?

7. (8.4) World coffee prices have fallen sharply in recent years as supply has increased. Can coffee producers learn anything from the actions of oil exporting nations in using OPEC as a cartel to raise oil prices?

8. (8.5) What can governments do to ease the distributional effects of trade within a country?

9. (8.5) Figure 8.10 suggests that trade makes wages reflect productivity within a country. Is this fair?

10. (8.6) Imagine a reunion in 10 years time with your classmates. Under one scenario, you find that although your income rose 50%, everyone else's income rose 100%. Under another scenario, your income fell by 25%, but everyone else's fell by 50%. Which of these scenarios do you prefer? What does this imply about competitiveness?

11 (8.7) An emerging market wishes to develop a presence in a key high-technology industry. It realizes that, at the moment, it could not possibly compete with existing firms, but it believes that if it were sheltered from competition via import restrictions for several years it could compete. (This is the *infant industry* argument for trade restrictions.) What are the likely problems with such an approach?

12. (8.8) Does popular resentment against free trade simply reflect economic illiteracy or more deep-seated political issues?

ANALYTICAL QUESTIONS

1. (Section 8.2) In country A, it is possible to produce a car with the same resources that would produce 1000 toy cars. In country B, producing a car uses resources that could produce 3000 toy cars. Show with a diagram how both countries can be better off if the international terms of trade between cars and toy cars is 1 car to 2000 toy cars. Suppose the country that is relatively good at making toy cars is poor and feels it cannot waste resources on consuming toy cars. Does this affect your analysis?

2. (8.2) Consider again the two countries in Question 1. Country A has a per capita GDP 10 times country B. The government of country B decides that concentrating on producing toy cars is harmful because it sees few countries in the rich, developed world that use more resources on building toys than on manufacturing automobiles. It places a 50% tariff on imported automobiles (so that if the world price of an automobile is $10,000, the domestic price will be $15,000). There is no change in world prices as a result of this. What is the impact of the tariff on the structure of domestic production? Is anyone better off? Is anyone worse off?

3. (8.5) A small industrialized country initially has no trading links with a large, but closed, centrally-planned economy that shares a border. Wages per hour for skilled and unskilled workers are $25 and $12, respectively, in the industrialized economy. The centrally-planned economy suddenly undergoes a peaceful revolution and the border with its industrial neighbor is completely opened to trade. In the former centrally-planned economy, skilled workers get paid $5 an hour and unskilled workers get paid $2 an hour. Productivity in the former centrally-planned economy is one-fifth that of the industrial country in all sectors and for all workers. What would factor price equalization imply happens to wages in the industrial country?

4. (8.7) How would the situation shown in Table 8.10 change if the EU increased its subsidy from $100 to $300? If you were the CEO of Airbus, how would you use this subsidy to improve your market position? How might Boeing respond?

Globalization

Overview

In economic terms, globalization is where barriers between national markets (whether for goods and services, capital, or labor) disappear and a single market with a single price is created. The first wave of globalization began in the early nineteenth century as transport costs fell, but it came to an end in the early twentieth century due to World War I and an increase in trade restrictions. After World War II, national governments coordinated to create international institutions such as the IMF, the World Bank, and GATT. The resulting decline in trade tariffs initiated a second wave of globalization that accelerated in the 1980s and 1990s as increasing numbers of emerging markets adopted trade-oriented policies.

Advocates of globalization argue that it brings many benefits—from world peace through the static gains of comparative advantage to beneficial effects on long-run growth. We review the evidence supporting these arguments and assess the benefits of trade liberalization for emerging markets. While economists tend overall to look kindly at globalization, there is also much vocal criticism. We consider these criticisms—including the loss of national sovereignty and cultural diversity, rising world inequality and poverty, the abuse of international institutions by multinational enterprises (MNEs), and environmental concerns. Many of these concerns raise the issue of what global governance and institutions there are in order to make global markets work beneficially. We end the chapter by studying the role of four major international financial institutions (IFIs)—the World Trade Organization (WTO), the International Monetary Fund (IMF), the World Bank, and the Organization for Economic Cooperation and Development (OECD).

Key Concepts

Bretton Woods Institutions
Conditionality
General Agreement on Trades and Tariffs (GATT)
Globalization
Import Substitution

Infant Industry
International Financial Institutions (IFIs)
International Monetary Fund (IMF)
Multinational Enterprises (MNEs)
Nontrade Barriers

Organization for Economic Cooperation and Development (OECD)
Tariffs
Trade Liberalization
World Bank
World Trade Organization (WTO)

9.1 Globalization—A Long-Term Perspective

Globalization refers to the way in which national economies are becoming increasingly interconnected with one another. This increasing interconnection reveals itself in three main markets:

- In 1990 total trade in *goods and services* (both exports and imports) amounted to 32% of GDP for OECD economies and 34% for emerging markets. By 2001 these numbers were 38% and 49% respectively. Figure 9.1 shows that around three-quarters of countries now have open trade policies, accounting for nearly half of the world population.
- Increased *capital* flows both between OECD nations and also between OECD and emerging markets. For example, Foreign Direct Investment (FDI) totalled $324bn in 1995 but had reached $1.5 trillion by 2000.
- While *labor* flows have not reached their nineteenth century highs, immigration has risen sharply in recent years.

WHEN DID GLOBALIZATION BEGIN?

World trade has been increasing for centuries as explorers have discovered trade routes and the technology of transport has improved. The great voyages of Christopher Columbus to the Americas in 1492 and Vasco da Gama to India in 1498 are dramatic examples of this long-running process of globalization. However, while these heroic journeys opened up new trading opportunities, the trade tended to be in high value added items that played a relatively small role in the economy. If trade is substantial, then prices for the same commodities should be similar in each location. Large price differentials can only persist if traders cannot buy commodities in the cheap location (which pushes up prices) and sell them in the more expensive location (which depresses prices). Trade forces prices to converge. Figure 9.2 shows evidence for this in a narrowing of price differentials during the nineteenth century in Amsterdam and Southeast Asia for three traded goods: cloves, black pepper, and coffee.

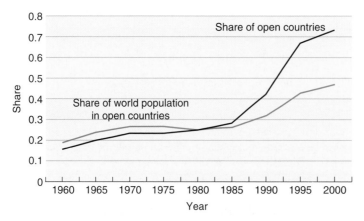

FIGURE 9.1 **World population living in open economies.** *Source:* Wacziarg and Welch, *Trade Liberalization and Growth: New Evidence*, NBER Working Paper 10152 (2003).

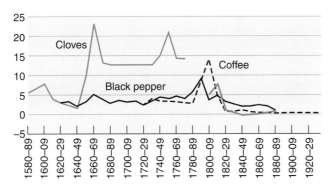

FIGURE 9.2   **Price differentials between Amsterdam and Southeast Asia (%).** As trade in many commodities increased sharply in the nineteenth century, international price differences fell. *Source:* Taken from material contained in *Southeast Asian Exports since the 14th Century: Cloves, Pepper, Coffee and Sugar* compiled by David Bulbeck, Anthony Reid, Lay Cheng Tan, and Yiqi Wu. Reproduced here with the kind permission of the publisher, Institute of Southeast Asian Studies Singapore, *www.iseas.edu.sg/pub.html.*

The driving forces behind this first age of globalization were dramatic declines in transportation costs. These declines were driven by the shift from sail to steam; larger, faster, and more reliable ships; the introduction of refrigeration for agricultural trade; the opening of the Suez and Panama Canals; and improvements in navigation, finance, and insurance. By the early twentieth century, this globalization process had led to high levels of integration, reflected in the following quote by John Maynard Keynes:

What an extraordinary episode in the economic progress of man that age was which came to an end in August 1914. . . . The inhabitant of London could order by telephone, sipping his morning tea in bed, the various products of the whole earth, in such quantity as he might see fit, and reasonably expect their early delivery upon his doorstep; he could at the same moment and by the same means adventure his wealth in the natural resources and new enterprises of any quarter of the world, and share, without exertion or trouble, in their prospective fruits and advantages. (The Economic Consequences of the Peace, 1920)

Figure 9.3 shows the annual growth in world trade over the last 100 years (excluding the World Wars of 1914–1918 and 1939–1945). Before 1914 world trade grew at an average of 5% per year, although it fluctuated widely depending on the business cycle. After the end of WWI in 1918, trade resumed but collapsed dramatically during the early 1930s. The United States and the rest of the world were in the midst of the Great Depression, and to prevent imports from capturing domestic demand, the United States enacted protectionist measures. Other countries retaliated, and trade declined.

By the end of WWII, most countries wanted to construct international institutions that would minimize the threat of conflict and foster international economic relations. To promote these goals, the International Monetary Fund and the World Bank were founded, and the General Agreement on Trade and Tariffs (GATT, which was later transformed into the World Trade Organization) was enacted. Through a

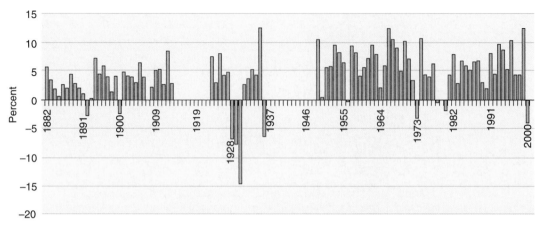

FIGURE 9.3 **Annual growth in world trade 1882–2001.** Since the end of WWII, the volume of world trade has risen at an annual rate of over 5%. *Source:* Maddison, *Monitoring the World Economy: 1820–1992* (1995). Copyright OECD. Updated using WTO data.

series of negotiations, GATT achieved reductions in trade tariffs and other barriers to trade, as shown in Figure 9.4. As a result, the world has witnessed a second wave of globalization that accelerated in the 1980s and 1990s as increasing numbers of emerging markets adopted trade orientated policies in an effort to boost their GDP growth.

DIFFERENCES BETWEEN TWO WAVES OF GLOBALIZATION

The first wave of globalization was driven by falling transportation costs and came to an end due to war and increasingly protectionist trade policies. By contrast, the second wave of globalization has been driven by a reversal of trade policies and increasing trade liberalization. The varying role of transport costs and trade policy in driving globalization is summarized in Table 9.1, which also documents the progress of globalization in labor and capital markets. According to the data, contemporary

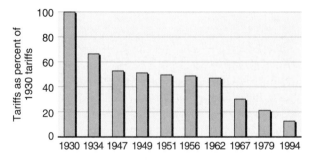

FIGURE 9.4 **Tariffs as percentage of 1930 levels.** The average tariffs on traded goods and services have steadily declined since the Depression. *Source:* Lavergne "The Political Economy of U.S. Tariffs" (Ph.D. thesis, University of Toronto, 1981), reproduction Robert E. Baldwin, "U.S. Trade Policy since World War II" in Baldwin and Krueger (eds.), *The Structure and Evolution of Recent U.S. Trade Policy* (Chicago: University of Chicago Press, 1986).

TABLE 9.1 **Two Waves of Globalization**

The first wave of globalization was driven by falling transport costs and the second and most recent wave by falling tariffs.

Epoch	Intercontinental Commodity Market Integration		Migration and World Labor Markets		Integration of World Capital Markets
	Change in Price Gaps between Continents	Why They Changed	How the Migrant Shares Changed in the Receiving Countries	Why They Changed	What Happened to Integration
1820–1914	Price gaps cut by 81%	72% due to cheaper transport, 28% due to pre-1870 tariff cuts	Rise in migrant shares (e.g. from 9.6% to 14.6% in U.S. 1850–1910)	Passenger transport cost slashed (Immigration policies remain neutral)	60% progress from complete segmentation toward market integration
1914–1950	Gaps double in width, back to 1870 level	Due to new trade barriers only	Drop in migrant shares (e.g. from 14.6% to 6.9% in U.S.)	Restrictive immigration policies	Revert to complete market segmentation
1950–2000	Price gaps cut by 76%, now lower than in 1914	74% due to policies, freeing trade, 26% due to cheaper transport	Rise in migrant shares (e.g. from 6.9% to 9.8% in U.S.)	Transport costs drop again (No net change in immigration policies)	Again 60% progress from complete segmentation toward market integration
Overall 1820–2000	**Price gaps cut by 92%**	**18% due to policies, 82% due to cheaper transport**	**No clear change in migrant shares**	**Policy restrictions, offsetting the transport improvements**	**60% progress from complete segmentation toward market integration**

Source: Lindert and Williamson, *"Does Globalization Make the World More Unequal?"* NBER Working Paper, WP 8228 (April 2001).

globalization in the goods market has passed the highs of the first wave of globalization to reach unparalleled levels. By contrast, while immigration has recently increased, it has not yet reached the levels of the end of the nineteenth century. Capital markets, on this measure, are of a similar scale, size, and role to those of the first wave of globalization.

There are other differences between these two waves of globalization. In the earlier wave, trade tended to be rather simple, with raw materials and agricultural goods going in one direction and finished manufactured goods in the other. The value-added chain today is, however, far more complex and involves many more stages. To exploit the comparative advantage of different countries, firms have sliced up the production process and located different stages in different countries. As a consequence, it is estimated that around one-third of all trade is intrafirm—that is, multinational enterprises (MNEs) with production distributed across many countries shipping products at various stages of completion to different parts of the company around the world. Not only does this make the structure of trade today different from the past but the existence of MNEs and strategic alliances amongst major companies creates large and powerful economic entities that governments have to deal with.

KEY POINT

Globalization began in earnest in the early nineteenth century driven by falling transport costs. WWI and increasing use of trade restrictions saw this first wave come to an end by 1914. A second wave began after WWII and has been mainly driven by falling trade tariffs due to international trade negotiations.

9.2   The Benefits of Trade Liberalization

The removal of trade restrictions, or **trade liberalization**, has been the subject of much criticism, and we shall review in the next section these arguments against globalization. For now we focus on the alleged advantages of trade liberalization.

TRADE, PEACE, AND COMPARATIVE ADVANTAGE

One long-running historical claim is that trade between countries helps reduce the risk of war between them. Montesquieu in his 1748 work *The Spirit of the Laws* argues that "commerce cures destructive prejudices" while Immanuel Kant argued that sustainable peace could be built upon a combination of democracy, international organizations, and economic interdependence. In a similar, but more jocular, vein Thomas Friedman in his best selling book *The Lexus and the Olive Tree* points out that no two countries that both have McDonalds in them have ever been to war with each other!

In Chapter 8, we reviewed the theory of comparative advantage, which argued that all countries benefit from free trade and the removal of trade restrictions. The essence of comparative advantage is that countries gain by focusing on producing goods they are most efficient at and purchasing other commodities more cheaply from abroad. These gains help produce an increase in the *level* of real GDP per capita. This is a *static* gain because once resources have been fully switched to the more efficient sector, the gains from trade are complete. The logic of comparative advantage implies that all countries gain although they do so in varying amounts. For instance, agriculture is a heavily protected sector across the world so there are significant gains for agricultural exporting nations. Figure 9.5 shows estimates of these static gains if countries were to remove all their existing trade restrictions. They are substantial—for both the EU and the United States static gains would exceed $500bn.

TRADE AND LONG-RUN GROWTH

A more controversial issue concerns the *dynamic* benefits of trade liberalization. Does the removal of trade restrictions influence the trend growth of an economy?

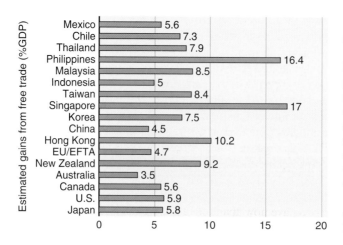

FIGURE 9.5 **Estimated gains from comparative advantage (%GDP) from eliminating trade barriers.** Substantial static gains may be realized from removing trade restrictions. *Source:* Brown, Deardorff, and Stern, "CGE Modelling and Analysis of Multilateral and Regional Negotiating Options" In Robert M. Stern (ed.), *Issues and Options for US–Japan Trade Policies* (Ann Arbor: University of Michigan Press, 2002).

As argued in Chapter 3, the welfare gains from boosting trend growth are enormous. Proponents of trade liberalization suggest that emerging markets should adopt outward looking policies based around free trade, exports, trade liberalization, and encouraging inward FDI. Opponents counter that they should adopt inward looking policies based around protective trade policies to encourage the development of domestic industries and **import substitution**, substituting imports with domestically produced goods.

During the 1950s, when many emerging markets were gaining colonial independence, inward looking strategies dominated. The overriding policy philosophy was well summarized by the Indian premier Jawaharlal Nehru when he said "I believe as a practical proposition that it is better to have a second rate thing made in one's own country than a first rate thing one has to import." The economic rationale behind this policy was a desire for countries to promote domestic high value added sectors, such as manufacturing, rather than relying on primary raw materials. This desire was driven by two concerns:

1. The Prebisch-Singer hypothesis, outlined in Chapter 8, that the terms of trade for agricultural products falls over time so the gains from trade will diminish.
2. A belief that technological progress and TFP growth occurs mainly in the manufacturing sector rather than agriculture. If, due to comparative advantage, the manufacturing sector of the economy shrinks, this would lead to a fall in TFP growth and slower long-term growth.

To avoid these concerns, manufacturing would be protected by trade barriers. This would give countries an opportunity to build up their proficiency in these industries until they were able to compete at a global level and trade protection could be removed. This is known as the **infant industry** justification for trade protection. A new industry in an economy cannot hope to compete with more experienced rivals in other countries, but through experience and learning by doing, it can become competitive.

As we mentioned, there are offsetting arguments that instead suggest that openness is good for the growth of emerging markets. These arguments point out that one problem with imposing high tariffs on importing manufactured goods is that it raises the price of capital machinery that domestic manufacturers need. A given amount of money for investment purposes will therefore buy fewer machines and lead to a smaller increase in the capital stock. The other problem with the infant industry/import substitution argument is that it ignores the fact that imports can be a source of TFP growth. By restricting imports, not only are domestic firms forced to pay higher prices for capital goods but they may have to utilize inferior domestic technology. This argument that imports can help boost TFP growth has recently been extended to the service sector. As we saw in Chapter 5, an efficient financial sector helps allocate investment funds more efficiently and boost TFP. This suggests that emerging markets with weak financial systems might benefit by allowing the import of more efficient financial services from advanced nations. The same argument also applies to other service industries such as airlines and telecoms.

Most emerging markets have now abandoned import substitution policies and lowered trade tariffs sharply (see Table 9.2). Why didn't import substitution work?

TABLE 9.2 **Trends in Average Tariffs Amongst Emerging Markets**

During the 1980s and 1990s, emerging markets moved away from import substitution and reduced trade tariffs sharply.

Country	Earliest (1960–70)	Earliest (1980–85)	Average (1986–90)	Average (1991–95)	Latest (1996–2002)
Argentina	181	28	25	11	14
Bangladesh		100	93	63	26
Bolivia		12	18	10	9
Brazil		44	42	17	13
Burundi		38	37	7	
Cameroon		28	32	19	18
Chile	83	35	17	11	8
China		50	39	40	14
Colombia	47	61	29	14	12
Costa Rica		21	19	12	7
Côte d'Ivoire		31	26	22	15
Egypt		47	40	33	30
Ghana		43	19	17	16
Guinea		76	10	11	17
India		74	94	54	40
Indonesia	58	29	26	20	7
Israel		8	7	8	8
Jordan		16	16	17	15
Kenya		40	40	30	20
Korea	40	24	18	10	9
Libya		13	23		20
Malawi		22	18	20	16
Malaysia		11	15	14	9
Mexico		27	14	13	17
Morocco		54	23	24	34
Nigeria		33	32	33	25
Pakistan		78	67	57	24
Peru	73	19	41	17	14
Philippines		41	28	23	8
Sierra Leone		26	31	30	16
Singapore	1	0	0	0	0
South Africa		29	15	9	13
Sri Lanka		41	28	24	16
Taiwan, Prov. of China		31	15	11	9
Thailand		32	40	32	17
Tunisia		24	26	28	36
Turkey		40	27	27	14
Uruguay	384	47	30	16	12
Average LDCs	**108**	**36**	**29**	**22**	**16**

Source: UNCTAD Trade Analysis and Information System.

- The infant industry argument needs to be applied selectively rather than applied in all sectors. If used selectively, it may occasionally work, as proven by our related discussion of strategic trade policy and Boeing/Airbus in Chapter 8 and by evidence in both the recent and historical experience of emerging markets. However, if it is applied generally to most industries, then governments end up paying too much in subsidies. This puts a strain on fiscal finances and leads to substantial rent seeking and inefficiencies in both industry and government.
- It led to high capital goods prices and domestic firms having to use low level technology.
- If an industry had not become competitive after several years, governments found themselves extending the protectionism rather than removing subsidies and tariffs and seeing the industry suffer from global competition.

KEY POINT

The link between trade openness and long-run growth is ambiguous from a theoretical perspective. However, in practice many emerging markets have moved away from import substitution policies towards export openness and trade liberalization.

TRADE LIBERALIZATION AND ECONOMIC GROWTH—THE EMPIRICAL EVIDENCE

As the previous section makes clear, theory is ambiguous about how trade liberalization affects long-run growth. Although most emerging nations are now pursuing policies of openness, we must review the empirical evidence to determine the effects of either closed or open trade policies.

Figure 9.6 shows there exists a strong negative correlation between tariffs and GDP—countries with low tariffs tend to have high GDP. But it is well known in economics that correlation does not imply causation. In other words, Figure 9.6 does not show conclusively that trade liberalization *causes* faster GDP growth. There are two main problems—omitted variables and simultaneity.

- *Omitted Variables* Countries that lower their tariffs may also introduce many other reforms. For example, they may improve education, reform institutions, improve their banking system, and so forth. It may be these other reforms that really improve GDP, rather than trade liberalization. Countries with high tariffs may

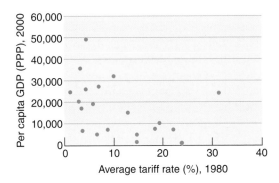

FIGURE 9.6 **Tariffs and GDP.** Countries with high tariffs tend to have lower GDP per capita. *Source:* Heston, Summers, and Aten, Penn World Table Version 6.1, Center for International Comparisons at the University of Pennsylvania (CICUP), October 2002, for GDP data; and UN Statistics Division Online Database www.unstats.un.org for tariff data.

have poor economic policies in other areas. For instance, many ex-communist economies have high tariffs and many market interventions and inefficiencies as well as having low GDP. Therefore, the strong correlation in Figure 9.6 might really reflect the influence of a third variable rather than trade liberalization itself.

To see the problems this causes econometrically consider the case where

$$\text{GDP per capita} = a \times \text{Financial Sector Reform} + b \times \text{Capital Stock} + c \times \text{Openness} + u$$

Where a, b, and c are positive coefficients and u is a random variable that on average equals zero. Let us also assume that countries tend to do financial sector reform at the same time as they reduce tariffs and increase openness so that Financial Sector Reform and Openness are correlated:

$$\text{Financial Sector Reform} = d \times \text{Openness}$$

If the econometrician mistakenly does not include Financial Sector Reform in the regression and instead estimates

$$\text{GDP} = b \times \text{Capital Stock} + f \times \text{Openness}$$

then the estimate of f will be $c + a \times d$. In other words, the econometrician will overestimate the effect of openness as $c + a \times d$ rather than the true value, c. If c were negative, i.e., trade liberalization decreases GDP, then this bias may even be large enough to think that trade liberalization was beneficial when it was actually harmful.

This omitted variable bias is an important problem as estimates of the impact of openness are sensitive to which other variables are included in the regression.

• *Simultaneity*   It may be the case that countries with high GDP have low tariffs. If this is the case, then we will once again overestimate c and the impact of trade liberalization. Why might countries with high GDP have low tariffs?

Poor countries tend to have weak systems for collecting taxes from labor income and so have to rely more on tariffs.

As we saw in Chapter 8, trade leads to some sectors expanding and some declining. Rich countries have more substantial welfare systems and so will be able to support the losers from free trade more easily and so will lower tariffs more. As a result, rich countries will have lower tariffs.

Both these problems can be overcome in our econometric estimation if we focus on a component of openness which is not affected by GDP (although it may in turn influence GDP) and is unlikely to be correlated with other policy variables. We can think of this as the *exogenous* component of openness—the portion of a country's openness that is unaffected by policy variables. Because this component is unaffected by GDP and uncorrelated with policy variables, we will be able to correctly estimate how openness affects GDP.

A natural way of estimating this exogenous component of openness is to focus on the role of geography. Countries that are physically near to other countries with large markets will have lower transport costs and so will do more trade than isolated countries *assuming the same tariff policy*. Using geographical proximity to large overseas markets to predict trade flows is called a *gravity* model approach to trade. If we find that countries that do more trade than others for geographic reasons also have higher GDP, we can be reasonably confident that openness boosts GDP. Using this approach, for instance, we find that Japan's trade (exports plus imports) should be around 40% of GDP due to its nearness to other countries whereas, in reality, trade is 25% of GDP. From this we can infer that Japan has relatively closed trade policies. By contrast, Singapore's geography predicts a trade share worth 108% of GDP compared to an actual trade share (in 1985) of 318% due to highly trade orientated policies. Using these trade shares as our measure of openness, we find that the more open countries do have higher GDP[1] and that the result is stable and significant.

Table 9.3 shows the role of trade policies in accounting for GDP growth across countries between 1960 and 1985. China over this time period achieved an increase in GDP per worker 16.7% larger than the average of other countries. Because of the low initial level of Chinese GDP, convergence factors would have explained growth 35% higher than the average. Improvements in education and high investment explain higher growth of 12.7% and 7.8% respectively. But the relatively closed nature of Chinese trade policy during this period *lowered* growth by 16%. In comparison, Hong Kong, Singapore, and Malaysia all enjoyed rapid growth in part because of their more open trade policies, which boosted growth by 49%, 86%, and 13% respectively over and above the effect of other variables.

TABLE 9.3   Impact of Openness on GDP Growth, 1960–1985
One reason for the fast economic growth in much of Southeast Asia was relatively open trade policies.

Country	Growth of Per-Worker GDP	Difference in Growth Above World Average	Contributions to Difference in Growth of Various Factors					
			Openness	Investment	Population Growth	Schooling	1960 GDP	Unexplained Factors
China	0.705	0.167	−0.164	0.078	−0.011	0.128	0.349	−0.213
Hong Kong	1.379	0.842	0.491	0.085	−0.038	0.181	−0.028	0.150
Indonesia	0.968	0.431	−0.084	0.015	−0.007	−0.049	0.229	0.319
Japan	1.329	0.792	−0.143	0.197	0.028	0.264	−0.079	0.525
S. Korea	1.350	0.813	0.003	0.098	−0.029	0.233	0.093	0.416
Malaysia	0.942	0.404	0.129	0.105	−0.041	0.144	−0.024	0.089
Philippines	0.353	−0.184	−0.073	0.026	−0.020	0.229	0.064	−0.411
Singapore	1.298	0.761	0.865	0.175	−0.040	0.208	−0.076	−0.371
Taiwan	1.326	0.789	0.095	0.102	−0.033	0.242	0.029	0.353
Thailand	0.928	0.391	0.054	0.046	−0.031	0.001	0.192	0.236

Source: Cyrus, Frankel, and Romer, "Trade and Growth in East Asian Countries: Cause and Effect?," Working Paper 5732 (1996).

[1] Frankel and Romer, "Does Trade Cause Growth?" *American Economic Review*, June, 89(3) pp. 379–399.

While this evidence is suggestive it is not immune to criticism. In particular, it is vulnerable to the criticism that perhaps openness induced by policy has a different effect on GDP than geography-induced openness. In other words, this result cannot be used to argue that lowering tariffs will increase GDP growth. However, a more recent study[2] of the link between trade liberalization and growth takes a different perspective, but finds similar results. On average, that study found that trade liberalization boosts GDP growth by around 1.5% per annum, suggesting substantial dynamic gains from trade. The interesting feature of this study is rather than just compare across countries and see how differences in trade policy influence GDP, it also focuses on how countries respond over time to changes in their own trade policy. Figure 9.7 shows the pattern of GDP growth after trade liberalization in a sample of countries. These charts show that on average trade liberalization leads to improved growth performance for emerging markets. However it is also clear that there is considerable variation across countries in the success of trade liberalization. Trade liberalization tends to boost growth but it is not an automatic panacea—in the case of several countries GDP actually falls after trade liberalization.

So what lessons can we learn from this empirical evidence?

- There is little evidence that supports the idea that inward looking high tariff policies boost growth. The econometric evidence tends to support the opposite—that open trade policies systematically boost GDP.
- The finding that trade liberalization tends to boost GDP growth does not imply that countries should rapidly remove trade restrictions across all sectors. It leaves open the issue of whether a gradualist or radical approach to trade liberalization is required.
- Exclusive focus on trade liberalization may be unwarranted. Although the data support trade liberalization as a means of boosting GDP growth, the same evidence can also be used to criticize governments and institutions that place an excessive faith in trade liberalization *alone* as a means of boosting GDP. Trade liberalization may work as an important component of a wide range of policy reforms.

TRADE AND POVERTY

A common criticism of globalization and trade openness is that it leads to increased poverty especially in nations that are already poor. However, we have just seen that trade liberalization tends to boost GDP and we also saw in Chapter 3 that GDP growth tends to reduce poverty. If we link these results together we see that trade liberalization lowers poverty.

If trade liberalization boosts GDP, then the only way that it will not reduce poverty is if there is an increase in inequality so that most of the GDP gains accrue to the wealthy. Figure 9.8 shows that, for a range of nations, there is clearly no systematic relationship between trade liberalization and inequality. On average, increasing openness should lead to reductions in poverty. From the perspective of comparative advantage, it

[2] Wacziarg and Welch, *Trade Liberalization and Growth: New Evidence* NBER Working Paper 10152 (2003).

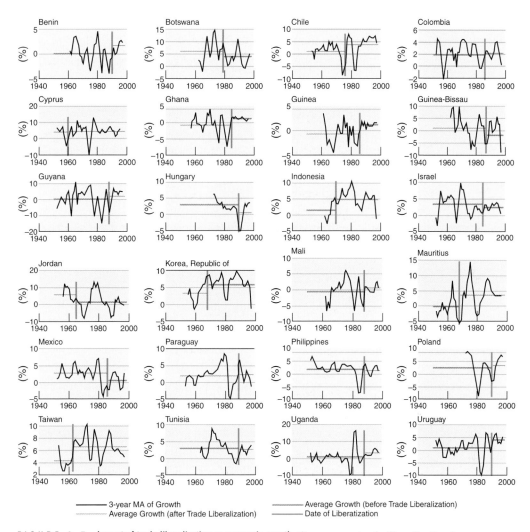

FIGURE 9.7 **Impact of trade liberalization on economic growth.** On average, trade liberalization increases GDP growth but not always. *Source:* Wacziarg and Welch, *Trade Liberalization and Growth: New Evidence* NBER Working Paper 10152 (2003).

is not surprising that increased trade does not systematically affect inequality. When countries trade more, some sectors expand and others contract. If poor people work in the sector that expands, then inequality will decline; if they are based in the sector that contracts, then inequality will rise. This pattern can be seen clearly in Figure 9.8—trade liberalization often has a marked impact on inequality, sometimes for the better and sometimes for the worse. Therefore, while trade liberalization will frequently benefit the poor through boosting GDP growth, governments also often have to worry about the adverse impact of trade liberalization on poverty.

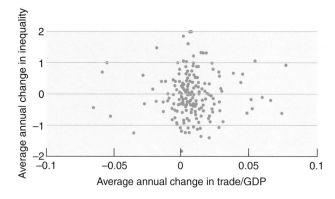

FIGURE 9.8 **Trade and inequality across emerging markets.** There is no relationship between changing levels of trade and changing levels of inequality. (Inequality is measured by the Gini coefficient—an increase in inequality shows as an increase in Gini coefficient.) *Source: Poverty in an Age of Globalization*, World Bank (October 2000).

KEY POINT

Econometric evidence suggests that increased openness to trade does raise the long-run rate of economic growth, although it is difficult to accurately isolate the impact that trade policy alone has on GDP. Although on average, trade liberalization boosts growth, success is not guaranteed.

9.3   Problems of Globalization

In 1824, the English historian Thomas Macauley noted that "Free trade, one of the greatest blessings which a government can confer on a people, is in almost every country unpopular." We have already noted the gains that lead from comparative advantage and trade liberalization, yet as trade has increased and emerging markets liberalized, there has been growing criticism of globalization and even riots on the city streets. In this section we focus on some of these criticisms and their validity.

DISTRIBUTIONAL IMPACTS AND INEQUALITY

As explained above and in Chapter 8, trade has important distributional effects with some sectors expanding and others contracting. Individuals in the contracting sector will have to find jobs elsewhere, assuming a constant natural rate of unemployment. This may involve relocating, retraining, or accepting a lower wage. (See Chapter 7 for a discussion of the natural rate of unemployment and the impact of trade on inequality.) Understandably, groups in society will resist these changes and so resist globalization. However, comparative advantage also makes clear that although this group loses, the benefits to society overall are positive.

Globalization has also been criticized for causing inequality and increased poverty in emerging markets. The argument is that with so many countries competing amongst themselves for the foreign direct investment (FDI) of large multinational enterprises (MNEs), wages will be bid down, which will lead to increased inequality and more poverty. We have already discussed in the previous section the relationship between trade liberalization and inequality. The most recent estimates[3] on poverty suggest that

[3] Sala-i-Martin, "The Disturbing Rise of Global Income Inequality," NBER Working Paper 8904 (April 2002).

between 1970 and 1998 the percentage of the world's population living on less than $1 a day has fallen from 16% to 5% while the proportion living on less than $2 has declined from 44% to 19%. In other words, during the period when globalization advanced rapidly, the world saw a *decline* in poverty.

MNES AND FDI

One of the major criticisms of globalization is the dominant role played by **multinational enterprises** (MNEs). Figure 9.9 shows the 100 largest economic entities in the world in 2001 as measured by the value added (not turnover) that they create. The largest company is Wal-Mart, which ranks forty-fourth, somewhat larger than Pakistan but smaller than Chile. With companies being larger than economies, there is a danger that trading rules will be set up to benefit corporations rather than citizens. One critic of globalization, Noreena Herz, says in her book *The Silent Takeover* that globalization leads to "a world in which the primary service that national governments appear able to offer their citizens is to provide an attractive environment for corporations or international financial institutions."

We will consider in a later section the influence that MNEs exert on trade negotiations. The other issue to consider here is whether countries and workers benefit by receiving FDI or if only MNEs do. In Chapter 6 we showed how countries benefit from FDI through an increase in capital and an improvement in TFP and how this leads to higher productivity and higher wages. Further, as shown in Figure 9.10, the other advantage of FDI is that, compared to alternative forms of foreign financing, it shows limited volatility. While bank lending and equity and bond finance flows in and out rapidly, FDI is more stable. Finally, it does not seem the case that FDI encourages greater corruption. As shown in Figure 9.11, FDI tends to flow to countries with *lower* levels of corruption. At the very least, this suggests that MNEs and related FDI bring some economic benefits to a country.

ENVIRONMENTAL DAMAGE

Critics of globalization fear it leads to environmental damage in two ways. First, due to the power of MNEs, governments abandon efforts to protect the environment through legislation. Second, increased levels of trade lead to greater use of fuel and more environmental damage. Further, much of this trade seems "pointless"—the United Kingdom, for instance, exports almost exactly the same number of pigs as it imports.

The need for governments to agree to global environmental standards to stop countries competing with one another along this dimension is connected to our next topic—the race to the bottom. The evidence regarding whether FDI worsens pollution is inconclusive, depending on which environmental indicator is considered. For instance, urban air pollution seems uncorrelated with FDI. Further, there is a strong correlation between GDP and environmental regulation, so that if FDI does raise GDP, it may also lead indirectly to improvements in the environment. There is also evidence that trade protectionism can damage the environment. Figure 9.12 shows that countries that protect agriculture and pay large subsidies are characterized by extensive use of fertilizers.

What about fuel arguments? That global trade leads to an increase in fuel use is undeniable. One cause of this is that airline fuel is frequently tax exempt so that the full cost of environmental damage is not paid by exporters and, as a result, trade is too extensive.

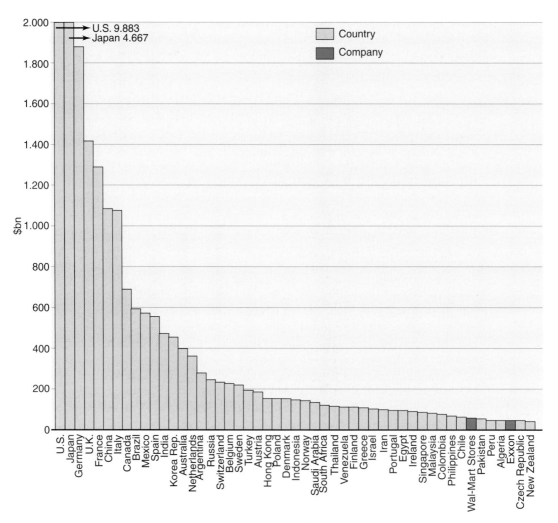

FIGURE 9.9   **100 largest global economic entities by value added, 2001.** Wal-Mart is the largest company by value added and is ranked forty-fourth in the world, slightly larger than Pakistan but smaller than Chile. *Source:* de Grauwe and Camerman, "How Big Are the Big Multinational Companies?" University of Leuven, mimeo 2002.

The other issue is whether or not the trade is "pointless." For instance, on average, every month Sweden imports 1305 metric tons of bottled water and exports 791 metric tons. Can this be justified? The main cost of this trade pattern is the additional transport costs—it would be cheaper for Sweden to consume its own water rather than ship it overseas and import other water. However, this cost can be offset by two factors. The first is that competition is increased through imports. This will lead to lower prices. Existing consumers of bottled water pay less. Because prices fall, more bottles are sold as consumption rises. The second benefit is that the variety of products available increases. If

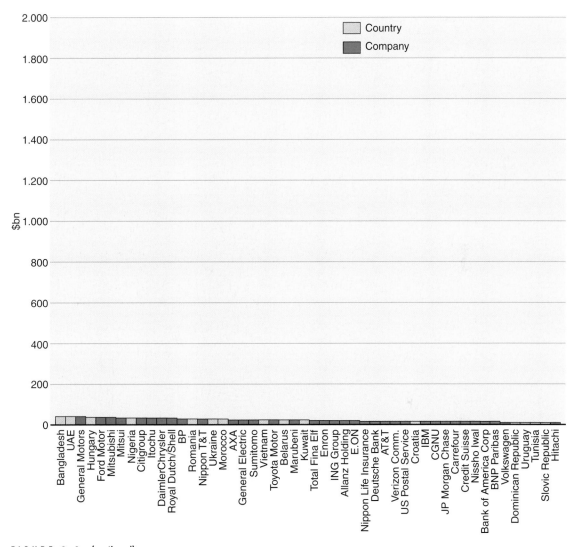

FIGURE 9.9   **(continued)**

consumers value variety, this will also boost welfare. If the competition and variety effects are large enough, they can offset the higher transport costs.

INSECURITY AND "THE RACE TO THE BOTTOM"

Comparative advantage means that a nation specializes in certain sectors so that it becomes vulnerable to adverse demand or price movements in that sector. In other words, workers face greater insecurity. This insecurity is further increased by the fact that MNEs and other firms can easily relocate to other countries. It is noticeable that countries that do more trade tend to have larger levels of government transfer payments, unemployment benefits, and welfare payments, which will help to offset this insecurity and cushion the volatility of employment.

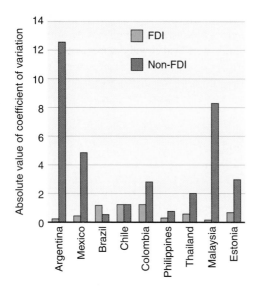

FIGURE 9.10 **Volatility of capital flows, 1990–1997.** FDI is a far more stable source of financing than other financial flows. *Source:* World Bank Global Development Report, p. 55 (1999).

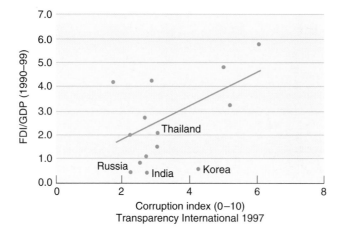

FIGURE 9.11 **FDI and corruption in emerging markets.** FDI tends to flow to emerging markets with better reputations for lack of corruption. *Source:* World Bank, *Global Development Finance* (2001).

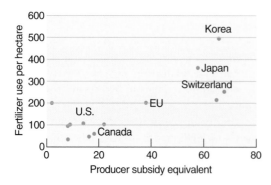

FIGURE 9.12 **Agricultural protectionism and environment.** Countries that subsidize and protect agriculture the most have worse environmental records. *Source:* Irwin, *Free Trade Under Fire* (Princeton: Princeton University Press, 2003).

However, while globalization may increase the need for governments to protect certain sectors of the population, the fear is it will reduce their ability to do so. MNEs can choose to locate around the globe, and so countries will compete to attract them by reducing corporate tax rates and offering large subsidies. This process is called "the race to the bottom" as governments compete with one another to offer the lowest corporate tax rates. If governments do cut corporate tax rates, then unless they can increase labor income taxes, they will not have enough revenue to finance the welfare state and will have to reduce their generosity. Globalization therefore may remove the ability to protect workers at the same time as it increases the need for this protection. The same argument can be applied to government regulations concerning environmental protection, working standards, and minimum wages. One way to overcome this problem is for governments to agree to common standards. For instance, the EU has rules restricting the subsidies that its member countries are allowed to pay to firms in order to prevent a race to the bottom, and efforts to create global environmental standards such as the Kyoto agreement are ongoing.

The race to the bottom argument rests on three assumptions:

1. MNEs do not have a strong reason to locate in one country rather than another, so they are easily tempted away by subsidies.
2. MNEs do not bring substantial spillover benefits to offset the lower tax rates they pay.
3. Corporate taxes are at the appropriate level to begin with and are not too high.

What is the evidence regarding the race to the bottom? Considering the overall tax burden paid by firms, expressed as a percentage of GDP, there is little support—the corporate tax take has not declined over time. This does not invalidate the threat of the race to the bottom; it just suggests that it has not yet operated strongly.

CULTURAL AND POLITICAL CONCERNS

We have focused above on the economic implications of globalization, but many of the criticisms are more politically focused. Globalization produces a greater role for markets, so naturally globalization is seen critically by those with anticapitalist views. Globalization also means that more resources are being allocated by market mechanisms and this may lack legitimacy. For instance, consider the case of a country that has banned child labor but now, because of globalization, finds itself importing textiles made using child labor. No democratic decision has been made in the importing country, yet market forces have brought about this change. This is also an example where countries begin to lose their national sovereignty—domestic rules cease to have jurisdiction. Other examples of this loss of sovereignty are connected to the power of MNEs and the rules of the World Trade Organization (WTO) that lead domestic governments to alter their policies. A loss of cultural sovereignty is also a common criticism of globalization. Globalization has led to a proliferation of global brands and an alleged homogenization of cultures—"Americanization" or "Europeanization."

This is a wide and varied list of criticisms of globalization. We have covered cultural change, environmental problems, inequality and poverty, the monopoly power of MNEs, instability, and insecurity. What is interesting is that these were precisely the criticisms made of industrialization in the nineteenth century as *domestic* markets began to grow and restructure the economy. Governments then realized that in order to bring out the best features of markets they would have to intervene to restrict industrial pollution, introduce town planning and health regulation, introduce schemes to help the poor, create government organizations to restrict monopoly abuse by firms and provide regulation and insurance to preserve stability in the banking system. In other words, in response to the growth of markets we saw the development of national governments, institutions and regulations to reduce the disadvantages of markets and support the advantages. What this argument suggests is that with the development of global markets we require national governments to agree to international standards and help construct global institutions in order to optimize the contribution that global markets make to welfare. In the next section we will review the global institutions that currently exist to support global markets.

KEY POINT

Global markets are raising many concerns relating to inequality, instability, the power of MNEs, environmental damage and the ability of governments to protect and offer social support to their citizens. Not all of these criticisms are supported by the evidence but for globalization to work efficiently, there is a need to develop global institutions and to coordinate national policies.

9.4   International Financial Institutions (IFIs)

In July 1944, a United Nations meeting held at Bretton Woods, New Hampshire, established two key institutions—the **International Monetary Fund (IMF)** and the **World Bank**. This meeting also tried to establish a third institution—an International Trade Organization (ITO)—but despite prolonged negotiations, this third pillar of the international community was not established. Instead, the trade agenda was pursued through the **General Agreement on Trade and Tariffs (GATT)**, which in 1995 evolved into the **World Trade Organization (WTO)**. Collectively, these three organizations are often referred to as the **Bretton Woods institutions** (although, strictly speaking, only the IMF and World Bank were successfully established at Bretton Woods). They attempt to govern global markets and, therefore, are the focus of much criticism.

The idea behind these global institutions was to avoid a return to the isolationism of the years between WWI and WWII in the belief that a vibrant interconnected world economy would reduce the likelihood of future conflict and help raise income standards. There was little desire to encourage global trade in labor and capital, so most of the initiatives focused on GDP growth and trade. To encourage trade there was a need to lower tariffs—either through an institution such as the ITO or through a series of negotiations such as GATT. Stable exchange rates were also deemed desirable both as a means to control inflation and also to boost trade. In order to produce stable exchange rates, it was recognized there would be a need for an organization that could provide short-term loans of foreign currency to governments, and this was the rationale behind the establishment of the International Monetary Fund. Because global capital flows were felt to be destabilizing for exchange rates, most countries still imposed restrictions on capital flows (capital account controls). However, this meant that poorer countries would not be able to get loans for development so the World Bank was established to provide long-term loans for countries to boost growth. The initial members of the Bretton Woods institutions were the richer nations but, over time, most other countries have joined. The **Organization of Economic Cooperation Development (OECD)** is the institution that focuses mainly on the economic agenda of the richer nations.

THE WORLD BANK

The World Bank has a membership of 184 countries with a staff of around 10,000. About 7,000 of the staff members are based in Washington, D.C., and the remainder in various countries around the world. Every member country contributes to the working capital of the World Bank in relation to the size of its economy. The larger the contribution a country makes to the World Bank's capital, the greater its shareholding in the Bank and so the greater its influence. As a result, the United States is the largest single shareholder (16.4%), followed by Japan (7.9%), Germany (4.5%), and France and the United Kingdom (4.3% each). The main focus of the World Bank is on poverty, and its general policy aim is to help the poorest parts of society in the poorest nations. These aims, summarized in the Millenium Development Targets agreed to by the United Nations in 2000, strive to reduce world poverty by half by 2015 and are based around 8 goals:

1. Eradicate extreme poverty and hunger.
2. Achieve universal primary education.
3. Promote gender equality and empower women.
4. Reduce child mortality.
5. Improve maternal health.
6. Combat HIV/AIDS, malaria, and other diseases.
7. Ensure environmental sustainability.
8. Develop a global partnership for development.

When it was first established, the World Bank was known as the International Bank for Reconstruction and Development (IBRD) and its aim was to make long-term loans to help countries grow in the aftermath of WWII. The IBRD still exists but it is now only one of five parts of the World Bank's operations. The IBRD focuses on making low interest loans to middle-income countries (less than $5300 GDP per capita). Often these countries will be able to borrow funds from private sector capital markets but World Bank loans have two substantial advantages:

- The World Bank offers more generous terms. The World Bank can borrow money at very low interest rates as it is ultimately backed by the rich countries that are its largest shareholders. It can then lend this money at low interest rates to countries who would otherwise have to pay higher interest rates if they borrowed directly from financial markets. As well as being able to borrow at lower interest rates, the World Bank also lends for longer, providing loans for around 15–20 years with a 3 to 5 year grace period before repayment of the loan must begin.
- Because of its focus on poverty, the World Bank will lend funds for specific projects related to poverty reduction or education that private sector capital markets will often not finance.

When the IBRD was established, substantial restrictions existed on money flowing from one country to another, and a significant amount of World Bank loans were for financing investment in infrastructure projects. However, as we shall discuss in Chapter 20, there are now very large-scale private sector capital markets that can potentially provide far more funding than the World Bank. This has led the World Bank to increasingly focus its lending in areas where private markets tend not to lend, including areas of market imperfections connected to poverty, environment, and gender inequality.

Another branch of the World Bank, the International Development Association (IDA), concentrates on the very poorest countries. These countries are so poor that they are often unable to borrow from commercial capital markets due to their lack of credit worthiness. (Currently 81 countries are eligible to borrow from the IDA.) The IDA provides grants/credits to these nations that are in effect interest free loans for around 35 to 40 years with a 10-year grace period. The hope is that these grants will relieve poverty and produce sustainable growth. Both through the IDA and the IBRD, the World Bank also offers considerable technical assistance in implementing economic policy. In 2002 the IBRD lent $11.5bn and the IDA $8.1bn.

THE INTERNATIONAL MONETARY FUND

The IMF was formally established in 1945: it now consists of 184 member countries. As shown in Figure 9.13, the number of member countries has grown significantly over time. Like the World Bank, it is based in Washington, D.C., but it has a much smaller staff of 2680. The IMF is essentially charged with achieving stability in the international monetary and financial system; this is reflected by the 5 main aims enshrined in its Article I:

1. Provide international monetary cooperation.
2. Facilitate expansion of balanced growth in trade.
3. Promote exchange rate stability.
4. Establish a multilateral payment system between countries and governments.
5. Make its resources available to member countries during a balance of payments crisis.

We will examine in detail balance of payments crises in Chapter 21, but these essentially occur when a country has run out of foreign currency and so wishes to borrow these funds from the IMF.

When a country joins the IMF it has to contribute a financing *quota* that is based on the size of its economy. As in the case of the World Bank, countries that make larger con-

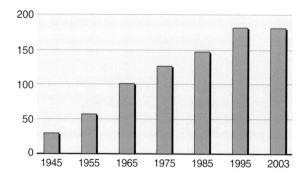

FIGURE 9.13 **IMF membership 1945–2003.** When the IMF was established, its membership was mainly rich nations, but it has since expanded to 184 countries covering both rich and poor. *Source:* IMF.

tributions get more of an influence in running the institution. Each IMF member country is given 250 votes plus additional votes depending on the size of their quota contribution. As a result, votes are unequally distributed—the largest voting bloc is the United States with a voting share of 17.1%, and the smallest is Palau with a voting share of 0.013%. For some issues, an 85% majority vote is required, giving the United States an effective blocking role.

When a country joins, it has to pay 25% of its quota to the IMF in terms of key stable international currencies, e.g., U.S. dollar, Euro, Yen, pound sterling, and so forth, and the remaining 75% can be paid in its own currency. This provides the IMF with readily available funds to lend to countries experiencing balance of payments problems. Every 5 years, quotas are reviewed and can be increased if the IMF requires more funds. The quota system is also used to determine how much a country can borrow. In any one year, a country can borrow up to 100% of its quota in the key international currencies up to a cumulative maximum of 300% of its quota. In exceptional circumstances, even these limits can be exceeded.

When it was established, the role of the IMF was purely to provide short-term loans to governments experiencing temporary balance of payments problems. In essence, the role of the IMF was to give countries a breathing space to make the required changes needed to resolve the problem. Based around this role the IMF has three main functions:

- *surveillance*—monitoring government policies to see if they are in danger of experiencing a balance of payments crisis
- *technical assistance*—the IMF helps governments implement economic reforms
- *lending assistance*—when countries experience a balance of payments crisis, the IMF lends funds

The emphasis in IMF lending has always been on repayment and the IMF will not loan funds unless a country accepts certain conditions on its future economic and financial policies (this is referred to as *IMF conditionality*). Negotiations over these conditions can be protracted and are invariably controversial. Acceptance of the IMF conditions is indicated when the country writes a *letter of intent* to the IMF requesting a loan and outlining how it attempts to meet the conditions set. The exact conditions imposed by the IMF will vary from country to country depending upon the circumstances. Suppose a country finds itself short of foreign currency and so it cannot purchase its imports due to a temporary fall in the price of its main commodity export. In these circumstances, the IMF could reasonably expect repayment of any loan to occur as soon as export prices recover. So the IMF conditions might be mild. They would in effect be an assessment that export prices are expected to increase and that the country is not importing an unsustainable amount of foreign goods. By contrast, if the fall in commodity prices is expected to be a permanent one, then more conditions would be imposed. The country will have been made poorer by the permanent fall in export prices and will either have to cut back on its expenditure and/or introduce reform policies to help restructure the economy and move resources away from the affected sector. Without these reforms, a country would be unable to repay the IMF and would be continually needing to borrow money.

The IMF has often found itself lending to governments who run out of foreign currency because they have been running unsustainable fiscal policy—that is, the government has been spending more than it brings in through tax revenue. In these situations, the IMF will focus conditionality on improvements in fiscal policy—making cutbacks in expenditure, removing subsidies, and raising taxes. Without these cutbacks, IMF lending will only temporarily solve a government's financing problem and the IMF is unlikely to get its loan repaid. This sort of conditionality has earned the IMF much criticism (and the nickname *It's Mostly Fiscal*), especially as expenditure cutbacks and removals of subsidies often affect the poor disproportionately.

Although the IMF was established to provide short-term financing to solve temporary balance of payments crises, it has found itself repeatedly drawn into long-term financing. The reason for this is that a number of countries have been unable to repay their initial IMF loans and, as these have been rolled over, the IMF has in effect found itself converting short-term debt into long-term loans. As the countries that find it difficult to repay tend to be those with poor GDP growth, the IMF has found itself increasingly involved with poverty issues and offering long-term advice on the supply side of a country, not just on its government expenditure and taxation programs. This focus on poverty has also been brought about because of sharp criticism that IMF fiscal policy recommendations, including removal of food subsidies, were substantially increasing poverty in countries in receipt of IMF loans. This extension of the IMF's role into long-term structural issues has brought about accusations of "mission creep" and complaints that **International Financial Institutions** (IFIs) are now dictating debtor nations' long-term structural policies concerning health, education, and the role of government.

Reflecting these developments, IMF lending is of two broad kinds. The first, typified by Stand By agreements, are funds that the IMF makes available to countries experiencing temporary but sharp balance of payments problems or currency crises. For instance, during the Asian crisis in 1997, Thailand and Korea received substantial loans through this channel as subsequently have Russia, Turkey, and Argentina. These loans tend to be extremely large (Korea, for instance, was allowed to borrow $40bn) and also are charged at a commercial rate of interest. In Chapter 21 we provide a detailed examination of currency crises and the record of the IMF in alleviating them. The second category comes under the Poverty Reduction and Growth Facility (PRGF). These loans are provided to countries with GDP per capita of less than $875. These loans are provided on concessionary terms—with an interest rate of only 0.5% and repayment between 5.5 and 10 years. These concessionary loans are not aimed at resolving short-run financing problems but at achieving sustainable long-run growth (the same role that the World Bank fulfills). The existence of such loans means that the IMF and World Bank have to coordinate their lending to these countries, and this is achieved in several ways, most notably through the Heavily Indebted Poor Countries (HIPC) initiative, established in 1996. The idea of HIPC debt relief is to help extremely poor countries burdened down with high interest payments on debt by reducing their debt. With less debt, the country will benefit from a fall in interest payments and so will have more funds available to focus on health, education, and the other factors we listed in Chapter 6 that were important for achieving long-run growth. To qualify for HIPC a country has to:

1. Face an unsustainable level of debt (i.e., interest payments are too high as a proportion of export earnings)
2. Establish a track record of economic reform
3. Have prepared a Poverty Reduction Strategy Program (PRSP) that has been developed through broad participation

The motivations behind these criteria are threefold: to minimize adverse incentive effects, debt relief is only given to those countries who are unable to repay; debt relief is only given to countries who have good policies aimed at producing sustainable growth (as we saw in Chapter 6, giving aid to countries with bad policies will not generate long term improvements); and, through a PRSP increase the chances that the resulting growth achieved through debt relief will be pro poor. So far a total of 27 countries have qualified for HIPC, 23 of them in Africa.

The IMF receives plenty of criticism for the way in which it operates. One major criticism is the standard complaint levied at IFIs—they represent a loss of national sovereignty as international institutions impose their will on individual nations. In the case of the IMF this criticism is combined with two further complaints:

- The IMF tends to act in the interests of the international financial community rather than the countries it lends to. For instance, critics of the IMF argue that by its insistence on repayment, it ensures that although the international financial companies are repaid their loans, poor countries are saddled with higher debts.
- The IMF is too rigid in the policy advice it offers countries and too focused on market based solutions. Nobel prize winner Joseph Stiglitz (and former chief economist at the World Bank) argues in his book *Globalization and Its Discontents* that forcing governments to cut back expenditure in order to receive loans worsens the economic crisis in a country. Further, he argues that the IMF focuses on pure market based policies, such as deregulation and privatization, which not only may adversely affect social order and poverty but are also more extreme than richer nations are prepared to implement themselves. Essentially this is a debate about the role of the government, with the IMF attempting to limit the role of governments through reduced expenditure and focusing mainly on economic efficiency but IMF critics arguing that successful development requires an active and extensive role for the government.

However, the IMF also gets criticism from another perspective—that it interferes too much with markets and creates instability. A common version of this criticism is that through offering loans to countries experiencing a balance of payments crisis, the IMF encourages countries to pursue unsustainable policies and persuades international banks to lend money knowing that eventually the IMF will bail out both the country and investors. As a result, the international financial system displays more volatility than if the IMF did not intervene.

WORLD TRADE ORGANIZATION

The failure to set up an International Trade Organization in the 1940s reflected a reluctance by many governments to hand over national sovereignty concerning trade to an international institution. However, there remained a desire amongst countries to reduce trade barriers and encourage trade. As a result, a series of trade negotiation rounds were instigated starting with Geneva in 1947, which became known as the General Agreement on Trade and Tariffs (GATT). Although based in a building in Geneva with staff, GATT was not a formal institution, but existed purely through the various trade negotiation rounds it instigated and advanced. Table 9.4 shows that GATT made considerable progress as increasing numbers of countries participated and average tariffs

TABLE 9.4   Impact of GATT Negotiations on Tariffs

Through a series of trade negotiation rounds, GATT achieved substantial declines in tariffs.

	Average Cut in All Duties (%)	Remaining Duties (% 1930 Level)	Number of Participants
Pre-GATT (1935–47)	33.2	66.8	23
First round 1947	21.1	52.7	23
Second round 1949	1.9	51.7	13
Third round 1950–51	3	50.1	38
Fourth round 1955–56	3.5	48.9	26
Dillon round 1961–62	2.4	47.7	26
Kennedy round 1964–67	36	30.5	62
Tokyo round 1974–79	29.6	21.2	99
Uruguay round 1987–94	38	13.1	125

Source: Yarbrough and Yarbrough, *The World Economy* (Ft. Worth, TX: Dryden Press, 1997).

declined as a result of negotiations, helping spur the growth in trade that we noted in Chapter 8. The early rounds of GATT were focused on reducing tariffs mainly in manufacturing. However, as many countries reduced tariffs, at the same time they began to increase nontariff barriers, e.g., introducing quotas limiting the total volume or amount of imports. Therefore, starting with the Tokyo round, increasing attention was placed on reducing not only tariffs but also nontariff barriers. With the Uruguay round, a much greater broadening of the agenda was achieved with attempts to extend negotiations to services, agriculture, intellectual property rights, dispute settlement, and the setting up of the World Trade Organization (WTO).

The WTO came into being on January 1, 1995, and, unlike GATT, it is formally an institution with its secretariat based in Geneva. WTO currently has a staff of 560. WTO was created to overcome two problems with GATT.

1. Under GATT, countries were not committed to agree to all rounds and so they could pick and choose which ones they wished to accept. By contrast, because the WTO is an institution, when a country joins it has to abide by all existing WTO rules and all future agreements. When countries join WTO, they negotiate the speed at which the 30,000 pages of WTO rules will be applied to different sectors. For rich nations, the rules apply almost immediately, but the poorer and more underdeveloped nations are given longer to comply. As of 2004, there are around 150 member countries—see Figure 9.14. These member countries account for 97% of world trade. A further 30 countries (including Russia and Saudi Arabia) are currently negotiating entry.

2. The second reason for establishing the WTO was that under GATT there was no enforcement mechanism. Countries that agreed to rules but then did not uphold them were subject to little formal punishment. By contrast, if the WTO decides that its rules have been breached, it allows the aggrieved nation to retaliate against the country concerned by imposing trade restrictions up to the value of

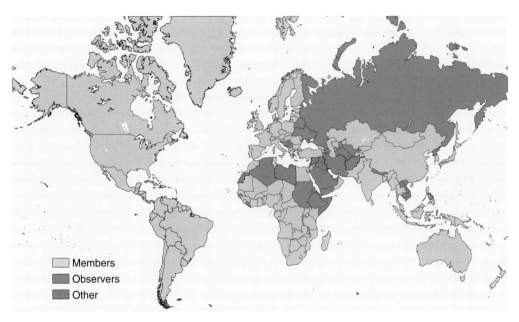

FIGURE 9.14 **WTO membership.** Most countries are now members of WTO. *Source:* WTO World Maps.

the damage it has suffered. However, this process is not a swift one—the WTO takes around a year to arrive at a decision on whether or not a country has been unfairly affected, and if the case goes to appeal, a further year can lapse.

Therefore the key difference between WTO and GATT is the institutional nature of WTO. The WTO has a broad role—to administer existing WTO (and GATT) agreements, to provide a forum for further trade negotiations, to deal with trade disputes, to monitor national trade policies, and to provide technical assistance and training to developing countries in trade related matters. The WTO is at pains to point out that it encourages not free, but *fair*, trade. The main idea of the WTO is that member countries have to give each other Most Favored Nation (MFN) status, the lowest level of trade tariffs a country offers. Joining the WTO means a country has to offer the same trade package to all trading partners who are members of WTO. Countries do not have to remove all trade restrictions but they have to treat all WTO member countries equally.

The WTO is based around three key pieces of legislation:

1. The agreements achieved through GATT
2. The General Agreement on Trade in Services (GATS). This seeks to extend the various tariff negotiations into services with agreements being made amongst some countries for limited liberalization in banking, insurance, telecoms, transportation, and tourism.
3. Trade Related Aspects of Intellectual Property Rights (TRIPs), which extended negotiations into Intellectual Property Rights, e.g., copyright, patents, and so forth. Attempts were made to limit differences in the ways that countries respect intellectual property rights and provide some minimum standards that member countries have to adhere to.

WTO is currently engaged in the ninth round of trade negotiations since GATT began—the Doha Development round, which was instigated in November 2001. Compared to previous trade rounds, the agenda for the Doha round is very broad and ambitious—to continue to reduce tariffs in manufacturing, to extend reductions into services and agriculture, to limit and reduce the role of nontariff barriers, to focus on intellectual property rights and environmental regulation, to improve transparency in government procurement and develop internationally minded competition policy, and a focus on a range of policies to try and make the benefits of trade negotiations more available to developing nations.

Progress with the Doha round to date has been limited. Not all countries accept the need for such a broad agenda and the United States, EU, and Japan show limited enthusiasm for removing agricultural protectionism, while many emerging markets are reluctant to liberalize their service sectors. As a consequence, in the biannual WTO ministerial meeting held in Cancun in 2003, negotiations seemed to come to an end. At the current time of writing, some efforts are being made to restart negotiations. It is unclear whether they will be successful; it seems unlikely that negotiations will be finished by the scheduled date of January 2005. However, as Figure 9.15 shows, GATT/WTO negotiations tend to be long-lasting, and as the number of participants increase, negotiations get longer. Viewed from this perspective, expecting to finish by 2005 looks extremely optimistic! One of the reasons why WTO negotiations are so long lasting is that they involve a broad agenda and many countries. Although this enables plenty of scope for negotiation trade-offs, it also leads to slow progress. By contrast, there are many regional trade bodies, such as the European Union, North American Free Trade Area, MERCOSUR, and so forth, in which similar negotiations can proceed faster due to the smaller number of countries.

Whilst WTO/GATT has made considerable progress in reducing trade tariffs, barriers still remain substantial. Table 9.5 shows the pattern of tariffs between countries on both agricultural and nonagricultural commodities. Agriculture tends to experience higher levels of protectionism (reflecting the effect of both tariffs and quotas), although average levels of protectionism are in general high. It is also noticeable that the industrial countries tend to charge one another lower levels of tariffs than they charge emerging markets. Figure 9.16 shows another problem for emerging markets, which is that richer nations tend to place higher tariffs on goods with a higher degree of processing. In other words, raw materials and intermediate products can be imported with lower tariffs

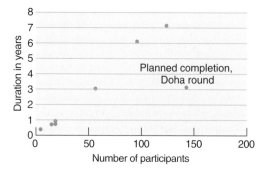

FIGURE 9.15 **Length of trade negotiations and number of participants.** As the number of country participants has increased, the length of trade negotiations has increased. *Source:* Authors' calculations from WTO data.

TABLE 9.5 **Tariff Structures between Countries**
The highest and richer countries tend to charge higher agricultural tariffs to emerging markets than to other rich countries.

Exporting Region	Importing Region						
	East Asia	Europe and Central Asia	Latin America	Middle East	South Asia	Sub-Saharan Africa	Industrial
Agriculture							
East Asia	31.0	30.3	15.5	45.3	38.4	19.0	30.5
Europe and Central Asia	24.2	36.4	23.8	55.3	34.2	12.7	35.1
Latin American and Caribbean	42.1	36.0	14.8	50.3	29.7	24.7	20.4
Middle East	23.0	43.4	14.9	76.4	31.8	18.9	23.4
South Asia	16.6	34.6	13.7	41.1	27.7	11.0	25.8
Sub-Saharan Africa	26.7	20.3	14.4	39.1	30.9	33.6	23.6
Industrial	33.3	43.7	20.1	65.4	16.4	24.0	15.3
Nonagriculture							
East Asia	8.2	13.8	15.1	12.2	28.1	14.5	5.1
Europe and Central Asia	6.4	6.4	11.4	8.6	25.8	12.8	5.9
Latin America and Caribbean	4.3	6.7	15.4	8.9	19.4	11.9	2.1
Middle East	5.4	11.5	8.8	11.4	33.6	11.7	6.0
South Asia	7.1	11.0	13.6	10.2	19.0	17.4	8.1
Sub-Saharan Africa	4.4	6.1	11.7	6.1	27.6	20.6	4.2
Industrial	7.4	9.6	8.5	10.4	25.2	12.2	1.0

Source: WTO, *Annual Report* (2003).

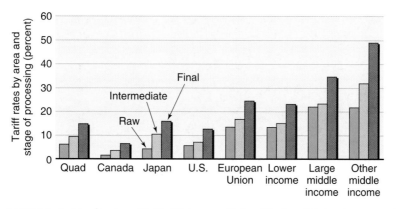

FIGURE 9.16 **Structure of tariffs.** Rich countries' tariffs rise with the degree to which imports are processed rather than raw materials. *Source:* WTO, *Annual Report* (2003).

than more high value added items, providing a barrier for economic growth in emerging markets. Tackling these features of trade restrictions that adversely effect emerging markets is meant to be a significant feature of the Doha Development round.

THE OECD

The final institution we examine in this section is the Organization for Economic Co-operation and Development (OECD). Unlike the World Bank or IMF, the OECD does not dispense money but instead combines a monitoring and advisory role for its 30 member countries. The origins of the OECD lie in the Organization for European Economic Co-operation (OEEC) which was set up by the United States and Canada to administer the Marshall Plan—an aid program to help with the reconstruction of Europe after WWII. With the end of the Marshall plan, the OECD was established in 1961 with the aim to help build strong market based economies amongst its members. Membership of the OECD is restricted to market economies with pluralistic democracies and tends to include the richest economies in the world. Its original membership of Western Europe and North America has extended to include Japan, Australia, New Zealand, Finland, Mexico, Korea, and the transition economies of the Czech Republic, Hungary, Poland, and the Slovak Republic. The OECD secretariat is based in Paris and has a staff of 2300. It has an annual budget of around $200 million funded by its member countries, with the United States providing around 25% of the budget.

Given its broad-based policy agenda, the OECD has a wide-ranging focus. Twice a year it produces *Economic Outlook*, which contains a forecast for its member economies and is also well known for its work on labor markets, technology, and corporate governance. As the OECD has no legislative role, it focuses on data collection, research, and analysis to help guide the policy of its members.

KEY POINT

Globalization has led to an increased role for the IFIs and growing controversy over their policies. The World Bank provides loans for long-term growth in poor countries with a focus on world poverty. The IMF provides loans to governments experiencing balance of payments problems but attaches conditions regarding the policies governments have to implement. The WTO is responsible for leading global trade negotiations and enforcing existing agreements. The OECD focuses on research and advice on the economic growth agenda of richer nations.

SUMMARY

Section 9.1 argued that globalization was the emergence of a single market in goods and services, capital, and labor. A first wave of globalization began in the early nineteenth century, due to falling transportation costs, and came to an end in the early 1900s due to WWI and growing trade restrictions. A second wave of globalization began after WWII due to a continual process of lowering trade tariffs amongst OECD nations. This process accelerated in the 1980s and 1990s as increasing numbers of emerging markets embarked on trade liberalization.

Section 9.2 reviewed the economic benefits of globalization. Increased economic interdependence is believed to reduce the chances of war and international conflict. Increased trade also enables a more efficient use of resources and achieves the static gains of comparative advantage. Economic theory is ambiguous as to whether openness to trade increases the long-term growth of an economy but, given the failure of import substitution policies, a number of countries have reduced trade barriers, a policy that econometric evidence suggests should boost growth.

Section 9.3 focused on the numerous criticisms that are made of globalization. These include fears of growing inequality and poverty; environmental damage; the abuse of power by MNEs; the loss of governments' ability to protect their citizens; and the lack of legitimacy of global markets, global firms, and international institutions. Many of these global problems have been addressed at a national level by national governments and regulations. Some problems require an increased role for global institutions if they are to be overcome.

In section 9.4 we considered the role of four particular IFIs: the World Bank, which focuses on poverty and growth in poor nations; the IMF, which focuses on stability of the international monetary and financial system; the WTO, which tries to ensure fair trade; and the OECD, which offers advice and research to the richer nations.

CONCEPTUAL QUESTIONS

1. (Section 9.1) What do you think the term "globalization" means? Is it just an economic phenomena?

2. (9.2) Trade liberalization shows that it is a mistake for policymakers to think that "exports are good and imports are bad." Discuss.

3. (9.2) Imagine that

$$GDP = 0.2 \times \text{Financial Sector Reform} + 0.4 \times \text{Capital Stock} - 0.05 \text{ Openness}$$

But that

$$\text{Financial Sector Reform} = 2 \times \text{Openness}$$

If an econometrician ran a regression of GDP on the capital stock and openness, what effect would they find from openness? Explain your answer.

4. (9.3) What are the limits and constraints to establishing global institutions and regulations? What does this imply about the process of globalization?

5. (9.3) To what extent does the focus by economists on the economic gains from globalization fail to recognize the concerns of noneconomists?

6. (9.3) What policies would governments need to focus on to make sure that trade liberalization did not adversely affect poverty?

7. (9.3) As an alternative to globalization, many critics are advocating a "buy local" campaign. Assess the merits and disadvantages of this policy.

8. (9.4) Does the world economy need stronger or fewer international financial institutions? Why?

Fiscal Policy and the Role of Government

Overview

In this chapter we consider the role of government and we ask why government spending varies across countries. We analyze the rationale behind government intervention and the public provision of services, and consider empirical evidence on government activities in different countries. We then discuss the implications of the size of government on taxation and how it can distort resource allocation. The structure of the tax system and how it can be designed to minimize distortions is analyzed. We consider the implications of governments running fiscal deficits, that is not covering their current expenditure out of tax revenue. We discuss how deficits and the stock of debt have evolved over the last century. We discuss the long-run implications of current deficits and show how the relative magnitudes of rates of return and growth of GDP are critical to the sustainability of the fiscal position. Finally, we discuss the empirical evidence for the link between the size of the public sector and long-run economic growth.

Key Concepts

Debt Sustainability	Laffer curve	Primary Deficit
Fiscal Deficits	Missing Markets Tax Distortions	Public Goods
Intertemporal Budget Constraint	Pareto Efficient	Tax Smoothing

10.1 Government Spending

Figure 10.1 shows that the size of the public sector varies considerably across countries. For instance, in Sweden over recent decades, government spending has accounted for around 60% of GDP, while in the United States it has been around 30%. Some things that governments do are both essential and could not be done by the private sector—it is hard to see how any entity but the government could be responsible for the legal system, the police force, and national defense. Some things that governments do in many countries are essential, but the private sector could do them. For example, in many countries, public sector health and education services comprise much of total

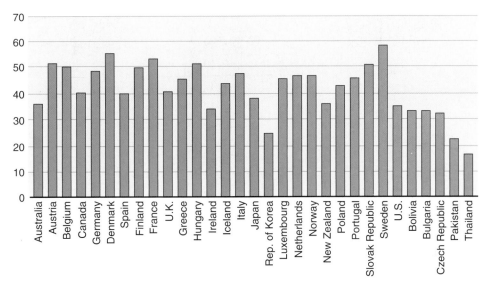

FIGURE 10.1   **General government spending (% GDP, 2002).** The size of government varies across countries, but in all developed economies the state plays a major role in economic life. *Source:* OECD Online Database and IFS Database (2003).

spending, but the private sector could provide these services. And some government activities need not be done, and until relatively recently, were not. For example, in most developed countries, governments provide various kinds of social security (unemployment and sickness benefits, old age pensions). This kind of social welfare provision, or social insurance, is a relatively recent phenomenon, but one that accounts for much of the rise in the role of government in market economies.

Not surprisingly, variability in the tax taken out of total incomes mirrors variations in the scale of government spending. Figure 10.2 shows the ratio between tax receipts by central governments and total GDP in 2002. If there were no corresponding differences in tax revenues, government debt would increase indefinitely in countries with a large public sector.

The public sector expanded in most countries during the twentieth century. Table 10.1 shows the share of government spending in GDP for 14 industrialized nations since the second half of the nineteenth century. In 1870, government spending as a percent of GDP averaged about 8% across these economies. Just after the end of World War I, expenditure had, on average, almost doubled to over 15% of GDP. By 1960, the average proportion of total spending that government accounted for had risen to almost 30% of GDP. Since then, expenditure has steadily increased in most countries, so that on average the public sector now accounts for over 40% of GDP in developed countries.

Much of the rise in government spending reflects growing government consumption; that is, government spending on wages (of civil servants, soldiers, police, and so forth) and on materials and supplies that public sector workers use (e.g., office supplies, arms, fuel, and electricity). This part of government spending absorbs or *directly* uses economic resources, but it excludes investment (e.g., road building). From the nineteenth century to

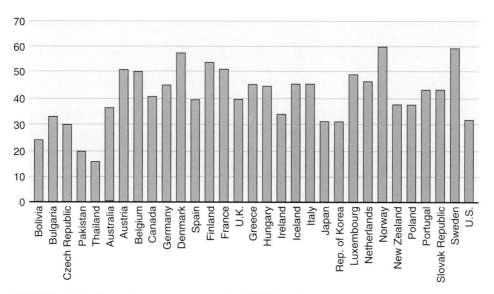

FIGURE 10.2 **General government current receipts (% GDP, 2002).** Tax receipts as a proportion of GDP, and therefore average tax rates, broadly reflect the scale of government spending. *Source:* OECD Online Database and IFS Database (2003).

TABLE 10.1 **The Increasing Share of Government Expenditure, 1870–2002 (% of GDP)**

	Late Nineteenth Century (about 1870)[1]	Pre-World War I (about 1913)[1]	Post-World War I (about 1920)[1]	Pre-World War II (about 1937)[1]	Post-World War II (about 1950)	1980	1990	2002
Austria	. . .	. . .	14.7	15.2	35.7	48.1	48.6	51.1
Belgium	. . .	. . .	. . .	21.8	30.3	58.6	54.8	50.2
Canada	. . .	. . .	13.3	18.6	28.6	38.8	46.0	40.4
France	12.6	17.0	27.6	29.0	34.6	46.1	49.8	54.2
Germany	10.0	14.8	25.0	42.4	32.4	47.9	45.1	48.1
Italy	11.9	11.1	22.5	24.5	30.1	41.9	53.2	47.7
Japan	8.8	8.3	14.8	25.4	17.5	32.0	31.7	38.3
Netherlands	9.1	9.0	13.5	19.0	33.7	55.2	54.0	47.2
Norway	3.7	8.3	13.7	. . .	29.9	37.5	53.8	46.4
Spain	. . .	8.3	9.3	18.4	18.8	32.2	42.0	39.4
Sweden	5.7	6.3	8.1	10.4	31.0	60.1	59.1	58.0
Switzerland	. . .	2.7	4.6	6.1	17.3	32.8	33.5	37.6[2]
U.K.	9.4	12.7	26.2	30.0	32.2	43.0	39.9	40.1
U.S.	3.9	1.8	7.0	8.6	27.0	31.8	33.3	35.0
Average	8.3	9.1	15.4	18.3[3]	28.5	43.3	46.1	45.1

Source: Data are from Tanzi and Schuknecht "The Growth of Government and the Reform of the State in Industrial Countries," IMF Working Paper, 1995; updated with OECD.

[1]Or nearest available year after 1870, before 1913, after 1920, and before 1937.

[2]1992

[3]Average; computed without Germany, Japan and Spain (all at war or preparing for war at this time).

World War II, the growth in overall government spending roughly mirrored the rise in government consumption. But since 1939, spending has outpaced direct government consumption. Now, on average, less than one-half of government spending in developed countries is consumption. The majority of government spending in developed countries now involves transfers, that is, various cash benefits, pensions, unemployment benefits, disability payments, and so forth. Unlike government consumption or investment, transfer payments involve the government spending money but without receiving any economic goods or services in exchange. Since the eve of World War II, this kind of transfer has been responsible for most of the growth of the government sector in developed countries. Across the seven developed countries for which reliable data are available, transfer payments relative to GDP averaged just under 4% in 1937. That figure had grown to over 15% by the end of the 1990s. Figure 10.3 shows the level of social benefits relative to GDP in 2002.

While there has been a common trend over the past century for the role of the government to expand, the extent of this role still varies among countries. Table 10.2 gives a broad breakdown of spending across six major economies for 2002, and Figure 10.4 shows a more detailed picture of how governments in the United States, Germany, and the United Kingdom spend money for a wide variety of programs. Nearly all the spending under the heading social security and welfare is transfer payments. In the United States, such transfers represent about 25% of government spending, while in most Continental European countries they are almost twice as large. In France and Germany, welfare payments make up about 40% of total spending. Japan spends a similar proportion. Public spending on health care also varies. In the United States, public health spending accounts for about 20% of all government spending. France, Germany, and

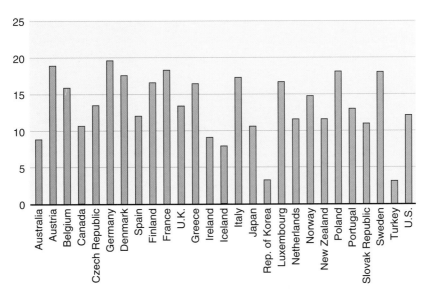

FIGURE 10.3 **Social benefits as percentage of GDP in 2002.** There is huge variability in spending on social benefits—in the United States spending represents about 10% of GDP. In many European countries it is over 50% larger relative to national income. *Source:* OECD, Economic Outlook (2003).

TABLE 10.2 Government Spending in Major
Economies, 2002 (% of GDP)

	Debt Interest	Social Security	Goods and Services	Total
Canada	2.5	10.6	27.5	40.6
France	3.0	18.3	32.8	54.0
U.K.	1.5	13.5	25.9	40.9
Italy	5.3	17.1	25.2	47.7
Japan	1.2	10.6	26.8	38.6
U.S.	2.0	12.1	21.5	35.6

Source: OECD, *Economic Outlook* (2003).

the United Kingdom spend a smaller percentage on health care; but because those countries have a bigger public sector, overall government spending on health care as a proportion of GDP is comparable. However, in Japan, Malaysia, and South Korea, government spending on health care is a much smaller proportion of total national income.

Defense spending also differs significantly across countries. The United States allocates around 10% of all its spending to defense; the fraction is not much lower in the United Kingdom. In Japan and Germany spending is much lower—largely as a legacy of World War II.

We have not distinguished in the figures between investment expenditure and current consumption. Although most governments do give some breakdown into capital and current expenditure, this does not correspond to the economic distinction between investment and consumption. This classification issue is acute for the public sector because governments call much of what they spend on goods and services "current expen-

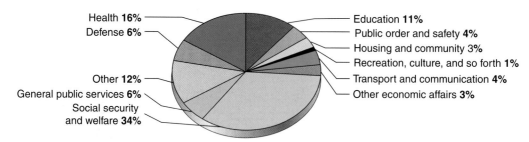

FIGURE 10.4 Composition of consolidated general spending—averages for Germany, United Kingdom, and United States, end 1990s. This is a detailed breakdown of current public spending, based on IMF statistics and a classification of government functions developed by OECD and the UN. The percentages here are percentages of government spending and give each country equal weight. These are figures for consolidated general spending, which is to say the combined expenditure of all levels of government (as recorded in IMF 2001), net of intergovernmental transfers. Subtracting these transfers avoids double counting. *Source:* Miles, Myles, and Preston, *The Economics of Public Spending* (Oxford: Oxford University Press, 2003).

diture" (which is often interpreted as consumption) when it is more like investment. Education expenditure helps enhance, or at least preserve, the national stock of human capital. The largest element of this expenditure is wages, but governments generally count them as current expenditure. We could make the same point about health expenditure. Firms count their expenditure to cover the depreciation of physical investment as investment; government health spending is, by analogy, a form of investment to cover depreciation of the national stock of human capital.[1]

These figures show that governments in all developed economies play a major role in the economy and that the range of government programs is wide. Why is this? In the next section, we discuss the rationale behind government spending on goods and services and, in particular, why transfer payments have grown.

KEY POINT

The size of the public sector varies greatly across countries but has tended to rise over time.

10.2 The Rationale for Government's Role and the Failure of the Invisible Hand

The political economist Adam Smith had a truly profound insight. The free operation of forces in decentralized markets would lead not to chaos but to order—resources would tend to be allocated to produce goods that society valued most. He likened the operation of these forces to the workings of an invisible hand. Smith argued that market mechanisms coordinate the actions of companies and households—all serving their own self-interest—to produce things that people want in the right quantities. It was as if some giant benevolent, but invisible, hand were guiding and coordinating the millions of economic decisions made each day. But market outcomes would only be efficient under certain circumstances: when agents understand the nature of the goods that are being offered for sale, when those agents behave rationally, when goods are produced under competitive conditions (i.e., no monopolies), and when all commodities that have value are offered for sale (i.e., when markets are "complete"). Efficiency here has a special, and unusual, meaning. The allocation of resources is efficient if a reallocation of resources (perhaps as a result of government intervention) is unable to make anyone better off without making someone worse off. We call such a situation **Pareto efficient**, named after the Italian economist Vilfredo Pareto (1848–1923).

The idea that market forces encourage the efficient use of resources is immensely powerful. There is also a simple intuition behind it: free markets tend to be efficient in this sense because if they were not, then profitable opportunities would not be exploited. But the conditions required to operate this invisible hand efficiently are demanding. And even if those conditions exist, the resulting allocation of resources could be hugely unequal, and unsustainable in a society in which citizens vote and governments respond to majority opinion.

---

[1] Of course, these issues also affect the classification of private sector spending into consumption and investment, but to a lesser extent.

Smith himself was aware that the conditions needed for *laissez-faire* (or totally un-regulated) capitalism to work well might not hold. He believed that government inter-vention when ideal free market conditions were not present *could* generate more desirable outcomes. Free markets might not produce certain goods that are desirable because it would be difficult to make people pay for them—some of these are so-called public goods; others are goods for which there are missing markets. For example, there may be no market in which I can insure myself against the risks of a permanent fall in my earning power. People might not fully take account of the consequences of produc-ing and consuming certain goods; irrationality can make free market outcomes subopti-mal and justify a paternalistic role for government. Finally, free market outcomes may generate an undesirable distribution of income. We will now consider the significance of these phenomena—we might call them market imperfections—and what they imply about the role of government.

KEY POINT

The "invisible hand" of the free market would lead to economic efficiency under ideal conditions. Governments play a role when ideal conditions do not exist.

PUBLIC GOODS

Even at the height of laissez-faire capitalism in the mid-nineteenth century, people rec-ognized that the state had to take responsibility for providing some things. These so-called "night watchman" duties of the state were largely concerned with ensuring law and order: the legal system (crucial to the functioning of any market economy based on exchange and property rights), policing, and national defense. A secure system of na-tional defense and a well-functioning legal system are goods in much the same way that a telephone is a good. But these goods are *nonexcludable*—it is hard to exclude any citi-zen from enjoying their benefits. If I live in a country in which crime is low, the legal system fair, and the borders secure, then I benefit even if I make no contribution to paying for the police force, the army, and the law courts. My consumption of these ben-efits, which are safe streets and peace of mind about the threat of invasion or arbitrary imprisonment, does not affect the cost of providing these services. We call goods that have this characteristic **public goods**.

The problem with public goods is that you cannot easily sell access to them: how can you get *individuals* to pay voluntarily for an army? People who live in the country benefit from the army whether they pay or not. So rational and nonaltruistic people would not pay for the service and, instead, hope to get a free ride from the contribu-tions of others. If everyone did this, the market would not provide an army.

It is the difficulty of preventing people from enjoying the benefits of these goods that makes providing them in a market problematic. When the cost of providing com-modities or services to another person is close to zero at the margin and the benefits of providing them cannot easily be blocked, it is hard for commercial enterprises to pro-duce them.

Moreover, markets for most standard (nonpublic) goods would not operate well unless some of these public goods were provided. Consider the importance of a police and legal system that is administered fairly and without corruption. This system is essential to the efficient running of an economy (see Chapter 4). We can see this most vividly by looking at cases in which respect for the law has broken down; such situations make the rewards of trying to expropriate the goods of others high and the benefits of actually producing goods (which are likely to be stolen) low. It is worth considering the costs of such situations and how they can trap standards of living at low levels. To do so, we introduce the notion of a Nash equilibrium.

PUBLIC GOODS AND NASTY NASH EQUILIBRIA

Most people who have read Joseph Heller's *Catch-22* remember the catch: if you were crazy, you could be declared unfit to fly dangerous bombing raids, but claiming insanity to avoid flying is the act of a sane man. In one of the scenes in the novel, a character is discovered committing a selfish act that could endanger others and is asked, "What if everyone did that?" After some thought, he answers, "Then I'd be a fool not to." Economists will instantly recognize a *Nash equilibrium* here (named after the mathematical economist and Nobel prizewinner John Nash). A Nash equilibrium is a situation in which, given everyone else's behavior, each person is acting in a way that is individually rational. The example from *Catch-22* suggests that such equilibria may not be pleasant places within which to get trapped.

In a nasty equilibrium, cheating, breaking conventions, or stepping outside the law are individually advantageous, though collectively costly. Laws and social conventions can prevent societies from being trapped in bad equilibria in which standards of living are low. It is useful that a convention forbids standing on your seat at a football game to get a better view—though doing so would be rational if people around you did it, even though it would be collectively self-defeating.

The football example is trivial, but the strength of social institutions (laws, conventions, how rules are enforced and changed) in preventing inefficient equilibria may help explain the massive differences in wealth and income across countries. As we saw in Chapter 3, the differences in output across countries are far more pronounced than the differences in capital stocks employed. Total factor productivity, in which social institutions and culture play key roles, is hugely important in explaining income differences.

So one of the primary roles of government is to try, in part through the legal and police systems, to reduce corruption, theft, and disrespect for the law. The World Bank also tries to reduce corruption, particularly in developing countries, because it sees how corruption can damage economic growth and standards of living.

PATERNALISM AND THE DISTRIBUTION OF INCOME: THE RATIONALE FOR THE WELFARE STATE

Many public goods (e.g., law and order, absence of corruption) are essential and the operation of markets cannot supply them. Until the middle of the nineteenth century, governments' almost exclusive role in the economy was to provide public goods. But Figure 10.4 shows that today only a small part of government spending represents the provision of public goods. In the developed countries, the emerging economies, and in the formerly centrally planned economy of Russia, spending on defense, public order, safety, and general public services does not exceed 25% of all government spending and is often lower. Starting in Bismarck's Germany, in the 1880s, governments in many countries began to provide social insurance, which almost always involved redistributing income among agents. In 1870 across the industrialized market economies, average spending on transfers was less than 1% of GDP. By the start of the twenty-first century, it was almost 20% of GDP.

Governments have come to play a bigger role here for many reasons. The first is a *paternalistic* one, reflecting the belief that, left to themselves, many people will not act in their own longer-term economic interests. For example, people may not perceive how education can benefit their future incomes and, if left to themselves, they would "underconsume" education. So governments subsidize education in most countries and force people to consume it by requiring that they stay in school until a certain age. People might also consume too much today and save too little for their old age—a decision that they might later bitterly regret. To protect people, governments in many countries force them to contribute to pension systems. And people might also fail to see the full benefits of health care, both for themselves and others, so governments subsidize health services.

These paternalistic arguments for the public sector providing some goods, and for the compulsory consumption of others, are partly behind the growth of the welfare state in many countries. Concern about the distribution of income is another reason for government involvement in the economy. The distribution of income that might arise from free market outcomes may be undesirable for many reasons. One may be that a majority of the population simply finds it ethically unacceptable that many of their fellow citizens should live in poverty. Another reason may be that risk-averse individuals, fearing the consequences of bad luck, bad genes, or bad schools, may want the state to offer them insurance against misfortune in their later lives. This can be a powerful, if not altruistic, force.

A third factor may also be important. You may not care that other people live in poverty or fear the risks of becoming poor yourself, but you may not like how other people's poverty affects you. Crime, delinquency, and disease are likely to be worse if a large economic underclass has poor economic prospects, bad schooling, and inadequate health care. The worse these problems are, the lower the quality of life for people in general—not just for those in poverty. Governments may take on social welfare roles with the aim of improve the quality of life for all their citizens. Some question, however, just how much of a role is appropriate for the government to take. In other words, as we discuss next, how big should the government be?

KEY POINT

There are many reasons why governments need to play a major role in the economy if markets are to work well.

10.3   Taxation and Distortions

We cannot answer questions about the appropriate size of government simply by focusing on the merits of different spending programs or the relative efficiency with which the private and public sectors provide services. It is also relevant to consider how public spending is financed. If government chooses to finance its spending mainly out of taxation, then we must take the economic costs of raising revenue into account when considering the optimal size of government.

TAXATION

Figures 10.5 and 10.6 show that there is a very high correlation between spending and the overall amount of tax revenue raised in both industrialized and developing countries. This is why we need to look at the costs of raising tax revenue when analyzing

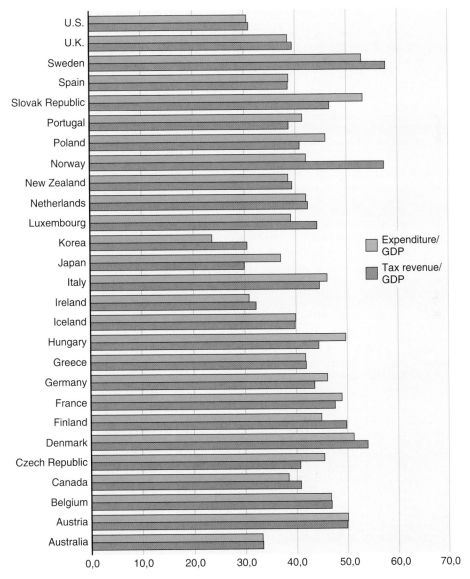

FIGURE 10.5 **Government spending and tax revenue in industrialized countries.** *Source:* OECD, *Economic Outlook* (2003).

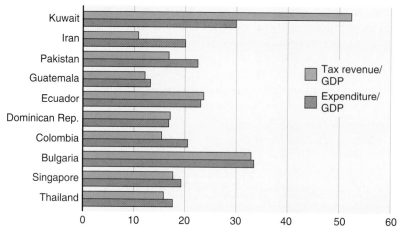

FIGURE 10.6   **Government spending and tax revenues in developing countries (% of GDP, 2003).**
Source: IFS Database (2003).

what is the right level of government spending. It is important to note that raising revenue is not the only reason governments tax. Taxes can be used to discourage the consumption and production of goods that have bad side effects for which consumers and producers may not pay all the costs. Taxes on tobacco, alcohol, gasoline, and the production of pollutants (carbon taxes) are examples of ways in which the government uses its tax powers to make market prices reflect some of the wider costs of certain activities.

But most taxes—and certainly all income taxes—are imposed to generate revenue to pay for government spending. Figure 10.7 shows how the largest OECD governments raised revenue in 2002. Taxes levied directly on individuals (on income, property,

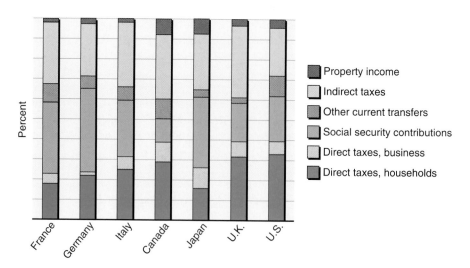

FIGURE 10.7   **Relative importance of different taxes, 2002.** *Source:* OECD, *Economic Outlook* (2003).

or goods and services consumed) have consistently been far more important than taxes raised from corporations. In those countries in which state pensions are generous and account for a big slice of government spending—Japan, Germany, France, and Italy—social security contributions are an important source of revenue.

There are economic costs associated with various methods of raising revenue. We do *not* mean simply how much revenue the government actually raises. There is no efficiency loss, *per se*, from raising the $500 million needed to build a new road by taxing people as opposed to charging fees for using the road. The costs of using one strategy or the other have to do with how particular revenue-raising schemes distort behavior. According to Smith's invisible hand, when markets are complete and competitive, the allocation of resources is efficient—prices signal to firms and workers the value that is placed upon the goods and services that they provide. Taxes drive a wedge—or create a gap—between what sellers receive for supplying goods and services and the prices that buyers pay. This can mean that highly valued activities will be underprovided if suppliers only receive a fraction of the value created. If labor income is taxed at 50%, workers only receive one-half of the price that buyers of labor pay; this is likely to affect labor supply. The higher taxes are, the more they will affect demand and supply decisions. This applies to direct taxes on labor incomes and profits and to indirect taxes on the sale of goods.

So the real cost of raising revenue through taxation is that it can distort patterns of spending and labor supply, savings behavior, or other aspects of economic activity. Virtually any form of tax alters economic behavior. Taxes on labor income are likely to influence people's choice of jobs, the number of hours they work, how hard they try to earn a bonus, or how much costly training and education they undertake. Taxes on corporate profits are likely to affect the investment that companies undertake. Social security contributions, levied either on workers or firms, will affect the cost of labor and the benefits of work and thus will tend to affect levels of employment, as seen in Chapter 7. Taxes on wealth and property influence people's incentives to save and allocate that saving. Taxes on consumption (indirect taxes) affect both the distribution of spending across commodities (because governments may tax commodities in different ways) and the supply of labor, because indirect taxes reduce the real spending power of wages.

DISTORTIONS

We can measure the costs of the *distortions* arising from taxes by thinking about how taxes affect the demand and supply for the taxed good. For taxes on earned income, the relevant good is labor. In Figure 10.8, the demand curve shows how many hours of work are demanded at different wages. Labor should be demanded up to the point at which the value of the extra output produced—which is the marginal productivity of labor (MPL)—equals the wage (see Chapter 7 for a full analysis). We can assume that the more hours worked—with a given amount of machines, computers, land, and so forth—the lower, eventually, marginal productivity will be. So, in Figure 10.8 we show a downward-sloping demand for labor. Because productivity declines with hours, the wage must fall if employers are going to buy more hours of labor.

The supply of labor schedule reflects the value people place upon the time they give up when they work one more hour. We can assume that, beyond some point, people place increasingly high values on the leisure they have to give up to work. The

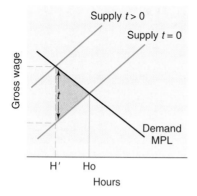

FIGURE 10.8   **Labor supply, labor demand, and taxes.**
Taxation (on wages) is distorting because it alters economic decisions relative to the invisible hand outcome. Hours worked fall from Ho to H' when tax rate t is levied.

When a person reduces hours worked:
- MPL measures the loss of output
- the height of a person's supply curve measures the value of the extra leisure gained from working less.

Thus the value of the distortion generated by a tax t is the gray triangle.

money value of the leisure given up will equal the wage a worker has to be paid to induce him or her to do the extra work. So we expect to see an upward sloping supply of labor schedule.

We also illustrate in Figure 10.8 the effect of taxing labor income. The vertical distance t is the tax on wages. This drives a wedge between the wage the employer has to pay and the net wage the worker receives. If we have the kind of demand and supply schedules that economists consider normal (downward sloping demand and upward sloping supply), the number of hours worked will fall at the same gross wage if the tax rate rises. The supply curve will move up by the amount of the tax, since workers' supply is based on their net, or after-tax, wages and in the figure we measure on the vertical axis gross wages, including taxes (which is what matters to firms).

The gray triangle in Figure 10.8, therefore, measures the cost of the distortion. It reflects the fall in the number of hours worked *and* the gap between the demand curve (the productivity schedule) and the supply curve (the value of leisure schedule) over that range of hours. This is a good measure of the distortions introduced by taxation because it measures the lost benefit of work: the difference between what workers actually produced (marginal productivity) and the value of what they gave up (leisure).

This diagram implies that the cost of the tax rises with the tax rate. Not only does the cost rise but, in fact, it will tend to rise more than proportionally because we are multiplying a reduction in hours worked (which depends on the tax rate) by a *widening* gap between productivity and the value of leisure—the distance between the demand and supply curves. In fact, as Figure 10.9 shows, the cost of the tax rises with the square of the tax rate.

A key insight into the economics of taxation is that the distortions to economic behavior that a rise in tax creates are likely to be greater the higher the tax is (Figure 10.10). This implies that the damage that a rise in the tax inflicts is greater the higher the level of that tax to start with. A simple example may help to illustrate this. A rise in the tax rate of 10 cents on the dollar of labor income may have relatively little impact on incentives to work if it takes the overall tax rate from 5% to 15%. Workers still get to keep 85% of the wages employers pay them. But suppose the tax rate was already at the high rate of 80% on marginal (or extra) income. If employers do not change the

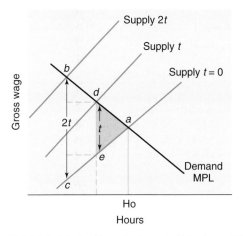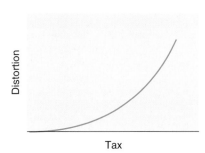

FIGURE 10.9   **Measuring the cost of labor taxes.** When taxes rise from t to $2t$ the cost of distortions more than doubles. The area *abc* is 4 times the area *ade*. Thus the cost of taxes is proportional to the square t. If tax t is doubled, the distortion will quadruple.

amount of wages they pay, then the extra 10 cents on the dollar tax cuts the after-tax earnings of a worker in half—from 20% of the gross wage to just 10% of the wage. This example may seem far-fetched but, in fact, marginal tax rates on labor income in several European countries have, at times, been in excess of 70%.

The revenue that the government raises from income taxes increases as the tax is increased from zero, but it will ultimately fall as taxes deter ever more workers from supplying hours. The curve describing this relation between tax revenue and the tax rate is shown in Figure 10.11. This hump-shaped curve is called the **Laffer curve**.

Notice in Figure 10.11 that there may be two different tax rates that generate the same level of overall revenue. The higher rate that generates a given level of revenue is one where the level of economic activity is relatively low and economic activity is taxed relatively heavily; the same level of revenue can be generated with a lower tax rate if, as a result of relatively light taxation, the amount of economic activity is higher. In Figure

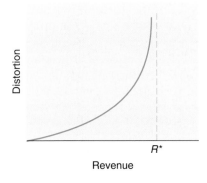

FIGURE 10.10   **Taxation theory.** Two important conclusions may be drawn from this figure.
- There is a limit to how much revenue that government can raise.
- The marginal cost of taxation, in terms of distortions, increases with revenue.

The cost approaches infinity close to R^*, *the maximum revenue*.

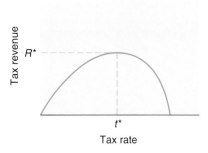

FIGURE 10.11 **The Laffer curve.** Beyond some point the rise in tax rates so discourages work that the overall tax revenue generated—the product of the tax rate, wages and hours worked—falls. That gives rise to the Laffer curve. The maximum tax revenue here is R* with tax at rate *t**.

10.11, the only level of tax revenue that can be generated by a single tax rate is the maximum amount of revenue R*. The tax rate that generates this level of revenue is denoted *t**.

Figure 10.11 suggests that it might be possible to cut the tax rate while boosting tax revenue—any cut in taxes from an original level in excess of *t** that takes the tax rate towards *t** will increase revenue and tend to boost economic activity. This argument for cutting taxes is often made by so-called supply-siders, who focus on the revenue advantages that lower taxes might generate as a result of workers' greater incentives to work and consume. The supply-side argument was the intellectual underpinning of the Reagan tax cuts in the United States during the 1980s and, to some extent, of the Bush income tax cuts in the 2000s. Figure 10.11 shows that its validity depends on taxes being beyond the level *t**. Whether that was the case in the United States in the 1980s or at the start of the 2000s is very far from clear.

What remains unclear, even after decades of intensive research, is the scale of the damage done to economies by government intervention. The average level of taxation that governments levy varies widely across the developed countries. If higher taxes had dramatic negative impacts on incentives, we would expect income levels, growth of productivity, and perhaps also levels of investment to be lower in countries with high levels of spending than in countries in which the government plays a smaller role. But if government expenditure helps boost education and health, then countries with higher taxes may have high growth. Figure 10.12 shows the relationship between government spending (as a percentage of GDP) and the growth of GDP per capita between 1970 and 2002. The relation between these variables is not strong. Nor have more sophisticated statistical techniques established a clear link between the size of the public sector and the rate of economic growth.[2] The absence of a clear link should not surprise us. What affects efficiency is how effectively the public sector provides goods and services and makes transfers. *Bad* government, not necessarily *big* government, damages a country. Furthermore, the distortions taxes generate depend on the structure of *marginal* tax rates, not on the average tax take out of GDP. A government can raise little revenue and yet impose damaging taxes. An example would be a situation in which revenue generated was small even though the marginal tax rates on income were 90% or more

[2] See Slemrod, "What Do Cross-Country Studies Teach about Government Involvement, Prosperity and Economic Growth?" *Brookings Papers on Economic Activity* (1995) vol. 2, pp. 373–431. See also *The Economic Journal* (1996) vol. 106, no. 439.

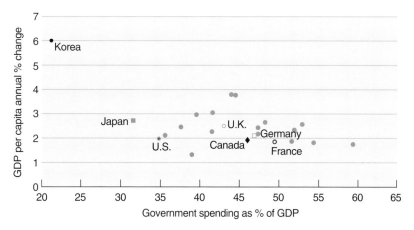

FIGURE 10.12 **Government spending and growth: Is there a relationship? (OECD countries, 1970–2002).** There is no obvious, strong link between growth and the share of output accounted for by government. *Source:* OECD Online Database and IFS Database (2003).

and incentives were badly damaged. The structure of the tax system probably matters more than the overall level of revenue that needs to be generated.

KEY POINT

The cost of taxes arises from the distortions to the allocation of resources that they almost invariably bring.

10.4 Deficits and Taxes

We have seen that there is a tendency for countries where the share of government spending in GDP is high to have high average tax rates. But taxes and spending do not typically match each other from year to year. Governments, like households and companies, can run deficits and incur debt. In fact, governments have far greater ability to spend more than they raise in tax revenue than individual households have to borrow to finance their current consumption. Governments can raise revenue in the future through the tax system and, unlike households and companies, they do not have to sell commodities at market prices to raise revenue. This means that governments can usually borrow more, and at lower cost, than companies or individuals can.

Figure 10.13 shows the difference between annual U.S. government spending and the revenue the government raised over 200 years from the 1790s to the 1990s (the total deficit). The size of the deficit is shown relative to gross national product (GNP). The three major peaks in deficits reflect wars: the Civil War of the 1860s, World War I, and World War II. For much of its history, except for during these wars, the U.S. government typically ran (close to) balanced budgets; indeed, after the Civil War and World War I, the government ran surpluses for several years and reduced the stock of debt. But for much of the period since the early 1970s, the U.S. government has run a

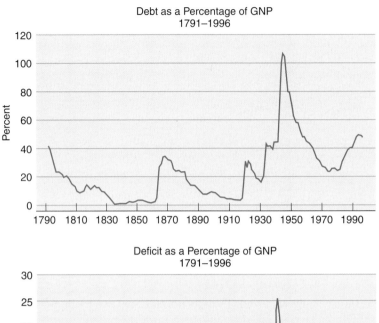

FIGURE 10.13   **Debt as a percentage of GNP, 1791–1996. Debt as a percentage of GNP, 1791–1996.** The U.S. government's stock of outstanding debt has fluctuated greatly over time while the deficit has shown even greater variability from year to year. *Source:* Elmendorf and Mankiw, "Government Debt" in *The Handbook of Macroeconomics*, vol. 1c (Amsterdam: North Holland, 2000).

deficit—the first sustained period in peacetime when the government did not balance expenditure against revenue. For most of the period from the mid 1970s to the end of the 1990s, the U.S. government ran deficits close to 4% of GNP. Only at the end of the 1990s did the U.S. government move back into surplus. But that proved to be a temporary phenomenon.

The experience of the United States since World War II is not unusual. Many governments in developed countries have run deficits on a scale previously only seen in wartime. In 1960, levels of government expenditure across the industrialized world were, on average, under 30% of GDP; by the end of the 1990s, expenditure was, on av-

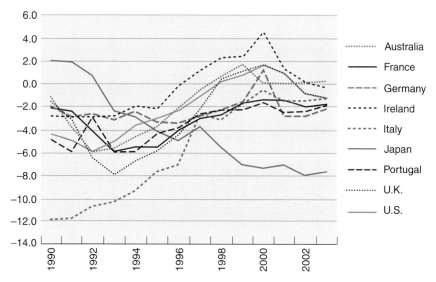

F I G U R E 1 0 . 1 4 **Fiscal surplus as % of GDP 1980–2003.** Budget deficits across the world's largest economies have fluctuated with the economic cycle: in the downturns in the early 1990s deficits rose sharply; in the upturns in the later part of the 1990s deficits fell. But with the slowdown after 2000, deficits have moved back up in many countries. *Source:* OECD, *Economic Outlook*, (2003).

erage, around 50% of GDP. Deficits have been generated consistently over the intervening period because the tax take out of GDP has not risen fast enough to offset increasing spending. Figure 10.14 shows the fiscal deficits of some of the largest economies from 1980 to 2003. Through several business cycles, the major economies, in aggregate, have consistently run deficits; over the 1980s and 1990s, deficits have averaged close to 3% of GDP. In 2003 nearly all of the large developed economies were running a fiscal deficit.

When a government is running a deficit, it is borrowing to finance the gap between expenditure and taxation. As a result, the stock of outstanding debt increases. Figure 10.13 showed how the stock of U.S. government debt relative to GNP has evolved. Again, major wars generated a sharp rise in the stock of debt relative to GNP and the stock of debt tended to fall in postwar periods until the mid-twentieth century. Since the 1970s, however, the stock of debt has increased steadily relative to GNP, at least until the end of the 1990s. Figure 10.15 examines recent decades in more detail and for more countries. The figure shows that the stock of net debt relative to GDP has risen in each of the biggest economies between 1980 and 2002, often sharply. Whether governments can continue to run deficits while preventing the stock of debt from rising continuously as a percentage of GDP is an important question, and we analyze it in detail later in this chapter.

This process can become unstable as interest payments on the accumulated stock of debt rise. In OECD countries, debt payments have risen sharply over the past 40 years, roughly tripling as a proportion of GDP since 1960, because stocks of debt have

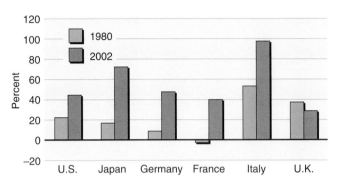

FIGURE 10.15   **Ratio of net government liabilities to GDP, 1980 and 2002.** For much of the 1980s and 1990s, most governments ran fiscal deficits and the ratio of net debt to GDP rose. *Source:* OECD.

increased. Table 10.3 shows the size of government deficits in 2002, again relative to GDP. The first column shows the overall balance between revenue raised and total spending. As we have noted, it is historically unusual that most governments in 2002 were running deficits at a time when no country was fighting a major war. The second column in Table 10.3 shows the *primary balance*—the difference between revenue and spending excluding debt interest. The difference between overall financial balances and primary balances reflects the importance of debt interest payments. The final column of Table 10.3 shows that in 2002 these annual interest payments were around 6% of GDP for Italy and averaged about 2.2% for developed countries as a whole.

Table 10.4 shows instead the stock of debt (in 2002) as a percentage of GDP for OECD countries. The figures reveal substantial variability across countries in the stock of debt. In Belgium, Italy, and Japan, for example, debt in 2002 was in excess of annual

TABLE 10.3   **Government Deficits, 2002**

	General Government Final Balances, 2002	General Government Primary Balances, 2002	General Government Net Debt Interest Payments, 2002
U.S.	−3.7	−1.4	2.3
Japan	−7.3	−6.0	1.4
Germany	−3.6	−0.8	2.8
France	−3.1	−0.2	2.9
Italy	−3.1	2.9	5.9
U.K.	−3.7	−1.4	2.3
Canada	1.0	3.8	2.8
All OECD	−0.7	1.5	2.2

Source: OECD, *Economic Outlook* (2003).

Column 1 = Column 2 − Column 3

TABLE 10.4 **Gross Government Debt, 2002 (% of GDP)**

Australia	22
Austria	68
Belgium	105
Canada	80
Germany	62
Denmark	52
Spain	66
Finland	47
France	67
U.K.	50
Greece	105
Ireland	34
Iceland	45
Italy	121
Japan	147
Republic of Korea	16
Luxembourg	6
Netherlands	53
Norway	24
New Zealand	41
Poland	45
Portugal	58
Slovak Republic	41
Sweden	60
U.S.	61
OECD Average	59

Source: OECD, *Economic Outlook* (2003).

GDP. But in Norway and Ireland debt was between only one-third and one-quarter of GDP. The figures show that the U.S. debt position in 2002 was not unusual; the ratio of debt to GDP of just over 60% is close to the average across all countries.

Financial markets do not seem to consider the rise in the stocks of government debt in developed countries to be an indication that governments are likely to default or go bankrupt. In most industrial countries, the cost of government debt, as measured by the interest rate that the government has to pay to sell bonds, has not increased over the past 30 years. If there was a perceived risk of governments defaulting on their debt, one would expect interest rates on government debt to be rising over time to compensate for increasing default risks. But, even if larger deficits have not significantly increased fears of default for most industrialized countries, those deficits nonetheless can affect the economy. In the next three sections of this chapter, we consider in detail how those effects may come about.

KEY POINT

In recent decades, governments across the developed world have run deficits more often than they have enjoyed fiscal surpluses. As a result, the stock of debt has risen in most countries.

10.5   Intergenerational Redistribution and Fiscal Policy

Government spending and taxing patterns often reallocate resources between people of different ages. They can also reallocate resources between people alive today and those not yet born. Laurence Kotlikoff[3] has studied countries to show the net impact of spending and taxing on people of different ages. He and his colleague Willi Leibfritz have developed a method that allocates elements of government spending (e.g., on health, education, pensions) to different cohorts, or age groups, of people. They also predict how tax rates will evolve in the future, calculating rates that ensure government debt remains sustainable. Using these tax rates and assumptions about who benefits from different types of spending, they work out the balance between payments of tax and receipts of benefits over the entire lives of people born at different times, known as net taxes. In this context, by net taxes we mean the difference between tax payments and receipts of benefits due to government expenditure (direct receipts in the form of pensions or unemployment benefits but also indirect receipts in the form of medical expenditure and government expenditure on education, for example).

Figure 10.16 shows estimates of the net taxes of different generations in the United States and Japan in 1995. It reveals that in both Japan and the United States those aged 60 or more in 1995 tended to be net gainers; that is, the present value of the benefits they receive from government spending programs exceeds the value of taxes they will pay over their lives. In contrast, those who were aged less than 50 in 1995 were likely to pay substantial net taxes over their lives.

If governments consistently ran balanced budgets and there were no intergenerational redistribution, then you would expect that net taxes paid over each individual's life would be roughly the same for people of different ages. But the United States and Japan, as well as most other developed countries, run pension programs on a pay-as-you-go (PAYGO) basis. Under such a scheme, pensions to the current generation of retirees are paid for by contributions from the current generation of workers. Such pension plans are also sometimes referred to as "unfunded." A combination of relatively generous unfunded pensions in the past and rising old-age dependency rates into

[3] Kotlikoff and Leibfritz, "An International Comparison of Generational Accounts," NBER Working Paper W6447 (March 1998).

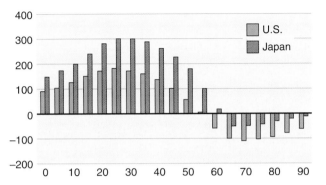

FIGURE 10.16   **Generational accounts (000s U.S.$, 1995).**[1] The young pay taxes and the old receive net benefits—therefore unchanged policies and demographic shifts mean large projected deficits. *Source:* Kotlikoff and Leibfritz, "An International Comparison of Generational Accounts," NBER Working Paper W6447 (March 1998).

[1]Present value of net tax payments (until death) by different generations indexed by age in 1995.

the future, due to burgeoning numbers of people entering old age, means that people now in their 20s and 30s are likely to have to pay far more in net taxes than those who were relatively young when unfunded pension systems were young themselves. The result will be substantial net intergenerational transfers from today's young (and those yet to be born) to today's old.

Figure 10.17 reveals the main factor behind intergenerational transfers in the United States. The projected dramatic increase in the size of federal government expenditure on social security, Medicare, and Medicaid reflects the aging of the U.S. population. Because it is likely that future workers will largely pay for this expenditure, it will redistribute resources from today's young to today's old.

Figure 10.18 illustrates that this kind of redistribution is not just a U.S. phenomenon. It shows that, for many countries, the total lifetime taxes of those born in 2015 are likely to be substantially higher than the present value of all the taxes paid by those born in 1995. Again, the large future tax increases awaiting younger generations are an implication of demographic change and reflect intergenerational redistribution.

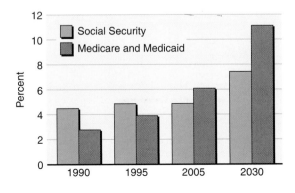

FIGURE 10.17   **U.S. social security spending, 1990–2030 (% GDP).** The aging population is likely to lead to large increases in pensions and health care. *Source:* Kotlikoff and Leibfritz, "An International Comparison of Generational Accounts," NBER Working Paper 6447 (March 1998).

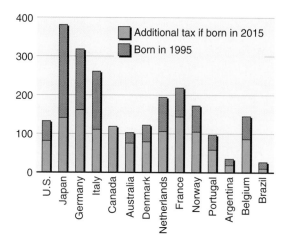

FIGURE 10.18   **Present value tax payments (000's U.S.$ 1995).** Large future tax increases await younger generations. *Source:* Kotlikoff and Leibfritz, "An International Comparison of Generational Accounts," NBER Working Paper 6447 (March 1998).

There are economic and moral reasons why redistribution toward today's old is reasonable. Many of the generations born in the first part of this century lived through World War I, the Great Depression, and World War II. In contrast, those people born since 1960 have enjoyed a substantially higher standard of living than their parents and grandparents and (at least at the time of writing!) have not faced the kind of world wars and economic depressions that occurred between 1900 and 1945. So it may be reasonable that people born after 1950 should make substantial transfers to those born earlier in the century.

These calculations of intergenerational accounts assume that the stock of debt, relative to GDP, does not rise dramatically over time. They also depend crucially on assumptions about the real interest rate and the growth of GDP. If GDP rises over the next 50 years substantially faster than it did over the past 50 years, then governments will have more scope to run deficits, while keeping the ratio of debt to GDP from rising. Were that to occur, governments would not need to raise taxes on today's young and unborn to anything like the extent that Figure 10.18 implies. So in thinking about the long-term implications of government spending and taxing, the relative magnitudes of the growth of GDP and the real interest rate on government debt are central. We consider these issues in more detail in the next section.

KEY POINT

Government spending, taxing, and deficit financing reallocate resources both between people of the same generation and across generations. The scale of intergenerational transfers can be very large.

10.6   Long-Run Sustainability

Every period the government runs an overall deficit, its debt increases—when spending plus interest payments on the existing stock of debt exceeds tax revenues, the stock of debt will rise. But it does not follow from this that governments cannot afford to run deficits for long periods. So long as the stock of debt does not rise relative to

GDP, then a government is likely to be able to keep paying the interest on its debt. At unchanged interest rates, the burden of paying interest would be constant relative to GDP if the debt to GDP ratio is steady. Since GDP—in nominal terms—is likely to rise over time, it follows that the nominal stock of debt can rise. For that reason, it can be sustainable for a government to consistently run overall deficits without finding its debt growing out of control. But there will be a limit to the sustainable deficit.

Let us examine the conditions under which a government can consistently run a deficit. Let D denote the stock of government debt and let GDP be denoted Y. The debt/GDP ratio is D/Y. If the government runs a primary deficit of zero (a zero deficit excluding interest payments), then debt increases because of the interest payments on its existing debt. These interest payments are the product of the interest rate (r) and the stock of debt (D). But offsetting this is the fact that the debt-GDP ratio falls because of GDP growth (g).

Debt is sustainable if D/Y is not changing. A change in the ratio of debt to GDP can result from any of three factors:

1. It rises because of interest on existing debt. This adds r (D/Y) to the debt to GDP ratio.
2. It falls because of growth of GDP. This reduces the debt to GDP ratio by g(D/Y).
3. Finally, debt changes by the size of the primary deficit relative to GDP.

Putting these three together we have:

Change in D/Y = $(r - g)$ D/Y + Primary Deficit/GDP

Therefore the debt/GDP ratio is constant when:

$(r - g)$ D/Y = Primary Surplus/GDP

If $r > g$, the government has to run a primary surplus in order to control the debt–GDP ratio. If $r < g$ then government can always run a deficit (of a certain size) without seeing debt/GDP ratio increase.

Table 10.5 illustrates the dynamics of debt by showing two situations. In both cases g exceeds r. This means that primary deficits can be sustained. Interest rates are 3%, while the growth in real GDP plus inflation (which is g) adds up to 5% (we assume 2% inflation, which implies real interest rates of plus 1%). In the first case, we start with a stock of public debt of $350 billion, and a primary deficit of $35 billion. The debt to GDP ratio is 50%, and the primary deficit to GDP ratio is 5%. But we see from the table that this level of deficit implies a rising stock of debt and a rising interest burden. The debt–GDP ratio would eventually settle down on this path, but at a much higher level than 50%. Only when the debt to GDP ratio is 250% is it sustainable. We know that the sustainable debt to GDP ratio is 250% because if we consistently run a primary deficit of 0.05 of GDP and with $r = 0.03$ and $g = 0.05$, the condition for unchanging debt to GDP ratio implies:

$(r - g)$ D/Y = Primary Surplus/GDP

which means:

$(0.03 - 0.05)$ D/Y = -0.05

This implies D/Y = $-0.05/(0.03 - 0.05)$ = 2.5 so that the sustainable stock of debt is 250% of GDP.

TABLE 10.5   Sustainable and Unsustainable Deficits

Because of output growth, a government can always run a deficit but its debt is sustainable (in the sense that D/Y stays at 50%). An economy with a 5% deficit eventually sees D/Y stabilize at 250%.

Unsustainable	GDP	Public Debt	Deficit	Interest	Debt/ GDP	Deficit GDP	Interest/ GDP
Year 1	$700bn	$350bn	$35bn	$10.5bn	50%	5%	1.5%
Year 2	$735bn	$395.5b	$36.8bn	$11.9bn	53.8%	5%	1.6%
Year 3	$771.8b	$444.1b	$38.6bn	$13.3bn	57.5%	5%	1.7%
Year 4	$810.4b	$496.0b	$40.5bn	$14.9bn	61.2%	5%	1.8%
Sustainable							
Year 1	$700bn	$350bn	$7bn	$10.5bn	50%	1%	1.5%
Year 2	$735bn	$367.5b	$7.35bn	$11.0bn	50%	1%	1.5%
Year 3	$771.8b	$385.9b	$7.72bn	$11.6bn	50%	1%	1.5%
Year 4	$810.4b	$405.2bn	$8.1bn	$12.2bn	50%	1%	1.5%

Assume 5% growth in money GDP - 3% real + 2% Inflation; interest rates are 3%.

The lower panel of Table 10.5 shows that if the deficit–GDP ratio were initially 1%, then although the stock of debt would continue to rise (because the government would consistently be running a deficit), the stock of debt to GDP would remain constant at 50%.

The key issue is whether the real cost of debt exceeds or falls short of the long-run, real sustainable rate of growth of GDP. This is because the key number for sustainable debt dynamics is $(r - g)$. Clearly whether g exceeds r matters. The sustainable rate of growth of real GDP (g) probably does not exceed 2.5% for mature, developed economies. What about the real rate of return on government debt (r)? One measure is to take nominal yields on government bonds and subtract inflation. But actual inflation over the last 20 to 30 years has probably, on average, exceeded expected inflation in many countries. So the ex-post (or realized) average real rate is a poor guide to the real cost of government borrowing going forward. Perhaps a better indication is to look at inflation proof (index-linked) bond yields. Few governments have issued index-linked bonds, but the biggest market, in United Kingdom government index-linked bonds, does provide some data. Since that market was created in the early 1980s, index-linked yields on medium-dated (10 year) government bonds have fluctuated, but the average has been close to 3%—above the likely sustainable long-run rate of growth of developed economies.

Most empirical evidence suggests that rates of return on assets in *general* do, over the long term, exceed GDP growth. That is, r does exceed g. This implies that sustainability of fiscal policies requires that governments do *not* consistently run primary deficits. *Governments with existing debt will need to run primary surpluses at some point to keep the debt-to-GDP ratio from exploding.* Indeed, if the interest rate on debt were to rise with the stock of debt, the need to offset current primary deficits with surpluses in the future becomes even more urgent. Failure to do that quickly could lead to an ever-rising interest rate. Investors can develop a fear that a government may have set off on an unsustainable path which, at some point, could trigger default on debt obligations because the government cannot raise sufficient revenues to even pay the interest on existing debt. That fear could cause interest rates to rise as investors need to be compensated for the risk of default on the bonds that they hold. It is easy to see how that fear could become self-fulfilling.

KEY POINT

In a growing economy, governments can run overall deficits consistently. But unless growth is high relative to the interest rate on debt, on average, primary surpluses are needed.

10.7 The Intertemporal Budget Constraint

We have seen that when r exceeds g a government will need, at some point, to run a primary surplus in order to avoid continually rising ratios of debt to GDP. This means that, if the government currently has outstanding debt, the government has to run a fiscal surplus at some point in the future so as to repay the debt.

The links between the stock of debt and future surpluses are easier to understand with a simple example. Imagine a two period model where the government has to balance its books at the end of two periods. Debt at end of first period (denoted period 0) is:

$$D(0) = G(0) - T(0)$$

where $G(0)$ is government spending in the first period and $T(0)$ is tax revenue in the first period.

To pay off the debt in the second period we need:

$$T(1) - G(1) = [G(0) - T(0)] \times (1 + r) = D(0) \times (1 + r)$$

so that debt equals the present discounted value of future primary surpluses:

$$D(0) = [T(1) - G(1)]/(1 + r)$$

This simple result can be generalized into an infinite number of periods. The more general result is that the stock of government debt today must equal the present discounted value of all future primary surpluses. This is the **intertemporal budget constraint**.

KEY POINT

The intertemporal budget constraint means that the current stock of debt should equal the present value of future primary surpluses. If that is not true, default will occur at some point.

The intertemporal budget constraint has huge implications. It implies that countries with high debt are either going to have to default or run tighter fiscal policy in the future. If a country has very good growth prospects, it can expect to be able to repay its debt; if growth is strong, it may do so without needing to raise tax rates. But if growth slows, then a country may need higher tax rates to generate fiscal surpluses. This may be politically difficult.

The intertemporal budget constraint tells us why it is problematic to have similar numerical targets for debt levels across countries. Debt sustainability means that, on the basis of existing government policies, the future will see sufficient fiscal surpluses to pay back current debt. Different countries have different future prospects and so should have different current levels of debt. Countries where future growth will be high can afford to have larger stocks of government debt than those where growth will be lower. Mature, developed countries cannot confidently expect future growth to be higher than the average over the past few decades. The implication is that, for mature economies who are unlikely to experience sustained shocks or changes in growth patterns, future prospects should be stable and so should debt levels. This is part of the logic behind the stability and growth pact of the European Union. This pact sets limits on the acceptable scale of fiscal deficits for European Community countries that have adopted the euro. The deficit limit is currently set at 3% (unless there is a temporary recession). There is also an upper limit of the acceptable debt to GDP ratio of 60%. The idea here is that, for the developed economies of the European Community, large deficits and high debt to GDP ratios cannot be sustainable because a long period of high growth of GDP is unlikely for any country.

But the intertemporal budget constraint implies that the purposes of deficits are as relevant as the size of the deficits. In drawing no distinction between deficits used to finance investment and those used to finance current spending, the growth and stability pact fails to allow for the fact that some spending may boost future tax revenues. The intertemporal budget constraint also makes it clear that running deficits and having the debt to GDP ratio rise sharply during a temporary slowdown—even if it a prolonged one—is not a problem, so long as future surpluses are large enough. The Stability and Growth Pact sets arbitrary limits—60% for the debt to GDP ratio and 3% for the deficit as a proportion of GDP. It is unclear whether those limits allow governments sufficient flexibility to keep their tax rates smooth (relatively unchanging) and for deficits, rather than taxes, to absorb the strain of temporary slowdowns in the pace of economic activity.

The intertemporal budget constraint also suggests that countries with a low current stock of debt but the prospect of high future deficits may have a real problem. This is relevant to many developed economies today where rapid aging of the population and generous state-run public pension schemes have the potential to generate large and sustained future deficits. As we noted earlier in this chapter, state-run pensions in most developed countries are run on a PAYGO basis, whereby pensions to the current generation of retirees are paid for by contributions from the current generation of workers. One indication of the scale of the problem with such systems is shown in Figure 10.19. This shows estimates of the present discounted value of all future deficits stemming from a gap between state payments of pensions and receipts of contributions if there is no change in contribution rates. The contribution rates are a form of tax. So, what the figure reveals is that at current tax rates if state pensions remain at the levels of generosity seen in recent years, and if there is no significant increase in retirement

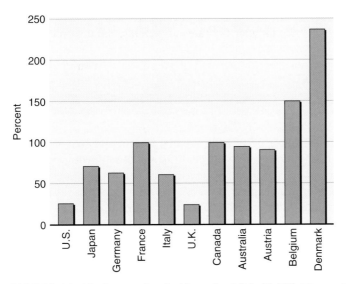

FIGURE 10.19 **Present value of public pension deficits (% GDP).** These values are based on a 5% discount rate and assume 1.5% productivity growth. *Source:* Roseveare, Leibfritz, Fore, and Wurzel, "Ageing Populations, Pension Systems and Government Budgets: Simulations for 20 OECD Countries," Economics Department Working Paper no. 168, (OECD, 1996). Copyright OECD.

ages, then deficits are likely to be generated by the government pension systems in most countries. The scale of these deficits could be very different across countries; in some cases, they could add up to the equivalent of more than 100% of current GDP. Such a rise in the scale of deficits would have to be ultimately offset by surpluses at later dates or by surpluses on the nonpension part of the government accounts. More likely is that future governments will have to head off the problem by further increases in the age at which state pensions are paid, some cut back in the generosity of pensions, and further increases in contribution rates. Indeed, in the period since the OECD made the initial forecasts shown in Figure 10.19, many of the countries have already announced some increases in future retirement ages and some cuts in the generosity of pensions.

KEY POINT

The intertemporal budget constraint has different implications for different economies, depending on the purposes for which they run deficits and their future prospects for growth.

10.8 Optimal Budget Deficits

Budget deficits can be a problem or a blessing. There are powerful justifications for governments running deficits. First, governments may be running deficits to finance investment. If debt is incurred to finance investment that will boost future GDP and enhance future tax revenues, it will be self-financing. Running deficits to pay for lavish presidential palaces—which are unlikely to boost future GDP and future tax revenues—is quite a different matter from government spending to improve the transport system. So we should always ask what governments are spending their money on. If net government investments in productive assets more than match a deficit, then such deficits need not be a problem. Certainly they need not be unsustainable, because the level of spending is likely to improve future government revenues and GDP growth itself.

Deficit financing can also be desirable when the economy suffers a temporary shock. Consider a major war, one of the biggest shocks that can hit any economy. Increasing taxation to balance a budget during wartime could be undesirable, for a variety of reasons. In terms of equity, the generation that is paying for the war—in the direct sense of fighting it—should not also have higher taxes reduce its net resources for consumption. So on a pure *equity* argument, there are grounds for running a sustained deficit during wartime. But there is also a **tax-smoothing** argument—an *efficiency* argument—about distortions.

Taxes distort individual behavior—they force people to do things differently, for example, work less hard, spend less, and so forth. These distortions discourage activities that are taxed heavily, even though using resources in those areas may be economically beneficial. Taxes move resources toward activities that are taxed less heavily, rather than toward those that are of greatest value. Moreover, as we showed in section 10.4, the level of the distortion typically rises more than proportionately with the tax rate. This implies that governments should keep taxes at a smooth average level, rather than change them every period in order to balance a budget.

To illustrate the point, consider the results of two tax policies. One would keep tax rates constant at 20% through booms and recessions. The other would raise tax rates to 30% in recessions (when tax revenue would otherwise tend to fall and unemployment benefit expenditure might be high) to avoid deficits and lower tax rates to 10% in boom times to stop a surplus from being generated. Under both policies the average tax rate over the cycle is the same, but because of tax distortions and inefficiencies, the constant 20% rule is better. Figure 10.20 shows why. Here the welfare loss from distortions due to taxation rises more than proportionately with the tax rate. Keeping tax rates constant at 20% would generate average welfare losses of level W_A. In contrast, setting tax rates sometimes at 10% and sometimes at 30% will generate an average welfare loss from

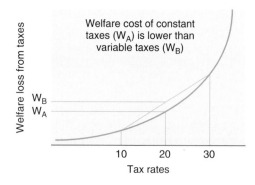

FIGURE 10.20 **Distortionary cost of taxes rises faster than tax rates.** Keeping taxes stable generates fewer distortions than having taxes sometimes well above, and sometimes well below, average.

taxation of level W_B—exactly halfway between the loss from a 30% tax and that from a 10% tax, which is greater than W_A.

If there are sharply rising distortion costs of tax changes, then to minimize the harm of taxation, governments should *not* try to balance the budget every period with different tax rates. Instead, they should try to keep tax rates steady over the business cycle and thereby ensure an average budget balance. If the economic cycle lasts for a long time, tax smoothing can justify prolonged periods of deficit, provided, of course, that the government expects offsetting surpluses in the future.

This tax-smoothing idea has strong implications for how to deal with unexpected expensive events, such as wars (or German unification). Governments should only increase tax rates by a small amount when faced with an expensive, one-time event, but keep them at this higher level for a long time. This will spread the burden across many periods. Governments have followed this policy during wartime. We noted earlier in this chapter that government deficits in the United States have risen dramatically during wartime, but that the stock of debt had tended to fall again after the war.

Tax-smoothing also has implications for long-term policy in the absence of unexpected events. *Governments should avoid changing taxes frequently.* Taxes should be set to ensure the long-run solvency of the government and not a balanced budget from year to year. Governments should expect to switch from surpluses during booms to deficits during recessions. Shifting tax rates over the economic cycle to ensure balanced budgets at all times would override automatic fiscal stabilizers and generate too much volatility in economic activity over the cycle. Raising tax rates at times of slow output growth (or falling output) and rising unemployment is likely to be destabilizing; it would aggravate recessions. Cutting taxes when demand in the economy is rising fast is likely to have a similar destabilizing effect, artificially stoking up demand in booms.

KEY POINT

Budget deficits are not something to avoid. Matching spending to revenue in each period will generate too many sudden changes in spending and in tax rates. But deficits need to be either temporary or balanced by investment that generates higher future taxes.

SUMMARY

Governments are important because their spending represents a high proportion of overall total expenditure—on average around 40% in the developed economies. In section 10.1, we saw that the range of activities undertaken by governments varies greatly across countries but, overall, government spending has been expanding in recent years.

If markets worked perfectly, and if the distribution of incomes created by the "invisible hand" of the free market were considered acceptable, there would be no role for government. But in section 10.2, we argued that if there are market imperfections, this invisible hand result no longer holds, and government can make the economy work more effectively. Governments provide public goods, play a paternalistic role, and attempt to correct undesirable distributions of income.

Financing government spending through taxes creates distortions—labor supply is affected by income taxes, and investment by companies and households is influenced by corporate taxes and taxes on saving. In section 10.3, we concluded that the optimal scale of government is one that perfectly trades off the benefits from government rectifying forms of market failure against the costs of raising the funds to finance spending.

Governments rarely match spending to tax revenue—fiscal deficits or surpluses are the norm. In section 10.4, we showed that in the period since World War II, deficits have been much more common than surpluses.

Government spending, taxing, and deficit financing reallocate resources both between people of the same generation and across generations. We showed in section 10.5 that the scale of intergenerational transfers can be very large. Pay-as-you-go state-run pension plans create a potential for immense intergenerational transfers in many developed nations.

The crucial determinants of the ability to run persistent primary deficits are the relative magnitudes of the interest rate and the growth rate of the economy. Evidence described in section 10.6 suggests that countries cannot persistently run primary deficits because the interest rate on debt is likely to be above the sustainable rate of growth.

Section 10.7 showed that the intertemporal budget constraint implies that if a country is not to default on its public sector debt, the current stock of debt should be matched by the present value of future surpluses.

Keeping tax rates smooth avoids excessive distortions in economic behavior. In section 10.8, we argued that governments should avoid rapid tax changes, aiming to balance deficits and surpluses over an entire economic cycle, rather than in each budgetary period.

CONCEPTUAL QUESTIONS

1. (Section 10.1) Figure 10.3 shows that the level of social benefits (e.g., unemployment benefits, retirement benefits, and income support) varies hugely across countries. Why might this be so? Consider whether differences in the degree of inequality of pre-tax incomes might be a factor.

2. (10.1) Some of the things that governments spend money on are luxury goods (goods for which the proportion of people's—or governments'—income that is spent on them is likely to rise as income grows). Health care and education may be such goods. If most goods that a government provides are of this type, the pressure for the share of government spending in total GDP to rise over time will grow. Should such pressures be resisted?

3. (10.2) Should governments force people to be in school? Why or why not?

4. (10.3) Resource allocation will be less distorted if taxes are levied on goods and services (including types of labor) that are in inelastic supply—that is, where changes in the price sellers receive does not change supply much. But would this generate a fair system of taxes? What conflicts might arise between the design of a tax system that generates small distortions and one that is equitable?

5. (10.5) Because future generations are likely to enjoy higher real incomes than the current generation, shouldn't we aim to run up the stock of debt so that those most able to pay face the higher taxes?

6. (10.7) Does it make sense for there to be any limits on the ability of a democratically elected government to run fiscal deficits? Does the fact that future generations cannot vote have any bearing on this issue?

ANALYTICAL QUESTIONS

1. (Section 10.2) Suppose the average value that a person in a certain city places on having 1000 extra police officers out on the streets for a year is $10. Some people have a higher value and some a lower value. The population is 7 million. The city government decides to ask people how much they value an extra 1000 police to see if it is worth spending the $50 million a year needed. Two questionnaires are proposed. The first version of the question-naire asks people to assess the value to them of the extra police and explains that people will pay whatever amount they answer—on the condition that the total of answers is at least $75 million. The second version of the questionnaire also asks people to reveal how much they value the extra police, but it says that everyone will pay the same amount if the police are hired, provided the sum of the personal valuations exceeds $75 million.

   (a) What would be the results of the different surveys?
   (b) Which is better?
   (c) Does either survey give people the incentive to tell the truth?
   (d) Can you devise a survey that does make people reveal the truth?

2. (10.2) Suppose that income is distributed within a country so that one-third of the popula-tion earns exactly one-third the average wage, one-third earn exactly two-thirds of the average-wage, and the richest one-third earn exactly twice the average wage. Initially there are no taxes and no benefits. The government then introduces a system of redistrib-utive taxes and benefits. Those earning more than the average wage are taxed at 25% on total earnings and those earning less than the average wage each receive the same flat rate benefit. Total taxes received and benefits paid are equal. Assuming no change in pre-tax wages, what is the new distribution of income? Now assume that one-half of those with above average incomes leave the country in response to the tax. What does the dis-tribution of income look like then?

3. (10.3) Suppose you had information on the impact of spending on public education on the productivity of the labor force. You also have information on how education spending re-duces crime. Finally, you have estimates of how raising extra taxes creates distortions to labor supply. Explain precisely how you would use this sort of information to help determine optimal spending on public education. What extra information would be valuable?

4. (10.4) A government is running a balanced budget. An election is approaching and the gov-ernment decides on a one-time, temporary massive tax cut that will cut tax revenue by $50 billion in one year; after the year is over, tax rates and tax revenue return to normal. The government decides to issue perpetual bonds of $50 billion to cover the cost of the tax cut. The interest rate on these bonds is constant at 6%. The tax to pay the interest in the future will be levied on the private sector. Suppose that one-half of the population plans ahead and wants to leave enough in bequests to the next generation so they are not harmed by future higher taxes. The other half of the population spends all they can now.

   (a) What is the impact of the tax cut on domestic saving?
   (b) What happens to consumption?
   (c) Who buys the $50 billion of debt?

5. (10.5) Suppose that the real interest rate in an economy is 6%. Real GDP grows by 2.75% a year. The new chief economic adviser to the government argues that a tax increase of $20 billion will generate huge benefits because the real interest rate is much larger than the

growth of GDP, so that tax rates will be lower on future generations forever. What is wrong with this argument?

6. (10.6) Consider the initial situation shown for the two economies in Table 10.5. Using a spreadsheet, calculate the evolution of the stock of debt, debt interest payments, and the overall deficit if interest rates are 4% rather than 3%. How much lower would the initial stock of debt need to be for the second country to generate a constant ratio of debt to GDP with a 4% interest rate?

CHAPTER 11

Money and Prices

Overview

This chapter focuses on the nominal side of the economy—the money and prices we use to measure economic activity. We examine the historical behavior of prices and the surge in inflation that occurred in the twentieth century. We consider how to measure prices and inflation and compare their different meanings. We discuss why policymakers want to control inflation and what are the costs of inflation.

Money is intimately linked to prices—after all, we quote prices of goods and services in terms of money. We review the historical development of money—from commodity money to paper money—and examine how governments and the banking sector create money and credit.

We then consider the interaction between money and inflation. We first discuss hyperinflations—inflations of more than 50% per month—and show that they really always originate in fiscal policy when governments print money to finance their activities. We review the concepts of seignorage and the inflation tax and compare them across countries. We then discuss a more general link between money and inflation and outline the quantity theory of money, which forms the basis of monetarism—the idea that inflation can be controlled by controlling the money supply.

Key Concepts

Hyperinflation	Monetarism	Quantity Theory
Inflation	Money Multiplier	Seignorage
Inflation Tax	Neutrality of Money	

 11.1 Rising Prices

THE HISTORICAL RECORD

Although historical evidence regarding the scale of economic activity is often obscure, we have much more evidence about the price of different items. The various receipts, invoices, and advertising leaflets that accumulate in pockets and wastepaper baskets amount to a substantial historical legacy. From these we can construct price indexes that reflect the costs of buying a representative collection of consumer goods over time. For example, we could go to a supermarket on January 1, 2004 and buy a typical household's weekly groceries for $120. When purchased on January 1, 2005, the same groceries might cost $125. With this information we can construct a *price index* that has a value of 120 in 2004 and 125 in 2005. This implies an **inflation** rate (the annual percentage change in prices) of 4.2% [100 × (125 − 120)/120]. Price indexes often are set at a value of 100 in a particular year—usually the year used to construct the average basket of goods. Therefore, in our example, the index would have been 100 in 2004 and 104.2 in 2005.

Figure 11.1 shows the behavior of U.K. prices between 1661 and 2002.[1] (A detailed examination and a cross-reference with U.K. history reveals many interesting events,[2] but we want to see the broad characteristics of price behavior.) Between 1661 and 1930, prices showed no persistent upward trend. Sometimes prices rose (1730 to 1820), but at other times, they fell (1820 to 1900). Similarly, prices sometimes rose sharply (e.g., during the Napoleonic Wars, 1790s to 1815, and World War I, 1914–1918) but then fell sharply. However, after 1930 things changed, and prices continued to increase—by twenty seven-fold between 1945 and 2000. As Figure 11.2 shows, after 1945 annual inflation was always positive. Before 1945 the United Kingdom had experienced extreme inflation, large deflations (falls in prices), and frequent small deflations, which all kept the price level reasonably constant over long periods.

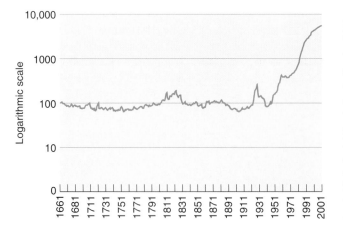

FIGURE 11.1 **U.K. prices, 1661–2002.** Until the twentieth century, prices showed no upward trend, experiencing both increases and decreases. In the twentieth century prices increased sharply. *Source:* Mitchell, *British Historical Statistics*, (London: Cambridge University Press, 1998) and updated using Office of National Statistics data.

[1] We have linked together a number of different price indexes because the average basket of goods has clearly changed over this time!

[2] See Fisher, *The Great Wave: Price Revolutions and the Rhythm of History* (New York: Oxford University Press, 1996), for an ambitious attempt to summarize 1000 years of inflation and its causes across a range of countries.

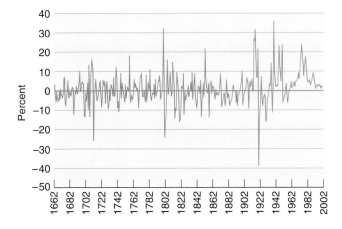

FIGURE 11.2 **U.K. inflation, 1662–2002.** Since 1955, inflation has been consistently positive. *Source:* Authors' calculations from Figure 11.1.

Although not all countries experienced the U.K.'s price stability between 1661 and 1930, most countries did see prices surge during the second half of the twentieth century—Figure 11.3 shows the same pattern for the United States.

KEY POINT

Most countries have experienced continuously rising prices since the middle of the twentieth century.

THE RECENT EXPERIENCE

Figure 11.4 shows the inflation experience among the seven leading industrialized nations over the last 30 years. We can note five distinct periods. The first covers 1973–1976 when inflation increased in all countries. Economists refer to this period as OPEC I. In October 1973 Arab nations, through a cartel of oil producers known as the Organization of Petroleum Exporting Countries (OPEC), embargoed oil sales as part of the Yom Kippur War with Israel. As a result, oil prices increased from $3 a barrel to $11.65

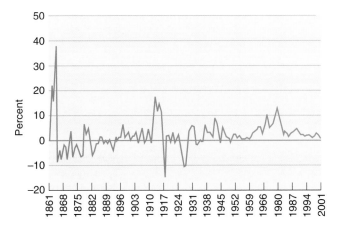

FIGURE 11.3 **U.S. inflation, 1861–2002.** U.S. inflation shows a familiar pattern—while prices rose and fell during 1800s, inflation has been consistently posititve since 1950. *Source:* www.nber.org historical data.

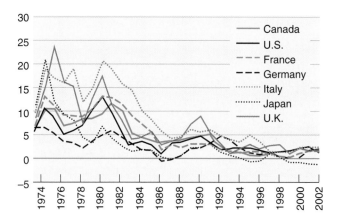

FIGURE 11.4   **G7 inflation, 1973–2002.** Inflation surged after increases in oil prices in 1973 and 1979 and after high global growth in late 1980s, but it was subdued by the end-of-the-century inflation. *Source:* IMF, *International Financial Statistics* (June 2003).

(see Figure 11.5 for the history of oil prices over this period). Industrialized nations were heavy importers of oil and had low oil stocks in the early 1970s, so the increase in oil prices led to a rapid increase in inflation.

By 1977 most countries had stabilized their inflation in response to OPEC I, but in 1979 OPEC again raised oil prices (OPEC II), which peaked at over $36 a barrel in 1980. Inflation surged again, although as Figure 11.4 shows, the increase was more restrained. The increase in oil prices and the associated rise in interest rates led to a global recession. This slowdown in the economy and a sharp fall in oil prices produced the third stage in Figure 11.4—lower inflation among the industrialized nations in the 1980s. Inflation fell and economic growth increased significantly in the industrialized world in the 1980s. The strength of this boom and the strong growth in all countries led to another increase in inflation by the end of the decade, so that governments again raised interest rates, and economic growth slowed. In the 1990s inflation continued to fall until, by 2000, it was at its lowest level since the 1970s. Since then inflation has remained low.

We have stressed the co-movements in inflation across countries, but differences are also significant. High inflation means something different to an Italian than to a German. These differences in annual inflation rates lead to big differences in price changes over long periods. Figure 11.6 shows how prices have changed across countries.

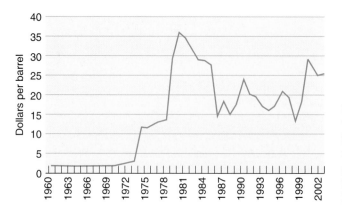

FIGURE 11.5   **Oil prices, 1960–2002.** In recent decades high inflation periods have followed big rises in oil prices. *Source:* BP Statistical Review of World Energy (June 2003).

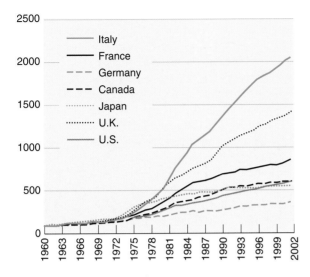

FIGURE 11.6   **G7 Price Levels, 1960–2002.** Persistent differences in average inflation rates have lead to big differences cross-country in how the level of prices have changed over time. *Source:* IMF, *International Financial Statistics* (June 2003).

Prices are set equal to 100 in each country in 1960, so that an index of 500 in 2000 means that prices have risen fivefold over that forty year period. Germany has had the lowest inflation over this time period, so goods that used to cost DM1 now cost the equivalent of around DM3 (though prices are now quoted in Euro). By comparison, Italy has seen large increases in prices—a commodity that used to cost 1000 lira now typically costs the equivalent of around 19,000 lira (though once again prices are now quoted in Euro).

> **KEY POINT**
>
> Global events, particularly changing prices of oil, have caused developed nations to experience similar patterns of inflation. But small differences in inflation rates can cause dramatic price differences between countries over time.

11.2 Measuring Inflation

Price indexes measure the cost of purchasing a bundle of commodities. However, different agents buy different bundles of commodities, and each bundle defines a different price index. The most important indexes are consumer price indexes (CPIs, which are sometimes called retail prices indexes (RPIs)), which measure the cost to the consumer of purchasing a representative basket of commodities. This basket includes both goods and services; commodities purchased in shops, through mail order or the Internet, and commodities produced either domestically or from abroad. Consumer prices also include any consumption taxes (e.g., general sales tax or goods and services tax (GST) or value added tax (VAT)). The CPI is the most important inflation measure because central banks often use it as a policy target.

Various countries and economies have different ways of measuring the overall index of consumer prices, which can make inflation measurements hard to compare. For example, the European Central Bank has an inflation target based on a measure called the harmonized index of consumer prices, which takes the geometric average of the prices of a wide range of individual goods. (The geometric average of a series of n numbers is nth root of their product). Until the end of 2003, the Bank of England had an inflation target based on the weighted arithmetic average of consumer prices, not the geometric average. This may seem an insignificant difference. But the geometric average price index always gives a lower level of inflation than one based on an arithmetic average and so, when the Bank of England switched to measuring inflation using geometric averages, the relevant rate of inflation fell. The difference was not small; simply averaging in a different way reduced measured inflation by around 0.5% when the switch was made. Given that the Bank of England had been using a central target of 2.5% inflation, a permanent reduction of 0.5% in measured inflation was significant

We can also construct price indexes for producers' input and output prices. Producer *input* prices measure the cost of the inputs that producers require for production. Industrialized nations import many of these raw materials, so that fluctuations in exchange rates will affect changes in producer input prices.[3] Producer *output* prices, or "factory gate prices," reflect the price at which producers sell their output to distributors or retailers. Factory gate prices exclude consumer taxes and reflect both producer input prices and wage and productivity terms.

Governments and central banks pay attention to producer prices because they can help predict future changes in consumer prices. Consider an increase in oil prices that increases producer input price inflation. Because the prices of commodities, such as oil, are volatile, the firm may not immediately change its factory gate prices—customers dislike frequent changes of prices. Instead, firms will monitor oil prices, and if they remain high for several months, eventually output prices will increase. This may not immediately result in higher consumer price inflation. Instead, retailers may decide to absorb cost rises and accept a period of low profit margins—they may think that the increase in output prices is only temporary or intense retail competition may mean they are unable to raise their own prices. However, if output prices continue to increase, eventually retail prices will follow.

The gross domestic product (GDP) deflator is another common measure of prices and inflation. In Chapter 2 we discussed the difference between nominal and real GDP. Changes in nominal GDP reflect changes in both output and inflation, whereas changes in real GDP only reflect changes in output. Therefore, we can use the gap between nominal and real GDP to measure inflation. We define the GDP deflator as nominal GDP/real GDP. Because it is based on GDP, this measure of inflation only includes domestically produced output and does not reflect import prices. Further, because GDP is based on the concept of value added, it does not include the impact of taxes on inflation.

Each of these different inflation measures reflects different commodities, so on a year-to-year basis, they can behave differently from each other. However, the various prices tend to move in a similar manner over long periods, as Figure 11.7 shows.

KEY POINT

The choice of index and method of calculation used to measure inflation can create significant differences in the measured inflation among economies, although most commonly used methods reveal similar trends.

---

[3] This is less important for the United States because many commodities are priced in U.S. dollars.

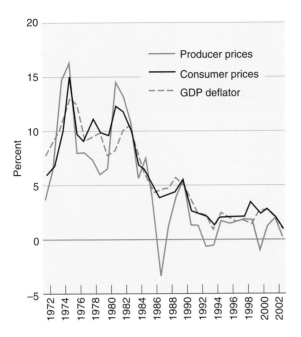

FIGURE 11.7 **Different measures of Danish inflation, 1970–2002.** Although inflation measures differ from one another each year, over time they show similar fluctuations. *Source:* IMF, *International Financial Statistics* (June 2003).

All measures of inflation tend to mismeasure actual inflation to some extent. Every year the quality of existing products improves, and firms introduce new products. If a toothpaste manufacturer increases its price when introducing a new tube that is easier to squeeze, how should our price index reflect this? The toothpaste costs more, but in part this reflects its improved quality. Therefore, some of the increased cost of purchasing the representative basket of goods reflects improvements in product quality rather than the increased cost of buying *exactly the same* commodity.

Improvements in computers and medical services illustrate this problem dramatically. Virtually no households had computers 40 years ago. Twenty years ago some households did have machines, but their capabilities were massively inferior to even the cheapest desktops available today. No PC today has as little computing power as a state-of-the-art machine had in the early 1970s. Medical services pose even deeper measurement problems. Some operations that are now relatively routine—cataract removals or hip replacements—were not feasible a few decades ago. Many drugs that exist today were not available even five years ago; how do we work out the impact of Viagra on average prices?[4] People might have paid fortunes for Viagra or hip replacements in the past, but the technology and know-how did not exist. In a fascinating article, Matthew Shapiro and David Wilcox show how issues around pricing medical services over time suggest that price indexes in the United States probably overstate inflation by around 1% a year.[5]

[4] See Krugman, "Viagra and the Wealth of Nations," *New York Times Magazine* (Aug. 23, 1998).

[5] Shapiro and Wilcox, "Mismeasurement in the Consumer Price Index: An Evaluation," NBER Working Paper W5590 (May 1997).

11.3   The Costs of Inflation and the Dangers of Deflation

As a result of the high levels of inflation in the latter part of the twentieth century, the control of inflation now dominates economic policy. Public opinion seems to support the notion that inflation damages an economy. Figure 11.8 shows evidence from a survey asking people in the United States, Germany, and Brazil whether they would prefer low inflation at the cost of high unemployment or low unemployment at the cost of high inflation. Except for Brazil, a high inflation economy, most people prefer low inflation even if it entails high unemployment.

IS MONEY NEUTRAL?

While public opinion seems firmly against inflation, economists find it more difficult to explain why people feel this way. Economists use money and prices as *nominal* measures of economic activity. This is analogous to using miles or kilometers to measure distance. Inflation means that something that cost $10 last year now costs $11; the commodity itself has not changed—only its price is different. To continue our analogy, it is as if the distance we use to define a mile has changed, so that one year (2004) we measured the distance between London and Boston as 3250 miles (using "2004 miles"), but in the next year we say it is 3500 miles (using "2005 miles"). Of course, the true distance has not changed at all; all that has changed is the units we use to measure distance—a "2005 mile" is a bit shorter than a "2004 mile." The same is true for inflation—after 10% inflation, a dollar buys 10% less.

Economists refer to money as "a veil"—it is merely a system used to price things and should not influence the real economy. It does not matter whether I measure the

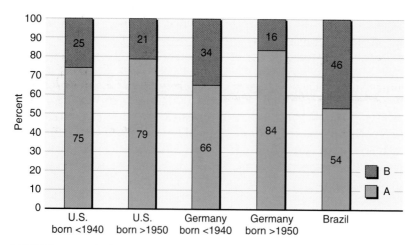

FIGURE 11.8   **Public attitudes to inflation.** Defeating inflation is seen as hugely important for the general population. A is the proportion of people who prefer 10 years of 2% inflation and 9% unemployment, and B is the proportion of those who prefer 10 years of 3% unemployment and 10% inflation. *Source:* Shiller, *Why Do People Dislike Inflation?* in Romer and Romer (eds.), *Reducing Inflation: Motivation and Strategy* (Chicago: Univ. of Chicago Press, 1997).

TABLE 11.1   **How Important is Preventing Inflation?**
Shows response to the question "Do you agree that preventing high inflation is an important national priority, as important as preventing drug abuse or preventing deterioration in quality of our schools?" While the general population believes defeating inflation is hugely important there is less consensus amongst economists.

	1	2	3	4	5
	Fully Agree		Undecided		Fully Disagree
All U.S. Citizens	52	32	4	8	4
Economists	18	28	11	26	18

Source: Shiller "Why do people dislike inflation?" In Romer and Romer (eds.), *Reducing Inflation: Motivation and Strategy* (Chicago: University of Chicago Press, 1997).

distance between London and Boston in miles or kilometers—the actual distance that needs to be traveled does not change. Similarly, it does not matter if we use 2004 prices or 1960 prices in the economy; the real side of the economy remains unaltered. This belief that, in the long run, money is neutral helps explain the different results shown in Table 11.1; 84% of ordinary citizens agree that preventing high inflation is as important as preventing drug abuse and deteriorating school standards. By contrast, economists are almost equally divided over the same question.

To understand why changes in prices should be neutral for the economy, consider the following example. Suppose that while you are reading this chapter, the government introduces a new law that doubles all prices and wages immediately. In other words, what used to cost $5 now costs $10, and if you previously earned $40,000, you will now earn $80,000. All bank accounts, loans, and asset prices will likewise be doubled. The exchange rate will depreciate by half, so that the price of imports or exports remains unchanged in real terms for their purchasers. A new currency will be introduced, and all old currency will be worth twice its face value. So all prices double,[6] but aside from causing confusion (which we will discuss later), how is it costly to society?

KEY POINT

Economists consider money to be a neutral, nominal measure of economic activity, rather than a measure of real changes.

COSTS OF INFLATION

However, this hypothetical example is unrealistic. One problem is that most tax systems are specified in nominal, not real, amounts. For instance, most countries do not tax income below a certain threshold. But as inflation increases, so do wages and income, and more people earn above the threshold and have to pay tax. Wages are only increasing in line with inflation; real incomes are not changing. But the increase in nominal income means that more people are paying tax, which actually makes them worse off.

[6] Technically this doubling of prices is not inflation—inflation is a *sustained increase* in prices.

The taxation of interest rates causes a similar problem. Tax is usually levied on the nominal interest rate, e.g., if interest rates are 10%, and the tax rate is 50%, the net of tax interest rate is 5% [10% × (1 − 0.5)]. However, two components make up the nominal interest rate—one term reflects expected inflation, the other reflects the real interest rate. The term reflecting inflation compensates the saver for rising prices. If inflation is 5%, then a good that costs $100 at the beginning of the year costs $105 by the end of the year. Therefore, investors need to earn at least 5% if they are not to lose by investing their money. The reward to saving is the difference between the nominal interest rate and ex-pected inflation. This is called the *real* interest rate. With an interest rate of 10% and an inflation rate of 5%, the real interest rate is 5%. After a year, the saver's $100 becomes $110, and after allowing for inflation (what used to cost $100 now costs $105), the real return is $5 or 5%. However, taxation applies to the whole nominal interest rate—even the part that compensates for inflation. For instance, with 50% tax rates, 5% interest rates, and 0% inflation, the pretax real interest rate is 5%, and net *of tax* is 2.5% [5 × (1 − 0.5) − 0 = 2.5]. If inflation and interest rates both increase by 5%, the pretax real interest rate remains unchanged, but the net of tax real interest rate falls to 0% (0.5 × 10 − 5 = 0). If interest rates and inflation reach 15% and 10% respectively, the pretax real rate re-mains 5%, but the net real rate is now −2.5%, i.e., 0.5 × 15 − 10.

Inflation also exerts a cost by reducing the value of cash. Unlike bank deposits, notes and coins do not earn interest, so there is no compensation for inflation. As a re-sult, the value of notes and coins falls as inflation increases (this is called the **inflation tax**, which we will return to later). As inflation increases, firms and individuals will hold less cash at any one time, so they will need to make more trips to the bank to withdraw cash, and spend more time keeping their cash balances at low levels. We call these costs "shoe leather costs." Taken literally, this phrase refers to the wear and tear that re-peated trips to the bank to withdraw funds exact on people's shoes! But it also captures a more general tendency to spend time managing finances (when inflation is 20% per month, unpaid invoices become urgent) rather than engaging in productive activity. De-spite the trivial sounding name, these costs can be substantial—shoe leather costs can exceed 0.3% of GDP when inflation is 5%.[7]

Another cost of inflation is *menu costs*. Changing prices is costly for firms. One ob-vious cost is physically changing prices—printing new menus or catalogs, replacing price labels and advertisements in stores and the media. The higher inflation is, the more often these prices have to change and the greater the cost to firms. Moreover, marketing departments and managers have to meet regularly to review prices, which is also costly. The lower is inflation, the less often these meetings need to be held.

Another unrealistic feature of our example of a costless increase in prices was that all prices simultaneously increased by exactly the same amount. As a result, there were no relative price changes, e.g., CD players did not become relatively more expensive than concerts, there was only a general increase in prices. In practice, although all prices might eventually increase by the same amount, they will not increase at the same time, which reduces the overall efficiency of the price system. For the market to work well, firms and consumers must respond appropriately to relative price changes. If the de-mand for a firm's product increases, the price of the product will rise. This will encourage

[7] Fisher, "Towards an Understanding of the Costs of Inflation II," *Carnegie Rochester Conference Series on Public Policy* (1981) vol. 15.

firms to produce more of that commodity and less of others. Prices therefore signal what consumers want. But inflation interferes with this signal. Producers may not know whether a price increase reflects increased demand for their product or just reflects a general increase in prices. Furthermore, some prices respond quicker than others, which redistributes income among individuals. For instance, if wages respond slowly to rising commodity prices, inflation will hurt consumers because their real income will fall. Table 11.2 suggests that this may help explain public resentment against inflation.

The volatility of inflation is also a problem because it leads to uncertainty—with very volatile inflation, firms and consumers do not know whether inflation will be 1% or 10%. If inflation is predictable, contracts can be written to minimize its costs. But if inflation is different from what was expected when contracts were written, the parties to the contracts will not get the return they were expecting. These are redistribution effects—some parties gain, others lose—but they can still have an overall impact on society. For instance, unexpectedly high inflation is particularly hard on retired people whose savings are invested in banks. Interest rates only compensate for expected inflation, so unpredictable inflation will tend to impoverish the elderly. No one knows whether inflation will be less than or greater than what they expected it to be. Volatile inflation makes writing contracts riskier, so fewer contracts will be written, and less money will be saved. All of this will hurt the economy. While these costs come from volatility in inflation, they are also indirectly related to the level of inflation. As Figure 11.9 shows, countries with high inflation tend also to have volatile inflation.

Inflation also harms long-run growth. Evidence suggests that an increase in inflation of 10% leads to a decline in growth per year of between 0.2 and 0.3% and a fall in investment/GDP ratio of 0.4–0.6%.[8] However, we can only identify these costs if we focus on countries whose inflation rates exceed 15%. At lower rates, inflation does not seem to adversely affect long-run growth.

Inflation may also seem costly for another reason—it complicates economic life. Imagine that every year the distance that we called a mile got smaller by a variable amount. This is analogous to how inflation every year reduces the value of what money can buy. Dealing with these changes would be a computational burden. What year was the atlas printed that tells you how far apart two cities are? In what year was the speed

TABLE 11.2   **Does Income Lag Inflation?**
Response to "How long will it be before your income catches up with inflation?" One reason individuals dislike inflation is a belief that their wages rise slower than inflation.

	Up to a Month	Next Negotiation	Several Years	Never	Don't Know
U.S.	0	7	39	42	11
Germany	0	8	40	40	12
Brazil	2	19	17	28	14

Source: Shiller, "Why do people dislike Inflation?" In Romer and Romer (eds.), *Reducing Inflation: Motivation and Strategy* (Chicago: University of Chicago Press, 1997).

[8] Barro, "Inflation and Economic Growth," NBER Working Paper 5326 (1995).

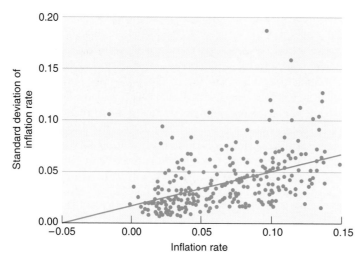

FIGURE 11.9 **Inflation and inflation volatility.** Countries with high inflation also have more volatile inflation. *Source:* Barro, "Inflation and Economic Growth," NBER Discussion Paper 5326 (1995).

control in your car installed or the speed limit signs on the highway erected? The scope for confusion and mistakes would be considerable. Not only do these annual changes in value lead to costly calculations, but people may not respond rationally to price changes. Table 11.3 shows that when people's salary rises by the same amount as inflation, so that their real income remains unchanged, nearly half of respondents would feel better off. Table 11.3 shows evidence of what economists call *nominal illusion*—people mistake nominal changes for changes in a real variable. If prevalent, this behavior will be another source of inflation costs.

KEY POINT

The costs of inflation include readily measurable penalties from taxes on wages and interest, and the inflation tax, as well as costs more difficult to measure, including complications, possible effects on long-run growth, uncertainty, menu costs, and lags in price or wage changes.

TABLE 11.3 **It's Just an Illusion?**
Responses to "I think that if my pay went up I would feel more satisfied in my job, more sense of fulfillment even if prices went up just as much." Individuals seem to react inappropriately to purely nominal variables.

	1	2	3	4	5
	Fully Agree		Undecided		Fully Disagree
All U.S. Citizens	28	21	11	14	27
Economists	0	8	3	13	77

Source: Shiller, "Why Do People Dislike Inflation?" In Romer and Romer (eds.), *Reducing Inflation: Motivation and Strategy* (Chicago: University of Chicago Press, 1997).

THE COSTS OF DEFLATION

It is not just rapid increases in the general level of prices that can cause economic damage. General declines in prices—deflation—can also pose problems. Indeed, the dangers of deflation became more of a concern in some developed countries in the early 2000s than the risks of inflation. In the United States, consumer price inflation fell to around 1% in 2003; with price indices probably overstating the effective inflation rate, it is possible that the general level of prices actually fell near that time in some quarters. Figure 11.10 shows that in Japan the general level of prices fell steadily from around the middle of 1999. And as prices fell, consumers became convinced that prices would continue falling.

Why should falling prices cause problems? There are two main reasons. First, what matters for real economic decisions is the real interest rate—the return on saving (or cost of borrowing) after accounting for inflation. When real interest rates are high, there is an incentive for people to save more and the cost of borrowing rises. This may mean weaker consumption spending and weaker investment by companies. Sometimes this is helpful—in an economy that is overheating and where inflation pressures may be high and rising, slowing the pace of spending is helpful. But when prices are already falling, cutting demand is not likely to be helpful. Yet falling prices will mean high real rate of interest unless nominal rates of interest can be taken to very low levels. Yet the level of nominal interest rates cannot fall below zero (or at least much below zero). If it did, people would just hold their savings in cash (which pays zero interest) rather than hold it in a bank where with negative interest rates, the money value of saving would

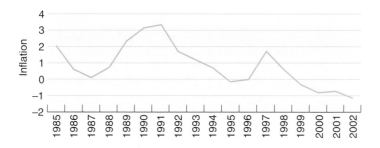

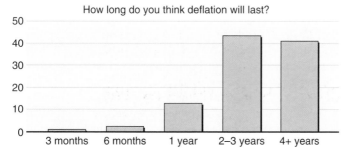

FIGURE 11.10   **Japanese consumer price inflation and survey results on attitudes toward deflation, 2002.** Japanese deflation has become entrenched—under these circumstances it is hard for monetary policy to work. *Source:* Bank for International Settlements, *Annual Report* (June 2003).

actually fall. So there is a potential for a vicious circle to develop with falling prices driving up real rates of interest in a way that cannot be offset (beyond some point) by easing monetary policy. This is because a natural floor has been reached for the nominal interest rate when it is near zero. Weak demand may generate even more rapidly falling prices, which further increases the real cost of debt.

A second, related, problem with deflation is that the real burden of debt—most of which is fixed in nominal terms—rises when prices fall. This makes those who have borrowed to finance spending less well off if prices fall. If the real burden of debt rises enough, bankruptcies will follow. Of course, there is another side of this: those who have lent money are—other things equal—better off when prices fall. But it is plausible that the cut in spending from those who lose out is greater than the rise in spending from those that gain. After all, the savers are those who have a tendency to save their resources while the borrowers have a tendency to spend what they can.

All these factors may have been at work in Japan at the end of the 1990s and into the 2000s—inflation became negative, the nominal interest rates fell to zero, bankruptcies increased, and the level of consumer and investment spending stagnated.

KEY POINT

Falling prices discourage saving, drive up real interest rates, and increase the real burden of debt.

11.4 The Nature of Money

In everyday conversation, when people talk about someone having lots of money, they really mean that she is rich—she has wealth. In calculating a person's wealth, we convert the components of that wealth—cars, stocks and shares, houses, gold, pension rights, yachts, works of art—into money values. But just because we can put a dollar value on your car or the current assets in your pension fund does not make them money, in the sense an economist uses the word. A car or a house is not money because money by definition can be used to make a transaction, which implies that it is an acceptable means of payment. Try paying for a pair of Nike sneakers with a few bricks from the side wall of your house!

What counts as money is a matter of convention and convenience. For instance, in North Carolina in 1715, 17 commodities were declared to be legal tender, including wheat and maize. Money is whatever people will accept in return for handing over goods. What is acceptable as money to *me today* depends crucially on what I expect its acceptability will be for *others tomorrow*. Acceptability limits what items can serve as money. Historically the need for acceptability led societies to use precious or rare commodities as money, but over time we have switched to money that has value only because government legislation says it has value, what we call *fiat money*.

Money makes an economy much more efficient. Suppose money did not exist and that people had to rely on barter—swapping goods directly rather than accepting money as payment for them. To get through the week in a barter economy, you would need to have some goods that the producers of gasoline, milk, electricity, bread, movies, newspapers, and so forth each wanted to swap with you. As economists, we make money by giving lectures, writing books, and thinking profound thoughts on, for example, the role of money. But how could we find someone willing to swap 10 gallons of gasoline on a wet night at 11:30 P.M. for some economics advice? And how does the person who sells gasoline buy this book (assuming we don't frequent the gas station)? She needs to find a bookseller who wants to trade a few cans of gasoline in exchange for this fine text. Tricky—to put it mildly.

Barter relies on a double coincidence of wants—you need to find someone who has the commodity you want and who also wants the good that you are willing to trade. This is costly in three ways:

1. Transaction costs are high; you have to find out what commodities people are willing to exchange and then you have to decide on a price.
2. When you go shopping, you have to carry around with you many different commodities in the hope that you can barter some of them.
3. You cannot consume this sample of commodities because you need them to make transactions.

KEY POINT

Any commodity may be acceptable as money, if people are confident they can use it to get something else they value. Using a common currency boosts this confidence and is an improvement over bartering.

THE ROLE OF MONEY

Money avoids these costs because everyone accepts it in exchange for commodities. The publisher sells this book for money and can then use money to buy gasoline. Note that the publisher values not the money itself but only what it can purchase. Similarly, the owner of the gas station accepts money for gas only because she can then use it to buy what she wants.

Money offers substantial efficiency gains over barter because it fulfills three key roles: it acts as a medium of exchange, a unit of account, and a store of value. We have already discussed the importance of money as a medium of exchange. But also important is its role as a unit of account—the language in which prices are quoted. We could measure the prices of commodities in terms of almost anything, for example, a loaf of bread. But it is bizarre to quote prices in terms of a commodity when transactions do not actually involve the exchange of that commodity. Why would we quote the price of boots, paper towels, computers, and motorbikes in terms of numbers of loaves of bread when nobody would pay for those things at a store with a truck full of loaves? It makes sense to quote prices in terms of what we will hand over when we purchase goods.

The final role for money is as a store of value—money needs to be a durable commodity that can transfer purchasing power from one period to another. Even in the simplest preindustrial societies, there was a gap between the times when people wanted to sell what they produced and the times when they wanted to buy what they consumed. As the local baker, I may want to sell all my loaves by 10 A.M. each day. Due to the drudgery of my life, I tend to want to spend much of the proceeds of my bread sales on alcohol, which I generally consume after 6 P.M.. So I need a means of holding the revenue from my bread sales until the bars open at 6 P.M. Holding my bread revenues in the form of money lets me do this.

COMMODITY AND PAPER MONEY

Until the nineteenth century, most money in most countries was commodity money, that is, money that itself was a durable and physical commodity as opposed to pieces of paper. To use money as a medium of exchange, the seller has to be persuaded that she is receiving something valuable. If the commodity used as money is scarce or not easily reproduced, then sellers are likely to be persuaded to accept it. Therefore common forms of money have been cowrie shells, gold, silver, and even stones (early Native Americans used *wampumpeag* as currency—strings of mainly white beads).[9]

Commodity money is a satisfactory way of establishing a medium of exchange because people will accept in payment a valuable commodity. But it also has disadvantages. First, because money is a valuable commodity, people like to use it for other purposes, e.g., gold can be used for jewelry or in industry or in dentistry. But because money is used as a medium of exchange, it will be in short supply for these other uses. For instance, during World War II, cigarettes were used as money in prisoner-of-war camps. This puts smokers in an expensive dilemma! Second, commodity money has intrinsic value. This gives individuals (or governments!) an incentive to adulterate coins with less precious metals and, as a result, the public loses faith in the value of money.

For these reasons, most countries over time moved from commodity money to paper money. To see how this process occurs, consider the practice on the Pacific islands of Yap where large circular stones (called feis) were for many centuries the only form of money.[10] Feis were so large that holes were drilled through them so that they could be carried around on poles. Because the stones were unwieldy, they were not carried around to pay for goods. Instead claims to the stones circulated as money. As long as you had a piece of paper that proved you owned a stone (which may be stored miles away and never moved), you had something valuable. If you could transfer that claim to another person, he should be willing to accept it in exchange for goods and services. So this is one (big!) step removed from pure commodity money. We are talking about a system in which paper claims circulate as money. The confidence in the pieces of paper ultimately rests on the knowledge that somewhere a stock of physical commodities could, in principle, be delivered when the paper claim is presented. Furthermore, the physical commodities are in limited supply and hard to counterfeit.

This describes a system of paper money in which people accept bits of paper as payment because they can go to the monetary authority and swap them for a precious commodity. However, in normal circumstances, people are too busy to keep swapping paper for the precious commodity. Therefore the paper money circulates with increasingly less use made of the underlying precious commodity. At this point, the government may be able to switch to a fiat currency by abolishing convertibility into the precious commodity and legislating that people *have* to accept intrinsically worthless pieces of paper as money. As long as everyone accepts this convention, and they

[9] See Davies, *A History of Money: From Ancient Times to the Present Day* (Cardiff: University of Wales Press, 1994) for a broad survey of the history of money.

[10] The rather unusual nature of currency in the Islands of Yap is a source of great fascination for numismatologists. A large sample of a fei stands in the courtyard of the Bank of Canada in Ottawa.

have done so historically, the fiat money system works as well as the commodity money system.[11]

The Chinese are widely believed to have been the first to introduce fiat paper money. Marco Polo lived in China between 1275 and 1292 and in Chapter XVIII, "Of the Kind of Paper Money Issued by the Grand Khan and Made to Pass Current throughout His Dominions," of his *Travels*, he writes:

> *In this city of Kanbalu is the mint of the grand khan, who may truly be said to possess the secret of the alchemists, as he has the art of producing paper money. . . . When ready for use, he has it cut into pieces of money of different sizes. . . . The coinage of this paper money is authenticated with as much form and ceremony as if it were actually of pure gold or silver. . . . and the act of counterfeiting it is punished as a capital offense. When thus coined in large quantities, this paper currency is circulated in every part of the grand Khan's dominions; nor dares any person, at peril of his life, refuse to accept it in payment. All his subjects receive it without hesitation, because, wherever their business may call them, they can dispose of it again in the purchase of merchandise they may have occasion for; such as pearls, jewels, gold or silver. With it, in short, every article may be procured.*

This captures the essence of paper money—note how the grand Khan enforces its acceptance!

Most countries now use fiat money. If you go to the European Central Bank or the U.S. Federal Reserve Board with a euro or a dollar you will not be given gold or silver. The one modern exception is countries that operate a currency board (see Chapter 21), such as Hong Kong, which is committed to swapping the national currency for dollars at a fixed rate. In this case, U.S. dollars fulfill the role of a precious commodity.

KEY POINT

Paper fiat money solves the key problems of using commodities as money, and most countries today use it.

11.5 The Money Supply

Typically, part of a person's wealth is in some form of money, but most of it is not. While people own bills (or bank notes) and coins, they may also hold part of their wealth in various types of bank deposits. In addition, they may hold stocks and shares, either directly or through pension plans. Many people also own their homes, though often they also have a large liability in the form of a mortgage. People can use some of the forms in which they hold wealth to quickly and easily buy other commodities. I can easily use money in my bank account to buy goods and services. But other financial assets are harder to exchange for

---

[11] Mankiw recounts another story from the Island of Yap. During a severe storm, some large feis were sunk irretrievably. It was agreed that the owners of the stones were not to blame and that their paper claims were still valid, *even though no feis backed them up*. This shows perfectly how an economy moves from commodity money, to paper money backed by commodities, to a system where the link between paper claims and the original commodity money becomes tenuous. (*Macroeconomics,* New York: Worth, 1992).

goods and services. I cannot easily get my hands on the assets in my pension fund until I retire. And if I own stocks and shares, I have to sell them and transfer the proceeds into a bank account before I can write a check on that account to buy goods.

Financial assets therefore have a spectrum of spendability, or *liquidity*. Some financial assets are readily available to use to buy goods and services—bills and coins, for example—and we will certainly want to call them *money*. Others (stocks and shares, life insurance policies, or pension fund assets) are less liquid and should not count as money. Somewhere in between bills and coins and stocks and shares held in pension funds, are assets whose availability to buy commodities is less clear. I cannot use a 90-day deposit with a bank to finance a last-minute weekend at a ski resort unless I can switch the deposit into a checking account. However, the 90-day deposit is clearly closer to being "money" than are the stocks and shares in my pension fund. So when we think about measuring the money supply, we should be aware that in modern economies the answer to the question "What is the money supply?" has no simple answer. It depends on what measure of money you want to use.

We can start with the narrowest definitions of money (bills and coins) and then add increasingly less liquid assets. Bills and coins are readily acceptable in exchange for goods and services almost anywhere. In fact, it is stated on most paper currency that people *have to* accept them, by law, in exchange for goods and services. But often people are less willing to accept a check. So checking accounts are *somewhat* less liquid than dollar bills. Other types of bank accounts that do not have checking facilities are even less liquid because we would usually need to transfer the money from them to a checking account, or else cash those deposits in (i.e., turn them into bills and coins), before we could use them to complete a transaction.

> ### KEY POINT
> Economists use several definitions of the money supply.

Table 11.4 shows increasingly wider definitions of the U.S. money supply and illustrates how the stock of different definitions of money stood in July 2003. The narrowest definition in the Table is M1, which is made up of currency plus demand deposits (that is, money available on short notice) and other deposits against which checks can be written (including traveler's checks). M1 represents funds that can readily be used to make transactions. Adding savings deposits to M1 gives us M2. (M2 includes other liquid forms of savings, including money market mutual funds and short-maturity eurodollar deposits.) If we add large denomination time deposits and other longer-maturity financial assets, we reach M3, a wider definition of the money supply.

DEFINITIONS:

M1 = currency + traveler's checks + demand deposits + other checkable deposits

M2 = M1 + retail money market mutual funds + savings and small time deposits + overnight repurchase agreements

M3 = M2 + large time deposits + term repurchase agreements + eurodollars + institutional money market mutual funds

TABLE 11.4 United States Money Supply ($bn), July 2003			
The U.S. money supply consists mostly of credit rather than currency.			
Currency in Circulation	M1	M2	M3
646	1277	6092	8934

Source: www.federalreserve.gov

TABLE 11.5 European Monetary Union Money Supply (Euro Bns), July 2003			
As in the United States, the European money supply is mainly made up of credit money.			
Currency	M1	M2	M3
355	2473	5101	6000

Source: European Central Bank, www.ecb.int

Table 11.5 shows the levels of M1, M2, and M3 in the European Monetary Union in July 2003. The definition of the various money stocks is close to, but not identical with, those used in the United States.

DEFINITIONS:

M1 = currency + overnight deposits

M2 = M1 + deposits with agreed maturity up to 2 years + deposits redeemable at notice up to 3 months

M3 = M2 + repurchase agreements + money market mutual funds + debt securities up to 2 years' maturity

11.6   How Banks Make Money—The Money Multiplier

As Tables 11.4 and 11.5 show, the stock of currency (that is, bills and coins) is a small part of the wider definition of the money supply in both the United States and Europe. Bills and coins are only 8% of total M3 in the United States, 7% in the European Monetary Union, and 3.5% in the United Kingdom. In this section we will show how, from a relatively small amount of currency, the commercial banking sector can create many more large bank deposits through a mechanism called the **money multiplier**. The money multiplier means that only a relatively small part of the money supply is under the *direct* control of the monetary authorities. In Chapter 15 we shall explain how central banks try to control the money supply and set interest rates. Here, however, we focus on how commercial banks create credit—literally how they make money, or create the gap between M3 and currency.

RESERVES

A critical variable for commercial banks is their reserves, which are either cash held in the banks' vaults or money the banks hold on deposit with the central bank. How much a bank can lend depends on its level of reserves. If a bank extends too much credit, it risks exhausting its reserves. If a high proportion of its customers simultaneously write checks or make payments from their accounts, the bank will not have the cash to honor its commitments to the other banks that have received these payments. Banks and the monetary authorities thus closely monitor the level of reserves. Most countries set a *reserve requirement*—a floor below which the ratio of reserves to checkable deposits must not fall. For instance, if the reserve ratio is 5%, a bank that has deposits worth $100 billion must have reserves of at least $5 billion. The value of the reserve requirement varies across countries. Some countries set a low ratio, and banks themselves often choose to use a higher one. Historically, many countries used the reserve requirement as a key part of monetary policy and used it to control the money supply. More recently, countries have used the reserve requirement to ensure a stable and prudent financial system.

Although the reserve requirement limits the ratio of reserves and deposits, in effect it also constrains banks' ability to issue loans because every time a bank issues a loan, *it also creates a deposit*. When you get a loan, the bank either sends you a check for you to deposit in another bank or credits your own account with the funds. This is how commercial banks create money—they essentially swap a loan note, which doesn't count as money, for a bank deposit, which does count as money. Therefore, a $10,000 loan creates a $10,000 deposit and, with a 5% reserve requirement, requires an additional $500 of reserves. If the bank already has a reserve-to-deposit ratio of 5% and cannot obtain new reserves, it cannot grant this additional $10,000 loan.

KEY POINT

Reserve requirements keep banks from loaning out all of their money.

THE MONEY MULTIPLIER

To see how the money multiplier works, consider the case of LoansR'us, which has reserves of $5 million and deposits of $100 million, so that it satisfies the minimum reserve requirement of 5%. The central bank purchases from LoansR'us $1 million worth of government bonds by placing $1 million in the LoansR'us bank account at the central bank. LoansR'us reserves are now $6 million against deposits of $100 million—it now exceeds the minimum 5% requirement, so it can lend $1 million to Greedyforfinance.com. It credits their account with $1 million. LoansR'us now has reserves of $6 million and deposits of $101 million. It has lent the full $1 million of extra reserves out, but the reserve requirement ratio is still close to 6%. LoansR'us can lend *another* $19 million until its deposits reach $120 million, and the reserve requirement reaches 5%. At this point Loans R'us can lend no more. Therefore, an extra $1 million of cash or reserves enables the commercial banking sector to create $20 million of additional deposits. In this example, the money multiplier is 20—$1 million of reserves is turned into $20 million of M3. The magnitude of the money multiplier depends on the reserve requirement. In fact, we have

money multiplier = 1/reserve requirement

so that a reserve requirement of 10% (0.1) would lead to a money multiplier of 10 (1/0.1).

The principle at work with the money multiplier is similar to our discussion of how the government issues paper currency backed up by its holdings of precious commodities. Because people only take a certain amount of paper currency a day to the central bank and demand to swap it for a precious metal, the central bank can issue more paper money than it has precious metal. For instance, if on average 5% of people want to swap paper for metal, then if the central bank has $5 million of gold, it can issue $100 million of paper money. This is exactly what commercial banks do. If, on average, only

TABLE 11.6 **The Money Multiplier**
Using a reserve requirement, banks can make loans and dramatically increase the money supply.

	Deposit	Reserves	Loan
Ms. A	$100	$5	$95
Mr. B	$95	$4.75	$90.25
Mrs. C	$90.25	$4.51	$85.75
Dr. D	$85.74	$4.29	$81.45
⋮	⋮	⋮	⋮
Total	$2000	$100	$1900

5% of their customers want to come and withdraw their account in cash, the commercial bank can issue $100 million of loans backed by its own reserves of $5 million.[12]

Table 11.6 shows this process. Ms. A deposits $100 in cash with LoansR'us, which increases its reserves by $100. But LoansR'us has to pay interest on this deposit and thus wants to lend money out to earn interest. However, LoansR'us cannot lend all $100 out because tomorrow Ms. A may wish to withdraw her cash. Based on its experience, LoansR'us calculates that, on average, its customers withdraw 5% of their deposits a day in cash, and therefore it decides that it can only lend out $95, which it does to Mr. B whose deposit increases by $95. However, on average, Mr. B will only want to withdraw 5% of these funds tomorrow (0.05 × 95 = $4.75), so LoansR'us can lend the remainder ($95 − $4.75 = $90.25) to Mrs. C whose account is credited with this amount. But like the other customers, Mrs. C will only withdraw on average 5% of her deposit (= $4.51), so that LoansR'us can lend another $85.74 to Dr. D. We could carry on this way for many pages (which would be very boring), but eventually we would find that from the original $100 deposit the bank increases the money supply by $2000.

KEY POINT

The money multiplier calculates the amount of money banks make by loaning money they are not required to keep on reserve.

Seignorage and the Inflation Tax—How Governments Make Money from Money

11.7

Issuing paper money is a high profit margin activity—the face value of currency normally far exceeds its production costs. The profit made from printing money is called **seignorage** and equals the amount of new currency that the monetary authority issues. Along with raising taxes and issuing debt, printing money is one of the three

---

[12] The money multiplier is not a modern invention. Sir William Petty, Professor of Anatomy at Oxford University, wrote in his 1682 work, *Quantulumcunque Concerning Money*, "We must erect a Bank, which well computed, doth almost double the effectiveness of our coined money."

ways in which a government can finance its activities.[13] Historically, seignorage was an important source of revenue for monarchs, whose one reliable source of revenue was the profit from minting coins.[14] However, in the modern economy, taxation revenues are much more substantial, and with highly developed government debt markets, seignorage for most countries is a relatively small source of finance. As Figure 11.11 shows, for most OECD nations, seignorage accounts for less than 1% of GDP, although it is more important for emerging markets in which tax and bond market infrastructure is less developed.

Closely related to seignorage is the **inflation tax**. Seignorage looks like a good way to raise revenue because it means that governments have to collect less revenue through taxes. However, this ignores a crucial link between issuing money and creating inflation—the subject of the rest of this chapter. Notes and coins do not earn interest; bank deposits do. Therefore inflation reduces the value of the cash holdings of individuals—after 10% inflation, a $10 bill is worth only $9 in real terms; it is as if the government has taken a dollar from your wallet. However, $10 in a bank account earning 12% interest (2% real interest and 10% for anticipated inflation) does not lose its value. Therefore

$$\text{inflation tax} = \text{inflation} \times \text{currency}^{15}$$

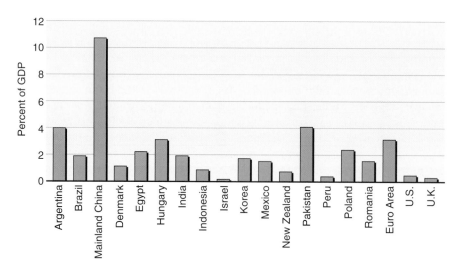

FIGURE 11.11 **Seignorage, 2001–2002 (%GDP).** For most countries seignorage is an unimportant source of revenue but for some countries it is substantial. *Source*: IMF, *International Financial Statistics* (June 2003). Calculated as change in monetary base divided by nominal GDP.

[13] Strictly speaking, a government finances its activities through taxation or by selling bonds either to the private sector or the central bank, with bonds being purchased by issuing new currency.

[14] Loans from the nobility were often politically costly, as was taxation. Plunder from wars and ransoms were other important sources of revenue.

[15] Strictly speaking, "currency" should read noninterest-bearing assets.

How is seignorage linked to the inflation tax? By definition

Seignorage = change in currency

Expressing everything relative to the size of the stock of currency, we have

inflation tax / currency = inflation rate

seignorage / currency = change in currency / currency

Therefore, if the inflation rate equals the growth in the money supply, then seignorage and the inflation tax are equivalent. In a later section, we outline a theory that makes exactly this claim—in the long run, changes in the money supply are proportional to inflation. Therefore, in the long run, the inflation tax is also proportional to seignorage.

This equivalence between seignorage and the inflation tax throws additional light on Figure 11.11. The amount of seignorage collected depends on the rate of inflation and on how much cash is circulating in an economy. China and Pakistan have a less developed credit industry, so cash is much more important in these societies than in the United States or the United Kingdom, and so, as a result, is seignorage.

KEY POINT

In developed countries, seignorage is not a major source of government revenue and is often linked to inflation.

11.8 Hyperinflation

In the rest of this chapter, we focus on the link between money and prices, and in particular, on whether inflation is always a result of increases in the money supply. However, before doing so, we discuss **hyperinflations** (technically when inflation is running at more than 50% per month) and show that these have their origins in fiscal policy (the government's decisions about spending and taxation) rather than monetary policy (the government's policies for investing and loaning money). While many countries have experienced hyperinflations, it has been a particular scourge recently in two regions—Latin America and the formerly socialist economies, as shown in Tables 11.7 and 11.8. In all these cases, the cause of high inflation was the same: a large fiscal deficit that, without tax increases or the ability to issue bonds, led governments to finance their activities through the inflation tax and by printing money. Unless a government reforms its fiscal position, it will have to print money and create inflation. Further, inflation will increase continuously while the authorities pursue this policy.

To see why inflation increases when the government resorts to seignorage, consider again the definition of the inflation tax as inflation multiplied by noninterest-bearing money. We can think of the inflation rate as the tax rate and the stock of noninterest-bearing money as the tax base, that is, the thing that is getting taxed. As tax rates increase, all other things being equal, the tax base shrinks as individuals shift to commodities with lower or zero taxes. Therefore, as inflation increases, people try to get rid of their cash holdings by spending them—in other words, the demand for money

TABLE 11.7   Latin American Inflation, 1981–2002

Latin America experienced numerous hyperinflationary periods during the 1980s.

	Argentina	Brazil	Bolivia	Nicaragua	Peru
1981	104.5	101.7	32.1	23.8	75.4
1982	164.8	100.5	123.5	24.9	64.4
1983	343.8	135	275.6	31.1	111.1
1984	626.7	192.1	1281.3	35.4	110.2
1985	672.2	226	11749.6	219.5	164.5
1986	90.1	147.1	276.3	681.6	78.0
1987	131.3	228.3	14.6	911.9	86.3
1988	343	629.1	16.0	14315.8	667.3
1989	3079.5	1430.7	15.2	4709.3	3398.5
1990	2314.0	2947.7	17.1	3127.5	7485.8
1991	171.7	477.4	22.4	7755.3	409.5
1992	24.9	1022.5	11.2	40.5	73.5
1993	10.6	1927.4	8.5	20.4	48.6
1994	4.2	2075.8	7.9	7.7	23.7
1995	3.4	66.1	10.2	11.2	11.1
1996	0.2	16.2	12.4	11.6	11.5
1997	0.5	6.9	4.7	9.2	8.5
1998	0.9	3.2	7.7	13.0	7.3
1999	−1.2	4.9	2.2	11.2	3.5
2000	−0.9	7.1	4.6	7.4	3.8
2001	−1.1	6.8	1.6	7.4	2.0
2002	25.9	8.4	0.9	4.4	0.2

Source: IMF, *International Financial Statistics* (June 2003).

falls.[16] When the demand for a good falls, its price also declines, which for money means it buys less as inflation increases the price of other goods. In other words, the real money supply falls. But the government has to raise all its revenue from the inflation tax so, as the real money supply falls, the inflation rate has to rise. But, of course, this only causes the demand for money to fall further and the inflation tax to rise. Lags in the collection of taxes exacerbate the situation. If inflation is running at 5000% per month, then tax revenues collected with a lag of a few months are effectively worthless, which increases the fiscal deficit. This is an example of the Laffer curve we documented in Chapter 10—a higher tax rate does not necessarily bring forth greater tax revenue.

[16] China has the strongest claim to have invented paper money and also had one of the first experiences of hyperinflation around 900 CE. China had a novel way to boost the demand for money in the face of hyperinflation: "a perfumed mixture of silk and paper was even resorted to, to give the money wider appeal, but to no avail; inflation and depreciation followed." Goodrich, *A Short History of the Chinese People* (London: Macmillan 1957).

TABLE 11.8 Inflation in Formerly Socialist Economies, 1990–2002

Reform in formerly socialist economies has been hampered by hyperinflation.

	Belarus	Bulgaria	Kazahstan	Romania	Russia	Ukraine
1990	9.4	23.9	5.6	127.9	5.6	4.2
1991	100.4	333.5	91	161.1	91.4	91.2
1992	969.3	82.2	1515.7	210.4	1734.7	1210.2
1993	1190.2	72.8	1662.3	256.1	878.8	4734.9
1994	2221.0	96.0	1879.9	136.7	307.5	891.2
1995	709.3	62.1	176.3	32.3	198	376.4
1996	52.7	123	39.1	38.8	47.9	80.2
1997	63.8	1061.2	17.4	154.8	14.7	15.9
1998	73	18.8	7.3	59.1	27.8	10.6
1999	293.7	2.6	8.4	45.8	85.7	22.7
2000	168.6	10.4	13.3	45.7	20.8	28.2
2001	61.1	7.5	8.3	34.5	20.7	12
2002	42.6	5.8	5.9	22.5	16	0.8

Source: IMF, *International Financial Statistics* (June 2003).

Therefore, hyperinflations create a vicious circle of inadequate tax revenue leading to a reliance on the inflation tax, which in turns leads to a decline in the demand for money and rising inflation. Rising inflation further reduces the real values of tax revenue collected and encourages the demand for money to fall further, leading to ever-rising inflation. The only way to end a hyperinflation is to solve the underlying fiscal problem.

The classic examples of hyperinflation are those that occurred in Central and Eastern Europe in the 1920s after World War I (1914–1918).[17] Figure 11.12 shows the *monthly* inflation rates between 1921 and 1925 for Austria, Germany, Hungary, and Poland. All these countries experienced horrendous hyperinflations. In Germany, inflation peaked at over 29,500% in October 1923.

These hyperinflations show all the signs that we documented above—large fiscal deficits, excessive reliance on monetary financing, and large reductions in the real money stock as people sought to avoid the inflation tax, which required even larger increases in inflation. For instance, in Austria between 1919 and 1920, the government issued currency to finance 63% of expenditure; in Hungary 48% between 1920 and 1921, in Poland 62% in 1923; and in Germany 88% between 1923 and 1924. Between the beginning and end of hyperinflation, the real money stock fell by 67% in Austria, 89% in

[17] See Sargent, "The End of Four Big Inflations," in *Rational Expectations and Inflation* (New York: Harper and Row, 1986).

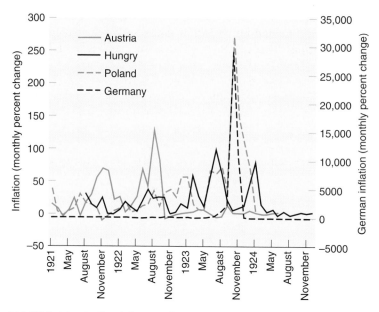

FIGURE 11.12 **Hyperinflations in Central and Eastern Europe, 1921–25.** Austria, Germany, Hungary, and Poland all resorted to printing money to finance expenditure in the 1920s, resulting in hyperinflation. *Source:* Author's calculations from data in T. Sargent, "The End of Four Big Inflations," in *Rational Expectations and Inflations* (New York: Harper and Row, 1986) pp. 41–98. Reprinted by permission of Addison, Wesley, Longman.

Hungary, 63% in Poland, and 99.9% in Germany. These hyperinflations ended the same way—with a new currency, fiscal reform, a return to a fiscal surplus that removed the need to print money, and the establishment of an independent central bank with the constitutional ability to ignore the demands of the fiscal authority.[18]

KEY POINT

Hyperinflation can result when governments have large fiscal deficits and try to resolve the problem by printing money rather than raising taxes or issuing bonds.

11.9 Monetarism and the Quantity Theory of Money

We have throughout this chapter been discussing the nominal side of the economy and referred often to the link between money and prices. We now focus on this in more detail by considering the claims of **monetarism**, the idea that money supply growth causes inflation. One of the famous concepts in economics—the **Quantity Theory of Money**—underpins this belief.

[18] Germany's fiscal problems were mainly a result of reparation payments to the Allies after its defeat in World War I. In 1921–1922, reparations amounted to 77% of all government expenditure. Refusing to pay reparations was a key part of German fiscal reform.

Nobel Laureate Milton Friedman is one of the most famous exponents of monetarism. In a seminal work, he and his co-author Anna Schwartz studied the relationship among money, output, and inflation.[19] Friedman concluded that "*Inflation is always and everywhere a monetary phenomenon.*" Some critics of monetarism argue that this statement is meaningless. Inflation is essentially a change in the price of money—a $10 bill buys less because of inflation. Therefore, to claim that inflation is always and everywhere a monetary phenomenon is as true, but as meaningless, as saying that, in the words of Frank Hahn, "The price of peanuts is always and everywhere a peanut phenomenon."

We start with a relationship that, by definition, has to hold—the *quantity equation*. Let M denote the stock of money, P the price level in the economy, and T the volume of transactions. In a monetary economy, money has to back transactions, but the money supply can be less than the value of all transactions if the same bills are used repeatedly. For instance, if I pay the baker $5, the baker pays the butcher $5, and the butcher pays the gas attendant $5, a single $5 bill can finance $15 worth of trade because it is used three times. Economists call the number of times that money is used for transactions in a period the velocity of circulation (V). By definition

$$M \times V = P \times T$$

Rather than focus on transactions, it will be easier to focus on the overall value added in the economy, in other words, the level of total output (GDP or Y). Value added is a different concept from the number of transactions, but the two are likely to be closely linked. We can therefore rewrite the quantity equation as

$$M \times V = P \times Y$$

which implies that

% change in money supply + % change in velocity

$\approx$ % change in prices (inflation) + % change in output

So far we have only developed an identity—a relationship that has to hold true by definition. To convert this into a theory of inflation, we need to make two more assumptions.

STABLE DEMAND FOR MONEY

The first is that the velocity of circulation does not change—the percentage change in velocity = 0. For the moment, assume that M measures a narrow monetary aggregate, such as M1, and that an individual wishes to keep two months of her annual expenditure in a checking account or in cash. Her annual expenditure is simply $P \times Y$, so money demand (M^d) = $(2/12) \times P \times Y$. But the quantity equation tells us that $M \times V = P \times Y$, so this assumption about money demand means that V = 6, which is, of course, a constant. Therefore, the percentage change in velocity = 0, and the quantity equation becomes

% change in money = % change in prices + % change in output

---

[19] Friedman and Schwarz, *A Monetary History of the United States 1867–1960* (Princeton, N.J.: Princeton University Press for NBER, 1963).

The same conclusion holds for any alternative assumption about how many months of expenditure the individual wants to hold in her bank account.[20]

LONG-RUN NEUTRALITY—OUTPUT INDEPENDENT OF MONEY

Assuming that the velocity of money is constant means that increases in the money supply feed through into increases either in prices or in output. Our second assumption is that changes in output are independent of changes in the money supply—in other words, **money is neutral**. In discussing the costs of inflation earlier in this chapter, we outlined the logic behind this argument. Money is a nominal variable that we use to measure economic value. Just as whether we use miles or kilometers does not influence the distance between Tokyo and New York, neither should it matter if things cost $10 or $20, as long as all prices double. Our analysis holds irrespective of whether things are priced in euros, dollars, Disney dollars, or whether things are priced as they were in 1950 or 2005.

Consider again our analysis in Chapters 3–7 of what determines a country's level of output. We discussed how, via the production function, capital, labor, and total factor productivity influenced output. These were links between *real* variables. We discussed many factors behind long-run growth, but did not mention the average level of prices or the money supply. Over the long term, the level of real output (Y) should be independent of shifts in the money supply and in prices. Instead, real factors like the efficiency with which machines are used, the numbers of new and useful inventions, the willingness of people to work, and so on determine a real magnitude like total output. We would not expect shifts in the price level or in the stock of money to substantially affect these factors. Instead, output grows at a rate (g) that is independent of the money supply but dependent on technology and other factors. This implies that the percentage change in output = g, so we can rewrite our quantity equation as

% change in money supply = % change in prices + g

or

% change in money supply − g = inflation

In other words, inflation should be strictly related to changes in the money supply. If the long-run growth rate does not change over time, every 1% increase in the money supply will increase prices by 1%. Therefore, by assuming that the velocity of money is constant and that money as a nominal variable cannot influence real output, we arrive at a version of monetarism—changes in the money supply directly affect inflation.

KEY POINT

Monetarism suggests that inflation is the result of changes in the money supply.

---

[20] Our result will also hold, with only minor modifications, even if there are predictable changes in velocity. Only large unpredictable changes in velocity undermine our results.

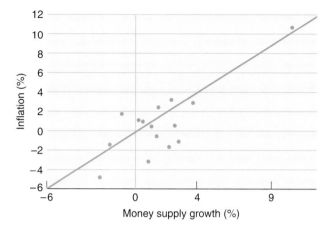

FIGURE 11.13 **U.K. money supply and inflation, 1799–1929.** Long-run U.K. data supports the notion that high money supply growth produces high inflation. *Source:* B. R. Mitchell, *British Historical Statistics* (London: Cambridge Univ. Press, 1988). Updated using Office of National Statistics Data.

Figures 11.13 and 11.14 support this monetarist view. Figure 11.13 shows money supply growth and inflation for each decade between 1799 and 1929 in the United Kingdom. Figure 11.14 shows inflation and money supply growth between 1980 and 2002 for a cross-section of 90 countries. Both figures support the conclusion of our monetarist argument—inflation is a monetary phenomenon, high money supply growth means high inflation. George McCandless and Warren Weber used data from a larger group of countries and for a slightly earlier period to assess the links between money, inflation, and output.[21] Table 11.9 shows their results: they found a very strong positive correlation between money and prices but essentially no correlation between money and real output. All this seems to give strong support to the quantity theory.

However, although Figures 11.13 and 11.14 support our quantity theory, they focus purely on long-run data. If we focus on the shorter term, the evidence is much less impressive. Figure 11.15 shows the same countries as in Figure 11.14 but focuses on money supply growth and inflation between 2001 and 2002. The evidence is less supportive—countries with low inflation have a range of outcomes for money growth. Therefore in the short run, money is a poor indicator of inflation trends.

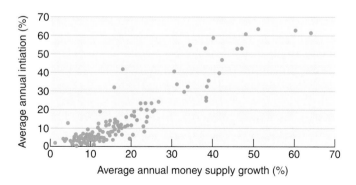

FIGURE 11.14 **Cross-country evidence on money supply growth and inflation, 1980–2002.** There is strong evidence that countries with the greatest money supply growth experience the highest inflation. *Source*: IMF, *International Financial Statistics* (June 2003).

[21] McCandless and Weber, "Some Monetary Facts," *Federal Reserve Bank of Minneapolis Quarterly Review*, vol. 19, no. 3 (1995).

TABLE 11.9   **Data for Inflation, Money Growth, and Output Growth Are Based on 110 Countries**

Correlation Coefficients for Money Growth and Inflation*
Based on Data from 1960 to 1990

Sample	Coefficient for Each Definition of Money		
	M0	M1	M2
All 110 countries	.925	.958	.950
Subsamples			
21 OECD countries	.894	.940	.958
14 Latin American countries	.973	.992	.993

*Inflation is defined as changes in a measure of consumer prices.

Source of basic data: International Monetary Fund

Correlation Coefficients for Money Growth and Real Output Growth* Based on Data From 1960 to 1990

Sample	Coefficient for Each Definition of Money		
	M0	M1	M2
All 110 countries	−.027	−.050	−.014
Subsamples			
21 OECD countries	.707	.511	.518
14 Latin American countries	−.171	−.239	−.243

*Real output growth is calculated by subtracting changes in a measure of consumer prices from changes in nominal gross domestic product.

Source of basic data: International Monetary Fund

Source: McCandless and Weber, "Some Monetary Facts," *Federal Reserve Bank of Minneapolis Quarterly Review*, vol. 19, no. 3 (1995).

Figures 11.13–11.15 tell us that the assumptions underlying our quantity theory—stable velocity of money and output being independent of inflation—are only true in the long run. Furthermore the theory may only be a good approximation to reality when there is significant inflation. Paul De Grauwe and Magdalena Polan, in a careful study of inflation across 160 countries, find that on average there is a very strong link between inflation and monetary growth.[22] But the average strong relation is largely accounted for by the close link in those countries where inflation has been high (on average more than 10%). Where inflation is lower—as it has been in most developed countries in recent years—the link between money and inflation is much less clear. And lessons from history also bring up instances inconsistent with the quantity theory. Bruce

[22] DeGrauwe and Polan, "Is Inflation Always and Everywhere a Monetary Phenomenon," CEPR Discussion paper no. 2841 (June 2001).

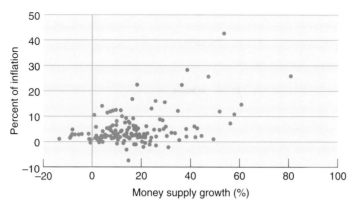

FIGURE 11.15   **Cross-country evidence on money supply growth and inflation, 2001–2002.** There is no evidence that in the short run money supply growth and inflation are strongly connected. *Source:* IMF, *International Financial Statistics* (June 2003).

Smith looks at the experience of North American colonies in the eighteenth century.[23] He finds that what happened then in New York, Virginia, Pennsylvania, and Massachusetts was quite inconsistent with the notion that movements in money and in inflation are closely linked and that output is unrelated to shifts in the money supply.

KEY POINT

Some economists suggest that the quantity theory may apply only over the long run or when there is high inflation.

In Chapter 15 we will examine why the quantity theory does not explain short-run inflation trends and show that, as a result, most governments have now moved away from the idea that they can control inflation by controlling the money supply. However, the lesson from this section is clear: as a long-run theory, the quantity equation goes a long way to explain inflation. Sustained, significant inflation is nearly always a monetary phenomenon.

SUMMARY

In section 11.1 we introduced the concept of inflation, which is defined as a sustained increase in prices. The twentieth century has witnessed dramatic inflation compared to previous periods. But inflation at the turn of the millennium was once more very low.

---

[23] Smith, "Money and Inflation in Colonial Massachusetts," *Federal Reserve Bank of Minneapolis Quarterly Review*, vol. 8, no. 1 (1984). See also Smith, "The Relationship Between Money and Prices: Some Historical Events Reconsidered," *Federal Reserve Bank of Minneapolis Quarterly Review*, vol. 12, no. 3 (1988).

In section 11.2 we noted that there are many different measures of inflation, reflecting both consumer and producer prices. Quality improvements and technological change make measuring inflation difficult, and it is widely believed that official statistics overestimate inflation.

In section 11.3 we discussed some reasons why the defeat of inflation is currently a main aim of macroeconomic policy, and one that receives widespread public support. Past experience of high inflation rates has convinced many people that it brings significant costs, including readily measurable penalties from taxes on wages and interest and the inflation tax, as well as costs that are more difficult to measure, such as possible effects on long-run growth, uncertainty, menu costs, and lags in price or wage changes. Falling prices—deflation—can also bring problems.

In section 11.4 we explored the nature and history of money. Money is an asset used for transactions. Originally money was a form of precious commodity, but over time the link with commodities has disappeared. Paper money now has value and is accepted in exchange as a result of government legislation and social convention.

In section 11.5, we considered the challenges of defining exactly what is, and is not, money. Economists have created several definitions of the money supply. In addition to paper currency issued by the government, the money supply also consists of credit created via the banking system, and different definitions of the money supply include increasingly less liquid forms of money.

We showed, in section 11.6, exactly how banks can add to the money supply by making loans of money they are not required to hold in reserve. The money multiplier varies in inverse proportions to a bank's reserves.

In section 11.7, we showed that the ability to issue paper currency provides governments with a source of revenue, called seignorage. Seignorage is equivalent to the inflation tax.

Section 11.8 described how hyperinflations are caused by governments resorting to seignorage as their main source of financing.

Finally, in section 11.9, we discussed monetarism. Monetarism derives from the quantity theory of money and states that sustained inflation is caused by increases in the money supply. Assuming that the velocity of money is constant and that output is not influenced by the money supply, increases in the money supply feed through into inflation. The long-run evidence behind monetarism is strong, but the short-run support is poor.

CONCEPTUAL QUESTIONS

1. (Section 11.2) Suppose a new drug can cure cancer. It costs a few cents to make the pill, and one pill can stop a malignant growth with zero side effects. The drug goes on sale for a few cents a pill, and although the manufacturer makes millions, the money value of the production is tiny. Is it right that GDP has not really changed much? What would the price index, both before and after the invention and sale of the drug, look like?

2. (11.3/11.9) Most economists—and nearly all central bankers—seem to think that inflation is costly. But the quantity theory asserts that there is no long-run link between money and output nor between inflation and output. Can inflation be costly if the quantity theory is true?

3. (11.4) Which of these is money: a credit card; lunch vouchers; a portfolio of blue-chip equities; a $100,000 revolving credit line; a $100 dollar bill in Moscow; one million Russian rubles in New York; one million Russian rubles in Des Moines, Iowa?

4. (11.4) Suppose people could walk around with electronic charge cards that they could use to buy anything; they never need to carry currency. People would have accounts that were invested in bonds, equities, and other financial assets into which their salaries, dividends, and interest were paid. The portfolio manager would automatically sell assets whenever the card was used. In such a world, would money exist? Would it matter?

5. (11.7) Rich people tend to hold more money than poor people; so is the inflation tax fair?

6. (11.9) Suppose thieves hijack a truckload of old paper currency on the way to the incinerator. The old currency is worth $1 billion. Who, if anyone, loses if the thieves get away with the cash?

ANALYTICAL QUESTIONS

1. (Section 11.2) The U.K. price index in Figure 11.1 has the value 109 in 1661, 83 in 1691, 81 in 1891, 231 in 1919, 208 in 1946, 1103 in 1975, and 5350 in 2000. Imagine a one pound note which is accidentally left in the attic of a stately home when it is built in 1661. Calculate the real value of this bank note for each of the years listed above.

2. (11.3) In the United States of Albion, expected inflation is 5% and the real interest rate is 2%.

   (a) What is the nominal interest rate?
   (b) If inflation turns out to be 10% instead, what is the *ex post* real interest rate? Who gains and who loses from this error in forecasting inflation?
   (c) Recalculate your answers for (a) and (b) for net interest rates when the tax rate is 50%.

3. (11.6) Main Street Bank sets its loans on the basis of a 5% reserve requirement and has $100 million cash in its vaults.

   (a) What is the maximum amount of loans the bank can make?
   (b) If the bank has made loans of $50 million to real estate firms and is required to keep a 50% reserve requirement against such loans, how does this change your answer?

4. (11.7) Let the demand for money in the economy be given by $150,000 - [\text{Inflation (\%)}]^3$. Calculate the amount of revenue raised through the inflation tax for inflation rates up to 50% (a spreadsheet would help!). What inflation rate maximizes revenue?

5. (11.9) The Central Bank of Arcadia has an inflation target of 2%, and forecasts real GDP growth of 2.5% with no change in the velocity of money.

   (a) What money supply growth should it target?
   (b) If the Central Bank revises its velocity forecast to 3% growth, what does this do to its money supply target?
   (c) Assume a forecast of no change in velocity. Interest rates are currently 4%, but inflation is 3% and the money supply is growing at 5.5%. Every 1% increase in interest rates leads to a 1% fall in money supply growth, a 0.5% reduction in output growth, and a 0.25% increase in velocity. What level do interest rates have to be to achieve the 2% inflation target?

Consumption

Overview

This chapter examines the determinants of consumption. Consumption is the largest component of demand in the economy and plays an important role in business cycle fluctuations. Saving is that part of income not spent on consumption. For this reason, analyzing consumption is also important for understanding capital accumulation and economic growth. We consider the influence of current and future income on consumption and how borrowing restrictions and financial deregulation influence savings. The response of consumers to uncertainty over future incomes, movements in interest rates, and expectations of future shifts in taxes and wages are key determinants of the impact of government policy. We also consider how concern for future generations and the desire to leave bequests can affect savings and wealth accumulation.

Key Concepts

Average Propensity to Consume (a.p.c.)

Borrowing Constraints

Intertemporal Budget Constraint

IS-LM Model

The Keynesian Cross

Marginal Propensity to Consume (m.p.c.)

The Multiplier

Permanent Income

Precautionary Savings

Substitution and Income Effects

12.1 The Importance of Consumption

Economists pay enormous attention to consumers' expenditure because they are interested in welfare which, to a significant extent, comes from the utility people get from consuming goods and services. Table 12.1 shows that the average U.S. household in 2001 spent around $40,000 on consumption. The two most substantial components were housing—including rent/interest payments, maintenance, and utilities—and transportation—including automobile expenses. The largest component of consumption is of services, with nondurable goods the next largest. The importance of consumer

TABLE 12.1   U.S. Average Household Consumption by Category, 2001

Food	$5321	Tobacco	$308
Housing	$13011	Apparel	$1743
Transportation	$7633	Health	$2182
Entertainment	$1953	Personal care	$485
Reading	$141	Education	$648
Miscellaneous	$750	Personal insurance pensions	$3737
Alcohol	$349	Total	$39518

Source: Bureau of Labor Statistics, Consumer Expenditure Survey (2001).

durables,[1] although lower, has risen over time. Whether it is televisions sets, computers, or cell phones, the relative price of consumer durables has tended to fall over time, which has boosted spending.

Consumption represents the largest part of overall spending and is a key determinant of gross domestic product (GDP). Table 12.2 shows the proportion of GDP accounted for by consumption in a sample of countries. The size of consumption varies across countries. For the majority of economies, it is around 50–70% of GDP. For the

TABLE 12.2   Consumption as a Proportion of GDP, 2002

Argentina	61.7
Bangladesh	77.5
Botswana	29.0
Brazil	59.2
Colombia	65.8
Czech Republic	52.7
Denmark	48.1
Kuwait	55.7
Norway	44.6
Philippines	69.0
Sweden	48.6
Thailand	56.4
U.K.	65.6
U.S.	69.9

Source: IMF, International Financial Statistics (June 2003).

[1] Durable consumption includes spending on motor vehicles, furniture, and household equipment; nondurables include food, clothing and shoes, gas and energy; services include housing, housing operations, transportation, medical care, and recreation.

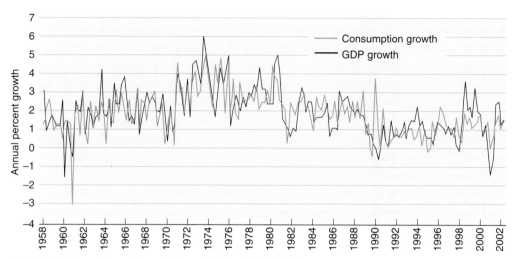

FIGURE 12.1a   **Consumption and GDP growth in Canada, 1958–2002.** *Source:* IMF, *International Financial Statistics* (June 2003).

developed economies, consumption averages around 65% of GDP. There is a greater range for the non-OECD economies—from 78% in Bangladesh to 29% in Botswana.

The importance of understanding the role of consumption in business cycle fluctuations is illustrated in Figure 12.1 where we see that the cyclical fluctuations in Canadian and Japanese GDP are closely mimicked by fluctuations in consumption. These figures also illustrate another fact—*while consumption closely follows GDP fluctuations, it is*

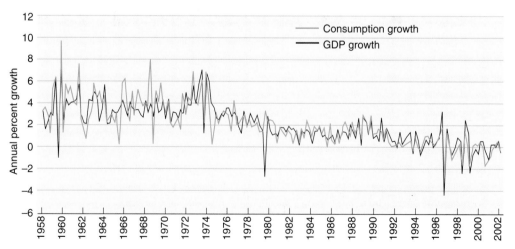

FIGURE 12.1b   **Consumption and GDP growth in Japan, 1958–2002.** Consumption tracks GDP very closely over the business cycle. *Source:* IMF, *International Financial Statistics* (June 2003).

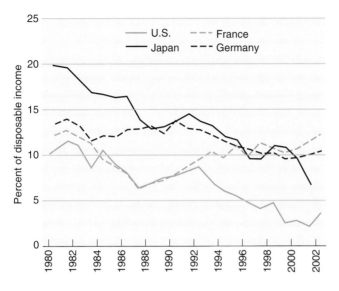

FIGURE 12.2 **Savings rates in United States, Japan, France, and Germany.** There are substantial variations in savings rate over time and across countries. *Source:* OECD, *Economic Outlook* (2003).

not quite so volatile. Consumption tends to be a bit smoother than income. Understanding why consumption changes are smoother than output changes will be a major focus in this chapter.

In understanding the determinants of consumption, we are also modeling saving decisions. What people do not spend out of their disposable income (that is, total income, including wages, interest payments and dividends, and social security payments, less tax payments), they must save. And, as we saw in Chapter 4, the level of savings in a country is a crucial determinant of its long-run steady state. Figure 12.2 shows that savings rates vary significantly both across countries and over time.

KEY POINT

Consumption is the largest part of GDP in nearly all countries. Saving—the difference between income and consumption—is the source of investment.

 The Basic Keynesian Model

The economist John Maynard Keynes stated that

The fundamental psychological law, upon which we are entitled to depend with great confidence both a priori from our knowledge of human nature and from the detailed facts of experience, is that men are disposed, as a rule and on the average, to increase their consumption as their income increases, but not by as much as the increase in their income.[2]

[2] *The General Theory of Employment, Interest and Money* (New York: MacMillan, 1936) p. 96.

In other words, we should expect to see a very close relationship between current consumption and current income—both for an individual and for an economy. Evidence in support of this can be seen in Figure 12.3, which shows that in the United States consumption rises closely in line with disposable income.

In Keynes' work an important concept is the **marginal propensity to consume**, or m.p.c. The marginal propensity to consume is the extra amount an individual will spend if you give them an extra $1. If the m.p.c. is 80%, or 0.8, then from every extra dollar of income, the individual spends 80 cents. A key task of this chapter is to examine the determinants of the m.p.c. The m.p.c. may not be constant—it may vary with income. But, for the moment, we will assume people spend a constant fraction of every dollar they receive.

However, the m.p.c. only tells us how much *additional* income an individual spends. What about someone who receives no income? This individual will still need to consume goods and services, whether financed by begging, borrowing, or stealing. Therefore, even at zero income, an individual will have positive levels of consumption. In Figure 12.4 we show how individual consumption is linked to income according to this simple Keynesian model.

At zero income the individual spends $A; A could be any amount, such as 100 or 1000. For every extra dollar, they spend b dollars, where b is the m.p.c. If they spend 80 cents out of every dollar, then $b = 0.8$. Therefore consumption is given by

Consumption = A + b × Disposable Income

or

C = A + b × Y

The m.p.c. is given by b, but we can also define the **average propensity to consume**—how much of an individual's total income he or she spends (recall that the m.p.c. is about how much of your *additional* income you spend). The average propen-

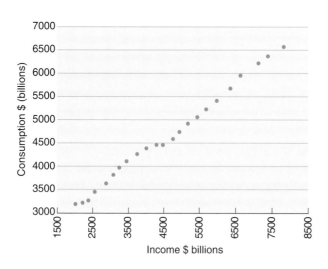

FIGURE 12.3 **Consumption and disposable income in the United States, 1980–2002.** Consumption tracks current income very closely. *Source:* OECD, *Economic Outlook* (2003).

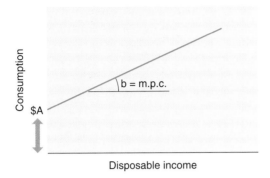

FIGURE 12.4 **The Keynesian consumption function.** The Keynesian consumption function has consumption rising with current income but by less than 1:1. The m.p.c. (*b*) is less than 1.

sity to consume (a.p.c.) is just consumption divided by income, or C/Y. Given our expression for consumption, this is

C/Y = A/Y + *b*

As income gets larger, the term A/Y goes toward zero so that eventually the a.p.c. is the same as the m.p.c. Because consumption plus savings equals income (C = S + Y), the a.p.c. equals 1 minus the savings rate (S/Y).

Why have we spent so much time outlining the concept of the m.p.c.? For Keynes, the level of demand in the economy is key to understanding business cycle fluctuations and, in turn, the m.p.c. is the key concept in influencing demand. To see why, consider again the national accounts identity from Chapter 2:

Output = Consumption + Government Expenditure + Investment

or

Y = C + G + I

where we have for ease of analysis ignored net exports (X − M). We showed in Chapter 2 how the income and output measure of GDP were equivalent, so using this fact and our expression for consumption we can rewrite this as

Y = A + *b*Y + G + I

which can be rearranged as

Y − *b*Y = A + G + I

or

Y = [1/(1 − *b*)] × {A + G + I}

In other words, GDP equals the sum of A plus government expenditure and investment all divided by (1 − *b*). If the government can increase G by $100 million, then according to this expression, GDP will increase *by more than $100 million*. If G increases by $100 million, then Y rises by $100 million/(1 − *b*). If *b* = 0.8, then GDP increases by $500 million, while if the m.p.c. (*b*) equals 0.9, GDP increases by $1000 million. The expression [1/(1 − *b*)] is called the **multiplier** and it represents the total impact on the economy of an initial increase in demand. The larger the m.p.c., the bigger the multiplier.

Why does this multiplier exist? When the government spends $100 million, it purchases goods with this money, which increases the incomes of the firms and workers that produce these goods. Because of the m.p.c. this extra income is spent on other goods and services, further increasing income and consumption elsewhere in the economy. But this additional income is also spent, so that the initial increase in government expenditure sets in motion a sequence of rising incomes and consumption throughout the economy, which serves to magnify the initial demand boost. The higher the m.p.c. the greater the impact on consumption at every stage of the process and so the greater the ultimate increase in demand.

KEY POINT

Keynes' concept of the m.p.c. is important in understanding demand in an economy because it contributes to a multiplier effect upon an initial increase in demand.

12.3 The Keynesian Cross

We can use this very simple framework for thinking about consumption to start to build up one side of the famous **IS-LM model**—a model designed to show how changes in elements of spending and in monetary conditions interact to drive the overall level of income in an economy.[3] We shall be developing the component parts of the overall IS-LM model over several chapters; we start here by considering further the implications of the dependence of consumption upon income.

At this early stage of developing the IS-LM model, we are assuming that only consumption varies with income and that all the other factors of demand (planned investment, government expenditure, and net exports) are exogenous, or given, amounts. Note that we refer to *planned* investment rather than just investment. From our analysis of GDP in Chapter 2, it will be remembered that investment equals investment in physical capital plus any increase in inventories, or unsold output. The latter will be important whenever overall spending in the economy differs from planned levels.

Assuming a closed economy and using our simple Keynesian consumption function, total planned expenditure (PE = C + G + I) in the economy equals:

$$PE = A + b(Y) + G + I$$

So planned aggregate spending depends upon actual income. Actual income has to be the sum of consumption, investment, and government spending. If actual income equals planned expenditure then PE = Y which implies:

$$PE = Y = A + b(Y) + G + I$$

---

[3] This is effectively a detailed way of modeling the aggregate demand side of the economy, which helps analyze how changes in fiscal or monetary policy can influence the economy. It was developed by John Hicks in the United Kingdom and Alvin Hansen in the United States and was based on their interpretation of Keynes' work.

Which, as before, implies:

$$Y = [A + I + G]/1 - b$$

So when planned aggregate expenditure equals actual income, the level of income is a multiple of the components of demand that are independent of income, the expression in curly brackets. Shifts in those components have a multiplied impact upon demand and income. As noted in the previous section, the multiplier is $1/1 - b$, which depends positively on the marginal propensity to consume.

What happens when planned expenditure and actual spending do not coincide? Consider Figure 12.5. On the horizontal axis we measure actual income, which, given GDP accounting, is equivalent to output. On the vertical axis we measure planned aggregate spending. A 45 degree line is drawn on the figure and when actual and planned spending are equal—which is something we will require for an equilibrium—we need to be on this line. The line PE-PE shows how planned spending varies with actual income. Because the propensity to consume is b, a number we plausibly take to be less than one but positive, the slope of the PE-PE line is less than 45 degrees. Its slope reflects how much planned spending rises as actual income goes up one dollar. Since we assume the only component of demand that depends on current income is consumption and that the marginal propensity to spend is b, then this slope is b—demand increases directly through increases in consumption of $\$b$ for every \$1 increase in output.

Suppose that firms assess that the level of output they should produce to satisfy planned spending is at level Y_1. This is in excess of the level of output consistent with output being equal to planned spending, which is level Y^*. If firms produce Y_1, they will find that, so long as the government spends G, then the overall level of demand, given firms' own planned investment, will fall short of Y_1. The vertical distance aB shows the difference between actual output and planned spending at a production level of Y_1. That distance is equal to unplanned inventory accumulation. Since we count inventory accumulation as a part of investment, then we can interpret the vertical distance aB as the difference between actual investment and planned investment.

Unplanned inventory accumulation is likely to encourage firms to reduce their output. Wise and far-sighted firms who could work out where they went wrong in the first period, when they expected planned spending to be at Y_1, might decide to produce Y^*

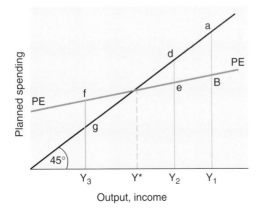

FIGURE 12.5 **The Keynesian cross.** Planned spending and actual spending only coincide at Y*.

in the second period. If so, we would then go straight to the equilibrium where plans and outcomes for spending are consistent. But maybe firms only scale back their plans partly and aim to produce Y_2 in the next round of production. In this case they would still accumulate unwanted inventories, but at the lower rate of de; eventually firms would converge on Y^*.

A similar story would unfold if firms had been too pessimistic about equilibrium output. Had firms anticipated that only at output level Y_3 would production match planned spending, they would have found that demand exceeded their expectations and that inventories would be drained by the amount fg. Only when they increased output up to level Y^* would unanticipated reductions in inventories cease.

In Figure 12.5, the point at which the 45 degree line and the planned expenditure line intersect is the point at which actual and planned spending coincide; this crossover point of the two lines is what gives the **Keynesian cross** its name. At this point the economy can be considered to be in equilibrium—planned output equals actual output. To demonstrate graphically how the multiplier works, we can return to our simple Keynesian cross model and show how important are shifts in investment, government spending, and the exogenous (to income) element of consumer spending (A) to the determination of income. Figure 12.6 shows that a given rise in G, I, or A has a long-run affect upon output that is much greater than the original stimulus—greater in fact precisely by the magnitude $1/1 - b$.

Figure 12.7 shows that if we look at two economies with different propensities to consume, the impact of extra investment or government spending will be greater in the economy with the larger propensity to consume. The economy with the larger marginal propensity to consume has a larger multiplier.

KEY POINT

The multiplier shows how much demand rises once all agents have adjusted to an event that generates a change in some component of demand. The multiplier depends upon the marginal propensity to consume.

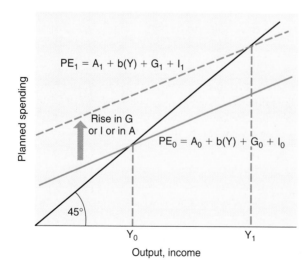

$$PE_1 = A_1 + b(Y) + G_1 + I_1$$

Planned spending

Rise in G
or I or in A

$$PE_0 = A_0 + b(Y) + G_0 + I_0$$

45°

Y_0 Y_1

Output, income

FIGURE 12.6 **The multiplier and the IS curve.** The rise in spending exceeds the initial rise in demand.

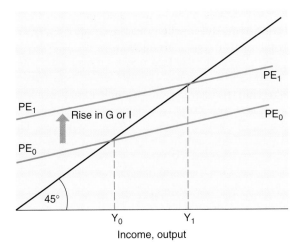

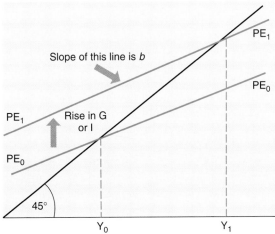

FIGURE 12.7 **The multiplier and the propensity to consume.** The larger is the propensity to consume, the steeper is the line PE and the greater is the multiplier.

12.4 The Permanent Income Model

Whereas current consumption undoubtedly does depend on current income, the model we have outlined is rather simplistic because it assumes nothing else matters. According to this model, an individual looks at his or her monthly salary check and spends a constant proportion of it. But consider whether this insight holds true for the following characters:

1. A senior in college has a current income of $3,000 from various part-time jobs, but Merrill Lynch offers her a job when she graduates with a starting salary of $80,000.
2. A bond trader at Goldman Sachs is currently earning $500,000 a year, but rumors of layoffs are rife.
3. The tax authorities refund $25,000 to someone in a steady job who has mistakenly overpaid taxes in recent years.

If we are thinking about how consumption is linked to current income, that is, the marginal propensity to consume, then in each of these three cases we would arrive at different answers. Although the student's current income is low, she will probably wish to spend substantially more than she is currently earning because of her high future income (assuming the bank will loan her the money). The Goldman Sachs trader has a very high current income, but uncertainty about the future will lead him to accumulate savings in order to prevent consumption from crashing if he loses his job. The third case involves a one-time windfall receipt of income which will not be repeated. The consumer therefore has to choose between spending it all today or spreading it out over several years.

All of these examples suggest, as does common sense, that when deciding how much to consume, households think about their income over the future as well as what they currently earn. These ideas lead us to a broader theory of consumption, called the *permanent income* theory,[4] which provides a much richer model of the determinants of the m.p.c. To understand this theory, we outline a simple and stylized model of income over a person's life.

THE INTERTEMPORAL BUDGET CONSTRAINT

Any model of consumption must contain two ingredients: the constraints consumers face and also their preferences. We focus first on their constraints.

Consider a person whose life consists of two periods (if it cheers you up, let the periods last for many years). Denote labor income in the first period by $Y(1)$ and in the second period by $Y(2)$. For instance, if the individual is a student in the first period, $Y(1) = 0$, but $Y(2)$ will be positive—her salary. If instead the individual is currently working but will retire next period, then $Y(1)$ is positive and $Y(2)$ zero. We shall denote consumption in the first period by $C(1)$ and in the second by $C(2)$. For ease of analysis, we also assume the individual has no wealth at the beginning of the first period. This means that at the end of the first period the individual's bank balance is $Y(1) - C(1)$. If the individual has saved money, $Y(1) > C(1)$, the bank balance is positive. If instead she borrowed money to finance high consumption $[Y(1) < C(1)]$, then she owes the bank money. Assuming the bank pays out interest r, (or charges an interest rate on loans of r), then at the beginning of the second period the bank account has funds worth

$$(1 + r) \times [Y(1) - C(1)]$$

Therefore, the maximum amount of money the individual has to spend in the second period is given by

$$Y(2) + (1 + r) [Y(1) - C(1)]$$

Assuming the individual does not wish to leave any inheritance she will spend this entire amount on second period consumption so that

$$C(2) = Y(2) + (1 + r) [Y(1) - C(1)]$$

---

[4] Developed by Milton Friedman, *A Theory of the Consumption Function* (Princeton, NJ: Princeton Univ. Press for National Bureau of Economic Research), 1957.

In order to arrive at the intertemporal budget constraint, we need to do a little re-arranging. First we collect on one side all the consumption terms and on the other all the income terms. This gives

$$(1 + r) C(1) + C(2) = (1 + r) Y(1) + Y(2)$$

If we finally divide through by $(1 + r)$ we have the **intertemporal budget constraint**

$$C(1) + C(2)/(1 + r) = Y(1) + Y(2)/(1 + r)$$

When we divide a number by $1 + r$ we *discount* the number. Discounting is a way of valuing future amounts of income or spending in terms of today's money. Imagine that I have $100 and the interest rate is 10%, i.e., $r = 0.1$. Therefore I can turn $100 of cash today into $110 in a year's time. This also means that if I were to calculate today the value of $110 received in a year's time, I would put it no higher than $100, i.e., 110/1.1.

KEY POINT

The intertemporal budget constraint says that current consumption plus discounted future consumption must equal the sum of current income and future discounted income.

The key constraint that the individual faces is a *lifetime* budget constraint. While in any one particular year an individual can save or borrow, over his or her lifetime total discounted expenditure must equal total discounted income. The intertemporal budget constraint reveals immediately the importance of the future. How much consumers can spend today, C(1), depends on their expectations of future income, Y(2), as well as future consumption, C(2), and current income, Y(1).

In the case of two periods, we can show the intertemporal budget constraint diagrammatically. Figure 12.8 shows the different combinations of first and second period

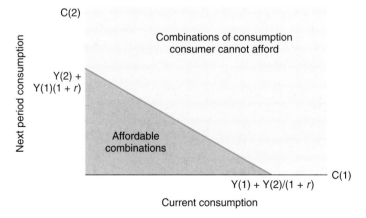

FIGURE 12.8 The intertemporal budget constraint. The intertemporal budget constraint shows combinations of first and second period consumption an individual can afford given lifetime income.

consumption the individual can afford on the assumption that today's income is $Y(1)$ and tomorrow's is $Y(2)$. Assuming individuals can borrow against future income, they could choose to consume the whole of today's income [$Y(1)$] plus an amount equal to the maximum they could borrow against tomorrow's income—$Y(2)/(1 + r)$. Therefore the *maximum* first period consumption is given by the point on the horizontal axis at which $C(1) = Y(1) + Y(2)/(1 + r)$ and $C(2) = 0$. At the other extreme, if an individual were to save all her current income, i.e., $C(1) = 0$, she would start the final period of her life with accumulated wealth of $Y(1) (1 + r)$, to which she would add final period income $Y(2)$ to enjoy a maximum final period consumption of $Y(2) + Y(1) (1 + r)$. These two extreme points involve setting consumption to zero in one period, but the consumer can, of course, reallocate consumption between time periods. Every $1 of reduced period 1 consumption translates into an extra $\$(1 + r)$ in period 2, so the slope of the line linking these two extreme points is simply given by one plus the interest rate. Any point on the straight line joining these two extremes or any point within the shaded triangle represents bundles, or combinations of consumption that the consumer can afford, given lifetime income.

CONSUMER PREFERENCES

The intertemporal budget constraint shows what the consumer can afford; it does not say what he or she prefers. To find this out we need to know about consumer preferences. Economists draw *indifference curves* to characterize preferences between commodities (and we can think of consumption today and consumption tomorrow as two distinct commodities). Indifference curves show combinations of consumption of the two commodities between which an individual is indifferent. Consider the points A and F in Figure 12.9. Point A involves high first period consumption but very little in the second period. By contrast, F involves a lot of second period consumption but not much in the first period. However, both points are on the same indifference curve, which means the consumer is equally happy with either bundle. The additional second period consumption that F implies just compensates for the loss of first period consumption compared to A.

The slope of the indifference curve tells us how willing a consumer is to substitute between first and second period consumption. Consider points A and B. At point A,

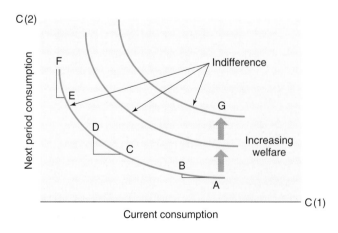

FIGURE 12.9 **Consumer indifference curves.**
Indifference curves indicate consumption bundles that yield equal pleasure.

the consumer has very little second period consumption but lots of first period consumption and we have drawn a very flat indifference curve. This means that the consumer is prepared to give up quite a lot of first period consumption in return for only a small amount of extra second period consumption. We are in effect assuming that when a consumer has a lot of one commodity but very little of another, he places a higher value on the scarce commodity. The same logic explains why the indifference curve is so steep between points E and F. In this case, the consumer has an abundance of second period consumption and so is prepared to forgo quite a lot of this in return for a small increase in initial consumption. Finally, between points C and D the consumer is willing to trade roughly equal amounts of first and second period consumption—when he has similar amounts of both commodities, they are valued roughly equally.

The previous discussion was about different combinations of first and second period consumption that yield the same welfare. However, comparing points A and G we see that they both have the same amount of first period consumption, but G involves more second period consumption. Therefore the consumer prefers bundle G to bundle A and these different combinations are on different indifference curves. The higher the indifference curve, the more the consumer prefers the consumption bundles.

THE CONSUMER'S CHOICE

If we put together the intertemporal budget constraint and the indifference curves, we have a complete analysis of the consumer's consumption decisions. Assuming that consumers want to maximize their welfare, they will want to choose the combination of first and second period consumption that puts them on the highest indifference curve that their intertemporal budget constraint makes feasible. This is shown in Figure 12.10 as point A—where the budget constraint just touches the highest achievable indifference curve. We have drawn Figure 12.10 to produce roughly equal amounts of first and second period consumption. This result is achieved by an indifference curve with the curved shape shown. As explained above, these indifference curves imply that consumers dislike volatile consumption—they prefer roughly equal amounts of consumption in each year. This is why they are prepared to give up a lot of second period consumption at F (see Figure 12.9) for only a small gain in terms of first period consumption.

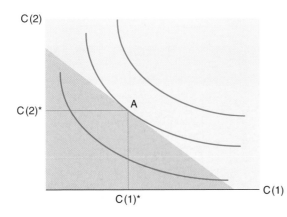

FIGURE 12.10 **Consumer's optimal choice.** Consumers choose the affordable consumption bundle that gives the highest welfare.

RESPONSE TO INCREASE IN CURRENT INCOME

Figure 12.11 shows how we can use our model to analyze the effect of a temporary one-time increase in current income. It considers the case in which current income is higher by $100,000 but no change is expected in period 2. If all income is used to finance current consumption, then instead of consuming $Y(1) + Y(2)/(1 + r)$ the consumer can now spend $Y(1) + 100,000 + Y(2)/(1 + r)$. Similarly, if the consumer saves everything, then maximum second period consumption rises from $Y(1) (1 + r) + Y(2)$ to $(Y(1) + 100,000) (1 + r) + Y(2)$. The effect in Figure 12.11 is for the whole intertemporal budget constraint to shift outward to the right. The increase in lifetime income means that consumption increases, but the increase in current income leads to a roughly equal increase in *both* first and second period consumption. This is because of our assumption about indifference curves—that the consumer prefers to divide consumption equally between both periods rather than experience substantial swings. This implies that, in response to a temporary increase in income, the m.p.c. in this two-period model will be approximately 50%—half the income is spent now and half later. The person who received the one-time tax refund would spend half the refund money now and the other half in a later period. Arguing analogously, we also note that if there are ten more periods, then the m.p.c. would be about 10%.[5]

> **KEY POINT**
>
> A one-time rise in income is likely to cause consumption to rise by less than it would with a permanent income increase, and the m.p.c. will be low.

RESPONSE TO INCREASES IN FUTURE INCOME

Now consider the case in which first period income remains unchanged but tomorrow's income is expected to be $100,000 higher. The maximum amount of first period consumption that can be financed (by borrowing on the basis of all future income) is

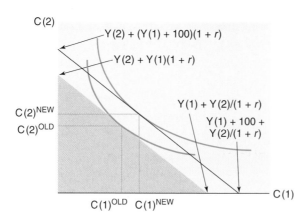

FIGURE 12.11 **Impact on consumption of increase in current income.** Both current and future consumption increase when current income rises in the forward-looking model.

[5] Because of discounting and interest rates, the increased lifetime income is not spread *exactly* equally between periods. The higher the rate at which people mentally discount future satisfaction, the more is spent today because consumers are impatient, and the higher the interest rate, the less is spent today because consumers have more of an incentive to save.

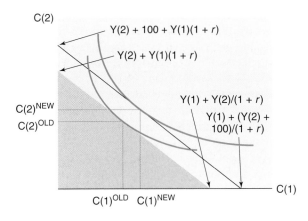

FIGURE 12.12 **Impact on consumption of increase in future income.** Because of borrowing, both current and future consumption increase when agent expects higher future income.

$Y(1) + (Y(2) + 100,000)/(1 + r)$ and the maximum second period consumption is $Y(1)$ $(1 + r) + Y(2) + 100,000$ (see Figure 12.12).

As in the previous case, the consumer's lifetime income has risen, and she responds by spreading the increase equally between both periods. The result is that current consumption rises even though current income has not changed. This would suggest that our graduating student will respond to her employment letter from Merrill Lynch by going out and spending, even though current income has not changed.

PERMANENT INCOME

Our previous two examples show that current consumption rises by a similar amount in response to an increase in current income and an increase in future income.[6] This is very different from the simple Keynesian model in which current income is all that matters. In the forward-looking model, the consumer sets consumption considering lifetime rather than current income and, given our assumptions on indifference curves, does so in a manner that tries to avoid large changes in consumption. Consider the extreme case in which the consumer wishes to set first and second period consumption to be the same. (For simplicity, assume that interest rates are zero.) Under these assumptions the intertemporal budget constraint is

$$C(1) + C(2) = Y(1) + Y(2)$$

If the consumer sets consumption to be the same in each period, then $C(1) = C(2) = C$ so we have

$$2C = Y(1) + Y(2) \text{ or } C = (1/2)\,[Y(1) + Y(2)]$$

that is, consumption is set equal to average lifetime income or what is called **permanent income**. Any change in permanent income is immediately reflected in current consumption. When first (or second) period income increases by $100,000, then permanent income (and consumption) increases by only $(1/2)$ ($100,000) = $50,000 and the m.p.c. is 50%.

---

[6] The reason why there will be a difference is due to interest rate effects. If interest rates are high, then the consumer will be tempted to save more of any first period increase in income. Similarly, it is more expensive to borrow against news of higher future income.

Therefore, the forward-looking model has as its main relationship the link between consumption and permanent, rather than current, income, and the m.p.c. is determined by the influence that current income has on permanent income. This permanent income model helps explain one of the key facts of Figure 12.1—in a recession, consumption does not fall as much as GDP does, nor does it rise as much in a boom. In a recession, GDP and income are temporarily low and so the fall in current income is greater than the fall in permanent income. As a consequence, the m.p.c. is low and consumption falls by less than income. Exactly similar reasoning holds during a boom so that, over the whole, business cycle consumption fluctuates by less than income.

The assumption of zero interest rates in our example means that permanent income only depends on labor income. However, with positive interest rates, consumers earn interest on their wealth and this has to be factored into our concept of permanent income. Once again, the principle of consumption smoothing dominates, so that the consumer spends from this wealth equally over time. In the extreme (and, sadly, unrealistic) case in which the consumer lives forever, this implies that the consumer spends only the interest payments, in order to maintain a constant level of wealth.

TEMPORARY AND PERMANENT INCOME CHANGES

We can combine our previous analysis of how current consumption responds to increases in current and future income to show how the m.p.c. out of permanent income shocks differs from that of temporary shocks. In response to a $100,000 increase in current income, we found the consumer would spend around 50% today and the rest tomorrow. In response to a $100,000 increase in *future* income, we suggested around 50% would be spent now and the rest tomorrow. A *permanent* increase in income of $100,000 is extra income today *and* next period; combining these two results, we conclude that the consumer has an m.p.c. out of additional permanent income of around 100% in the current period as well as the next period.

KEY POINT

The m.p.c. out of shocks to permanent income is much greater than out of temporary shocks. In the case of permanent shocks to income, the implications of the forward-looking model and the Keynesian consumption function are very similar—consumers will spend most of any increase in current income.

SAVING FOR A RAINY DAY

The permanent income model has important implications for savings. Consider the case in which savings are negative; that is, consumption is greater than current income. This, in turn, implies that average lifetime income is greater than current income, such as when the individual feels that his or her income will rise in the future. By contrast, consider the case in which savings are positive, so that current income exceeds consumption and average lifetime income. In these circumstances, the individual thinks his or her income will fall in the future. Therefore, according to the permanent income model, savings is for a "rainy day"—people only accumulate assets if they believe their income is going to fall. For instance, if the individual is retiring from work in the next period, his income will fall to zero and he should be saving now in order to finance his retirement. Conversely, as we saw, the student who is waiting to begin employment with Merrill Lynch should be borrowing heavily and then using her high future income to repay her bank loan.

12.5 The Importance of Current Income Revisited

The forward-looking model of consumption is not consistent with the central assumption of the Keynesian consumption function that there is a simple and stable relationship between current consumption and current income. Instead it emphasizes the importance of future income in influencing current consumption decisions. In this section, however, we add two different features to the forward-looking model, each of which reinstates the importance of the link between current income and consumption. The first factor we add is consumer uncertainty about future income; we then examine the implications of constraints on how much individuals can borrow.

THE IMPORTANCE OF UNCERTAINTY

So far we have been assuming that people have knowledge of current and future incomes. In practice, however, future earnings are highly uncertain. This is likely to affect savings and consumption decisions through influencing the m.p.c. One recent study[7] suggests that as much as 46% of personal sector wealth is the result of higher savings aimed at insuring against future income uncertainty.

Let's consider two different people. Mr. Gray has taken a safe job with the IRS that pays a steady income forever. He is a reliable and boring type—a James Stewart character from a Frank Capra film. Then there is Ms. Purple who has piled all her savings into setting up a software company that has generated her a first-year income of $90,000, but whether she will even have a company in two or three years is anyone's guess—she is more a Sharon Stone type in a late 1980s thriller. Let's assume that Mr. Gray also earns $90,000 doing his repetitive tasks. Mr. Gray should not worry about volatility in his future income and as a result will be inclined to spend more—in other words, he will have a high m.p.c. By contrast, the entrepreneur must remember that her income could fall to zero any day. Since dramatic swings in consumption are unpleasant for consumers, Ms. Purple will likely save in order to accumulate assets for precautionary reasons. Note that these savings are for precautionary reasons and are different from the rainy day savings we mentioned above. You save for a rainy day because your best guess is that your income will fall. In contrast, **precautionary savings** provide individuals insurance against their income turning out worse than they forecast. The more uncertainty there is about income and the more risk averse consumers are, the greater is precautionary savings.[8]

KEY POINT

Introducing precautionary savings makes current income more important than future income.

---

[7] Carroll and Samwick, "How Important Is Precautionary Saving?" *Review of Economics and Statistics* (1998) vol. 80, no. 3, pp. 410–419.

[8] You may have spotted an obvious problem with this argument. Running a company attracts risk-lovers and working for the tax authorities attracts the risk-averse. James Stewart was the worrying type (which is why he takes the safe job with the IRS), while Sharon Stone doesn't give a damn about tomorrow and loves risk. So maybe Stewart saves more than Stone. This is an example of *sample selection bias*. The point we make in the text, however, relies on holding attitudes to risk constant. Thus the person in the safe job would save less than the person running the new company. Our James Stewart character will save more if he is starting up a new firm than if he is employed with the IRS.

Future income is uncertain—I may fall ill and be unable to earn, my boss may be replaced by my arch rival who forces me out of the firm, and so forth. Given news about a $100,000 increase in both current and likely future income, the m.p.c. will be a lot higher out of the former. There is no need to do any precautionary savings in respect to current income.

BORROWING CONSTRAINTS

There is another way of reinstating the close link between current consumption and current income that characterizes the basic Keynesian model. For the forward-looking model to be relevant, individuals must not be affected by **borrowing constraints**. Consider again the student with a job offer from Merrill Lynch. The only way she can spend more than her current income is if a bank is persuaded to loan her funds. If banks refuse, then it does not matter what the student's permanent income is—she can only finance consumption equal to current income. This situation is shown in Figure 12.13. If the consumer could borrow from the bank, her budget constraint is given by the line ABC. However, if the bank does not grant her credit, then first period consumption cannot exceed first period income and the budget constraint becomes ABD. With this budget constraint, the consumer chooses first period consumption $C^*(1)$ and consumption during the next period of $C^*(2)$. Therefore, she consumes too little in the first period and then too much in the second period. The inability to borrow reduces her welfare because she is on a lower indifference curve.

We can use Figure 12.13 to examine the impact of credit liberalization on an economy. During the 1980s a number of European economies instituted a process of financial deregulation. The result was a much greater degree of competition between financial institutions and the introduction of overseas banks eager to grab market share. The consequence was a surge in bank lending as banks competed among each other for new customers. In order to attract market share, banks became willing to lend on anticipation of future incomes and large loans were offered for house purchases. The budget

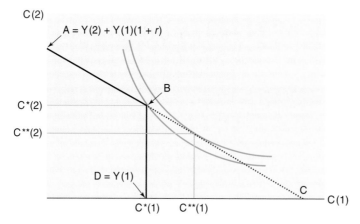

FIGURE 12.13   Borrowing constraints make consumption equal to current income. If consumers are unable to borrow, then current consumption depends on current rather than permanent income. If there were no borrowing constraints consumption in period one would be $C^{**}(1)$, which is greater than $Y(1)$.

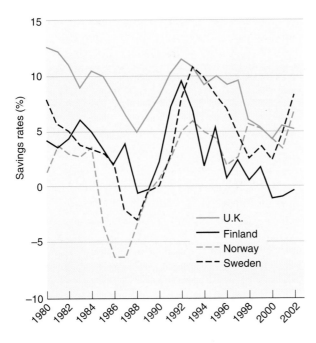

FIGURE 12.14 **Impact of 1980s financial deregulation on U.K. and Scandinavian savings.** Increased ability of banks to lend in the 1980s led to dramatic falls in the savings rate in U.K. and Scandinavian economies. *Source:* OECD, *Economic Outlook* (2003).

constraint thus shifted from ABD to ABC and current consumption rose strongly. Further, if consumers expect rising future income, then according to our "rainy day" story, savings will go negative as consumers avail themselves of the opportunity to smooth their consumption over time. Figure 12.14 shows this is exactly what happened in Sweden, Norway, Finland, and the United Kingdom—countries where rapid financial deregulation took place in the 1980s.

In the case of borrowing constraints, the m.p.c. is very high—individuals have too low first period consumption and too high second period consumption. They would like to reallocate this consumption but cannot because they cannot borrow. Therefore, when they receive more current income they will spend most of it—there is no point in saving money when consumption next period will already be too high. This situation is shown in Figure 12.15 where the increase in current income shifts the budget constraint

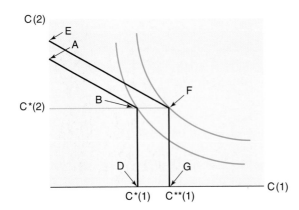

FIGURE 12.15 **Increases in income create high m.p.c. under borrowing constraints.** With borrowing constraints, increases in current income feed through into current consumption only.

from ABD to EFG. In this case, the increased income leads entirely to higher extra first period consumption and has no effect on second period consumption.

KEY POINT

If borrowing constraints are important, it is current income rather than future income that matters.

12.6 The Influence of Interest Rates

Because of the importance of consumption as a component of GDP, the influence of interest rates on consumption is an important aspect of monetary policy. In the basic Keynesian model, all that matters for consumption is current income so that interest rates have only an indirect effect. For savers, a higher interest rate means greater income because of higher interest payments. However, for debtors the higher interest rates reduce their income available for discretionary consumer spending. The extra income gained by creditors should equal the income loss to debtors so overall aggregate income has not changed. However, there may still be an influence on consumption. Creditors tend to have low m.p.c.—they do a lot of saving—whereas debtors have a high m.p.c.— this helps explain why they are debtors. The interest rate increase therefore leads to a redistribution of income from those with a propensity to spend toward those with a tendency to save. The result will be a fall in consumption. This fall in consumption, via the multiplier effect outlined at the beginning of the chapter, will lead to a fall in GDP and rising unemployment, potentially generating a further fall in consumption.

In the forward-looking model, the effect of interest rates is more direct but also more ambiguous, as shown in Figure 12.16. An increase in interest rates leads the

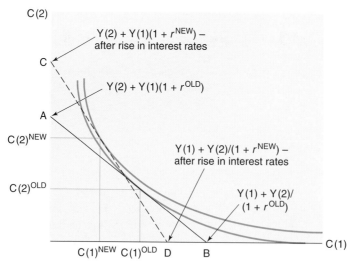

FIGURE 12.16   **Impact of interest rates on consumption.** Increases in interest rates lead to lower consumption as a result of income and substitution effects.

budget constraint to tilt from AB to CD. Higher interest rates mean that, for the same second period repayment, the consumer can afford a smaller loan in the current period—more money has to be spent on interest payments. Therefore, on the horizontal axis, the budget line shifts inward. However, if the consumer saves his or her first period income, then the higher interest rates lead to greater second period interest income and lead the budget line to shift *up* on the vertical axis. Because the budget line tilts, interest rates have two conflicting effects on consumption. One impact, called the *substitution effect*, causes a fall in first period consumption and is best reflected in the inward shift on the horizontal axis from B to D. The interest rate is an intertemporal price for the consumer—every $1 of current consumption means $(1 + r) less future consumption. If the interest rate increases, this makes first period consumption more expensive and so the consumer substitutes away toward second period consumption by saving more. The other influence is the *income effect*. When interest rates increase, savers receive higher interest payments and can afford to spend more—this is the reason the intercept on the vertical axis shifts up from A to C. This higher income means the consumer can spend more over his or her lifetime and, because of consumption smoothing, this will lead to an increase in first and second period income.

For savers, the income effect leads to higher current consumption. However, for debtors, the higher interest rates mean higher debt interest payments and so *lower* lifetime income and lower current consumption. Therefore, for debtors, the income effect of higher interest rates leads to lower current consumption. For borrowers, the effect of higher interest rates is unambiguous—current consumption falls. For savers, however, consumption can either rise or fall depending on the relative strength of income and substitution effects. In Figure 12.16 we have shown the substitution effect dominating so that consumption falls; this outcome is also supported in the aggregate consumption data. However, the impact of interest rates on consumption is relatively small, partly due to offsetting income and substitution effects.

KEY POINT

Under both Keynesian and forward-looking models, interest rates affect debtors and savers differently. In forward-looking models, the effects on savers are complicated by substitution and income effects.

12.7 Building Up the IS Curve

In the Keynesian cross diagram shown in Figure 12.5, we focused on shifts in consumption induced by changes in disposable income. Let us assume that, in aggregate, consumption is negatively affected by a rise in the interest rate—an assumption that is consistent with empirical evidence from developed countries. It is the influence of interest rates on the components of aggregate demand that leads us to the IS curve we mentioned earlier in this chapter.

We can expect not only consumption, but also investment and perhaps net exports, to be negatively affected by interest rates. We would certainly expect that overall

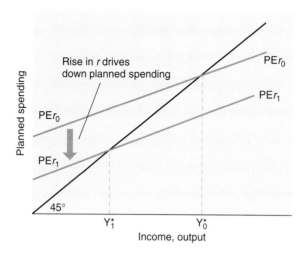

FIGURE 12.17   **Aggregate demand and a rise in interest rates.** A rise in interest rates reduces some components of spending and causes equilibrium income and output to fall.

planned spending would decline with higher interest rates. Figure 12.17 shows that in the Keynesian cross diagram, the implication of this is that the higher are interest rates then, other things being equal, the lower will be the equilibrium level of output. When interest rates increase from r_0 to r_1, the aggregate spending schedule shifts down from PE_{r0} to PE_{r1}—in part because consumption is likely to be lower. As a result, the equilibrium level of output falls from Y_0 to Y_1. If we vary the interest rate and calculate the equilibrium level of output for each rate, we would trace out a negative relation, shown in Figure 12.18. Figure 12.18 is the IS curve—it is built up by using Figure 12.17 to draw a PE schedule at various interest rates and calculating the equilibrium level of income consistent with actual and planned expenditure being equal for each interest rate. The IS curve gives policy makers an indication of the effects of interest rates on economic output.

KEY POINT

The negative relation between the level of interest rates and the level of equilibrium demand for goods in the short run is the IS curve.

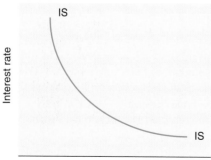

FIGURE 12.18   **The IS curve.** The IS curve shows combinations of interest rates and income consistent with equilibrium in the demand for goods and services.

12.8 | The Role of Wealth and Capital Gains

We have so far focused only on income and interest rates as influences on consumption, but another important influence is wealth. The household sector does not hold all its money in a bank account but also owns stocks, bonds, and real estate. Changes in the value of these other assets will affect consumer wealth and also consumer spending.

What is the marginal propensity to consume out of wealth? The analysis closely parallels that for the m.p.c. out of income. Assuming consumers are forward looking, they will not consume all their wealth today but only a small proportion of it—the rest they will leave for later years. We can expect the m.p.c. of wealth to be much lower than that for income. Income is a *flow*, something that is received every year, whereas wealth is a *stock* and needs to be maintained if it is to last for many periods. The result is that consumers spend a much higher proportion of their annual income than of their current wealth.

The existence of capital gains raises issues about how to measure the savings rate. The savings rate is defined as unspent income divided by income and, as measured by the national accounts, income *excludes* capital gains but *includes* interest payments and dividends. As we saw in Figure 12.2, in the late 1990s the U.S. savings rate fell dramatically, as measured by the national accounts, but at the same time the U.S. stock market boomed. Between 1989 and 1999 the Dow Jones index of U.S. stock prices increased fivefold. Consumers borrowed from banks using these capital gains as collateral in order to finance consumption, and the result was a sharp fall in savings. But does this give a misleading impression of household finances?

National accounts measures of savings ignore the financial resources available to the consumer through capital gains. Including capital gains dramatically changes the performance of the U.S. savings rate. Figure 12.19 shows the national accounts (NIPA) measure of savings along with an alternative measure that includes realized capital gains (i.e., capital gains that have been banked via selling stock) in its concept of

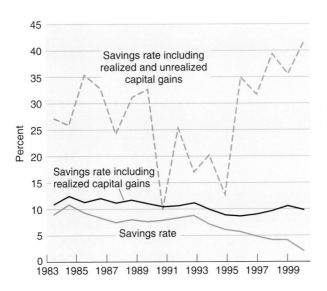

FIGURE 12.19 **U.S. savings rate and importance of capital gains.** The U.S. savings rate in the 1980s and 1990s would have been much higher if capital gains were factored into the concept of disposable income. *Source:* Peach and Steindal, "A Nation of Spendthrifts?" *Current Issues in Economic and Finance* (September 2000), vol. 6, no. 10, pp. 1–30.

income. This adjusted series suggests that U.S. consumers save a much higher proportion of their income and that this proportion has changed very little. Figure 12.19 also shows the savings rate for U.S. consumers including unrealized gains in the measure of disposable income. Far from showing a dramatic decline in U.S. savings in the 1990s, the chart suggests that, until the bear market that started in 2001, *savings* had actually increased so that U.S. consumers were being cautious in the rate at which they were spending these capital gains. Given the very sharp falls in stock prices in 2001 and 2002, such caution was amply justified by subsequent events.

It is now clear that many of the apparent gains in wealth that seemed to have been generated by stock price rises in the late 1990s evaporated in the bear market of 2001 and 2002. Those households that borrowed on the basis of apparent stock market wealth in 1998 and 1999 may well have regretted their decisions by 2002 when stock prices were around 50% lower. Because of this sort of stock price volatility, how much of a rise in stock prices to treat as real income is very hard to gauge. The same issue is true of gains in wealth for owners of real estate. In fact, there is an added factor here. Even if a big rise in house prices is permanent and not reversed in future years, it is unclear how much of a real gain this generates for a homeowner. If there is a general rise in prices of properties in areas where I want to live, then I may be no better off. I would certainly be overestimating my wealth if I counted all the rise in the value of my current house as a gain without taking account of the fact that, if I buy a new house, I will have to pay inflated prices for my new property. And if I never plan to move, in what sense am I really better off if my property is worth more? Problems in measuring wealth and the issue of how changes in the market value of tangible assets might affect consumption are hard to figure out.

POLICY PROBLEMS

Earlier in this chapter we outlined the key role of the m.p.c. in determining the efficacy of government spending in influencing GDP. If the m.p.c. is a stable and large number, then governments have a powerful influence on the economy that they can use to try to stabilize the business cycle. However, the forward-looking permanent income model illustrates some of the problems policymakers face.

KEY POINT

The dependence of the m.p.c. on consumers' expectations of future income, whether they perceive income increases to be temporary or permanent, the importance of uncertainty, and the variable impact of capital gains, combined with the issue of whether they have access to credit—all make the m.p.c. a difficult number to pin down. This suggests that governments have limited ability to reliably influence consumption by shifting taxes or moving interest rates.

12.9   Demographic Influences in the Life Cycle Model

We have omitted much of the richness of individual lives in the simple two period models that we looked at earlier in this chapter. But this richness affects both consumption and savings. The profile of income over individual lives is likely to be uneven and, as a consequence, we can expect people's savings behavior to be different at different points in their *life cycle.*Most people earn low amounts in their teens and often into their twenties as they get a formal education. They then (usually) start work, and their income tends to rise as they become better at what they do and get promoted. At some point, productivity declines and earnings fall. The profile of earnings over working life depends on the work people do. Professional football players' productivity declines sharply in their 30s, but a professor of English literature might not peak until her late 50s (at which point she can understand *Finnegan's Wake*). The Rolling Stones' earnings seem to rise as they move into their 60s. But usually income tails off sharply as people move near or into retirement.

Consumption is also likely to vary dramatically over the life cycle. Most people are single in their early adult life, during which period consumption is relatively low. However, as they become older they may have a family, with consumption increasing as a result. Eventually children grow up, leave home, and (hopefully) stop relying on parental income, at which point household consumption falls. During retirement, consumption tends to continue to fall (perhaps the desire for extravagant skiing holidays in Aspen declines as the ability to get out of bed in the morning diminishes).

Support for these demographic shifts in consumption and income is shown in Figure 12.20 and Table 12.3 and 12.4. These show how consumption and income vary across a large sample of 107,000 U.S. households as the age of the reference adult in the household varies. The income profile is exactly what we outlined, except that income remains significant at the end for people older than 75 because measured income in this survey includes interest earnings and pension payments.[9]

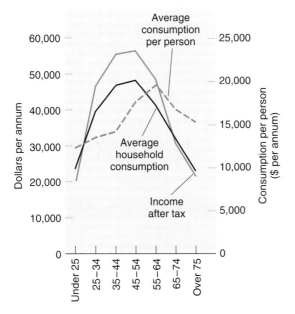

FIGURE 12.20 **Consumpton and income over the life cycle—average U.S. consumer, 2001.** Consumption and income vary with age—peaking in the middle age and then declining. *Source:* Bureau of Labor Statistics, *Consumer Expenditure Survey* (2003).

[9] It is important to note that Figure 12.20 is based on data covering different individuals of different ages and not consumption over a single individual's life. Because of productivity growth, income differs across generations.

TABLE 12.3   Average Household Size and Number of Children, 2001

	Under 25	25–34	35–44	45–54	55–64	65–74	Over 75
Persons	1.9	2.9	3.3	2.7	2.1	1.9	1.5
Under 18	0.3	1.1	1.4	0.6	0.2	0.1	0.0

Source: Bureau of Labor Statistics, *Consumer Expenditure Survey* (2001).

This survey data is based on households and the number of individuals in the household changes over time. Table 12.3 shows that household size peaks during the 35–44 age band as children per household peak at 1.4. To avoid any confusion from changes in the size of households, Figure 12.20 also shows average consumption per household member. Household consumption peaks during the 45–54 age band, as does income, but individual consumption peaks during the "golden years" of 55–64 when children have left home. After this point, consumption continues to decline, as does income.

With income and consumption following such different paths, the household has to use savings to offset the differences. Table 12.4 shows the savings that accompany Figure 12.20: early in adult life consumers borrow and then repay their loans and accumulate funds, which they then run down slightly during retirement.

Although the life cycle model achieves many empirical successes, it does have some problems. In particular, older generations tend not to spend their savings at a very rapid rate, if at all. Two possibilities are frequently stressed to account for the reluctance of older generations to reduce their savings dramatically: uncertainty and bequests. First, uncertainty is critical. People don't know exactly when they are going to die. So the simple life cycle theory that says that people should decumulate wealth in retirement and have negative savings rates do not translate easily to a model in which people are uncertain about how long they will live. You may be afraid that you will live too long and run out of money, so you try to avoid exhausting your stock of wealth during retirement. And, of course, many people want to hand over substantial bequests to their heirs. The relative importance of uncertainty over longevity and the desire to leave a bequest are controversial as explanations for the surprisingly high savings rates of retired individuals, with some studies suggesting these motives account for more of U.S. wealth than life cycle savings.

KEY POINT

Because savings is likely to vary substantially over people's lives, changes in the overall demographic structure of a country are likely to have a significant impact upon its aggregate rate of saving.

TABLE 12.4   Savings Rates by Age, 2001

Under 25	25–34	35–44	45–54	55–64	65–74	Over 75
−13.3	20.2	20.4	21.6	20.2	1.1	−3.4

Source: Bureau of Labor Statistics, *Consumer Expenditure Survey* (1991).

SUMMARY

In section 12.1, we discussed the importance of consumption. Consumption accounts for around 60% of GDP and is closely tied to GDP growth over the business cycle. Consumption decisions also determine savings, which is a key determinant of the long-run standard of living.

In section 12.2, we saw that, traditionally, Keynesian economics has given a key role to consumption in influencing how fiscal policy impacts the economy. The key concept is the *marginal propensity to consume*—how much of an extra dollar of income is spent by an individual. In section 12.3, we examined the role of the m.p.c. and planned expenditure in creating a multiplier effect on output in an economy and looked at the Keynesian cross diagram, which relates planned expenditure and output.

The basic Keynesian model has consumption depending on current income. In section 12.4, we introduced the permanent income model, which offers a richer framework and has consumers smoothing their lifetime income by setting consumption equal to permanent income. The m.p.c. then depends on whether changes in income are perceived as temporary or permanent. In section 12.5, we saw that it also explains savings as dependent on future income expectations—if income is expected to grow, then savings are negative.

In section 12.6, we examined how the forward-looking model can produce a close relationship between current consumption and income, like the Keynesian model, but for different reasons. One reason is that individuals are sometimes unable to borrow; the other, that individuals are unsure of future income expectations and so base their current expenditure decisions on current income. In the forward-looking model, the impact of interest rates is ambiguous depending on the relative strength of income and substitution effects. For borrowers, the effect is for current consumption to fall, but for savers, the net effect is indeterminate.

Tracing through the impact of shifts in incomes and in interest rates upon consumption and the overall level of demand allows us to build up a simple model of the demand side of the economy. In section 12.7, we saw that the Keynesian cross and the IS curve are useful building blocks in this analysis.

In section 12.8, we examined the additional role of wealth in consumption choices and noted the difficulties for policy makers in predicting m.p.c. that are introduced by capital gains and consumers' expectations and uncertainty levels.

Finally, in section 12.9, we noted that, as well as depending on future income expectations, the pattern of consumption is also influenced by demographic considerations—in particular, the number of children in a household. Profiles of both income and consumption vary systematically with age, meaning that savings rates are also age dependent.

CONCEPTUAL QUESTIONS

1. (Section 12.1) Is there a useful distinction to be made between consumers' expenditure and consumption for (a) services, (b) nondurable goods, (c) durable goods? Might spending on these different components react very differently to changes in income and to interest rates?

2. (12.3) Use the Keynesian cross diagram to show how a fall in government spending can affect consumption.

3. (12.4) Draw indifference curves for a patient consumer compared to an individual with a need for instant gratification.

4. (12.4) What would the budget constraint look like if it were only possible to borrow at an interest rate higher than the deposit rate?

5. (12.4) When inflation increased sharply in the 1970s, the savings rate increased. Evaluate the role of interest rates and current and future income in explaining this phenomenon.

6. (12.4) The permanent income model assumes that you treat your current financial wealth and the present value of your discounted future income in the same way. Discuss the plausibility of this result.

7. (12.5) In practice, the m.p.c. out of current income is very high—is this necessarily inconsistent with the forward-looking model?

8. (12.5) What would be the impact on savings if the government introduced an unemployment insurance scheme?

9. (12.9) In the two-period model the consumer aimed to die with zero assets. What would be the planning horizon of parents who wished their children to enjoy the same standard of living they experienced? What is the planning horizon if every generation feels this way?

10. (12.9) How would an increase in the popularity of annuities affect levels of inheritances in a country? (Annuities are contracts where in exchange for handing over a lump sum of money today, a person receives a certain [known] amount of money each year until death.)

ANALYTICAL QUESTIONS

1. (Section 12.2) A consumer expects to earn the following sequence of income over the next five decades

   4   7   10   19   0

   (a) Using the forward-looking consumption smoothing model, calculate consumption, savings, and wealth for the consumer in each decade (assuming interest rates are zero).

   (b) The government introduces a tax system to pay benefits to all those earning less than 8. As a result, the net of tax income the individual earns (including benefits) changes to

   8   8   10   14   8

   Recalculate consumption, savings, and assets for each decade. What impact does the benefit system have on consumption?

2. (12.2) Consider an individual who is planning his consumption over five periods during which he expects his income to be 4, 10, 16, 12, and 8.

   (a) What is his permanent income?

   (b) What is his marginal propensity to consume out of a temporary increase that boosts first period income to 6?

   (c) What is the m.p.c. if the income increase of 2 is expected to continue into period 2?

   (d) What is the m.p.c. if the income increase of 2 is expected to continue for every period of the consumer's life?

3. (12.3) Suppose C = 100 + 0.7 Y, G = 50, I = 120

In a closed economy Y = C + I + G

(a) What is the equilibrium level of Y ?
(b) What happens if the level of consumption becomes C = 130 + 0.7 Y?
(c) What happens if the level of consumption becomes C = 120 + 0.85 Y?

Illustrate your answers using the Keynesian cross diagram.

4. (12.6) Consider the same consumer as in question 1, but now the consumer is unable to borrow—wealth always has to be positive.

(a) How does your answer to question 1a change?
(b) How does your answer to question 1b change?
(c) What difference is there in the way fiscal policy influences the economy in these two situations? Why?

5. (12.6) Consider a consumer who expects to receive income in five periods of 4, 12, 23, 16 and 0. In response to 5% interest rates, the consumer defers savings and aims for her consumption to grow by 1 every period. If interest rates are 10%, then she wishes her consumption to increase by 2 every period.

(a) Calculate consumption and savings in each period when interest rates are 5%.
(b) Repeat these calculations for interest rates at 10%. Comment on the relative income and substitution effects.

6. (12.7) Using the same simple model of the economy as in question 3, now allow for the impact of interest rates on consumption. The consumption function is:

$$Y = 120 + 0.7 Y - 10r$$

where r is the level of interest rates.

Calculate the equilibrium level of income when interest rates are 1, 2, 3, 4, 5, 6, 7, 8, 9 and 10% Draw the resulting IS curve.

CHAPTER 13

Investment

Overview

In this chapter we focus on capital spending in economies—investment in machinery, plant, buildings, and infrastructure. We also look at investment in intangible assets. Investment is the means by which a country preserves and enhances its productive potential; it is also a major source of demand for output. Investment expenditure, especially when it is taken to include the accumulation of inventories of goods (stockbuilding), is not only a significant element of overall demand, it is also a volatile one. Because investment also tends to be procyclical, it is a force behind business cycle fluctuations. We explore the determinants of investment expenditure and analyze why it is volatile. We also look at the distribution of spending among different types of capital goods and where that spending is done—domestically or overseas. Overseas investment (sometimes called foreign direct investment) has become more important to both developed and developing countries over the past 30 years, and we discuss this trend and its implications.

Key Concepts

Cost of Capital	Optimal Capital Stock	q Theory of Investment
Intangible Assets	Procyclical	Tax Wedges

13.1 Introduction: Investment and the Capital Stock

We have noted several times the staggering differences in standards of living across countries. Income per head in the United States is over 40 times as great as in many African countries. One factor behind this is differences in capital per worker. What we mean here is capital in the form of physical assets (steel mills, PCs, laboratories, trucks, buildings, telephone systems). Differences in the overall value of physical capital among countries can account for a substantial part—but by no means most—of the dif-

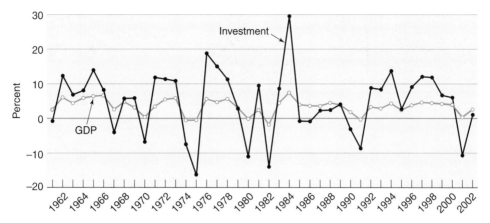

FIGURE 13.1   **Percent change in U.S. GDP and private sector investment.** Investment is procyclical and much more volatile than GDP. *Source:* OECD, *Economic Outlook* (2003).

ferences in standards of living.[1] The value of intangible assets—copyrights, brands, secret formulas, knowledge about how to organize physical capital to create value—is also great and possibly even more unequally distributed across countries. Calculations by Robert Hall suggest that perhaps 40% of the value of corporate assets in the United States reflects the worth of intangibles.[2]

The variability in physical capital per worker is itself marked; in some African countries, capital per worker is only a few hundred dollars; in the richest countries in the world it is close to $100,000. There is a clear, positive correlation between output per head and capital per head. This suggests that the accumulation of capital is a critical determinant of the standard of living. But there is almost certainly also a feedback from income to investment. Rich countries tend to invest a higher proportion of their output than do poor countries. This is particularly noticeable at low levels of income, where some countries are so poor that they can hardly set aside any income for capital accumulation.

Understanding what drives investment is critical not only for understanding movements in the standard of living of countries, but also for understanding the volatility of activity from year to year. Movements in investment expenditure tend to be sharper than shifts in other components of expenditure. Figure 13.1 shows a time series of the percentage change in real GDP and private sector investment for the United States.

---

[1] We are careful to use the term "account for" rather than "causally explain." The level of capital available to workers is an important factor behind productivity. But unless we understand how capital comes to be accumulated and the link between accumulation and incomes, we will not have an explanation of why labor productivity differs among countries.

[2] Hall, "The Stock Market and Capital Accumulation" NBER Working paper 7180 (June 1999). See also the later version of that paper with the same name that appeared in the *American Economic Review* (2001) vol. 91, pp. 1185–1202.

TABLE 13.1   **The Volatility of Investment**
Investment is more than twice as volatile as GDP.

1960–2002	% Change GDP (Standard Deviation)	% Change Investment (Standard of Deviation)
Germany	2.87	5.72
France	1.82	4.33
U.K.	1.94	5.31
U.S.	2.15	5.34

Source: OECD, *Economic Outlook* (2003).

Table 13.1 summarizes investment and GDP information for a range of developed economies. Here we define investment broadly to include spending on new plant and machines, buildings (including residential homebuilding), and inventory. The long-run trend in investment expenditure and in GDP is similar in all of these economies. But investment is much more volatile than GDP. In the big economies, changes in investment are more than twice as volatile as changes in GDP.

Changes in investment and GDP are highly correlated; investment is **procyclical**. That is, when output in the economy as a whole is rising rapidly, investment expenditure tends to increase sharply; when output growth falls, investment expenditure tends to decline markedly. Movements in investment expenditure may be disproportionately important in driving the business cycle.

When we talk about investment, we should be precise about what we mean. In Figure 13.1 and in Table 13.1, investment means the accumulation of physical capital. We are not talking about expenditure on the education system or on research and development. What we mean is investment in machines, buildings, and so on—tangible assets used in the production process. Expenditure on these kinds of capital assets is extremely important. Figure 13.2 shows investment as a proportion of GDP in some of the major economies since 1980. It is clear from the figure that investment expenditure is a substantial proportion of overall spending in developed economies—accounting for around one-quarter of GDP. In some developing nations, the ratio is even higher—in Korea in the 1990s and in China for the last 10 years, the investment to GDP ratio has been close to 40%. The part of overall production that is set aside for capital accumulation clearly differs across countries. In Japan, China, and South Korea, between 30 and

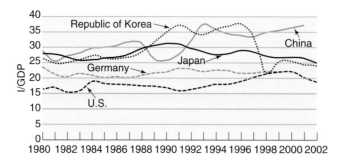

FIGURE 13.2   **Total fixed investment as percent of GDP.** *Source:* OECD, *Economic Outlook* (2003) and IMF, *International Financial Statistics* (2003).

40% of GDP has been used for investment during most of this period. In the United States and the United Kingdom, investment in physical capital has been only around half as much. But investment in intangible assets is both important and very hard to measure and it is possible that, once we account for intangible assets, the difference in overall investment rates between the United States and some other countries is not so great. We will return to this issue at the end of the chapter.

The figures we have looked at so far are for total (or gross) expenditure on investment. This is not the same as the net addition to the capital stock. Physical assets wear out, and much of total (or gross) investment simply replaces worn out capital. In developed economies, the stock of physical capital often has a value of around three times the value of annual output. Many machines become obsolete or just wear out within 10 to 20 years. Suppose we are looking at an economy that has a ratio of physical capital to annual GDP of 3, and where the typical machine has a useful economic life of about 20 years. With 20-year lives, about 5% of machines, on average, need to be replaced in any one year. With a ratio of the total capital stock to GDP of 3, this means that 15% of annual output would need to be set aside for investment simply to preserve the value of the capital stock. Given the substantial growth in physical capital over time, it is not surprising that investment relative to GDP is in excess of 15% in most developed countries, and often is double that level.

KEY POINT

A high level of gross investment is needed in developed countries just to prevent the capital stock from falling.

Even in the United States, where investment relative to GDP has been lower than in most other developed countries, the scale of net accumulation of capital has been substantial in the postwar era. Figure 13.3 shows the path that the measured market value of capital per worker in the United States took over this period. Between 1965

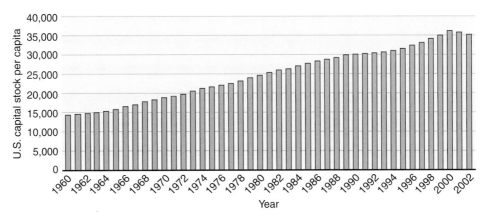

FIGURE 13.3 **U.S. capital stock per person.** The per capita stock in the United States has risen steadily over time. *Source:* OECD, *Economic Outlook* (2003).

and the early 1990s, the value of the physical capital per worker in the United States roughly doubled from about $15,000 to $30,000 (at 1985 prices). Capital per worker continued to rise through the 1990s. In fact, investment increased particularly fast in the 1990s as output and corporate profits grew rapidly. By the end of the century, the average U.S. worker had significantly more than three times the capital that was available in 1945 at the end of the World War II.

Such figures almost certainly underestimate the growth of effective machine power. Consider, for example, how computers have changed over the past 40 years. At the end of the 1940s, the largest computers could perform a few thousand floating point operations per second (flops). Such machines were enormous—the largest was so big and used so much electricity that, when it was running at full power, street lights in neighboring areas were often dimmed. Such machines were housed in large buildings and were valued at hundreds of thousands of dollars. Today, the most basic desktop PC can outperform these giants of the postwar period. Supercomputers today have teraflop power; they can perform one *trillion* flops per second. The power of machines has increased by a factor of about 1000 every 20 years since the 1940s. But the price of machines (which reflects how they get accounted for in valuing the capital stock) has plummeted. If you were to calculate what it might have cost in 1945 to build and run a computer with the same capacity as today's $1000 desktop PC, you might find that it would have cost several percentage points of GDP.

In countries where the investment to GDP ratio has been substantially higher than in the United States—Japan, Germany, South Korea—the rate of increase of capital per worker over the past few decades has been much faster. This reflects, to a large extent, their position in the aftermath of the World War II. As we noted in Chapter 4, in Japan and Germany war damage had decreased capital per worker by the end of the 1940s to low levels. Pictures of Tokyo, Berlin, Dresden, and Hiroshima from 1945 reveal the almost complete destruction of infrastructure, buildings, and factories. And South Korea was starting from a highly underdeveloped position when industrialization began to accelerate a few decades ago. So much of what we see in recent trends in investment in these countries reflects "catch-up." By contrast, the capital stock of the United States was unscathed. Of course, in the war years, U.S. military expenditure increased sharply, which probably squeezed out some domestic investment.

The notion of catch-up, which seemed plausible for Germany and Japan in the decades after World War II and seems plausible for China today, is based on a simple idea: at any point in time, there is a capital stock that is optimal and reflects the relative cost of machines against the extra profits that could be earned from their installation. This optimal capital stock level is likely to be different from the actual stock of capital in place in the economy. For a country emerging from a devastating war—where the capital stock has plummeted—the desired, or optimal, capital stock is likely to be substantially more than the actual capital stock. For a country with a huge workforce which is disciplined and educated and where the existing capital stock is low—China in the late 1990s—the same is likely to be true. Because installing new capital is costly and time consuming, it may take years to close most of the gap between the actual capital stock and the desired capital stock. So one would expect that levels of investment would remain high for a prolonged period. This simple idea doesn't seem controversial. But we have not yet specified in detail the key element: namely, the determinants of the optimal, or desired, stock of capital. In the next section, we will consider this in detail. For the moment, we note that the idea that a gap between the cost of machines and their rate of return drives investment is most readily applied to the private sector, where maximization of profits seems natural. Private sector capital accumulation is really the main focus of this chapter.

KEY POINT

When countries that might desire similar long-run capital stocks start from very different initial levels, investment ratios will be markedly different for many years.

13.2 The Optimal Stock of Capital

It makes sense for a company to expand its stock of capital if the cost of the additional investment turns out to be lower than the value of the extra profit the new machines generate. But it makes no sense to continue investing if the extra revenues from the new machine do not at least cover its cost. So we can think of the **optimal capital stock** as being that level beyond which extra returns are lower than cost, and below which extra returns exceed cost. Figure 13.4 shows a simple illustration of the determination of the desired capital stock. On the horizontal axis, we measure the total value of the machines that are already in place (that is, "the capital stock"), and on the vertical axis, we measure costs and marginal rates of return. It is important to be clear about the units in which we are measuring costs and returns here. When we think about costs, we are measuring the *extra* resources that are used over a particular period as a result of installing one extra unit of capital. Let us think of that period as one year. We can then measure the cost of capital as the resources that a company has to come up with to enjoy the use of a particular lump of capital for 12 months. And we measure the marginal product of capital as the *extra* profit that the company derives from having that capital in place over that period.

Of course, it is arbitrary to think of the period over which we measure extra profits, and the cost, as precisely 12 months. We should really think about how long the capital is in place and the stream of extra profit that it can generate over that period. You can hire, or rent, some pieces of capital for a day. If I hire a van to help me move furniture into my new house, then the relevant cost of capital is the one-day

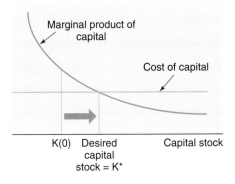

FIGURE 13.4 **What determines investment?** The optimal level of the capital stock is where the cost of capital just equals the marginal productivity of capital.

rental cost, and the gain is whatever money value I can put on the benefits of using a van for 24 hours. If we can buy a machine today and sell it again in a few months, then the relevant period to calculate profits against cost is a few months. Many machines remain in place for longer periods, perhaps 10 or 20 years. When we think about the extra profit that such a machine can earn and about its cost, then we may need to form expectations of those benefits and costs over many years. So, although we have simplified the time period to one year for our example, in practice the type of capital we are talking about greatly affects the time period for measuring costs and benefits.

Let us, for the moment, return to the somewhat abstract world depicted in Figure 13.4 and focus on how we actually measure the cost of capital. We need to think about the extra resources that using a piece of capital for "a period" consumes. This cost reflects several things. First, there is the cost of the funds tied up in the machine. Suppose that you bought a piece of capital machinery on January 1 and borrowed the money to finance the purchase. A major element of the cost of capital would then be the interest rate on the borrowed funds. If you sold the machine again at the end of the year, a second element of cost would be the change in its value, which itself reflects both depreciation (or wear and tear) and the change in the market price of that sort of capital.

So two of the major elements in the **cost of capital** are changes in the value of the machine and the cost of using funds. That second element—the cost of funds—is more subtle than simply the rate of interest. Most corporations, in fact, do not finance their investment expenditure by borrowing from banks, so we need to think about more than just a bank interest rate. Companies finance investment from many sources: they issue shares, retain profit, issue bonds, and sometimes rely on credit from suppliers of capital goods. The cost of capital should reflect the cost of each type of finance and its relative importance. Table 13.2 shows that, in the last quarter of the twentieth century, companies in Germany, Japan, the United States, and the United Kingdom, in aggregate, re-

TABLE 13.2   The Financing of Investment: Flow-of-Funds Estimated (%)

	Germany	Japan	U.K.	U.S.
Internal finance	78.4	69.9	95.6	94.0
Bank finance	12.0	30.1	15.0	12.8
Bond finance	−1.0	3.4	3.8	15.3
New equity	−0.02	3.4	−5.3	−6.1
Other	10.6	−6.8	−9.1	−16.0
Data sample	1970–94	1970–94	1970–94	1970–94

Note: Internal finance comprises retained earnings and depreciation. The "Other" category includes trade credit and capital transfers. The figures represent weighted averages where the weights for each country are the level of real fixed investment in each year in that country.

Source: Corbett and Jenkinson, "How Is Investment Financed?" The Manchester School (1996) vol. LXV, pp. 69–94.

lied on internal funds for a far higher proportion of their investment than borrowing from banks or issuing new debt or equity.[3] Of course, internal finance is not free!

When a company uses some of its profits to finance investment, there are opportunity costs involved. The company is using money that it could otherwise pay out to shareholders as dividends. And once the dividends are distributed to shareholders, they could earn a rate of return that reflects the investment opportunities open to investors. So we should think of the cost of internal finance as reflecting the rates of return that investors might earn on the funds if they were available to them. Those funds could be invested in the stock or bond markets or put in banks, so the overall cost to a firm of using internal finance should reflect the varying rates of return that could be earned on a whole range of financial assets.

And then, of course, there is risk. The shareholders in a company may perceive investments in that company as more risky than putting money in the government bond market or buying a diversified portfolio of equities. In this case, the cost of capital to the individual firm will reflect not just the rates of return that could be earned on other assets, but also a risk premium to reflect greater uncertainty over returns.

In figuring out the cost of capital, as well as the required rates of return that investors might expect on different assets, we must also consider the impact of the tax system. Interest on debt is usually tax-deductible to corporations, so this helps determine both the relative attractiveness of debt and equity to companies and the overall level of the cost of capital. Tax also plays a key role in calculating the marginal product of capital. Companies pay tax on profits that they earn, and these taxes are a deduction from the available profits. In fact, the tax system is much more complicated than this. Depreciation of capital is often tax-deductible, and companies may enjoy tax incentives to undertake investment.[4] We shall see below that the impact of taxes on investment differs in important ways across countries.

KEYPOINT

The optimal amount of capital is that level above which additions to the stock increase costs more than they increase revenues. At this point, the marginal product of capital equals the marginal cost of capital; the latter is often called the marginal user cost of capital.

PUTTING IT ALL TOGETHER . . .

An example may help to draw together some of the key factors that determine the cost of capital and the marginal returns on extra investment, the factors we expect to influence optimal capital accumulation. Suppose a company is trying to figure out how many new PCs to buy for its workforce. First, let us look at the returns from this company's investment in PCs. It reckons that 1000 computers would increase productivity such

---

[3] Internal funds means profit not paid out to shareholders that is available to finance expenditure.

[4] Governments in developed countries have often introduced tax breaks to encourage investment expenditure, especially when investment looks low and the economy is in a slump. The effectiveness of tax breaks, which may prove temporary, is questionable given the length of life of much capital equipment. Temporary tax breaks may also affect the *timing* of investment expenditure more than the *amount* of capital accumulation.

TABLE 13.3

| Number of New PCs | Estimated Net Extra Revenue ($ Million Over a Year) | |
	Gross	After Tax
250	937,500	703,125
500	1,650,000	1,237,500
750	2,250,000	1,687,500
1000	2,800,000	2,100,000
1250	3,100,000	2,325,000
1500	3,200,000	2,400,000
1750	3,250,000	2,437,500

that gross revenues would be $3 million higher over a year. In addition to paying for the PCs themselves, the company would need to hire people to provide software and hardware support and probably do some training of the existing workforce. After subtracting these extra labor costs, the company still expects to generate net higher revenues of $2.8 million. More computers would probably generate yet more revenue; fewer would probably give less revenue. Table 13.3 shows the extra gross revenues that the company can expect to achieve by buying various numbers of PCs. We are concerned with extra after-tax profit, so we need to take account of extra taxes that will have to be paid on increased revenues. Let us assume the corporate tax rate is 25%. The right-hand column in Table 13.3 shows the extra post-tax revenues.

Next, let's consider the extra costs of the PCs. The machines cost $1000 dollars each and will be sold at the end of the year. The resale price of a PC is estimated to be $500 dollars. The company will be able to deduct the depreciation of 50% (or $500 dollars) from its taxable profit, so we must take this into account in calculating the cost of having the machines for one year. The gross cost of each machine is $500, but the post-tax cost is $0.75 \times \$500 = \$375$. The company still needs to find $1000 dollars to pay for each machine bought at the start of the year. Suppose that the investment cost will come from retained profit and that shareholders (who would otherwise get the funds) can earn a nominal rate of return of 12%. The cost of using $1000 of shareholders' funds for a year is, therefore, the $120 dollars they could have earned on the cash. So the overall cost of each machine over one year is this $120 dollars plus the $375 coming from the depreciation; this generates a flat per-machine cost of $495. We can now draw up a schedule of the extra cost of installing various numbers of machines versus the extra net revenues they generate; this makes it easy in Table 13.4 to see the optimal level of investment.

The best bet would be to buy about 1250 machines. Buying this many PCs generates a net gain, having taken account of all the costs of using the machines for a year, of about $1.71 million; this is more extra profit than when fewer or more new machines are purchased.

A useful way to find the same answer is to draw up a schedule showing the extra cost, and extra after-tax revenues, of having a *further* 250 machines starting from differ-

TABLE 13.4

Number of New PCs	Extra After Tax Revenue	Extra Cost	Net Gain
250	703,125	123,750	579,375
500	1,237,500	247,500	990,000
750	1,687,500	371,250	1,316,250
1000	2,100,000	495,000	1,605,000
1250	2,325,000	618,750	1,706,250
1500	2,400,000	742,500	1,657,500
1750	2,437,500	866,250	1,571,250

ent points. You can easily calculate the schedule from the last one by simply taking the difference between successive entries in each column. This generates *marginal* (or incremental) revenue and *marginal* cost for each *marginal* 250 machines. The first two columns in Table 13.5 correspond to the marginal product and cost of capital schedules in Figure 13.4 (the latter is constant in this example). So long as marginal product exceeds marginal cost, expanding the number of PCs generates a net increment to profit, so the total profit figure will increase. Between 1250 and 1500 machines, net revenue from the extra machine dips below the extra cost. So total profit is maximized when the firm buys a few more than 1250 machines, at a point where the cost of a machine (the cost of capital) equals the extra revenue it generates (its marginal productivity, or marginal revenue).

Figure 13.4 depicts a situation that is consistent with our numerical example and where the marginal product of capital itself falls with the value of the capital stock. This is probably plausible for an individual company. The greater the capital stock, the larger the level of output and, beyond a certain point, price probably has to fall to sell more of a product, so marginal profitability declines. If the cost of capital is either flat or increasing, and the marginal product of capital schedule, at least beyond some point, begins to decline, then there will be a unique desired capital stock. In Figure 13.4, initial capital is at level K(0) and desired capital is at level K(*). If there are costs in adjusting

TABLE 13.5

Number of New PCs	Marginal Revenue	Marginal Cost	Net Marginal Profit
250	703,125	123,750	579,375
500	534,375	123,750	410,625
750	450,000	123,750	326,250
1000	412,500	123,750	288,750
1250	225,000	123,750	101,250
1500	75,000	123,750	−48,750
1750	37,500	123,750	−86,250

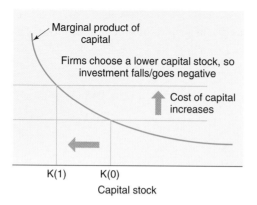

FIGURE 13.5 **What happens when interest rates increase?** A rise in the cost of capital, other things remaining equal, reduces the optimal capital stock.

the capital stock quickly, then investment will be undertaken to close the gap between K(0) and K(*) over some period; but we will not jump straight to the new level. The amount of time taken to close the gap between current capital and optimal capital reflects the size of the gap and the costs of installation of capital.

We can use this framework to analyze the impact of changes in some of the main determinants of the capital stock. Figure 13.5 shows what happens when the cost of capital increases. If firms were initially at their optimal capital stock, so that K(0) coincided with K(*), then anything that causes the cost of capital to increase will take the new optimal level of capital *beneath* the current level (to K(1)). Many things could increase the cost of capital. Investors may suddenly come to see the risks of investing in corporations as having increased, in which case the risk premiums on corporate capital will rise, meaning that the required rates of return on new investment need to be higher. Or, the monetary authorities may increase interest rates, which may cause bond prices to fall, thereby increasing companies' nominal cost of borrowing. (The lower are bond prices, the greater is the cost for firms in selling bonds to finance investment; we explore the link between bond prices and the required rates of return of investors in Chapter 18). Unless there is an offsetting increase in expectations of inflation, then the *real* cost of borrowing has risen, and the cost of the capital schedule will move up. The negative impact of a rise in interest rates upon investment is one of the important factors that lies behind the IS curve that we built up in section 12.7. We might, in fact, expect investment to be more sensitive to a change in interest rates than is consumption expenditure. In addition, because the user cost of capital depends upon much else besides interest rates, other factors will also drive investment. Changes in the tax system (for example, reductions in the generosity of deductions of interest charges against taxable profit) could have the same impact as a movement in interest rates.

If the cost of capital increases, for whatever reason, then the optimal stock of capital will be lower. However, companies may not be able to reduce their capital stock instantly to a lower level. The transition from K(0) to K(1) following a rise in the cost of capital could, in fact, take years. If a firm finds that its optimal capital stock is substantially beneath its current level of capital, then it may decide to undertake zero *gross* investment for some years and allow depreciation to gradually reduce its capital.

Note that all this tends to make investment expenditure volatile. Small movements in the cost of capital could take the equilibrium level K* from being slightly in excess of K(0) to well beneath it. If a company found that K* was in excess of K(0), it would want to undertake positive net investment, which, given depreciation, could imply substantial levels of *gross* investment. But if K* then dipped beneath K(0), the firm might find it optimal to reduce gross investment to *zero*, as we have noted. This is one reason why investment expenditure might be more volatile than consumption expenditure. It would be unusual for an individual to decide to cut consumption to *zero* in response to news about interest rates or future incomes, but it is not unusual for firms to move from substantial *net* investment to zero *gross* investment from one year to the next.

KEY POINT

Investment expenditure is likely to be much more volatile than consumption. The sensitivity of investment to the cost of borrowing is an important factor behind the shape of the IS curve.

One of the main driving forces behind investment expenditure is technological advances. Many companies spend a lot of money on computer systems because computer hardware and software technology has advanced so dramatically in the last 20 years that one generation of machines is virtually obsolete within a few years. Again, we can use the simple framework we have developed to analyze the impact of technological breakthroughs. If a new invention dramatically increases the productivity of capital, then the marginal product of capital schedule will shift significantly outward. Figure 13.6 illustrates this. After a technological breakthrough, you might expect dramatic investment for substantial periods of time. You might also expect existing machines that have become obsolete to be scrapped. Technological progress can simultaneously increase both gross investment and the scrapping of existing machines. So its overall impact on the value of the net capital stock may not be dramatically positive. But its impact on productivity may, nonetheless, be profound. We see here another reason why investment expenditure is likely to be more volatile than consumption expenditure. Technological breakthroughs often profoundly affect the structure of the capital stock and can be sudden and hard to predict.

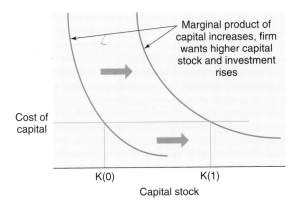

FIGURE 13.6 **What happens with technological breakthrough?** An increase in productivity raises the optimal stock of capital.

13.3 Investment and the Stock Market

We noted above that in the largest developed economies, corporations finance most of their investment expenditure from internal resources; ultimately this is shareholders' capital. The stock market valuation of companies' existing capital reflects the return that shareholders might earn on funds. So we should expect to see a link between levels of investment companies undertake and the stock market. In fact, the link was elegantly and formally set out many years ago by James Tobin, who developed the so-called **q theory** of investment. Tobin noted that if the value of a company on the stock market was substantially more than the replacement cost of the assets that the firm employs (most of which we will assume are some form of capital equipment), then in principle that company has a major incentive to increase investment. When we think about the replacement value of capital here, we mean the current cost of buying the sorts of machines that the company uses. If the ratio between the value of its shares and the replacement cost of that firm's capital stock is greater than 1, then the stock market is valuing the firm at more than it would cost to replace all its capital by buying new machines. If that were the case, a company would have an incentive to replicate itself by expanding its capital stock, and its stock market valuation would rise by more than the cost of the investment. The company could finance the purchase of the new machines from its existing shareholders who would enjoy immediate gains as the firm's stock market value increased by more than the cost of the new machines. The ratio between the value of a firm's shares (or its stock market valuation) and the replacement cost of its capital stock is Tobin's "q."

Consider the example of a small company that produces specialized pistons for high-performance car engines. Suppose the stock market valuation of this company is $200 million. The assets of the company are really of two sorts: (1) the physical plant, machinery, and buildings with which it produces pistons and (2) its less tangible assets, like the experience of its workforce and the value of the techniques that the firm has developed. Suppose that the firm can hire more workers with the same skills and at the same cost as the current workforce, and that it can sell more pistons on the same terms as existing output. This means that doubling the productive capacity—buying new machines, getting new buildings, hiring more workers, and so on—should double the value of the firm. Suppose that the existing machines, buildings, and such have a replacement cost of $150 million. Because the existing company is valued at $200 million, and it costs $150 million to double productive capacity, the company could increase its market value by $200 million by spending $150 million; obviously this is a good deal.

In this example, Tobin's q is well in excess of 1 (it is 200/150 = 1.333), so there is a clear incentive to invest. Note that we specified that the firm could expand production by taking on extra workers who were no more costly and no less productive than the existing ones. We also assumed that the firm could sell the extra pistons at no lower a price and, further, that the techniques they had developed (whose worth the market value of the existing firm reflected) could be applied as productively to the operation of the new machines as the old ones. These assumptions ensured that the value of existing assets was a guide to the increase in value that expanding capacity would bring. (Put more technically, we needed to ensure that the average q on the existing assets was equal to the marginal q on new investments.)

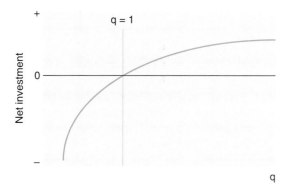

FIGURE 13.7 **The q theory of investment.** When q is above 1 there is an incentive to undertake net investment because the rate of return on capital is larger than cost of capital.

The q theory has a simple prediction for the relationship between the level of investment and the value of the stock market, and Figure 13.7 depicts it. If the q of a company exceeds 1, that company should find that the cost of buying machines is below the value that the stock market will then place on those machines. This is an incentive for a firm to expand and start investing, which will be in the interest of its shareholders. By the same token, if Tobin's q is less than 1, then the stock market is valuing the capital of a company at less than its replacement cost. This means that, were a company to undertake investment, it would find that the cost of buying the machines was greater than the value the market placed on those machines. Firms would have no incentive to invest under such circumstances. In fact, they should start selling their capital because they would get more for it on the secondhand market than the value shareholders placed on it.

KEY POINT

The q theory of investment implies that we should expect to see a strong link between movements in the stock market value of firms and their levels of investment.

The q theory is closely linked to the idea that firms should invest if the rate of return on new capital exceeds the cost of capital. To see this, assume that a firm can get a return on new investment that is close to the return on its existing capital. Then a good way to measure the marginal rate of return is to take the ratio between the profits earned on the existing capital and the replacement cost of that capital. (For simplicity, we assume here that it is an all-equity-financed firm, but this is not essential to the logic of the argument.) This ratio tells you the average rate of return given the actual purchase price of machines, and this is the relevant number when considering buying a new machine. So our measure of the rate of return is

profits / replacement cost of capital

What about the cost of capital? If a firm is generating just enough profits to satisfy its shareholders, we would expect that the ratio of profits to stock market value is equal to shareholders' required rate of return. So a measure of the cost of capital is

profits / stock market value of firm

The ratio of our measure of the rate of return to the cost of capital is therefore

[profit / replacement cost of capital] / [profit / stock market value of firm]
= stock market value of firm / replacement cost of capital = q

Thus q is the ratio of the rate of return to the cost of capital. As noted above, if $q > 1$, the rate of return exceeds the cost of capital, and the capital stock should be expanded. If $q < 1$, the rate of return falls short of the cost of capital, and the capital stock should not be expanded.

The q theory of investment implies that there should be a positive link between stock market valuations (relative to the purchase cost of plant, machines, buildings, and so forth) and the level of investment. But empirical evidence suggests that there is not such a clear link. Figure 13.8 plots changes in the level of investment expenditure in the United States charted against the change in stock prices. While the two move roughly in line, the correlation between them is low. Similar pictures could be drawn for all the major economies.

What are we to make of the relatively weak link between stock prices and levels of investment? The most natural interpretation may be that corporations do not find sudden shifts in stock market valuations informative when it comes to predicting rates of return they can earn on new investment. Given the volatility in stock prices, often apparently unrelated to shifts in fundamental factors that might influence profitability, they may be right. If stock prices have a tendency to become unconnected with fundamental economic forces—supply and demand for goods—then firms would not be helping their shareholders by undertaking massive bouts of investment every time the stock market moved up sharply, only to slam on the brakes when stock prices plummet.

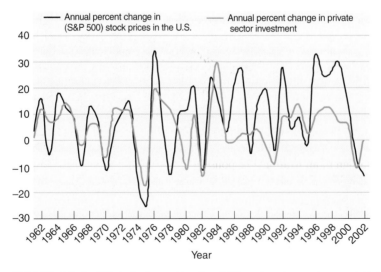

FIGURE 13.8 **U.S. stock prices and investment.** There is at best only a weak link between movements in stock prices and changes in investment. *Source:* OECD, *Economic Outlook* (2003) and Thomson Financial Datastream.

Paradoxically, in the light of the failure of q theory to account for much of the variability in investment, many commentators have blamed relatively low levels of investment in the United States and the United Kingdom over the past 40 years on the greater role that stock markets might play in allocating resources in those countries. During the 1980s and for much of the 1990s, the "short termism" hypothesis gained ground in those countries. Its advocates claimed that in countries where the stock market was really significant (for example, where the total values of stocks were large relative to GDP) and where takeovers often shifted corporate control, that firms had to pay too much attention to their stock price and that short-term movements in equity prices had undue influence. Furthermore, they argued that companies in the United States and the United Kingdom were far less inclined to think about long-term profitability of investment expenditure and had a tendency to underinvest as a result. In contrast, companies in Germany and Japan, where it appeared that stock market values were less important and borrowing through the banking system relatively more important, were more inclined to invest in the long term.

The British finance minister Nigel Lawson asserted in the 1980s that

The big institutional investors nowadays increasingly react to short-term pressure on investment performance . . . (and) . . . are increasingly unwilling to countenance long-term investment.

At about the same time as Lawson made his claim, the actor Michael Douglas, playing the role of Gordon Gekko in the film *Wall Street*, was asserting that greed was good and was the ultimate driving force behind the efficient allocation of resources.

In the 1980s many agreed with Lawson and felt that Gekko was trying to defend the indefensible (which is what the film's director, Oliver Stone, believed). However, the depression into which Japan fell in the early 1990s, and sustained expansion in U.S. output and stock prices throughout the 1990s, reduced the popularity of the short termism hypothesis. In fact, the tone of much popular comment on the role of stock markets and the efficiency of corporations in the United States and the United Kingdom relative to Germany and Japan was transformed. By the end of the 1990s, the United States had enjoyed an almost unprecedented period of sustained and high GDP growth and in contrast, Japan was suffering an unprecedented period of stagnant (indeed falling) output and rising unemployment. In the United Kingdom, where Germany had long been a point of comparison for economic performance, unemployment had fallen to about one-half the German rate. Suddenly all the short termism seemed to be in Japan, and in Europe the creaking inefficiency seemed to be in Germany, not the United Kingdom! In Japan, the government seemed incapable of stimulating consumption or investment expenditure, and the media now interpreted the high levels of investment undertaken there in the 1980s more as a sign of an irrational response to a speculative bubble in asset prices than as level-headed and far-sighted investment in projects with solid long-term payoffs.

In fact, the whole short-termism debate now seems wrongheaded. The United States, the United Kingdom, Japan, and Germany have far more in common in financing and investment than is generally perceived. Table 13.2 showed that in all four countries *new* equity finance[5] was, in aggregate, unimportant and that debt finance was also

---

[5] As opposed to retained profit, which we can think of as *old* equity finance, i.e., funds that shareholders allow the company to use to finance company expenditure that could otherwise have been paid to them as dividends.

TABLE 13.6   **Balance Sheet Measures of Gearing (%)**

	Germany	Japan	U.K.	U.S.
Market value				
Median	15	17	11	23
Aggregate	6	28	13	31
Book value				
Median	18	37	16	33
Aggregate	10	49	19	45

Notes: Estimates for 1991. Gearing is measured broadly as total debt over total assets. The sample of firms comprises those nonfinancial companies covered by the Global Vantage data set that reported consolidated balance sheets in 1991. Adjusted liabilities are defined as total liabilities, less pension liabilities (in Germany), less cash. Adjusted debt is measured as the book value of debt, less cash and marketable securities. Adjusted assets are total assets, less cash and short-term securities, less pension liabilities (in Germany), less intangibles. Adjusted book value of equity is book equity, plus provisions, plus deferred taxes, less intangibles.

Source: Rajan and Zingales, "What Do We Know About Capital Structure: Some Evidence From International Data" *Journal of Finance* (1995) vol. 50, pp. 1421–1460.

much less important than internal funding. Table 13.6 shows that gearing—the ratio between a company's debt and its overall assets—does not vary much across countries. The United Kingdom and Germany have similar corporate balance sheets, at least in terms of the relative use of debt and equity. The same is true of the United States and Japan.

If the short-termism debate seems to have missed the point, we are still left with a puzzle as to why there is apparently such a weak link between movements in stock market value and investment. One factor that may be crucial is the role of intangible assets and investment in them. We return to this issue in the final section of this chapter.

13.4   Cash Flows and Investment

Relatively heavy reliance on internal resources to finance investment suggests that shifts in current profits may have more influence on levels of investment expenditure than do movements in stock prices, or even shifts in expectations of future profits. Of

course, this isn't how we analyzed investment expenditure in the abstract models outlined above. There, what really mattered was the relative magnitude of the cost of capital and the marginal rate of return on new investment. Current cash flow or the amount
of internal revenue that the company generated played no role. Investment depended
completely on the *potential* returns and costs of new investment rather than on the revenue generated by existing capital. If current profits were, in fact, a key determinant of
investment expenditure, it would not only be in marked contrast to the simple model, it
would also suggest that resources could become significantly misallocated. If existing
cash flow, rather than potential profitability, determines investment, then in periods of
buoyant profits, companies might tend to overinvest and they might underinvest when
current profits were low. Investment could also destabilize the macroeconomy. Corporate profits and revenues would tend to be high during booms, and if investment also
tended to be high, it would exacerbate the economic cycle; similarly, corporate revenues would tend to fall in recessions, and investment expenditure might also decline.

Because of the influence on business cycles, it is important to find out whether or
not the cash flow story of investment is correct. This is a controversial area, and the evidence is not straightforward. The problem is that movements in current profits not only
generate shifts in available resources (i.e., in cash flow), they also, plausibly, should influence expectations of the *future* profitability of investment expenditure. Even a high
correlation between current profits and levels of investment would not prove that available cash flow is the key variable that drives investment. It could simply reflect a strong
correlation between expectations of high future profitability on capital and high current
profitability. Indeed, it would be bizarre if such a correlation did not exist.

So an apparent link between current cash flows and investment expenditure does
not indicate that something has gone wrong with how corporations make investment
decisions. There are, nonetheless, worrying signs. Surveys in the United States[6] and in
the United Kingdom[7] in the 1990s revealed that companies seemed to apply unusual
criteria in deciding whether to undertake investment projects. Specifically, they appeared to require rates of return on investment expenditure that are often dramatically higher than the rates of return that investors typically receive on funds. It looks,
at face value, as if firms are requiring hurdle rates of return[8] on potential new investment projects that are much larger than rates of return that you might expect investors
to be content with. Could this affect the relatively low levels of investment expenditure
in the United Kingdom and in the United States? Again, the evidence is far from conclusive. Managers of corporations, who are used to inflated forecasts of profits about
projects from those in the company who have the most to gain from expansion, may
tend to correct for this excess optimism by applying a higher discount factor. Of
course, this isn't the right way to handle excess optimism: a better strategy would be to
scale back the inflated expectations of profits that come from the planning department.
But, as a rough and ready response to institutionalized excess optimism, it is at least
understandable.

[6] By Jim Poterba and Lawrence Summers.

[7] By the Bank of England.

[8] That is, minimum required rates of return on new investment projects

13.5   Lumpy Investment and Business Cycles

We have assumed that if a firm finds a gap between its existing and desired stock of capital, it will aim to close it through new investment. But how quickly will the gap be closed? This depends on the costs of installing new machines. Consider this description of retooling in the U.S. auto industry:

> *When the line was stopped at the end of the model run, the bulk of the production force would be laid off, new machinery would be installed, new dies moved into place, and the assembly line rearranged for the production of the new model.*[9]

The auto industry evidently has major costs updating and replacing machines—production is disrupted (indeed it halts!). This is likely to be true in many companies. If the disruption costs of installing capital are high, then it makes sense for companies to concentrate their investment in particular periods; better to do a major overhaul of equipment once every three years and close down production for a while than to have production continually disrupted by installing some new capital every month.

Empirical evidence supports the idea that investment is lumpy. In the United States a study of plant-level investment in the 1970s and 1980s showed that companies concentrated their spending on particular plants and in particular periods. U.S. economists Doms and Dunne found that firms tended to do more than 50% of their total investment over a 17-year period in the years on either side of their peak spending year. Figure 13.9 indicates how bunched expenditure can be. It shows the proportion of total investment a sample of U.S. firms undertook per year over 20 years. Across the sample of firms, almost 17% of investment over the 20-year period was, typically, undertaken in the year of heaviest investment. Less than 1% of investment was typically undertaken in the year when spending was lowest.

This bunching of investment would not have any obvious macroeconomic significance if different firms bunched spending at different times. Aggregate investment would be smooth even if company-level expenditure was irregular, as long as all companies did not tend to bunch their spending at the same time. But in fact, companies will tend to bunch spending together if common factors are driving the optimal level of capital. Shifts in interest rates set by the central bank or tax rates set by government will move the cost of capital for all companies in the same direction at the same time and will also move their optimal (or target) capital stocks in the same direction. General productivity shocks (such as advances in technology) will have common effects and will also tend to make investment procyclical, because improvements in productivity will boost current output and simultaneously increase the desired capital stock, which encourages new investment. Firms in general are also likely to become more optimistic about the future when aggregate output is growing fast.

The lumpiness of investment, its concentration in particular periods, and its tendency to be high when output is already rising mean that movements in investment expenditure significantly affect business cycle fluctuations, as we saw in Figures 13.1 for

---

[9] Sidney Fine, quoted in Cooper and Haltiwanger "The Macroeconomic Implications of Machine Replacement: Theory and Evidence" *American Economic Review* (1993) vol. 83, pp. 360–382.

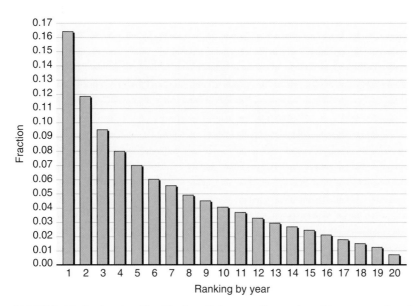

FIGURE 13.9 **Investment bunching in particular years.** Proportion of investment done in different years ranked from heaviest to lightest years by form. *Source:* Cooper, Haltiwanger, and Power, "Machine Replacement and the Business Cycle: Limps and Bumps," *American Economic Review* (September 1999) vol. 89, no. 4, pp. 921–946.

the United States. That role is greater when companies' expectations about future demand are more volatile, and when companies' expectations are more sensitive to shifts in current spending. There are different possible explanations for this effect. Keynes argued that those expectations of future demand conditions were unstable and that waves of optimism and pessimism among firms generated investment booms and slumps that exacerbated business cycle fluctuations. The evidence of the volatility of investment, and its procyclicality, supports the Keynesian view. But if shifts in technology, which generate surges in productivity, are the real force behind business cycle fluctuations, then this would offers an alternative explanation for why investment is volatile and procyclical.

KEY POINT

Bunching of investment stems from many forces, one of which might be that optimism and pessimism are contagious, self-reinforcing, and perhaps also self-fulfilling.

13.6 Foreign Direct Investment and the Global Capital Market

Increasingly firms in the developed world make their investment decisions by asking not just what the optimal stock of capital is, but also where in the world that capital should be installed. Over the past 30 years, corporations in the developed economies

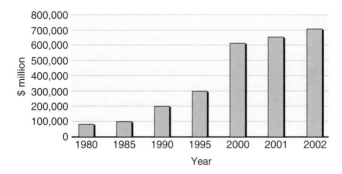

FIGURE 13.10 **World foreign direct investment.** World stock of Foreign Direct Investment ($ millions). *Source:* UNCTAD, *World Investment Report* (2003).

have channeled an increasing proportion of their capital expenditure overseas; these economies have been sending more investment to other countries *and* have been receiving more inward investment from abroad. Figure 13.10 shows the stock of foreign direct investment (FDI) relative to GDP for the industrialized countries. Over the past twenty years there has been a huge increase in the stock of foreign direct investment. This represents a huge increase in the internationalization of investment flows. Although the scale of this investment has risen sharply over the past twenty-five years, it is certainly not unprecedented. In the nineteenth century, much of the investment that made the United States an industrial superpower was FDI.

KEY POINT

Flows of foreign direct investment (FDI) have increased greatly since the late 1980s. An increasing proportion of world investment is now undertaken by multinational companies.

There are obvious reasons why both the marginal productivity of capital and the cost of capital can differ across countries. If technology is common across countries (and a multinational corporation can use the same know-how in Mozambique as in Manhattan), then differences in capital–labor ratios and wages can generate big differences in the marginal returns on new investment. Differences in taxation can also be a big factor, both on the cost side (e.g., differences in the rate at which interest payments can be deducted against the company tax bill) and on the revenue side (e.g., differences in tax rates on profits).

Figures 13.11*a, b,* and *c,* show an estimate of different overall tax rates on various sorts of capital investment across developed countries. These calculations take into account the taxation of corporate income and the value of allowances that companies can claim against tax. They also reflect the tax treatment of income to those who provide funds, that is, the investors. Because the tax that investors pay generally depends on their income, we have to make some assumption about who the investor is before we can calculate the overall impact of the tax system on the incentives to invest in different types of physical capital. The OECD data in the figures assume that the investor is someone earning average income for that country. The figures show the so-called **tax wedge** on various types of capital investment relative to a bank deposit. This is the difference between the required pretax return on the relevant capital (machinery, buildings, or inventories) and the interest rate required from a bank deposit, so as to generate the same after-tax return.

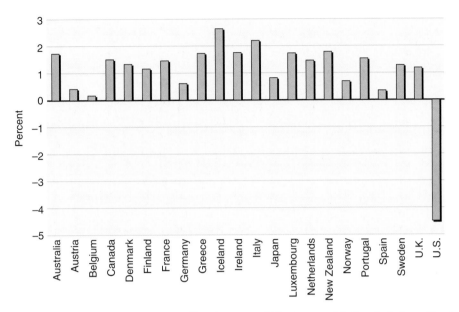

FIGURE 13.11a   **Tax wedges on machinery investment, 1996.** *Source:* OECD calculations (Gordon and Tchilinguirian, "Marginal Effective Tax Rates on Physical, Human and R&D Capital," OECD Discussion Paper 199, 1988). Copyright OECD.

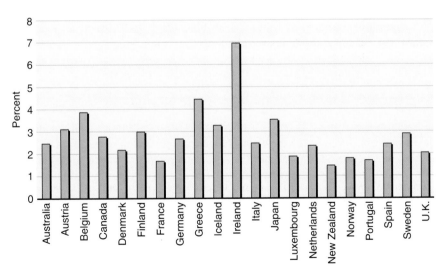

FIGURE 13.11b   **Tax wedges on inventory investment, 1996.** *Source:* OECD calculations (Gordon and Tchilinguirian, "Marginal Effective Tax Rates on Physical, Human and R&D Capital," OECD Discussion paper 199, 1998). Copyright OECD.

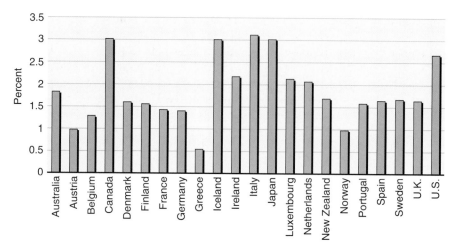

FIGURE 13.11c **Tax wedges on building investment, 1996.** Tax systems differ greatly across countries, creating a wide range of incentive and disincentives to invest. *Source:* OECD calculations (Gordon and Tchilinguirian, "Marginal Effective Tax Rates on Physical, Human and R&D Capital," OECD Discussion Paper 199, 1998).

Figure 13.11a shows that the tax system in the United States made investment in machinery profitable even though the machines might have generated a pretax (gross) return 4.5% below the return on a bank deposit. So in 1996, the United States effectively subsidized investment in machinery. Figures 13.11b and 13.11c show that investment in buildings and inventories in the United States was, in contrast, taxed more heavily than bank deposits. These figures reveal that tax on various types of capital investment varies across countries, which has influenced cross-border flows of investment. Careful empirical research by Cummins, Hubbard and Hassett suggests that tax factors are powerful influences upon investment.[10]

13.7 Intangible Assets and Investment in Intangibles

We noted that the q theory of investment, although theoretically compelling, did not seem to match the facts very well. The match between movements in q (the ratio of the stock market value of firms and the replacement cost of their capital) and the level of investment in physical capital was not a close one. We must remember, however, that the value of a firm reflects not just the physical assets it has, but also the value of other factors—brands, copyrights, and know-how embedded in the work practices of a company and not easily transferred to other companies. These **intangible assets** do not just fall from heaven—research and development, staff training, and trial and error in management practices and design all go into building up a stock of intangible assets. Expen-

---

[10] Cummins, Hassett, and Hubbard: "Tax reforms and Investment: a Cross Country Comparison," NBER Discussion paper 5232 (August 1995).

diture on that kind of activity to enhance the value of the firm is really a form of investment, but it is hard to measure. By their very nature, intangible assets are not easy to put a price on. There is, however, an indirect means of measuring the value of intangible assets and the scale of investment in them. We could subtract from the market value (that is the stock market value) of a firm the value of its physical (tangible) assets. Whatever is left over is the value of intangibles. We can infer from changes in that value what the scale of investment in intangibles has been.

This is the technique followed by Robert Hall in his analysis of the U.S. stock market and corporate capital.[11] He argues that the differences between the market values of U.S. corporations and plausible assessments of the cost of their physical assets provide a good estimate of the value of their intangible assets. Figure 13.12 shows Hall's estimate of the ratio of the stock market value of U.S. companies to the replacement cost of their plant and equipment. This is often interpreted as Tobin's q, a number that we expect to be around one. Hall interprets the deviations of this ratio from unity as reflecting the value of intangible assets. In the 1960s and again in the late 1990s, the ratio was around 1.4. Hall interprets this as implying that the value of intangible assets was around 40%, on average, of the value of the tangible assets of U.S. companies. Hall suggests that the big increase in the ratio in the 1990s reflects massive investment by U.S. companies in intangible assets—largely related to the acquisition of know-how in the use of information technology (which he argues was much larger than the value of physical capital in IT goods such as computers).

In some way this is a non-testable theory. We cannot easily measure the value of intangible assets except by looking at the difference between the stock market value of firms and the value of their tangible assets. But suppose stock market values are volatile creatures that are sometimes driven by waves of excess optimism and pessimism rather than by a cool assessment of the true worth of the know-how of a company? In that case, Hall's measure of intangibles will bear little relation to something of real value. As Jason Cummins notes in a recent paper,[12] according to this market-based approach, Yahoo's intangible assets were worth about $100 billion in 2001 and worth less than a tenth of that number in 2003. Is that really plausible?

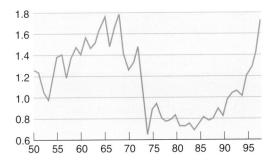

FIGURE 13.12 **Tobin's q—ratio of market value to reproduction cost of plant and equipment.** *Source:* Hall, "The Stock Market and Capital Accumulation" NBER working paper 7180 (June 1999). See also the later version of that paper with the same name that appeared in the *American Economic Review* (2001) vol. 91, pp. 1185–1202.

[11] Hall, "The Stock Market and Capital Accumulation," *American Economic Review* (2001) vol. 91, pp. 1185–1202.

[12] Cummins, "A New Approach to the Valuation of Intangible Capital," NBER Discussion paper 9924 (2003).

We return to this profound question of what stock market valuations really reveal in Chapter 17.

SUMMARY

At the beginning of the chapter, in section 13.1, we discussed two reasons why investment expenditure is important: it is the means whereby the capital stock grows (or at least is preserved) and it is a significant, volatile, and procyclical element of overall spending. We explored the procyclical nature of investment further in section 13.5, when we discussed the forces that tend to cause bunching of investment.

In section 13.2, we suggested that investment depends upon expectations of the profitability of new capital relative to its cost. The cost depends upon interest rates, the tax system, depreciation, and movements in the price of capital goods.

In section 13.3, we explored Tobin's q theory. According to this theory, there should be a link between the stock market value of firms and their incentives to invest—summarized in deviations in Tobin's q from unity. But, in section 13.4, we saw that financing constraints are one reason why that theory may not really be very satisfactory. More important, assessing how good the q theory is runs into problems because intangible assets, and investment in them, are very hard to measure, as we discussed in section 13.7.

We saw in section 13.6 that firms are increasingly undertaking investments that produce, or are designed to produce, abroad as well as in the domestic economy. Investment has become increasingly footloose and therefore sensitive to cost and rate of return differences across countries.

CONCEPTUAL QUESTIONS

1. (Section 13.1) Can a country invest too much? How might you assess what is too much?

2. (13.2) Suppose firms extrapolate from recent growth in demand to future growth in demand. They invest when capital is insufficient to meet projected demand. If current capital exceeds what is required to meet expected demand, investment is cut to zero. How could an economy that worked like this generate investment-led business cycles?

3. (13.2) Suppose interest rates rise sharply but are expected to fall again in a year or so. How do you think this would affect the level of investment in machines with short lives and those with very long useful lives?

4. (13.3) Suppose an invention renders much of existing production techniques in a sector of the economy obsolete. What would happen to the stock prices of firms and to investment in the sector? What does this tell you about q theory?

5. (13.7) Should governments give incentives to overseas firms to invest in the economy? Should incentives be the same for domestic firms? What if other governments offer incentives?

6. (13.7) How much production in your country is undertaken by foreign multinationals? Consider the reasons why those companies chose to locate investment and production in your country. Are they the same factors that have made companies that are based in your country invest abroad?

ANALYTICAL QUESTIONS

1. (Section 13.1) The capital output ratio in an economy is 2.5. Capital depreciates at 6% a year. Output grows at 3% a year. What is the ratio of gross investment to output that keeps the capital–output ratio constant?

2. (13.2) A delivery company can buy a new van for $50,000. It can finance the purchase with a bank loan. The annual interest rate is 12%. Interest payments are tax deductible and the corporate tax rate is 30%. The company estimates that it will be able to sell the van a year later for $30,000. Any capital loss is tax deductible. What is the annual user cost of a van?

3. (13.2) Consider again the delivery company in question 2. The company estimates how much extra pretax income a given number of new vans will bring in. Here is the schedule:

Extra Vans	Extra Income (pretax $)
10	300,000
20	570,000
30	840,000
40	1,000,000
50	1,150,000

How many vans should the firm buy?

4. (13.2) Suppose that the corporate sector in an economy aims to do enough investing to preserve a ratio of the capital stock to output of 3. If the capital stock is less than 3 times output, firms invest; if the capital stock is above 3 times output, firms do not scrap capital or sell it because the scrap, or secondhand values, are very low. Instead, companies can cut gross investment so net investment can be negative. Capital wears out and companies need to invest 4% of their existing capital just to preserve the value of capital. Initially, companies expect output to grow at 2% a year next year and plan their investment accordingly. What will be the level of investment if total current output is $1000 billion? Firms suddenly change their view on output growth cutting expected growth from 3% to 0. What happens to investment? Finally, firms become despondent and expect output to fall by 3%. In each case calculate the ratio of investment to output.

5. (13.2) Suppose companies can deduct interest payments on their debt against their taxable income: they pay tax on profits, *net* of interest payments on debt. The revenue that a company generates from some new investment is taxed, but it can be offset by depreciation of the capital. Suppose the government introduces a 100% deprecation allowance so that companies can immediately deduct all investment spending from taxable profit. But to offset this very generous measure, they set the corporate tax rate at a high level of 60%. Is the resulting tax system advantageous or disadvantageous to investment—take as your benchmark a situation with no taxes at all. Assume companies use debt to finance investment.

6. (13.3/13.7) An all-equity company (which has no debt) has a stock market value of $540 million. Its tangible assets comprise land, buildings, and machines. The land is worth $100 million. The buildings are worth $120 million. The replacement value of the machines is $300 million. What is Tobin's q? Why might q differ from unity? The intangible assets of the company include the value of its reputation. Does the fact that these assets might have value imply that the company should expand?

Business Cycles

Overview

Business cycles are medium-term fluctuations in the economy; that is, fluctuations that are normally completely contained within a decade. The business cycle involves oscillations between periods of high and low activity, or expansions and contractions. In this chapter, we outline the main statistical facts that characterize business cycles—how the business cycle affects different industries and different individuals. We consider whether business cycle fluctuations are bad for the economy or whether they may have beneficial effects. Understanding the business cycle requires identifying the shocks that trigger fluctuations and the various economic mechanisms that propagate these shocks over time. We view a range of different business cycle theories, outlining the shocks and propagation mechanisms they assume and reviewing the evidence in support of each. We describe a simple supply and demand model with which to analyze the effects of these shocks and propagation mechanisms.

Key Concepts

Business Cycle	Frisch-Slutsky Paradigm	Real Business Cycle Theory
Depression	Propagation Mechanism	Recession

14.1 What Is a Business Cycle?

One way of defining the business cycle is that it is the fluctuations in output around its trend. The production function tells us that, for a given level of capital, labor, and technology, a certain amount of output can be produced. This is what we have referred to as the trend level of output. However, at any point in time, output does not have to equal its trend value. Firms can always produce less output if they do not work at full capacity or if they do not work their labor force at full efficiency during its working shift. Therefore, output can always be below this trend level. But output can also exceed the trend level predicted by the production function. For instance, workers can be persuaded to work overtime for short periods and machines can be utilized at more than full

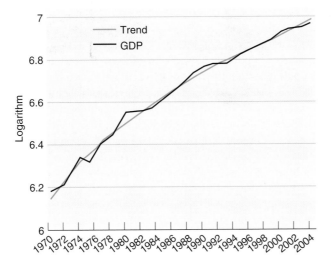

FIGURE 14.1 **Italian GDP and trend GDP.** GDP isn't always equal to its trend level but fluctuates around it—these are business cycle fluctuations. *Source:* OECD, The World Economic Outlook Database (September 2003).

capacity during intense periods of production. Firms cannot maintain these high levels of activity indefinitely—eventually the workforce needs a rest, and if machines are used too intensively they will break down and there will be stoppages. However, for short periods, this intensive use of factors of production enables output to be above its trend. These fluctuations of output above and below the trend level provide one definition of the **business cycle**. Figure 14.1 shows an estimate by the OECD of the trend (or potential) level of output for Italy, as well as its gross domestic product (GDP). Figure 14.2 shows the gap between Italian GDP and potential output, which is one measure of the business cycle. When output is above trend, the economy is in the boom phase of the cycle, and when it is significantly below trend, the economy is in **recession**.

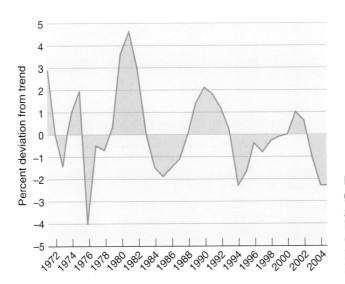

FIGURE 14.2 **Italian output gap, 1970–2004.** The output gap is a measure of the business cycle. *Source:* OECD, The World Economic Outlook Database (September 2003).

The measure shown in Figure 14.2 is sometimes referred to as the "output gap"—the distance between potential output and current GDP. The output gap is a popular concept used to explain how monetary policy operates. When the output gap is large and negative, GDP is far below its potential level and factors of production are not being used intensively. By contrast, when the output gap is positive and large, GDP exceeds potential output by a large margin. This can only be the case if factors of production are being used intensively, so that overtime is high and machines are operating a full shift. In these circumstances, inflation is likely to be rising. If firms are already at full capacity when they receive additional orders, these orders cannot easily be met, so the firm will start to increase prices to choke off demand. In addition, overtime costs more than normal working hours, so costs will increase, which also puts upward pressure on prices. Therefore, a large positive output gap is associated with either high or rising inflation, while a large negative gap leads to subdued inflation.

As Figures 14.1 and 14.2 make clear, business cycles are only temporary—whether in an expansion or a recession, output is eventually expected to return to its trend level. However, the economy can remain either above or below its trend level for several successive years. In other words, expansions last for several years and then are replaced by recessions, which are also persistent. In this chapter we will try to explain why the economy experiences these oscillations and also try to document how persistent each stage of the business cycle is.

KEY POINT

The business cycle is the continual process whereby the economy enjoys an expansion, endures a recession, and then again experiences an expansion.

14.2 Measuring the Business Cycle

We do not actually observe the business cycle—we only observe GDP. To measure the business cycle, we have to make assumptions about trend output. To further complicate matters, economists use a variety of terms when discussing business cycles—booms, recessions, expansions, contractions, depressions, growth recessions, and other expressions. What do these terms mean?

One often cited definition of a recession, particularly in the United States, is when an economy has experienced two successive quarters of negative growth. Therefore, if an economy grows by -0.3% and -0.5% in two quarters, it is in recession. Unfortunately this definition is somewhat restrictive. Imagine that over the last three quarters output growth had been -15%, 0.01%, and -35%. This economy is clearly in recession but does not conform to our two consecutive quarter ruling. We need a more flexible way of defining recessions. The authoritative National Bureau of Economic Research in the United States provides one such definition. A business cycle committee, which examines recent trends in output and other variables as well as different sectors of the economy, decides whether the economy is in recession. They declare a recession if economic activity contracts across a wide range of variables and a broad range of sectors. Table 14.1 shows the NBER estimates of the phases of the U.S. business cycles over the past 150 years.

TABLE 14.1   Dating of U.S. Business Cycles
U.S. business cycles vary in their duration—on average, contractions are shorter than recessions.

Trough	Peak	Duration (in months) of		
		Contraction	Expansion	Business Cycle
12/1854	6/1857		30	
12/1858	10/1860	18	22	40
6/1861	4/1865	8	46	54
12/1867	6/1869	32	18	50
12/1870	10/1873	18	34	52
3/1879	3/1882	65	36	101
5/1885	3/1887	38	22	60
4/1888	7/1890	13	27	40
5/1891	1/1893	10	20	30
6/1894	12/1895	17	18	35
6/1897	6/1899	18	24	42
12/1900	9/1902	18	21	39
8/1904	5/1907	23	33	56
6/1908	1/1910	13	19	32
1/1912	1/1913	24	12	36
12/1914	8/1918	23	44	67
3/1919	1/1920	7	10	17
7/1921	5/1923	18	22	40
7/1924	10/1926	14	27	41
11/1927	8/1929	13	21	34
3/1933	5/1937	43	50	93
6/1938	2/1945	13	80	93
10/1945	11/1948	8	37	45
10/1949	7/1953	11	45	56
5/1954	8/1957	10	39	49
4/1958	4/1960	8	24	32
2/1961	12/1969	10	106	116
11/1970	11/1973	11	36	47
3/1975	1/1980	16	58	74
7/1980	7/1981	6	12	18
11/1982	7/1990	16	92	108
3/1991	3/2001	8	120	128
11/2001		8		

Source: NBER www.nber.org

TABLE 14.2
Percentage Output Declines During the Great Depression
Depressions are characterized by dramatic and long lasting falls in output.

Argentina	−13.72
Australia	−5.78
Austria	−19.79
Belgium	−7.09
Canada	−24.08
Chile	−30.02
France	−14.66
Germany	−23.50
Mexico	−17.66
New Zealand	−14.64
U.K.	−5.09
U.S.A	−26.99
Venezuela	−21.20

Source: Maddison, *Monitoring the World Economy 1820–1992* (OECD Paris, 1995).

In many economies, recessions—that is, genuine falls in output—are quite rare. However, growth recessions are more common. A growth recession occurs when, although the economy is still expanding, the growth is less than the economy's long-run trend rate. The output gap is increasing during a growth recession. For instance, growth may slow down to 1% even though over the last three years it has been expanding at 5% per year. Such a slowdown is a growth recession, but not a recession itself—the economy is still expanding, but not as fast as previously.

Another term used when the economy is performing weakly is **depression**. As with much business cycle terminology, depression does not have a precise definition.[1] Loosely speaking, it signifies a bad recession—one that is both long-lasting and in which output declines substantially. This does not specify how bad or long-lasting a recession has to be to be called a depression. Probably the key difference between a recession and a depression is that, as Figure 14.2 shows, recessions tend to be short-lived and output soon returns to its trend value. The economy shows momentum between good and bad periods. However, in a depression the economy seems to have lost all momentum—the downturn lasts so long that the economy seems unable to recover on its own without a dramatic policy intervention.

The most famous example of an economic depression is the one that affected many countries between 1929 and 1932. Table 14.2 shows the percentage decline in output between 1929 and 1932 of the countries that were most affected by the Great Depression. Throughout this three-year period, output in these countries fell sharply. Both the extent of these declines and the duration of the contraction make this period a depression rather than a recession.

14.3 Characterizing Business Cycles

Business cycles are not just a feature of modern OECD economies—even the Bible describes seven years of feast followed by seven years of famine. Figure 14.3 shows annual growth in real GDP since 1980 in Germany and Peru. It reveals a pattern of oscillation between periods of high and low growth.

The nature of these fluctuations differs across countries—for instance, Peruvian growth varies much more than that of the postwar United States—but they all show the general pattern of expansions followed by contractions. Why do such different economies experience business cycle fluctuations? Later we will provide a model to explain these fluctuations, but for now we shall use a simile. The economy is like a reservoir. With no wind or disturbance, the water will be still. However, as soon as something is thrown into the water, it sets in motion a wave-like pattern on the surface. If a pebble is thrown in, the waves will be small and will not extend far. If an automobile is thrown in, the waves will be bigger and more pronounced. In other words, different disturbances evoke different fluctuations in the water, but all disturbances evoke a wave-like motion. Economists think in a similar way about the economy. Its structure is

---

[1] Although it is sometimes said that a recession is when you know someone who has become unemployed and a depression is when you become unemployed!

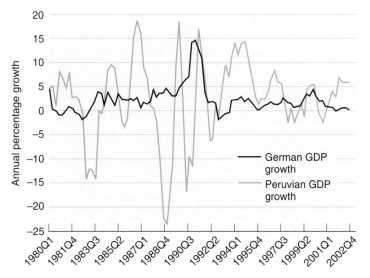

FIGURE 14.3   **Annual GDP growth in Germany and Peru, 1980–Q1 2003.** Although their frequency and amplitude changes, all countries in all historical periods have experienced business cycle fluctuations. *Source:* IMF, *International Financial Statistics* (November 2003).

such that any disturbance, such as an increase in the price of oil or in interest rates, sets in place a long-lasting reaction in which output fluctuates between high and low periods of activity.

KEY POINT

Different economies will experience different shocks, and the magnitude and duration of business cycles may vary, but such fluctuations are inevitable.

WHAT DO BUSINESS CYCLES LOOK LIKE?

We have said that a business cycle consists of two stages: an expansion and a contraction. There are many differences between these two stages of the business cycle. The first is that expansions tend to last longer than recessions. Table 14.3 shows estimates from the IMF of the patterns of recessions and expansions in 16 industrialized countries since 1881. Expansions last three to four times longer than recessions—recessions last around 12 to 15 months and expansions 4 to 7 years in most countries. Note that these are averages—each business cycle may be different.

Although recessions are shorter than expansions, they have at times seen more dramatic changes in output. This was particularly marked in the interwar years. In the period 1919–1938, output declined by an annual average of 8.1%; in the shorter period shown in Table 14.3, output declined dramatically in many countries. There have not, however, been any corresponding episodes where output has risen so sharply in a short period. During expansions the economy regains the losses of output that occurred during recessions, but at a more leisurely pace.

TABLE 14.3   **Recessions and Expansions, 1881–2000**

	Prewar 1881–1913	Interwar 1919–38	Bretton Woods 1950–72	Post-Bretton Woods 1973–2000
Recessions				
Decline in output				
Average decline in output (percent)	−4.3	−8.1	−2.1	−2.5
Proportion with a decline in output of:				
0–2 percent	29.4	23.5	50.0	57.5
2–4 percent	33.3	17.6	44.4	30.0
> 4 percent	37.3	58.8	5.6	12.5
Length of recessions				
Average length of recessions (years)	1.3	1.8	1.1	1.5
Proportion that were:				
One year in length	79.4	60.8	94.4	60.0
Two years in length	16.7	15.7	5.6	32.5
Three years or more in length	3.9	23.5	0.0	7.5
Proportion of years in recession	24.7	29.4	5.2	13.4
Proportion associated with a decline in investment	58.9	77.4	63.6	96.2
Expansions				
Increase in output				
Average increase in output (percent)	19.8	34.6	102.9	26.9
Length of expansions				
Average length of expansions (years)	3.6	3.7	10.3	6.9
Proportion of years in expansion	75.3	70.6	94.8	86.6
Average number of years until previous peak is reached	2.0	2.7	1.1	1.7
Memorandum				
Average growth rate (percent)	2.8	3.8	5.3	2.6

Source: IMF staff calculations.

14.4   Business Cycles as Aggregate Fluctuations

CO-MOVEMENT ACROSS VARIABLES AND ACROSS SECTORS

In Chapter 1 we defined macroeconomics as focusing mainly on aggregate uncertainty, that is, events that many agents tend to experience. The business cycle is a prime example of a macroeconomic phenomenon. In a recession many firms and industries will be performing poorly. As we saw in Chapter 1, this doesn't mean that all firms are doing badly—in a recession, bankruptcy advisers' workload will soar, and firms can still get lucky by introducing a new product consumers really want. In other words, idiosyn-

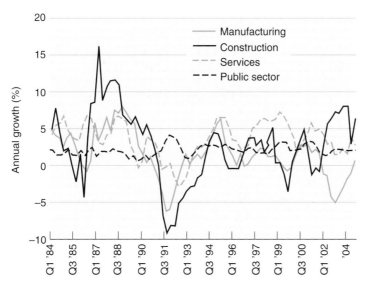

FIGURE 14.4   **U.K. output growth by industrial sector, 1984–Q2 2003.** All sectors rise and fall together over the business cycle but volatility is most pronounced in manufacturing and construction. *Source:* Economic Trends Annual Supplement, National Statistics Online, http://www.statistics.gov.uk/statbase/tsdtimezone.asp?vlnk=etas

cratic uncertainty is important. However, most firms in most industries will be performing below average in a recession.

Figure 14.4 shows this common aggregate experience by examining the four main productive sectors of the U.K. economy: manufacturing, services, construction, and the public sector. These figures show that normally when one sector is doing well, so are the others—all four sectors' output tends to move together. However, although output moves in a similar direction across industries, the magnitude of the fluctuations differs greatly.

The sector most exposed to the business cycle shown in this figure is construction—output growth in this industry has hit peaks of 17% and declines of 9% in a year. The manufacturing sector is also as volatile—over the same time period, both growth and declines reached as much as 8%. By contrast, the service and public sectors show muted business cycle fluctuations. Output growth in the public sector has varied between 4% and 0%, although for most of the time it lies in the range of 0 to 2%. The service sector shows more variability, with fluctuations between 7% and −7%, but this is still less volatile than either manufacturing or construction output. Therefore, while most sectors show a business cycle pattern, some are more exposed than others.

Like business sectors, most aggregate economic variables display a strong cyclical pattern, but some do not. For example, wage growth displays little volatility over the business cycle and a much lower correlation with GDP than other economic variables. Trying to explain why wages show such a weak cyclical pattern when unemployment and employment are so strongly cyclical is a key challenge to business cycle theorists and an issue we will examine in section 14.7 of this chapter. Other variables, such as GDP and unemployment, cycle in opposite directions When GDP growth is strong, unemployment falls, but when the economy moves into recession, unemployment starts to rise (and employment falls). The labor market is normally a lagging indicator of the business cycle—it usually takes around six months for a rise in the rate of GDP growth to have an affect on employment or unemployment.

CO-MOVEMENTS ACROSS REGIONS

Regions within a country are strongly connected, so we would expect to find positive co-movement between them. Table 14.4 shows the correlation of output across U.S. states between 1986 and 2001. If the correlation is positive, then output growth tends to be high in each state when overall U.S. output growth is high. The closer the correlation is to 1, the stronger the co-movement. If the correlation is negative, then output in the state tends to be low when the rest of the economy is doing well. If the correlation is zero, then there is no consistent pattern between how output at the state level varies with the national business cycle. Table 14.4 shows that the majority of regions face similar business cycle experiences—over half the states have a correlation coefficient greater than 0.6 and many have a correlation coefficient above 0.8. Only Hawaii and Delaware have negative correlation coefficients.

T A B L E   1 4 . 4   Output Correlations across U.S. States, 1986–2001

Alabama	0.59	Kentucky	0.69	North Dakota	0.04
Alaska	0.32	Louisiana	0.31	Ohio	0.83
Arizona	0.63	Maine	0.84	Oklahoma	0.46
Arkansas	0.25	Maryland	0.75	Oregon	0.63
California	0.80	Massachusetts	0.91	Pennsylvania	0.83
Colorado	0.56	Michigan	0.72	Rhode Island	0.74
Connecticut	0.84	Minnesota	0.87	South Carolina	0.83
Delaware	−0.02	Mississippi	0.41	South Dakota	−0.16
District of Colombia	0.25	Missouri	0.68	Tennessee	0.46
Florida	0.90	Montana	−0.14	Texas	0.58
Georgia	0.82	Nebraska	0.25	Utah	0.33
Hawaii	−0.02	Nevada	0.49	Vermont	0.64
Idaho	0.39	New Hampshire	0.76	Virginia	0.84
Illinois	0.91	New Jersey	0.82	Washington	0.54
Indiana	0.74	New Mexico	−0.32	West Virginia	0.18
Iowa	0.52	New York	0.85	Wisconsin	0.78
Kansas	0.69	North Carolina	0.83	Wyoming	−0.07

Source: Author's calculations from data from Bureau of Economic Analysis, www.bea.doc.gov.

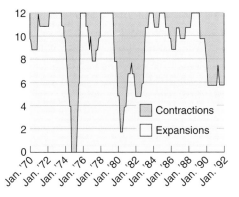

FIGURE 14.5 **Number of countries in recession or expansion.** Business cycle conditions tend to be similar in different economies.

CO-MOVEMENT ACROSS COUNTRIES

It is understandable why sectors within an economy tend to share a common business cycle. If the manufacturing sector is doing well, it will generate demand for new buildings that will encourage the construction industry and will also generate increased demand for the service sector (increased realtor services, mortgage demands, insurance policies, and so forth.). National economies are also linked together—when the U.S. economy is growing fast, it generates demand for non-U.S. goods and that helps output grow faster in other countries. As a result, we should expect to see signs of a common business cycle across countries.

Figure 14.5 shows how many of the 12 largest developed economies in the world have been in expansions or contractions at the same time between 1970 and 1992. It is very rare for only a few economies to be in recession; normally several countries experience a downturn simultaneously. However, while national economies tend to experience similar business cycle timings, this is not inevitable. For instance, in 2000 the United States had been experiencing a long and sustained economic boom; Continental Europe experienced modest growth and Japan was mired in recession.

KEY POINT

The key feature of business cycles is that they are an aggregate phenomenon. Co-movement characterizes them; that is, many economic variables from different sectors and regions of the economy, and also from different countries, display similar behavior at roughly the same time. In this section we have documented this co-movement.

14.5 Have Business Cycles Changed?

While business cycles have been a feature of economies for most of recorded history, their nature is not constant. Table 14.3 suggests that volatility (as measured by the standard deviation of output growth) has declined sharply since 1950. Both the frequency of recessions and the scale of falls in output during recessions have dropped in recent decades.

The abrupt change in the nature of this volatility and the much reduced frequency and depth of recessions has lead to considerable discussion among policy makers and economists—particularly because from 1950 onwards, many governments used fiscal and monetary policy to try to reduce business cycle volatility. Table 14.3 supports the idea that governments succeeded in reducing this volatility.

One key question is whether or not the business cycle volatility has really declined. A study by Christina Romer of Berkeley suggests that it has not.[2] The reason lies in how we measure the economy. Before 1950, governments did not measure GDP. Instead, economists monitored the behavior of a wide range of different industries. Historical series of GDP are therefore constructed after the event—economic historians use the measured output of industries for which there are data and combine them to estimated GDP. However, the GDP data measured from 1950 are based on many more industries than economic historians have data for before 1950. Because GDP data before 1950 is an average of a smaller range of industries, we would expect it to be more volatile. Imagine estimating the average height of the population by measuring only the people living in your household. This is unlikely to be close to the national average, and comparing estimates across different households will yield widely varying results. However, if we take averages of households in each street or even in each town, then these averages will get closer to the national average and will show much less variation across streets or towns. In the same way, measuring GDP by sampling only a few industries will lead to much more volatility in GDP than when we sample many industries.

Romer showed that this measurement difference can account for the reduced volatility in U.S. GDP. To examine whether volatility has declined in the U.S. economy, she considered only the industries for which there are data before and after 1945 (40 in all), and then compared the volatility of industry output both before and after 1945. Using midpoints of the intervals as measures of volatility, we find that 22 industries have a pre-1939 volatility of output the same or less than post-1945. In other words, no strong evidence suggests that U.S. GDP fluctuations are less dramatic after 1945.

However, while we cannot conclude that the volatility of business cycles has fallen, the nature of U.S. business cycles has changed. Table 14.1 shows the dates for U.S. expansions and contractions and the duration of each. The table illustrates a point we made earlier—business cycles are not uniform in length. The table also shows, however, that expansions have been longer since 1945, while contractions have become shorter. This experience is common to industrialized countries.

Recent research by James Stock and Mark Watson suggests that in the United States, business cycle variability declined sharply after 1984.[3] From 1960 to 1983 the standard deviation of annual growth in real GDP was 2.7%; between 1984 and 2001 it was 1.6%. Before World War II it was much greater. This is illustrated in Figure 14.6. Stock and Watson estimate that between 20% and 30% of the reduction in volatility was due to improved monetary and fiscal policy. A further 20% to 30% was due to

---

[2] Romer, "The Cyclical Behavior of Industrial Production Series 1889–1984," *Quarterly Journal of Economics* (February 1991) pp. 1–31.

[3] Stock and Watson, "Has the Business Cycle Changed and Why?" NBER working paper 9127 (September 2002).

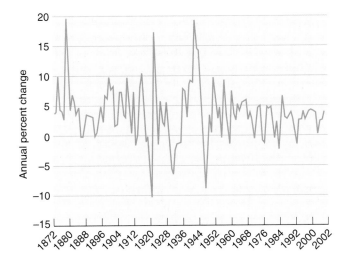

FIGURE 14.6 **U.S. output growth, 1871–2004.** There has been a sharp decline in volatility of measured U.S. output. *Source:* From data used in Basu and Taylor, "Business Cycles in International Historical Perspective," *Journal of Economic Perspectives* (1999) pp. 45–68 and updated using OECD, The World Economic Outlook Database (September 2003).

identifiable good luck in the form of productivity and commodity price shocks. The rest (40% to 60%) was due to smaller unforecastable shocks.

KEY POINT

Business cycles may have grown less volatile since the middle of the twentieth century, and have definitely shown longer periods of expansion with shorter contraction during the same time period.

14.6 Are Business Cycles Bad?

In Chapter 3 we outlined an argument of Nobel Prize winner Robert Lucas that said that the benefits to boosting the long-run rate of economic growth were enormous and that the gains from eliminating business cycle fluctuations were fairly small. In this section we reexamine this argument. Lucas is correct in saying that the benefits from boosting long-run growth are large *relative* to the gains from removing business cycles. However, are the gains from eliminating business cycles so small?

In essence, Lucas' argument is that consumption does not vary much over the business cycle, and that according to some measures, investors do not need to be compensated much for bearing risk (although our analysis of equity markets in Chapter 17 suggests that this is not uncontroversial). Lucas' conclusions are based on fluctuations in *aggregate* consumption. However, business cycle volatility affects some sectors more than others. Therefore, for some individuals, consumption volatility may be greater than Lucas' calculations suggest. Figures 14.7 and 14.8 show that this is indeed the case. These are taken from a study of U.K. households that examined the impact of the 1990–1991 recession on consumption of different individuals and households. Recessions hit the young and the unskilled much more than they affect prime working-age professionals. Therefore, focusing on aggregate consumption underestimates the volatility some consumers face.

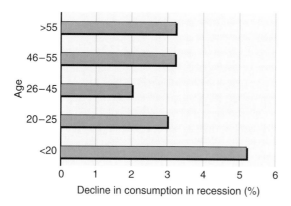

FIGURE 14.7 **Impact of recession on consumption by age.** The impact of recession is felt the most by the young and the least by those of prime working age. *Source:* Clark, Leslie, and Symons, "The Cost of Recessions," *Economic Journal* (1994), vol. 104, pp. 10–37. Reprinted with permission of Blackwell Publishers.

KEY POINT

Although the long-run impact of business cycle volatility on aggregate economic performance may not be dramatic, the short-run effect on the welfare of households may be significant because the impacts of recessions are not shared equally. They hit certain households disproportionately hard.

Table 14.5 shows how the consumption costs of recession are distributed across the population. Most of the population (57.7%) experiences small declines in consumption as a result of recession—between 0 and 2%. In all, nearly three-quarters of the people suffer, at most, a 4% decline in their consumption. For this group, Lucas' calculations would seem to apply—business cycles involve relatively small variations in consumption. However, a small group suffers disproportionately. For 1% of the population (and, if the sample is representative of the U.K. population, that is 600,000 people), consumption declines more than 10%, and for 15% of the population, it falls more than 6%. Figure 14.8 also suggests that those who suffer the most tend to be the poorest in society, unskilled workers rather than professionals, which suggests that these declines in consumption will substantially affect their standard of living.

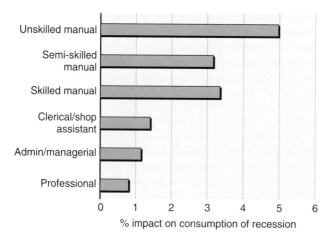

FIGURE 14.8 **Impact of recession on consumption by occupation.** Recessions are particularly costly for those with fewer skills. *Source:* Clark, Leslie, and Symons, "The Cost of Recessions," *Economic Journal* (1994), vol. 104, pp. 10–37. Reprinted with permission of Blackwell Publishers.

TABLE 14.5 **Distribution of Consumption Costs of Recession**
The majority of individuals suffer very little from recessions but a sizeable minority are badly hit.

0–2%	2–4%	4–6%	6–8%	8–10%	10–12%	12–14%	>14%
57.7	16.5	13.4	5.4	3.4	0.3	0.3	0.3

Source: Clark, Leslie, and Symons, "The Cost of Recessions," *Economic Journal* (1994) 104, 10–37.

Recent research by Justin Wolfers, based on survey evidence of what makes people happy and depressed, also suggests that business cycle volatility be might more costly than the Lucas calculations imply.[4] Wolfers finds evidence that people are much more averse to spells of unemployment than to inflation. He finds that the levels of volatility in developed countries in recent years reduced well-being by the equivalent of raising unemployment by a quarter of a percentage point.

Business cycles may also be costly because the volatility of business cycles may be connected to the long-run growth rate. Business cycles create volatility not just in output but also in other variables, such as corporate profits and firm cash flow. This volatility may retard investment. Firms will be reluctant to commit cash or borrow funds to finance investment if there is a substantial risk of a serious downturn in the economy. Therefore the greater the magnitude and duration of recessions in an economy, the lower the investment rate and, potentially, the lower the long-run growth rate. Business cycle volatility may also hinder growth through other channels. During recessions, unemployment increases. If learning by doing is important, then those who become unemployed will lose certain skills, and their productivity will decline. This will hinder their efforts to regain employment when recovery occurs and may permanently diminish output.

Nonetheless, it is not obvious that business cycle volatility is bad for growth. Indeed, recessions may even be good for the average growth rate. In an expansionary phase, when the economy is growing strongly, it is costly for firms to stop production and add new machinery or rearrange the production process to boost efficiency. However, during a recession machines are idle and workers have spare time; this is a good time for firms to restructure and try to boost productivity. Intense competition during recessions also gives firms the incentives to reorganize. In other words, recessions may act like a pit stop for the economy during which efficiency and productivity improve, so that growth can accelerate when the economy recovers.

Figure 14.9 shows the volatility of output growth between 1961 and 2001 for 154 countries plotted against the average growth rate for each country over this time period. Overall the data suggest a weak, but negative, relationship—in other words, volatile business cycles are probably bad for growth—although clearly other things also affect growth. One study finds that every 1% increase in business cycle volatility leads to a 0.2% reduction in growth.[5] This implies that if Portugal could reduce its business

[4] Wolfers, "Is Business Cycle Volatility Costly? Evidence from Surveys of Subjective Well-being", NBER discussion paper 9619 (April 2003).

[5] Ramey and Ramey, "Cross-country Evidence of the Link between Volatility and Growth," *American Economic Review* (1995) vol. 85, pp. 1138–1151.

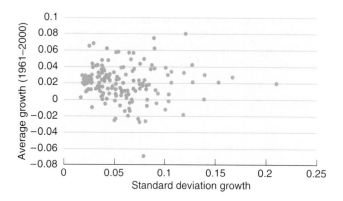

FIGURE 14.9 **Trend growth rates and business cycle volatility, 1961–2001.** There is some evidence that volatile business cycles lead to low growth, but it is very weak. *Source:* Heston, Summers, and Aten, Penn World Table Version 6.1, Center for International Comparisons at the University of Pennsylvania (CICUP), October 2002, http://datacentre2.chass.utoronto.ca/pwt/

cycle volatility to the U.S. level, its trend growth rate would be 0.4% higher, or if the United States could reduce its business cycle volatility to that of Sweden, U.S. trend growth would be higher by 0.15%.

14.7 The Frisch-Slutsky Paradigm

We have already implicitly discussed the main ideas behind the **Frisch-Slutsky paradigm** when we drew an analogy between business cycles and reservoirs.[6] The Frisch-Slutsky paradigm identifies three components in business cycle fluctuations—as shown in Figure 14.10.

The first component is an impulse or a shock that triggers business cycle fluctuations. In terms of our metaphor, the impulse is the pebble or automobile that is thrown into the reservoir. However, as in our metaphor, the fluctuations that are produced may have a different pattern from the impulse that started them. This is because the impulse acts through a **propagation mechanism** that converts one-time shocks into persistent business cycle fluctuations—the pebble interacts with the structure of water to produce a wave.

Most economists agree about what business cycles, the third part of the model, look like. Therefore, debate focuses on the first two components of the Frisch-Slutsky paradigm—which shocks are most important and what economic factor converts these shocks into the business cycles we observe. Although economists disagree over which of them is most important in explaining observed output fluctuations, there is broad agreement over which shocks are candidates for causing business cycles. These include monetary and fiscal policy shocks, shifts in desired consumption and investment, terms of

FIGURE 14.10 **Frisch-Slutsky business cycle paradigm: a theoretical characterization of business cycles.**

[6] Named after two 1930s economists: Norwegian Ragnar Frisch and Italian Eugene Slutsky.

trade shocks (including oil prices), technology shocks, and shocks to the financial structure. But the most substantial debate is over what mechanism propagates business cycles. This is because the nature of the propagation mechanism determines how policymakers should respond. Policymakers can do little to reduce the likelihood of technology or terms of trade shocks. The issue is, instead, whether policymakers can, or should even try to, offset the business cycle fluctuations these shocks cause.

In the rest of this section, we outline two different views of business cycles. One says that business cycles are the efficient response of markets to shocks that have affected the economy—in other words, business cycles are a sign that the market is working correctly. The other viewpoint, which we shall call Keynesian, is that business cycles are a sign that the market is failing to operate.

REAL BUSINESS CYCLE THEORY

The last 20 years have seen substantial debate in academic journals about business cycles. **Real Business Cycle theory** has generated much of this debate.[7] Real Business Cycle theory created several controversies, but here we focus on only two:

- The first is its claim that technology (or more generally total factor productivity, TFP) shocks cause business cycles. Traditionally economists believed that variations in demand caused business cycles and that changes in TFP drove long-run growth but not business cycles. Real Business Cycle theory's rejection of demand shocks and its use of the same model to explain growth *and* business cycles are therefore radical.
- The other controversy concerns the propagation mechanism. Real Business Cycle theory says that the profit maximizing decisions of consumers and firms convert technology shocks into business cycle fluctuations. When technology improves, firms want to hire more workers and capital. The capital stock cannot be increased instantaneously but, once in place, it leads to high demand for labor and rising wages. This, in turn, leads to higher personal income and thus higher consumption. The effect of the positive technological development is thus spread over several periods.

This view that the propagation mechanism is the efficient operation of the market is particularly controversial. In essence Real Business Cycle theory says that booms are a time of high productivity and good technology shocks. As a result, firms want to produce high levels of output, to employ many workers, and to invest in new machinery. Because productivity is high, firms will pay high wages. So economic expansions happen because it is a good time to be economically active. By contrast, recessions happen because productivity/technology is poor. It is a bad time to produce, and firms will not wish to pay high wages, invest, or hire workers. With wages low, workers will not be eager to work. Recessions are simply bad times to be economically active. Note that in this theory, individuals make the decision not to engage in high levels of economic activity based on the market prices in the recession, the "invisible hand." This result tells

---

[7] Many have contributed to Real Business Cycle theory, but its origins are in the work of Finn Kydland and Ed Prescott, "Time to Build and Aggregate Fluctuations," *Econometrica* (1982). Far more sophisticated Real Business Cycle theories have been developed than that we outline here.

us that the market is efficient. Of course, this doesn't mean that recessions are good—everyone would prefer to be in a boom than a recession. It does, however, mean that because the economy is experiencing low productivity, it is optimal for the economy to be in recession—in other words, governments should not try to kickstart the economy.

As an analogy, consider agricultural production and employment, which vary substantially over the year, reaching a peak at harvest time and a trough during the winter. Governments do not respond to the dramatic decline in output, investment (sowing), or employment during these winter months by aggressively cutting interest rates or trying to boost government expenditure. They recognize that winter is a bad time for farmers and employees to work, so output is low. Real Business Cycle theorists make essentially the same argument regarding business cycle fluctuations. Although recessions may be bad in the sense that we would rather not have them, given the circumstances (bad weather, adverse technology shock), the economy is inevitably in recession, and the government should not try to alter output or employment.

This claim that recessions are optimal market responses to bad economic events is understandably controversial. As our seasonal analogy suggests, it also raises interesting issues. In Chapter 2 we saw that economies experience substantial seasonal fluctuations that are actually more dramatic than those observed over the business cycle. However, governments do not express concern over seasonal downturns, and economists rarely use anything other than seasonally adjusted data. This suggests that volatile output is not necessarily bad—the key issues are what produces this volatility and how the economy responds to it.

Are Real Business Cycle theorists correct in their claims that recessions are an optimal response by the market to bad technology shocks? To answer this question we need to look more closely at Real Business Cycle theory by focusing on its model of the labor market. As we noted earlier in this chapter, wages fluctuate relatively little, but employment fluctuates a lot. Over the business cycle, we see volatility in output, employment, and investment, but much less volatility in interest rates, inflation, and wages. In other words, quantity variables are more volatile than price variables. To explain this, we have two main camps. One camp, which includes the Keynesian models we will soon discuss, says that markets sometimes do not work well and that prices are sluggish. As a result, the economy can only respond to adverse shocks through big changes in output or employment. The other camp, which the Real Business Cycle model belongs to, says that markets work well and that individuals are very responsive to changes in prices.

How does Real Business Cycle theory explain this? When the economy experiences a positive technology shock, then the marginal product of labor is high. At a given wage, firms now want to hire more workers, so the labor demand curve shifts to the right. How this increase in labor demand affects wages and employment depends on the slope of the supply curve. Figure 14.11 shows two different possibilities. In Figure 14.11a the labor supply curve is steep—even with higher wages, firms are not able to employ more people. In this case, fluctuations in labor demand lead to large changes in wages, but no change in employment. However, this is inconsistent with the business cycle facts we documented earlier. But if we assume a flat labor supply curve, so that in response to small changes in wages individuals are prepared to dramatically change their hours worked, then this model can explain the high employment variability and low wage movement that we see over the business cycle. To explain business cycle fluctuations, therefore, the Real Business Cycle model needs to assume that labor supply is very responsive to changes in wages, as in Figure 14.11*b*; individuals are highly responsive to market prices. Are Real Business Cycle models justified in assuming such a flat labor supply curve as in Figure 14.11*b*? This flat labor supply curve assumes that individuals want to work an average number of hours over the business cycle. However, they will work more hours when wages are high and will reduce their hours when wages are below average. As we've seen, according to Real Business Cycle theory, recessions are periods of low total factor productivity, which means a low marginal product of labor, so firms are not prepared to pay high wages. The theory suggests that people respond to these low wages by choosing not to work many hours, which leads to a fall in employment and a rise in unemployment.

However, studies suggest that people are not very responsive to changes in wages. In fact, studies of the responsiveness of prime working-age males reveal that their labor supply hardly varies with changes in wages—Figure 14.11*a* would capture their behavior much better. Other demographic groups show more responsiveness, but never enough to justify the flat labor supply curve in Figure 14.11*b*. We see some support for Figure 14.11*b* when we consider those who change their employment status over the business cycle rather than just vary the hours they work. For instance, some people may not find it worthwhile to seek employment when wages are low because they have to pay for, say, daycare for their children. However, when wages rise above a certain level, these people do find it profitable to work a full shift. As a result, their employment is very responsive to changes in wages. However, even this variation of employment does not empirically account for the business cycle facts—most people's labor supply decisions are just not responsive enough to changes in market prices. As a result, Real Business Cycle theory has had to develop and extend the model of Figure 14.11*b* by introducing other impulses, such as changes in tax

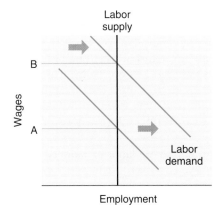

FIGURE 14.11a **Business cycles with inelastic labor supply.**

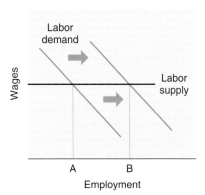

FIGURE 14.11b **Business cycles with elastic labor supply.** To explain the observed business cycle pattern of employment and wages requires an elastic labor supply curve.

rates, that in addition to technology shocks lead to shifts in the labor supply curve. More recently, this field of theory has started to incorporate demand shocks as an important source of business cycle fluctuations. It has also started to adopt a different view of why we see such little price variability and such large fluctuations in output and employment. It assumes not that people are very responsive to prices, but that prices do not change much because they are fixed or sticky. This leads us to a different view of business cycles.

THE KEYNESIAN VIEWPOINT

In 1936 John Maynard Keynes (1883–1946) published *The General Theory of Employment, Interest and Money*. This was a defining moment for macroeconomics. Keynes wrote his masterpiece in the wake of the Great Depression of 1929–1932. His basic message was that, in certain circumstances, the market mechanism may not work. For various reasons, he argued that prices, wages, and interest rates might be unable to change, or to change enough, to prevent the economy getting caught in a period of low output and high unemployment. If the market works well, then prices and wages should fall until demand and employment increase. Keynes argued that prices may not be able to fall and, even if they did, it may exacerbate matters. Keynes was essentially arguing that microeconomics—the study of the marketplace and how prices and individuals interact—may not be relevant for studying the aggregate economy. In other words, macroeconomics needed different models and tools.

The General Theory was innovative not just in its analysis of the Great Depression but also in its suggested remedy. If markets could not restore prosperity on their own, then governments had to. If prices could not be relied on to change to create demand, then government had to pump demand into the economy by raising government expenditure, cutting taxes, or lowering interest rates. The differences between this approach to business cycles and that of Real Business Cycle theory are many. This Keynesian perspective says that recessions are caused not by adverse supply shocks, but by too low a level of demand. Further, recessions are not occasions when individuals optimally choose to produce low output, but periods when the market does not work properly, leading to suboptimally low output. In other words, recessions are bad, and the government should and can improve things.

The General Theory is a fascinating book. However, Keynes tended to prefer words to diagrams and math. As a result, it is not always clear what he means, or how the effects he describes operate. The book has so many ideas that it is not always obvious which idea Keynes put most emphasis on. As a result, a huge literature is dedicated to sorting out what Keynes really meant to say. Given that Keynes died in 1946, however, it is hard to reach a definitive view on this issue, so the literature has recently focused less on what he meant to say and more on developing his insights into how market failures may lead to business cycles.

Essentially Keynesian economics is about malfunctioning markets. Of course, a market can fail in many ways, and there are many different markets to fail. As a result, Keynesianism has many different strands—some Keynesians think that it is the labor market that does not function well and that wages do not change, so unemployment can become too high. Others argue that product market monopolies keep prices too high and output too low, so that unemployment is too high. Another camp argues that flaws in the credit markets and banking sector produce fluctuations and recessions. Of course, all three markets could operate poorly, and the interactions among them could produce large fluctuations and inefficient business cycles.

Keynesian models are therefore many and varied, linked by the common theme of market failure. In many of these models, the market failure is of a particular form—what economists call a "strategic complementarity"—a situation in which whether a person acts in a particular way depends on whether someone else is also acting that way. Consider whether you want to go to a party this evening. You are probably more likely to go if you think that your friends will be there. Just knowing the cost of attending the party, e.g., cab fares, gifts, and so forth—does not provide enough information to make a decision. This is an example of a strategic complementarity, in which you are more likely to do an action if others are as well.

Keynesian models invariably involve strategic complementarity. Consider the example of an economy dominated by two large industries—A and B. Each industry is contemplating a major investment program that will substantially increase productivity and output, but will be extremely costly. The investment will only prove profitable if the economy has enough demand to purchase the extra output. If each industry makes the investment, productivity and wages will be so high the economy will have enough demand to make the investment profitable. If only one industry undertakes the investment, demand will not be high enough, and the expanding industry will make a loss. In this situation, each industry will only undertake the investment if it thinks the other industry will, too. As a result, the invisible hand does not work—firms cannot simply look at the market price and make their decisions; they also need to know what other industries will be doing. This raises the possibility of a coordination failure—what if each industry wants to make the investment but thinks the other industry won't? Then neither industry will invest and the economy remains at a low level of output. If each industry could be persuaded that the other will invest, then the economy would be at a high level of output.

This example introduces another common feature of Keynesian models: multiple equilibria. This example has two outcomes—either both industries invest, and the economy booms, or neither does, and the economy remains at low output. This offers a different perspective on business cycles—expansions are periods when everyone is confident, and the economy performs well, but recessions are periods of coordination failure when pessimism takes hold, and the economy is at a low activity level. In this case recessions are clearly bad—it is better to be at the high output level. What should the government do? In our example the solution is simple. The government has to promise that it will always provide enough demand in the economy to purchase the production of firms. Then each industry knows that if it makes the investment, it can sell its output and make profit, no matter what other industries do. As a result, all industries make the investment and the government never actually needs to buy anything— because all firms expand, there is enough demand from the private sector.

A popular strand of Keynesian thought is that prices and wages are sticky—that they do not adjust in response to changes in output or employment. As a result, over the business cycle, we get large fluctuations in output and employment, but little fluctuation in prices and wages. One explanation for this price stickiness is that firms are monopolists and set too high a price—as a result, their output is lower and they need fewer employees, so unemployment will be higher.

To see how this fits in with our discussion of strategic complementarities, consider that the demand for a firm's product depends essentially on two factors: the price of the product relative to other commodities and the total amount people want to spend. The latter factor depends on the stock of money in the economy. However, what this money can buy depends on the price level. The higher the price level, the fewer commodities this money can buy. When a firm sets its price, it tends to think only of how its price affects its attractiveness relative to other commodities. This gives it an incentive to lower its price, but it ignores an additional channel. If a firm lowers its price, then it increases the amount that individuals are prepared to spend on all commodities—the amount of money they hold can now buy more. However, this effect is small if only one firm lowers its price, and it boosts demand for all products (this is the strategic complementarity), not just those of the firm itself. Therefore, the firm ignores this additional benefit from cutting prices when it selects its own price and as a result sets prices too high. But the same reasoning leads all firms to set prices too high, so that output and employment are too low.

If somehow all firms could be persuaded to lower their prices, then the economy would have more demand and output and employment would be higher. This problem can only be overcome if government tries to boost the demand for all commodities. In this simple model, if firms won't lower prices, then the government should increase the money supply.

KEY POINT

In Keynesian models, markets do not function well, individuals may act in an uncoordinated way and arrive at a bad equilibrium, and in these circumstances, the government can and should improve things.

14.8   Aggregate Demand and Aggregate Supply

Broadly speaking, two categories of impulses might trigger business cycle fluctuations: aggregate demand shocks and aggregate supply shocks. In this section we use fluctuations in the aggregate supply and demand curve to construct a simple way of thinking about business cycle fluctuations.

AGGREGATE DEMAND

Aggregate demand measures the claims made on output produced. We saw in Chapter 2 that we can categorize the use made of output produced into four components: consumption, investment, government expenditure, and net exports. As Table 14.6 shows (for Canada), consumption is the largest component of demand, net exports the smallest, and investment the most volatile domestic component.

TABLE 14.6 **Canadian National Accounts**
Percent of GDP is calculated for 2002 and standard deviation from annual change of quarterly data between 1961 and 2002.

	% of GDP	Standard Deviation
Consumption	57%	1.92
Government expenditure	19%	2.80
Investment	19%	4.09
Exports	41%	4.05
Imports	37%	4.47

Source: IMF, *International Financial Statistics* (November 2003).

To construct our model of business cycles, we need to use the concept of an aggregate demand curve. Figure 14.12 shows this negative relationship between demand and prices. When prices are high, demand is low—output is too expensive. We are interested in shifts in the demand curve, that is, changes in the amount of demand in the economy even without a change in prices. Figure 14.12 shows the example of an increase in aggregate demand that shifts the demand curve to the right. This means that at the price P, demand in the economy is now Y(1) and not Y(0). Note that this shift has nothing to do with changes in prices—at unchanged prices, individuals wish to buy more.

What might cause such a shift? Aggregate demand consists of consumption, government expenditure, investment, and net exports. We are looking for shocks to aggregate demand—unexpected increases in any of these components. For instance, consumers may decide that they would rather save less out of their income than they have previously—perhaps because the population is getting younger on average, or social forces glamorize conspicuous consumption, or the population just feels more optimistic about the future. Any of these events would lead to an increase in aggregate demand through a

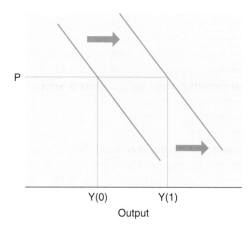

FIGURE 14.12 **Shifts in aggregate demand curve.** The aggregate demand curve shifts right when, at a given price, the level of demand increases.

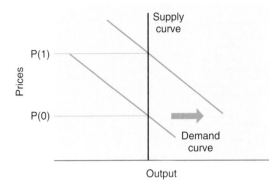

FIGURE 14.13 **Business cycles with vertical supply curve.** With a vertical long-run supply curve, an increase in demand only raises prices and leaves output unaffected.

shift in consumption. Similarly, an increase in the optimism of firms regarding invest-ment prospects, a change of government to a party that favors increased government ex-penditure, or a sudden shift in world demand towards the products a country produces will all lead to shifts in aggregate demand and affect business cycle fluctuations.

However, a complete model of business cycles needs to contain both supply and de-mand features. Chapters 3 through 7 outlined in detail the development of the supply side of the economy. There we listed the determinants of supply as the capital stock, employ-ment, and total factor productivity (TFP). However, our analysis omitted prices—if all prices are doubled (including wages and the rental cost of capital), then this should make no difference to the capital stock, employment, or TFP, and so no difference to output. In other words, Chapters 3 through 7 suggest that the supply curve should be vertical. We il-lustrate this in Figure 14.13. There is a fixed level of output that can be provided, which the capital stock, employment and TFP determine, regardless of the price level.

However, Figure 14.13 shows that, with this model of the supply side, we cannot ac-count for the business cycle properties we observe through shocks to aggregate de-mand. When the demand curve shifts out, this means that at a given price the economy has more demand. However, firms cannot provide any more output to meet this extra demand—they can only produce their full capacity output and no more, and capital, labor, and TFP pin this level of output down. The extra demand only pushes up prices—from $P(0)$ to $P(1)$. As prices rise, they choke off demand until demand equals the output that firms can produce. This model implies that when demand varies output does not change, only prices fluctuate—clearly this is no good as a model of business cycle fluctuations. However, if the supply curve is not vertical but upward sloping, then changes in demand evoke both changes in output and changes in prices—as in Figure 14.14. The flatter the supply curve, the more output varies and the less prices change—similar to what we observe over the business cycle.

Figure 14.14 implies that when firms start to receive increased orders, they meet this extra demand by some combination of raising prices and increasing output. There-fore Figure 14.14 can account for business cycles, but its plausibility depends on the an-swers to two questions: Are firms prepared to meet increases in demand by expanding output rather than just raising prices? And why would firms not just raise prices when demand increases?

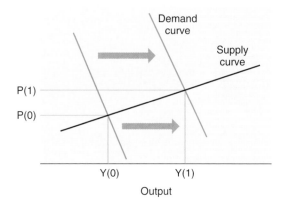

FIGURE 14.14 **Business cycles with short run supply curve.** With an upward sloping short-run supply curve, firms respond to increases in demand by raising output.

Figure 14.15 shows the results of a Bank of England survey that asked firms how they respond to increases in demand. The huge percentage of respondents who would increase output even if this means working more overtime, hiring more workers, or increasing capacity is striking. Only 12% of firms gave increasing prices as one of their main responses. Figure 14.15 gives very strong practical justification for the flat supply curve in Figure 14.14.

There are two reasons why firms seem willing to increase output rather than raise prices when demand increases. The first is that firms only periodically review prices, so that for significant periods prices are fixed. For instance, mail order firms and restaurants print catalogs and menus in advance and cannot alter prices between printings. This makes prices sticky and costly to change, an example of what economists call "nominal rigidities." Figure 14.16 shows that firms from the same Bank of England survey only occasionally review their prices—the rest of the time prices are fixed, and either output or delivery lags vary when demand changes. While 22% of firms review their prices daily, over a quarter review them once a month, and another 19% only once a quarter. Therefore, firms may not change prices in response to every change in demand—prices are sticky.

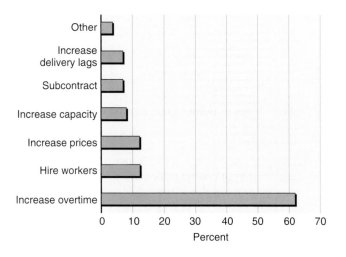

FIGURE 14.15 **How firms respond to increased demand.** Survey evidence suggests most firms respond to higher demand more by raising output than increasing prices. *Source:* Hall, Walsh, and Yates, "How Do U.K. Companies Set Prices?" Bank of England Working Paper 67 (1997). Reprinted with the permission of the Bank of England.

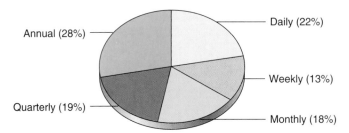

FIGURE 14.16 **Frequency of price reviews.** The majority of firms review their prices once a month or less. *Source:* Hall, Walsh, and Yates, "How Do U.K. Companies Set Prices?" Bank of England Working Paper 67 (1997). Reprinted with the permission of the Bank of England.

Prices are also sticky because firms may be unable to change them, or may choose not to change them. Figure 14.17, also from the Bank of England survey, shows the number of price changes firms made in a year. Even though 22% of firms review their prices daily, only 6% change their prices more than 12 times a year. In total, 80% of firms change their prices only every six months or more—firms do not adjust prices only frequently in the short run.

But if we assume that firms are maximizing profits, why don't they increase prices by more when they have the opportunity to increase them? Firms don't raise prices for many reasons. The first is that, when firms raise prices, they lose customers and thus revenue. If the firm has many competitors, none of which has raised prices, then the firm will be wary of doing so itself for fear of losing revenue and profit. The second reason is costs. A standard result in microeconomics is that firms maximize their profits when they set price equal to a markup over their marginal cost, where the markup depends on how much monopoly power the firm has. According to this formula, firms should only change prices when either the markup they demand, or their costs, change. Therefore, the behavior of marginal costs is crucial in determining the slope of the supply curve. If marginal costs do not alter much when the firm increases output, then it should increase output, not change its prices. Therefore it can be profit maximizing for firms not to increase prices even if they have the opportunity—this is what economists call "real rigidities." Similarly even if marginal costs increase with output, firms may not

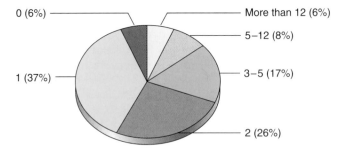

FIGURE 14.17 **Frequency of price changes over one year.** But the majority of firms change prices twice a year or less. *Source:* Hall, Walsh, and Yates, "How Do U.K. Companies Set Prices?" Bank of England Working Paper 67 (1997). Reprinted with the permission of the Bank of England.

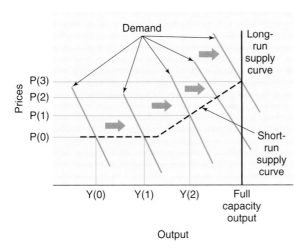

FIGURE 14.18 **Supply and demand model of business cycle.**

change prices if they are prepared to take a lower markup. Therefore, a combination of nominal rigidities (that is, firms cannot change prices because of fixed contracts, existing advertising, or price stickers), and real rigidities (that is, firms not wanting to raise prices even when they make a price review), means that in the short run the supply curve is not vertical and variations in demand lead to changes in output and prices, as in Figure 14.18.

RELATIONSHIP BETWEEN SHORT-RUN AND LONG-RUN SUPPLY CURVES

Doesn't this contradict our supply side model outlined in Chapters 3 through 7? The answer is no, because the analysis in those chapters focused on long-run developments in the economy, how the level of output varied from decade to decade. However, when we analyze business cycles, we are considering fluctuations that complete themselves within a decade. We can therefore think of the vertical supply curve of Figure 14.13 as being a long-run supply curve and the flat curve of Figure 14.14 as a short-run supply curve.

The long-run supply curve shows the level of output that an economy can produce when machines and labor are working at full capacity for a given level of TFP. As Figure 14.18 shows, demand increases at this full capacity level produce price increases because firms cannot produce any more output—the marginal cost of output soars as firms find it increasingly difficult to produce any more, so prices rise.[8] However, firms are not

---

[8] Another way of drawing the long-run supply curve is for it to be placed just before the short-run supply curve becomes vertical. In other words, price increases occur when firms try to produce too far above the full capacity level by utilizing machines more than is sustainable or by using too much overtime.

always at this full capacity output. Machines may be lying idle, and employees may not have enough work to keep them fully occupied. In these circumstances, when a firm receives new orders, it has the spare resources to boost output without increasing costs—the machines and workers are already there and are not being used. As a result, the supply curve will be flat, and as Figure 14.18 shows, any increases in demand boost output rather than prices. However, as output increases, fewer machines are idle, and all potential employee hours are being used. Under these circumstances, firms will have to use overtime, hire more workers, or invest in new machinery to meet rising orders. As a result, marginal costs begin to increase, and the firm responds to extra demand by a combination of raising output and raising prices. The supply curve is no longer flat but increasingly slopes upwards.

Figure 14.18 suggests the following pattern for prices and output over the business cycle. Consider an economy in recession with output $Y(0)$—the economy has a large negative output gap because GDP is far below its capacity level. However, as demand increases, the economy grows to $Y(1)$ but experiences little inflation—firms meet the increase in orders by boosting output, not prices. At $Y(1)$ the output gap has shrunk, so that when demand continues to increase, firms still increase production but also start to pass along price increases to customers. Output rises to $Y(2)$ and prices to $P(1)$, and the economy grows until it reaches full capacity output, and prices are at $P(3)$. At this point the economy is on the long-run supply curve, and firms cannot boost output—any additional increase in demand feeds straight through into inflation. Therefore, in the latter stages of an expansion, output growth slows and inflation increases. Policymakers will try to allow growth during the recovery stage but prevent demand from increasing when the economy is at full capacity. Figure 14.18 shows why central bankers analyze information about the output gap so closely—it indicates potential inflation.

WHEN DOES THE SHORT RUN BECOME THE LONG RUN?

How do we link the short- and long-run supply curves? The long-run supply curve moves over time as the capital stock and the level of technology changes, so that the full capacity level of output increases. However, the capital stock and technology change slowly and only increase substantially over decades. Within a business cycle, which tends to last less than a decade, they change little, so that the full capacity output level is roughly fixed—in other words, over the business cycle, the long-run supply curve does not move. This is consistent with the definition of business cycles as medium-term fluctuations around the trend level of output.

DO SUPPLY SHOCKS CAUSE BUSINESS CYCLES?

Figure 14.18 shows fluctuations in demand causing business cycles while the supply curve remains fixed. However, supply shocks can also affect business cycle fluctuations. When we discussed Real Business Cycle theory, we mentioned one source of supply shock: technological innovations. There are, however, many other sources of supply shock. The most obvious example is an increase in the price of commodities such as oil. As Figure 11.5 showed, the price of oil has varied considerably over the last 30 years, with particularly large increases in 1973 and 1979.

Oil is an important input into the production process of many commodities. If the price at which firms sell their product does not change, but their input costs have risen,

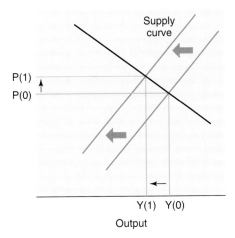

FIGURE 14.19 **Adverse supply shock causes recession.**

then the profit margin will decline and the firm will start to scale back production. For the same price, firms will now want to supply less output, and the supply curve shifts in, as in Figure 14.19. As a result of this adverse supply shock, output falls, and the economy goes into recession. However, while a demand shock moves the economy into recession, a negative supply shock also increases prices. In other words, with oil price increases, producers cut back on production but also try and recapture their profit margins by raising prices.

There are wider sources of supply shocks than oil price increases—anything that alters the output firms provide at a given price shifts the supply curve. For instance, increases in indirect taxes will act as a negative supply shocks because for the same retail price, firms now receive a lower profit margin. Another source of supply shocks is structural reform—collapsing output and rising inflation, as you might expect following a negative supply shock, characterized the early years of economic reform in Central and Eastern Europe.

14.9 So What Causes Business Cycles?

In outlining the Frisch-Slutsky approach to business cycles, we commented that although there was broad agreement over the list of candidate shocks for explaining the business cycle, there was no consensus over which of these many shocks is most important. The problem is partly that we have to infer from the data which shocks are hitting the economy, and different assumptions lead to different conclusions about the importance of shocks. Table 14.7 shows the results of one study that attempted to discover the ultimate source of business cycles in the three largest European nations. It distinguishes among three distinct causes of business cycle fluctuations: nominal demand shocks (due to variations in the money supply), real demand shocks (shifts in consumption, investment or fiscal policy not related to monetary policy), and supply shocks. The results vary from country to country but essentially show that demand shocks tend to cause most business cycle volatility.

TABLE 14.7 **Causes of G7 Business Cycles, 1973–1995**
Demand shocks explain the majority of business cycle fluctuations.

	Percentage of Nominal Demand Shocks	Output Volatility Real Demand Shocks	Explained by Supply Shocks
U.S.	37	52	11
Germany	98	2	
U.K.	57	43	
France	3	67	30
Italy	35		65
Canada	45		55

Source: Canova and Nicolo, *On the Sources of Business Cycles in the G7*, Universitat Pompeu Fabra mimeo.

KEY POINT

While economists accept a role for supply side shocks in the business cycle, they see fluctuations in demand as the major source of business cycle volatility.

SUMMARY

In section 14.1, we described business cycles as medium-term fluctuations in the economy around its long-run trend rate of growth. Business cycle fluctuations are normally, although not always, finished within a decade. In section 14.2, we saw the difficulty of developing definitions for recessions and expansions. In section 14.3, we discussed measuring business cycles and reviewed evidence that expansions tend to last longer than recessions, although the economy changes more dramatically each period in a recession.

In section 14.4, we noted that the key feature of the business cycle is co-movement—economic variables tend to move up and down together as do different sectors and regions of the economy. To a lesser extent, countries also tend to show similar cyclical movements, although this is not always the case. In section 14.5, we saw that there is some evidence that business cycle expansions have become longer since 1945.

In section 14.6, we discussed the benefits from eliminating business cycle fluctuations. These are not trivial, and they arise from the beneficial impact on growth through encouraging investment by reducing uncertainty. Because the impact of recessions tends to fall disproportionately on the poorer members of society, reducing business cycle fluctuations also reduces inequality.

In section 14.7, we examined two major theories about the origins and meanings of business cycles. For Keynesians, the business cycle reflects a market failure, and recessions are a time of suboptimally low output. The market failure can be caused by numerous factors and often relates to coordination failures in either the product, labor, or asset market. In contrast, Real Business Cycle theory says that recessions are the result of bad technology shocks that make it optimal for firms to produce little and workers not to work many hours. However, to account for the observed high variation in output and employment but low volatility in prices and wages, the Real Business Cycle model has to rely upon an implausibly high sensitivity of individuals' labor supply to changes in market prices.

In section 14.8, we showed how a simple supply and demand model can be used to account for business cycle fluctuations, although to account for the low variability in prices but high volatility in output, we have to utilize a short-run supply curve. The short-run supply curve describes the fact that in response to new orders, firms may not just increase price but will also boost production. We argued that there are real and nominal rigidities such that firms decide only infrequently whether to change prices and often decide not to. Finally, in section 14.9, we saw that research suggests the most important sources of business cycle fluctuations are changes in demand with variations in supply playing only a supporting role.

CONCEPTUAL QUESTIONS

1. (Section 14.3/14.5) Why are recessions shorter than expansions?

2. (14.6) Are recessions a good time for reorganizing and improving the efficiency of firms?

3. (14.6) If the economy goes into recession, how will it affect you? Consider not just your income but the prices of any assets you might own or commodities you purchase. How can you minimize this impact?

4. (14.6/14.7) In a recession, share prices tend to be low and companies can be bought at low prices and workers hired for low wages. Given that recessions are only temporary, what stops you from buying loads of stocks in a recession and then selling them during an expansion?

5. (14.7) If rising inflation after an oil price increase leads the Central Bank to dramatically increase interest rates, what is the impulse behind this business cycle and what is the propagation mechanism?

6. (14.7) How much of your weekly shopping is on commodities with "sticky" prices—prices that firms cannot immediately change? Are these sticky prices relevant or can they be negotiated? How do you think the introduction of barcoding and computer pricing have influenced price behavior?

7. (14.7) Travel on a train between Paris and Madrid and the view from the window changes—fluctuating between green land and a heavy concentration of economic activity. What explains this bunching of activity over space? Could similar factors explain the bunching of activity over time (the business cycle)? If so, how should governments respond to the business cycle?

8. (14.7) What role do you think consumer and firm psychology has in driving the business cycle through fluctuations in demand?

9. (14.7) What are the impulses and propagation mechanisms of Real Business Cycle theory and Keynesian models?

10. (14.8) Real Business Cycle theory implies that negative total factor productivity shocks cause recessions. What do you think such shocks might be?

ANALYTICAL QUESTIONS

1. (Section 14.1) Output in an economy is given by the following numbers

Year	1	2	3	4	5	6	7	8	9	10
Output	1	1.2	2.8	4.3	5.2	6.1	6.7	7.4	8.9	10

(a) Assume a simple straight line between Year 1 and Year 10 is a good estimate of trend GDP. Calculate the output gap.

(b) In Year 11 output is measured at 10.5. How does this change your estimate of trend output? What about your estimated output gap in Year 10?

(c) In Year 11 output is instead measured as 12. What happens now to your estimate of trend output and the output gap? Discuss the problems this suggests in using the output gap to measure the current state of the business cycle.

2. (14.1/14.7) You will find a spreadsheet useful in answering this question. Let the output gap in Year 0 and Year 1 be 0. Further, let the output gap today equal 0.9 of yesterday's output gap less 0.9 of the output gap two periods ago, e.g., $Y(t) = 0.9*Y(t-1) - 0.9*Y(t-2)$.

(a) Calculate the output gap for Years 1 to 20.

(b) An unexpected shock in Year 2 increases the output gap to +1. What happens to the output gap now until Year 20?

(c) What happens to the amplitude and duration of business cycles when the shock is 12 instead?

(d) What happens to the amplitude and duration of business cycles when the output gap follows the rule $Y(t) = 0.5Y(t-1) - 0.5*(Y(t-2)$?
When it is $Y(t) = 0.1Y(t-1) - 0.1Y(t-2)$?
What about $Y(t) = Y(t-1) - Y(t-2)$?

(e) Consider again the case where $Y(t) = 0.1Y(t-1) - 0.1Y(t-2)$. What happens to fluctuations when $Y(2)$, $Y(3)$, and $Y(4)$ are increased by 1 and $Y(5)$, $Y(6)$, and $Y(7)$ are lowered by 1 and the same three-period oscillatory pattern is imposed for the remaining years? What does this tell you about the relative role of propagation and shocks in explaining persistent business cycle fluctuations?

3. (14.7) Consider the Real Business Cycle model of Figure 14.11a. How does the labor supply curve need to shift for the model to explain business cycle fluctuations? What might cause such a shift?

4. (14.7) An economy is dominated by two industries, both of which are considering whether to initiate a major investment project. If both industries invest, then employment and productivity are high and each industry makes profits of $5 billion. However, if neither industry invests, the economy is weaker and each industry makes $1 billion profit. If only one industry invests, then the industry that doesn't makes $2 billion profit but the additional costs of the investing industry mean that it loses $1 billion.

(a) If each industry assumes the other one will not invest, what is their optimal course of action?

(b) What if they assume the other industry will invest?

(c) What is the role of changing business optimism in this economy?

(d) How do your answers change when government offers an investment subsidy worth $3 billion to each industry? Is society better off?

5. (14.8) Use a supply and demand model to analyze the impact of an oil price shock on the economy. After an increase in oil prices, what is likely to happen to profits, unemployment, income, and consumer confidence? How will this further affect your analysis? How useful is the distinction between supply and demand shocks?

Monetary Policy

Overview

By the end of the twentieth century, monetary policy was, almost always and almost everywhere, aimed at control-ling inflationary pressures. Most governments in the industrial world had ceased using fiscal and monetary policy to fine-tune the economy, that is, to try and keep output close to a target path. Governments no longer saw fiscal pol-icy as an effective tool for manipulating short-term demand. Instead they saw monetary policy—and specifically short-term interest rates—as an instrument they could use to try and dampen inflation. How this situation came to exist and whether it will last are important questions we address in this chapter. We also consider how governments operate monetary policy, what they try to target, how they seek to achieve this, and how monetary policy affects the economy. We consider what problems are created in an environment where inflation is low, and may become nega-tive. Finally, we consider how monetary policy may be affected by developments in the banking sector.

Key Concepts

Credit Channel
Inflation Targeting
Intermediate Target

LM Curve
Open Market Operations

Taylor Rules
Transmission Mechanism

15.1   The Influence of Central Banks

The number and power of central banks have never been greater than they are today. Before the twentieth century, the United States did not even have a central bank. Now most countries have a central bank that implements a form of monetary policy. Many more of these central banks are now independent of government than was the case even 10 or 15 years ago.[1] The Bundesbank in Germany and the Federal

---

[1] "Independent" is a somewhat slippery concept. What we mean here is that the central bank does not merely implement monetary policy decisions that have been made by the government. Full central bank independence means that the bank sets its own targets and chooses monetary policy accordingly. However, in some cases the target is set by government, and the central bank is independent in its choice of monetary policy to meet that target.

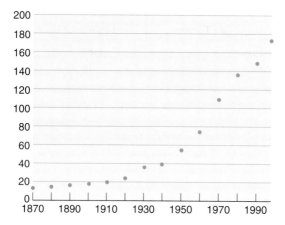

FIGURE 15.1 **Number of central banks, 1870–1999.** In the twentieth century the shift away from commodity money has increased the importance and number of central banks. *Source:* King, "Challenges for Monetary Policy: New and Old," paper presented at New Challenges for Monetary Policy conference at Jackson Hole, Wyoming, 1999.

Reserve in the United States had considerable independence over monetary policy for decades. But until recently, that was the exception rather than the rule. Within the last 20 years, several major central banks—the Bank of England, the Reserve Banks of Australia and New Zealand, the European Central Bank (responsible for setting monetary policy in the euro area)—have gained substantial autonomy to set monetary policy. Furthermore, most of these central banks set policy explicitly to control inflation.

Why have central banks become influential in setting monetary policy and why has monetary policy become so focused on controlling inflation? Until the breakdown of the gold standard because of World War I, the operation of monetary policy was of limited significance because in most countries money had always been commodity money (as described in Chapter 11), and the central banks that then existed had little discretion and few policy choices open to them. (This, of course, was why so few central banks existed, as Figure 15.1 shows.) The breakdown of the gold standard marked the end of the long centuries of commodity moneys. For the first time, central banks, usually under the control and instruction of governments, could influence monetary conditions and faced real choices.

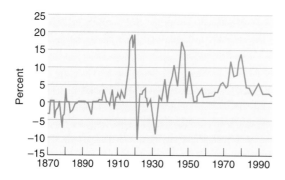

FIGURE 15.2 **Global Inflation, 1870–1999.** High levels of inflation have been a recurring global problem in the twentieth century. *Source:* King, "Challenges for Monetary Policy: New and Old," paper presented at New Challenges for Monetary Policy conference at Jackson Hole, Wyoming, 1999.

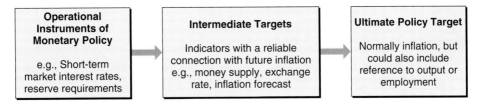

FIGURE 15.3   **The three aspects of monetary policy.** The central bank uses instruments of monetary policy to achieve an outcome for an intermediate target and in that way control its ultimate target, usually inflation.

But as Figure 15.2 illustrates, for much of the twentieth century, inflation in the world was far from insignificant. The monetary history of the twentieth century was a long process of learning the appropriate institutional and operational structure for monetary policy.

To understand monetary policy we have to distinguish among three different elements, as shown in Figure 15.3.

1. The first is the **ultimate policy target**, whether that target be inflation, output growth, or employment. However, monetary policy does not affect the economy immediately, but with a lag.
2. In order to achieve their ultimate target, therefore, central banks have to try and achieve an **intermediate target**, a variable that, if it can be controlled by the central bank, will enable it to achieve its ultimate target. Central banks have used numerous intermediate targets. Money supply growth and exchange rates are popular options. If the ultimate target of the central bank is to control inflation, then we can think of these intermediate targets as a nominal anchor—if the bank successfully meets its intermediate target, then it will keep the price level under control.
3. Finally, there are the **operational instruments of monetary policy**,—what the central bank uses to implement monetary policy. For most countries this is the level of short-term interest rates.

In the next section we develop a simple framework for thinking about how monetary policy can affect the level of demand in the economy, introducing the concept of the LM curve and using the IS curve first introduced in Chapter 12 to show how shifts in monetary policy can affect the wider economy. We then focus on how monetary policy is actually implemented.

KEY POINT

Central banks set monetary policy instruments to try to hit targets. Increasingly in the developed economies, central banks have come to adopt formal targets for the rate of inflation, though the U.S. Federal Reserve does not have a formal inflation target.

15.2 Monetary Policy and the LM Curve

The IS curve shows combinations of interest rates and levels of output (or income) such that the spending plans of households and firms are fulfilled (*Investment* is consistent with *Savings*). However, when interest rates change, they affect not just plans on spending but also the desirability of holding different types of financial assets. The cost of holding non-interest bearing money [notes (or bills), coins, and highly liquid bank deposits that pay close to zero interest] rises with the level of interest rates for opportunity cost reasons—the higher the level of interest rates, the more costly is it to hold cash that yields no interest. Further, the use of money for transactions purposes suggests that as GDP rises, so too will the demand for highly liquid assets, such as cash.

To see this, consider the case of an individual choosing between holding her wealth in the form of a non-interest bearing checking account or in bonds which yield a return (in Chapter 18 we analyze the bond markets in detail). Imagine that GDP rises. So does the income of the investor, which will boost her consumption and so increase her demand for liquid assets. This will cause her to move her wealth from bonds and into cash. But by selling bonds, she will affect bond prices, and bond yields also influence interest rates. Therefore, we cannot just focus on combinations of interest rates and income levels (which is what we are looking at when we consider points on the IS curve) in isolation from conditions in the financial markets. To see how monetary policy affects demand, we need to introduce the **LM curve**, which focuses on equilibrium in the money market. In particular it focuses on the demand and supply of money provided by the central bank. For the moment, we will assume that the central bank can control the supply of money; later in this chapter, we describe what this means and explain how open market operations work in practice.

KEY POINT

The LM curve shows equilibrium in the money market where money supply equals money demand.

Let us return to the quantity equation we introduced in Chapter 11. This says that

$$MV = PY$$

Consider the case where M denotes non-interest bearing forms of money. We know that in equilibrium money supply equals money demand so that $M = M^s = M^d$. With a little rearrangement, we therefore have

$$M^d/P = (1/V)Y$$

So that the demand for real money balances depends inversely on the velocity of circulation (V) and positively on the level of GDP, or income, (Y). As explained in Chapter 11, the velocity of circulation is a measure of how frequently money is used for transactions. The velocity is likely to depend on the level of interest rates; when interest rates are high, then holding cash is expensive (due to the foregone interest). Individuals will economize on their cash balances and the velocity of circulation will rise, so that at a given level of income, M^d/P will fall. Therefore we can expect increases in interest rates

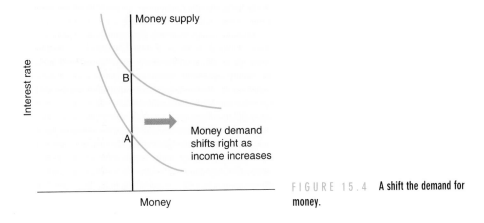

FIGURE 15.4 **A shift the demand for money.**

to *lower* the demand for money and increases in income to *increase* the demand for money.

In considering the supply of money, we shall first consider the case where the central bank sets a fixed level for the money supply. Combining this with our demand for money, we have the situation shown in Figure 15.4, with equilibrium shown at A. We can use this to derive the LM curve, which is a curve showing the relationship between interest rates and income. When income increases, for a given level of interest rates, this will increase the demand for money. But if the central bank does not alter the supply of money, then the market is not in equilibrium. The only way equilibrium can be restored is if interest rates rise so that a new equilibrium is restored at B. Therefore money market equilibrium involves a *positive* relationship between interest rates and GDP; this is the LM curve shown in Figure 15.5.

The LM curve helps show how monetary policy affects the economy. As shown in Figure 15.6, when the central bank increases the money supply from M_0 to M_1, this leads to a fall in interest rates—assuming income remains unchanged, the only way for

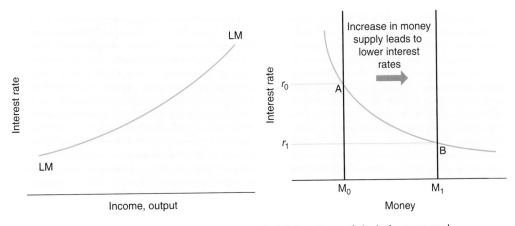

FIGURE 15.5 **The LM curve.**

FIGURE 15.6 **A rise in the money supply.**

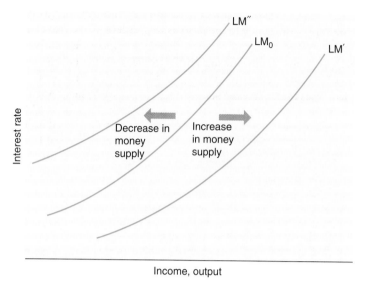

FIGURE 15.7   **Changing the money supply.**

money demand to equal the new higher level of money supply is if interest rates fall to encourage higher demand. In other words, an increase in the money supply is equivalent to a rightward shift in the LM curve, as shown in Figure 15.7. In contrast, a reduction in the money supply involves the LM curve shifting leftwards.

Having developed both the IS and LM curves, we can finally complete our analysis by bringing them together, as shown in Figure 15.8. In this figure the only combinations of interest rate and output consistent with simultaneous equilibrium in the goods market (the IS curve) and the money market (the LM curve) are r^* and Y^*.

KEY POINT

Where the IS and LM curves cross, we have simultaneous equilibrium in the markets for goods and money.

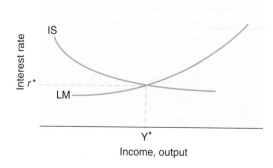

FIGURE 15.8   **Equilibrium in the goods and money market.**

Suppose, however, that the central bank does not have a target for the supply of money but instead allows the supply of money to move so as to preserve a given level of the interest rate. Interest rate setting is now much more common among central banks than fixing the money supply. For instance, in the United States, the Federal Reserve uses purchases and sales of treasury bills—open market operations—to achieve its Federal Funds *target rate*. How does that affect the shape of the LM curve? The upward slope of the LM curve when supply is fixed reflects the fact that interest rates (r) need to go up or down as income rises or falls, so as to keep money demand (M) constant as Y fluctuates. But if M fluctuates so as to preserve a given level of r, then there will be no relation between Y and r—the LM curve will be flat at the targeted level of interest rates. So we can always think of the LM curve as showing consistent combinations of r and Y for equilibrium in the money market.

Figure 15.9 illustrates the impact of a relaxation in monetary policy. In the top panel we show a situation where there is a money supply target and the target is raised (that is, the central bank allows a larger money supply). This shifts the upward sloping LM curve to the right. Output is higher, interest rates are lower, and demand and

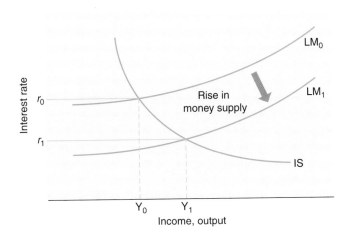

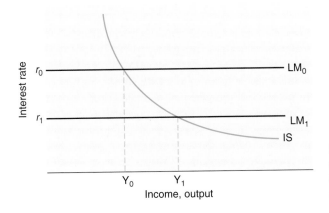

FIGURE 15.9 **The top panel shows an increase in the target for money supply. The bottom panel shows a cut in the target for interest rate.**

output expand as interest sensitive components of demand—investment, exports, and consumption—react to a lower cost of funds. Looser monetary policy operates here by inducing a move down an IS curve; in contrast, easier fiscal policy operates by shifting the IS curve. The lower panel of Figure 15.9 shows a situation where the central bank operates a target for the interest rate and reduces the target level (from r_0 to r_1). In effect, the impact on the economy is the same—interest rates fall, output rises, and we move down an IS curve. The distinction between the two panels of Figure 15.9 is, in some sense, not very significant. As noted above, in a world where there is no uncertainty about the demand for money schedule (and therefore no uncertainty about the position of the LM curve), the same effect can be achieved by moving the target for the supply of money by a given amount or shifting the price of money in a way that leads people to want to hold that amount more money.

15.3   What Does Monetary Policy Target?

In the twenty-first century the most popular type of target adopted by central banks is not for some measure of the money supply nor for a given level of interest rates. Rather it is an explicit inflation target. The Reserve Bank of New Zealand, for example, in 2000 had an inflation target range of 0% to 3%. The Bank of England's inflation target was then 2.5% per year, which was changed in 2004 to a target of 2%. The European Central Bank sought to limit inflation to no more than 2%, and to try to keep the rate of inflation close to the 2% level.

As these examples show, many governments ask their central banks currently to target inflation of around 2% per annum. Inflation is costly, as we saw in Chapter 11, so achieving a low level of inflation is desirable. But why do many governments aim at 2% inflation—if inflation is costly, why not aim for price stability and inflation of 0%?

One reason is because we mismeasure prices. As discussed in Chapter 11, official price indexes do not adequately abstract from quality improvements. Therefore, some of the increases in prices reflect an improvement in quality rather than exactly the same good selling at a higher price. The extent of this bias varies across countries, depending on how price indexes are constructed, but it is believed to be typically worth somewhere between 0.5% and 2%. Therefore, aiming for an inflation rate of 2% may in effect be the same as aiming for price stability if there is a 2% overstatement of inflation due to measurement problems.

Another reason why aiming for zero inflation may be undesirable has to do with the labor market. Individuals are very reluctant to accept wage cuts, although they will sometimes accept a wage freeze, that is, 0% increase in nominal salaries. Evidence for this can be seen from wage bargaining data which reveals a cluster of wage settlements near 0%. If employees will not accept wage cuts, then the only way that real wages can fall is if inflation is positive. If the central bank targets 0% inflation, then even this channel is not feasible and real wages may remain too high in a recession, leading to increases in unemployment. By allowing for a modest amount of inflation, the central bank can achieve some variation in real wages even if nominal wages are sticky.

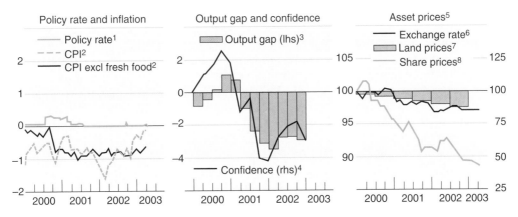

FIGURE 15.10   **Japanese monetary policy and the wider economy, 2000–2003.** *Source:* BIS Annual Report (2003).

[1]Uncollateralised call money rate, in percentages.

[2]Annual percentage changes in consumer price index.

[3]As a percentage of potential output.

[4]Consumer confidence: assessment balance, in percentage points.

[5]Last value of 1999 = 100.

[6]Nominal effective rate.

[7]Residential.

[8]Nikkei Index of stock prices.

Source: Bank for International Settlements 73rd Annual Report (2003).

Further support for not attempting to target price stability comes from the experience of Japan since 1990. The Japanese economy remained in recession for most of the 1990s even though the Bank of Japan reduced interest rates to virtually zero. Figure 15.10 shows that, between 2000 and 2003, even though the level of interest rates set by the Japanese central bank was zero, the output gap rose, confidence fell, and land and share prices fell. Inflation remained negative so that even though nominal interest rates were zero, real rates were positive. As we saw in our analysis of consumption and investment, low interest rates should stimulate output growth, but this did not happen in Japan. Interest rates cannot go below zero, and if the rate of inflation is less than, say, 1%, then real interest rates cannot be below a certain level (in this case −1%). The optimal level of real interest rates for an economy in a slump may be substantially negative. This implies that monetary policy cannot be set optimally unless inflation is substantially positive because there is a floor of zero on the nominal interest rate.

How serious a problem is this zero lower limit on the level of interest rates that the central bank can maintain? Figure 15.11 and the data in Table 15.1 suggest that the problem is only likely to arise rarely. Figure 15.11 shows that in the 150 years from the middle of the nineteenth century to the end of the twentieth century there was only one period in the United States where the level of short-term nominal interest rates fell to zero. This was during the 1930s and in the early 1940s. Table 15.1 shows that periods

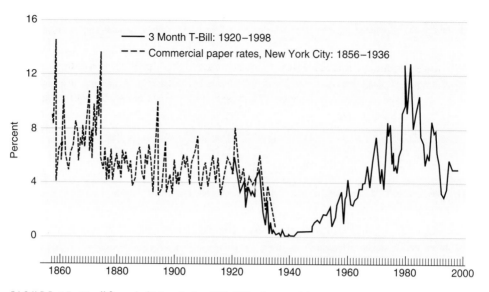

FIGURE 15.11   **U.S. nominal interest rates, 1856–1998.** *Source:* Clouse, Henderson, Orphanides, Small and Tinsley, "Monetary Policy When the Short Term Nominal Interest Rate is Zero," *Topics in Macroeconomics*, vol. 3, Issue 1, (2003).

TABLE 15.1   **Frequency of Effective Deflation, 1960 Q1–2002 Q4[1]**

	1960–69	1970–79	1980–89	1990–99	2000–01	2002
Headline inflation	13.7	3.0	7.5	11.8	22.1	28.9
GDP deflator[2]	8.7	2.0	5.3	15.4	32.3	34.7
Core inflation[3]	3.5	1.6	3.4	14.7	31.3	17.9
Services less housing[4]	4.0	1.3	2.2	12.2	28.6	16.1
Wholesale inflation[5]	27.6	7.6	23.1	35.2	25.0	57.3

[1]The frequency of effective deflation is defined as the percentage of quarters with yearly inflation less than 1% for each type of price index from Argentina, Belgium, Brazil, Canada, Chile, China, Colombia, France, Germany, Hong Kong SAR, Indonesia, Italy, Japan, Korea, Malaysia, Mexico, the Netherlands, Peru, Singapore, Sweden, Switzerland, Taiwan (China), Thailand, Venezuela, the United Kingdom and the United States.

[2]Excluding Argentina, Chile, China, Colombia, Peru, Singapore and Venezuela.

[3]Excluding the countries in footnote 2 and Brazil, Hong Kong SAR, Indonesia, Malaysia and Taiwan (China).

[4]Excluding the countries in footnote 2 and Hong Kong SAR, Malaysia, Taiwan (China) and Thailand.

[5]Excluding China and Hong Kong SAR.

Source: Bank for International Settlements 73rd Annual Report (2003).

when inflation has been less than 1% are rather rare. But the period from 2000 to 2003 was a period of low inflation in many countries, and it was a period where the level of short-term nominal interest rates in the United States fell to 1%. So, although the zero lower bound on interest rates might not have been a problem for most of the past 150 years, it has in recent years become more of a concern. The experience of Japan since 1990 suggests that rare events do happen, and the lower bound on interest rates may prevent monetary policy from assisting output growth in some circumstances. But the consensus is that such events are sufficiently rare that they should not unduly influence the inflation target.

KEY POINT

Because inflation is costly, central banks wish to achieve a low inflation rate. However, for measurement reasons and in order to provide them with some flexibility in how they use monetary policy, central banks do not target a zero inflation rate but somewhere between 2% and 3%. Such low rates achieve what Federal Reserve Chairman Alan Greenspan calls "price stability"—"price levels sufficiently stable . . . that expectations of change do not become major factors in key economic decisions."

15.4 What Intermediate Target Should Central Banks Use?

In trying to achieve a given inflation target, the central bank has to use an *intermediate target*. An intermediate target is a variable which reliably tracks future inflation and which the central bank can control. The need for the intermediate target to track *future* inflation is because of the lags involved between changing monetary policy and its effect on inflation. If the central bank only responds when it sees actual inflation increasing, then by the time the policy response has an effect, inflation may be even further out of control. However, if an intermediate target—for instance, the money supply—increases, this means that future inflation will probably be high. By tightening monetary policy preemptively today in response, the central bank can then avoid the higher future inflation.

There are three main forms of intermediate targets currently in use: money supply targets, an exchange rate target, and an inflation target—and we explain each in detail below. Central banks can consider using these intermediate targets individually or in combination. Figure 15.12 shows the type of intermediate targets in use over the 1990s for a sample of 91 central banks. Over the whole decade, an increasing number of banks adopted some form of explicit target for monetary policy. Several banks use more than one intermediate target, and over time the reliance on using just monetary targets has declined. Inflation targeting is growing in popularity, as is the use of exchange rate targets, although the latter is normally used in conjunction with another indicator. The European Central Bank (ECB) uses both an inflation target and a money supply target; the Federal Reserve in the United States is one of the few central banks with no explicit target; the Bank of England, the central banks of Sweden and Switzerland, and the Reserve Banks of Australia, Canada, and New Zealand have purely an inflation target; and Argentina and Hong Kong have an exchange rate target.

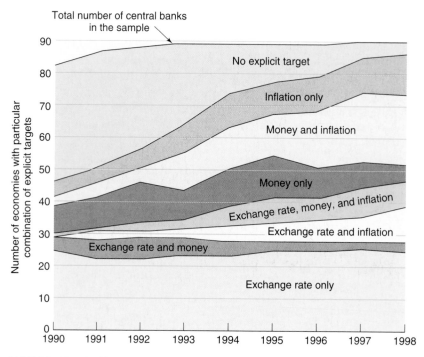

FIGURE 15.12   **Monetary policy targets for 91 countries.** The use of explicit monetary targets has increased over time, with inflation and exchange rate targets becoming more popular and money supply targets less so. *Source:* Sterne, "The Use of Explicit Targets for Monetary Policy: Practical Experience of 91 Countries," *Bank of England Quarterly Bulletin* (August 1999) vol. 39, no. 3. Reprinted with permission from the Bank of England.

15.5   Money Supply Targeting

Chapter 11 outlined in detail the quantity theory of money, which states that by definition

percentage change in the money supply − percentage change in velocity of circulation = inflation − percentage change in real output

If we add the assumption that the velocity of money is constant (or at least predictable) and that the growth of output is given by the real factors considered in Chapters 3 to 8, then we have a simple relationship between money supply growth, and inflation. If velocity is constant and real output grows at a trend rate of 2.5%, then money supply growth of 4.5% will produce inflation of 2%. Therefore, using a money supply growth rate of 4.5% as an intermediate target should mean we hit a target of 2% inflation.

In the 1980s such monetarist policies were implemented in many advanced economies. While inflation did decline (see Figure 15.2), the reliance solely on monetary targets was not seen as successful. In Chapter 11, we showed how the quantity theory was excellent at explaining long-run inflation but not very successful in explaining

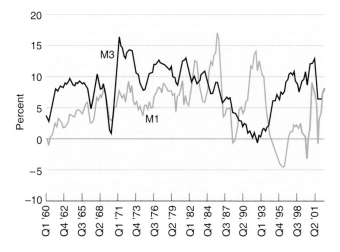

FIGURE 15.13 **U.S. money supply growth, 1960–Q3 2003.** Different money supply measures show very different behavior. *Source:* Federal Reserve Board, http://www.federalreserve. gov/releases/H6

short-run inflation. Purely relying on money supply targets to control short-run inflation proved difficult for five reasons.

1. WHICH MONEY SUPPLY?

As described in Chapter 11, there are several different monetary aggregates, or money supplies. If all monetary aggregates behave similarly, then it does not matter which monetary aggregate the central bank targets. However, in practice, different monetary aggregates behave in different ways. Figure 15.13 shows the behavior of U.S. M1 and M3 growth. Until the late 1970s, M1 and M3 showed fairly similar behavior, but not afterwards. Frequently while one aggregate is showing rapid growth, the other is slowing down. In 1992 should the Federal Reserve have been relaxed about inflation because M3 growth was falling to zero or deeply alarmed that M1 growth was close to 15%? Heated debate occurred during these years as to the relative merits of each monetary aggregate, and often central banks would switch from one intermediate target to another. However, in the end, none of them proved reliable and *Goodhart's Law* was established—this states that any observed regularity between a monetary aggregate and inflation will break down when central bankers try and exploit it for policy purposes.

2. THE VELOCITY OF MONEY IS NOT PREDICTABLE

One reason why the monetary aggregates behaved differently was because of large changes in the velocity of circulation. Figure 15.14 shows the velocity for a narrow and a broad measure of money for the United Kingdom between 1983 and 2002. During this period, the introduction of ATMs (automatic teller machines) led to a large increase in velocity for narrow money. Because it was easier to get hold of cash, people reduced the amount they withdrew from their bank on each trip and held less cash in their wallet. As a result, the velocity of narrow money increased substantially. At the same time, however, the velocity of broad money fell. Changes in legislation meant that more financial institutions could make loans and the result was intense competition and an increase in credit and broad money, which lowered the velocity of broad money. If these trends were predictable, then allowance could be made for them when setting the

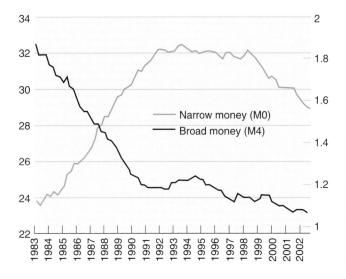

FIGURE 15.14 **U.K. velocity of money, 1983–2002.** Velocity of money has shown large and hard-to-predict changes. *Source:* Economic Trends, U.K. Office for National Statistics, http://www.statistics.gov.uk/

money supply target, but they were not predicted. No one knew when these changes would come to an end nor what would happen in the year ahead. The result was to weaken considerably the link between the money supply and inflation.

3. CAN THE CENTRAL BANK CONTROL THE MONEY SUPPLY?

In Chapter 11 we outlined the money multiplier, which implies that the great majority of broad money is the creation of commercial banks through their credit policies, rather than something that is under the direct control of the central bank. As we shall see later, a central bank can use interest rates only to influence the cost at which a commercial bank can borrow. The central bank cannot be certain whether this cost increase is passed on to a bank's loan customers or whether its increase in lending rates will affect demand for loans. Without a predictable link between changes in interest rates and changes in the money supply, it is problematic to use monetary aggregates as a reliable intermediate target.

4. IS THE SUPPLY CURVE VERTICAL?

Our example of a 4.5% money supply target producing a 2% inflation rate was based on stable output growth of 2.5% per annum. In Chapter 11 we explained the idea of a vertical long-run supply curve that shifts out over time because of technological progress and capital accumulation. With a vertical supply curve, any increase in the money supply will raise aggregate demand but lead only to higher prices and no extra output, as shown in Figure 15.15. However, firms do not usually immediately increase prices in response to an increase in demand. Either because of real or nominal rigidities (as described in Chapter 14), firms choose to keep prices fixed initially and increase output. While this policy is not sustainable, in the short run, while it lasts, the supply curve will not be vertical but have a flatter slope. The result is, as shown in Figure 15.15, that increases in the money supply lead to higher output and inflationary pressure in the short run. Therefore, any attempt at controlling inflation via money supply targeting

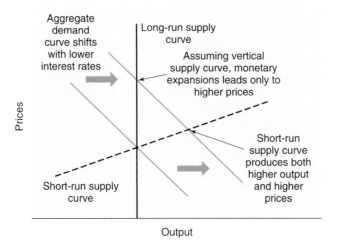

FIGURE 15.15 **Effects of monetary expansion on prices and output.** Assuming a long-run vertical supply curve, monetary expansions produce only inflation. With a short-run supply curve, output and prices both increase.

must make an assumption about the current slope of the supply curve and how long it will take for the inflationary pressures to emerge. To achieve a 2% inflation target will take different money supply growth depending on whether output is growing at 1% or 4% this year.

5. SUPPLY SHOCKS

Even if the velocity of money is constant and the money supply is under control, this does not mean that inflation will be on target. Figure 15.16 shows the case of an adverse supply shock, such as an oil price increase. Even if the money supply is controlled so the demand curve remains fixed, the oil price increase will produce higher inflation and lower output. If these effects are only temporary, then it is less important. But if the supply shocks occur over a long period of time (for instance, a sustained improvement in technology), then the effects on inflation will be long lasting and must be taken into account.

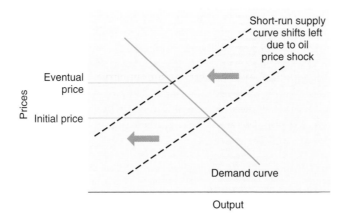

FIGURE 15.16 **Inflation and supply shocks.** Adverse supply shocks will also cause inflation to rise even if the money supply is under control.

While the long-run performance of the quantity theory in explaining inflation is impressive, each of these five factors meant that simple reliance on monetary aggregates was insufficient to control inflation in the short run. As a former governor of the Bank of Canada said, "We didn't abandon the monetary aggregates, they abandoned us." As a consequence, very few countries still maintain such a pure version of money supply targeting. This does not mean that the money supply numbers are uninformative for inflation. It simply means that central banks have to monitor other variables and use additional or alternative intermediate targets.

One country that did profess faith in money supply targeting was Germany. The German enthusiasm for monetary targeting was important in establishing the "twin pillar" approach of the ECB to monetary policy—to use both inflation targeting and monetary indicators in setting interest rates. Even in Germany, however, the use of money supply targeting was not as simple as the approach outlined above. The Bundesbank would only set its money supply target after it had considered in detail the likely behavior of velocity and gross domestic product (GDP) growth over the next year. Changes in these forecasts would lead the Bundesbank to revise its money supply targets. This focus on a wide range of variables rather than just the money supply is more characteristic of inflation targeting than straightforward monetarism.

> **KEY POINT**
>
> Money supply targeting is now much less common than it was in the 1980s and 1990s. This is largely a reflection of the instability in the relation between measures of the money supply and inflation.

15.6 Exchange Rate Targets

An alternative nominal anchor to money supply targets is to set monetary policy in order to achieve a target exchange rate. By dedicating monetary policy to fixing the exchange rate, the hope is to achieve inflation control. In Chapters 19 and 20 we examine in detail the behavior of exchange rates and the links between inflation and interest rates and the relative merits of fixed exchange rates. For now, we take a more informal approach and note that if the central bank achieves a fixed exchange rate, then it is likely that over the medium term it will achieve the same inflation rate as the country with which it has a fixed rate of exchange (see the detailed discussion of *purchasing power parity* in Chapter 19).[2] In order to achieve its exchange rate target, a central bank can raise interest rates if it wants the currency to appreciate or lower them if it wishes the currency to fall (see the discussion of *uncovered interest parity* in Chapter 20).

As Figure 15.12 shows, many countries use exchange rates as a guide to operating monetary policy. However, exchange rate targets can also be costly. The main cost is that if monetary policy is used to fix the exchange rate, it cannot also be used to influ-

---

[2] The intuition is as follows: If one country has a higher inflation rate than another, then its currency will buy fewer items in that country. Therefore people will sell the high inflation currency, leading it to depreciate. If the exchange rate is fixed, it must be because individuals are indifferent as to which currency they hold—they buy both in the same amount. This means inflation must be equal in the two countries.

ence the domestic economy. This lack of an independent monetary policy was at the heart of the United Kingdom and Italy's exit from the European Exchange Rate Mechanism in 1992. The Bundesbank was raising interest rates to control German inflation at this time, and other countries in the group had to follow in order to maintain a fixed exchange rate. However, with other countries in recession, this increase in interest rates was unwelcome, and as a result of these tensions the pound sterling and the lira were forced to leave the fixed exchange rate system. For small open economies whose economy is closely tied to that of the country whose exchange rate they are targeting, fixed exchange rates seem to work well. For larger economies they are more problematic.

15.7 Inflation Targeting

The problem that many central banks encountered with money supply or exchange rate targets is their inflexibility—policymakers only focus on one statistic, be it the money supply or the exchange rate, in order to control inflation. No other information can be used to override the rule. Consider again the case of the United Kingdom and the exchange rate mechanism. While Germany was expanding rapidly and seeing inflation increase, the United Kingdom was in recession and faced no inflationary pressures. If the Bank of England could give weight to a wide range of evidence, then it might conclude that even if sterling depreciated against the deutsche mark this would not threaten higher U.K. inflation. As a result, it might be able to leave interest rates unchanged. By contrast, under a fixed exchange rate the central bank does not have this discretion—regardless of what the data for output or inflation says, the central bank would have to respond to a devaluation in sterling by increasing interest rates to maintain the exchange rate target.

This example suggests the desirability of adopting a monetary policy rule that utilizes a wide range of information and that is flexible enough for policymakers to respond differently to different circumstances. However, no rule could be written down that describes how policy would be set in all possible outcomes. This leaves two alternatives. First, choose a simple rule—such as a money supply or exchange rate target—and face the occasional risk of having to abandon the rule in certain circumstances, leading to some loss of credibility within the country. Alternatively, develop a framework that offers the central bank some discretion in how it responds to the data but also provides a clear objective to which policy is directed and against which the performance of monetary policy can be assessed. This latter option is referred to as "constrained discretion."

Inflation targeting is an attempt to achieve this constrained discretion. Inflation targeting involves the central bank stating explicit quantitative targets (or ranges) for inflation for a specific time horizon. The central bank also dedicates monetary policy to achieving a low inflation rate and no other purpose. The intermediate target in this framework becomes the central bank's own inflation forecast. If the forecast is for inflation to exceed its target, the central bank has to raise interest rates accordingly. By using the forecast rate of inflation as an intermediate target variable, the central bank can take into consideration a huge range of information. Any variable that influences inflation should be considered, including the exchange rate and the money supply. No one variable is dominant and the net effect of all of them is considered.

This obviously provides the central bank with a large amount of discretion, so in order to preserve credibility, inflation targeting is characterized by vigorous efforts at communicating with the public. Through publications and speeches, the central bank reveals the logic behind its deliberations and actions, and publishes its forecasts and its analysis of how it thinks the economy and monetary policy operate. After decades of acting with the utmost secrecy, the adoption of inflation targeting has brought about a dramatic change in the behavior of central bankers.

The belief is that by explaining in a consistent and logical manner the reasons behind monetary policy decisions, the public will appreciate that inflation targeting is desirable, should be supported, and will be consistently followed. Further, if this is understood, the public will not fear the central bank using its discretion to risk high inflation but will instead expect it to use discretion to set monetary policy in a flexible manner. Indeed, some advocates of inflation targeting argue that it should increase credibility. Simple inflexible rules will inevitably be abandoned in certain circumstances, but not flexible approaches like inflation targeting.

KEY POINT

Inflation targeting is a framework for monetary policy, not a rule—it occupies a midpoint on the rules versus discretion spectrum. It provides a forward-looking discipline that should enhance credibility, but allows flexible responses to events (such as shocks to the demand for money). Inflation targeting does not provide mechanical instructions to the central bank, but allows it to use its discretion in the short run.

Inflation targeting has been enthusiastically adopted by central banks. Starting with New Zealand in 1990 and subsequently Canada, the United Kingdom, Finland, Sweden, Australia, Israel, Chile, Mexico, and Brazil, inflation targeting has become a common *modus operandi*. The European Central Bank also operates a form of inflation targeting, although it continues to place a special—though probably diminishing—emphasis on the money supply figures.

In adopting inflation targeting, numerous operational issues have to be determined. What measure of inflation should be used? Which inflation rate should be the target? Should a range be targeted or a specific value? What horizon should the central bank focus on? Most countries focus on increases in consumer prices (sometimes extracting volatile components) and a target of around 2%. Some countries specify that inflation should be below a certain limit (the ECB sets a target of 2% or less), while others allow deviations from the target rate within a narrow band (from 2004 the Bank of England targets 2.0% inflation around a band of 1% either side, New Zealand, a range of 0–3%).

15.8   The Operational Instruments of Monetary Policy

As well as the ultimate and intermediate targets, the other key component of monetary policy is the instruments the central bank has at its disposal. Currently the key tool of monetary policy is the short-term interest rate.

How can central banks, with limited resources, control almost exactly the level of short-term interest rates? The answer is that, at least in the current state of monetary arrangements and transactions technologies, money remains essential. The central bank is the monopoly supplier of so-called *base money*, that is, the cash plus reserves that the commercial banking system holds.

The monetary system in most developed economies is, ultimately, similar. At its center stand commercial banks, which take deposits from the private sector, make loans, and, crucially, help facilitate transactions by honoring checks and other payment instructions from their customers. If the customers of a bank write more checks in a working day than the bank receives in payment, that bank may have to make a net transfer of funds to another bank. For example, suppose that the customers of Deutschebank write checks that the receivers deposit into Dresdnerbank and that compensating flows in the other direction do not match them. At the end of the day, Deutschebank needs to transfer, say, 50 million euro to Dresdnerbank. Both banks will typically have accounts with the central bank; the central bank will hold accounts for the major commercial banks that allow them to settle transactions with each other. Central banks severely limit the ability of private banks to overdraw these accounts or take their reserves below a critical threshold (the reserve requirement). This means that if, toward the end of a working day, Deutschebank has insufficient funds to transfer the necessary amount to the Dresdnerbank account, Deutschebank will need to do something.

The interbank market allows Deutschebank to borrow money from another commercial bank overnight, so that it does not go into deficit at the central bank. But suppose that most major banks are going to be overdrawn at the end of the day and that the system does not have enough funds to allow individual banks to borrow from others that had a surplus at the central bank. Suppose, for example, that a large corporation pays its tax bill on a particular day. When it pays its tax bill, it transfers a large quantity of funds from its account at a commercial bank to a government account. Government accounts are normally held with the central bank, so that clearing the check will result in a net drain of funds from the pool of money available to private banks. If the central bank did nothing to alleviate this shortage, private banks would be bidding for funds on the interbank market and would begin to drive interest rates up.

In this system, central banks operate by providing reserves, mainly through so-called **open market operations** or through lending at the discount window. During a working day, a central bank may realize that the money market will run short of funds unless it acts. The central bank will then signal that the system is likely to run short of funds that day and that it will buy short-term securities[3] in exchange for cash at a specified interest rate. Every time the central bank buys a security from a private bank, that bank's reserves with the central bank are credited with the sale proceeds. So by buying securities (that is, engaging in open market operations), the central bank can help regulate

---

[3] Short-term securities are certificates that represent ownership of loans to government (treasury bills) or companies (commercial paper) where the loans are less than 6 months.

the quantity of reserves in the system. Central banks can also control reserves by directly lending funds to the private banks that require funds. In the U.S. system, such loans are called *discount window lending*.

The key thing to remember about all this is that the central bank has rules about how much funds the private sector banks have to hold with it. The private sector banks will, in certain circumstances, find that there is a shortage (or sometimes a glut) of reserves. If the central bank were to do nothing, the level of money market interest rates would move. The central bank can prevent significant movement in these money market rates by buying or selling securities or by lending money at the discount window. The central bank has enormous influence over the level of money market interest rates because it can supply almost unlimited quantities of funds to the market or, by selling securities, it can drain enormous quantities of reserves from the market.

KEY POINT

Central banks decide the terms at which they will purchase or sell securities and lend them at the discount window.

Note that if commercial banks were not required to hold reserves at the central banks, the central banks would not have the power to alter interest rates. The precise nature of the reserve requirements the central bank requires differs from system to system. In the United States, commercial banks that hold accounts at the Federal Reserve for settlement of flows are required not to be in deficit, on average, over a two-week period. Other systems require that individual banks not be overdrawn on a daily basis. Regardless of the specific detail, the key point is that failure to meet these reserve requirements is penalized by the central bank and only the central bank can supply reserves to the banking system. This is the reason behind the central bank's influence over short-term interest rates.

15.9   Controlling the Money Supply or Interest Rates?

Earlier in this chapter, we reviewed how central banks have tended to move away from trying to control the money supply to a framework of inflation targeting. We also introduced the concept of the LM curve. In doing so, we began with a simple assumption that the central bank controls the money supply. But as Figure 15.9 showed, we can just as well use the IS-LM apparatus to illustrate the much more relevant case where the central bank sets an interest rate and allows the money supply to adapt to its new target rate of interest. Here we return to this important issue.

Figure 15.17 illustrates a situation in which the central bank has a target for some measure of the money supply. As before, we assume a negative relation between the level of the short-term nominal interest rate and the stock of money. The higher the interest rate, the more expensive it is to hold cash, the more narrow money demand falls; and the more expensive it is to borrow, the more credit and broad money decline. M* is

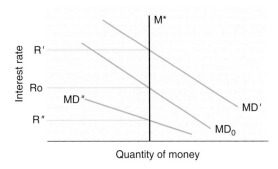

FIGURE 15.17 **Monetary policy when targeting the money supply.** Money supply targets imply volatile interest rates if money demand is unstable.

the target level, and MD_0 illustrates the expected position of the money demand curve. If demand for money turns out to be what the central bank anticipated, then interest rates will be R_0. But if the demand for money is either higher or lower than the central bank anticipates, interest rates will deviate from R_0. If demand is at level MD' and the target does not change, monetary conditions will be tighter, and interest rates will rise to R' to reflect the scarcity of funds. But if demand for money is lower than the central bank anticipates, at MD'', interest rates will fall to R''. With higher demand for money, the central bank will be offsetting expansion in banks' balance sheets by selling securities (that is, entering into contractionary open market operations). This will drain reserves from the banking system and cause interbank interest rates to be bid up as the commercial banks vie to attract funds. In this case, in which the central bank is targeting the money supply, fluctuations in money demand produce considerable volatility in interest rates.

Under inflation targeting, the central bank sets interest rates to achieve a particular inflation target. This case is shown in Figure 15.18. Again, MD_0 denotes the level of demand for money that the central bank anticipates. If the central bank aims to keep interest rates at R^* *and* if demand turns out to be MD_0, the money supply will be at M_0. But if demand deviates from MD_0 and interest rates are kept at level R^*, the supply of money will deviate from M_0. So, for example, if the money demand

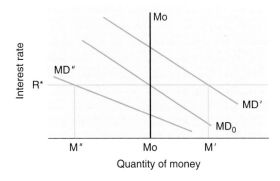

FIGURE 15.18 **Monetary policy when central bank sets interest rates.** When the central bank sets interest rates, volatility occurs in the money supply.

schedule is to the right of MD_0, the quantity of money will exceed M_0. And if the demand for money balances is substantially lower than MD_0, then so will be the stock of money.

If the demand for money schedule is predictable, there is no substantive difference between interest rate targeting and money supply targeting. The central bank could choose to specify a money supply target or a particular level of interest rate, and the two would be equivalent because each interest rate corresponds to a particular (known) level of money demand. As we discussed earlier, it was unpredictable shifts in money demand, due to technological developments and financial innovation, that contributed to central banks looking for alternatives to targeting the money supply.

15.10 How Monetary Policy Affects the Economy— The Transmission Mechanism

We have outlined the aims of a central bank and how it adjusts the instruments of monetary policy to achieve them, but we have not yet outlined in any detail how changes in interest rates affect inflation and output. This is called the **transmission mechanism** of monetary policy—the link among changes in interest rates, changes in components of demand within the economy, and how such changes in demand can affect inflation pressures.

KEY POINT

It is the nature of the transmission mechanism that determines the slope of the IS curve.

Figure 15.19 outlines the main links through which the transmission mechanism works. When the central bank increases official interest rates, this will begin to have an effect on interest rates of all maturities and will influence asset prices. Assuming inflation in the short term is relatively unchanged, short-term *real* interest rates will be higher. If the markets believe the higher interest rates are not purely transitory, this will also increase longer-term bond yields. These increases in interest rates will have a direct effect in lowering demand. As we saw in Chapter 12, increases in interest rates lead to reductions in consumption. In addition, higher interest rates will affect the cost of borrowing and the real rate of return that needs to be earned on investments projects, leading to a fall in investment spending. The higher interest rates will also lead to a fall in asset prices (see Chapters 17 and 18) and further reductions in consumption and investment through wealth effects and the q theory of investment (see Chapter 13). If higher interest rates are expected to lead to a future slowdown in the economy, consumer and producer confidence will also fall, which in turn will lead to retrenchment of consumption and investment plans.

The increase in interest rates will also affect external demand in the economy. As we noted earlier, higher interest rates lead to an increase in the exchange rate. The higher exchange rate makes imports cheaper, which may place downward pressure on

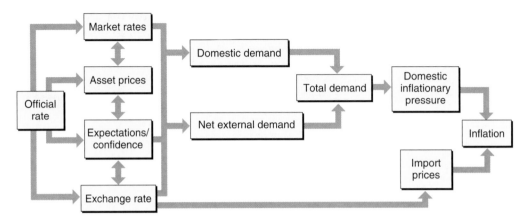

FIGURE 15.19   **The transmission mechanism of monetary policy.** Interest rates affect output and inflation through numerous channels. *Source:* Monetary Policy Committee, Bank of England, *The Transmission Mechanism of Monetary Policy* (1999). Reprinted with permission from the Bank of England.

domestic inflation. Further, the higher exchange rate makes exports more expensive and so reduces demand in the economy. The overall impact of the increase in interest rates is therefore to reduce demand in the economy.

Figure 15.19 focuses on how increases in the price of money, the interest rate, affect the economy. However, in some cases monetary policy operates less as a result of changes in the *price* of money and more through the *quantity* of lending banks undertake. This is known as the **credit channel** of monetary policy. Increases in interest rates can produce declines in real estate and equity prices, which reduce the collateral firms can offer banks. As a consequence, banks reduce their loans to the corporate sector, which has a direct effect on consumption and investment. It has been argued that the credit channel, rather than inappropriate levels of interest rates, was responsible for the severity of the Great Depression. The credit channel occurred through the failure of the Federal Reserve to offset the dramatic decline in the stock of money by providing banks with cash that they could lend.[4] The Federal Reserve could have done this by buying securities from the banking sector and providing it with loanable funds.

Figure 15.19 only outlines the channels through which interest rates effect output and inflation, not the magnitude of the effects nor how long the impact takes. Figure 15.20 shows empirical estimates of how the U.S. economy is affected by a 1% increase in the main federal funds interest rate. As our analysis predicts, the higher interest rates lead to a fall in the money supply, increases in unemployment, and lower prices and output. At its peak, output falls by about 0.7% after about two years. Prices are lower

[4] Friedman, M. and Schwartz, A. (1963) *A Monetary History of the United States 1867–1960,* Princeton University Press.

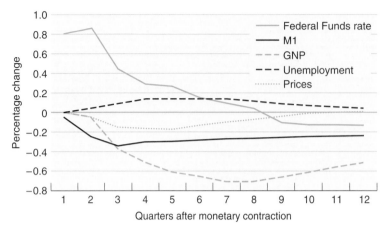

FIGURE 15.20   **The impact of a 1% increase in interest rates on the U.S. economy.** Higher interest rates lead to declines in prices, output, and the money supply and to higher unemployment. Their effect on prices and on output peaks after two years. *Source:* Christiano, Eichenbaum, and Evans, "The Effects of Monetary Policy Shocks: Evidence from the Flow of Funds," *Review of Economics and Statistics* (1996) vol. 78, pp. 16–34. © by the President and Fellows of Harvard College and the Massachusetts Institute of Technology.

by around 0.2%, with the effect peaking after a year. These long lags in the transmission mechanism show the importance of using a forward-looking intermediate target when setting interest rates.

The magnitude of interest rate effects and how quickly they impact the economy depends on the economy's financial structure. Monetary policy will be particularly effective if many domestic firms and households rely strongly on banks for credit, as the interest rate on bank loans varies closely with changes in the short rates under the control of the central bank. In contrast, the cost to companies of issuing equity is likely to be less affected than the cost of borrowing on a loan from a bank. If some firms and households find it difficult to substitute other forms of finance (for example, issues of equities or long-dated bonds) for bank loans, shifts in monetary policy are likely to hit them hard. The degree of substitutability between bank finance and other forms of finance will also be an important influence on the scale of the credit channel. Because financial structure varies across countries, so does the monetary policy transmission mechanism. Figure 15.21 shows how the impact of higher interest rates varies across countries. The overall shape of all the responses is the same, but the size and timing of the impacts vary.[5]

---

[5] Figures 15.20 and 15.21 are taken from different studies covering different time periods. For this reason, the results for the United States are not identical.

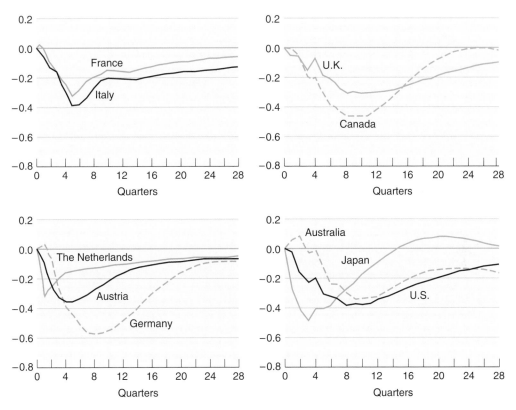

FIGURE 15.21 **Impact of 1% higher interest rates on GDP.** *Source:* Mihov, "Monetary policy implementation and transmission in the European Monetary Union," INSEAD mimeo (2000).

15.11 Monetary Policy in Practice

Let's assume, as is the case in most developed countries, that the central bank sets monetary policy. In general terms, how central banks set policy is uncontroversial. The central bank will first analyze the economy and then consider how best to set the policy instruments that it has, usually short-term money market interest rates. Central banks act in light of the current economic situation and base their assessments on such crucial factors as how the policy instrument will affect the overall level of demand in the economy and how demand is linked to the ultimate policy target. A stylized description of this process is shown in Figure 15.22.

As this discussion and our earlier one regarding inflation targeting reveal, setting interest rates to control inflation is a complex activity. A useful way of summarizing the way interest rates are set are **Taylor rules**.[6] Taylor rules specify a link between the level

[6] After the Stanford economist, John Taylor. See his "Discretion versus Policy Rules in Practice," Carnegie-Rochester Conference Series on Public Policy (November 1993) vol. 39, pp. 195–214.

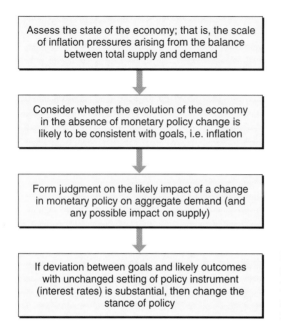

FIGURE 15.22 **Stylized description of behavior of central bank.** Central bankers have to process a wide range of information and form views of future inflation when setting interest rates.

of the short-term interest rate and output and inflation. Some proponents of Taylor rules advocate them for use in setting interest rates in practice. However, our discussion of inflation targeting outlined some problems with using fixed rules. Here we simply propose Taylor rules as a way of approximating what central bankers try to do when setting rates. A number of studies have found such rules provide a reasonably good explanation of actual central bank behavior.

The following equation gives the typical structure for a Taylor rule:

nominal interest rate = equilibrium nominal interest rate + λ × output gap + α × (inflation − inflation target)

where the equilibrium nominal interest rate is the real interest rate plus the inflation target and λ and α are positive numbers. The Taylor rule says that if the output gap is positive (GDP is above its trend value), then the central bank should raise interest rates. Similarly, if inflation is above its target, then interest rates also should be increased. A variety of versions of the Taylor rule exist. Some use the gap between expected future inflation and the inflation target, rather than current inflation. Also, interest rates from the last period are often included in order to smooth the changes in interest rates, something that central banks appear to do.

The positive coefficients λ and α reflect an assessment of the sensitivity of inflation and output to shifts in monetary policy *and* to the chosen tradeoff between inflation volatility and output volatility. If inflation is very sensitive to changes in interest rates, then other things being equal, α will be small, similarly for λ. If the central bank will not tolerate much volatility in inflation, then α will be large, similarly for λ and output volatility. For the United States, the values of λ and α that best account for the behavior of interest rates are about 0.5 and 1.5, respectively. This says that in response to a

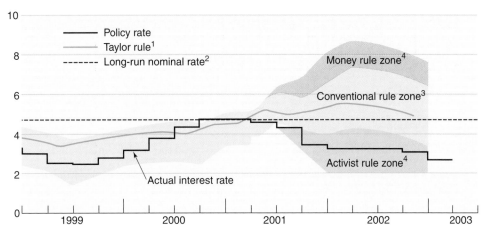

FIGURE 15.23   **ECB interest rate policy and estimates of policy under various forms of Taylor rule.** *Source:* BIS *Annual Report* (2003).

[1](Baseline) Taylor rule = $r^* + \pi_t + \alpha (\pi_t - \pi^*) + \beta\chi_t$, where π_t is HICP inflation, x_t is the output gap, $r^* =$ 3.2% (mean ex post real policy rate over the period 1982–2002), $\pi^* = 1.5\%$, $\alpha = 0.5$ and $\beta = 0.5$

[2]Equal to $r^* + \pi^*$ (baseline).

[3]Range of Taylor rules with r^* set to 2.5 or 3.5%, α set to 0.5 or 2 and β set to 0.5 or 1.

[4]Money rule zone: upper bound is baseline Taylor rule plus 0.5 $(\Delta m_t - \Delta m^*)$, where Δm_t is M3 growth and $\Delta m^* = 4.5\%$ (ECB reference value). Activist rule zone: lower bound is baseline Taylor rule plus the difference between the federal funds rate target and a baseline Taylor rule for the United States. These rule zones are calculated from 2001 onwards.

Source: Bank for International Settlements 73rd Annual Report (2003).

1% increase in the output gap the Federal Reserve tends to raise interest rates by 0.5%. In response to inflation being 1% above its target, the Federal Reserve raises interest rates by 1.5%. It cuts them by 1.5% when inflation is 1% below target. Broadly similar values are obtained for other countries, although differences in attitudes toward inflation mean there are some variations.

If α equals 1, then nominal interest rates would only rise in line with inflation and the real interest rate would not alter. When α exceeds 1, then the central bank responds to higher inflation by increasing the real interest rate—it is the increase in real interest rates that makes the policy contractionary. The Taylor rule, and its ability to track actual changes in interest rates, suggests that central bankers translate the various messages conveyed by a wide range of macroeconomic variables into movements in the output gap and inflation relative to the target. Then, having formed these views, they adjust interest rates accordingly.

The Taylor rule can be used to assess how tight monetary policy has been. The ECB was accused by many of running too tight a monetary policy between 2001 and 2003. Figure 15.23 shows the level of short-term interest rates set by the ECB and compares it with rates that might have been expected based on a Taylor rule and other interest rate setting rules. The figure shows that the ECB actually appeared to be setting a level of interest rates below that which might have been anticipated based on typical relations between conditions in the wider economy and monetary policy.

15.12 The Future of Central Banks

In 1999 Mervyn King, then deputy governor of the Bank of England, noted:

The future of central banks is not entirely secure. Their numbers may decline over the next century. The enthusiasm of governments for national currencies has waned as capital flows have become liberalized and exchange rates more volatile. Following the example of the European Central Bank, more regional monetary unions could emerge. Short of this the creation of currency boards, or even complete currency substitution, might also reduce the number of independent national monetary authorities.[7]

Fewer central banks does not imply a reduction in the power of monetary policy. But the forces that King describes—liberalization of capital flows in particular—may undermine the influence of the few remaining central banks. We noted above that central banks get their power to set short-term nominal interest rates because commercial banks need to hold funds at the central bank to settle transactions among themselves and central banks are the only institution that can provide settlement balances. But for how long will this remain true? The Internet and other types of electronic transfer of information may allow companies and individuals to settle transactions instantaneously and without using what we normally think of as money.

Suppose, for example, that an efficient and highly liquid market exists for a range of securities in which prices are known second by second across the globe. For some assets we are almost in that situation already. The prices of bonds and equities that large companies and governments in developed economies issue are known instantaneously and more or less 24 hours a day across the world. Suppose it were also known, and could be verified, what the value was of the portfolio of such assets that individuals or corporations held. We could then imagine that buyers could purchase commodities and services by immediately transferring claims to such assets to the accounts of sellers.

We might go further and imagine that the ultimate means of settlement was not the monetary unit of account of one country but rather a universal unit of account that could be some sort of commodity money in which the underlying commodity, rather than being gold or silver, was a collection of financial assets. Suppose, for example, our unit of account was a composite equity. Imagine that the world currency, call it the Global, is equal to one share in IBM, one long-dated U.S. government bond, one share in Microsoft, one share in Shell, and one share in Deutschebank. One Global is that collection of assets. The prices of all commodities could then be quoted in terms of Globals.

[7] "Challenges for Monetary Policy: New and Old," a paper prepared for the Symposium on "New Challenges for Monetary Policy," Jackson Hole, Wyoming (August 27, 1999).

Suppose I want to purchase music over the Internet. Its price is one-hundredth of a Global and my Internet account publicly reveals that I have 3,000 Globals. The seller of the music is happy to accept marketable securities whose value is the equivalent of one-hundredth of a Global, and by pressing a button, securities of that value are immediately transferred to the seller's account. There are no reserve balances of money with central banks and, as a result, central banks do not set interest rates because there are no open market operations. This brave new world would also not have generalized price inflation, unless the supply of the equities and bonds that make up the Global were to increase.

Under such a scenario, we would have returned to a sort of gold standard, one based on the value of corporations and bonds. Further, this system need not operate in just a few developed countries; it could be a truly global system and one in which monetary policy would play no role.

SUMMARY

In section 15.1, we saw that the twentieth century has experienced a large increase in the number of central banks as the move away from commodity-based money has given governments more discretion over monetary policy. Monetary policy consists of three main components: an intermediate target the central bank tries to control in order to meet its ultimate target; the instruments of policy the central bank has at its disposal; and the ultimate policy target the central bank wishes to achieve.

In section 15.2, we described how the IS-LM apparatus can be used to depict how changes in monetary policy affect the level of demand in the economy. Although it is common to think of shifts in monetary policy in the context of the IS-LM apparatus as stemming from changes in the money supply, in practice central banks actually control the level of the short-term interest rate. But this is not inconsistent with the IS-LM framework.

We saw in section 15.3, that a belief in a vertical long-run supply curve, pessimism over the ability to fine-tune the economy, and a belief that following rules will improve credibility and achieve lower inflation have all combined to persuade many central banks to target inflation, which most try to keep at around 2%.

In sections 15.4–15.7, we noted that countries have experimented with a range of intermediate targets; money supply, fixed exchange rates, and inflation targeting are the most common. In the 1980s a number of countries attempted to control inflation via controlling the money supply. However, this proved unsatisfactory in practice so that now setting targets for inflation or for the exchange rate are the most common policies. Inflation targeting is attractive to central banks because it provides discretion as to how to respond to economic events while still providing a rules-based framework to help promote credibility.

In section 15.8, we saw that central banks invariably use short-term market interest rates to implement monetary policy. The central bank has control over these because it is the only supplier of reserves to the banking system. In section 15.12, we explored projections from some commentators who believe that technological developments may remove this monopoly position and undermine central banks' role in monetary policy.

In section 15.10, we described a model of the transmission mechanism by which monetary policy affects demand directly by changing interest rates, asset prices, exchange rates, and affecting consumption, investment, and exports. Additional effects work through changes in producer and consumer confidence. Further, a credit channel is believed to sometimes affect the economy. This operates through changes in the supply and demand for credit that are not directly related to interest rates. Empirical estimates suggest that the effect of changing interest rates accumulates over time and takes between 18 months and 2 years to have its peak impact.

In setting interest rates, central bankers monitor a wide range of statistics. In section 15.11, we introduced Taylor rules as a useful way of conceptualizing this process. Interest rates increase when the output gap is large and when inflation exceeds its target.

CONCEPTUAL QUESTIONS

1. (Section 15.1) Should something that has such a large impact on the economy as monetary policy be handed over to a central bank rather than decided by elected politicians?

2. (15.1) Central banks control short-term interest rates because they control the supply of base money, which is the ultimate, final form of settlement for transactions. Are central banks abusing this power by using it to determine interest rates?

3. (15.4–15.7) Why not specify a goal for the monetary authorities that included both a price level and an unemployment target?

4. (15.7/15.11) Should measures of inflation include asset prices (e.g., stock prices and house prices), so that inflation targeting would require the monetary authorities to act when asset prices rise dramatically?

5. (15.11) At Christmas and Easter the public withdraws large amounts of cash from their accounts. What should central banks do during these periods to stabilize interest rates?

6. (15.12) In a world in which electronic transfer of funds is becoming easier and the value of more and more people's assets is easier to ascertain, is the power of central banks doomed to decline? Is this worrisome?

ANALYTICAL QUESTIONS

1. (Section 15.2) Use the IS-LM apparatus to show how the change in the level of interest rates needed to bring about a given change in demand is greater the less responsive are investment and consumption to the cost of borrowing.

2. (15.2) Use the IS-LM framework to show that the level of interest rates needed to preserve demand at some given level might require negative interest rates.

3. (15.11) The Federal Reserve Bank of Albion operates a Taylor rule of

interest rate = inflation target + equilibrium real interest rate + 0.5 × (output gap)

+ 1.5 × (inflation − inflation target)

It has an inflation target of 2% and believes the equilibrium real rate to be 3%. Currently the output gap is zero and trend output growth is 2% per annum.

(a) If output growth is predicted to be 4% this year and inflation 3%, what level should interest rates move to?

(b) How does your answer change if the central bank changes its inflation target to 3%?

(c) Consider again the economy in (a). What should the central bank do if it thinks that trend output growth may have increased to 3.5%? What would happen if it was wrong?

4. (15.11) The Community of Pacific States (CPS) operates a Taylor rule of

interest rates = 5% + A × (output gap) + B × (inflation − inflation target)

Inflation is determined by a Phillips curve so that

inflation = inflation target + *0.5* × output gap last year

And interest rates impact on the output gap so that

output gap = −0.5 × (interest rates last period − 5%)

The output gap is currently 2% and inflation is 3% with a target of 2%. The central bank of the CPS is considering two alternative policy rules. One sets A = 0.75 and B = 1, whereas the other sets A = 0.25 and B = 2.

(a) Compare the behavior of interest rates, inflation, and output over the next five years for both rules.

(b) How does the volatility of inflation and output vary in each case?

(c) Examine how your answers change when the slope of the Phillips curve and the sensitivity of interest rates change.

(d) How would your answers change if inflation = last year's inflation + 0.5 × output gap last year.

5. (15.11) The League of Big States (LBS) has inflation expectations of 5% and an estimated natural rate of unemployment of 5%. A 2% rise (fall) in unemployment leads to a 1% fall (increase) in inflation.

(a) What is inflation when unemployment equals 5%?

(b) What is inflation when unemployment falls to 3%?

(c) If unemployment falls to 3% but the Central Bank of LBS thinks that the natural rate has also fallen to 3%, what will happen to inflation?

(d) How will the behavior of interest rates differ in your answers to (b) and (c) if the Central Bank uses higher interest rates to keep inflation at 5%?

(e) The Central Bank is not sure whether or not the natural rate of unemployment has changed. How will its behavior vary depending upon whether its goal is (1) to achieve inflation of 5% or less, (2) try and maintain stable inflation and unemployment, or (3) inflation should be in the range of 4.5–5.5%?

(f) Let inflation expectations be equal to last period's inflation. Unemployment is currently 5%, the natural rate is 5%, and last year inflation was 5%. The Central Bank wants to lower inflation from 5% to 2%. Compare how unemployment and inflation vary over the next four years when (1) the government wants to achieve 2% inflation next year, (2) the government wants to achieve 2% inflation by lowering inflation by 1% each year.

Stabilization Policy

Overview

In this chapter we ask a big question: Can governments use fiscal and monetary policy to stabilize the economy? We saw in Chapter 14 that economies do not grow smoothly. Most advanced industrialized countries go through periods when economic growth is above the long-run average, unemployment falls, and inflation is high. In other periods, output is far more sluggish, unemployment rises, and inflation falls. In this chapter we consider whether fiscal policy and monetary policy can be used to make the path of output, unemployment, and inflation smoother than it otherwise would be. We analyze whether tradeoffs between inflation and output exist. We consider whether governments and central banks operate macroeconomic policy better when they have maximum flexibility (or discretion) or whether binding rules exist that generate better long-run outcomes although they reduce discretion in the short run.

Key Concepts

The Phillips Curve	Ricardian Equivalence	The Sacrifice Ratio
Policy Credibility	Rules and Discretion	Time Inconsistency

16.1 Output Fluctuations and the Tools of Macroeconomic Policy

In Chapter 14, we introduced the concept of the output gap—the difference between gross domestic product (GDP) and its trend level. The volatility of an economy's output gap is one measure of the strength of its business cycle fluctuations. These business cycle fluctuations can be large, as Figure 16.1 shows. What can the government do to reduce these fluctuations? Can the government stabilize the economy by using fiscal and monetary policy?

We can use the aggregate demand and supply analysis of Chapter 14 to show what might be feasible. Consider Figure 16.2, which shows the case of an economy that has experienced a positive aggregate demand shock (e.g., an investment boom, a consump-

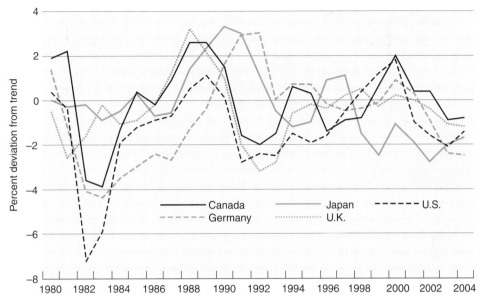

FIGURE 16.1   **Output gaps in industrialized nations, 1980–2004.** Output shows substantial volatility over the business cycle. *Source:* OECO, *The World Economic Outlook Database* (September 2003).

tion surge, or an increase in government expenditure). In the short run, the economy moves from A to B—prices rise and output increases. However, at B the economy is producing above its trend level—the output gap is positive—so prices are rising. As prices increase, demand and output fall until the economy reaches C. The result is an increase in prices but no long-run increase in output. While moving from A to C, output and prices show considerable volatility. If the government could control the demand curve, it could reduce demand—for instance, by raising taxes, reducing government expenditure, or increasing interest rates—and shift the demand curve back again. Prices would remain at A and output would not change. A similar logic holds for negative

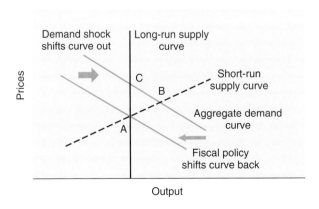

FIGURE 16.2   **Stabilization policy with demand shocks.** By changing monetary and fiscal policy, government may be able to adjust demand to stabilize prices and output in the face of aggregate demand shocks.

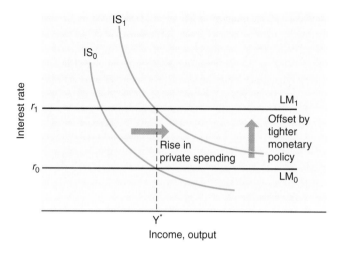

FIGURE 16.3 **Using monetary policy to offset higher spending.**

demand shocks. In this case, by boosting demand (through interest rate and tax cuts, or increases in expenditure) the government could avoid recession. By using fiscal and monetary policy to change demand, Figure 16.2 suggests that governments might be able to stabilize output and prices.

Figure 16.3 illustrates how monetary policy operated by the central bank setting the interest rate can play this role using the IS-LM framework. Here the target for income is Y^*. Initially, planned spending generates an IS curve at IS_0. A surge in optimism in the private sector boosts household and corporate spending plans, so the IS curve moves to IS_1. A tightening of monetary policy is required to offset the expansionary impact of this wave of optimism. The LM curve moves up from LM_0 to LM_1 as the central bank responds to the strength of demand by raising interest rates from r_0 to r_1—exactly what is required to keep income constant.

Figure 16.4 illustrates another example of counter-cyclical monetary policy. Here, monetary policy is loosened to offset a decline in planned private sector spending that has pushed the IS curve to the left (from IS_0 to IS_1). The LM curve shifts from LM_0 to

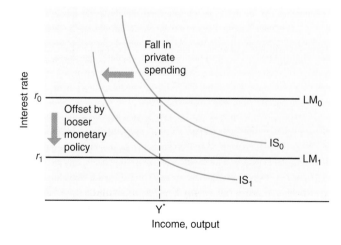

FIGURE 16.4 **Using monetary policy to compensate for a fall in spending.**

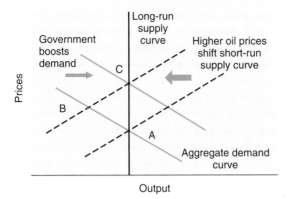

FIGURE 16.5 **Stabilization policy and supply shocks.** Using fiscal and monetary policy to boost demand helps stabilize output and avoids the need for prices to fall.

LM_1 as interest rates fall from r_0 to r_1—exactly enough to boost interest sensitive spending so as to offset the fall in other components of demand.

Figure 16.5 shows the role of stabilization policy after an adverse supply shock—for instance, an increase in oil prices. The increase in oil prices causes the supply curve to shift leftwards, which produces an increase in prices and a fall in output as the economy moves from A to B. B is below the trend level of output and so is not a long-run equilibrium. For the economy to return to equilibrium, either prices have to fall and the economy moves from B to A (which, given price stickiness, could take a long while), or the government boosts demand and shifts the economy from B to C. If the government does the latter, it will be stabilizing output but destabilizing prices.

Events in the 1970s and 1980s substantially reduced this optimism. Later in this chapter we will outline a powerful argument that says governments should *not* try to use fiscal and monetary policy in such a discretionary way. Instead, they should follow fixed rules and avoid the temptation to try to stabilize the economy. We shall show that, in certain cases, we reach the counterintuitive result that by doing so the government achieves a better outcome than if it tried to manipulate the economy. This is a positive argument for not using stabilization policy—there are better ways of doing things.

There are also negative arguments—that stabilization policy will not work if it is tried. These negative arguments apply to both monetary and fiscal policy. They are based both on the fact that policymakers have only limited information at their disposal and on the time lags involved between the economy experiencing a problem and a policy response having its effect. We explore these arguments further in the next section.

General Arguments against Stabilization Policy

16.2

UNCERTAINTY

In Figures 16.2 and 16.5, we assumed that the government knew by exactly how much the demand or supply curve had shifted and also what the trend level of output was. However, one of the key problems of stabilization policy is figuring out what is happening in the economy. Figure 16.6 shows a variation on Figure 16.2. In this case, the long-run supply curve has shifted out, presumably because of some technological development, at the same time as the positive demand shock has happened. The government needs to decide how much of the increase in output has been caused by demand factors and how much by permanent supply changes. If it mistakenly assumes that the cause is nearly all demand shocks, then fiscal and monetary policy will be tightened too much and the economy will experience a sharp recession. Therefore, the government runs the risk of being the source of volatility if it uses stabilization policy when it is uncertain of the structure of the economy.

POLICY-MAKING LAGS

Monetary and fiscal policy are also subject to long lags. Stabilization policy faces three types of lag: informational lags, decision lags, and implementation lags. Informational lags arise because economic data are published only with a delay and even then are normally revised after publication. For example, in December we usually only have provisional estimates of what GDP was in June. Therefore, governments will only have statistical evidence of a boom or a recession several months after the fact. Decision lags arise because, even when it has obtained the data, the government has to decide how to respond. For monetary policy, when all that has to be decided is the interest rate, this can be done relatively quickly. However, fiscal policy involves many different tax rates, tax thresholds, and thousands of government procurement decisions; fiscal policy cannot be adjusted so rapidly.

Finally, even when a government has identified an economic problem and adjusted its policy accordingly, it will take several periods before the change has its full impact on the economy. This is the implementation lag. First, the policy actually has to be

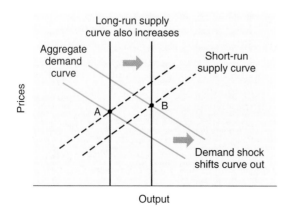

FIGURE 16.6 **Business cycle expansion due to demand and supply boost.** Stabilization policy is complicated by the need to work out whether fluctuations are caused by temporary demand shocks or permanent supply improvements.

changed. In the case of interest rates this can be done swiftly, but for tax and expenditure plans, the process is more cumbersome and may even require legislation. Second, once policy has been changed, it has to have an effect on the economy. Empirical estimates suggest that it takes around two years before the peak impact of changing fiscal and monetary policy is achieved. Long, uncertain lags mean that stabilization policy may actually be destabilizing. By the time a government has boosted demand in response to a recession, the economy may well have recovered, thus the policy is simply adding demand to an already strong recovery.

PROBLEMS WITH FISCAL POLICY

Fiscal policy is not a very flexible tool. Changes in taxes are administratively difficult and take time. Government expenditure cannot be turned on and off like water from a tap. Government departments have to plan in advance. No one could run a government department of transportation in which expenditure on road maintenance fluctuated massively from year to year as the government tried to fine-tune the economy with sharp movements in the overall level of spending. The same is obviously true of defense, health, and education spending. There is a tension, then, between sensible long-run planning for providing public sector services and using the overall level of government spending to regulate demand in the economy. An additional problem for fiscal policy is that governments wish to achieve many objectives through tax and expenditure policies—long-run growth, redistribution, environmental concerns, and political ends. These aims may conflict with the role of fiscal policy in stabilizing business cycles. This is different from monetary policy, in which the sole instrument is interest rates and the government seeks to achieve only limited aims.

The other complication in using fiscal policy is uncertainty over the impact that changes in taxes or increases in expenditure will have on demand. There are three channels through which attempts by the government to boost demand may be offset by the behavior of the private sector: Ricardian equivalence, consumer expectations, and crowding out.

RICARDIAN EQUIVALENCE

The eighteeth-century English economist David Ricardo (1772–1823) argued that whether a government financed spending by raising taxes or by issuing debt would have little impact upon demand if people were forward looking. The idea was that if debt was issued, people would see that this was just storing up more tax for the future. The **Ricardian equivalence principle** says that the impact of government expenditure on the economy does not depend on whether higher taxes or government debt is used to finance it. In other words, government deficits have no effect on the economy. Ricardian equivalence is a special result which relies on several strong assumptions. Ricardian equivalence is unlikely to hold exactly. However, it is the case that sometimes increases in fiscal deficit have little effect on demand because of increases in private sector saving. Unless the multiplier effects of fiscal deficits are predictable, using fiscal policy to stabilize the economy can be destabilizing.

CONSUMER EXPECTATIONS

As we saw in Chapter 12, how consumers respond to tax cuts depends on whether they perceive them as transitory or not. If consumers believe tax cuts will be reversed as soon as the economy recovers from recession, consumption will respond only weakly to a tax cut, if at all. Only if the tax cuts are perceived as being permanent will consumption respond strongly. As tax cuts made to stabilize the economy are only temporary, this not only suggests they will have only a small effect on the economy, it also adds an additional element of uncertainty as to how fiscal policy will work.

CROWDING OUT

There are a variety of different ways in which "crowding out" works, but all have the same essential mechanism: increases in the fiscal deficit lead to higher interest rates and lower private sector demand. If the government is trying to stimulate demand with spending that enlarges the deficit, the drop in demand due to higher interest rates "crowds out" the government's efforts. If private sector demand is highly sensitive to interest rates, these crowding out effects can be substantial.

The classic way in which crowding out operates is through a larger fiscal deficit reducing the amount of funds available to other borrowers, including the corporate sector. This leads to higher interest rates, which leads to lower investment and consumption. The expenditure plans of the private sector have to be reduced in order to provide the financing for the fiscal deficit. For this channel to work, the fiscal deficit must be large relative to the amount of funds available in the loan market. In the 1950s and 1960s, when global capital flows were very small, deficits had to be financed largely through the domestic loan markets and so this channel would have been important. Given the size of global capital markets today, however, very few economies are likely to have a large enough fiscal deficit for crowding out to work through this channel. This argument is probably only relevant for the case of an extremely large U.S. fiscal deficit. But this is a relevant case, since the U.S. deficit in the early 1990s and again ten years or so later was large and growing.

There are, however, alternative ways that crowding out can happen. Monetary policy is set mostly by independent central banks, which may be persuaded to raise interest rates in order to reduce inflationary pressures if governments run large fiscal deficits. A non-accommodating monetary policy designed to keep the level of output steady in the wake of a rise in spending triggered by a laxer fiscal policy will generate a rise in rates. The higher rates can crowd out extra demand by curtailing interest-rate sensitive spending. Figure 16.3 illustrated just such a case. These higher interest rates would lower consumption and investment and, through a higher exchange rate, lead to lower exports.

MONETARY POLICY

In many ways, monetary policy is a more useful tool for stabilization. Central banks can change interest rates at very short notice. The U.S. Federal Reserve, the European Central Bank, and central banks in Japan, Australia, New Zealand, and in the United Kingdom have regular meetings to discuss monetary policy after which, literally within minutes, the decisions on interest rates that have been made are implemented. The lag between a decision and the implementation of monetary policy is virtually zero.

Nonetheless, many of the problems with fiscal policy are common to monetary policy. Private sector expectations about the aims of policy are critical. Time lags between the implementation of policy (a change in interest rates) and its impact upon expenditure decisions are long and variable. Most of the effects of interest rates on output and inflation may only come through after two or three years.

Finally, although the ability to move official interest rates and other short-term interest rates is substantial, central banks do not control *real* interest rates of any maturity. So when they set monetary policy, central banks have a very indirect impact on the prices that really matter for many private sector spending decisions. One would expect that investment decisions, precisely because they have long-term implications, would be most sensitive to shifts in long-term, real interest rates. But central banks only set short-term, nominal interest rates. This means that unless movements in interest rates set by the central bank can influence expectations of inflation and of future interest rates, they are unlikely to have a substantial impact upon spending.

KEY POINT

Using stabilization policy is problematic and assumes a great deal of knowledge and proficiency among economic policymakers. Fiscal policy is not flexible enough and its impact too uncertain to be extensively used for stabilization purposes. Although monetary policy also has drawbacks, it is more suitable as a short-term demand management tool.

We shall now examine whether, using monetary policy, governments should seek to stabilize output. The answer to that question depends, in part, on whether there is a trade-off between inflation and unemployment.

16.3   The Inflation Output Tradeoff

Historically there has been a correlation in most developed economies between the rate of unemployment and the rate of inflation. Bill Phillips, who spent most of his life as a professional economist at the London School of Economics, first noted this link.[1] Phillips observed an empirical regularity between unemployment and inflation. Specifically, he documented a negative correlation between the level of unemployment and the rate of increase in prices and wages. The lower unemployment, the higher inflation tended to be. The data he considered and the curve that explains this data is shown in Figure 16.7.

To understand this correlation, let's suppose that at some point in time people expect that inflation will be 3%. We will assume that the labor market is in equilibrium (at the existing level of real wages, all those who want to work can, and firms are employing precisely the number of people that maximizes their profits). In this case, if unemployment remains constant, wages should be increasing at the rate of expected inflation, so that real wages are expected to be steady (for the moment we ignore technological progress, which would allow wages to grow by inflation plus the rate of productivity growth). Suppose that instead of wages and prices both increasing at 3%, as people had

---

[1] Alban William Housego "Bill" Phillips was an inventive man (as well as being a polymath, a crocodile hunter, and a school dropout at the age of 15). He built probably the first working model for macroeconomic experiments. The machine was made up of tanks and pipes with different colored water to represent levels of consumption and exports; a variety of taps and plugs showed how demand circulated through the economy. For a fascinating account of Phillips and his life, see Leeson, "A.W.M. Phillips MBE (Military Division)," *The Economic Journal* (May 1994).

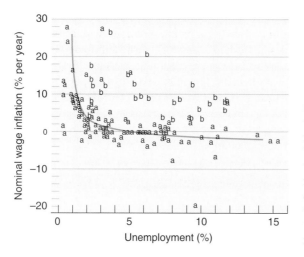

FIGURE 16.7 **Wage inflation and unemployment, U.K. 1856–1997.** Phillips used U.K. historical data and found a negative relationship between (wage) inflation and unemployment. *Source:* Reprinted from Haldane and Quah, *Journal of Monetary Economics* (1999), vol. 44, pp. 259–278. Copyright 1999. Reprinted with permission from Elsevier Science.

anticipated, demand for the output of firms turned out to be higher than producers had anticipated and, in response, companies increased their prices by more than 3%. If wages are fixed in nominal terms in the short run, then real wages will have fallen (nominal wages will have risen at 3% while the prices of goods will have increased by more than 3%, so real wages—the ratio of nominal wages to the price level—will have fallen). Because labor is now cheaper, firms will hire more workers to supply more output, particularly when demand is high. The end result is a negative correlation between inflation and unemployment, as illustrated in Figure 16.8.

Figure 16.8 depicts the Phillips curve for a given level of inflation expectations; that is, the relation between unemployment (horizontal axis) and inflation (vertical axis) holding anticipated inflation constant. We can represent the Phillips curve in a simple formula

inflation = inflation expectations + A × (natural rate

of unemployment − actual unemployment)

where A is a positive number. This version of the **Phillips curve** states that actual inflation will equal expected inflation if output and unemployment remain at their equilibrium levels (see Chapter 7 for a full analysis of the natural rate of unemployment). This

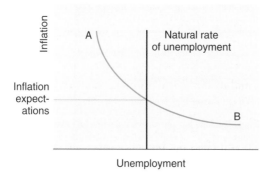

FIGURE 16.8 **The Phillips curve.** The Phillips curve shows a negative relationship between inflation and unemployment. Unemployment equals the natural rate when inflation equals inflation expectations.

means that the point at which the Phillips curve crosses the line depicting the natural rate of unemployment gives an inflation rate equal to inflation expectations. If the level of inflation expectations changes, then the Phillips curve will shift to a new position.

Suppose A = 0.5 and the natural rate of unemployment is 6%. Suppose, too, that everyone thinks that inflation is going to be 5%, and unemployment is 6%. The Phillips curve says that in these circumstances, inflation will turn out to be 5%. But if unemployment were 2%, inflation would need to be 7%, that is, the 5% expected inflation plus an extra $0.5 \times (6 - 2)$.

In explaining why there is a negative relationship between inflation and unemployment, we made the assumption that wages could not adjust as rapidly as prices. It was because of this that the real wage changes, which in turn affects labor demand and unemployment. However, as soon as wages do adjust, the real wage returns to a value consistent with unemployment being at its natural rate. That is, the negative relationship between inflation and unemployment is only a short-run phenomenon—it is only while wages are sticky relative to prices that this tradeoff between inflation and unemployment exists. When wages and prices have both fully adjusted, unemployment will be at its natural rate. Therefore only in the short run can governments use demand management to affect unemployment.

Unemployment is a real variable that ultimately must be explained by real factors, not nominal forces. As Chapter 7 showed, the natural rate of unemployment depends on real factors such as the tax and benefits system, the power of trade unions, employment protection legislation, and monopoly power in firms. The original Phillips curve contained no reference to inflation expectations or the natural rate; it simply envisaged a negative relationship between inflation and unemployment. It was through the work of Edmund Phelps and Milton Friedman that these additional aspects of the Phillips curve were introduced. As we shall see, the introduction of expectations and the natural rate profoundly changes the government's policy options.

There is one further addition to the Phillips curve that we have to make. We saw in Chapter 14 that supply shocks also contributed to inflation through adverse shifts in the supply curve. Further, these negative supply shocks cause output and employment to fall. We need therefore to amend our Phillips curve to

inflation = inflation expectations + A × (natural rate of

unemployment − actual unemployment) + supply shocks

Supply shocks introduce another reason why the Phillips curve can shift. The negative tradeoff between inflation and unemployment only exists for changes in demand—adverse supply shocks cause inflation and unemployment to rise together. *Therefore the Phillips curve exists as a short-run tradeoff the government faces when it uses demand management; it is not necessarily a strongly observed relationship in the data.* Figure 16.9a, b, c show inflation and unemployment for the United States, Japan, and France between 1980 and 2004. For Japan, and to some extent France, a negative relationship exists, but certainly not for the United States during this time period. However, this does not mean the Phillips curve does not exist. Any changes in inflation expectations, the natural rate of unemployment, or supply shocks will shift the Phillips curve but, at any moment in time, the government still faces the Phillips curve tradeoff in operating demand management policies.

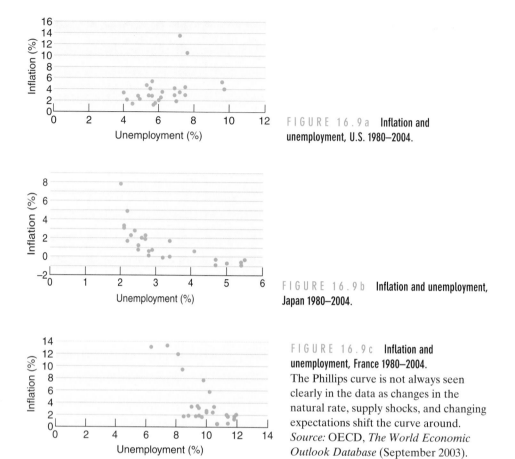

FIGURE 16.9a   **Inflation and unemployment, U.S. 1980–2004.**

FIGURE 16.9b   **Inflation and unemployment, Japan 1980–2004.**

FIGURE 16.9c   **Inflation and unemployment, France 1980–2004.**
The Phillips curve is not always seen clearly in the data as changes in the natural rate, supply shocks, and changing expectations shift the curve around. *Source:* OECD, *The World Economic Outlook Database* (September 2003).

If there is a known, stable, and predictable Phillips curve, governments have a tool to help operate stabilization policy. Using Keynesian demand management, it seems that the government could usefully increase or reduce demand depending upon events in the economy. Therefore, it appears possible to achieve a preferred level of unemployment. The role of the Phillips curve is to tell policymakers the costs of a particular unemployment rate in terms of the inflation it will generate. If governments want to reduce unemployment and are prepared to pay the price of higher inflation, they simply need to increase demand within the economy, which will bid up prices and generate more inflation. To the extent that this inflation is unexpected, unemployment will be lower as we move along the Phillips curve from a point like B to one like A in Figure 16.8. Alternatively, a government may decide that inflation is too high, and the Phillips curve will tell the policymakers how much unemployment they have to accept to reduce inflation. If governments believe that the inflation and unemployment combination of point A in Figure 16.8 is suboptimal and inflation too high, then the level of unemployment at B might be a price they would pay to reduce inflation.

16.4 The Phillips Curve and Shifting Expectations

During the 1950s and 1960s, the Phillips curve was crucial to understanding how governments ran fiscal and monetary policy in an effort to stabilize the economy. However, Milton Friedman warned that the Phillips curve could not be used for this purpose and, if it were, the result would be ever higher inflation rates.[2] Key to Friedman's analysis is the fact that a different Phillips curve exists for each level of inflation expectations. If inflation expectations increase, then the Phillips curve shifts upwards, while a decrease in expectations leads to a downward shift. Figure 16.10, which shows U.K. wage inflation and unemployment, indicates that such shifts do occur. Between 1856 and 1957 (points labeled *a*), inflation was low and so were inflation expectations. However, between 1957 and 1997 (points labeled *b*), U.K. inflation increased substantially and so did expectations. The result was the Phillips curve shifting upwards.

Figure 16.11 illustrates Friedman's powerful argument. Suppose initially that inflation expectations are 2% and unemployment equals its natural (equilibrium) rate. The government, however, wishes to achieve lower unemployment and so increases demand by raising government spending. This leads to higher prices and inflation moves above

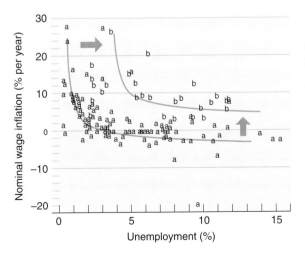

FIGURE 16.10 **U.K. Phillips curve and shifting expectations.** Increases in inflation led U.K. inflation expectations to rise and the Phillips curve to shift outwards. Point *a* denotes observations in period 1856–1956; point *b* from period 1957–1997. *Source:* Reprinted from Haldane and Quah, "The U.K. Phillips Curve and Monetary Policy," *Journal of Monetary Economics* (1999), vol. 44, pp. 259–278. Copyright (1999). Reprinted with permission from Elsevier Science.

[2] Friedman, "The Role of Monetary Policy," *American Economic Review* (1968), vol. 68, pp. 1–17.

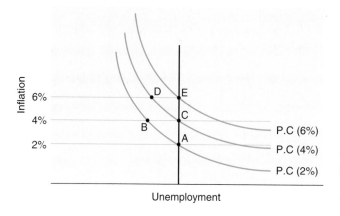

FIGURE 16.11 **The long-run Phillips curve.** Because inflation expectations adjust to higher inflation outcomes, the government does not face a usable trade-off between inflation and unemployment.

2%. Because of wage sluggishness, the real wage falls. This lower real wage leads to a fall in unemployment. The economy moves along a short-run Phillips curve to a point such as B—with lower unemployment and inflation above 2% (we have assumed it at 4%).

At point B one of three things will happen. First, wages may never adjust; the real wage remains permanently lower and unemployment stays at this low level. However, for this to happen we have to discard our analysis of the natural rate as an equilibrium concept and assume that unemployment, a real variable, is determined by nominal demand rather than real supply side factors. Second, nominal wages could adjust to the higher inflation level; the real wage returns to its equilibrium level and the economy returns to A. However, for this to happen, individuals have to display slightly strange behavior. At B, inflation is at 4% and the economy can only be at A if individuals expect inflation of 2%. In deciding what level of wages to bargain for, workers have to form an expectation of inflation. In doing so, surely they will consider the current level of inflation. The government has already revealed it prefers B to A, so if workers negotiate wages on the basis of 2% inflation expectations, inflation is once again likely to be 4%. The third possibility therefore is that workers revise upwards their inflation expectations to 4% and the Phillips curve shifts upwards to the line we have marked PC 4%. If that happens, then if inflation remains at 4%, unemployment will move back to its natural rate (point C).

If the government wants to keep unemployment beneath its natural rate, it must increase demand again. But now, it has to generate inflation *above* 4% in order to lower the real wage. So we could move to point D with unemployment beneath its natural rate, but the inflation rate now has to be higher again, at 6%. But if the economy remains at point D, we would have to assume that workers begin to anticipate 6% inflation and inflation remaining at 6% would then imply that unemployment would move back to its natural rate at point E.

Therefore, if individuals adapt their inflation expectations in response to changes in observed inflation, attempts by governments to exploit the Phillips curve produce only higher inflation and no long-run benefits in terms of unemployment. There is a *vertical* long-run Phillips curve positioned at the natural rate. Friedman's crucial insight is that there is no usable long-run tradeoff between inflation and output. The key assumption is that the natural rate of unemployment is itself independent of nominal variables and is determined by fundamental supply side factors.

KEY POINT

Friedman's analysis of the Phillips curve is a forceful argument against using demand management to achieve "full" employment. If full employment is incompatible with the natural rate of unemployment, then attempts at demand management will just result in higher inflation. However, Friedman's argument does not necessarily imply that stabilization policy must fail. After all, stabilization policy is designed to stabilize output and unemployment around some long-run trend rather than to try to drive the level of output (or unemployment) permanently above (or below) that long-run trend.

The Friedman argument showed how important the private sector's expectations are in determining the short-and long-run response to shifts in demand induced by movements in government policy. We will develop this theme in the next section of the chapter, when we examine the role credibility plays in setting monetary policy. Friedman's argument also illustrated the enormous importance of the difference between shocks that might affect the natural rate of unemployment (and certainly would then affect the long-run sustainable rate of output or unemployment) and shocks that affected short-run demand. This distinction is critical to stabilization policy. Governments should not try to offset supply side shocks that affect the natural rate of unemployment. If shocks occur that mean that unemployment can now safely be 2% rather than 4% without inflation accelerating, governments should not try to tighten policy and reduce the level of demand in the economy when unemployment falls beneath 4%. But if a temporary demand shock (for example, stock prices are bid up irrationally or consumers start spending in a wave of optimism) drives unemployment beneath its natural rate of 4%, governments might want to head off incipient inflation by reducing demand. The dilemma faced by the U.S. Federal Reserve under Alan Greenspan in setting interest rates in the late 1990s was to identify which of these scenarios was the most likely.

16.5 Policy Credibility—The Good News about Shifting Expectations

Friedman's analysis suggests governments should not try to exploit the Phillips curve in a regular manner, and it implies that demand-side policies cannot affect the level of unemployment. The reason for this pessimism is the fact that inflation expectations change with observed inflation. However, the importance of shifting inflation expectations also brings good news for monetary policymakers. Shifting expectations may lead to the ability to lower inflation without large increases in unemployment.

From the Phillips curve, we have that every 1% increase in unemployment produces an A% decline in inflation. Therefore, to reduce inflation by 1% we need to increase unemployment by (1/A)%—this is called the **sacrifice ratio**, how much unemployment needs to be generated to lower inflation by 1%. If, however, the government can persuade the private sector that inflation will be reduced, then inflation expectations will fall

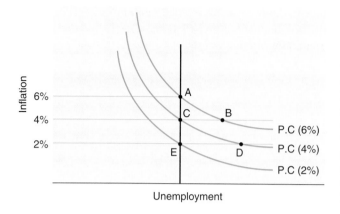

FIGURE 16.12 **Disinflation when expectations are slow to change.** The central bank can lower inflation either by moving along a Phillips curve by achieving higher than expected inflation (i.e., A to C) or by lowering inflation expectations (A to C) and shifting the Phillips curve down.

and so will inflation *without any need for higher unemployment*. Therefore, the more that inflation expectations change, the less disinflationary work unemployment has to perform.

To see how this argument works, consider Figure 16.12. Suppose that the private sector—either through inertia and myopia, or through scepticism about what government policy can actually achieve—believes that the current inflation rate is likely to stay the same. Suppose also that inflation is higher than the government wants it to be. To be specific, suppose that the inflation rate is 6% and everyone thinks that it will stay there. Suppose now that the government tries to reduce inflation. We can use the Phillips curve to work out how the economy might evolve. We start at point A in Figure 16.12. The government now tightens policy—by having the central bank increase interest rates, by cutting government spending, or by increasing taxes—and by doing so lowers inflation to, say, 4%. But because people still expect that inflation will stay at 6%, they do *not* respond to this tougher policy by lowering their anticipation of future price rises, and wage settlements continue to run at a level that reflects expectations of a 6% rise in general prices. This means wages are set too high relative to inflation, the real wage is high, unemployment increases, and we move to point B.

If the economy remains at B for long enough, then eventually the private sector will adjust its inflation expectations. It will realize that the government is serious about producing low inflation and is even prepared to accept high unemployment in order to do so. If people now believe that inflation will stay at 4%, the Phillips curve shifts down and we move toward point C. But suppose the government really wants to cut inflation to 2%. With actual inflation now at 4%, it has to again announce a tough policy of relatively high interest rates and/or relatively tight fiscal policy. If people continue to believe that inflation will stay at its current rate (4%), we have to endure again the pain of higher unemployment to drive the inflation rate down. Given expectations of 4% inflation, unemployment must rise to point D for actual inflation to be 2%. Only after another spell of unemployment do we eventually drive expectations of inflation down to 2%. Then we can return to the original level of unemployment, but with inflation at 2% rather than 6%. The government has achieved its planned disinflation but only at the cost of a prolonged period with unemployment above its natural rate. The longer that inflation expectations take to fall, the more prolonged is this period.

But now suppose that the private sector was rational, forward-looking, *and*, crucially, believes that the government will ultimately bring the inflation rate down to 2%. Then as soon as the government announces its intentions, expectations of inflation move down from 6% to 2%. The unemployment rate does not have to increase at all. Instead, wage bargains immediately reflect expectations of 2%, rather than 6%, inflation. We move directly from point A to point E in Figure 16.12. The credibility of the government's policy, and the forward-looking nature of price setting in labor and goods markets, means that the sacrifice ratio is zero!

KEY POINT

The more that disinflation can be achieved by lowering expectations (shifting the Phillips curve down) rather than raising unemployment (moving along a given Phillips curve) the lower the sacrifice ratio.

Whether inflation expectations shift downward depends on the credibility of the government's announced disinflation plan. Governments cannot just announce a policy of being tough on inflation and expect that inflation will immediately fall at zero cost. The private sector may have good reason *not* to believe the government. If this is the same government that started out with low inflation, but through its misguided attempts to lower unemployment raised inflation to 6%, the private sector will be extremely skeptical if the government announces a plan to reduce inflation to 2%. That was, after all, where inflation started out! In order to gain credibility, governments have to earn it—either by making tough decisions, for instance demonstrating the need to accept high unemployment in order to lower inflation, or by having a track record of always achieving low inflation. As we saw in Chapter 11, the Bundesbank achieved low inflation by international standards between 1960 and 1999 (at which point the European Central Bank took over interest rate setting) and as a result enjoyed substantial credibility. The Bank of Italy and the Bank of England have less impressive inflation records and their attempts at lowering inflation were hampered by credibility problems in the 1970s and 1980s.

Figure 16.13 shows estimates of the sacrifice ratio for OECD countries over the period 1985 to 1999. Over this period, inflation was brought down in nearly every country. But the cost of doing so varied greatly. In part this was because the degree of credibility over policy at the start of this period varied significantly across countries. There is also evidence that those countries that reduced inflation the fastest (what is known as the "cold turkey" approach to disinflation) achieved the lowest sacrifice ratios, i.e., the smallest increases in unemployment.[3] When countries implement a sharp tightening of monetary policy, unemployment will rise substantially. However, this signals to the private sector the determination of the government to lower inflation regardless of the unemployment cost. As a result, inflation expectations adjust swiftly, the Phillips curve moves down, and inflation falls. By contrast, if disinflation occurs slowly, expectations do not adjust quickly and the government comes under prolonged political pressure in the wake of a slow and long-lasting increase in unemployment.

[3] See, for example, Ball, "What determines the sacrifice ratio?" in G. Mankiw (ed.), *Monetary Policy*, (Chicago: Univ. of Chicago Press, 1994) pp. 240–281.

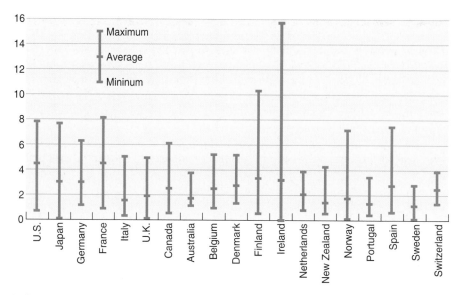

FIGURE 16.13 **The sacrifice ratio in developed economies, 1985–1998.** The cost of bringing down inflation differed substantially across countries in the 1980s and 1990s because the credibility of policy was diverse. *Source:* Andersen and Wascher, "Sacrifice Ratios and the Conduct of Monetary Policy in Conditions of Low Inflation," BIS working paper no. 82 (1999).

16.6 Time Inconsistency

A feature of our analysis in this chapter is the importance of expectations in determining the success of policy. In particular, we have found that the success of government actions *today* depends on the private sector's beliefs about what the government will do *tomorrow*. For instance, the success of an anti-inflation policy depends on whether the private sector believes inflation will be low in the future. This dependence of the current situation on expectations of the future raises the problem of **time inconsistency**; that is, when the future arrives, it may no longer be optimal to carry out your plan. If people are aware of this problem, then they have no reason to believe your predictions.

The problem of time inconsistency arises in many settings—monetary policy, threatening punishments to children if they don't carry out chores, or more seriously, governments dealing with terrorists. Every government would like every potential hostage taker to think that it will never negotiate. If that really were credible, terrorists would never hijack airplanes because they would know, in advance, that governments would not give way. But after the hijack, when the plane is stuck at the airport with bombs onboard and 80 million people watching on TV, the government has a strong incentive to negotiate. This is an example of time inconsistency.

KEY POINT

A time inconsistent policy is one in which a rule that seemed optimal at one time (e.g., we do not negotiate with terrorists) subsequently becomes undesirable. When the government announces its non-negotiating stance, it genuinely believes it will follow this strategy. However, talk is cheap and, unless other actions are taken to make this a credible strategy, the stance will be ignored.

Time inconsistency is a major problem for governments when they wish to achieve low inflation. Consider again Figure 16.12 and a government that finds itself at A, with 6% inflation. If it successfully persuades the private sector that inflation will be 2%, then the economy will shift to E. However, if inflation expectations have fallen to 2%, why not generate inflation of 4%? This will produce a fall in inflation (from 6% to 4%) as well as a fall in unemployment as real wages are pushed down by unanticipated inflation. If the private sector realizes that if it expects inflation will be 2%, then inflation will actually be 4%, then it won't adjust its expectations and inflation will not fall. If the government cannot credibly commit to producing low inflation, inflation will remain high.

MONETARY POLICY AS A GAME

We can show this more formally in the context of a very simple game between the private sector and the government. Consider the case in which the government can produce either low or high inflation. Table 16.1 shows the various possibilities for unemployment in this game, depending on whether inflation is greater than, less than, or equal to inflation expectations.

Before we can analyze what choices the government and private sector will make, we have to know their preferences. We assume that the government likes low unemployment and low inflation, but has a stronger preference for low unemployment. Its most preferred outcome is scenario C (inflation higher than expectations and unemployment below the natural rate). Its next best outcome is A (low inflation and unemployment at the natural rate), followed by D (high inflation and natural rate unemployment), and its least preferred is B (low inflation, high expectations, and unemployment above the natural rate). In Table 16.2 we show these preferences and we attach numerical values to each outcome, reflecting the value government places on each. The first number in each cell is the payoff to the government, and the second is

TABLE 16.1 **Possible Outcomes in Monetary Policy Game**
The level of unemployment depends on whether inflation expectations hold or not.

Scenario	Inflation	Inflation Expectations	Unemployment
A	Low	Low	Natural Rate
B	Low	High	Above Natural Rate
C	High	Low	Below Natural Rate
D	High	High	Natural Rate

TABLE 16.2   **Payoffs to Government and Private Sector**

The first number in each cell is the return to the government; the second is the return to the private sector.

Governments will always choose high inflation, regardless of inflation expectations of the private sector.

		Private Sector Inflation Expectations	
		High	Low
Governments	High	−3, 0	3, −3
Inflation Choice	Low	−5, −3	0, 0

that to the private sector. We assume that the private sector dislikes having its expectations turn out to be wrong; in other words, it finds only unexpected levels of inflation costly. Therefore it is indifferent between low or high inflation so long as expectations are in line with outcomes. (This could be modified to have a preference for low inflation without altering our conclusions.) The private sector does not value unemployment below the natural rate because this is only achieved by real wages being low as a result of false expectations.

We can now examine the equilibrium of this game between the private sector and the government. The structure of the game is as follows: first, the private sector negotiates wages on the basis of its inflation expectations, and then the government decides the level of inflation. It is crucial that the private sector makes its decision first—time inconsistency only arises because agents' expectations of the future influence the success of events today.

Consider first the actions of the government. If the private sector has high inflation expectations, then the best course of action for the government is to produce high inflation. With this outcome, unemployment equals the natural rate. If instead the government produces low inflation, then real wages will be too high (because they have been set assuming high inflation) and unemployment will be above the natural rate. Because the government places a higher weight on unemployment, the low inflation in this scenario does not compensate for the higher unemployment. Therefore if the private sector has high inflation expectations, in this model the government will deliver high inflation. If instead, inflation expectations are low, the government will still find it optimal to produce high inflation. With low inflation expectations, high inflation leads to a low real wage and lower unemployment below the natural level. The government preference for low unemployment means this outweighs the high inflation. The other alternative would be to have low inflation, but this would lead unemployment to be equal to its natural rate which is not optimal for the government. *Therefore, regardless of the private sector's inflation expectations, the government will choose high inflation.* Knowing this, the private sector sets its expectations for high inflation.

The situation is illustrated in Figure 16.14. Notice that the outcome of the game is inefficient—society prefers the low inflation, natural rate unemployment outcome (A in Table 16.1) to the high inflation, natural rate unemployment outcome (D). However, it

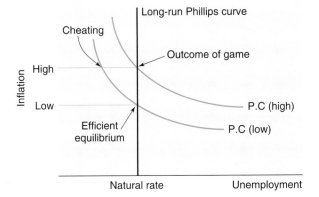

FIGURE 16.14 **Inflation bias.** Because the government has a preference for low unemployment it cannot achieve a low inflation equilibrium; inflation is too high.

is not possible to be at A because even if the government claims it will produce low inflation, as soon as the private sector lowers its expectations, the government has an incentive to cheat, produce high inflation and lower unemployment. Sticking to a low inflation policy is a time inconsistent promise by the government and so the economy stays at a high inflation outcome. The mere fact that a Phillips curve exists and may be exploited by governments creates an inflationary bias in the economy.

KEY POINT

If governments could remove the option to use discretionary policy and abandon the opportunity to exploit the Phillips curve, this inflationary bias would disappear. But so long as governments have a preference for lower unemployment, they will be tempted to use this option. Notice that this preference for low unemployment is futile—in equilibrium unemployment is at its natural rate, so the government never benefits from low unemployment. In other words, it might as well just focus on low inflation.

CENTRAL BANK INDEPENDENCE

How can governments overcome this problem of time inconsistency? As our analysis suggests, the answer is to give up the option of discretion and instead follow certain rules. One way this can be achieved is to hand control of inflation policy over to an independent central bank and give it the goal of controlling inflation *with no reference to unemployment*. By setting up incentives that penalize the central bank when inflation exceeds its target and by not making its prestige depend upon unemployment, the government effectively changes the preferences of the policymaker. We saw in the previous chapter that many central banks have now become independent and that many of these have adopted some form of inflation target. Table 16.3 shows how we can incorporate this change into our theoretical game analysis. Assume that the central banker has no preference regarding unemployment but simply prefers low to high inflation. The central bank is then indifferent between scenarios A and B (low inflation; natural rate unemployment and low inflation; unemployment above the natural rate, respectively) but prefers these to C and D (high inflation, below natural rate unemployment; high inflation; natural rate unemployment, respectively). Repeating our earlier analysis, we find that with these preferences *the central banker will always choose low inflation, regardless*

TABLE 16.3 **Payoffs to Independent Central Bank and Private Sector**
The first number in each cell is the return to the central bank; the second is the return to the private sector.

By appointing an independent central bank to control only inflation, the preferences of the policy authority change and now can achieve the low inflation outcome.

		Private Sector Inflation Expectations	
Central Bank		High	Low
Inflation Choice	High	−3, 0	−3, −3
	Low	0, −3	0, 0

of the private sector's expectations. Given this, the private sector will set their expectations for low inflation. As a result, the inflationary bias disappears and the economy will be in a low inflation equilibrium.

This result is obviously a paradox—by setting monetary policy without worrying about unemployment the outcome is better than if you are allowed discretion. However, there are many examples in which denying yourself certain options in the future actually generates better outcomes. The classical reference here is to Homer's *The Odyssey*. Odysseus knew that if he allowed himself to hear the Sirens' songs while he was still in command of his ship, the sound and sight of the Sirens would lure him toward them where he would meet a horrible death. So he had his crew stop up their ears with wax and tie him to the mast, so that he could neither persuade the crew to change direction nor steer the ship himself. As a result, he could hear the beautiful singing of the Sirens without losing his ship or his life. This classic example illustrates the advantages of "tying ones hands"—by denying yourself short-term flexibility, a better outcome is achieved.

The ability of independent central banks to overcome the inflationary bias of monetary policy is given substantial support in Figure 16.13. Countries with strong, independent central banks achieve substantially lower inflation. Some economists argue that all Figure 16.13 shows is that countries that have a strong dislike of inflation achieve low inflation and have independent central banks. It is the dislike of inflation that matters rather than whether the central bank is independent. These economists argue that if society does not strongly dislike inflation, then an unelected central bank that pursues severe anti-inflationary policies will not exist for long. However, the logic of the time inconsistency argument and the evidence of Figure 16.13 have been extremely influential over the last decade, with many governments granting substantial independence to central banks.

KEY POINT

It may seem strange for governments to hand such an important policy instrument over to an unelected group of officials and to ask them to target only inflation. However, our analysis shows that the fact the central bankers are unelected and do not have a policy goal of achieving low unemployment is crucial in achieving a better outcome for society.

16.7 Rules versus Discretion

We have outlined three broad sets of arguments that suggest in operating monetary and fiscal policy governments may find it preferable to follow fixed rules rather than discretionary policies.

1. Pragmatic concerns regarding whether the authorities have enough up-to-date and reliable information about the state of the economy and whether inevitable lags in the system will make stabilization policy actually destabilizing.
2. Concerns over whether the government really has the ability to control the level of demand. The impact of fiscal deficits will, at least in part, be offset by the actions of the private sector as we saw with crowding out and Ricardian equivalence. Further, the central bank can only set the short-term nominal interest rate. The important long-term real interest rate is not under its control.
3. Time inconsistency arguments suggest that by denying themselves discretion and following fixed rules, governments can achieve better outcomes.

In combination, these three arguments have been so persuasive that most governments no longer try to use fiscal and monetary policy to fine-tune the economy. As we saw in Chapter 15, monetary policy is now based on achieving announced targets for inflation and is operated mostly by independent central banks whose overriding aim is the control of inflation. Similarly, fiscal policy is rarely used in a conscious way to influence the business cycle. The exception is Japan in the late 1990s where, as a result of a severely depressed economy, the authorities pursued policies to handle the depression. Although automatic fiscal stabilizers operate and help inject demand when the economy is weak and remove it when growth is strong, governments now rarely adjust tax rates and expenditure in an effort to control the business cycle.

However, whereas the rules for operating monetary policy are now well established, this is not the case for fiscal policy and we expect this to be an area of considerable research over the next decade. Just like monetary policy, fiscal policy suffers from problems of time inconsistency. In Chapter 10 we saw that tax smoothing was an optimal policy. Tax smoothing implies that governments only need to worry about balancing their budget over a long run. Therefore fiscal deficits are allowable today, so long as they are followed by future surpluses. Governments can therefore justify not raising taxes today because of expected higher revenues in the future. But when the future occurs, the government may decide that it would rather spend these additional revenues, or even reduce taxes, rather than run a surplus. The result is that deficits are not matched by surpluses and government debt increases continually.

The perception that governments may face incentives to spend more than they raise in taxes lies behind the various balanced-budget amendments to constitutions that have been advocated in some countries (most notably the United States). The logic behind these amendments is similar to the arguments for central bank independence: governments (or politicians), if left to themselves, face too many temptations to cut interest rates or taxes, or to boost expenditure, in order to gain electoral popularity.

There are a variety of ways in which the discretion of governments in setting fiscal policy could be reduced. A particularly draconian form would be a requirement that government expenditure (or planned expenditure) could never exceed taxation in any year. In practice, to avoid the penalties of breaching this requirement, governments would generate surpluses almost every period so as to avoid even the smallest chance of not covering spending out of current taxation. A more modest balanced budget requirement would have the government balance its budget over a longer planning horizon (maybe five or seven years, or some period reflecting the average duration of the economic cycle). The U.K. government takes this approach with its Code for Fiscal Stability. Alternatively, restrictions could be placed on the size of fiscal deficit that a country can run. This was supposed to be the approach of countries in the European Monetary Union with the Growth and Stability Pact. But when France and Germany ran large deficits in 2003, they effectively ignored the rules of the pact. This illustrates the problem of time inconsistency.

Although there are analogies between balanced-budget amendments and governments handing over control of monetary policies to central banks, we should not take these too far. As we saw in Chapter 15, granting control over monetary policy to even the most independent central bank does *not* mean that monetary policy should be set to preclude stabilization. In fact, any central bank that was pursuing a target for inflation would almost certainly be loosening policy when unemployment was rising above, and output falling beneath, its equilibrium level and tightening monetary policy when the opposite was happening. The same would *not* be true, however, with a tightly specified balanced budget amendment.

KEY POINT

If governments could never run a budget deficit, they would have to cut spending in a recession (when tax revenues tend to fall) and cut taxes or increase spending in a boom (when revenues tend to rise). So a tightly specified balanced budget requirement is almost certainly inconsistent with a stabilizing role for fiscal policy.

SUMMARY

In section 16.1, we discussed how output and inflation fluctuate substantially over the business cycle. If this volatility is undesirable, governments can try and manage the level of demand in the economy using fiscal and monetary policy. This is stabilization policy.

However, we saw in section 16.2 that achieving successful stabilization policy is fraught with problems. Knowledge about the economy and how it operates is imperfect, and macroeconomic data is only available with a delay of several months. Further, the instruments of stabilization policy operate with long and uncertain lags. There exists uncertainty over the impact of these policy instruments on the economy, as the efforts of the government can be offset by the actions of the private sector. The delays and uncertainty over impact are particularly problematic for fiscal policy.

In sections 16.3, 16.4, and 16.5, we explored the implications of the Phillips curve. The Phillips curve is a negative relationship between inflation and unemployment. In the 1950s and 1960s, it was believed this offered governments a tradeoff between inflation and unemployment. However, recognizing the importance of inflation expectations and how they change over time led to a belief that the long-run Phillips curve was vertical. This also raised awareness of the importance of inflation expectations in achieving low inflation outcomes.

In section 16.5, we showed that, because expectations of the future influence events today, monetary policy suffers from a problem of time inconsistency. Governments may not find it optimal to deliver the low inflation that they promise. We showed how this leads to an inflation bias in the economy which can be removed if the government follows rules rather than a discretionary approach to policy. Handing control of monetary policy to an independent central bank is a way of overcoming this bias and has been widely adopted.

In section 16.7, we saw that the preference for rules rather than discretion is now firmly based among macroeconomic policymakers. Whereas the rules and operating procedures are well developed for monetary policy, governments are only just beginning to investigate the fiscal rules they should follow.

CONCEPTUAL QUESTIONS

1. (Section 16.1) How might a big hike in oil prices affect the natural rate of unemployment in a country that relies heavily on imported fuel and where oil is an essential input into the production of many goods? How might things be different for an oil-producing country?

2. (16.1/16.2) The natural rate of employment depends on the stock of capital, which in turn obviously depends on investment expenditure. The natural rate also depends on technical progress, which is also likely to depend on levels of investment and research and development spending. Suppose that governments can affect investment in the short term by demand management policies. Does it follow that demand management must have long-term impacts on the level of employment?

3. (16.2) Think of how lower prices (or lower inflation) may generate greater overall demand within the economy. Could these mechanisms be more powerful than forces that reduce overall demand when prices (or inflation) rise?

4. (16.2) Fiscal and monetary policy in small open economies with fixed exchange rates are not likely to significantly influence the level of demand for the output of domestic producers. Why are things different in a country like the United States, which is not very open and has a floating exchange rate?

5. (16.2) In the 1990s as output fell and unemployment rose in Japan, the level of interest rates was cut to zero and the government ran large deficits; output remained depressed. Does this show that stabilization policy is ineffective?

ANALYTICAL QUESTIONS

1. (Section 16.2) The economy responds to changes in interest rates with a lag. Suppose that aggregate demand for goods is given by the equation

$$Y_t = A + bY_{t-1} - cr_{t-2} + e_t$$

where Y_t is demand in year t; r_{t-2} is the interest rate in year $t - 2$; and e_t is a shock to demand in period t. A = 200; b = 0.7; and c = 10.

(a) Suppose that the economy goes through many years in which interest rates are steady at 6 and there are no shocks. What is the equilibrium level of demand?

(b) Now there is a sudden, one-time shock to demand in period t of -30 ($e_t = -30$). Show what happens to demand over the next five years if there is no monetary policy response. (Assume that e returns to zero after the first year.)

(c) Now assume the government immediately reduces interest rates from 6% to 3% to offset the shock. Show how the economy responds over the five years after the shock when interest rates stay at 3%.

(d) Can you devise a better response to the shock than cutting interest rates to 3% and leaving them there?

2. (16.3) Imagine the Phillips curve is

inflation = inflation expectations + 0.5 × (natural rate of unemployment − unemployment)

Over the next 10 years the data is as follows

Year	1	2	3	4	5	6	7	8	9	10
Inflation Expectations	3	3	4	4	4	4	3	3	3	3
Natural rate	5	5	5	5	5	6	6	6	7	7
Unemployment	5	3	4	5	5.2	5.7	6.1	6.4	6.8	7.2

(a) Calculate inflation in each year.

(b) Draw a chart showing inflation and unemployment over these periods. What evidence do you have for a Phillips curve?

(c) Can you explain your answer to (b)? Can you rescue the Phillips curve?

3. (16.3) Consider the following two specifications for the Phillips curve:

inflation = 5 − 0.3 × (natural logarithm of unemployment rate)

and

inflation = 5 − 0.3 × (unemployment rate)

(a) Graph each of these Phillips curves over the range of unemployment from 1 to 10.

(b) What is the difference between the two curves? Which do you think is more plausible?

(c) How does the sacrifice ratio differ in each case?

4. (16.6) Consider the monetary policy game between the government and the private sector described in section 16.6, but this time assume that the private sector dislikes high inflation, even if it is expected, and also values low unemployment. The payoff matrix is now

Governments	Private Sector Inflation Expectations	
Inflation Choice	High	Low
High	−3, −1	3, −2
Low	−5, −3	0, 1

(a) How does this alter your analysis?

(b) How would you construct the payoff matrix for the case in which the government, rather than make the central bank independent, appoints a central bank chairman with a pathological hatred of inflation?

(c) What about if the government appoints a trade union leader as chairman?

CHAPTER 17

Equity Markets

Overview

How stock prices are determined and why they move are issues of major economic importance. Shifts in equity prices affect the value of wealth, influence the new investment decisions of firms, and can trigger restructuring of companies if they lead to takeovers. We first develop a way of valuing equities based on the earnings potential of a firm's assets—these assets can be machines, buildings, the experience of the workforce and management, the value of brand names, or the future advantages of market dominance. There is controversy, however, about whether a valuation model based on these fundamentals can explain the observed volatility of equity prices. Therefore, we will also consider other factors that play a role in making stock prices volatile, including speculative bubbles, irrational herd-like behavior by investors, and myopia in forecasting the future. We will also consider whether equities in general may become mispriced for long periods relative to other assets.

Key Concepts

Asset Market Bubbles	Dividend Discount Model	Equity Risk Premium
Capital Gain	Dividend Yield	Fundamental Value
Coefficient of Relative Risk Aversion (CRRA)	Equities	Mean Reversion

17.1 What Are Equities?

A company consists of assets. These, of course, include physical capital but company assets also encompass less tangible things that, for many firms, may have more value than physical capital, such as brands, monopoly power, patents, or a good reputation. **Equities**, or shares, are claims to own these assets; in effect, they are claims on the future stream of profits that these assets may generate. Trade in shares enables sellers to swap a claim on a flow of future (and uncertain) income from corporate assets in

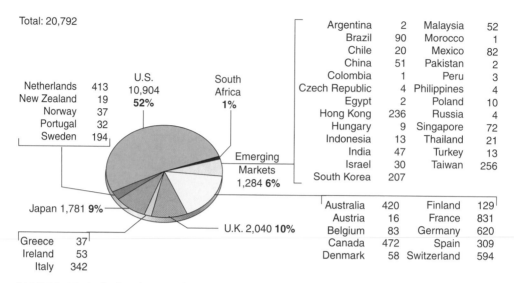

Total: 20,792

Argentina	2	Malaysia	52
Brazil	90	Morocco	1
Chile	20	Mexico	82
China	51	Pakistan	2
Colombia	1	Peru	3
Czech Republic	4	Philippines	4
Egypt	2	Poland	10
Hong Kong	236	Russia	4
Hungary	9	Singapore	72
Indonesia	13	Thailand	21
India	47	Turkey	13
Israel	30	Taiwan	256
South Korea	207		

Australia	420	Finland	129
Austria	16	France	831
Belgium	83	Germany	620
Canada	472	Spain	309
Denmark	58	Switzerland	594

Netherlands 413
New Zealand 19
Norway 37
Portugal 32
Sweden 194

U.S. 10,904 **52%**

South Africa **1%**

Emerging Markets 1,284 **6%**

Japan 1,781 **9%**

U.K. 2,040 **10%**

Greece 37
Ireland 53
Italy 342

FIGURE 17.1   **Stock markets around the world, 2003 data.** Values are $ million; figure in parentheses are % of total. *Source: Financial Times*, (February 2004).

exchange for immediate funds; buyers acquire a claim on a future flow of income in return for cash. In essence, equity markets are where a significant part of the value of the assets of the world's largest economies are continually put up for sale. In most developed countries, on average about two-thirds of the value of the flow of output goes to labor as wages; the rest goes to providers of equity and debt capital. Because equities are claims on much of this flow, the total value of such claims is large. Figure 17.1 shows the total value of the stock markets in the major economies at the end of 2003. In the United States, equities were worth well over one year's gross domestic product (GDP). In the United Kingdom, the market value of equities was close to one-and-a-half years' annual GDP. In the 1980s and early 1990s, the value of Japanese equities was sometimes in excess of annual GDP—though it was much lower by 2003 after 3 years of very poor stock market returns. Annual turnover in equity markets is also enormous. Transactions in the major stock markets in the world in 2000 typically added up to around 50% of the value of the outstanding stock; in other words, shares changed hands on average about once every two years.

Share prices themselves fluctuate widely. Even if we look at averages of the share prices of many companies, which smoothes out a lot of volatility, variability is substantial. Figures 17.2 through 17.4 show the history of the main national stock price indexes for the three largest stock markets in the world over the last few decades. In the United Kingdom and the United States, stock prices over this period show an upward trend, though one that is far from steady and that saw major price falls after the peak of the bull market in 2000. In Japan, prices rose and fell on either side of the peak in the market at the end of the 1980s. In all countries, short-term volatility was considerable; in the United States, the market fell over 20% in one day in 1987!

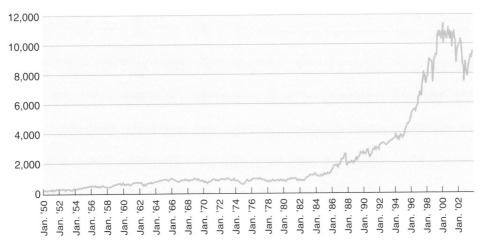

FIGURE 17.2   **Dow Jones industrial stock index.** *Source:* Thomson Financial Datastream.

Even if we look at longer periods, and adjust for the impact of general price inflation by measuring stock prices in real terms, the strong upward trend in prices and the high volatility of those prices remain. Figure 17.5 measures real (inflation adjusted) U.S. stock prices and real dividends from 1871.[1] Both series are on a rising but variable trend. Stock prices are noticeably more volatile than the flow of dividends those stocks generate.

FIGURE 17.3   **Financial Times stock exchange 100 share index.** *Source:* Thomson Financial Datastream.

[1] Robert Shiller of Yale University compiled the series. It has been the basis for much work on long-run stock price trends. Called the Shiller index, it is based on the values of the Standard and Poor's stock price index.

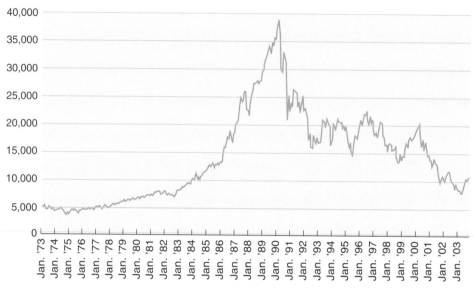

FIGURE 17.4   **Nikkei 225 stock index.** *Source:* Thomson Financial Datastream.

The pattern of stock prices revealed in the figures and the data on the overall value of the stock markets across different countries raise several questions: Why do share prices move? Are the substantial fluctuations we observe in the stock market related to economic fundamentals or the whims of speculators? How important are equities in the portfolios of the private sectors across different countries? Why have equities in the past tended to yield greater returns than those earned on most other assets? Can we expect this excess return on equities to continue into the future?

FIGURE 17.5   **U.S. real stock prices and dividends: The Shiller data.** *Source:* Robert Shiller data; see Shiller, *Market Volatility* (Cambridge, MA: MIT Press, 1989), Chapter 26, for details of the construction of the data. Data updated by authors.

Economists have thought a lot about these questions. Equity markets fascinate them, partly because these markets seem to meet many of the strong assumptions that standard economic theory often makes: they are markets with many participants, none of whom has much monopoly power, all of whom have access to a lot of information, and most of whom want to make money. Does such a market really function well—do prices reflect a sensible judgment on the future earnings power of the underlying assets of corporations? Because stock markets are so important, this is not just an academic question. We saw in Chapter 13 that investment expenditure should depend on stock prices. And we saw above that, in many of the major economies, total stock market values are large relative to the size of the economy. For both these reasons, how equity markets work has great economic significance.

As well as trying to answer some of these fundamental questions about how equity markets work, we also hope to help you make sense of the massive amount of commentary on stock markets in the media. This commentary often addresses another set of issues, usually why the market went down or up yesterday. For example, a recent report we read on the day's trading in the U.S. stock market said, "On a wave of buying, U.S. stocks rallied 220 points in early trading on Wall Street today."

However, because every transaction involves a seller as well as a buyer, this statement makes about as much sense as, "On a wave of selling, U.S. stocks rallied 220 points."[2] The financial pages also often contain quotes from celebrated market gurus who will make comments such as, "If the market moves below 6500 it will break a key resistance point and will then fall to 6000." Such a statement seems to imply that stock prices are subject to external pressures like the unknowable forces of nature, but what are they, and what economic factors lie behind them?

Our own favorite piece of misleading "analysis" is the almost universal tendency of media commentators to want to identify a single piece of news as responsible for the movement in a stock price index. Remember that an index is an average of prices based on companies in completely different sectors of the economy and often (effectively) in different countries. We are routinely told things such as, "News of the latest comments from the chairman of the U.S. Federal Reserve sent stocks tumbling in Europe, but was already discounted in Wall Street prices." This confident type of assertion about a causal link between two events that happened at about the same time cannot be proved or refuted. These assertions are unverifiable stories, not economic analysis.

Therefore, this chapter will provide a more formal analysis to help you understand how equity markets operate. This is worth doing because how these markets work is important. It matters greatly whether stock price movements are the result of rational and reasoned responses by investors to information on the long-term economic prospects of firms or whether they are the result of a whim or of herd-like behavior that is triggered by sports results, the weather, or blind panic.

KEY POINT

The investment decisions of firms are likely to depend to some extent on movements in financial asset prices, so it would be worrisome if those financial market valuations were dissociated from fundamental determinants of corporate profitability. When markets work well, they reward those who are most efficient at producing what society wants and punish those who are not.

---

[2] Although the market can fall by 220 points without any trades.

The price of buying a company's equity is the cost of acquiring the right to take over the management of a collection of corporate assets. To put resources to their most productive use, the equity price should be highest when the best managers are in charge. So it would be worrisome if the price at which firms can be taken over—possibly changing how they are run—bears little relation to their earnings prospects. If there was only a weak link between the efficiency with which a company was run and its stock price, good managers would be as likely to lose their jobs after a hostile takeover deal as bad ones. And if stock price movements bear little relation to underlying economic conditions in the corporate sector, it would be folly for former centrally planned economies to be reshaped to give the stock market a key role in allocating resources.

17.2 | International Comparisons of Equity Markets

The importance of equity markets varies greatly across countries. For instance, in continental Europe stock markets have played a smaller role in funding companies than in the United States or the United Kingdom and the aggregate value of equities has constituted a smaller part of the total stock of financial assets. Where companies rely heavily on banks and bond issues to finance investment, and less on new equity issues and retained profits, the value of the equity market relative to GDP will tend to be smaller. And where private firms that are not quoted on a stock market account for a substantial part of economic activity, the importance of publicly traded stock is correspondingly lower.

One reason why stock markets have been more important in the United Kingdom, the United States, Ireland, and (to a lesser extent) the Netherlands is because a substantial part of the incomes going to the retired come from funded pensions in these countries. Funded pensions are those where contributions are invested in assets and pensions paid from the accumulated value of the resulting fund. In most continental European countries, unfunded state pensions, financed by taxes on current workers, have generated a much higher proportion of income for the elderly. Pension funds are long-term investors, and over the long term, equities in the biggest stock markets have substantially outperformed other asset classes, causing pension funds to invest huge amounts of money in equities.

KEY POINT

Over the long term, equities have generated higher returns than nearly all other assets.

Figure 17.6 shows the nominal returns on U.S. stocks, bonds, bills, gold, and cash since 1800. The figure shows how assets would have risen in value before we adjust for inflation. But adjusting for inflation is important. A dollar bill held since 1800 would have been worth about 7 cents, in real terms, by the end of the twentieth century; inflation has eroded more than 90% of its value. Gold, which is often thought to be a safe long-term investment, would have done better and been worth about $1.20 by the end of the period—still a miserable return over 200 years. Bonds would have done better

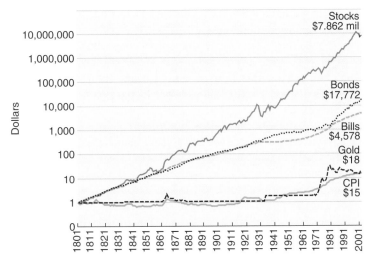

FIGURE 17.6   **The value of $1 invested in 1800.** Equities have massively outperformed other investments in the United States over the past 200 years. *Source:* Siegel, *Stocks for the Long Run*, 3rd edition (New York: McGraw Hill, 2002).

still; $1 invested in the bond market in 1800 would have been worth about $1000 200 years later. But equities do very much better. Despite big falls in 1929 and in the early 1970s, the equity line consistently rises faster than any of the others. Note how even big shocks—like the 1987 stock market crash—have been washed away by the overwhelming tendency over the longer term for stock prices to rise faster than the prices of bonds, bills, and gold. That same $1 invested in 1800 would have been worth almost $8 million in nominal terms and over $500,000 in real terms by the end of the period if put into U.S. stocks. Furthermore, in almost none of the 20-year intervals from 1800 do cash (dollar bills), gold, or U.S. bonds or bills outperform U.S. stocks.[3]

The average time lag between when a pension fund receives money to invest on behalf of a worker and when it pays that money back to the worker might be 30 years. Therefore, pension funds will be particularly attracted to the exceptional long-run performance of equities, and pension funds in the United States and the United Kingdom have typically held between 60% and 80% of their overall portfolios in equities, though that percentage has fallen since 2000.

As we saw in Chapter 10, the aging population of OECD countries could put intolerable strains on state pensions systems within Europe because, for Europe as a whole, the ratio of those of retirement age to those of working age will roughly double by 2040. This may force governments to reduce the value of the state pension, which might encourage rapid growth of private, funded pensions, stimulating the demand for equities. Whether that would be beneficial depends on whether the signals that stock prices give provide accurate information for investors to guide resource allocation. So how equity prices and rates of return are determined will be critical. But how are those prices determined?

[3] The exception is the 20 years starting just before the Wall Street crash of 1929.

17.3   The Determination of Stock Prices

Our analysis of what determines share prices starts with a model in which fundamentals pin down equity prices—that is, expectations of the future profitability of the companies whose stocks are being valued. Later we will consider additional factors, including market psychology.

When someone buys a share, that investor has in mind a required rate of return. If, at the current market price of the share, it seems likely to generate a return at or above the required level, it is worth buying. If the price is so high that the share seems unlikely to earn a return at the required rate, it is not worth buying. The required rate of return will depend on a number of factors. How risky is it to hold the share? What rate of return could you earn on other, perhaps safer, investments? How easily can you sell the share at short notice, i.e., how liquid is the market? The more risky the share, the higher the return available on other assets, and the less liquid the market, then the higher the required rate of return the investor will demand from the share.

Let's start out with a simple case and suppose that you can trade the share in a deep and liquid market easily (and that's pretty much the case for the equities of large firms in developed countries). Take a particular stock, say an IBM share. If you hold this share for a year, you get two sorts of return. First, if IBM pays a dividend, you will get some cash. Second, by the end of the year, the price will almost certainly be different from the price at the beginning of the year. The change in price generates a **capital gain** or loss that is also part of the return.

If the stock market is working efficiently, the rate of return (or yield) people *expect* to get from an asset should just equal the required rate of return that they demand. Consider the case in which the typical (or representative) investor would hold the share if it was expected to deliver a return of 15% over the next year. At the existing market price, however, the investor currently thinks that the share is likely to yield 18%. In these circumstances, the share is a good buy and remains so while the expected return is above the required return. However, as the typical investor buys more and more of the share, its current price will tend to rise. Assuming that expectations of next period's price do not change, then a rise in the current price reduces expectations of future capital gains. In other words, the expected return on the share declines. Eventually the current price will rise until the expected and required rates of return are equal. At this point the investor will stop purchasing shares, and the price will stop rising. By contrast, consider the case in which the expected return is 12%—below the required return of 15%. In this case, the investor will start to sell her share holding. This will tend to lower the share price. As the share price falls, the investor increases her expectation of future capital gains. This leads to a higher expected rate of return until eventually the share price falls to a level at which the expected and required rates of return are equal.

The expected rate of return from holding a share is equal to the expected capital gain plus any dividend payments (all expressed as a percentage of the original share price). For simplicity, assume that investors' required return is the same from period to period and is equal to r. We need the expected return (capital gain plus dividend) to be equal to r. Let's write today's share price as $P(0)$ and the expected share price one period (say a year) ahead as P(1). Let the expected value of dividends paid this year be D(1). We require that

expected capital gains + dividend yield = required rate of return
$$[P(1) - P(0)]/P(0) + D(1)/P(0) = r$$

Figure 17.7 shows the relation among P(0), P(1), D(1), and *r*. On the horizontal axis, we measure the expected return from holding a share given the price at which we can buy it. That price is P(0) and is measured on the vertical axis.

The left-hand side of the equation above gives the return. For a given set of expectations about the price one year ahead and about the dividends to be paid, then the higher is the current price, the lower is the expected return. Keeping expectations of the future constant, a higher current price means lower capital gains and a smaller dividend yield. Therefore, there is a negative relationship between the expected rate of return and the current price that the downward-sloping line in Figure 17.7 shows. The required rate of return does not depend on the current price, so we draw it as the vertical line at *r*. Equilibrium in the market requires that the expected rate of return equals the required rate of return. This occurs when the downward-sloping expected returns schedule intersects the vertical required rate of return line. This therefore determines the current share price for given expectations about equity prices next period and for given expectations of dividends and a particular required rate of return.

Anything that changes expectations of capital gains, dividends, or the required rate of return will affect the current price. For instance, imagine that the investor revises upwards her expectation of next period's stock price, P(1)—she expects a larger capital gain. For a given level of current prices, this would lead to a rightward shift of the expected return line (as in Figure 17.8) and so to a higher level of current prices. Investors would buy the stock today in expectation of a higher price tomorrow. This leads to a higher price today until the expected return on the stock is again equal to the required rate of return.

Consider the implications of some good news that raises people's expectations of the dividend to be paid this year—D(1) increases. If this does not change people's expectations of *next* period's price, the current share price must rise. Figure 17.8 illustrates why. The sloping line shifts up if D(1) rises, so the equilibrium share price today must increase from P(0) to P(0)′. Before the increase in forecast dividends, investors were

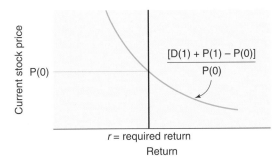

FIGURE 17.7 **Share prices and expectations.** D(1) is the anticipated per share dividend at the end of the year; P(1) is the expected share price one year ahead; *r* is the required expected return over a year.

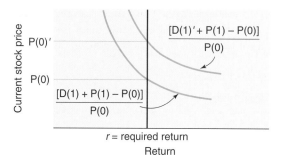

FIGURE 17.8 **An increase in expected dividends.** D(1) is the initial value of the expected dividend per share for the year ahead; D(1)′ is the revised, and more optimistic, expectation for the dividend.

happy to hold the share because it offered a rate of return equal to r. Assuming the current market price did not change, then the increase in dividends will lead to a rate of return in excess of r. As a result, the investor will buy more of the share, which will push prices up. Eventually prices will rise until the expected return is no longer in excess of the required rate of return. This is why good news about future corporate profits and dividends leads to an increase in current share prices.

What if the required rate of return were to increase? Suppose, for instance, that the central bank raises interest rates, so that investors can now get a higher return on relatively safe investments such as bank deposits. Investors would want a higher return in exchange for putting their money into the riskier investment of stocks; this is known as an **equity risk premium**. For simplicity, suppose that this rise in interest rates is expected to be temporary and only last for one year. It might then be reasonable to expect no change in the share price at the end of the year. The increase in current interest rates leads to a rightward shift in the required rate of return line. (Remember, this is the required rate of return over one year.) Assuming that both P(1) and D(1) were unchanged, then the current share price must fall—as Figure 17.9 shows.

Before the interest rate increase, the share was offering a rate of return just equal to the desired rate of return. However, the increase in interest rates led to an increase in the required rate of return, which means that at its current price, the stock would fail to meet the investor's target. The investor would no longer wish to hold the share and would sell it. This pushes the share price down until eventually the expectation of increased capital gains (because the share price has fallen) and the higher dividend yield, i.e., $D(1)/P(0)$, means that the expected return on the stock has risen to a level consis-

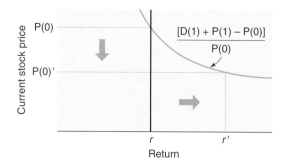

FIGURE 17.9 **An increase in the required rate of return.** r is the initial value of the required rate of return; $r′$ is the new, higher rate of return.

tent with the investor's new required rate of return. This model therefore implies that when governments increase interest rates (or when economic data are released that suggest that the government will have to raise interest rates) then, all else being equal, the share price will have to fall.

It should be obvious from all this that stock prices are forward-looking variables. The value of the share now should depend on your judgment about the dividend that will be paid this year and on what you think the share might be worth at the end of the year. To see this, we can simply rearrange our earlier equation. First, we know that the expected amount of money earned on holding the share is the rate of return times the purchase price of the share—that is, $r P(0)$. This must equal the anticipated capital gains from holding the stock plus the dividends earned: $P(1) - P(0) + D(1)$. Therefore

$$r P(0) = P(1) - P(0) + D(1)$$

which can also be written as

$$(1 + r)P(0) = P(1) + D(1)$$

or

$$P(0) = [P(1) + D(1)]/(1 + r)$$

This shows us that the current share price is equal to the expectation of next period's stock price plus the expected dividend all divided by (or more accurately *discounted* by) 1 plus the required rate of return.

This may not appear too helpful; after all, it simply says that today's price should depend on what people expect the price will be tomorrow, and that hardly seems to be a theory that ties down where prices should be. The message seems to be that if people expect a share price to be fantastically high in a year's time, then it should be fantastically high today. And that theory seems to allow share prices to be pretty much anywhere at all. To make this more useful, we need to work out what people's expectations of next period's price will be.

In fact, we can make a lot of progress toward answering this if we think about how prices will be valued a year ahead. We can apply exactly the same reasoning as lies behind Figure 17.7 to argue that the share price a year from now should depend on the anticipated dividend in the year *after that* plus the expected share price one year on (i.e., two years from now). In other words

$$P(1) = [P(2) + D(2)]/(1 + r)$$

So the stock price *next* period should equal the sum of the discounted values of the expected stock price and dividend in *two* periods' time. If that is right, then today's share price should depend positively on expected dividends over the next *two* years plus the expected value of the share price two years ahead. Imagine investors increasing their forecast of dividends two years hence, that is, an increase in $D(2)$. This will therefore lead to an increase in $P(1)$ in Figure 17.8. But Figure 17.8 also implies that if next period's stock price increases, a rise in $P(1)$, then so does the *current* price, $P(0)$.

We can use the same argument again and think of the share price two years from now as reflecting what people expect the dividend to be the year after *that* and their expectations of what the price will be *three* years from now. If we apply this argument over and over, we can write the share price as being equal to the discounted value of the stream of dividends up to some point far in the future *plus* the discounted value of the price at that point in the future.[4]

However, note that while the current stock price reflects information about all future dividends, all dividends are not equally important. Because of discounting, current dividends influence the current stock price more than dividends in the far future. The discounting works as follows. The current stock price depends on the discounted expected price and dividends next period, $P(0) = [P(1) + D(1)]/(1 + r)$. We also know that next period's price equals the discounted value of expected prices and dividends in period 2. Therefore, in influencing today's stock price, current dividends are discounted only once, $D(1)/(1 + r)$, but dividends expected in period 2 are discounted twice. That is because we have to discount $P(1)$ when considering its influence on $P(0)$ and because $P(1)$ itself depends on discounted dividends in period 2. Therefore, the influence of period 2 dividends on the current stock price is twice discounted, $D(2)/(1 + r)^2$. Because $(1 + r)^2$ is greater than $(1 + r)$, future dividends drive the current stock price *less* than current dividends do. In fact, the further ahead we look, the less influence dividends have on current prices.

We have therefore shown that the current share price depends on the discounted sum of future dividends. This is why we called this approach a means of valuing shares that depends on **fundamental value**. Under this model, how much you are prepared to pay for the stock depends on the underlying profitability of the company and the dividends it pays. It does not depend on whether the Dow Jones has fallen below 6000 on the third Tuesday of a month with an R in its name—the price you should pay depends only on the profitability of the underlying asset. However, we still need to tie up a loose end here. We have shown that the current share price depends on the discounted stream of dividends *and the discounted expected stock price several periods in the future.* In other words, the current share price, $P(0)$, depends on all discounted dividends over the next, say, 40 years, $D(1)/(1 + r) + D(2)/(1 + r)^2 + \ldots$ all the way to $D(40)/(1 + r)^{40}$, but it also depends on the discounted value of the share price in 40 years' time: $P(40)/(1 + r)^{40}$. We still need to solve the problem that if stock prices are forward-looking, then the current stock price must depend on both future dividends and how much investors think the stock will be worth in the future. Unless we can somehow get round this dependence on future prices, we will have a circularity that we cannot solve.

---

[4] We have that $P(1) = [P(2) + D(2)]/(1 + r)$ and that $P(0) = [P(1) + D(1)]/(1 + r)$. Therefore, we can write $P(0) = [[P(2) + D(2)]/(1 + r) + D(1)]/(1 + r) = P(2)/(1 + r)^2 + D(2)/(1 + r)^2 + D(1)/(1 + r)$. However, we also have that $P(2) = [P(3) + D(3)]/(1 + r)$, so we can use this to write $P(0) = P(3)/(1 + r)^3 + D(3)/(1 + r)^3 + D(2)/(1 + r)^2 + D(1)/(1 + r)$. If we continue in this manner, we would arrive at $P(0) = P(40)/(1 + r)^{40} + D(40)/(1 + r)^{40} + \ldots + D(2)/(1 + r)^2 + D(1)/(1 + r)$. We could, of course, carry on like this indefinitely and arrive at an expression $P(0) = P(N)/(1 + r)^N + D(N)/(1 + r)^N + \ldots + D(2)/(1 + r)^2 + D(1)/(1 + r)$, where N is any large integer you want to specify.

However, we can probably ignore this discounted future price term—that is, we can expect that $P(40)/(1 + r)^{40}$ is small. So long as the average annual growth in share prices over the next 40 years is less than r, then $P(40)$ is less than $(1 + r)^{40}$ times its value today; if that is true over any long horizon, $P(n)/(1 + r)^n$ eventually goes to zero.

But would the share price in the distant future be small relative to the discount factor? The answer is basically—yes. The reason is straightforward. The real rate of return on relatively safe assets (like inflation-proof government bonds) has been around 3–4% over the past 20-odd years (the only period when bonds guaranteeing a real rate of return have existed). This means that a typical share (which is riskier than these safe assets) is likely to have a required real rate of return in excess of 3–4%. In other words, the value of r in equation (1) is likely to be greater than .03, and probably significantly greater (note that we are talking in *real* terms). The sustainable, or long-run, rate of growth of real GDP in nearly all developed economies is under 3%. So now consider what would happen if the price of an IBM share were expected to consistently rise in real terms by more than r, when r itself is in excess of the growth of GDP. This would mean that the value of one share in IBM would, eventually, be larger than the whole GDP of nearly any advanced economy. This seems implausible, so it seems sensible to assume that share prices ultimately grow at a slower rate than r. If this is the case, then the discounted share price eventually tends to zero, and we can write the current share price as depending *only* on the discounted sum of future dividends.

This implies that share prices can, indeed should, move in response to anything that changes the expected value of dividends at any point in the future (such as new products or inventions, changes in regulatory rules, increases in corporate taxes) *or* anything that causes people to change their required rates of return over any period in the future (changes in interest rates, changes in how investors assess risk). Anything that causes the expectation of the dividend to be paid in the future to rise will cause stock prices to rise *now*. And anything that causes investors to require a higher rate of return causes share prices to fall *now*. Therefore, we can begin to see why stocks might be so volatile and dependent on rumor and information.

The idea that the value of a share should equal the discounted value of expected future dividends has a powerful logic behind it. But is it right? After all, some companies pay no dividends, show no inclination to do so, and yet have high share prices. Microsoft has been one of the star performers in the U.S. stock market over the past 20 years; yet until the end of that period, it did not pay one cent in dividends. But the dividend/discount account of stock prices is not, at least in principle, inconsistent with how Microsoft was valued for all those years when it paid no dividends. The **dividend discount model** says that the expectation of a dividend being paid *at some point in the future* generates value today. That point could be 20 years off; as long as the eventual payoff is big, so is the stock price today. In fact, the payoff need not actually come as a dividend. Share repurchases by the company, or purchases of stock by another company that launches a successful takeover bid, are other means of distributing cash to shareholders. (We can think of these as forms of dividend payment; in a takeover, the purchase of stock is really a final dividend payment to the holders of shares in the company that is taken over.)

So, in principle, the massive valuations of some dot.com (Internet) companies that were seen at the end of the 1990s and the notion that stock values reflect the present discounted value of future cash distributions by the company are not inconsistent. In practice, however, most stock valuations in the Internet frenzy at the end of the 1990s were hard to reconcile with rational valuation, and their stock values subsequently slumped. Consider what happened to the Internet stock At Home:

> *At Home went public at $17 per share, and its stock valuation went through the roof. At the time of its IPO [initial public offering of shares] in July 1997, At Home's revenue was only $750,000 but its market capitalization was $2.6 billion. By the summer of 1998 its market capitalization was up to $5.6 billion, even though in the previous 12 months its revenue was only $12 million. And by the time At Home announced the acquisition of Excite in January 1999, At Home capitalization was all the way up to $12.4 billion, even though in its most recent quarter the company posted a loss of $7.6 million. "You'd think you'd do forward earnings estimates based on the year 2000," quips one venture capitalist. "I guess I was wrong—it's actually based on the year 3000."[5]*

Startup companies certainly do have uneven profiles for dividends. This is less true for mature companies or for the market as a whole. Figure 17.5 showed that an index of real dividends paid on all industrial stocks since 1871 is fairly steady; certainly it appears less volatile than the index of stock prices themselves. If dividends—either on an individual stock or the aggregate of all companies—grow at a roughly constant rate, we can use simple algebra to come up with a useful way of expressing share prices.

First, recall what the dividend discount model predicts for the price today of a stock, denoted P(0)

$$P(0) = D(1)/(1 + r) + D(2)/(1 + r)^2 + D(3)/(1 + r)^3 + \cdots + D(N)/(1 + r)^N$$

where for any value of j, $D(j)$ is the expected dividend to be paid in period j. We assume here that the required rate of return does not change from period to period.

Suppose dividends grow at a constant rate g, so that

$$D(2) = (1 + g)D(1)$$
$$D(3) = (1 + g)D(2) = (1 + g)^2 D(1)$$
$$D(4) = (1 + g)D(3) = (1 + g)^3 D(1) \text{ and so forth}$$

We can then write the stock price

$$P(0) = [D(1)/(1 + r)]* \{1 + (1 + g)/(1 + r) + [(1 + g)/(1 + r)]^2$$
$$+ [(1 + g)/(1 + r)]^3 \cdots + [(1 + g)/(1 + r)]^N\}$$

This messy looking formula is just an infinite geometric progression. Each term in the final set of braces is a constant multiple of $(1 + g)/(1 + r)$ times the previous term, and there are an infinite number of such terms to be added. As long as g is less than r (and we argued above that this is plausible), such a sum has a finite limit of $(1 + r)/(r - g)$, which gives a value for P(0) of

$$P(0) = D(1)/(r - g)$$

---

[5] Perkins and Perkins, *The Internet Bubble* (New York: Harper Collins, 1999) p. 169.

If we rearrange this equation we get

$$D(1)/P(0) = r - g$$

This equation says that the ratio of the next dividend paid to the current stock price, which is called the (prospective) **dividend yield**, is the difference between the required rate of return and the long-run growth of dividends. Because we can measure the dividend yield on a stock, or on an index of the stocks of many companies, accurately, we now have a way of judging what the gap between the required rate of return and the anticipated growth of dividends is. We just take the latest stock price and dividends, and by forming the dividend yield, we can measure the implied expected excess return over and above the anticipated growth of dividends. This simple and useful relation says that if the dividend yield is low, either the required rate of return on equities is itself low or the anticipated growth of dividends is high.

We can try applying this relation to real-life data. Figure 17.10 shows the dividend yield on the Shiller index of U.S. stock prices from 1871. In 1929, on the eve of the massive fall in U.S. stock prices, the dividend yield on U.S. stocks was around 4%. This was significantly below the average from the previous 50 years. Recall that our relation says that if the dividend yield is low, either the required rate of return on equities is itself low or the anticipated growth of dividends is high. In 1929, short-term nominal interest rates were about 4%, and inflation had been low. So real interest rates might have been just under 4%. If we add an equity risk premium of about 3% to a real interest rate of just under 4%, we generate a required real return on stocks of about 7%. Now if we suppose that people expected dividends to grow in real terms by about 3%, we can explain a dividend yield of around 4%. Because the U.S. economy had been growing steadily for much of the 1920s, an expectation of 3% real growth of dividends might not have seemed unreasonable. Certainly the great U.S. economist Irving Fisher believed on the eve of the stock market crash that U.S. equity prices were sustainable. In fact,

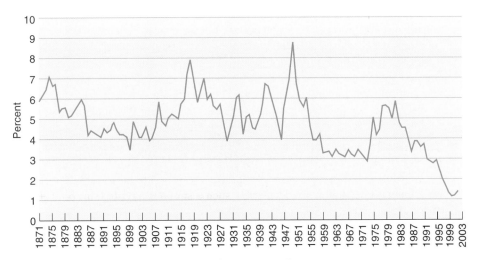

FIGURE 17.10 **Dividend yield on U.S. stocks (Shiller estimates).** *Source:* An update of data shown in Chapter 26 of Shiller, *Market Volatility*, (Cambridge, MA: MIT Press, 1989).

U.S. real GDP has not grown by 3% a year over the long term since the 1920s, and because dividends tend to grow in line with output, at least over the long term, the belief that dividends would grow 3% over the long term was, *in retrospect*, too optimistic. In 1929 prices fell, the dividend yield rose sharply, and the implied anticipated growth of dividends (given stock prices) probably moved down sharply. Note from Figure 17.10 how low the U.S. dividend yield fell during the 1990s.

> **KEY POINT**
>
> One interpretation of a low dividend yield is that people became more optimistic about long-run economic growth and the growth of dividends. Another explanation, which is not inconsistent with the first, is that people come to see equities as less risky, so their required rate of return falls.

Either of these forces could account for a decline in the dividend yield during the 1990s. We will consider the risk premium issues in more detail shortly. But another explanation is that stock prices were just far ahead of their fundamental value by the end of the 1990s—for some reason, share prices had become higher than would be predicted by companies' earnings. In the light of the large falls in stock prices in 2001 and 2002, this now looks more likely.

17.4   On the Unpredictability of Share Prices

We have offered a theory of what determines share prices based on fundamentals—the anticipated value of future corporate dividends. But can we use this theory to make money? That depends on how predictable stock price movements might be, which, in turn, depends on what drives share values. Our examples so far have focused on changes in stock prices that are driven by news about economic fundamentals. But rational expectations of current and future economic conditions are not the only determinants of stock prices.[6] Expectations do not have to be formed in a scientific, logical, coherent, consistent way. Indeed, many puzzles about stock market prices and movements in returns on equities are hard to square with the view that prices are the discounted value of expected future earnings *and* that people form rational and coherent expectations. We will look at some of that evidence shortly.

But even our theory of rational investors evaluating the fundamentals before purchasing a stock is consistent with volatile and unpredictable movements in share prices. Indeed, we shall now show that if the world is peopled by rational, calculating individuals, movements in stock prices over short periods should appear to be random and unforecastable. If that is so, even smart people won't be able to make money by predicting movements in stock market prices.

---

[6] We are using a technical definition of rational expectations—that agents use all the information at their disposal and the appropriate model of the economy and of share prices in forming their guesses of what the future holds. This does not mean that agents do not make mistakes—it just means that they cannot forecast their own mistakes.

Assume that stock prices are equal to the discounted values of the sum of future expected dividends. We could then think of the *change* in the price of an equity over a short period of time as simply being equal to the *change* in the expectation of the (discounted) stream of future dividend payments—assuming that the required rate of return does not change. If this is the case, then rational behavior makes those changes unforecastable. In other words, share prices should be unpredictable.

We should dwell on this point for a moment and illustrate it with an example. Suppose I asked you now what your best guess was for the temperature at noon in New York City on Christmas Day, 2050. Let's say your answer is 30 degrees Fahrenheit. Now suppose I ask you a different question: "What do you expect your answer will be if I ask this same question again a year from now?" Any answer other than 30 degrees Fahrenheit would be illogical. It would make no sense to say that your best guess now about the temperature in New York City at Christmas in 2050 is 30 degrees but that you also expected that your best guess about the answer to the *same* question a year from now would be different. That is not to say that when I ask you *in a year's time* that you must still answer 30 degrees. In the meantime, you may have all kinds of news about global warming and how it will affect New York, and if so, you would be perfectly reasonable to change your answer. But the key point is that you cannot *now* expect your best guess to be different in the future. Any change in expectations must be unforecastable if you are using information sensibly. In other words, while you will quite likely change your forecast of the temperature in New York at Christmas in 2050 over the coming years, you cannot predict how you will revise your forecast. That is, you should not be able to forecast changes in your own forecast.

The same logic applies to your best guess about future dividends. We have shown that the current stock price depends on your current forecast of all future dividends. Similarly the stock price in a year will reflect your forecast in a year of all future dividends. Therefore, the difference in the share price today and next period will reflect how your forecasts of future dividends have altered. If you revise your forecasts of future dividends upwards, the share price will rise; if you revise your forecast downwards, the share price will fall. However, *you cannot today forecast how you will change your forecast—just as with the New York temperature example, this would be irrational.* Therefore, your current best guess of the next instant's stock price must be today's price—changes in stock prices should be unpredictable. Technically this means that stock prices should follow what is called a "random walk": whatever the past path of the price, the next move is as likely to be up as down.

KEY POINT

Random fluctuations in stock prices rather than necessarily being the result of chaos, irrational behavior, indecision, inconsistency, bubbles, or other hiccups in the market are more or less an implication of rational and efficient behavior.

In fact, stock price changes do look random. Figure 17.11 shows the annual percentage change in U.S. stock prices from 1870. The year-to-year fluctuations in prices have no obvious pattern. This is at least consistent with the notion of a rational and efficient market. (But apparent unpredictability does not *imply* that the market is rational

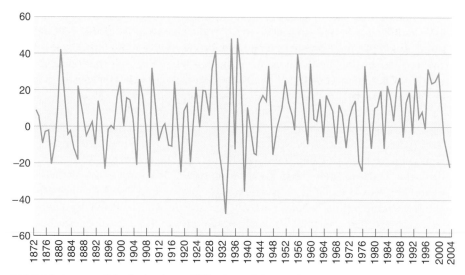

FIGURE 17.11   **% Stock price change (Shiller data on U.S. market)**. *Source:* An update of data shown in Chapter 26 of Shiller, *Market Volatility*, (Cambridge, MA: MIT Press, 1989).

and efficient—it is a necessary but not sufficient condition. If a flip of a coin governed stock price changes, they would look random, but such changes have nothing to do with revisions to future forecasts of company earnings.)

This combination of rationality and the forward-looking nature of stock prices also explains other features of stock prices that might appear puzzling. When the central bank cuts interest rates or a firm announces an increase in dividends, the share price often falls. How can this be? We have just shown at great length that lower interest rates or higher dividends should *boost* the current stock price. However, the market expectation of future events affects share prices. Imagine that the market expects the central bank to cut interest rates by 0.5% or expects a firm to announce a 10% increase in dividends. The market will therefore price stocks based on these assumptions. If the government only cuts interest rates by 0.25%, or the firm announces only a 5% rise in dividends, the market will have to change its forecast. The market now sees that interest rates will not be as low as it thought or that dividends will be lower than forecast, so the price of shares will fall. Similarly, if the government cut rates by 1%, or the firm announced dividend growth of 20%, the stock price would rise. Finally, if the interest rate cut was 0.5% or dividend growth was 10%, nothing would happen—the market had already forecast this, so these announcements contain no information, and the market has no reason to change its forecast. As a result, the stock price does not alter.

17.5   Risk, Equity Prices, and Excess Return

We noted above that, at least in the United Kingdom and the United States, the rate of return on equities over the last 100 years had, on average, substantially exceeded the rate of return available on government bonds. This makes perfect sense as long as the risk on equities substantially exceeds the risk of those other investments. But what do we mean by risk here, and how might we measure it? The answer to these questions matters a lot, because movements in the risk premium can dramatically affect stock prices. If people come to think of equities as much more risky, they might require that, on average, they yield 10% more than government bonds, rather than, say, 5% more. Discounting future dividends at a rate that is higher by 5% could easily generate 40% or 50% falls in the price of equities. We can see, in principle, why this is so if we look again at Figure 17.7. Anything that causes the required rate of return to increase will decrease share prices unless there are compensating shifts in future dividends. Therefore, increases in risk premiums will lead to sharp falls in share prices *even if investor forecasts of future dividends do not change.*

The simple dividend discount model for stock prices, combined with an assumption of anticipated steady dividend growth, generates a link between stock prices, the latest dividend payment, and the relative magnitudes of the overall required return and the expected growth in dividends

$$P = D/(r - g)$$

The required return on equities, r, is the sum of a safe rate and the risk premium. Let's consider some plausible magnitudes for a developed economy. The safe (real) rate might be around 3%. With a risk premium of 4%, $r = 7\%$. If dividends grow in line with GDP, 2% a year might be plausible, giving a value for $(r - g)$ of 5%, so that the price to dividend ratio is 20. Suppose that the risk premium falls to 2%; $(r - g)$ is now 3% and the price to dividend ratio rises to 33—an increase in stock prices of 65%!

As long as investors perceive that equities are riskier than other assets, they will have to yield a higher rate of return. Can we therefore use this perspective to explain Figure 17.6, which shows by just how much equities have outperformed rates of return than other conventional assets? The first issue to consider here is whether equities really are riskier than most other investment categories.

It may seem obvious that equities are riskier than bank deposits or government bonds. But that is a hasty conclusion. What matters are *real* rates of returns, that is, the proportionate increase in the money value of the asset less the rise in the general cost of living. Most government bonds guarantee a nominal rate of return, and even then, that return is only guaranteed if you hold the debt until maturity and if the government has a zero probability of default. Holders of U.S., Italian, and U.K. government bonds found that those assets generated substantial negative real returns through much of the 1970s because inflation was higher than expected. Holders of Russian government bonds had a much nastier shock in 1998; their market value fell by about 80% during the year. Nor do bank deposits generate predictable real rates of return; inflation is unpredictable even over a five-month horizon, let alone over five or ten years. These facts should make us think harder about the relative riskiness of equities and other assets.

To gauge whether the extra return over bonds or bank deposits that investors in U.S. or U.K. equities have got over the last century is a fair compensation for risk, we need to use a more formal apparatus. In 1985, Raj Mehra and Ed Prescott published an influential paper on the "equity premium"; that is, the extra return that equities yield over risk-free assets.[7] Using past data, Mehra and Prescott estimated that the U.S. risk

[7] Mehra and Prescott, "The Equity Premium: A Puzzle," *Journal of Monetary Economics* (1985), vol. 15, pp. 145–161.

TABLE 17.1   **The Equity Premium in the United States**

Time Periods	Return on "Riskless" Asset (Commercial Paper Rate)	Return on S&P Stocks	Risk Premium
1900–2000	4.10%	10.10%	5.80%

Source: Dimson, Marsh, and Staunton, *Triumph of the Optimists: 101 Years of Global Investment*, (Princeton, NJ: Princeton University Press, 2002).

premium was about 6%. Another team of researchers, Dimson, Marsh, and Staunton, examined excess return on equities over the past 100 years. As summarized in Table 17.1, they also found an average excess return on equities of nearly 6%.[8]

Mehra and Prescott's paper suggests that the equity premium has been too high. In other words, investors have been overcompensated for the higher risk that equities involve. Mehra and Prescott call this the "equity premium puzzle"—the puzzle is, why do equities yield such a high rate of return?

Of course, whether this is a puzzle depends on how investors—ultimately you and me—feel about taking risks.[9] The measure of risk aversion economists most frequently use is called the **coefficient of relative risk aversion (CRRA)**. Mehra and Prescott argued that unless for the typical investor this measure is well above 2 (and probably nearer 10), standard economic theory cannot account for the observed magnitude of the equity premium.

But what does a CRRA of 2 or 10 mean, and are people this averse to uncertainty? Suppose you have been offered a job that is potentially lucrative but risky. If the job goes well, you will get an average annual income over the next 20 years (in present value terms) of $80,000. The value of your human capital (the present value of future labor income) would then be $1.6 million (20 × $80,000). We will assume that this is your only source of wealth. But there is a 50% chance that the risky job will go badly—there are spells of unemployment and you have to change firms. These factors will have a negative impact on your reputation and your resumé. If the job goes badly, your average income over the next 20 years would be only $20,000 (in present value), so that the overall value of human capital would be $400,000 (20 × $20,000).

We can work out how risk averse you are by knowing what certain level of income in a completely safe job gives you the same utility, or happiness, level as accepting this risky job. If you would consider a safe job earning an average salary of $50,000 a year as giving you the same welfare as the risky job, you have no aversion to risk; your CRRA is 0. This is because the expected value of the average annual salary in the risky job is $50,000—halfway between the good outcome ($80,000) and the bad outcome ($20,000)—which is exactly the same as the guaranteed income in the safe job. A CRRA of 0 therefore indi-

---

[8] Dimson, Marsh, and Staunton, *Triumph of the Optimists: 101 Years of Global Investment* (Princeton, NJ: Princeton University Press, 2002).

[9] As well as depending on risk aversion, the magnitude of the equity premium should also depend on how much risk there is in the world. Focusing on aggregate consumption changes, Mehra and Prescott argue that measured in this way risk is fairly small—consumption changes fluctuate between −2 and +4% per year. Therefore, we can only account for the equity premium if agents are highly risk averse because measured risk is too small to play a substantial role.

cates that individuals are indifferent between certain outcomes and risky outcomes with the same average value.

However, if an investor has a CRRA of greater than zero, she would rather take the certain salary than a risky one that is only on average the same. This also implies that she would prefer a slightly lower salary if it was guaranteed rather than a higher but riskier salary. The degree of risk aversion determines exactly how much lower the guaranteed salary can be for the person to be indifferent. For instance, if you think a job that guarantees you an annual salary of $48,000 gives you the same utility as the risky job in our example, your level of CRRA is 0.21—this is close to being indifferent to risk, certainly not very risk averse. As we increase the level of risk aversion, the guaranteed income the person requires falls—for instance, with a CRRA of 0.4, the fixed income falls to $46,000. By the time the CRRA rises to 4. It implies a safe salary of only $25,000.

Remember that Mehra and Prescott concluded that unless CRRA was greater than 5, standard economic theory could not account for the observed historical equity premium. As our example shows, this implies that investors would need to be incredibly risk averse. As a result, Mehra and Precott conclude that U.S. equities have yielded far too much for the excess returns just to reflect a risk premium.

If Mehra and Prescott are right, the market has mispriced equities in the largest stock market in the world for over 100 years and by a huge magnitude. The scale of that mispricing is staggering. Suppose that equities, on average, should not yield any more than "safe" government debt—perhaps around 2% per year in real terms. In that case $1000 invested in 1870 in the stock market should have generated a value by 2000 of about $(1.02)^{130}$, which is about $13,122. In fact, the rate of return was more like 8% a year, so that the real value of $1000 invested in equity was by the end of the period about $22,135,000. This is 1686 times its assumed fair value, which by any criteria would imply colossal market error and overcompensation for risk bearing.

Since Mehra and Prescott published their article, a huge academic debate has occurred about whether the equity premium really poses a puzzle. Perhaps the most interesting counter to the Mehra and Prescott argument is to question whether the *ex post* (or actual) average excess rates of return in the United Kingdom and the United States over the last century really do measure the equity premium. In assessing the equity premium, the *ex ante* (or expected) return on equities, not the *ex post* excess return, is important. In other words, what is relevant is the excess return investors expected they were going to earn, rather than what they actually did obtain. The problem may be that the United States is not a representative economy, so that returns on equity may have been much higher than elsewhere. After all, the United States is the most successful capitalist nation and emerged relatively unscathed from two major world wars. But would an investor have predicted this in 1870 when the United States was still in its economic adolescence? Was it really so clear to U.S. investors in 1932 that the stock market would rise strongly over the coming decades? Or on the morning after Pearl Harbor? And what about investors in Tsarist Russia in 1870—would they feel that equity investors have been overcompensated for the risk they have borne? They lost everything with the Russian Revolution in 1917. In other words, focusing on the United States may make it look like the market has overcompensated equity investors, but this is misleading—equities really are risky, and examining other countries and other periods of time suggests that not all investors have benefited from an equity premium. History offers many examples of investors who have lost fortunes by buying bonds and equities issued by companies operating in countries where returns looked to be fabulous, but where the economy subsequently performed dreadfully as a result of war or catastrophic mismanagement.

KEY POINT

One needs to remember just how much more successful than other countries U.S. economic performance has been over the past 150 years before assuming that the equity premium on U.S. equity indicates the average outcome for equity investments.

Figure 17.12 and the data in Table 17.2 also indicate that this focus on the United States might be misleading. They show rates of return across many economies for various time intervals over the last century. If you take the excess rate of return of equities over debt including all the countries in Table 17.2, the figure is not as high as the 6% that puzzled Mehra and Prescott. If one includes countries that were defeated in world wars (Germany, Japan, and those countries that were occupied), the overall rate of return on equity looks to be substantially lower than the U.K./U.S. average. Figure 17.12 brings this point out clearly. It shows a positive relation between the amount of time a stock market has traded more or less continuously and the average return over that period. So in countries where there was discontinuity in the stock market (generally because of economic disintegration, often as the result of war), average rates of return tend to have been lower. This implies that focusing on those stock markets that have traded continuously for the longest period may introduce a systematic upward bias to rates of return. This is a problem of survivorship bias.

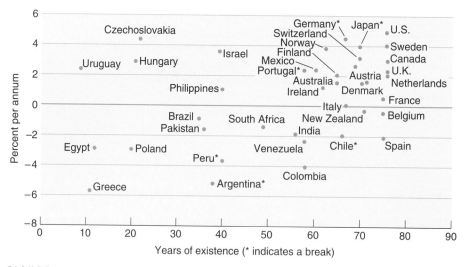

FIGURE 17.12 **Real returns on global stock markets sorted by years of existence.** *Source:* Goetzmann and Jorion, " Global Stock Markets in the 20th Century," *The Journal of Finance* (1999), vol. 54, no. 3, pp. 953–980. Copyright American Finance Association.

TABLE 17.2 **Average Equity Returns, 1900–2000**

Country	Nominal Rate of Return	Inflation	Real Rate of Return
Australia	11.9	4.1	7.5
Belgium	8.2	5.5	2.5
Canada	9.7	3.1	6.4
Denmark	8.9	4.1	4.6
France	12.1	7.9	3.8
Germany	9.7	5.1	3.6
Ireland	9.5	4.5	4.8
Italy	12.0	9.1	2.7
Japan	12.5	7.6	4.5
Netherlands	9.0	3.0	5.8
South Africa	12.0	4.8	6.8
Spain	10.0	6.1	3.6
Sweden	11.6	3.7	7.6
Switzerland	7.6	2.2	5.0
U.K.	10.1	4.1	5.8
U.S.	10.1	3.2	6.7

Source: Dimson, Marsh, and Staunton, *Triumph of the Optimists: 101 Years of Global Investment,* (Princeton, NJ: Princeton University Press, 2002).

Sample selection for countries also affects how we interpret the investment performance of individuals. The financial pages of newspapers love stories about star investors who have outperformed the market over the past 1, 5, 10, or even 20 years. Should these stars impress us? Probably not. Newspapers focus on winners and tend to ignore the average performers or those who did even less well than that. Some investor will always have the best record over the past 10 years, and their return will be much higher than the average if they are the best performers out of a sample of 10,000 investors. But there would be a "best investor," with an apparently fantastic ability to pick winners, even if every investor chose stocks by throwing a dart at a dartboard. Our advice is not to be too impressed by fantastic past performance.

Sample selection is important and may explain the Mehra and Prescott puzzle. So maybe the equity premium puzzle is not a puzzle after all. This may reassure academics, but it is sobering if you are thinking about rates of return that you might earn in stock markets in the future. The sample selection story suggests that measuring the average rate of return over the last century by focusing on the United Kingdom and the United States (which looks sensible given that they are big markets that have existed for a long time) inflates the estimate of the likely rates of return in the future.

17.6   Are Stock Prices Forecastable?

Belief in efficient (or rational) stock market pricing has taken big blows over the last 20 years. Robert Shiller led the intellectual assault on belief in stock market efficiency in a series of papers written more than 20 years ago.[10] In 1981 Shiller argued that stock prices in the United States over the 100-year period starting in 1870 were far too volatile to be consistent with a rational evaluation of the fundamental value of the corporate sector.[11]

Shiller wanted to compare the volatility of stock prices observed in practice with the volatility of share prices if they are based on rational forecasts of future dividends. However, we cannot recreate *now* what rational forecasts of future dividends were in 1870. Therefore, Shiller focused instead on the volatility of share prices assuming that the investor had perfect foresight about future dividends. If you had known in 1870 what dividends U.S. companies would pay over the next 100 years, then using the logic of Figure 17.7, you could work out what the price of equities should have been over this period on the basis of this perfect foresight. (Of course, this depends on choosing a discount factor *r*.) Shiller argued that the actual path of dividends that companies paid over that 100-year period should have been *more* volatile than the path that it was rational to expect in 1870. In other words, if actual share prices are more volatile than Shiller's perfect foresight share price, then they must also be more volatile than share prices based on forecasts of fundamentals.

Crucial to Shiller's argument was the claim that the share price based on perfect foresight should be more volatile than the share price based on rational forecasts. The argument was subtle, some would say intellectually dangerous. An analogy might be helpful in understanding it.

Suppose I asked you what you expected to be the average outcome of tossing an unbiased coin 100 times. You would probably say that you would expect 50 heads and 50 tails. Suppose now I actually tossed a coin 100 times. The outcome is unlikely to be exactly 50 heads and 50 tails. I could repeat the same question to you over and over again, and toss a coin 100 times after each answer. We would find significant variability from one occasion to the next in the actual outcome of tossing a coin 100 times, but no variability in your expectation of what the result would be (you keep saying 50 heads and 50 tails). Shiller argued analogously that the expectation of future dividends should be less variable than actual future dividends. This implied that the price calculated by discounting the actual future course of dividends (the perfect foresight price) should be more volatile than the share price that would result from people forming rational expectations of the present value of future dividends. This meant that Shiller expected the perfect foresight share price to be more volatile than the actual history of share prices. Figure 17.13 shows what he saw.

---

[10] For an excellent review of this work, see Shiller, *Market Volatility* (Cambridge, MA: MIT Press, 1989).

[11] Shiller, "Do Stock Prices Move Too Much to Be Justified by Subsequent Changes in Dividends?" *American Economic Review* (1981), vol. 71, pp. 421–436.

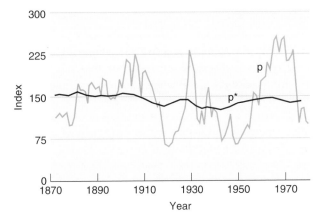

FIGURE 17.13 **Share prices more volatile compared to those constructed using actual dividends paid.** Reproduced with permission from MIT Press from Robert Shiller, *Market Volatility* (Cambridge, MA: MIT Press, 1989) Chapter 5.

The p line is actual share prices, and the line marked p* is the perfect foresight path. Remember, the perfect foresight line should be *more* volatile than the actual prices. Clearly it is not! Shiller concluded that sensible reactions to news about future economic fundamentals were not driving variability in stock prices; if they were, we could expect the perfect foresight path to be much more variable relative to the actual path for prices.

If Shiller is right, things are rather worrying. Big swings in prices either up or down might have much more to do with irrational sentiment than with changing expectations of future profits. But is he right? The jury is still out on this question. The statistical issues are subtle and still not resolved. Furthermore, sample selection bias, which we argued was relevant to the equity premium puzzle, is also relevant to the Shiller story. In a sense, the 100-year period between 1870 and 1970 that Shiller used for his original work was not a large sample of observations. It was one run of history for one country. And one observation is a small sample on which to base a devastating hypothesis.

In defense of Shiller, you could argue that dramatic volatility in stock prices is not confined to the United States. Huge swings in prices occur in stock markets in most countries: in the United Kingdom, share prices dropped by 35% in 1973 and by 55% in 1974. In Russia, the stock market index fell by over 80% between January and September 1998. Between 1990 and 1992, the Japanese stock market fell by 50%.

But stock price volatility, and more specifically big drops in prices in short periods, are not inconsistent with an efficient market. If news arrives that causes a substantial change in expected future profits (on which dividends are based), prices should move a lot. Smart economists can construct stories around the events in Russia, Japan, and the United Kingdom at the time of big market falls that are consistent with efficient markets. Despite this, the work of Robert Shiller began to undermine faith in efficient markets.

KEY POINT

An important insight of Shiller's was to note that although efficient markets might imply near-random behavior in asset prices (under certain circumstances), such randomness did not imply efficiency; it was a necessary but not sufficient condition for efficiency.

17.7 Speculation or Fundamentals?

The efficient market view that movements in stock prices are unpredictable has also been assaulted. Many respectable academic papers argue that asset price movements are predictable in ways that are difficult to square with an efficient market. Jim Poterba and Lawrence Summers, for example, have presented evidence of **mean reversion** in stock prices.[12] Mean reversion is a statistical concept that implies that a variable tends to return to some long-term value. For instance, the average temperature in New York City in January may be 30 degrees Fahrenheit, although in any one year it may be colder or hotter. For several consecutive years the weather may be warmer in January. However, if the temperature is mean reverting, eventually the temperature in January in New York will revert back to around 30 degrees Fahrenheit.

If mean reversion exists in share prices, it implies that when prices have moved up substantially, relative to some underlying trend, they are more likely to fall; and when asset prices have moved down sharply relative to some longer-run trend, they are more likely to rise. It might seem like common sense that asset prices would behave in this way, but if they consistently did, smart traders could consistently make big profits. If there is mean reversion, then as the price of an asset falls further below some underlying path, it becomes increasingly likely that it will return toward it, thus generating capital gains. But if that were so, wouldn't the buying and selling decisions of smart speculators prevent the price moving far from the underlying equilibrium? They would be bidding the price up when it was below equilibrium and driving it down (by selling) when it was above. This is a form of arbitrage—a process whereby traders aim to take advantage of mispricing by buying undervalued assets and selling overvalued assets. So how can any significant mean reversion persist?

It has been suggested that although arbitrage arguments like this might remove mispricing of assets relative to others that were close substitutes (what is called pure arbitrage), they were not relevant for equities in general. The idea that a small group of smart investors could, by their seeking to take advantage of mispricing, drive prices back to "*fundamental value*" depends on an infinitely elastic demand (i.e., investors undertake unlimited purchases when they see a price discrepancy). This is plausible (just!) for pure arbitrage, when no risk is involved in the trade, but not when risky speculative positions have to be taken. Some researchers have argued that there is no equivalent arbitrage argument applicable to equities in general—to bet against the level of the market means taking big risks.

Shleifer and Summers have argued that the amount of capital that could be gambled against general, and potentially persistent, mispricing of assets (e.g., equities) is small.[13] Regular monitoring of fund managers by their clients may make it risky for the

---

[12] See Poterba and Summers, "Mean Reversion in Stock Prices: Evidence and Implications," *Journal of Financial Economics* (1988), vol. 22, pp. 27–60; Summers, "Does the Stock Market Really Reflect Fundamental Value?" *Journal of Finance* (1986), vol. 41, pp. 591–601; Cutler, Poterba, and Summers, "Speculative Dynamics," *Review of Economic Studies* (1991*a*), vol. 58, pp. 529–546; Cutler, Poterba, and Summers, "Speculative Dynamics and the Role of Feedback Traders," *American Economic Review* (1991*b*), vol. 80, pp. 63–68.

[13] Shleifer and Summers, "The Noise Trader Approach to Finance," *Journal of Economic Perspectives* (1990), vol. 4, no. 2, pp. 19–33.

funds to follow a strategy of betting against the market—*relative* underperformance in the period before their bet comes good may cost them their jobs/mandates.

Shiller, Shleifer, Summers, and others have also argued that fads, rumors, and group pressures can make deviations from fundamental values substantial and prolonged. Evidence from psychological experiments shows that people have a tendency to extrapolate from recent trends even when no link to the future exists. Experiments also show strong tendencies for groups to influence each other and make common mistakes (peer group errors) or display *herding behavior*.

The many historical examples of massive price rises followed by sharp falls provide the strongest evidence that these factors are sometimes at work. Two that have received considerable attention from economists are the tulip mania of the seventeenth century and the South Sea bubble of the eighteenth century.

- Early in the seventeenth century, the price of tulips in the Netherlands rose dramatically before collapsing. Garber reports that a single Semper Augustus bulb sold for 2000 guilders in 1625.[14] In late 1637 prices surged again and continued rising fast until February 1639. But then they collapsed, and bulbs could not be sold at even 10% of their values of a few weeks earlier.
- Shares in the now infamous South Sea Company (which aimed to buy British government debt in the 1720s and fund the purchases by issuing equity) were dramatically volatile. Between February and July 1720, the company's share price increased about eightfold. But by the end of September, the price was back at its original level.

Both these cases—that of tulip mania and the South Sea bubble—saw a dramatic clamor for assets once prices had begun to rise fast. Investors trying to calculate potential future returns seem to have attached much more weight to recent high returns than to the future earnings power of the underlying assets. If speculators do that, their actions can clearly be destabilizing—falls in price generate more selling, while rises in price only generate higher demand.

Summers and his coauthors show evidence of mean reversion across a range of markets, which suggests persistent and predictable deviations from fundamentals. Over short time horizons, they find positive correlations between excess returns on stocks and more excess returns. Over the long-run, however, they find negative correlations, suggesting that values do revert toward a long-term value. This is consistent with people following trading rules based on extrapolation so that deviations from fundamentals are exacerbated rather than eradicated quickly.

Of course, all arguments that prices can deviate in systematic (i.e., partly predictable) ways from their longer-term trend are open to the counterargument that smart gamblers will start trading, taking prices back to fundamental value. But if the length of deviations from fundamentals is uncertain, and potentially long, gambling against those who have driven prices away from fundamentals is risky. Any investor who sold Japanese stocks in 1985 when the market-price-to-earnings ratio was 30 would have lost his or her shirt in 1986 when price-to-earnings ratios went to 60.[15] Smart speculators might do better to try to "ride" deviations from fundamental value, and time

---

[14] Garber, "Famous First Bubbles," *Journal of Economic Perspectives* (1990), vol. 4, no. 2, pp. 35–54.

[15] That is the average ratio of company stock prices to latest annual corporate earnings.

their exit from the bubble, rather than just trade against deviations from fundamental value. Of course, if speculators do that, their activities may not help bring prices back to fundamental value.

This leaves the efficient market enthusiasts with awkward facts to explain. Nonetheless, the proponents of the efficient markets view have cast doubt on the validity of much of the "evidence" against efficient markets.

KEY POINT

Many events that matter hugely for stock prices are unique, or at least have not happened often—wars, monetary unions, the invention of cheap computing, and the Internet. Forming expectations about how these things affect corporate profits and dividends is hard, so it is tough to be sure that some market movement is inconsistent with investors behaving sensibly.

17.8   Bubbles

A form of market inefficiency that has interested economists is **asset market bubbles**. A bubble occurs when an asset price is different from its fundamentals, and this difference does not disappear even if investors know the price is above its fundamental value.[16]

With bubbles, if the deviation in the asset price is to be sustainable, the deviation from fundamentals must become even more pronounced. We can demonstrate this with an example. Suppose prices start out 20% above "fundamentals" with a 1 in 10 chance of dropping back to their equilibrium level. To generate an annual average return of, say, 15%, the following equation must hold

$$15\% = x\,\%(0.9) - 20\%(0.1)$$

where x is the proportionate rate of price increase *if* the bubble does not burst—which is 90% probable. There is a 1 in 10 chance that the price will fall back to its fundamental value, which is 20% lower, hence the final term in the equation. The solution to this equation is $x = 18.9\%$. Therefore, even though the price starts off 20% overvalued in a bubble, we can expect to see it rise by almost 19% more. This means that prices are even further above fundamentals if the bubble persists; and next period's value of x needs to be even higher because if prices crash, they fall further.

In provocative research, Peter Garber has argued that when you look at events that researchers have universally accepted as asset price bubbles, a bubble may not really have existed.[17] Indeed, we have already mentioned the events he looks at—the tulip mania of the 1630s and the South Sea bubble of the 1720s. In each case, he cannot rule out nonbubble explanations for the massive price movements—in other words, given what it was reasonable for people to believe on the basis of what they then knew, the prices may not have been crazy.

[16] By the "fundamental value," we mean the value based on the discounted sum of expected future earnings that the underlying productive asset generates.

[17] Garber, "Famous First Bubbles," *Journal of Economic Perspectives* (1990) vol. 4, no. 2, pp. 35–54.

17.9 Market Efficiency—What Should We Think?

We have seen that, from the perspective of standard economic theory, equity markets have several puzzles. So what! Does it matter if stock market prices sometimes are substantially above, and sometimes substantially below, valuations that would more accurately reflect the fundamental economic value of corporations?

We think that these things do matter. Prices are supposed to guide the allocation of resources. The q theory of investment, which we discussed in Chapter 13, links the amount of new investment undertaken to stock market valuations of existing assets. If stock market values do not reflect a rational assessment of future profits and dividends of companies, the life of investors becomes tricky, and companies cannot rely on the signals stock markets give to guide their investment; new investment based on stock prices will misallocate funds. So whether stock prices really do reflect fundamental profitability matters. If they do not, economists would say that the market displays a form of inefficiency.

So in principle, substantial and prolonged asset price deviations from fundamental values are significant. Of course, people who actually allocate resources are generally not economists, do not believe the efficient markets theory, and probably would not look to the stock market to help them decide whether to build a new factory or open a new shop. Companies probably do not base investment decisions on the current level of their stock price, a proposition consistent with the failure of q theories to explain actual movements in physical investment. Here is the founder of the Internet company Yahoo, billionaire Jerry Yang, on how stock market valuations of his company affect his business decisions:

> We're on the field, we're playing the game, and it's probably the bottom of the third inning. I have no idea what the spectators are doing. They could be selling tickets for this game, even at the scalper's prices. I have no control over that. We've just got to win this game.[18]

But if the prices of financial assets do not much influence resource allocation within a capitalist economy, this is hardly comforting. After all, market prices are *supposed* to guide the allocation of resources. And evidence on how companies actually make investment decisions is worrisome: they often use payback periods as an investment criterion (which is anathema to economists), and they often seem to confuse nominal and real discount rates.

Even if it did not affect new investment, excess price volatility in equity markets, or sustained persistence of price deviations from fundamentals, can be costly for other reasons. Asset price movements shift the distribution of wealth. They make saving over a person's lifetime more difficult (although paradoxically they may actually increase saving). Volatile asset market prices may put people off funded pensions. They can generate risk premiums that are too high in terms of fundamentals. Asset price volatility may cause unnecessary takeovers and make it more difficult to monitor company management because investors cannot confidently assess the true worth of the company by reference to market values. Volatility unrelated to fundamentals can makes portfolio allocation more difficult.

---

[18] Quoted in Perkins and Perkins, *The Internet Bubble* (New York: Harper Collins, 1999), p. 163.

So it matters that asset prices might move much more than fundamentals would justify—it certainly matters if you have to sell most of your portfolio of equities and the market drops 30%! In a world in which most people are risk averse, it also matters if diversifiable sources of risk are not diversified away. And all this will matter even more if equity markets become a more important source of funds for corporations in the world and account for an increasing share of portfolios of wealth.

So what should we think? The idea that stock market prices—or indeed prices in any asset market—become *permanently* dissociated from fundamental values strikes us as implausible. If stock prices were several times greater than a plausible assessment of their worth based on likely future corporate earnings, eventually even the most slow-witted, or most irrationally optimistic, investors would catch on. But that process can take a long time, so mispricing of a large margin can last for several years.

This sort of mispricing is likely to be larger and persist longer if many investors base their judgment on future returns on current movements in share prices rather than on an assessment of corporate incomes. Robert Shiller has collected valuable information on the tendency of investors to do just this. He sent out about 2000 questionnaires after the October 1987 stock market crash in the United States to try to find out what investors were thinking on the day of one of the largest price changes in history. On October 19, the Dow Jones industrial average fell 508 points, a drop of 22.6%. Shiller's survey results suggest that rather than being a response to news about fundamentals, investors' reactions to the most recent price changes drove changes in sentiment about prices. In summarizing the survey results Shiller observed:

> Since no news story or any other recognizable event outside the market appears to be immediately responsible for the crash, we will . . . turn to considerations of a theory of the crash as being determined endogenously by investors: that the . . . crash was related to some internal dynamics of investor thinking, investors' reactions to price and to each other . . . There were two channels by which price declines could feed back into further price declines: first a price-to-price channel—investors on October 19 were reacting to price changes; second, a social-psychological channel—investors were directly reacting to each other. From the information collected on the frequency with which investors checked prices and talked with each other on October 19, both feedbacks were happening.[19]

We think that prices in stock markets often reflect a tendency of investors to infer something about true value by looking at prices themselves rather than the fundamentals and that, as a result, prices can move away from fundamental value. It can also make sharp price falls or rises self-reinforcing. But if investors only gauged fair value by reference to actual price, prices could rise or fall without limit—we certainly could not expect to see the mean reversion in asset prices that does, in practice, seem to exist.

KEY POINT

This suggests that the pull of fundamental value—that is, of assessments based on expectations of the future path of the earnings of the underlying assets being valued—is powerful in the longer term.

---

[19] Shiller, *Market Volatility* (Cambridge, MA: MIT Press, 1989), Chapter 23.

Jeff Bezos, founder of Amazon.com, sums this view up succinctly:

I subscribe to . . . the view that there is no correlation between great companies and short-term stock prices. But in the long term there is 100% correlation.[20]

SUMMARY

In sections 17.1 and 17.2, we explored the nature of equities and compared their importance to various nations. Stock prices are important because they give an indication of the value of firms and help guide investment decisions. Fluctuations in prices also generate big movements in the wealth of the private sector and are likely to cause movements in spending.

In section 17.3, we suggested that the value of a company's equity should reflect the expected value of the earnings that it will generate into the future, earnings out of which dividends can be paid.

If this is how stock prices are determined, we explained in section 17.4 why we should not be surprised by the fact that changes in stock market values appear random. Shifts in expectations and movements in required returns will drive shifts in stock prices.

In section 17.5, we saw noted that stock returns in the United States have exceeded returns on bonds and most other assets by a large margin over the last 200 years. This creates another puzzle: the excess return puzzle. In part this may reflect a systematic sample selection problem—history records the deeds of the winners. If that is so, the past returns in the world's most successful large capitalist country give an exaggerated estimate of the likely returns on equities in the future.

In section 17.6, we saw that, while volatility of stock prices, per se, is not inconsistent with the efficient functioning of the market, the degree to which prices fluctuate may be. In 17.7, we explored further the idea that stock price gyrations often appear hard to reconcile with the notion that cool-headed investors make rational assessments of future earnings of companies and discount those earnings appropriately. Some analysts suggest that herding behavior and extrapolations from recent price movements may play a role. Asset market bubbles are another interesting market phenomenon, which we explored in section 17.8.

Despite the various forces pushing equity prices away from their fundamentals-based values, we concluded in section 17.9 that, over the long run, fundamentals still exert a pull on equity pricing.

CONCEPTUAL QUESTIONS:

1. (Section 17.1) Firms tend to use retained earnings rather than issue new shares to finance a higher proportion of new investment. Does this mean the stock market is largely irrelevant for companies?

2. (17.3) Suppose a company cuts its dividend today to finance more investment from retained current profit. Under what circumstances would this increase, decrease, and leave unchanged the share price?

---

[20] Quoted in Perkins and Perkins, *The Internet Bubble* (New York: Harper Collins, 1999), p. 159.

3. (17.4) "Share price changes are volatile and unpredictable, therefore the stock market is un-related to what happens in the rest of the economy; it's just a casino."

"Share price changes are volatile and unpredictable; therefore the stock market is efficient and helps allocate resources effectively."

What is wrong with each of these propositions?

4. (17.5) How would you judge what the equity risk premium is today? How would you assess whether it was adequate?

5. (17.6) Suppose stock prices are more variable than efficiency implies, in the sense that stock prices vary more than do rational expectations of discounted future dividends. What implications does this have about the efficiency of the takeover mechanism as a means to discipline the managers of companies?

6. (17.7) Suppose you know that some other people know some things that are relevant for predicting future corporate earnings. You do not know what these things are nor who knows them. How does this affect your response to a rise in demand for stocks and big price increases? Is it rational to follow the herd?

ANALYTICAL QUESTIONS

1. (Section 17.3) Investors expect that a company will pay dividends per share of $1.50 for each year over the next five years. The next dividend is due a year from now. They also anticipate that the share price at the end of five years will be $17. They require an expected rate of return of 9%.

   (a) What is the current share price?
   (b) What happens to the share price if anticipated dividends over the next five years rise to $2.00 but this is viewed as temporary so there is no change in the anticipated share price five years ahead?
   (c) What happens if the required rate of return falls to 8%, and as a result, the five-year ahead anticipated share price rises to $18.75?

2. (17.4) Suppose that the price of a share always either goes up by 20% or falls by 30% over the next year whatever its current level. The chances of an up move are 0.75 and the chances of a down move are 0.25. The stock pays no dividends. Suppose you know nothing about the recent performance of the stock. What is the expected rate of return on the stock? Suppose you now discover that over the past five years the returns on the stock have been: +20%, +20%, −30%, −30%, −30%. What do you now think the expected return for the next year is?

3. (17.5) In an economy, aggregate dividends paid by companies are expected to grow in line with GDP. The trend rate of growth of GDP is 2.5% per annum. The required rate of return on equities equals a safe rate plus a risk premium. The safe (real) rate is 3%, and the risk premium is 5%. What would you expect the dividend price ratio (or the dividend yield) to be? By how much would stock market prices change if the risk premium increased to 6%?

4. (17.5) Suppose you are risk neutral, so that your coefficient of risk aversion is 0. You are on a game show where you have already won $500,000. You can quit now with the $500,000 or take a chance by answering a question you are not sure of. If you guess right, your winnings go to $1,000,000, and you walk away a millionaire. If you guess wrong, you get to keep a mis-

erable $50,000. You assess that there is a 50:50 chance of guessing right. Should you gamble? What would the odds need to be on a correct guess to make you indifferent between gambling and quitting? Suppose the fall-back prize if you guess wrong is $250,000. How does this change your answers to the first two questions?

5. (17.6) Suppose your weight fluctuates randomly from month to month; it is as likely to go up as down. Your current weight is 161 pounds. Looking back at records of your weight over the past year the pattern is:

Jan.	Feb.	Mar.	Apr.	May	June	July	Aug.	Sep.	Oct.	Nov.	Dec.
150	145	148	153	157	155	158	160	161	159	159	161

What is your best guess on the profile of monthly weights over the next 12 months? How volatile is the path of actual monthly weights over the next year likely to be relative to your estimated profile?

6. (17.7) A stock is expected to pay a dividend of $3.00 each year forever. You assess that the expected return is 10% and from this you conclude that the fair price should be $30. But you know that stock prices sometimes deviate from fair value by significant amounts. When those deviations occur, you believe that prices do revert back to fair value, but not immediately. You calculate that one quarter the discrepancy between the current price and the fundamental price is closed each year. If the current price is $22, what do you calculate the expected return on the stock will be over each of the next five years?

CHAPTER 18

The Bond Market

Overview

Companies and governments borrow to finance investment and cover current expenditure—households, ultimately, provide the funds. The household sector's stocks of financial assets are—either directly or indirectly—claims on future revenues of corporations and governments. Those claims come in many forms. Broadly speaking, they are of two sorts: debt and equity. In this chapter, we focus on a particular type of debt: bonds. The bond market is important because it is where interest rates on medium and long-term debt are determined. We will discuss how bonds are used, how they are priced, what their risks are, and how shifts in bond values affect the wider economy. The links among monetary policy, the cost of borrowing, and the value of bonds are significant; we will see how governments and central banks through their influence on the bond market can affect the wider economy. These effects can be positive, but often they are negative, sometimes disastrously so.

Key to understanding the significance of the bond market is the relation among bond prices, rates of return (or yields), and expectations of future short-term interest rates. Central banks implement monetary policy by controlling short-term interest rates. But longer-term interest rates, that is the rates of return required on investments over horizons of 5, 10, or 20 years, are probably more important for private sector saving and investing decisions than the interest rates on 1-month bank loans or deposits that central banks directly influence. Short-term rates and longer-term rates are linked, and one of the aims of this chapter is to explain and then assess this link.

Key Concepts

Coupons

Duration

Face Value

Fixed Income Securities

Leverage

Maturity

Modigliani-Miller Theorem

Par Value

Redemption

The Yield Curve

18.1 What Is a Bond?

A bond is basically an "I owe you" (IOU). When a company or a government issues a bond, it promises to repay certain amounts of money at specific dates in the future. Most bonds specify the precise cash values of the repayments, and their timing, in advance.[1] These IOUs often have long lives; many governments want to borrow money for 20 or 30 years, and debt issued today may not finally be repaid until 2020 or 2030. Indeed, the U.K. government issued bonds to help finance World War I (1914–1918) that have an indefinite life—they are promises to pay a certain amount of cash to the holder each year until the end of time (or until the end of the United Kingdom!). Like equities, bonds are traded in a secondary market—holders of bonds can sell their claims to third parties and liquidate their holding without recourse to the issuer. For this reason, a 30-year bond—one that the issuer will not finally repay for three decades—can nonetheless be a highly liquid asset.

Bonds are traded in securities markets (the bond market); this distinguishes bonds from bank debt—claims held by banks cannot, in general, be sold to a third party. And the debts that banks issue directly to the public—that is, deposits—are also not traded in a secondary market. When you want the cash you have lent a bank, you get it from the bank rather than by selling your deposit to someone else. In this sense, bonds have more in common with equities than with bank debt because both bonds and equities are traded securities that you can cash in by selling to other investors; the original issuer is not involved. If I own bonds issued by a company, I can sell their claims to you and liquidate my holdings without involving the company.

Bond prices are set, on a minute-by-minute basis, by market makers who typically work for large financial institutions like Morgan Stanley, Merrill Lynch, or Goldman Sachs. They quote prices at which they will buy and sell bonds. These prices reflect the flow of buy and sell orders they receive. As always, the forces underlying demand and supply generate prices. Expectations about whether bondholders will really receive the money bond issuers have promised them are crucial, as are the ways in which people value money that will only be paid 5, 10, or 20 years ahead. As people's views on these factors change, demand and supply curves shift, which generates changes in prices. The prices reflect the cost of borrowing money for various time periods and are a major factor behind corporate investment decisions.

The big distinction between bonds and equities is that the repayment schedule for bonds is specified in great detail, whereas equities merely represent a claim on some unspecified fraction of whatever corporate profits (after tax and interest payments) happen to exist in the future. As a result, bonds have different risk characteristics.

Bond markets are certainly big news. Table 18.1 indicates the size of the global market. In the middle of 2003, bonds that governments and companies in the major developed countries had issued had a market value of nearly $50 trillion. The U.S. bond market rivals the size of the U.S. stock market. In June 2003, the total value of bonds

---

[1] The cash (or nominal) values are usually known, though the *real* value of those payments is not because inflation is uncertain. Some bonds pay future amounts that are linked to inflation outturns and generate cash flows with known real values.

TABLE 18.1 Size and Structure of the World Bond Market, June 2003 (Nominal Value in Billions of U.S. Dollars)

Country	Total Out- standing	Percent World Bond Market	Domestic US$ bn	Percent of Domestic	International US$ bn	Percent of International	Government US$ bn	Percent of Government	Corporate* US$ bn	Percent of Corporate	Financial Institutio US$ bn	Perce of Finan Instituti
Developed Countries												
U.S.	19874	41.1	17041	46.3	2833	27.6	4782	26.3	2882	47.1	12211	54.
Japan	7319	15.1	7072	19.2	246	2.4	5281	29.0	732	12.0	1305	5.
Germany	3624	7.5	1915	5.2	1709	16.6	1009	5.5	166	2.7	2450	11.
Italy	2312	4.8	1877	5.1	436	4.3	1367	7.5	185	3.0	761	3.
France	2258	4.7	1647	4.5	611	5.9	923	5.1	438	7.2	898	4.
U.K.	2118	4.4	1162	3.2	956	9.3	471	2.6	513	8.4	1135	5.
Netherlands	997	2.1	493	1.3	503	4.9	224	1.2	126	2.1	646	2.
Canada	923	1.9	669	1.8	254	2.5	572	3.1	172	2.8	179	0.
Spain	863	1.8	551	1.5	312	3.0	408	2.2	107	1.7	348	1.
Belgium	619	1.3	400	1.1	220	2.2	337	1.8	33	0.5	249	1.
Australia	414	0.9	256	0.7	158	1.5	94	0.5	86	1.4	234	1.
Sweden	384	0.8	242	0.7	142	1.4	146	0.8	44	0.7	194	0.
Denmark	373	0.8	335	0.9	38	0.4	113	0.6	26	0.4	234	1.
Austria	363	0.7	217	0.6	146	1.4	194	1.1	10	0.2	159	0.
Switzerland	331	0.7	200	0.5	132	1.3	83	0.4	32	0.5	217	1.
Greece	218	0.4	151	0.4	67	0.7	202	1.1	6	0.1	10	0.

rtugal	188	0.4	107	0.3	81	0.8	93	0.5	20	0.3	75	0.3
land	160	0.3	92	0.2	68	0.7	104	0.6	20	0.3	37	0.2
rway	142	0.3	87	0.2	55	0.5	37	0.2	24	0.4	81	0.4
land	138	0.3	57	0.2	81	0.8	37	0.2	35	0.6	66	0.3
xembourg	28	0.1			28	0.3	0	0.0	2	0.0	26	0.1
w Zealand	9	0.0			9	0.1	4	0.0	3	0.0	3	0.0
eland	7	0.0			7	0.1	2	0.0	1	0.0	4	0.0
btotal	43662	90.3	34570	93.9	9093	88.6	16482	90.5	5661	92.5	21520	96.5
shore Centers	120	0.2			120	1.2	20	0.1	22	0.4	78	0.3
veloping Countries												
ica and Middle East	100	0.2	62	0.2	37	0.4	68	0.4	12	0.4	20	0.1
ia and Pacific	1436	3.0	1276	3.5	160	1.6	660	3.6	276	4.5	500	2.2
rope	366	0.8	267	0.7	99	1.0	334	1.8	14	0.2	19	0.1
tin America and Caribbean	677	1.4	397	1.0	280	2.7	499	2.7	64	1.0	114	0.5
ternational Organizations	479	1.0			479	4.7						
orld Total	48363	100.00	36829	100.00	10268	100.00	18213	100.00	6117	99.0	22289	99.5

cludes private and public sector.

rce: Bank for International Settlements (BIS), *BIS Quarterly Review* (December 2003). Table 12 (A–D) and Table 16 (A–B).
://www.bis.org/statistics/secstats.htm

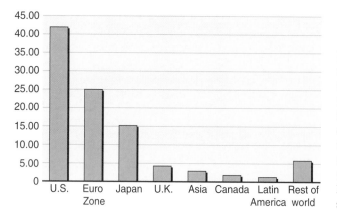

FIGURE 18.1   **Shares of the world bond market, June 2003.** Shares in total world stock of bonds by country of origin of issuer. *Source:* Author's calculation with data from the BIS *Quarterly Review* (December 2003). Table 12 (A–D) and table 16 (A–B). http://www.bis.org/statistics/sectats.htm

that the U.S. government and big U.S. corporations had issued was almost $20 trillion; at that time U.S. equity market capitalization was about $12 trillion. The U.S. bond market is also far larger than any other market (Figure 18.1).

In many countries, as Table 18.1 shows, the government dominates the bond market. The importance of government debt reflects two factors. First, governments often need to borrow on a large scale because they cannot cover their expenditure out of tax revenue—sometimes by choice and sometimes of necessity. This is particularly true during war. The stock of government debt outstanding has often increased massively because of long and expensive conflicts. Second, governments issue bonds because they cannot issue equities. Corporations have a wide choice of financing techniques; governments do not. If you think about the difference between bonds and equities, this makes sense. The returns that shareholders get from holding equities depend on the profits that companies earn, and these, in turn, reflect a company's efficiency and skill in producing things that people want. Governments, in contrast, do not aim to make profits. If they did, life would be strange. After all, governments can (in most developed countries at least) raise taxes further and thus can (within limits) generate a surplus of revenue over spending. If governments really decided to maximize the excess of their revenues over their expenditure, they could generate huge "profits." If governments considered it their duty to maximize profits to generate returns to shareholders, taxpayers would suffer. Furthermore, shareholders might only be willing to buy equity in governments if, in exchange, they had a say in how government was run. This is hard to square with "one person, one vote" democracy!

So when governments want to borrow, they typically look to the bond market. Table 18.1 shows that among the developed countries, the government issues far more bonds than non-financial corporations. But corporations are also big players in the bond market; this has long been true in the United States, and in the 1990s, European companies also became significant issuers of bonds. When companies issue bonds, they are, like governments, issuing IOUs that give the holder of the bond the right to some portion of future corporate revenues.

The prices at which companies and governments can issue bonds are crucial because they reflect the rate of return that investors demand to hand over cash now in exchange for the promise of repayment in the future. This is a key determinant of the level of corporate investment. The price at which governments can issue bonds determines the cost of the national debt. The cost of debt to companies and governments is, of course, the mirror image of the return savers earn.

KEY POINT

Bond prices reflect the balance of supply and demand for debt. The flow of new bonds coming on to the market depends on the level of investment that companies wish to undertake and the needs of government to borrow.

The demand for new bonds reflects the desired level of saving of households and companies. Both demand and supply in the bond market depend on returns on other financial assets—for example, equities and bank deposits. To understand how these factors affect bond prices and the volumes of debt issued, we need to understand the link between returns, or yields, and bond prices.

18.2 Prices, Yields, and Interest Rates

If you buy a bond, you hold a piece of paper that gives you the right to receive cash flows at specified dates in the future. The expectation of receiving those cash flows gives your piece of paper some value today. Because there are alternatives to holding bonds—for example, putting the money in a bank where it will earn a particular rate of interest—bonds have to generate a positive expected return to make them worth holding. We can think of the price of a bond as simply reflecting the value today of all the streams of cash that it will generate in the future. Because we value the cash paid to us tomorrow less than the cash that is in our pocket today, we will discount those future receipts of cash that a bond entitles us to. So the *price* of a bond is the appropriately discounted value of all the repayments on the bond until it is finally redeemed. Those repayments come in two forms: regular **coupon** payments, plus a final payment in the last period of the bond's life (its **face value**) at the **redemption** date (when the bond matures). The *yield* on a bond is simply the rate of return that, when used to discount future cash receipts, makes their total value equal to the current market price of the bond.

We need to be more precise about these relations. If we denote the yield on a bond by y and its price by P, then the relationship between the price and the yield on a bond with n periods to maturity is given by:

$$P = \frac{C}{1+y} + \frac{C}{(1+y)^2} + \cdots\cdots + \frac{C}{(1+y)^n} + \frac{F}{(1+y)^n}$$

where C is the regular annual coupon payment on the bond, and F is the face value. Here we assume that coupon payments come at 12-month intervals, and the first coupon is paid exactly a year from today. (In practice, some bonds pay coupons more than once a year, while others only make a final repayment.) The bond **matures** (or is redeemed) n years from now. Such a bond has a residual maturity of n years; obviously as time passes, n falls. So a bond issued in 1985 with an original maturity of 30 years,

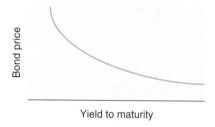

Yield to maturity

FIGURE 18.2   **Bond price/yield to maturity relationship.**
There is a negative, non-linear relation between the yield on a bond and its price.

and a face value of $100, will guarantee to its holder in 2015 a final payment of $100. By 2005 the bond's residual maturity is 10 years.

You can see from the relation in the equation above that the prices of bonds and their yields have an inverse relationship. The higher is the yield to maturity y, the lower is price. Figure 18.2 shows that relationship.

KEY POINT

The yield to maturity is a measure of the average rate of return a buyer will earn on a bond if the buyer holds it to maturity.

If you buy a bond at a low price, then given that the issuer will make regular payments each year of $C and the bond also will generate a final payout of $F when it matures in n periods' time, the bond will generate a high return over its entire life. The higher the price you have to pay for the bond today, the less, *on average*, you will earn on it, year by year, over its life. The key point is that the amount of money you get back from holding the bond is fixed in advance. This is why bonds are sometimes described as **fixed income securities**.[2] By paying more now to get the right to those fixed future amounts, you are getting a worse deal, i.e., a lower yield.

Let's take a concrete example of bond pricing: a bond with a face value of $100, a maturity of four years, and a coupon rate of 8%. The issuer promises to pay $8 (the coupon rate times the face value) each year and to make a final (or redemption) payment of the full face value ($100). Suppose the next coupon payment is due a year from now, and the final coupon payment is made at the time of redemption exactly four years from now. Finally, suppose that the required yield on the bond is 6%. This means that the rate of return needed over a four-year horizon, expressed as an annual rate, is 6%.

The value of the bond will be the sum of the present values of each of the cash flows using a 6% discount rate to calculate those present values.

The first coupon is worth today: $8/(1.06)
The subsequent coupons are worth: $8/(1.06)^2$; $8/(1.06)^3$; $8/(1.06)^4$
The final repayment of the face value is worth today: $100/(1.06)^4$

[2] Not all bonds pay amounts fixed in advance. For example, inflation-protected bonds (sometimes called index-linked bonds) pay coupons and have a final redemption payment that depends on what happens to inflation between the time the bond is bought and its maturity. Such bonds have guaranteed real repayments but uncertain nominal repayments. Other bonds have cash flows that vary in line with movements in interest rates (floating rate bonds).

Evaluating each of these terms and summing them give us the bond price today:

$$P = \$7.55 + \$7.12 + \$6.72 + \$6.34 + \$79.21 = \$106.94$$

Note here that because the yield on the bond (6%) is less than the coupon rate (8%), the price exceeds the face value. If you paid the face value of $100 (this is sometimes called the **par value**), you would be earning 8% a year because that is what the coupon rate is. But the required return is only 6%. So you are willing to pay more than $100 to buy the bond. The price will be driven up from a face value of $100 to $106.94 to generate a return of 6%. If the yield (or required return) were to coincide with the coupon rate, the annual coupons would generate a return equal to the yield as long as the price stayed at $100. If the yield were in excess of the coupon, the price would be below the face value. When governments and companies issue bonds, they typically set the coupon rate at close to what they expect the yield on the bond to be, so that bond prices are usually around face values near to the issue date; such bonds are said to be trading at par.

Figure 18.2 reveals an important fact about bonds: not only is the relation between price and yield *inverse*, it is also nonlinear. An increase in yields of a given amount has a smaller negative impact on price at high yields than at low yields. We will see below that a given shift in yields also has different impacts on the prices of bonds of different maturities.

So far we have just defined what we mean by the yield on the bond—it is simply the average return you will earn from holding the bond *until the time at which the debt is finally repaid*. This is why we sometimes call yields "yields to maturity" or "redemption yields." We do not really know yet what will determine those yields and tie down bond prices. This is a crucial and difficult question, but expectations of future short-term interest rates, which central banks largely control, should be a key part of the story. To see the link more clearly, suppose you wanted to invest some money for 10 years. You could buy a 10-year bond. For simplicity, let's assume that this bond will make no payments until the end of the 10 years when the issuer—a government or a company—will send you a check for $100 for every bond that you own. (In other words, the coupon rate is zero; such bonds are called zero-coupon bonds or sometimes "zeros.") Buying and holding such a bond would clearly be one way to invest money for 10 years. You could also put the money in a bank savings account in which interest was reset every month in line with money market interest rates. Those money market interest rates will be closely linked to the rates of interest that the central bank will fix (see Chapter 15).

As shown in Figure 18.3, we now have two options:

1. to buy now, at its current market price, a government bond that has 10 years still to run until maturity; or
2. to put your money in a bank and leave it there for 10 years, accruing interest each month at a rate that will be reset at the beginning of each month in line with whatever short-term interest rates then rule.

Suppose that we do not care too much about the uncertainty of future short-term interest rates. Then in order to be indifferent between these two investment strategies, the yield on the 10-year government bond, a number that we know for sure today, should be nearly the same as to the average interest rate we think we are going to earn

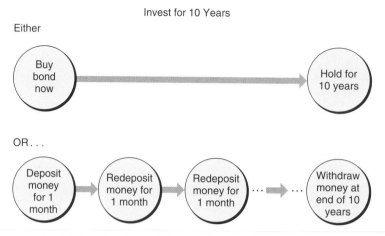

FIGURE 18.3 Alternative strategies for an investor with a ten-year horizon.

on those bank deposits if we hold them for a decade. If that was not true, then one or the other of the two strategies would clearly be dominant, and if enough people agreed that one of these strategies was better than the other, there would be either massive movements of funds out of bank deposits and into bonds or huge selling of government bonds and a massive inflow of funds into banks. Such large movements would generate price changes that would eventually make the two investments similar again. Suppose that 10-year bond yields were substantially higher—given current bond prices—than people's expectations of what the average interest rate would be on bank deposits over the next 10 years. People would have an incentive to buy bonds and write checks on their banks to pay for them. The massive increase in demand for bonds would boost their price which, as saw in the equation above, would reduce their yields. Meanwhile the big outflows of money from banks would encourage banks to increase their deposit rates. This process would continue until the 10-year bond yield was close to the average expected interest rate on bank deposits over the next 10 years.

Let's take a concrete example. Suppose the U.S. Federal Reserve funds rate was 3%, and the rate on Treasury bills with one month to maturity was at the same level—reflecting an expectation that over a one-month horizon, at least, the Federal Reserve was likely to hold rates steady. Now 3% is an unusually low rate for the United States, and if the Federal Reserve had engineered short rates down to that level, investors would not expect them to keep them there for long. Let's assume that investors thought that rates on one-month Treasury bills would have moved up to 4% by 12 months ahead because the Federal Reserve was set to increase rates. Suppose further that the Federal Reserve was expected to raise rates gradually to 5% by two years ahead and to 6% by three years ahead. After that, the consensus view was that the Federal Reserve would leave rates at 6%. Figure 18.4 shows the path along which the one-month Treasury bill rate is expected to evolve. Now consider what the yield on a bond with one year to maturity should be. If one-month Treasury bill rates are now 3% and are expected to gradually move up to 4% by a year from now, then the average of one-month rates over the next 12 months is 3.5%. This is approximately where the yield on one-

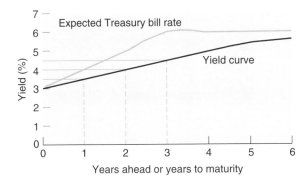

FIGURE 18.4 **Expected Treasury bill rate against yield curve.** The anticipation of rising short-term interest rates generates an upward sloping yield curve.

year bonds should be. If you kept investing in one-month Treasury bills and as each bill matured you bought another, the average interest rate you would earn, over the year, is 3.5%. The one-year bond yield is, by definition, the return you get from holding a one-year bond to maturity, so this should be close to the 3.5% you expect to earn from buying a series of one-month bills.

What about two-year bonds? The average Treasury bill rate over the first year is expected to be 3.5%, and the average over the second year is expected to be 4.5% [(4 + 5)/2)]. The simple average of short rates over the whole two years is expected to be 4%, which is about where two-year bond yields should be. A similar argument shows that the average of one month rates over the next three years is expected to be 4.5%. As we consider bonds with longer and longer maturities, the average of expected one-month Treasury bill rates over the time to their redemption gets closer and closer to 6% (though it always remains below 6%). The yield curve, which shows the relation between yields to maturity and time to maturity, would be upward sloping toward 6%, as Figure 18.4 shows.

KEY POINT

The yield curve shows the average return that is expected to be earned holding bonds of different maturities.

Now consider what would happen if the chairperson of the Federal Reserve announced that in the view of the Federal Reserve inflationary pressures in the U.S. economy were likely to remain low over the foreseeable future and that there was no reason to expect that the Federal Reserve would significantly increase interest rates. Assuming that the chairperson had at least some credibility, expectations of future short-term interest rates would come down. If the chairperson had complete credibility, expected future one-month rates would fall to 3%, the current Federal Reserve rate. As long as future expected short rates fall, so do longer-dated bond yields; in the extreme case of complete credibility, all bond yields would fall immediately to 3%.

So one would expect that bond yields will be sensitive to expectations of where short-term interest rates will be moving in the future. Bond yields thus tend to move around a good deal over time. Figure 18.5 shows the yield on long-dated U.S. government bonds

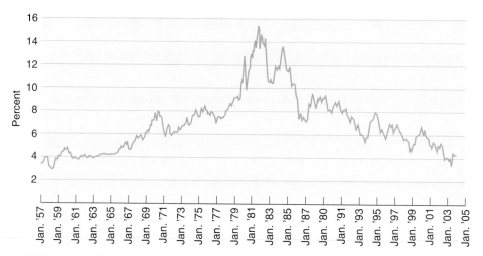

FIGURE 18.5   **U.S. long-term bond yield.** Yields rose sharply in the 1970s as inflation in the United States increased to high levels. *Source:* Thomson Financial Datastream.

between 1957 and the end of 2003. Over that period, yields have varied dramatically. In the mid-1970s and early 1980s, when inflation and short-term interest rates were high, bond yields were frequently in double figures. By the mid 1990s, government bond yields had moved down substantially. Yields were almost 9% in January 1990; they fell to 7% by early 1993 and to under 6% by early 1998. By early 2003, yields were down to about 4%. In Europe, yields in the 1990s declined even more. Italian government bond yields moved down sharply as expectations rose that Italy would be among the first countries to join a monetary union and that its short-term interest rates would move down to the much lower German levels.

Note that for a given change in yields, the movement in price tends to be greater for longer-dated bonds. We can illustrate this with zero-coupon (or *pure discount*) bonds. Suppose initially that the yield curve is flat at 5%. Column 1 in Table 18.2 shows the prices of bonds of various maturities, all with face values of $100. Column 2 shows how prices would move if yields rose by 10 basis points (ten basis points equals one-

TABLE 18.2   **The Relation between Prices and Yields**

	Price at 5% Yield	Price at 5.1% Yield	Percent Change in Price
1-year bond	95.24	95.15	−0.1
2-year bond	90.70	90.53	−0.19
5-year bond	78.35	77.98	−0.48
10-year bond	61.39	60.81	−0.96
15-year bond	48.10	47.42	−1.44
20-year bond	37.69	36.98	−1.92
30-year bond	23.14	22.49	−2.90

tenth of one full percentage point), to 5.1%. Column 3 shows the percentage change in the price. Note that the percentage impact on price is greater the longer the maturity of the bonds. In fact, the percent change is roughly proportional to maturity. This is a special feature of zero-coupon bonds. More generally, how a yield change affects the price depends on both coupon and maturity. To be more specific, the relation between price change and yield change depends on the **duration** of a bond, which is a measure of the average time that your money is tied up in a bond if you hold it to maturity. For coupon-paying bonds, duration is less than maturity because you get cash back before the redemption date. For zero-coupon bonds, duration and maturity coincide, which is why the link between the percentage price changes in Table 18.2 and the maturity of the bonds is so close.

KEY POINT

Prices and yields are inversely related and prices are more sensitive to yield the longer you lend your money to the issuer of the bond.

18.3   The Bond Market in February 2004

The concept of the yield curve that we introduced in the last section is straightforward—it is the relation at a point in time between the yields to maturity on bonds and time to maturity. But in practice, no *single* yield curve exists because a huge number of companies and governments issue bonds. Bonds differ by type of issuer (government and corporations), by currency of issue, and by maturity. The market is global—bonds are issued in all major currencies (and many minor ones); corporations from all developed countries and governments from both developed and less developed countries issue them. Well-established, large corporations that are household names around the world issue them, but so do largely unknown start-up companies that may not survive for five years.

Prices of bonds with the same coupon rate and maturity can differ if they are issued in different currencies because people expect currencies to shift in value. Bonds denominated in the same currency can have different prices (or yields) because people do not consider all promises to pay coupons and make final redemption equally good. Both governments and corporations can default on the promises implicit in those IOUs. People who held bonds issued by the Tsarist regime that ruled in Russia until 1917 would testify to this. For developed countries at least, governments are usually considered better risks than corporations. This does not mean that the market thinks that governments are better run than companies! It reflects governments' ability to raise taxes to generate more revenue. Companies cannot do that, and if their debt is large relative to their assets, they may be unable to generate enough revenue in competitive product markets to pay bondholders. Because of the higher risk of default, corporate bonds generally need to offer a higher rate of return than government debt. In the major economies, the difference between the return promised on a company's bonds and the yield on government debt is a common measure of a company's credit-worthiness.

As we shall see, there are huge differences in credit-worthiness. Spreads over government bonds—that is, the amount by which corporate bond yields exceed those on government debt of similar maturity—can be as low as 10 basis points; with this tight a spread, if a government bond is paying a return of 9%, a corporate bond would need to offer an average return over the bond's life of 9.10%. Spreads can also be many thousands of basis points. In early 1999, Russian government bonds yielded 38%, while U.S. Treasuries yielded around 5%; this is a spread of 3300 basis points!

KEY POINT

For bonds of a given currency, the yield on domestic government bonds is generally the benchmark against which other issuers are compared.

Table 18.3 shows the yield to maturity in February 2004 on medium-dated bonds that various governments had issued in their domestic currency. These are 10-year bond

TABLE 18.3   **10-Year Benchmark Spreads, February 9, 2004**
Annualized yield basis.

	Bid Yield	Spread vs. Euros	Spread vs. T-Bonds
Australia	5.61	+1.47	+1.55
Austria	4.23	+0.09	+0.17
Belgium	4.27	+0.13	+0.21
Canada	4.44	+0.30	+0.38
Denmark	4.31	+0.17	+0.25
Finland	4.11	−0.03	+0.05
France	4.15	+0.01	+0.09
Germany	4.14	—	+0.08
Greece	4.35	+0.21	+0.29
Ireland	4.10	−0.04	+0.04
Italy	4.27	+0.13	+0.21
Japan	1.28	−2.86	−2.78
Netherlands	4.14	—	+0.08
New Zealand	5.95	+1.81	+1.89
Norway	4.34	+0.20	+0.28
Portugal	4.20	+0.06	+0.14
Spain	4.13	−0.01	+0.07
Sweden	4.57	+0.43	+0.51
Switzerland	2.61	−1.53	−1.45
U.K.	4.82	+0.68	+0.76
U.S.	4.06	−0.08	—

Source: Financial Times (February 10 2004).

TABLE 18.4   Emerging Market Bonds, December 15, 2003

	Redemption Date	S&P Rating	Price	Yield	Spread vs. U.S. Dollar
EUROPE (EUROS)					
Croatia	02/10	BBB−	98.63	4.88	+1.32
Slovenia	04/11	A+	106.73	4.28	+0.48
Hungary	01/13	A−	99.33	4.59	+0.43
LATIN AMERICA DOLLAR					
Argentina	02/07	D	25.40	80.36	+76.14
Brazil	01/11	B+	105.00	8.53	+4.64
Mexico	03/33	BBB−	102.08	7.46	+2.25
ASIA DOLLAR					
China	10/13	BBB	98.88	4.95	+0.65
Philippines	01/14	A−	98.25	8.69	+4.23
South Korea	05/13	A−	95.25	4.94	+0.71
AFRICA/MIDDLE EAST DOLLAR					
Lebanon	07/06	B−	109.32	6.68	+4.39
South Africa	04/08	BBB	109.78	4.45	+1.46
Turkey	01/14	B+	115.34	7.45	+3.04

Source: Thomson Financial Datastream.

S & P ratings reflect perceived credit quality.

S & P ratings range from AAA (highest quality) to D (bonds in default).

yields; that is, (roughly speaking) the average annual rate of return that could be earned from buying a 10-year IOU from the government and holding it until repayment in early 2014. The second column in the table shows how the yield of the bond (in the currency of the issuing government) differs from the yield on euro bonds that the German government issued. The third column shows the yield relative to the dollar yield on 10-year U.S. government bonds (which are known as Treasuries or T-bonds). Table 18.3 shows that yields on different government bonds vary a lot—even when we focus only on bonds issued by governments in developed and relatively stable (politically and economically) countries. Ten-year Swiss government bonds in February 2004 were yielding around 2.6%; Japanese government bonds were yielding about half this (1.28%); in contrast, U.S. Treasuries offered just over 4%, but in a different currency.

When we look at yields on bonds that emerging countries issue, the spread in rates of return becomes much more dramatic. Table 18.4 shows that Brazilian government bonds, denominated in U.S. dollars, were yielding over 8.5%—well over double the yield on U.S. Treasuries. Argentinian government bonds (again denominated in dollars) yielded about 80%—reflecting great uncertainty over whether the government would be able to repay the debt in full. Clearly, yield differences of this magnitude affect the incentives to borrow, the levels of expenditure that government and firms finance by issuing debt, and their willingness to default.

TABLE 18.5   U.S. Corporate Bonds, February 9, 2004

	Red Date	Coupon	S & P Rating	Moody's Rating	Price	Yield	Spread vs. Governments
UTILITIES							
Pac Bell	03/26	7.13	A+	A1	112.88	6.06	+1.15
American Elec	05/06	6.13	BBB	Baa3	107.80	2.55	+0.40
FINANCIALS							
Morgan Stanley	04/06	6.10	A+	Aa3	107.89	2.36	+0.61
JP Morgan	02/11	6.75	A	A2	114.14	4.37	+1.31
INDUSTRIALS							
Ford Motor Cr	02/06	6.88	BBB−	A3	106.51	3.43	+1.68
Unilever	11/10	7.88	A+	A1	117.56	4.11	+1.05

Source: Financial Times (February 10, 2004).

Table 18.5 shows details of bonds that large U.S. corporations issued in U.S. dollars. The spread of maturity dates in the first column is large; in February 2004, Pacific Bell had issued bonds that had over 20 years more to run until final repayment. The second-to-last column of the table shows the yields on the bonds at the close of business on February 9, and the final column shows the difference in yield from U.S. government bonds. The Pacific Bell bonds were offering yields close to 6%, around 1.2% above U.S. government bonds of long maturity.

18.4   Inflation and the Bond Market

By now, you should understand why people who hold conventional (fixed rate) bonds are hit hard when inflation rises unexpectedly. An inflationary environment erodes the real value of fixed income securities, and persistent and unanticipated inflation can inflict enormous damage to returns on bonds. The inflation rate in the 10 years from January 1970 to January 1980 was, in almost every developed country, higher than the 10-year bond yield at the start of the decade. Investors in government bonds who bought in the early 1970s invariably earned negative real returns. But the losses on bonds that the developed countries issued in the 1970s pale alongside the much greater losses on the debt of emerging countries that occurred in the 1980s and 1990s. Russia is a case in point. Yields on ruble bonds moved up sharply during the 1990s as inflation in Russia reached hundreds of percent a year. Faced with hyperinflation, the government pushed up ruble short-term interest rates sharply, generating massive increases in bond yields and causing huge falls in bond prices that all but wiped out the value of investments.

KEY POINT

The inverse relation between yields and prices makes inflation, which nearly always brings higher short-term interest rates, the enemy of the bond holder.

That inverse relation also explains what might otherwise appear puzzling. You often hear descriptions of activity in the bond market that sound something like this, "Yesterday was a good day for the U.S. bond market as yields on long-dated Treasuries fell 20 basis points on expectations of further Fed easing." Bonds are debt, and people that hold bonds own IOUs. So why are bondholders laughing when interest rates come down, which is normally thought to be bad for people who hold debt? The reason is that bonds, as we noted above, are typically *fixed income securities*. In other words, the amount of cash that you are going to get in the future from holding a bond does not change when interest rates and yields move, *but the present value of that cash does*. In other words, bond prices rise leading to capital gains for bondholders.

All this is in marked contrast to the situation in which holders of bank debt (or bank deposits) find themselves. Depositors with banks are, other things equal, better off when central banks push up interest rates because most bank deposits are earning interest at rates that typically move closely in line with shifts in central bank rates. Note the contrast here with conventional bonds, which are fixed income securities, and where the coupon payments are usually fixed in nominal terms in advance. The fixity of the nominal repayment schedule on bonds means that bond prices have to move when required rates of return shift. With bank deposits, the interest stream (analogous to coupons on bonds) is generally not fixed, and as the general level of interest rates moves, the stream of interest income that the deposit generates also moves, so that the value of the underlying deposit does not change. The absence of sharp changes in capital values distinguishes bonds from bank deposits and makes the return on fixed income assets more volatile. It also means that the link between changes in monetary policy, both actual and anticipated, and the price of bonds is important. We discuss this link next.

18.5 Government Policy and the Yield Curve

We argued above that yields on long-dated bonds are likely to reflect expectations of future short-term interest rates. This is the essence of the so-called expectations theory of the yield curve. In this section we discuss in more detail the link between what governments and central banks do, particularly in setting short-term interest rates through monetary policy decisions, and the longer-term interest rates that are likely to be important for private sector saving and investment decisions.

Figure 18.6 shows the yield curve on U.S. government bonds in early February 2004. (Note that we always have to give a particular date to the yield curve; hence it only makes sense to talk about "the U.S. government bond yield curve" on a specific day.) The figure shows that U.S. government bonds that only had a year or so still left to run were yielding about 1.0%. Bonds with about five years still to run were yielding about 3%, and bonds that had 20 or 30 years still to run were yielding just under 5.0%. Yield curves can slope up sharply, slope down sharply, or be flat. Again, the main factor is expectations about future short-term interest rates. At this time, it was widely believed that the U.S. Federal Reserve would need to increase interest rates—the Federal Reserve funds rate was close to 1% but was expected to rise over the course of the next few years.

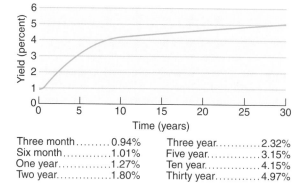

FIGURE 18.6 **U.S. yield curve.**
With short-term interest rates in early 2004 at unusually low levels, there was a widespread perception that the next movements in short rates would be up. *Source:* Thomson Financial Datastream.

Three month	0.94%	Three year	2.32%
Six month	1.01%	Five year	3.15%
One year	1.27%	Ten year	4.15%
Two year	1.80%	Thirty year	4.97%

Suppose, for example, that short-term (say three-month) interest rates were currently high but were expected to fall gradually over the next 5 to 10 years. (This happened for many European countries before the monetary union at the start of 1999.) If you expect short-term interest rates to decline gradually, then the average of the interest rates over the next year will be greater than the average of the interest rates over the next three years, which, in turn, will be greater than the average of short-term interest rates over the next five years. Because the yield on one-year bonds should be linked to average short-term interest rates over a year, and the yield on five-year bonds should be linked to the average of short-term interest rate over five years, one would expect that five-year bond yields would be substantially lower than one year bond yields. In other words, the yield curve would be sloping downwards. Clearly, if you expected short-term interest rates to rise over the next five years, then five-year bonds would tend to have much higher yields than one-year bonds. In that case, the yield curve would slope up.

Is this expectations theory consistent with the evidence? If it is, and assuming that expectations of future short-term interest rates and inflation are rational, the shape of the yield curve should help predict changes in inflation and short-term interest rates. The evidence supports this view. Figure 18.7 estimates what you would have predicted the change in interest rates to be, given the yield curve (forward spread), and what subsequently happened to (one-year) interest rates over the next year (spot change). There is some correlation between these lines for the four countries. But clearly one would only have predicted the general shape of changes, and even then only been right on average, rather than have an accurate measure of the future course of short-term interest rates. The predictive ability of the forward spread is modest.

The yield curve appears to be slightly more informative in predicting inflation than in predicting interest rates. When two-year bond yields exceed (fall short of) one-year yields, evidence shows that inflation is higher (lower) two years ahead than one year ahead. Figure 18.8 shows the actual change in inflation against the predicted change, based on the slope of the yield curve (as measured by the term spread between two-year and one-year bonds). Clearly the two are significantly correlated.

The close correlation means that the slope of the yield curve tends to change over the business cycle. When an economy emerges from a recession, short-term nominal in-

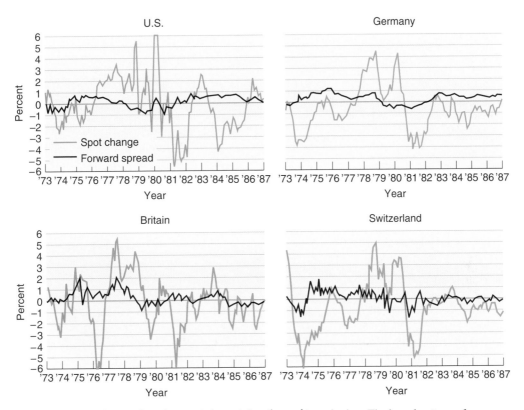

FIGURE 18.7   **Some evidence in support of expectations theory of term structure.** The broad pattern of movements in short-term interest rates is explained moderately well by looking at the slope of the yield curve. *Source:* Jourion and Mishkin, "A Multicountry Comparison of Term Structure Forecasts at Long Horizons," *Journal of Financial Economics* (1991) vol. 29, no. 1, pp. 59–80. Reprinted with permission from Elsevier Science.

terest rates are generally low; but central banks should be expected to increase rates gradually as growth picks up and the economy moves back to full capacity. With low current interest rates and the expectation of higher rates to come, the yield curve will tend to slope upwards. During a boom, in contrast, the central bank may have raised short-term interest rates to levels substantially above the long-term average. If tightening monetary policy is effective, the market will anticipate slower growth and falling inflation, which would allow the central bank to reduce interest rates in the future. In this environment, longer-dated bonds will tend to have yields *below* short-term interest rates, and the yield curve will slope down. Inversions of the yield curve—that is, downward-sloping curves—are common, though over the long run, yields on long-maturity bonds tend to be higher than yields on short-dated bonds and Treasury bills.

Because yields on bonds reflect expectations about future monetary policy, they give us useful information about the future of the economy. This information has at least three elements.

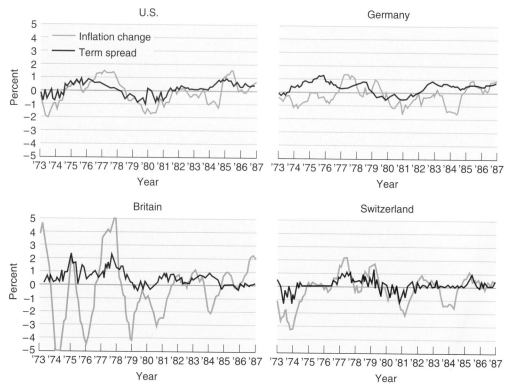

FIGURE 18.8 **Yield spread useful in predicting inflation.** The shape of the yield curve also gives some information about changes in future inflation—when the yield curve slopes up more than usual inflation tends to be on the increase. *Source:* Jourion and Mishkin, *Journal of Financial Economics* (1991) vol. 29, pp. 59–80. Reprinted with permission from Elsevier Science.

- First, we might focus on the *absolute levels* of government bond yields of different maturities. This tells us something about the level of short-term interest rates that we can expect in the future, and those levels are likely to reflect demand pressures in the economy, the strength of output growth, and inflation pressures. So, for example, if 10-year bond yields are at 15%, this is likely to reflect a strong belief that inflation is going to be so consistently high that the central bank will need to set short-term nominal rates at double digit levels.

- Second, as noted above, the *slope* of the yield curve is likely to reveal something about how monetary policy will be *changing*, and that, in turn, should reflect whether the economy is slowing down or accelerating.

- Third, we can learn something about shifts in perceptions of bankruptcy risk from movements in the average *spreads* between government and corporate bonds. After the major sell-off in emerging market bonds (particularly in Russian government bonds) in mid-1998, spreads between corporate and government bond yields in the United States widened as fears about default risks for highly indebted companies increased.

Evidence shows that bond prices, specifically the shape of the yield curve, do provide useful information for predicting movements in output. For example, economists have found that when the yield curve has a shallow slope (or slopes down), recession is more likely. Under the expectations theory, a downward-sloping yield curve suggests that short-term interest rates are falling, which is likely if the economy goes into a recession.

KEY POINT

The sensitivity of bond prices to expectations of what the central bank will do in the future gives monetary policy real teeth. Even in countries in which individuals and companies do not borrow money at short-term variable rates of interest, the central bank can still significantly affect the cost of borrowing.

Remember, central banks only have *direct* influence over short-term interest rates. If individuals borrow at long-term fixed rates of interest (e.g., by taking out mortgages), or if companies issue long-dated bonds to finance investment, governments and central banks might not seem to have much influence on the relevant cost of borrowing. Not so! Long-dated bond yields depend on expectations of short-term interest rates into the future. So by influencing expectations about their *future* actions when setting short-term interest rates, central banks can *today* influence the cost of borrowing money for long periods ahead. They can also generate big swings in bond prices. The expectation that a central bank might have to increase short-term interest rates sharply in the future can cause bond prices to decline. Given the value of the total stock of debt outstanding (Table 18.1), big percentage changes in bond prices can significantly change the total wealth of the private sector, which, in turn, can cause major changes in consumption. In the United States the value of bonds in 2004 was about twice annual GDP. Therefore an important element in the transmission mechanism of monetary policy is the induced impact on bond yields and bond prices of central bank actions.

18.6 Deficits and Bond Prices

In all financial markets, prices reflect the interaction of demand and supply. In focusing on expectations of future interest rates as the key determinant of bond prices, we have implicitly assumed that these are the driving forces between movements in demand and supply curves, and that seems sensible. Why would a company issue 10-year bonds at a yield of 9% if it expected over the next decade to be able to borrow from a bank at an interest rate that varied around an average of 6%? And why should a pension fund buy five-year bonds with yields of 4% if three-month interest rates on large deposits are 6% and are not expected to fall? So both the supply and demand for bonds are sensitive to expectations of future interest rates. However, governments may have to issue large quantities of debt from time to time, even though yields may be temporarily high.

Governments have been issuing bonds for centuries. The U.K. government, for example, started issuing bonds just over 300 years ago to help finance a war. (Figure 18.9 shows what has happened to yields on long-dated U.K. government bonds over those three centuries.)

KEY POINT

Because most governments now have large stocks of debt outstanding, and because a good chunk of that debt matures in any one year, they are constantly rolling forward the debt by issuing new bonds.

We have mentioned wars already: Figure 18.10 shows the outstanding stock of U.K. government debt over a 300-year period. (The United Kingdom is one of the few countries that has an uninterrupted history of trading in a large stock of government bonds; other countries' financial markets collapsed often because of hyperinflation, revolution, invasion, or civil war—sometimes all four!) The stock of debt here is measured relative to GDP. The Napoleonic Wars of the early nineteenth century and the World Wars of the twentieth century increased the stock of U.K. government debt enormously.

To finance these expensive struggles, the U.K. government could not rely on tax revenues. It would not have been feasible to finance such massive increases in military expenditure by increasing tax revenues in a short period. Indeed, any temporary increase in government expenditure is probably best met by increasing government debt rather than increasing taxes only to reduce them again in a year or two. Sharp fluctuations in tax rates are likely to disrupt the economy more than sudden increases or decreases in the amount of new government debt that is to be sold. A sudden increase in the corporation tax rate that was expected to be followed by future reductions might give companies major incentives to push receipts of revenue into future periods. Big in-

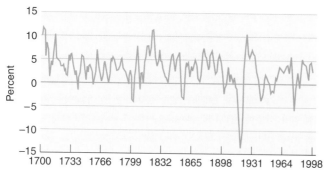

FIGURE 18.9   U.K. long-term real interest rate, 1700–1998 (yield on medium dated government bonds minus moving average of inflation). Real interest rates on U.K. government bonds have moved around a great deal—but much of the fluctuation has been due to unanticipated inflation rather then shifts in expected real returns on bonds. *Source:* Miles, "Interest Rates from the 17th to the 21st Century," Merrill Lynch Report (June 1998).

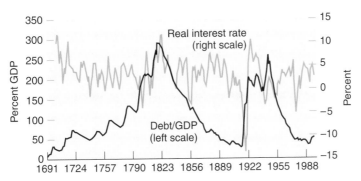

FIGURE 18.10   **Stock of U.K. government debt/GDP (1691–1998) and real interest rate (medium-dated bond yield minus five-year moving average of inflation).** In the U.K. over a 300-year period there has been little relation between movements in real interest rates and shifts in the stock of government debt. *Source:* Miles, "Interest Rates from the 17th to the 21st Century," Merrill Lynch Report (June 1998).

creases in income tax that people expect to be reversed would encourage them to work less today, and more in the future. These kinds of tax arbitrage cause costly revisions to plans. Therefore, governments should use bond issues as a safety valve to smooth out temporary differences between revenues and expenditures. But does issuing more bonds affect yields?

In most countries, the level of government borrowing in the bond market varies from year to year. Over the long-term, at least in Europe, the stock of government debt has increased. Government debt outstanding at the end of 2003 in Europe was substantially higher than it was 20 years earlier. Table 18.6 shows the sharp rise in outstanding government bonds. But the effect of this on yields is unclear. We have already discussed Ricardian equivalence—the argument that the private sector perceives government debt as simply deferred taxation. If people themselves (or their children or their children's children or . . .) have to repay government debt in the future by paying higher taxes, they will want to save more now to generate enough income for that future tax. This suggests that the demand for financial wealth from the private sector goes up exactly in line with increases in the supply of government bonds. After all, the value of the government bonds sold equals the present value of the future tax that governments will need to levy to buy those bonds back in the future.

If this consideration is relevant, we might not expect to see a strong relation between the stock of government debt outstanding and the price of that debt. In effect, both the supply and demand curves will shift by precisely the same amount in response to higher government deficits. Indeed, economists have had difficulty finding a significant and consistent relation between bond prices and the stock of government debt. Figure 18.10 shows the stock of U.K. government debt (relative to GDP) outstanding since the end of the seventeenth century and a simple measure of the *real* yield on that debt. That yield measure simply subtracts the 10-year moving average of actual inflation from the nominal bond yield. The figure shows no clear relation between these series, and formal statistical tests also show little link. What has happened in Japan over the past 10 years also suggests that there is no clear link between bond yields and

TABLE 18.6   **Stock of Government Debt Relative to Annual GDP (%)**

	1981	1991	2003
U.S.	42.5	69.2	62.5
Japan	56.1	68.2	166.8
Germany	34.9	41.4	63.1
France	21.9	37.5	61.3
Italy	59.7	100.6	106.6
Spain	24.6	49.9	63.3
U.K.	50.8	34.2	39.0

Source: World Economic Outlook, OECD (2003).

deficits. Table 18.6 shows that there has been a huge rise in the stock of government debt in Japan since the early 1990s. But Japanese government bond yields in 2004 were the lowest in the world.

But government debt issuance involves more than simply deciding how many bonds to issue. Governments have at least three dimensions of choice even after deciding what the overall level of bond issuance will be. Government bonds differ by (1) maturity, (2) by currency, and (3) whether payments are fixed in nominal terms (conventional bonds) or real terms (index-linked bonds). Historically, governments have issued by far the largest part of their stock of debt in nominal bonds in the domestic currency. This is surprising. You would expect that savers would find index-linked debt attractive, especially since 1945 when inflation has been higher, more variable, and more persistent than before. And governments can offer indexed debt because the source of revenue from which future payments on bonds will be made—that is, tax revenue—tends to naturally move in line with the level of prices. So on risk grounds, both governments and investors might be better off if most government bonds were inflation-proof. Yet most government debt is nominal (or fixed rate) bonds issued in domestic currency. Short-dated government debt—Treasury bills—makes up a significant part of the stock of debt in only a few countries; governments have usually preferred to issue longer-term paper. Indexed bonds remain relatively unimportant.

18.7   Bond Yields and Equity Yields

We have focused on the level of bond yields and how they vary both by maturity and over time. Now we consider how bond yields compare with returns on equity. This comparison is important because it may affect how companies finance their investment and how households structure their portfolios. One might expect that over the long term, bonds tend to generate lower returns than equities. Equities represent a claim on the *residual* profits of companies after interest and capital repayments on debt have been made. The money that equity holders put into a firm helps prevent bad outcomes from eroding the value of bonds. This tends to make the flow of returns to shareholders more volatile than the flow of returns to bondholders. Empirical evidence backs up this simple point. Government bond yields over the long term have typically been well beneath the rates of return that equities have generated. Of course, government bonds tend to be the least risky type of bonds, so it is interesting to compare corporate bond yields with equity returns. In the United States, most large companies can borrow at yields that are somewhere between 0.05% and 3% above yields on government debt. If we added 2% to the average return on U.S. government bonds over the last 100 years we would have a very crude estimate of the type of return we could have gotten on a portfolio of corporate bonds issued by large companies. In the United States, over the last 100 years, equities have yielded about 6% more a year than government bonds; so the excess return on corporate equity over corporate bonds might be about 2% lower, leaving a still hefty 4% risk premium on equity.

If we look at even longer horizons, the yield differences are no less dramatic. We saw in Chapter 17 that Jeremy Siegel estimates that $1 invested in U.S. equities in 1802 would have been worth about $7.8 million by 2003 (if dividends were re-invested). One dollar put into bonds in 1802 would have been worth a paltry $18,000 in comparison. Over that period, equities generated an average annual real return of about 7%, while bonds generated a return of about 3.5%. How much of this yield difference is due to a rational reaction by investors to differences in risk and how much to misperceptions of inflation is moot. The whole of the yield gap probably does not reflect risk premiums; remember, these bonds were not inflation proof, so their real return would have been diminished if inflation turned out higher than people had expected when they bought bonds. For much of the period since 1945 in the United States, inflation has been significantly higher than it was between 1845 and 1945, so on average, inflation has probably exceeded expectations.

Table 18.7 shows how the recent value of the U.S. equity premium over bonds squares up against the type of excess returns earned in other countries.

TABLE 18.7 **Arithmetic Average Real Returns on Equities and Bonds, 1900–2000.**

	Equity Return 1900–2000 (1)	Bond Return 1900–2000 (2)	(1) − (2)
Germany	8.8	0.3	8.5
Italy	6.8	−0.8	7.6
Japan	9.3	1.3	8.0
France	6.3	0.1	6.2
U.S.	8.7	2.1	6.6
U.K.	7.6	2.3	5.3

Source: Dimson, Marsh, and Staunton, *Triumph of the Optimists* (Princeton NJ: Princeton University Press, 2002).

Differences in actual excess returns of equities over bonds across countries is not surprising. First, unexpected inflation has probably been different across countries since the 1940s. Second, companies and governments typically have different levels of debt in different countries. The higher the level of debt a company has, the more it is unlikely to be able to repay all its debt in a downturn—it will default. The greater the default risk, the lower will be the price of bonds, and the higher will be their yield. So in countries in which corporate debt is high and in which corporate revenues vary greatly from year to year, we would expect corporate bonds to yield more, and perhaps the gap between corporate debt and the return on equity to be lower.

Another factor could explain differences in return across countries: global bond markets (and equity markets for that matter) may not be well integrated. We hear a lot of talk about globalization, which implies that financial markets are almost fully integrated everywhere. In fact, the portfolios of investors in most countries tend to be dramatically nondiversified (geographically). We would not therefore expect rates of return to be equalized across countries.

Exchange rate variability might help explain the lack of integration. A U.S. investor will generally be concerned with returns in U.S. dollars, so buying a German government bond exposes that investor to variability in the euro–dollar exchange rate. If exchange rate variability does partly explain the lack of integration in financial markets, we would expect asset prices and rates of return to move more closely together when that variability is removed. This happened to government bond yields in Europe in the run up to the creation of monetary union at the start of 1999. Figure 18.11 shows yields to maturity on 10-year bonds issued by the major European countries. The yields are shown from 1991 up to August 2003. Yields on 10-year government bonds were es-

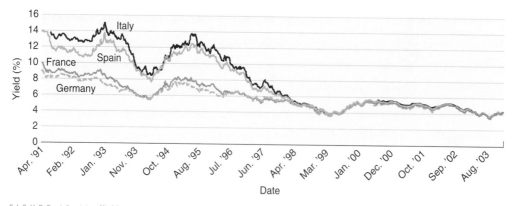

FIGURE 18.11   **Yield to maturity on ten-year government bonds in France, Germany, Italy, and Spain, 1991–2003.** In the lead up to the launch of the European Monetary Union, yields on government bonds issued by countries thought likely to be initial members converged. *Source:* Thomson Financial Datastream.

sentially equal from early 1999 when the Euro came into existence. As it became clearer that many countries would join the monetary union from the outset, the yields on European government bonds that matured well after the creation of the currency union moved closely together. This fits in neatly with our observation that the yields on longer-term debt should be highly sensitive to expectations of future interest rates. All countries in the European Monetary Union face the same set of central bank interest rates. There is only one European central bank and it determines a single set of interest rates in the wholesale money markets. Bonds that European governments issued prior to monetary union were redenominated into euros from January 1999. Once the European Monetary Union was formed, the only difference among a French government bond, a German government bond, and an Italian government bond was due to differences in probabilities of default of those governments and a residual possibility that the monetary union would fracture and that the lire, the deutsch mark, and the French franc would again become three separate currencies. Figure 18.11 implies that by the middle of 1998 people thought monetary union was a certainty *and* that it would prove sustainable.

18.8   Corporate Bonds and Leverage

We noted above that the link between the stock of government debt outstanding (relative to GDP) and the yield on government bonds did not appear to be strong. At the corporate level, we would, however, expect to find a substantial relation between bond prices and outstanding debt (or **leverage**). This is not because any one company can dramatically affect the overall stock of debt outstanding in the world—no company is that big (although governments certainly are—the Japanese and U.S. government stock of debt is huge relative to the overall world stock). Instead, a company's decision to issue more debt will affect the price of its existing bonds to the extent that it influences the perceived probability that it may default.

There are, in fact, dramatic differences in the market's view of default risks. So-called credit spreads—differences in the yields on bonds that share a common currency and maturity but are issued by different entities—can be enormous. Table 18.8 lists the details of bonds that both corporate and sovereigns (i.e., governments) had newly issued in international bond markets in February 2004. In addition to illustrating how international the bond market is, Table 18.8 shows that different issues of bonds face different costs of borrowing.

The tables in this chapter illustrate how the bond market offers investors many choices—about the maturity of bonds, about the currency of the bonds, and about the creditworthiness of the borrower. In part, borrowers can control their creditworthiness. The more debt a company has, the lower, other things being equal, its credit rating will be, and the higher the yield on its bonds will be. A large issue of debt could cause an issuer's perceived credit rating to slide and its bond prices to fall.

Of course, we would not expect a switch from one *form* of debt to another to have this impact. So, for example, if a company issued bonds to repay bank debt, we would not expect this to substantially affect the default premium on its bonds. Indeed, assuming that the corporation did this to reduce its overall cost of borrowing, we might expect

TABLE 18.8   New International Bond Issues, February 2004

U.S. DOLLARS	Amount	Maturity Years	Coupon (%)	Yield (%)	Launch spread over government bonds (basis points)
Citigroup Inc	$1.00bn	5	3.625	3.678	+53
EIB	$1.00bn	2	2.000	2.086	+30
Freddie Mac	$5.00bn	2	1.875	1.997	+22.5
Wachovia Corp	$1.25bn	5	3.625	3.675	+58
Federal Farm Credit Banks	$1.00bn	2	2.125	2.206	+46
EUROS Laender No 17(b)	E1.50bn	5	3.500	3.528	+13.5
Landesbank Berlin	E1.25bn	7	4.125	4.175	+26.4
KFW	E5.00bn	5	3.500	3.531	+21
STERLING EIB	£100.0m	1	6.125	4.561	+12
RMPA Services Plc	£579.9m	34	5.337	5.374	+59

Source: Financial Times (February 7, 2004).

its perceived chances of default to be reduced. So there is a big difference between companies switching from one form of debt to another and increasing their overall indebtedness.

Switching from bank to bond debt has been increasingly important in the United States for several decades and could become more important in Europe. Until recently, corporations in Europe have not relied much on issuing bonds to finance investment. Nonfinancial companies have relied almost exclusively on the banking system to fund debt. But times change, and monetary union in Europe brought with it a deeper, more liquid, and more integrated market in corporate bonds.

Let's suppose that companies increasingly use corporate bonds instead of bank debt and perhaps also equity. Would that have wider economic significance, beyond its influence on the relative job prospects of bank managers and bond traders? The theory of corporate finance as it has developed over the past 40 years says that if markets work in an efficient and frictionless way, and the tax system does not distort investing and borrowing decisions, whether firms finance investment from issuing bonds, borrowing from banks, or selling equities should not matter. The celebrated **Modigilani-Miller theorem** states that the structure of corporate financial liabilities does not matter; firms cannot be better off (nor can they do any harm) by switching from one form of debt to another or from changing the ratio of debt to equity. This is not the place to prove that result, but the intuition is clear: if a firm switches its debt to equity ratio or alters the type of debt it issues, it will be allocating its future revenue stream to different kinds of investors and in different ways. But unless it simultaneously changes its capital stock of productive machines and buildings, or changes how much research and development it does, or alters its pricing or employment, the value of those future company revenues will not change. As long as the revenues do not change, the fundamental factor behind the overall value of the company has not altered. So neither should the way the market values the whole firm.

This is a powerful and intuitive result. But it relies on smooth and efficient markets in which all the players involved—investors and those that run companies—know and understand what each other is doing. And, of course, that is unrealistic. The people who run companies sometimes have incentives to conceal things from shareholders, banks, and bondholders. They may want debtors to believe that the firm is acting one way while the firm is actually doing something different to benefit shareholders. Both shareholders and bondholders can often legitimately fear what is being done with their money. In those cases, the differences among equities, bonds, and bank debt matter a lot. With equity funds the company—once it has issued shares—has no obligation to give the money back; shareholders can try to sell their shares to other investors, but they cannot ask the company for their own money back—companies do not have to buy back their own shares. By contrast, the bondholder lends funds for a finite period. This may keep those who run companies "honest" because they know that even if they do not need *net* new funds they will have to keep returning to the bond market to sell more bonds as old debt matures.

With bank debt, a company owes the money it raises to one institution that will have its own techniques for assessing risk and monitoring the performance of the company. Bond markets do their monitoring in different ways, often relying on the influence of bond rating agencies, such as Moody's and Standard and Poor's, whose judgments profoundly and immediately affect the yield that companies have to pay on bonds.

SUMMARY

In Section 18.1, we saw that bond markets are where borrowers (governments and companies) meet savers (ultimately households). The prices that match supply and demand in this market reflect the required rates of return for lending money in different currencies, for different time periods, and to borrowers of different credit quality. In Sections 18.2 and 18.3, we argued that these prices significantly affect the investment decisions of firms and the cost for government of running fiscal deficits. Sections 18.4 and 18.5 showed how shifts in prices reflect changing expectations about monetary policy and inflation. Those changes in price can generate big gains or losses to bondholders and the movements in wealth cause further shifts in spending and saving.

It is in the bond market that much of the impact of changes in monetary policy is transmitted to the wider economy. Bond prices are strongly influenced by the interest rate set by the central bank. Where short-term interest rates are, and how they are expected to move, are the key determinants of longer-term yields. Central banks only control very short-term interest rates. Spending and borrowing decisions by the private sector are likely to depend on longer-term rates that are only indirectly influenced by monetary policy. But the expectations theory of the yield curve suggests that this indirect influence is likely to be very strong.

CONCEPTUAL QUESTIONS

1. (Section 18.2) What do you expect to happen to short-term interest rates when the yield curve is unusually steep? Would you expect an inverted yield curve, where longer rates are below shorter rates, to be sustainable?

2. (18.2) Suppose yields on one-year bonds are at 6%, on two-year bonds are at 7%, and on three-year bonds are at 6.5%. What does this imply about future short-term interest rates if the expectations theory of the yield curve is valid?

3. (18.4) How would you expect a rise in inflation to affect the yields and prices of nominal, fixed-rate bonds? Distinguish between an anticipated and unanticipated shock to inflation and between one that was expected to persist and one that was temporary.

4. (18.4) Consider the kind of inflation shocks described in question 1 and analyze how they would affect yields for inflation-proof (indexed) bonds.

5. (18.6) "Ricardian equivalence implies that the supply and demand curves for government debt move by the same amount." What does this statement mean? Is it likely to be true?

6. (18.7) On risk grounds, should governments continue to issue fixed-rate, nominal debt when their sources of revenue are, largely, linked to inflation? Would they not be better off issuing inflation-proof debt?

7. (18.7) Suppose that two-year bonds the U.S. government issues yield 1% *less* than bonds the U.K. government issues but that yields on 10-year U.S. debt are 2% *more* than 10-year U.K. debt. What might this tell you about what direction people think the dollar–pound exchange rate is going?

ANALYTICAL QUESTIONS

1. (Section 18.1) Assume short-term interest rates are set in the way outlined in question 5. Investment expenditure is sensitive to yields on five-year bonds. For every 1% (100 basis points) rise in yields, investment expenditure falls by 0.5%. Consumption expenditure is also sensitive to yields. For every 1% rise in yields on five-year bonds, consumption falls by 0.25%. Government expenditure is unaffected by changes in yields. Initially investment spending and government spending are each 20% of GDP; consumption is 60% of GDP. There is no trade. Calculate the impact on aggregate spending if the central bank raises interest rates from 8% to 10%.

2. (18.2) Using a spreadsheet, calculate the price of the following bonds on the assumption that yields to maturity are 7% for all maturity dates:

   (a) a bond with exactly 10 years to maturity that pays no coupon and has a face value of $100

   (b) a bond that pays an annual coupon worth 5% of face value and will pay a coupon every year for 10 years and then be redeemed for $100

   (c) a bond that pays an annual coupon worth 7% of face value and will pay a coupon every year for 10 years and then be redeemed for $100

   (d) a bond that pays an annual coupon worth 9% of face value and will pay a coupon every year for 10 years and then be redeemed for $100

   What is the percentage change in the price of each bond if yields move up from 7% to 7.5%?

3. (18.2) Consider each of the bonds you priced in question 1. Calculate the percentage change in the price of each bond between the start of one year and the start of the following year. Assume yields to maturity remain at a constant level of 7% throughout. Now add the coupon yield (the ratio of coupon to price) to the percentage change in price. What do the one-year returns on each bond look like? (The one-year returns are the percentage change in price plus the coupon yield.)

4. (18.4) The central bank in a country has set the short-term interest rate at 6%. It is widely expected that the short-term rate will stay at this level for a year and then rise to 7% for a year before moving back to an equilibrium level of 6.5%, where it is expected to remain from two years ahead indefinitely. Assuming that the expectations theory is true, what would you expect the yield to be on government bonds of maturities from 1 year up to 10 years?

5. (18.4) Suppose it is believed that the U.S. dollar will steadily depreciate against the euro at a rate of 2% a year over the next three years. After that, people expect the dollar–euro rate to be steady. Ten-year U.S. government dollar bonds yield 8%. What would you expect the yield to be on 10-year euro government bonds? Assume risk neutral behavior.

6. (18.4) Suppose that short-term interest rates in an economy fluctuate as the central bank tries to keep inflation stable in the face of various types of shocks. People anticipate that short-term interest rates will fluctuate around 6%, but that deviations from that level will be persistent. Specifically, they expect the three-month interest rate will follow the process:

$$R_{3t} = R_{3t-1} + 0.2(6 - R_{3t-1})$$

Where R_{3t} is the three-month rate in quarter t and R_{3t-1} is the three-month rate one quarter earlier. If three-month rates are initially at 11%, calculate the expected path of three-month rates over the next 40 quarters. (Use a spreadsheet for this.) Calculate the yield on zero-coupon 10-year bonds assuming the pure expectations theory is correct. What happens if the three-month interest rate suddenly drops to 9%?

CHAPTER 19

Exchange Rate Determination I— the Real Exchange Rate

Overview

The nominal exchange rate is the rate at which the currencies of two countries can be exchanged, whereas the real exchange rate is the ratio of what a specified amount of money will buy in one country compared with what it can buy in another. This chapter focuses on explaining changes in the real exchange rate. We first consider the law of one price, which says that, in the absence of trade restrictions and transportation costs, the same commodity should have the same price wherever it is sold. We use the law of one price to derive Purchasing Power Parity (PPP), which says that identical bundles of goods should cost the same in different countries. This implies that the real exchange rate should be constant and equal to one and that changes in the nominal exchange rate are driven by inflation differences. Reviewing the empirical evidence suggests that only in the very long run does PPP hold and that the real exchange rate is more volatile than inflation alone would suggest. To explain this volatility, we focus on the current and capital accounts of a country. The current account reflects trade in the goods and services of a country, and the capital account reflects the trade in assets. Finally, we review the factors that influence the capital and current accounts and how those factors can explain some, but not all, of the volatility in the real exchange rate.

Key Concepts

Balance of Payments

Balassa-Samuelson Effect

Bilateral and Effective
  Exchange Rates

Capital Account

Current Account

International Investment
  Position (IIP)

Law of One Price

Nominal and Real Exchange Rates

Purchasing Power Parity (PPP)

19.1   Types of Exchange Rate

Exchange rates can be confusing. Pick up any financial paper, and you will see various exchange rates quoted. There are many countries, many different exchange rates, and also many terms—bilateral and effective exchange rates, and real and nominal rates. In this section, we clarify these terms.

BILATERAL AND EFFECTIVE EXCHANGE RATES

A **bilateral exchange rate** is the rate at which you can swap the money of one country for that of another. For instance, if one euro can be swapped for $1 U.S., then the exchange rate is 1:1. If the euro *appreciates*, then it rises in value—it becomes more expensive to buy euros if you are holding dollars. For instance, if it now takes $1.10 to buy a euro, then the euro has appreciated by 10%, whereas if it costs 90 U.S. cents, the euro has *devalued or depreciated* by 10%. The exchange rates of major currencies (U.S. dollar, euro, and U.K. sterling) are generally quoted in terms of units of foreign currency required to purchase $1, €1, or £1. For example, if 100 yen are required to buy one dollar, the dollar/yen exchange rate is 100.[1]

Bilateral exchange rates only measure the behavior of one currency against another. But what if the euro rises against the U.S. dollar and the pound but depreciates against the Canadian dollar and the Japanese yen? Has the euro appreciated or depreciated? To answer this question, we need a measure of how the currency has done on average against *all* countries, rather than just one. The **effective exchange rate** measures this average performance. When calculating the effective exchange rate, it is necessary to recognize that certain currencies are more important than others. For instance, in assessing the average performance of the euro, it is more important to know how the euro has done against the U.S. dollar than against the Thai baht because Europe trades far more with the U.S. than with Thailand. We can measure a currency's performance by calculating the effective exchange rate on a *trade weighted basis*. If a country's trade (the sum of imports and exports) with the United States is ten times more than with Thailand, the dollar will get a weight 10 times higher. As a result, if the euro appreciates against the dollar by 1% but depreciates by 1% against the Thai baht, while remaining unchanged against all other currencies, the effective exchange rate will rise. Figure 19.1*a, b* shows the trade weights used in calculating the effective euro and dollar exchange rate.

The effective exchange rate is expressed in an index form, so that in one particular year (usually the year that the trade weights refer to) it has a value of 100. Therefore, if the effective exchange rate appreciates on average by 10% from that date, the index will be 110, whereas if it depreciates by 10%, it will be 90.

KEY POINT

Bilateral exchange rates record the behavior of one currency against another. Effective exchange rates record the average behavior of a currency against a basket of other currencies where each currency is weighted by its importance in trade.

[1] There are exceptions to this generalization. As far as the U.S. dollar is concerned, the exceptions to this are sterling, the euro, the Australian dollar, and the New Zealand dollar, all of which are quoted the other way (e.g., euro/dollar at 0.9 means that 1 euro is worth 90 U.S. cents).

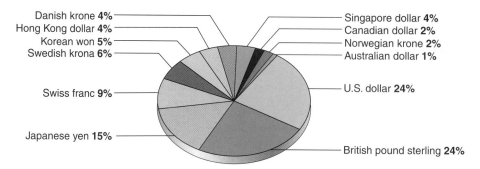

FIGURE 19.1a **Trade weights for euro effective exchange rate, January 2001.** *Source:* European Central Bank, http://www.ecb.int/stats/eer/eer.shtml

REAL VERSUS NOMINAL EXCHANGE RATES

Throughout this book we have distinguished between *real* and *nominal* variables—real variables reflect quantities or volume measures, while nominal variables reflect money values. The **nominal exchange rate** is the rate at which you can swap two different currencies—this is the exchange rate we have just been discussing. If, at an airport, you wish to swap Australian for Canadian dollars, you can do so at the nominal exchange rate. In contrast, the **real exchange rate** tells you how expensive commodities are in different countries and reflects the competitiveness of a country's exports.

Suppose, for example, a cup of coffee costs 200 yen in Japan and $1 in the United States, and the nominal exchange rate is ¥100 to $1. You can swap $1 for ¥100, but in Tokyo ¥100 only buys half a cup of coffee. The real exchange rate (for coffee) is therefore 0.5—you can only purchase half as much with your money in Japan as you can in the United States. A New Yorker returning from a vacation who says that Tokyo was expensive is essentially saying that the yen–U.S. dollar real exchange rate is low—goods in the United States are cheap by comparison.

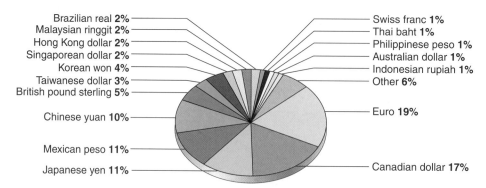

FIGURE 19.1b **Trade weights for U.S. dollar effective exchange rate, January 2004.** The U.S. effective exchange rate is more influenced by Asian currencies than the Euro for which sterling has a major impact. *Source:* Federal Reserve Board, http://www.federalreserve.gov/releases/h10/Weights/

However, the real exchange rate is not just about *one* commodity—it reflects all the goods you purchase in a foreign country. In other words, it is about the overall price level in a country and not just the cost of a cup of coffee. It can be expressed as:

real exchange rate = nominal exchange rate
$$\times \text{ domestic price level/overseas price level}$$

Consider a case in which what costs \$1 in the United States costs 3 pesos in Argentina and where the nominal exchange rate is 3 (3 pesos buys \$1). In this case we have:

$$\text{real exchange rate} = 3 \times \frac{\$1}{3 \text{ pesos}} = 1$$

The real exchange rate is 1—you can buy exactly the same amount for your money in either country. If, instead, everything that costs \$1 in the United States costs 5 pesos in Argentina, then we have:

$$\text{real exchange rate} = 3 \times \frac{\$1}{5 \text{ pesos}} = 0.6$$

so that in Argentina you can buy only 60% of what the same money (in dollars) buys you in the United States.

Historic data shows that fluctuations in the real exchange rate track movements in the nominal exchange rate quite closely. Explaining this similarity in behavior is a substantial challenge for economists. One argument says that real and nominal exchange rates behave similarly because the real exchange rate is just the nominal exchange rate multiplied by the ratio of domestic to overseas prices. Every minute of the day, the nominal exchange rate changes, often substantially. However, prices in a country change only slowly—as we showed in Chapter 15, prices are sticky. If prices hardly change, then movements in the nominal exchange rate will lead to fluctuations in the real exchange rate. An alternative view suggests that the key factors that determine the real exchange rate are volatile, causing volatility in the real exchange rate that leads to a volatile nominal exchange rate. We will evaluate the strength of these arguments over the next two chapters.

KEY POINT

The nominal exchange rate is the rate at which one currency can be swapped for another. The real exchange rate is a measure of competitiveness and records how much the same amount of money can buy in different countries. When the real exchange rate equals 1, goods cost the same in each country.

19.2 Law of One Price

In this section, we begin to build a model of real exchange rates by introducing the **law of one price**. This states that identical commodities should sell at the same price wherever they are sold—the same model of television set, for example, should cost the same whether it is sold in Madrid or Barcelona. The basis of the law of one price is *arbitrage*. If the television is cheaper in Barcelona, a firm can buy televisions in Barcelona, sell them in Madrid, and pocket the difference. This would increase the demand for television sets in Barcelona and their supply in Madrid. It would thus push up the price of televisions in Barcelona and lower them in Madrid, reducing the price discrepancy between the two cities. According to the law of one price, arbitrage will continue until the price of the television is exactly the same in each city—one price prevails.

The law of one price can also be applied across different economies. Once prices are expressed in a common currency, identical commodities should sell in different economies at the same price. Imagine that the television set retails in Barcelona for 150 euros, and let the U.S. dollar be worth 1 euro. Arbitrage should ensure that in America the television set costs $150 (150/1 = 150). In other words, the law of one price says:

dollar price of television in U.S. = dollar/euro exchange rate

× euro price of television in Barcelona

Does the law of one price hold? The answer is basically no—except for a few commodities, little evidence supports the law of one price. There are several real-life factors that prevent the ideal of one price:

- transportation costs
- the border effect
- pricing to market

TRANSPORTATION COSTS

The law of one price says that identical commodities should sell for identical prices. But if transport costs matter, then location is an important feature of a commodity. If transport costs are high and the distance between markets is great, the same commodity will sell for different prices in different locations. We can measure transport costs by comparing the prices of goods when they leave a country as exports to their cost when they arrive at their destination as imports. Exports f.o.b. (free on board) refers to the value of commodities when they are loaded on board a ship or plane. Imports c.i.f. (cost, insurance and freight) refers to the value of imports when they arrive, including the cost of insurance and freight. Figure 19.2 shows estimates of transport costs using this difference between f.o.b. and c.i.f. Costs vary from around 2% for tobacco and transport equipment to around 9% for oil and stone. Figure 19.2 focuses on a few aggregate industries covering all global trade. Figure 19.3 shows the distribution of transport costs for over 25,000 manufacturing industries to a single country, the United States.

For most industries, transport costs are under 10%. However, for a minority of industries, transport costs are over 25% of value. Figure 19.3 is also based on goods that are actually traded—there are many other goods with transport costs so high they are effectively nontradeable. With transport costs of this magnitude, identical commodities will sell for very different prices in different locations.

KEY POINT

The existence of transportation costs mean that location is a key characteristic of a commodity, and so goods will sell at different prices in different countries.

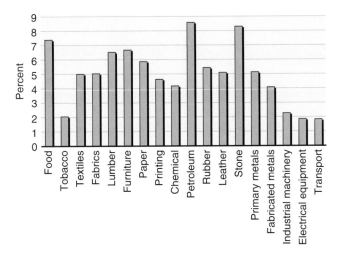

FIGURE 19.2 **Estimated transport costs for global trade.** The transport costs of tradeable commodities are significant. *Source:* Ravn and Mazzenga, "Frictions in International Trade and Relative Price Movements," London Business School Working Paper (1999).

THE BORDER EFFECT

Transportation costs matter both between and within countries. San Francisco is a long way from Boston so we can expect that the prices of televisions will be different in these cities just as they are between New York and Barcelona. However, close examination reveals that differences in prices for the same commodity between cities in the *same*

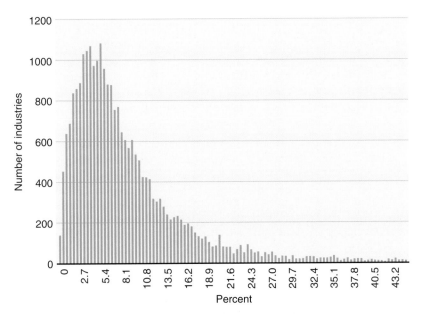

FIGURE 19.3 **Estimated transport costs for U.S. manufacturing imports.** Some industries have very large transport costs which partly explains why the law of one price does not hold. *Source:* Ravn and Mazzenga, "Frictions in International Trade and Relative Price Movements," London Business School Working Paper (1999).

country are tiny compared to the differences in price for the same commodity in *different* countries. The difference in prices for the same commodity increases not just with distance and transport costs but also when the commodity crosses a national border. This suggests that border effects are another reason why the law of one price fails to hold.

To see how important this border effect is, consider Figure 19.4, which shows the volatility, or dispersion, of prices across cities in the United States and Canada between 1978 and 1994. The higher the measure, the greater the discrepancy between prices in different cities. If prices were exactly the same in each city, volatility would be zero. Except for three categories, the discrepancies in prices between Canadian and U.S. cities are larger than those between U.S. cities or between Canadian cities. The data in Figure 19.4 show that crossing a national border substantially increases price differences—it is equivalent to adding an additional 1800 miles of transport costs over and above the actual distance between a U.S. and Canadian city.

Why does the border matter so much? One reason is tariffs (as defined in Chapter 8, tariffs are taxes on imports). Tariffs prevent arbitrage and are one reason why the law of one price fails to hold. There are other reasons too—technical requirements (U.S. and Spanish television sets work on different electrical voltages, cars in the United Kingdom need to be right hand-drive but are left-hand drive in the United States and continental Europe) or attempts by firms to obtain regional monopoly power (if a European buys a camera in the United States, for example, warranties are only valid in the United States). These factors reduce the role of arbitrage in establishing the law of one price.

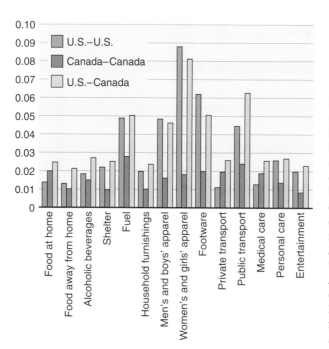

FIGURE 19.4 **Price differences between U.S. and Canadian cities.** Price differences between cities cannot be explained just by transport costs—differences in prices between U.S. and Canadian cities are greater than differences within countries regardless of distance apart. *Source:* Engel and Rogers, "How Wide Is the Border?" *American Economic Review* (1996) vol. 86, pp. 1112–1125. Reprinted with permission from American Economic Association.

KEY POINT

The border effect shows that transportation costs alone cannot explain why prices differ so much across regions. Goods sold in different countries or denominated in different currencies show large variations in prices unrelated to distance.

PRICING TO MARKET

Consider again the television set that costs 150 euros in Spain. When the exchange rate is 1 euro to 1 dollar, the law of one price says that the television should retail for $150 in the United States. If, instead, the exchange rate is 1.5 euros to the dollar, the U.S. price should be $100. But what happens when the currency changes, but the U.S. price is sticky and remains $150? At the new exchange rate of 1.5 euros to the dollar, the cost of the television in the United States translates into 225 euros—much more expensive than the price in Spain. The law of one price fails to hold, and the volatility in the exchange rate directly affects the volatility of relative prices across countries.

Table 19.1, which focuses on 65 European cities between 1981 and 1997, shows evidence for this relative price volatility. The first two rows indicate that relative prices between *different* countries (*international*) are far more volatile (by around 20 to 50 times) than relative prices *within* a country (*intranational*). The last row of the table shows why—the volatility in relative prices, or real exchange rates, between countries is almost exactly the same as the volatility in nominal exchange rates. Therefore, because prices tend to be sticky in each country but nominal exchange rates tend to be volatile, as we discussed earlier in the chapter, the real and nominal exchange rates tend to move together in the short run.

One reason why the relative price of a television set varies between countries is that firms may be *pricing to market*. Consider the case of a U.S. television manufacturer who sells to Spain. When the exchange rate is 1 euro equals 1 dollar, its television set retails at $150 in the United States and 150 euros in Spain. When the exchange rate goes to 1.5 euros to the dollar, the firm should charge 225 euros in Spain to preserve the same equivalent dollar price. But this is a huge increase in price, which will undermine

TABLE 19.1 **Relative Price Volatility between and across European Cities**

	Variance of Change in Relative Prices		
	1 Month	1 Year	4 Years
Intranational	0.17	0.96	2.83
International	2.76	52.3	159.8
	Variance of Change in Exchange Rates		
International	2.62	53.1	159

Source: Engel and Rogers, "Deviations from Purchasing Power Parity: Causes and Welfare Costs," Reprinted from Journal of International Economics (2001) Vol. 51, no. 1, with permission from Elsevier Science.

the competitiveness of U.S. products. Therefore, the U.S. producer may keep the Spanish retail price at 150 euros and sell the product for the equivalent of $100 in Spain but $150 in the United States. The U.S. producer is pricing to market—the price in the Spanish market is set taking into account Spanish circumstances rather than the domestic costs of production and the domestic selling price of the U.S. producer.

As this example makes clear, if firms price to market, then fluctuations in exchange rates bring about large swings in profit margins. This is why exchange rate fluctuations matter to exporters—a low exchange rate and a pricing to market strategy mean high profit margins, but when the exchange rate is high, the firm may even lose money if it keeps its foreign currency denominated export prices fixed.

Pricing to market also opens up another issue—exchange rate pass-through. When the exchange rate depreciates (the euro depreciates in our example when it goes from 1 euro equals 1 dollar to 1.5 euros equals 1 dollar), imports become more expensive when converted into domestic prices. The $150 television rises in retail value from 150 euros to 225 euros in Spain if the law of one price holds. Therefore a depreciating exchange rate may lead to higher import prices and put upward pressure on wages and inflation. However, if pricing to market occurs, then exchange rate changes need not lead to inflation—if the U.S. producer prices to the Spanish market, it charges 150 euros no matter what happens to the exchange rate. The exchange rate change is not "passed-through" to the Spanish consumers.

The precise amount of pass-through varies for different countries and different industries. If no European-based television producers rival the U.S. firm, it is not constrained by competition. It will pass through a larger portion of exchange rate changes, and euro prices will rise as the euro depreciates. Studies suggest that pass-through is never complete. For instance, one study finds that only around 50% of exchange rate volatility is passed through in changed prices of imports in the United States. For Germany, the estimate is 60% pass-through; for Japan, 70%. For Canada and Belgium, smaller economies and smaller markets, the pass-through is about 90%.

KEY POINT

Firms set prices based on local conditions and prices set by rivals. These prices tend to be sticky, but nominal exchange rates are very volatile. As a result, nominal exchange rate changes feed into real exchange rate changes and the law of one price fails to hold.

19.3 Purchasing Power Parity

The law of one price is a key part of our first theory of real exchange rate determination—**Purchasing Power Parity (PPP)**. The law of one price refers to particular commodities. PPP applies the law of one price to *all* commodities—whether they are tradeables or not. Imagine going shopping in Germany and buying commodities that cost 100 euros. If in Japan, the same purchases cost ¥5000, then according to PPP, the yen-euro exchange rate should be 5000/100 = 50. At this exchange rate, the yen price of your shopping trip equals the euro cost of the same items in Germany. Therefore PPP says:

PPP nominal exchange rate (yen/euro) = Japanese price / German price

If the German price increases to 110 euros and the Japanese cost to ¥6000, then PPP implies that the exchange rate should adjust to 54.54 (= 6000/110).

It is worth going back to our definition of the real exchange rate to grasp the implications of PPP. We have:

Real ¥-euro exchange rate = nominal ¥-euro exchange rate
× German Prices / Japanese Prices

But according to PPP, the nominal ¥-euro exchange rate equals Japanese prices divided by German prices. Putting this into our definition of the real exchange rate results in the value 1—things cost the same in each country.

PPP real Nominal ¥-euro exchange rate = (Japanese prices/German prices)
× (German prices / Japanese prices) = 1

Therefore, PPP implies that all countries are equally competitive, that commodity baskets cost the same the world over, and that the real exchange rate is forever equal to 1.

Further, the PPP definition of the nominal exchange rate implies that

Change in Nominal ¥-euro exchange rate = Japanese inflation − German inflation

In other words, PPP implies that currencies depreciate if they have higher inflation than other countries and appreciate if they have lower inflation. We showed above that when the shopping cost 100 euros in Germany and ¥5000 in Japan, PPP implies an exchange rate of 50. If German inflation is 10%, so that costs increase to 110 euros, but Japanese inflation is 20%, so the price rises to ¥6000, PPP implies an exchange rate of 54.54.[2] This is an appreciation in the euro of around 10%—or the difference between German and Japanese inflation.

How well does PPP agree with historical evidence? We have already shown evidence that suggests that PPP will perform poorly—we saw that the real exchange rate is volatile and that the law of one price (the basis for PPP) holds for few commodities. However, PPP does have some successes—in particular, PPP appears to be a useful model for explaining long-run data.

We can see the relative successes and failures of PPP in Figure 19.5a–c, which compares for a broad range of countries the behavior of bilateral exchange rates and inflation differentials over various time horizons. If PPP holds, the relationship should be one for one—for every 1% higher inflation a country has compared to the United States, its exchange rate should devalue by 1% against the dollar. In Figure 19.5a, which shows inflation and exchange rate depreciations over 2003, we see no evidence in favor of PPP. Over this period, exchange rate fluctuations appear to have nothing to do with inflation differences. Figure 19.5b, which looks at the period 1999–2003, shows a stronger relationship between countries with high inflation and depreciating currencies but the relationship is still not reliable. Only in Figure 19.5c, which shows changes in the exchange rate from 1984 to 2003, are the implications of PPP strongly observed—inflation differentials and exchange rate changes are closely connected.

---

[2] Although Japanese inflation is 10% higher than German inflation, the exchange rate does not depreciate by exactly 10% but by the factor (1.10/1.20)—this is approximately 10%.

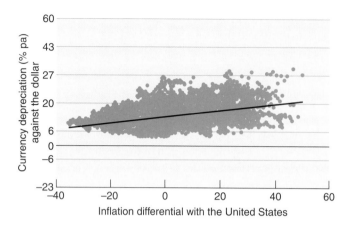

FIGURE 19.5a **Annual change in exchange rates and inflation, 2003.** *Source:* Global Financial Data.

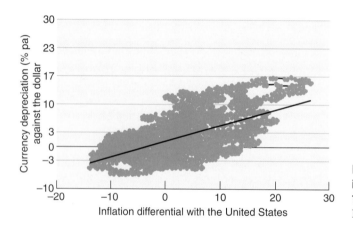

FIGURE 19.5b **Change in exchange rates and inflation, 1999–2003.** *Source:* Global Financial Data.

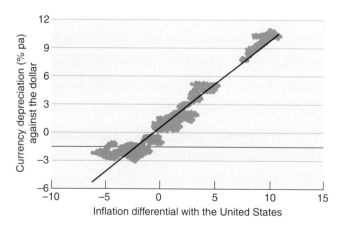

FIGURE 19.5c **Change in exchange rates and inflation, 1984–2003.** In the long run, the implication of PPP that inflation differentials equal currency depreciation is a good approximation, but in the short run the success of the model is very weak. *Source:* Global Financial Data.

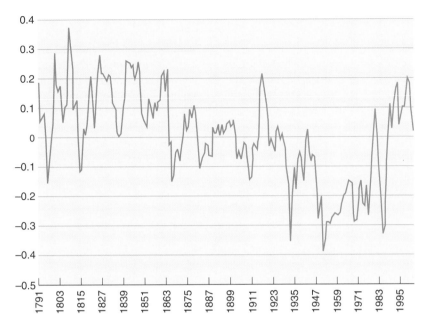

FIGURE 19.6   **Sterling/dollar real exchange rate, 1791–2001.** PPP holds in the very long run, but real exchange rates return to their PPP values very slowly. *Source:* Lothian and Taylor, "Real Exchange Rate Behavior: The Recent Float from the Perspective of the Past Two Centuries," *Journal of Political Economy* (1996) vol. 104, pp. 488–509. Updated by Mark Taylor.

Figure 19.6 plots the real exchange rate between the United Kingdom and the United States from 1791 to 2001 and offers further support for the long run validity of PPP. Figure 19.6 supports the weakest implications of PPP—there is some average value to which the real exchange rate eventually returns. The exchange rate may not re-turn to this long-run average value for decades, but eventually it does—a country does not stay forever overpriced. However, the correction in the real exchange rate overval-uation is not immediate, and before the real exchange rate declines, it may rise further, making the country seem even more expensive. The forces that bring about equality of prices are weak and take a long time to work. As a result, the real exchange rate shows large and persistent fluctuations, in contradiction to the implications of PPP.

We should not discard PPP completely—over decades, depreciations of nominal currencies are related to inflation differentials. However, PPP does not offer a reliable guide to the short-run volatility of real and nominal exchange rates.

KEY POINT

PPP assumes the cost of living is the same across all countries so that the nominal exchange rate should equal the ratio of prices and the real exchange rate should be 1. As a consequence, high-inflation countries should have depreciating currencies. As a long-run theory, PPP performs well but has limited validity in the short run.

THE BIG MAC INDEX

The Economist magazine popularizes a version of PPP with its Big Mac index ("in an effort to make exchange rate theory more digestible"). PPP posits that identical commodities should sell for the same price wherever they are sold. *The Economist* therefore uses a ratio of the domestic price of Big Macs in different countries to estimate PPP exchange rates. For instance, if a Big Mac costs $1 in the United States and A$3 in Australia, the implied Big Mac exchange rate is A$3:$1. If the actual exchange rate is A$2:$1, then the Australian currency is overvalued—Australian Big Macs are more expensive than American ones.

Table 19.2 shows actual exchange rates and the Big Mac PPP exchange rates in January 2003 and the implied over- or undervaluation. If we use the Big Mac rates as a

TABLE 19.2   **The Hamburger Standard, January 15, 2003**
Using the Big Mac to calculate PPP exchange rates.

Country	Big Mac Price in Local Currency	in U.S. dollars	Actual Exchange Rate 1 USD=	Over(+)/ Under(−) Valuation against the dollar, %	Purchasing Power Price
U.S.	$2.65	2.65	1		
Argentina	Peso 3.85	1.31	2.95	−50.78	1.45
Australia	A$3.20	2.46	1.30	−12.16	1.14
Brazil	Real4.50	1.58	2.84	−40.18	1.7
U.K.	£1.99	3.63	1.83‡	36.96	0.75
Canada	C$3.20	2.43	1.31	−7.93	1.21
China	Yuan9.95	1.20	8.29	−54.75	3.75
Euro area	2.75	3.46	0.79	29.66	1.03
Hong Kong	HK$11.25	1.49	7.77	−45.43	4.24
Hungary	Forint 492	2.37	207.92	−10.54	186
Indonesia	Rupiah 16,155	1.92	8424.70	−27.64	6,096
Japan	¥263	2.46	106.83	−6.95	99.4
Malaysia	M$5.10	1.34	3.81	−49.58	1.92
Mexico	Peso22.0	2.02	10.90	−23.83	8.3
New Zealand	NZ$3.95	2.65	1.49	0.08	1.49
Poland	Zloty 6.30	1.69	3.72	−36.04	2.38
Russia	Rouble 40.00	1.40	28.52	−47.09	15.09
Singapore	S$3.30	1.94	1.70	−26.89	1.24
South Africa	Rand14.05	1.96	7.17	−26.11	5.3
South Korea	Won3,211	2.68	1198.30	1.06	1,211
Sweden	Skr30.0	4.13	7.27	55.84	11.32
Switzerland	SFr6.35	5.11	1.24	93.08	2.4
Taiwan	NT$70.55	2.09	33.71	−21.03	26.62
Thailand	Baht55.0	1.40	39.19	−47.05	20.75

Source: The Economist, January 16, 2003.

guide to PPP, the currencies in Argentina, China, Malaysia, and Russia appear substantially undervalued. The Swedish krona and the Swiss franc were overvalued, and restoration of PPP would involve their depreciation. Unfortunately, a trading strategy based on the Big Mac index is unlikely to make you rich. As we have stressed, PPP is a long-run influence on exchange rates, and PPP rates exert only a weak short-run influence on exchange rates. In the short term, an undervalued currency can become even more undervalued according to PPP measures, and it may take decades to return to its PPP level. While the currency becomes more undervalued, the Big Mac inspired trade will be losing money.

The Big Mac index has other problems over and above failures of PPP. First, the Big Mac has more to do with the law of one price than with PPP—it refers to one commodity rather than a basket of goods. Second, the Big Mac may be identical across countries, but it is not tradeable—a freshly cooked Big Mac in London is a different commodity from a reheated one imported from China. Third, Big Macs are not identical—a Big Mac consumed in Tokyo reflects the cost of rent for a retail outlet in Tokyo plus various local labor and indirect taxes. This makes it a different commodity from a Big Mac sold in Manila. For these reasons, the Russian price of a Big Mac may always be lower than that of one in Copenhagen without affecting the ruble-krona exchange rate.

WHY DO RICH COUNTRIES HAVE HIGHER PRICES?

One systematic deviation from PPP is that prices tend to be higher in industrial economies than in emerging nations—as Figure 19.7 shows. This is known as the **Balassa-Samuelson effect**.

To explain this, we assume that productivity growth in the service sector (which is substantially nontradeable) is lower than in the tradeable sector. In other words, it is harder to boost the productivity of hairdressers than manufacturing firms. With rising productivity in the tradeable sector, wages will be increasing in these industries. If the nontradeable sector is to continue to hire workers, then wages in the nontradeable sector will also have to rise. However, the nontradeable sector does not benefit to the same extent from productivity improvements, so the only way to finance higher wages is to charge a higher price for services, which can be done because there is no threat of foreign competition. The result is higher prices, originating from the nontradeable sector, in countries with high levels of productivity in the tradeable sector.

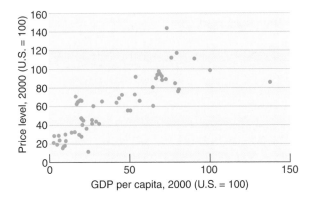

FIGURE 19.7 **Wealthy countries have high prices.** *Source:* Heston, Summers, and Aten, Penn World Table Version 6.1, Center for International Comparisons at the University of Pennsylvania (CICUP), October 2002.

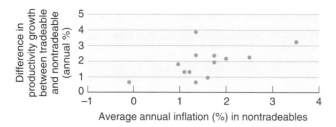

FIGURE 19.8 **The Balassa-Samuelson effect, OECD 1960–1998.** High productivity in the tradeable sector leads to high inflation in the nontradeable sector as wages rise across the economy.

According to the Balassa-Samuelson theory, countries with higher productivity growth in their tradeable sectors will have to have higher nontradeable wage increases and thus higher nontradeable inflation—this is exactly what Figure 19.8 shows. As a result, fast growing economies tend to have higher inflation than slower growing ones.

KEY POINT

Nontradeable commodities are a key reason why the law of one price does not hold. Countries with high productivity in their tradable sector tend to have high prices for nontradeables so that rich countries are more expensive than poor ones.

19.4 The Balance of Payments

The previous sections have shown that real exchange rates are too volatile for PPP to explain, so we need to develop alternative models. To do this we have to introduce some important concepts. In particular, we have to discuss a country's balance of payments, which is made up of its *capital account* and *current account*. The **balance of payments** is a statistical record, covering a particular time, of a country's economic transactions with the rest of the world. The **current account** records the net transactions in goods and services while the **capital account** records transactions in assets between countries. The relationship between these concepts is:

balance of payments = current account surplus + capital account surplus = 0

In other words, if the current account is in surplus (deficit), the capital account should be in deficit (surplus) by an equivalent amount.

KEY POINT

The current and capital accounts should sum to zero (the balance of payments has to balance).

THE CURRENT ACCOUNT

The current account measures the net flow of goods and services between a country and the rest of the world. It consists of four main categories: goods, services, income, and transfers.

current account = balance of trade (exports of goods − imports of goods)

$$+ \text{ balance on services (exports of services − imports of services)}$$
$$+ \text{ investment income and dividends}$$
$$+ \text{ net transfers}$$

- *Goods* Countries both export and import goods (automobiles, wheat, oil, and so forth). For instance, in 2002 (see Table 19.3) the United States exported to the rest of the world $685.4bn worth of goods and imported $1164.8bn. Therefore its net exports of goods were −$479.4bn—what economists term a *balance of trade* deficit.
- *Services* Services account for a broad collection of activities—such as transport services, telecommunications, legal, and financial services—and in 2002, U.S. exports of services were $288.7bn against imports of $227.4bn providing a surplus on services of $61.3bn and a balance on goods *and* services of −$418bn (−$479.4bn + $61.3bn).
- *Income and Dividends* Japan, as a result of previous investment, owns assets overseas but also foreign companies and investors own assets in Japan. For instance, Japanese pension funds and insurance companies have invested in the U.S. stock market, and firms such as Citibank and Merrill Lynch own offices in Japan. The Japanese funds invested overseas earn interest and dividends that are

TABLE 19.3 **Capital and Current Account Flows, 2002 ($bn)**
Argentina and Japan ran current account surpluses in 2002, and the United States ran a deficit. The United States and Japan saw an increase in their foreign currency reserves, but Argentina saw a fall.

	U.S.	Argentina	Japan
Balance on Goods	−479.38	17.24	93.83
Balance on Services	61.34	−1.60	−42.23
Balance on Goods & Services	**−418.03**	**15.64**	**51.60**
Net Investment Income	−3.97	−6.47	65.77
Net Transfers	−58.85	0.41	−4.92
Current Account	**−480.85**	**9.59**	**112.45**
Capital Account	−1.29	0.04	−3.32
Net Direct Investment	−98.20	1.42	−22.93
Net Portfolio Investment	437.24	−6.10	−105.97
Net Other Investment	192.64	−18.77	63.04
Financial Account	531.68	−23.46	−65.86
Net Errors and Omissions	−45.84	−1.55	0.39
Overall Balance	**3.69**	**−15.38**	**43.65**
Reserve Assets	−3.69	15.38	−43.65

Source: IMF, *International Financial Statistics* (September 2003).

paid to Japanese investors. Similarly Citibank in Japan sends profits and dividends back to Citibank in the United States. The current account records these income flows. In 2002, Japan received $91.5bn in income on its current account and paid out $25.7bn, for a balance of $65.8bn. For the United States, investment income received was $255.5bn but investment income paid out $259.5bn.

- *Transfers* Transfer payments occur when no asset or good is provided in return for money paid. For instance, if the United States donates resources to Sub-Saharan Africa for Overseas Development Assistance (ODA), this is a transfer payment because either goods or money flows in one direction only. Similarly, the remittances that U.S.-based Mexicans send back to Mexico would enter as a transfer debit on the current account. In 2002, the United States paid out $59.15bn in net transfers.

If we add transfers to the balance on goods, services, and income, we have the total current account for the United States in 2002—a $480.9bn deficit.

THE CAPITAL ACCOUNT

The current account records transactions in goods and services between a country and the rest of the world. The capital account records transactions in assets—both financial and nonfinancial. Strictly speaking,[3] we should refer to the *capital and financial account*. However, this distinction is rare, and we normally refer to the whole of the capital and financial account as just the *capital account*. We shall follow this practice throughout this chapter, except in the next few paragraphs, where we distinguish between the capital and financial accounts.

$$\text{capital and financial account} = \text{capital account} + \text{financial account} \\ + \text{errors and omissions}$$

- *Capital Account* The capital account refers to capital transfers (such as debt forgiveness) as well as the acquisition or disposal of nonproduced, nonfinancial assets (like copyright ownership and patents). If the U.S. government were to cancel $2bn of debt that was owed to the U.S. by the Iraqis, this would show up as −$2bn in the capital account. If a Japanese investor were to buy the copyright for REM's songs, this would show up as a surplus on the U.S. capital account.

- *Errors and Omissions* The balance of payments has to balance so that the current and capital account surpluses add to zero. However, logging all the financial transactions between a country and the rest of the world is a Herculean task. First, some transactions, such as money laundering, are illegal and will not be registered, so these transactions will be excluded from the balance of payments. Second, even legitimate transactions will not always come to the attention of statisticians. For these reasons, the capital and financial account will not always exactly offset the current account, and the size of the discrepancy is a measure of the magnitude of the errors and omissions made in the calculations. For the United States in 2002, these errors and omissions amounted to $45.8bn.

---

[3] For those of you who wish to speak strictly on balance of payments accounting issues, there is no better place to learn than the IMF's *Balance of Payments Textbook*. This offers a complete overview of the structure of balance of payments accounting as well as detailed definitions of various terms.

- *Financial Account* The financial account refers to the acquisition and disposal of financial assets and is by far the largest component of the capital and financial account. The financial account is made up of four different categories:

$$\text{financial account} = \text{net direct investment} + \text{net portfolio flows}$$
$$+ \text{net other investment} + \text{change in reserve assets}$$

- *Direct Investment* Direct investment occurs when an individual or firm in one country acquires a lasting interest in an enterprise resident in another economy. Direct investment implies a long-term relationship between the investor and the recipient firm, where the investor has significant influence over the enterprise.[4] For instance, if Coca-Cola opens a bottling factory in the Philippines, it would count as U.S. foreign direct investment abroad. If Toshiba opens a production factory in California, it would count as Japanese foreign direct investment abroad. As well as including such "greenfield" investment, FDI also includes mergers and acquisitions. We need to be careful about what signs we use when we measure the financial account. When Coca-Cola opens its Philippine bottling plant, it is in effect purchasing or "importing" an overseas asset. Therefore U.S. investment overseas counts as a negative for the U.S. financial account. Table 19.3 shows that in 2002, the United States had a deficit of $98.2bn on direct investment (consisting of $137.8bn of foreign investment compared to investment in the United States by foreign firms of $39.6bn).

- *Portfolio Investment* The portfolio assets section of the financial account refers to trade in various assets, but mainly equities (stocks) and bonds. In 2002 for the United States, this part of the financial account saw a surplus of $437.24bn—the United States sold this many more equities and bonds than it bought from overseas. In contrast, Japan purchased $106bn of overseas equities and bonds, including purchasing U.S. assets.

- *Other Investment* Another part of the financial account is investment in other assets. As its name suggests, it reflects a range of different transactions (such as trade credit), but its most important category is bank deposits and bank loans. When a U.S. investor places funds on deposit in a London account, the funds will appear in the "other investment" category (with a negative sign for the United States—the United States is acquiring an asset in the United Kingdom). When a Korean firm borrows from a New York-based bank, the loan will also show up in this category (as a positive term—the Korean economy has increased its liabilities to the rest of the world). In 2002, the United States had a surplus (i.e., was borrowing money) of $192.6bn on this other investment category while Argentina had a deficit of $18.8bn.

- *Reserve Assets* The final part of the financial account is the reserve asset category. This reflects mainly the government's financial interactions with the rest of the world and in particular with other governments. Consider the case of Argentina in 2002 (see Table 19.3), which had a current account surplus of $9.6bn. Counting trade in goods and services, and allowing for income and

---

[4] The investor does not, however, have to have majority control—a 10% stake or more is normally enough. See IMF *Balance of Payments Textbook*, p.107.

transfers, the Argentine economy sold $9.6bn more commodities abroad than it purchased from foreign countries. The logic of the balance of payments requires a matching deficit in the capital and financial account of $9.6bn. A capital and financial account deficit means that investors were pulling money out of Argentina and accumulating assets overseas. For Argentina in 2002, the capital and financial account (including errors and omissions) was a deficit of $25bn—far in excess of the current account surplus of $9.6bn. Argentina had an *overall balance* (current account + capital and financial account + errors and omissions) of −$15.4bn. Without any government intervention, this imbalance should lead to a sharp fall in the peso—the capital account outflow of funds far exceeds the current account surplus, so too many people are trying to sell the peso.

Governments have various means to try to resolve this balance of payments problem and avoid a sharp currency depreciation. If the Argentinean central bank had stocks of dollars and yen, it could intervene in the market and sell them (thus providing the desired foreign currency) and buy pesos to try to increase their value. If the central bank has sold all its reserves of foreign currency, then it has to finance the balance of payments in other ways. This is where the IMF and other international institutions play a role. By transferring funds to Argentina and arranging exceptional financing (i.e., Argentina can borrow foreign currency from other central banks), they can use reserve assets to finance the balance of payments. In 2002, the official financing of $15.4bn in Argentina was made up by $4.5bn of reserve sales by the central bank, and exceptional financing of $10.9bn (loans from IMF and other central banks).

19.5   Which Countries Are Rich and Which Are Poor?

The capital account records disposals and acquisitions of assets within a particular period. If a country is running a capital account deficit (buying overseas assets), then its *stock* of overseas assets is rising. The net **International Investment Position** (IIP) measures this stock of external wealth. If this is a positive number, then a country has more foreign assets than it does liabilities; if it is negative, then the country owes the rest of the world money. Further, if this stock of wealth is invested in assets that increase in value, then the wealth is increasing *even if there is no further capital account deficits/overseas investment* because of capital gains.

Figure 19.9 shows the net IIP (expressed as a percentage of GDP) for the United States, Japan, Germany, and the United Kingdom between 1970 and 1999. Throughout this period Germany and Japan had net overseas assets, while the United States and the United Kingdom acquired more liabilities than assets. The United States and United Kingdom switched from being creditor to debtor nations. The slow deterioration of the U.S. position from a positive stock of around 10% of GDP to a net debt of 19% reflects the years of persistent current account deficits. By contrast, the Japanese graph shows a continual increase in overseas assets from a stock of around 3% of GDP in 1970 to over 30%, due to the ability of the Japanese economy to generate current account surpluses.

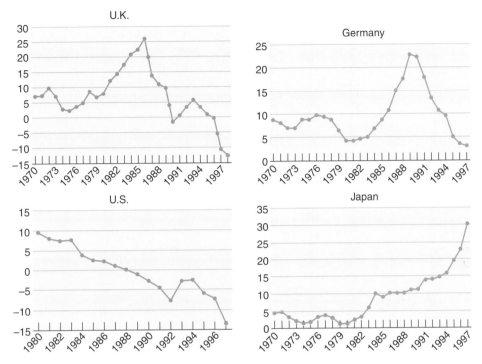

FIGURE 19.9   **Net foreign assets (% GDP)**. Germany and Japan are important global creditors, the U.S. is a debtor. *Source:* Lane and Milessi-Ferretti, "The External Wealth of Nations," CEPR Discussion paper (2000).

Until 1989, Germany experienced a similar pattern of rising foreign assets caused by several years of current account surpluses. However, German reunification transformed the German current account, and Germany began to sell its overseas assets/borrow from overseas to finance its reunification program. As a result the current account moved into deficit, and net foreign assets declined.

Table 19.4 shows the net foreign asset position of a range of countries in 1998. Does it matter if a country is a net creditor or debtor? As so often in economics, the answer is that it depends on the circumstances. Sustained periods of negative net foreign assets may be optimal when there are exceptional domestic investment opportunities. For instance, if a country is starting from a low level of capital, then our analysis in Chapters 4–6 suggests that investors could earn a high return from investing in that country. As a result, the country will borrow from overseas (run a capital account surplus), and as long as the money is invested appropriately, the country's economy will grow fast, which will allow the loans to be repaid. However, if a country is running a current account deficit because of high consumption (rather than high investment), then selling off its foreign assets is a cause for more concern because eventually foreign assets cannot fall further, and consumption will have to be curtailed.

TABLE 19.4   **Net Foreign Asset Position (% GDP) 1998**

Creditors	Debtors (0–20%)	Debtors (20–40%)	Debtors (40–60%)	Debtors (over 60%)
Botswana (120)	China (−8)	Argentina (−33)	Algeria (−49)	Cote d'Ivoire (−139.1)
Oman (15)	Egypt (−19)	Brazil (−30)	Bolivia (−52)	Jamaica (−79)
Singapore (210)	El Salvador (−9)	Costa Rica (−37)	Chile (−48)	Jordan (−70)
South Africa (16)	India (−17)	Colombia (−32)	Ecuador (−57)	Trinidad (−80)
Taiwan (49)	Israel (−12)	Dominican Republic (−36)	Indonesia (−54)	
Uruguay (11)	Korea (−5)	Guatemala (−28)	Malaysia (−45)	
Venezuela (16)	Austria (−10)	Mauritius (−33)	Mexico (−43)	
Netherlands (27)	Belgium (−9)	Paraguay (−21)	Morocco (−41)	
Norway (19)	Spain (−18)	Philippines (−32)	Pakistan (−50)	
Switzerland (48)		Sri Lanka (−38)	Peru (−47)	
France (3)		Syria (−22)	Thailand (−47)	
		Turkey (−30)	Tunisia (−43)	
		Finland (−21)	Zimbabwe (−55)	
		Greece (−40)	Australia (−55)	
		Canada (−24)		

Source: Lane and Milesi-Ferretti, "The External Wealth of Nations: Measures of Foreign Assets and Liabilities for Industrial and Developing Countries," CEPR Discussion Paper 2231 (1999).

Note also that a stock of overseas assets enables a country to potentially run a continual current account deficit. A country can always maintain a current account deficit if it also has a capital account surplus. A capital account surplus means that a country is selling its assets to overseas investors. If the Netherlands has a stock of overseas assets, then these will be increasing every year either through interest and dividends or because of capital gains. If the Netherlands every year sells foreign assets equal to these gains while maintaining a constant level of foreign assets (it only sells the gains it realizes from the assets, not the capital itself), then it will create a capital account surplus (it is selling Dutch assets). It can thus maintain a continuous current account deficit if it desired.

KEY POINT

If a country runs a capital account deficit (surplus), then it is acquiring foreign assets (liabilities). The level of these foreign assets is measured by a country's net IIP.

19.6 Current and Capital Accounts and the Real Exchange Rate

We focused above on the accounting definitions behind the balance of payments. Before we can use these concepts to explain real exchange rate movements, we need also to consider the balance of payments using the national accounts framework of Chapter 2.

The previous section stated that a country running a capital account deficit is acquiring foreign assets. In order for this to happen, the country must be doing more savings than investment. That is

$$\text{capital account deficit} = \text{savings} - \text{investment}$$

Consider the case where net savings is positive—savings within a country exceed investment. The banking system can therefore finance all the domestic investment needs of a country and still have surplus deposit funds left over. But banks want to make a profit and will not simply sit on these surplus funds. Instead, they will lend them overseas and earn profit on them. If the surplus savings are invested in overseas equity markets, then the portfolio asset part of the capital account will show a deficit. If instead, the bank lends the money to an overseas firm, then the other investment category of the capital account will show a deficit. In all these cases, the level of net savings is equal to the capital account deficit.

In Chapter 2, we showed how GDP is a measure of income—the total of wages and salaries and capital income. We also showed how GNI was equal to GDP plus the net income earned on foreign assets, e.g., GNI = GDP + NIFA. The income that the economy earns is used by the personal sector in one of three ways: it is spent as consumption (C); it is used to pay taxes (T); or it is saved in the financial system (PS). Therefore

$$\text{GDP} + \text{NIFA} = \text{C} + \text{T} + \text{PS}$$

So that savings equals

$$\text{PS} = \text{GDP} + \text{NIFA} - \text{C} - \text{T}$$

Chapter 2 also showed how GDP was used in one of four ways: as consumption (C); investment in physical machinery or buildings (I); as government expenditure on goods and services (G); or as net exports (X − M). Therefore

$$\text{GDP} = \text{C} + \text{I} + \text{G} + (\text{X} - \text{M})$$

Using this in our expression for savings gives

$$\text{PS} = \text{I} + \text{G} - \text{T} + \text{X} - \text{M} + \text{NIFA}$$

Or

$$\text{PS} + (\text{T} - \text{G}) - \text{I} = \text{X} - \text{M} + \text{NIFA}$$

PS is the savings of the personal sector while T − G is the savings of the public/government sector (the fiscal surplus). Therefore S = PS + T − G is savings for the whole economy. Therefore the national accounts implies

$$\text{S} - \text{I} = \text{X} - \text{M} + \text{NIFA}$$

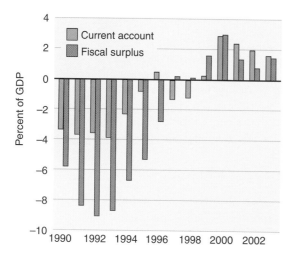

FIGURE 19.10 **Canadian fiscal and current account surplus.** The current account is strongly affected by fluctuations in the fiscal surplus. *Source:* IMF, *International Financial Statistics* (September 2003).

As we have just shown, $S - I$ is the capital account deficit, $X - M$ is the balance of trade on goods and services, and NIFA is net income and dividends on overseas assets. Therefore $X - M + \text{NIFA}$ is the current account surplus. Once again we have derived the result that the capital account plus the current account have to sum to zero. However, we can now convert that into a more meaningful economic statement—net savings in an economy has to equal net exports. Using this net savings–net export approach enables us to explain why the real exchange rate fluctuates.

Consider the case of an economy that starts to run a large fiscal deficit. If net savings by the personal sector do not increase, the larger fiscal deficit means a lower level of net national savings $(S - I)$. This, in turn, means that the capital account deficit will reduce in size and may even become a surplus as the government's borrowing needs leave less funds available for overseas investment. The improvement in the capital account (i.e., a move into surplus) means a growing current account deficit, so that a fiscal deficit will worsen the current account and an improvement in government finances will be associated with an increase in the current account. This positive relationship between the fiscal and current account surpluses is shown for Canada during the period 1990 to 2003 in Figure 19.10.

KEY POINT

The balance of payments implies that net savings (the capital account deficit) must equal net exports (current account surplus) or $S - I = X - M$.

THE ROLE OF THE REAL EXCHANGE RATE

PPP was rejected by the data because the real exchange rate was too volatile. We will now use this balance of payments framework to show that changes in the real exchange rate are needed to achieve balance between net savings and net exports.

As outlined at the beginning of this chapter, the real exchange rate reflects a country's competitiveness—the higher its real exchange rate, the more expensive its commodities are to overseas residents. With a high real exchange rate, a country's exports

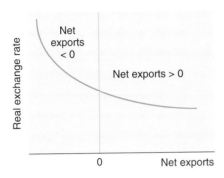

FIGURE 19.11   **Real exchange rate and net exports.**
Net exports improve when the real exchange rate
falls.

will be low and imports high because foreign goods are cheap. Therefore the higher the
real exchange rate, the lower the level of net exports and the higher the current account
deficit. Figure 19.11 shows this negative relationship between the real exchange rate
and net exports.

Figure 19.11 suggests that when countries experience a real depreciation their current account should ultimately improve. However two points need to be stressed:

1. It is the *real* exchange rate that matters. If the nominal exchange rate falls but is
   offset by higher domestic inflation so that the real exchange rate is unaltered,
   then there is no effect on net exports.
2. The beneficial effect of the depreciation may not be immediately felt. In fact in
   the short term, the current account may worsen due to the *J-curve* shown in Figure 19.12.

To understand the second point, consider the case when the real exchange rate depreciates so much that the cost of imports rises in domestic currency terms. Eventually this
higher import cost will lead to lower demand, and net exports will improve. However,
in the short run, firms and individuals may be contracted to purchase, at specified *foreign currency* prices, goods from overseas. While these contracts are in force, the costs
of imports will rise without any offsetting benefits from reduced demand. Of course, as
contracts come up for renewal, the extra cost means that many will be cancelled, and
net exports will improve. It may take 6 months or more before the improvement mani-
fests itself. Economists call this delayed beneficial effect on the current account the
J-curve effect, for reasons that should be obvious from Figure 19.12.

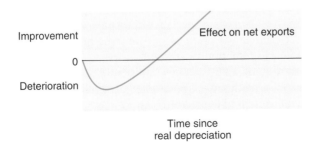

FIGURE 19.12   **J curve.** The
current account initially worsens
before improving after real
depreciation.

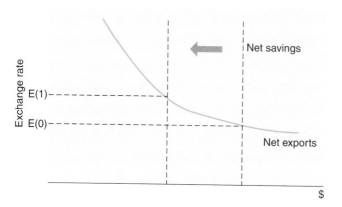

FIGURE 19.13   **Real exchange rate appreciation from investment boom.** An increase in investment reduces net savings and leads to real exchange rate appreciation.

Having described how the real exchange rate affects net exports, we need to make an assumption about how exchange rates affect net savings to complete our model. In the rest of this section we assume that net savings do not depend on the exchange rate—whether the currency is high or low, savings and investment decisions are unaffected. This assumption means that net savings is given by a vertical line, as in Figure 19.13.

We can now use this framework to consider the case of a country embarking on an investment boom that leads to a fall in net savings. This causes the net savings line to shift left in Figure 19.13. Lower net savings means a larger capital account surplus, as the investment boom needs to be financed by overseas funds (assuming domestic savings does not change). A larger capital account surplus requires an increased current account deficit and for this to happen, the exchange rate has to appreciate in real terms—from E(0) to E(1). With a higher real exchange rate, exports become uncompetitive and fall, while imports increase.

This analysis explains why the U.S. dollar saw a real appreciation in the 1990s (see Table 19.5). U.S. firms increased investment substantially to benefit from the New Economy (see Chapter 5) and this was financed by significant foreign investment. This produced a large capital account surplus (see Table 19.3) and a large current account deficit. The larger current account deficit was produced as the capital account inflows led to an appreciation of the dollar real exchange rate. Between 1995 and 2001 the dollar appreciated by 34%.

Anything that shifts the net export schedule will also change the real exchange rate. Consider what happens when Mediterranean goods suddenly become fashionable. At any particular real exchange rate, exports from Italy will be higher than before—the net export schedule shifts to the right, as in Figure 19.14. However, net savings have not altered and at the existing exchange rate, net exports will be greater than net savings. This cannot happen—the current and capital accounts must sum to zero—so the real exchange rate will have to increase to choke off the demand for Italian goods. Figure 19.14 shows this case—where the increased demand for Italian goods leads to an appreciation of the exchange rate from E(0) to E(1).

TABLE 19.5   **U.S. Investment and the Dollar in the 1990s**

The U.S. investment boom in 1990s led to a fall in net savings and a larger current account deficit through an appreciating real exchange rate.

	Investment (% GDP)	Current Account (% GDP)	Real Effective Exchange Rate
1990	14.6	−1.4	104.8
1991	13.4	0.1	103.7
1992	13.5	−0.8	101.3
1993	14.1	−1.2	104.8
1994	14.7	−1.7	103.5
1995	15.0	−1.4	100.0
1996	15.5	−1.5	104.3
1997	16.0	−1.5	111.9
1998	16.7	−2.3	119.9
1999	17.0	−3.1	119.1
2000	17.2	−4.2	124.9
2001	16.3	−3.9	134.2
2002	15.2	−4.6	133.6

Source: IMF, *International Financial Statistics* (September 2003).

Note that we can use the same diagram to examine import controls. If a government introduces import controls, then for a given real exchange rate, the level of imports is reduced, but exports are unchanged, so that net exports increase. As a result, the real exchange rate has to rise to reduce exports in line with the reduction in imports.

This simple model suggests that there are good reasons (shifting net export and net savings curves) for expecting fluctuations in the real exchange rate. However, the key question here is one we posed earlier about PPP: How well does it agree with the data?

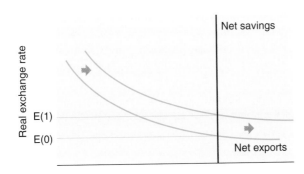

FIGURE 19.14   **Shift in export demand and real appreciation.** An increase in demand for a country's net exports leads to appreciation.

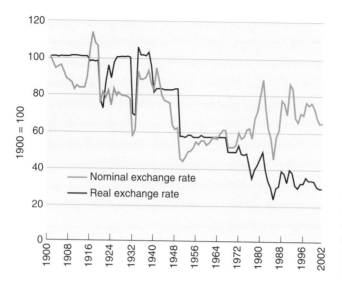

FIGURE 19.15 **Nominal and real dollar–sterling exchange rate.** The short-run volatility of nominal exchange rates is shared by the real exchange rate. *Source:* Bank of England Historical Data.

Examination of the nominal and real exchange rate (see Figure 19.15) shows them both to be volatile and their general fluctuations show a similar pattern. These facts have two potential explanations:

- First, as we suggested in this section, the real exchange rate changes, and the factors that lead it to change are volatile. According to this account, volatile economic fundamentals lead to a volatile real exchange rate which, in turn, produces a volatile nominal exchange rate.
- The alternative explanation is the idea mentioned earlier in the chapter that, because prices in a country are relatively sticky, changes in the nominal exchange rate feed through into changes in the real exchange rate. According to that analysis, we need to focus on the nominal exchange rate, and in particular monetary models, to understand the volatility of the real exchange rate.

Which of these two explanations is correct? While opinions differ, the general consensus is that real exchange rates are far too volatile, especially in the short run, to be explained by changes in the macroeconomic fundamentals that underpin the net exports and net savings curve. As our analysis of the United States in the 1990s shows, we can use changes in macroeconomic fundamentals to explain some of the medium-run fluctuations in the real exchange rate. However, as we see in Figure 19.15, the real exchange rate is too volatile in the short run to be explained by variations in fiscal policy, savings, investment, and so forth. For that reason, in Chapter 20 we will move on to discuss changes in the nominal exchange rate.

KEY POINT

Fluctuations in net savings and net exports can be used to partially explain why the real exchange rate is so variable compared to the predictions of PPP. However, these fluctuations in economic fundamentals are not large enough or frequent enough to explain more than 3–10 year swings in the real exchange rate.

SUMMARY

In section 19.1, we defined various concepts of exchange rates. The bilateral exchange rate is the rate at which two particular currencies are exchanged, and the effective exchange rate reflects the behavior of a currency against a trade-weighted average of all currencies. The nominal exchange rate reflects the rate at which you can swap different currencies whereas the real exchange rate represents the relative cheapness of one country compared to another.

In section 19.2, we discussed the law of one price—the idea that the same commodity should sell for the same price in all countries due to arbitrage. We showed that there are substantial deviations from the law of one price due, in part, to tariffs and transportation costs but also due to border effects and pricing to market on the part of firms.

In section 19.3 we applied the law of one price to all commodities by using Purchasing Power Parity. PPP implies that the real exchange rate should equal one, as all countries should have the same prices, and that the nominal exchange rate should equal the ratio of prices between countries. As a result, countries with high inflation should have depreciating currencies. In the very long run (over 10 years), PPP describes the data well, but in the short run it performs poorly.

In section 19.4, we introduced the balance of payments—a statistical record of a country's dealings with the rest of the world. The balance of payments equals the sum of the current and the capital account. The current account details trade in goods and services between countries, while the capital account shows trade in assets. The balance of payments has to balance so that a current account surplus must be matched by a capital account deficit and vice versa.

Section 19.5 showed how, over time, the capital account of a country determined its net foreign assets or International Investment Position. Countries that run large capital account deficits are purchasing foreign assets and so will have a positive IIP, while capital account surplus countries will owe money.

In section 19.6, we discussed how well the balance of payments framework works to explain variations in the real exchange rate. An increase in the real exchange rate reduces net exports and performs a key role in ensuring that the capital account deficit (which equals net savings) equals the current account surplus (net exports). This approach can help explain 3–10 year general shifts in exchange rates, but it cannot plausibly explain the magnitude of short-run fluctuations in the real exchange rate. Instead, the consensus view is that short-run fluctuations in the real exchange rate reflect variations in the nominal exchange rate.

CONCEPTUAL QUESTIONS

1. (Section 19.1) The nominal exchange rate between Eurasian and Oceanian dollars is 3:1. The average shopping trip costs E$400 in Eurasia and O$75 in Oceania. Which country is cheapest? What is the real exchange rate?

2. (19.2) What does the increasing impact of the Internet imply for the law of one price?

3. (19.3) You have been hired as a statistician by an international economic institution and asked to construct estimates of PPP exchange rates. What data do you need and what problems would you expect?

4. (19.3) A multinational company has asked you for a thirty-year forecast of various African exchange rates against the U.S. dollar. The firm will give you any macroeconomic forecasts you need. What data would you ask for?

5. (19.4) A German investor places some funds with an emerging market stock market fund and intends to leave it there for 5 years and have all dividends paid into a Munich bank account. How will this affect the German current and capital account in each of the next five years?

6. (19.4) Assuming in Table 19.3 that "Net Other Investment" covers volatile short term financing that is easily reversed and that Central Banks cannot continuously use reserves to fund their balance of payments, assess the vulnerability of each country's capital account position.

7. (19.5) Figure 19.9 shows the United States is a net debtor to other countries, yet Table 19.3 shows that its investment income position in the current account was nearly in balance. What might explain this?

8. (19.6) The Hong Kong dollar depreciates by 5% against the U.S. dollar, but Hong Kong inflation also rises by 5%. What will happen to the Hong Kong current account? How would your answer differ if the authorities managed to prevent inflation from increasing?

9. (19.6) In 2003, several European nations were running large fiscal deficits. What would our net savings = net exports analysis predict should happen to the euro?

ANALYTICAL QUESTIONS

1. (Section 19.1) The United States of Albion does 30% of its total trade with the Republic of Oz, 25% with the Federation of Tropical States, and 45% with the Banana Republic. Over the last three years the exchange rate changes against the U.S. dollar have been

	Republic of Oz	Federation of Tropical States	Banana Republic
Year 0	−4%	−3%	+8%
Year 1	+2%	−1%	+4%
Year 2	+2%	−1%	+5%

Calculate the effective exchange rate for the United States of Albion dollar.

2. (19.3) Calculate the purchasing power parity exchange rate between the following countries (where all goods are purchased in equal amounts).

Commodity	United States of Albion	Republic of Oz
Gasoline	120	180
Meat	80	140
Books	20	33
Fruit juice	40	40
Coffee	15	10
Clothes	70	160

3. (19.5) The New Economic Republic has a Net Foreign Asset position of $0 in 2003 but runs capital account deficits of 3% in 2004, 2005, and 2006. The capital account deficit is used to purchase overseas equity.

    (a) Assuming no GDP growth, no capital gains, and no change in the exchange rate, what is the IIP in 2004, 2005, and 2006?

    (b) Assume no GDP growth or changes in the exchange rate but that the equities purchased experience capital gains of 10% per annum. Recalculate your answer to (b).

    (c) In addition to the assumptions in (b), assume that the New Economic Republic currency depreciates by 10% per annum. How does this change your answer to (b)?

4. (19.6) (a) Use the model of real exchange rate determination in section 19.6 to analyze the impact on the dollar of a fall in U.S. investment.

    (b) Use the same model, but where the net savings line depends positively (e.g., is upward sloping) on the real exchange rate, to analyze the impact of import controls.

5. (19.3)/(19.6) What slope does the net export schedule in question 4(a) have to be in order to account for purchasing power parity? What is the economic justification of assuming this slope?

Exchange Rate Determination II—Nominal Exchange Rates and Asset Markets

Overview

This chapter focuses on explaining the volatility in nominal exchange rates. It does so by examining asset markets and capital flows and the relation between nominal exchange rates and interest rates. We outline the theory of uncovered interest parity (UIP), which implies that when interest rates increase, currencies should appreciate immediately but that, over time, high interest rate currencies should experience a depreciation. UIP also implies that exchange rates are affected by the whole expected path of future interest rates, which helps to explain why exchange rates are so volatile. While UIP captures well the response of exchange rates to interest rate changes, it is in conflict with the data in many other dimensions. The focus of UIP is to use macroeconomics to explain exchange rates, but in the short run this is unsuccessful, as exchange rates seem to be driven by other factors. To understand the short-run behavior of exchange rates, economists are placing increasing focus on the microstructure of markets and transaction order flows. We conclude the chapter by focusing on the magnitude of capital account flows from both contemporary and historical perspectives. We assess their economic function and consider the issue of whether there really is a single global capital market.

KEY CONCEPTS

Covered Interest Parity (CIP)	Market Microstructure	Spot and Forward Exchange Rates
Global Capital Markets	Order Flows	Uncovered Interest Parity (UIP)
Home Bias	Risk Premium	

20.1 The Importance of Asset Markets

In this chapter we explain how international asset markets, or investment opportunities, influence the nominal exchange rate. We focus particularly on differences in interest rates between countries. Just as we did with the law of one price and purchasing power parity (PPP) in Chapter 19, we consider what arbitrage implies for exchange rate fluctuations. However, whereas with PPP we focused on arbitrage in goods and services, we now focus on arbitrage between investment opportunities in different economies.

The importance of asset markets in explaining exchange rates is evident when the size of daily market transactions is considered. Figure 20.1 shows daily turnover in foreign exchange markets between 1989 and 2001. Both **spot** transactions (for immediate delivery of one currency in exchange for another) and **forward** transactions (where exchange rates are fixed today but delivery is in the future) have increased substantially over time, although the introduction of the euro in 1999 did lead to a fall in turnover. By 2001, the combined level of *daily* turnover was approximately $1.2 trillion, equal to the *annual* GDP of Italy. Less than 5% of these exchange rate transactions are related to trade in goods and services, the focus of Chapter 19. The majority of these transactions are for investment in asset markets.

Not surprisingly, the world's three largest economic areas (the United States, Euroland, and Japan) have the three most heavily traded currencies.[1] The most traded combination is U.S. dollar/euro, which had a daily trading volume of $354bn, followed by U.S. dollar/yen ($231bn) and then U.S. dollar/U.K. sterling ($125bn). Table 20.1

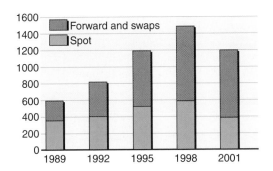

FIGURE 20.1 **Average daily turnover ($bn) in foreign exchange markets.** Foreign exchange market turnover has increased substantially over time. *Source:* Bank for International Settlements "*Central Bank Survey of Foreign Exchange and Derivatives Market Activity in April 1998*" and "*Triennial Central Bank Survey: Foreign exchange and derivatives market activity in 2001*" (March 2002).

TABLE 20.1

Geographical Distribution of Foreign Exchange Market Activity
London is the main foreign exchange market.

U.K.	31.1
U.S.	15.7
Japan	9.1
Singapore	6.2
Germany	5.4
Switzerland	4.4
Hong Kong	4.1
France	3.0

Source: Bank for International Settlements, *Triennial Central Bank Survey: Foreign exchange and derivatives market activity in 2001*, (March 2002).

[1] These percentage shares add to 200% because a dollar–yen trade is recorded as both a dollar share of transactions and a yen share.

shows where these currency trades occur. Even though the British pound accounts for only around 13% of total trade in foreign exchange, London accounts for a third of all turnover.

20.2   Covered Interest Parity

The aim of this chapter is to explain how variations in interest rates and asset returns lead to fluctuations in exchange rates. We start our analysis with **covered interest parity** or CIP. Consider a Japanese investor deciding whether to invest in a yen or a dollar bank account. The yen account pays interest of 1%, the dollar account 4%, and the current spot rate is ¥100:$1. For the Japanese investor, the return on the yen account is straightforward—it is simply the Japanese interest rate. However, the return on the dollar account consists of two factors—the dollar interest rate (4%) plus any appreciation of the dollar against the yen. What the investor does depends on what she expects the yen–dollar exchange rate to be.

The Japanese investor has to compare two different investments (as outlined in Figure 20.2). The first is investing ¥100,000 for one year in a yen account and earning interest i^J, which in our example is 1%, or 0.01. The alternative is to invest in a dollar bank account. Assume the current exchange rate is $S(0)$. (The notation $S(0)$ reminds us that we are talking about today's *spot* rate. In our example, $S(0)$ is ¥100:$1.) The Japanese investor would deposit $(100,000/S(0))$ in the dollar account. This pays inter-

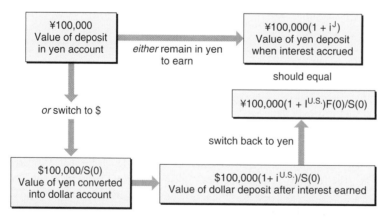

FIGURE 20.2   **Covered interest parity.** Covered interest parity implies that the difference between forward and spot exchange rates compensates for any interest rate differential.

est at the rate i^{US} (4% or 0.04), so that at the end of the year, the account is worth $\$100{,}000(1+i^{US})/S(0)$.

However, this is a dollar amount, and to compare it with the yen investment, we need to convert it back into yen. With CIP we do this by using the forward rate. The forward rate is the rate at which you can purchase currency at specific future dates at an exchange rate that is fixed today. Our Japanese investor wishes to know the future yen value of $\$100{,}000(1+i^{US})/S(0)$. If she signs a one year forward contract today at a rate of $F(0)$, then in one year's time, the investor is guaranteed $¥100{,}000(1+i^{US})F(0)/S(0)$. Note there is no uncertainty here because all transactions are made today. Therefore, whether the investor chooses a yen or a dollar account, she faces no exchange rate risk if she uses forward contracts. The exchange rate risk is *covered* by the forward contract.

Over the year, the ¥100,000 converted into dollars increases by a factor of $(1+i^{US})F(0)/S(0)$. If $F(0) > S(0)$ then the dollar is said to have a forward premium—the forward rate includes a dollar appreciation (i.e., at the forward date more yen are paid out for dollars than at the current spot rate). If $F(0) < S(0)$, then there is a forward discount as the dollar depreciates. We can therefore write $F(0)/S(0)$ as $1 + fp$, where fp denotes the forward premium. If the forward rate is 5% above the spot rate, then $fp = 0.05$. Using this notation, the return on the U.S. dollar investment for the Japanese investor is $(1+i^{US})(1+fp)$ and the return on her yen investment is $(1+i^{J})$.

If $(1+i^{US})F(0)/S(0)$ exceeds $(1+i^{J})$, the dollar investment is more profitable than the yen investment. The investor will sell yen in the spot market (to open a dollar account) and will buy yen in the forward market (to convert the dollar account back into yen). As the investor sells yen today, it will drive up the spot value of the dollar and so increase $S(0)$. As the investor buys yen forward, it will tend to push up the future price of yen and lower $F(0)$. As this happens, the advantage of investing in the dollar account diminishes as $F(0)/S(0)$ (the forward premium) falls. The investor will switch her funds into dollars as long as the return on the dollar investment exceeds the yen return. But eventually, by switching her funds, the return on the dollar and yen accounts will become the same. That is eventually

$$(1 + i^{US})(1 + fp) = (1 + i^{J})$$

which is approximately the same as

$$i^{US} + fp = i^{J}$$

Thus, CIP says that as a result of arbitrage, the return on the dollar investment will equal the return on the yen investment when evaluated using the forward rate. That is, the forward premium is equal to the difference in interest rates. For a Japanese investor, the return on a U.S. account consists of interest earned plus the forward premium on the dollar. In our example, U.S. interest rates were 4%, and Japanese rates were 1%. In this situation, covered interest rate parity implies there is a forward dollar discount of 3%—the forward rate should be 3% lower than the current yen–dollar rate. In order for the return on the two investments to be the same, it must be that the currency that offers a higher interest rate has to be priced at a forward depreciation. CIP therefore pins down a precise relationship between interest rate differentials and the spot and forward exchange rates.

Does CIP hold? The answer is a resounding "yes." If it did not hold, investors could make infinite amounts of money at no risk by switching funds between currencies. There is, however, one caveat. CIP only holds exactly if there is absolutely no risk to either the yen or dollar side of the transactions. Imagine a Japanese investor considering a yen deposit account in Tokyo with the Bank of Sashimi or a dollar account based in Moscow with the Russian Samovarbank. Because the accounts are based in different countries and with different banks, their risk characteristics may not be identical. One country might impose capital controls, or one of the banks might be almost insolvent, in which case the investor will lose his money. In this case, the investor may place funds in the account that offers a lower return because it is less risky. If, instead, we concentrate attention on deposits in the same country with the same bank, these risk differences do not exist and CIP holds exactly.

20.3   Uncovered Interest Parity

A key feature of CIP is the use of a forward contract so that the investor faces no uncertainty when comparing the return on yen and dollar accounts. By contrast, with **uncovered interest parity (UIP)**, the investor does not buy forward but waits before converting dollars into yen at the future spot rate. In other words, instead of comparing ¥100,000$(1 + i^J)$ with ¥100,000$(1 + i^{US})$ $F(0)/S(0)$, the investor compares it with ¥100,000$(1 + i^{US})S^e(1)/S(0)$ where $S^e(1)$ is what the investor expects the spot exchange rate to be one period in the future. Of course, the investor could be wrong—$S^e(1)$ may not equal $S(1)$; the outcome may be different from the investor's forecast. But this is the risk the investor takes because he does not cover his position by a forward transaction.

Under UIP, investors rearrange their portfolio until the return on the yen account is equal to the expected return on the dollar account. In the case of UIP, we have:

expected appreciation of dollar $[S^e(1) - S(0)]/S(0)$

= Japanese interest rate − U.S. interest rate

In other words, if U.S. interest rates are higher than Japanese interest rates, investors must be expecting a depreciation (or negative appreciation) of the dollar. If Japanese interest rates are 2% and U.S. interest rates are 6%, then the market must be expecting a 4% depreciation in the dollar. Imagine instead that at these interest rates the market expects the dollar to remain unchanged. Investors will shift funds into U.S. dollar accounts in order to earn 6% compared to 2%. Investors buying dollars will lead to an increase in the dollar so that (assuming an unchanged forecast) the dollar is now overvalued and expected to depreciate. If the dollar is expected to depreciate by only 1%, it is still worthwhile shifting funds into dollars that earn 5% (6% interest less 1%

depreciation), compared to 2% on yen. Investors will therefore continue to buy dollars until the dollar has risen so far they expect it to fall by 4%. At this point, the interest rate differential is completely offset by the expected depreciation on dollars. UIP therefore offers a theory to explain expected changes in exchange rates—interest rate differentials.

THE RISKS OF INVESTING IN HIGH YIELDING COUNTRIES

UIP helps explain why investors do not place all their funds in countries offering high interest rates. In Figure 20.3 we show Turkish and U.S. interest rates for the period 2000–2003. On the basis solely of interest rates, putting funds in Turkish accounts was the best move. Turkish interest rates were frequently 50% above those in the United States, and in February 2001 they were nearly 400% higher. Why shouldn't United States investors take advantage of this huge difference and invest in Turkish lira? The reason is that U.S. investors placing funds in a Turkish bank account need to worry about the future lira–dollar exchange rate. Figure 20.3 also shows the annual depreciation of the lira against the dollar. Every single month shows the lira depreciating against the dollar, partly offsetting the higher Turkish interest rates. Frequently the decline in the exchange rate is not enough to offset the enormous interest rate differential, and the Turkish lira investment still earns higher returns. At other times, however, the depreciation is larger than the interest rate differential and the U.S. dollar investment dominates. Potential fluctuations in the exchange rate are an important component of investors' expected return.

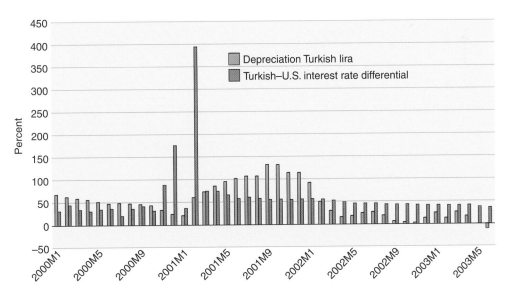

FIGURE 20.3 **Turkish and U.S. interest rates.** Turkish interest rates are always higher than those in the United States but this is often offset by lira depreciation. *Source:* IMF, *International Financial Statistics* (September 2003).

KEY POINT

Uncovered interest parity says that currencies with high interest rates should see their value depreciate and should not offer superior investment performance.

20.4   Pinning Down the Exchange Rate with UIP

In this section, we use UIP to develop a model of what determines the current *level* of the exchange rate. A key feature of this model is to work out today's exchange rate *taking as fixed expectations of where the exchange rate will be tomorrow*. In other words, we reverse the flow of time and take a forward looking approach. Rather than try to work out expectations of where the exchange rate will be tomorrow by reference to the current exchange and interest rates, we do the opposite—*we calculate the current exchange rate by reference to interest rates and where we expect the exchange rate to be in the future*.

In Figure 20.4 we consider again the case of a U.S. and Japanese investment and use UIP to derive the yen–dollar exchange rate. For the Japanese investor, the yen–denominated return on the Japanese investment is i^J and does not depend on $S(0)$, the current spot rate. For example, if $i^J = 2\%$, then the return on the yen account is 2%—whatever happens to the dollar. The return on the yen account is therefore given by the vertical line in Figure 20.4.

The return on the dollar account for the Japanese investor is $i^{US} + [S^e(1) - S(0)]/S(0)$. The higher are U.S. interest rates and $S^e(1)$, the expectations of future spot rate, the greater the return on the dollar account. For a given $S^e(1)$, the U.S. return is *decreasing* in $S(0)$. The reason is simple—by keeping fixed the forecast of the future exchange rate but increasing the current strength of the dollar, there is less dollar appreciation and as a result, a lower return on dollars. Therefore, the U.S. dollar return is shown in Figure 20.4 as a downward sloping line—for given expectations of the future spot rate, the higher the current spot rate, and the lower the dollar return.

UIP says that in equilibrium, the return on the yen account equals the expected return on the dollar account. This occurs at the point where the two lines in Figure 20.4 intersect, and this determines the current exchange rate—shown as $S^*(0)$.

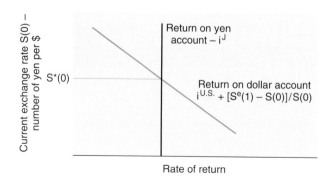

FIGURE 20.4   Determining the nominal exchange rate. Domestic and overseas interest rates and expectation of future exchange rates determines current exchange rate.

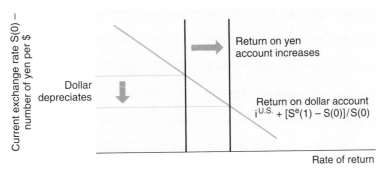

FIGURE 20.5   **Increase in Japanese interest rates leads to dollar depreciation.** Higher domestic interest rates means currency appreciates.

We now use this analysis to model exchange rate fluctuations in response to:

- changes in Japanese interest rates
- changes in U.S. interest rates
- revisions to expectations of the future value of the dollar

IMPACT OF HIGHER JAPANESE INTEREST RATES ON THE DOLLAR

As shown in Figure 20.5, an increase in Japanese interest rates leads to a rightward shift in the yen return curve and a decline in $S^*(0)$, so that a dollar buys fewer yen. Therefore, *an increase in Japanese interest rates leads to a depreciation of the dollar and an appreciation of the yen.*

IMPACT OF HIGHER U.S. INTEREST RATES ON THE DOLLAR

Figure 20.6 shows the impact of an increase in U.S. interest rates on the dollar. For a given current exchange rate, an increase in U.S. rates leads to an increase in the return on dollar investments, so the dollar return line in Figure 20.6 shifts right. As a result, the yen–dollar rate increases—the dollar strengthens and can be used to buy more yen per dollar. Therefore, a rise in U.S. rates leads to a dollar appreciation/yen depreciation.

Consider the case where U.S. interest rates are 4%, Japanese rates 1%, and investors expect the yen–dollar rate to be 97 in a year's time. Because U.S. interest rates

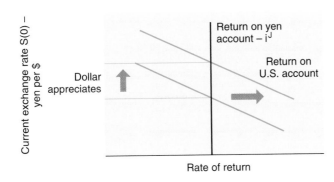

FIGURE 20.6   **Increase in U.S. interest rates leads to dollar appreciation.**

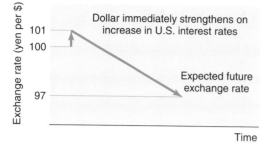

FIGURE 20.7 **Appreciation of dollar after increase in U.S. interest rates.** Exchange rate jumps in response to higher interest rates.

are 3% higher, UIP implies an expected dollar devaluation of 3%, which gives a current exchange rate of 100 (3% higher than the expected future value of 97). If U.S. interest rates increase to 5%, UIP now implies an expected 4% devaluation of the dollar, so the current exchange rate should be approximately 101—as shown in Figure 20.7. In response to the 1% increase in U.S. interest rates, the dollar *strengthens* from 100 to 101.

UIP says that countries with high interest rates should see their currencies depreciate, but we have just shown that an increase in U.S. rates leads to an *appreciation* of the dollar. However, this immediate increase in the dollar in response to higher interest rates is necessary for UIP to hold—over the next year the higher U.S. interest rates are offset by a larger dollar depreciation, as shown in Figure 20.7. If the dollar did not rise today then, for a given forecast of the future exchange rate, superior returns would be available on the dollar. Therefore, in using UIP it is important to separate out the immediate response of exchange rates from the future effect.

IMPACT OF CHANGED EXPECTATIONS OF THE DOLLAR

We have so far concentrated on how interest rates influence the current exchange rate. However, expectations of future exchange rates are also important, because they influence the expected return on the overseas investment.

Figure 20.8 shows the case where the market revises upwards its expectation of future dollar strength—this increases the expected return from the dollar investment and shifts the return schedule on the U.S. investment for the Japanese investor to the right. The result is an increase in the current value of dollars—*market expectations of future dollar strength lead to an immediate appreciation of the dollar*. This makes sense—if investors think the dollar will be strong in the future, they will wish to buy dollars now to benefit from this, which will lead to an appreciation today.

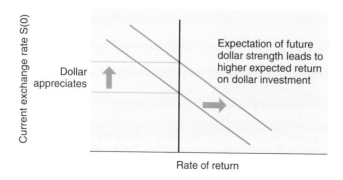

FIGURE 20.8
Expectations of future dollar strength lead to dollar appreciation. Expectations of future high currency leads to an appreciation today.

20.5 The Role of Expectations

UIP tries to explain exchange rate volatility through interest rate differentials. However, expectations of the future are critical to UIP. We now show how changing expectations can lead to considerable volatility in exchange rates. In other words, the current exchange rate displays considerable volatility in response to *unanticipated* events. We first discuss changes in expectations concerning interest rates, and then consider changes in expectations about future exchange rates.

INTEREST RATE EXPECTATIONS

Consider the case where the market thinks that the yen–dollar exchange rate will be 100 next period, $S^e(1)=100$. U.S. interest rates are 4% and Japanese rates 1%. However, the market is expecting that today's meeting of the Federal Reserve Board will raise U.S. rates to 6%. On the basis of this expectation, the current exchange rate is 105—at 6% interest rates, UIP predicts a 5% decline of the dollar to a level of 100 in a year's time. However, the Federal Reserve surprises the market and only increases interest rates from 4% to 5%. With a 5% U.S. interest rate, UIP predicts only a 4% devaluation, so that the dollar falls from 105 to 104, giving it scope to depreciate by 4% to 100. *Note that even though U.S. interest rates have increased, the currency has immediately depreciated.* However, this does not contradict our previous analysis—the key point is that U.S. interest rates in this example are lower than what the market expected, which is why the dollar falls.

EXPECTATIONS OF FUTURE EXCHANGE RATES

Crucial to our modelling of the exchange rate was an expectation for future exchange rates, $S^e(1)$. Without knowing how to model $S^e(1)$, however, we have not really arrived at a model that explains the current exchange rate. However, modelling $S^e(1)$ is easy—we can just use UIP again!

We have shown how to determine the current exchange rate, $S(0)$, based on current interest rates and a forecast of the future exchange rate $S^e(1)$. However, this analysis should hold for all periods, not just today. In other words, we could use the same analysis to deduce the expected exchange rate tomorrow, $S^e(1)$, given expectations of interest rates tomorrow and the exchange rate two periods from now, $S^e(2)$.

What determines $S^e(2)$? Again we can use UIP and derive $S^e(2)$ as depending on interest rates two periods from now as well as on expectations of the exchange rate in three periods time, $S^e(3)$. We can keep performing this trick until we have expressed the current exchange rate in terms of the expectation of some long-run equilibrium exchange rate ($S^e(LR)$) that will occur at some distant future point and *the whole intervening course of domestic and foreign interest rates*—as shown in Figure 20.9.

How can we pin down this long-run equilibrium exchange rate? In Chapter 19, we showed that, over several decades, purchasing power parity seemed a reasonable guide to how nominal exchange rates behaved. This suggests we can use PPP to pin down $S^e(LR)$. For instance, if over the next twenty years U.S. inflation is expected to be 40% higher than Japanese inflation, then PPP would suggest that over the next twenty years the dollar will depreciate against the yen by 40%—this pins down $S^e(LR)$. However, the dollar will not experience a straight line depreciation over this 20-year period; differences between U.S. and Japanese interest rates will add additional exchange rate dynamics.

This dependence on the whole future path of interest rates can potentially account for substantial volatility in exchange rates. Consider the case where the market expects only a temporary increase in U.S. interest rates over the next year. This does not affect $S^e(LR)$ (a temporary increase in interest rates is unlikely to affect long-run U.S. inflation) or even $S^e(1)$ (unless it influences interest rates more than one period from now). Therefore the effect on the current exchange rate is relatively small—the dollar appreciates by the amount of the interest rate increase.

However, compare this with the case where the United States increases interest rates and the market expects them to stay permanently higher. In this case, the dollar

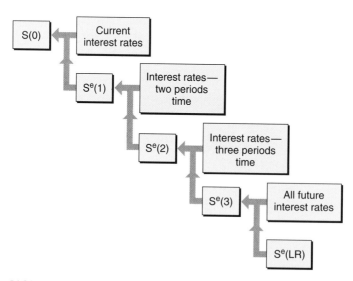

FIGURE 20.9   **Dependence of current exchange rate on all future interest rates.** Because the exchange rate depends on interest rates and exchange rate forecasts, the current exchange rate depends on all future interest rates.

will appreciate substantially. First, the permanently higher interest rates should lower long-run U.S. inflation. As a result, S^e(LR) will increase because PPP implies that the dollar depreciates less in response to the lower long-run U.S. inflation. Second, the whole future path of U.S. interest rates is now expected to be higher, so that according to UIP, the dollar now has to *depreciate* by more over the coming years. This faster depreciation is not just in the next year but in every subsequent year. To provide room for this depreciation, the dollar has to appreciate immediately and substantially relative to S^e(LR), which has itself increased anyway. As a result, a permanent change in monetary policy will exert a substantial impact on the current exchange rate and create volatility in the current exchange rates. Therefore, UIP implies that rational, forward-looking investors should generate a highly volatile exchange rate if changes in monetary policy are highly persistent.

KEY POINT

UIP explains exchange rate volatility by suggesting that changing expectations about current and future interest rates and inflation are likely to lead to substantial unpredictable changes in exchange rates.

20.6 Does UIP hold?

We have spent a lot of time outlining UIP, but we have not yet assessed the empirical validity of the model. Figure 20.10 shows the U.S.–Japanese interest rate differential between 2000 and 2003, as well as the monthly depreciation of the dollar against the yen. If UIP is to be a useful guide, on average the dollar should depreciate when U.S. interest rates are higher than those in Japan.

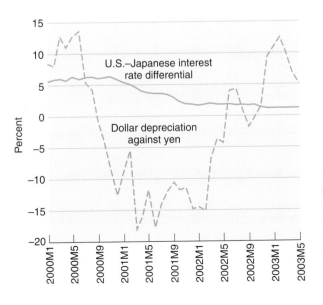

FIGURE 20.10 **Do interest rate differentials predict exchange rate depreciations?** If evidence for UIP is weak, countries with high interest rates often experience an appreciation. *Source:* Federal Reserve Board www.federalreserve.gov/releases

Throughout this entire period, U.S. interest rates were higher than Japanese rates, albeit at a diminishing rate. UIP would therefore predict a depreciation of the dollar over the entire period, but between January 2000 and July 2003, the dollar actually *appreciated* by 2%—from 116 to 119. In other words, not only would an investor have attained higher interest rates on dollars, they also would have benefited from an appreciation on the dollar.

Figure 20.10 is not just an isolated failure of UIP. It reflects something more systematic. We can examine this failure of UIP another way if we consider what happens when an econometrician runs the regression:

% depreciation of currency = constant + β × (domestic interest rate − overseas rate)

If UIP is correct, the interest rate differential should have a coefficient of one (β = 1). However, one survey of 75 published estimates of this regression found the average value was −0.88.[2] In other words, contrary to the implications of UIP, the currency of countries with high interest rates tends to *appreciate*.

KEY POINT

UIP is correct in predicting how exchange rates respond immediately to interest rates and monetary policy, but it is wrong in forecasting the exchange rate forward. Instead, high interest rate currencies tend to appreciate.

The result that high interest rate currencies tend to appreciate suggests that it may be possible to earn superior returns by investing in them. Support for this is shown in Figure 20.11, which compares cumulative returns to a U.S.-based investor with $1 in 1964 from three alternative investment strategies.

1. *U.S. Investment* Simply deposit $1 at U.S. interest rates and reinvest interest income.
2. *Lowest Interest Rate Currency* Place funds in whichever country has the lowest prevailing interest rate out of the five most heavily traded currencies (U.S. dollar, Japanese yen, German DM, U.K. pound, or Swiss franc). As well as earning interest, a nondollar investment is exposed to currency fluctuations.
3. *Highest Interest Rate Currency* Place funds in whichever country has the highest prevailing interest rate out of the five most heavily traded currencies (U.S. dollar, Japanese yen, German DM, U.K. pound, or Swiss franc). As well as earning interest, a nondollar investment is exposed to currency fluctuations.

If UIP holds, the three strategies should deliver roughly the same returns (since low interest rate currencies should tend to appreciate against high interest rate currencies). In practice, the failure of UIP means that investing in high interest currencies is a simple and profitable strategy. Note, however, that both the high and low interest rate currency strategies expose the investor to currency fluctuations, so the returns are volatile and risky. As our example of the Turkish lira earlier in this chapter suggests, this risk is

---

[2] Froot, "Short rates and expected asset returns," NBER Working Paper 3247 (1990).

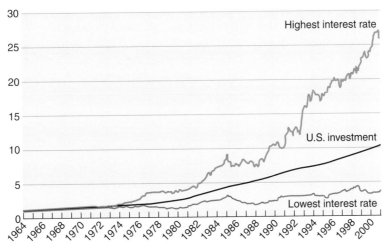

FIGURE 20.11   **Investment return on alternative currency strategies.** In contradiction to UIP, high interest rate currencies frequently earn a higher return. *Source:* Authors' calculations using IMF data.

substantial. Investors will need to assess whether or not the extra returns shown in Figure 20.11 compensate for this higher risk.

20.7 Introducing Risk Averse Investors

In an effort to make UIP fit the data better, this section modifies one of its assumptions—that investors ignore risk. When we moved from CIP to UIP, we stressed that the investor no longer covered the future exchange rate risk by buying forward. As a result, the exchange rate uncertainty makes the U.S. investment more risky for a Japanese investor than the yen investment. If Japanese investors are *risk neutral*, the extra risk/variability involved in the dollar investment does not influence their decisions. The investor only compares the expected return on the yen investment to the expected return on the dollar investment and does not worry about the uncertainty of the latter.

However, if Japanese investors are *risk averse*, then when given the choice between two assets with the same expected return, but where one is more risky, they will choose the less risky one. This means that to be indifferent between the yen and dollar investments, the Japanese investor will require a higher return on the U.S asset. This additional return required to compensate for higher risk is the **risk premium**. In this case we have to modify UIP so that

U.S. return = U.S. interest rate + expected dollar appreciation

= Japanese interest rate + risk premium

Imagine that Japanese investors require a risk premium of 2% on U.S. investments. Then if the Japanese interest rate is 1% and the U.S. interest rate is 4%, this equation tells us that the market is expecting a 1% fall in the dollar.

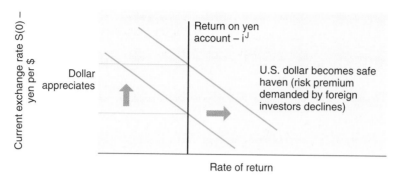

FIGURE 20.12   **Risk premiums and exchange rate fluctuations.** Introducing risk premiums produces a more volatile exchange rate.

So far we have only been considering the case of Japanese investors, but U.S. investors will also require a risk premium if they are to invest in yen accounts. Obviously, both U.S. and Japanese investors cannot simultaneously achieve a positive risk premium, so the sign and size of the risk premium will depend on the relative risk aversion of each group of investors and the perceived risk in each country.

Figure 20.12 shows the implications of introducing a risk premium into our UIP analysis. Consider the case where the risk premiums that Japanese investors demand from overseas investments decline—in this case the United States becomes like a "safe haven." For a given current exchange rate and unchanged U.S. interest rates, this is equivalent to boosting the risk adjusted return from investing in dollar accounts, so the overseas return schedule shifts to the right. This immediately strengthens the dollar. Therefore the perception that a currency is now less risky, or has become a "safe haven," will lead the currency to appreciate even if interest rates have not altered. Similarly, an increase in perceived risk will lead to a depreciation of a currency.

A risk premium adds an additional source of exchange rate volatility and can *potentially* explain why the currencies of countries with high interest rates tend to appreciate over time. If, when U.S. interest rates increase, the required risk premium for holding dollar assets increases by *more*, then our risk-adjusted UIP implies that the dollar should appreciate over the coming period. Consider the case where U.S. interest rates are 4%, Japanese interest rates are 1%, and the required risk premium on dollar assets is 2%. Our risk-adjusted UIP implies that the market is expecting a 1% depreciation of the dollar. However, if U.S. rates rise to 5% and, at the same time, the required risk premium *increases* to 5%, then our risk-adjusted UIP implies a dollar *appreciation* of 1%.

Do the data support this potential explanation of exchange rate volatility? The answer is no. Empirical studies based on interest rate data and market expectations of future exchange rates reveal that although a risk premium exists, and that it varies over time, it is neither large enough to account for the magnitude of exchange rate volatility nor correlated with interest rate differentials in the way UIP requires. The second problem is that, at least in the short run, exchange rate changes appear to be uncorrelated with macroeconomic developments, which rules out any role for risk premiums linked to macroeconomic variables. As one recent study concludes, "*the exchange rates of low-*

inflation countries are almost unrelated to macroeconomic phenomena."[3] Indeed, a seminal study in 1983 (whose results have remained essentially unchallenged) concluded that a wide variety of economic models of the exchange rate were unable to outperform the simple forecasting rule that the future exchange rate over the next year would remain unchanged.[4] In other words, macroeconomic data is not useful in forecasting short-run changes in the exchange rate. Despite an exhaustive hunt, researchers have struggled to overcome this result. PPP and inflation differences help to predict very long-run changes in exchange rates; the net savings/net exports approach helps explain medium-run changes in the real exchange rate and, using UIP, interest rates have some role to play in explaining how exchange rates respond to monetary policy. However, the majority of the substantial short-run fluctuations in exchange rates seem unrelated directly to macroeconomics.

As a result, exchange rate economists are pursuing new avenues. One of the most promising is to concentrate on the microstructure of exchange rate markets. This approach focuses on how currencies are actually traded and how their prices are set by market makers and how this may influence the behavior of exchange rates. We discuss this approach further in the next section.

KEY POINT

Introducing risk premiums into UIP can help explain more of the volatility in exchange rates, but ultimately UIP fails to successfully account for short-run fluctuations in exchange rates. While it correctly predicts how exchange rates react to interest rate changes, there seem many other factors that drive exchange rates that are not reflected in UIP. Over a six-month horizon there seems little role for macroeconomics in predicting exchange rates.

20.8 What Are Exchange Rate Markets Really Like?

To understand the way FX (Foreign Exchange) markets work, we focus on a survey of the London market.[5]

The first revealing feature is how quickly the market responds to economic information (see Table 20.2). Two thirds of respondents suggest that the market assimilates new information about interest rates within 10 seconds, and the overwhelming view is that markets have incorporated all macroeconomic developments within one minute.

The survey also tells us which economic variables FX dealers think most influence exchange rates. Figure 20.13 shows that the most significant variable is the interest rate, offering some support for UIP. Also important are unemployment and inflation, which are key determinants of monetary policy. Output and trade deficits have little impact.

---

[3] Flood and Rose, "Understanding Exchange Rate Volatility without the Contrivance of Macroeconomics," *The Economic Journal* (1999) vol. 109, pp. F660–F672.

[4] Meese and Rogoff, "Empirical Exchange Rate Models of the Seventies : Do They Fit Out of Sample?" *Journal of International Economics* (1983) vol. 14, pp. 3–24.

[5] Cheung, Chinn, and Marsh, "How do UK Based Foreign Exchange Dealers Think Their Market Operates?" NBER Working Paper 7524 (2000).

TABLE 20.2 **Responsiveness of Exchange Rates to Macro Information**
Proportion of respondents answering the question "How fast do you believe the market can assimilate the new information when the following economic announcements from the major developed countries differ from their market expectations?"

	<10 seconds	<1 minute	<10 minutes	<30 minutes	>30 minutes
Unemployment rate	51	44	10	1	1
Trade deficit	45	46	13	1	2
Inflation	49	40	14	2	2
GDP	29	50	23	1	3
Interest rates	65	30	9	0	3
Money supply	22	61	20	2	2

Exchange rates respond swiftly to macroeconomic data.
Source: Cheung, Chinn, and Marsh, "How Do U.K.-Based Foreign Exchange Dealers Think Their Market Operates?" NBER Working Paper 7524 (2000).

The survey offers little support for PPP. When asked the following:

In your opinion, the purchasing power parity condition
(a) can be used to compute the fair spot exchange rate
(b) proposes national price levels, once converted to the same currency via the appropriate exchange rate, should be the same
(c) is only an academic jargon and has no practical relevance to the FX market
(d) Other

sixty percent of respondents chose (c). Furthermore, 70% of respondents said they would take no trading action if PPP calculations indicated the dollar was overvalued; only 29% would sell the dollar. This all confirms what we saw in Chapter 19—PPP is a poor guide to short-run exchange rate developments.

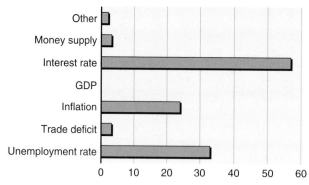

FIGURE 20.13 **Impact of economic data on exchange rates.** Proportion of respondents answering question "In your opinion, which one of the following economics announcement from the major developed countries has the biggest impact on the FX market?"
   Interest rates are the most important macroeconomic variable for the markets. *Source:* Cheung, Chinn, and Marsh, "How Do UK- Based Foreign Exchange Dealers Think Their Market Operates?" NBER Working Paper 7524 (February 2000).

TABLE 20.3   **What Drives Exchange Rates?**

Proportion of respondents answering the question "Select the single most important factor that determines exchange rate movements in each of the three horizons listed."

	Short Run Intraday	Medium Run (up to 6 months)	Long Run (over 6 months)
Bandwagon effects	51	13	1
Over reaction to news	57	1	0
Speculative forces	44	42	3
Economic fundamentals	1	43	80
Technical trading	18	36	11
Other	3	2	2

In the short run, macroeconomics has little influence on market participants.

Source: Cheung, Chinn, and Marsh, "How Do U.K.-Based Foreign Exchange Dealers Think Their Market Operates?" NBER Working Paper 7524 (2000).

The most informative part of the survey asks dealers what factors they think drive exchange rates at different horizons (see Table 20.3). Hardly anyone gives much of a role to macroeconomic fundamentals in the short run. Instead, the momentum of the market and the beliefs of dealers dominate (bandwagon effects, speculative forces, and overreaction to news). Over the medium run (up to 6 months), economic fundamentals play a bigger role, and bandwagon effects and overreaction cease to matter. But even at this horizon, speculative forces are just as important as macroeconomics. Only in the long run (over 6 months), do the macroeconomic fundamentals exert the main influence.

The idea that noneconomic factors may influence exchange rates in the short run has encouraged researchers to look at how the FX markets operate as a way to try to explain exchange rate volatility—economists call this the **microstructure** approach. A key variable in all microstructure models (whether it be equity markets, housing markets, or exchange rates) is **order flow**, which is used as a measure of buying and selling pressure. Order flow is the difference between buyer-initiated orders and seller-initiated orders. For instance, if an exchange rate dealer quotes an exchange rate of ¥100:$1 and receives $10mn orders purchasing dollars and $2mn selling dollars, the order flow would be +$8mn.

Figure 20.14 shows how order flows and exchange rates move closely together over time. Using order flow dynamics, the exchange rate becomes predictable over short time horizons, and the forecast produced is better than a "no-change" forecast that simply uses the current exchange rate as the future forecast. Although macroeconomic factors (in particular the interest rate) still play a role, it is small compared with the impact of order flows.

Although these results are striking, they are simply a statistical fact and raise the question *why* order flows matter so much for exchange rates. If macroeconomic factors were the only thing that determined exchange rates, and if this information were fully publicly available, then exchange rates would change even without order flows or

 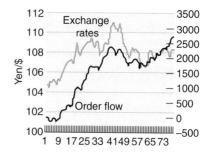

FIGURE 20.14   **Exchange rates and order flows, August 1999.** Buying and selling pressure closely mimics exchange rate fluctuations. *Source:* Evans and Lyons, "Order Flows and Exchange Rate Dynamics," NBER Working Paper 7317.

transactions. As soon as data were released, everyone would be aware of it, and the exchange rate would adjust immediately. Order flows start to matter when some information is not publicly available and is only revealed through trading. Even if all information is publicly available, investors may differ in their interpretation of what this data means for future exchange rates and interest rates. For instance, as more investors buy dollars, the market gets information that the dollar is underpriced and starts to increase its demand for dollars. The apparent significance of order flows in predicting exchange rates suggests that these effects are important.

KEY POINT

Microstructure models, which focus on the detail of how currencies are traded and their prices set, seem able to explain significant amounts of short-run exchange rate volatility and high levels of trading volumes. Order flows reveal information to market participants about market sentiment and how other participants view economic fundamentals.

20.9   Global Capital Markets

This chapter has focused on how the substantial flow of capital between countries influences exchange rates in response to differences in interest rates and asset returns. In this remaining section we focus on the economic rationale behind these capital flows.

As shown in Figure 20.15, the size of these capital flows has increased substantially over the last ten years. There are three reasons for this dramatic increase:

1. Advances in communications and large cost reductions. International telephone calls are less than 1% of their cost 30 years ago, and improvements in information technology will lower them further.
2. Removal of capital control constraints. Starting with the more developed economies, and now many emerging markets, capital account liberalization—the removal of restrictions on the inflows and outflows of capital between countries—has grown.

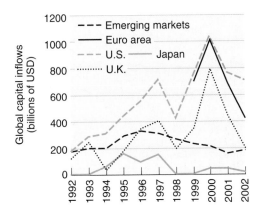

FIGURE 20.15 **Global capital flows.** Global capital flows increased substantially over the last decade. *Source:* IMF, *Global Financial Stability Report* (2003).

3. Deregulation of the domestic financial system. Over the last twenty years, many countries have deregulated their domestic markets and removed the monopoly power that providers of financial services enjoyed. This enables overseas financial institutions to enter and compete for market share.

HISTORICAL PRECEDENT

The huge capital flows we observe today tend to be seen as unprecedented. In terms of their absolute size in billions of dollars, this is true, but not when they are measured as a proportion of the economy. Around the end of the nineteenth century, capital flows between economies were enormous. Many economies that are now rich and part of the OECD were then emerging markets and were the recipients of huge capital inflows. This is shown in Figure 20.16, which plots the average capital account position (as a percentage of GDP) for 12 countries between 1870 and 2002.[6] To focus on the magnitude of the flows between countries, we show only the *absolute* value of the capital account—whether a

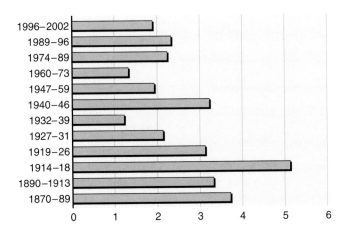

FIGURE 20.16 **Average absolute capital account surpluses (%GDP) for 12 OECD economies, 1870–2002.** Peak years for global capital flows were around the turn of the nineteenth century. *Source:* Obstfeld, "The Global Capital Market: Benefactor or Menace?" *Journal of Economic Perspectives* (1998) vol. 12, 4, pp. 9–30 and IMF, *International Financial Statistics*, 2003.

[6] Argentina, Australia, Canada, Denmark, France, Germany, Italy, Japan, Norway, Sweden, United Kingdom and United States.

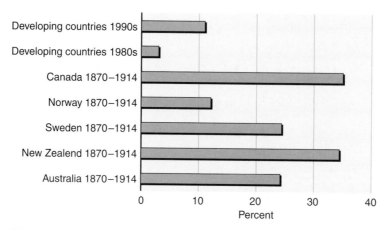

FIGURE 20.17   **Capital account flows to emerging markets as percentage of investment.** Compared to the past, only relatively small amounts of investment are financed through global capital markets. *Source:* Obstfeld, "The Global Capital Market: Benefactor or Menace?" *Journal of Economic Perspectives* (1999).

country has a capital account surplus of 5% of GDP or a deficit of 5% of GDP, it appears as 5% in Figure 20.16.

Figure 20.17 indicates the amount of investment in a country that the capital account has financed. Even after the surge in capital flows to developing economies in the 1990s, overseas capital financed proportionately less investment than 100 years ago.

SAVINGS AND INVESTMENT CORRELATION

The fact that so much investment is financed by domestic savings rather than through the capital account raises questions over the role of **global capital markets**. Capital markets use funds from savers and lend them to individuals/firms/countries that can invest them profitably. Therefore, countries that invest do not have to be the same as those who save. Indeed, if capital markets work well, we should not expect to find any cross-country correlation between savings and investment. However, Figure 20.18 shows that, among OECD countries, savings are strongly correlated with investment.

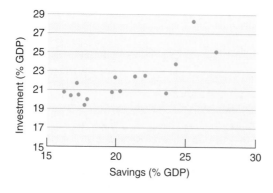

FIGURE 20.18   **OECD cross-country savings-investment correlations, 1980–2002.** High saving economies also have high investment. *Source:* Authors' calculations from OECD, *Economic Outlook* (June 2003), OECD database.

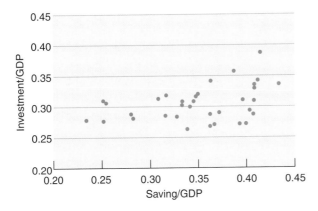

FIGURE 20.19 **Savings and investment correlation in Japanese prefectures, 1985–1990.** No correlation across Japanese regions between savings and investment means that the market works well. *Source:* Hess and Van Wincoop, *Intranational Macroeconomics* (Cambridge: Cambridge University Press, 2000)—Chapter 1, "Intranational versus International Saving-Investment Correlations."

Figure 20.19 shows the same calculation of the correlation between savings and investment, but for Japanese prefectures. Regions in Japan show very little correlation between savings and investment. This suggests that, within a country, the domestic banking system allocates funds from savers to investors on a much larger scale than occurs between countries. Even though flows between countries are large and growing, they do not lead to the kind of separation between savings and investment that we observe *within* a country.

A CONSUMPTION PUZZLE

As well as help finance investment, financial markets also finance people through bad times. Consider a construction worker whose income is seasonal—low in the first and fourth quarter of the year but high in the second and third quarter. To maintain consumption, the worker should borrow from the bank during the low-income quarters (see Chapter 13 for a full analysis). For this example to work, the bank must have funds to lend, and it will if there exists a retail worker who works hard during the Christmas quarter and in the New Year sales period but not for the rest of the time. Therefore in the first and fourth quarter, the retail worker, through the bank where she saves, lends the construction worker money. In the second and third quarter, the construction worker repays the retail worker and helps to maintain her consumption during her low-income periods. As a result, when financial markets help smooth out income fluctuations, individual consumption should show no correlation with individual income on a quarterly basis.

The above system works only for idiosyncratic income fluctuations, that is, changes that not everyone experiences. Consider, however, the case where the economy moves into recession and the income of both the retail *and* the construction worker falls. Both of them wish to keep consumption high in the recession, so both want to borrow. But because the income of both has fallen, the banking system cannot borrow money from one and lend to the other. As a result, the consumption of both workers will fall. The financial system can help smooth consumption against idiosyncratic shocks to income but not in response to aggregate income shocks that affect everyone. So with an efficient financial system, every person's consumption should rise or fall depending on what is

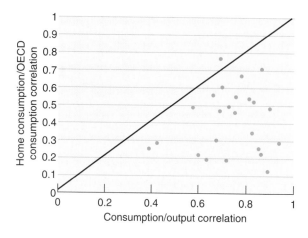

FIGURE 20.20   **Risk sharing amongst OECD nations, 1960–2003.** For OECD countries, output is more closely correlated than consumption over the business cycle. *Source:* Authors' calculations using IMF, *International Financial Statistics* (September, 2003).

happening to aggregate income, but individual consumption should not show any response to purely idiosyncratic fluctuations in income.

Applying this logic to countries suggests that national and world consumption should be strongly correlated and that this should be higher than the correlation between national consumption and national GDP. If, for instance, German GDP is weak today while French GDP is high, then France can temporarily lend money to Germany (Germany has a capital account surplus), which is then reversed when German GDP is stronger than French GDP in the future.

The evidence, however, suggests that global capital markets achieve only limited consumption smoothing with respect to country-specific output fluctuations. Figure 20.20 shows that for only 1 out of 28 countries is the correlation between national and OECD consumption greater than the correlation between national consumption and GDP.

KEY POINT

Global capital markets have shown substantial increases over the last twenty years due to declining costs and capital account liberalization. However, compared to 100 years ago, a larger proportion of investment is financed domestically. Further, national consumption is closely tied to fluctuations in GDP suggesting limited consumption smoothing across countries.

20.10   A Home Bias Puzzle

We have shown that even though capital markets are large and growing rapidly, evidence suggests that they are not as good as domestic institutions at performing the functions we expect capital markets to do, namely financing investment and smoothing consumption. In this section we show the reason for this—investor portfolios are heavily biased towards their home economy, they show a **home bias**. In other words, holdings of overseas assets are small, so domestic savings has to finance much domestic

TABLE 20.4 **Overseas Assets as Proportion of Private Sector Total Financial Wealth, 1998.**
Private sector portfolios are strongly biased towards domestic assets.

Country	Percent (%)	Country	Percent (%)
Australia	13.4	Japan	6.0
Austria	13.7	Netherlands	18.2
Belgium	15.0	Norway	5.6
Canada	7.2	Spain	2.3
Denmark	5.5	Sweden	10.0
France	4.2	Switzerland	14.5
Germany	6.7	U.K.	16.4
Ireland	28.0	U.S.	9.4
Italy	4.8		

Source: Data collected and kindly made available by Intersec, London.

investment. Savings and investment track each other closely over the business cycle; and each country's consumption relies heavily on its own output because portfolios are not sufficiently diversified.

Table 20.4 shows the percentage of the total financial wealth of the private sector held in overseas assets and shows evidence of limited international portfolio diversification.

Why are investment portfolios so internationally undiversified? Each of the following factors helps explain the lack of portfolio diversification we observe.

- Capital market restrictions
- Measurement issues
- Asymmetric information

CAPITAL MARKET RESTRICTIONS

Many OECD economies did not substantially remove capital controls until the 1980s, and only in the 1990s did several emerging markets follow this policy. Restrictions on capital account flows dramatically reduce holdings of overseas equity and can help account for the home bias in portfolios. However, capital controls cannot fully account for the magnitude of the home bias. For instance, there are few capital controls between France and Germany, but equity cross-holdings between these nations are still low.

MEASUREMENT PROBLEMS

Table 20.4 might overstate the lack of international diversification in portfolios. Consider a Finnish investor holding a large portfolio of Finnish equities. This may appear to be an instance of home bias, but closer inspection reveals that Nokia, the telecommunications company, accounts for more than 80% of the Finnish equity market. Nokia is an international firm and earns its profits around the world. Therefore, by buying shares in

Nokia on the Finnish exchange, the investor is diversifying her portfolio away from the Finnish economy. Such international diversification through holding domestic equity somewhat (but not completely) alleviates the home bias problem.

ASYMMETRIC INFORMATION

If you are a U.S.-based investor, you can easily gain information about U.S. firms and economic developments—trading screens, newspapers, television advertisements, and even conversations with taxi drivers are all potential sources of information. Getting this information is much more costly for non-U.S. based investors. Therefore, U.S. equity will be cheaper for U.S. investors, and they will have a much greater U.S. portfolio holding than non-U.S. investors. A close examination of OECD cross-border equity flows between 1989 and 1996 supports informational asymmetries as an explanation of the home bias puzzle. Table 20.5 shows the results of an econometric study of equity investment from country i into country j. First, the study indicated that a well-developed market system was needed for international capital investment. The larger the equity markets in country i and country j, the greater the equity investment from country i into country j. Further, the more sophisticated the financial markets of country i, the greater the outward investment it makes. Three key variables that reflect information flows between nations also affect overseas equity investment. The evidence suggests that the further apart two countries are geographically, the less equity flows between them. However, equity flows increase with the number of telephone calls between the two countries and with the number of bank branches the investing country has in the recipient country. Obviously the more telephone calls and the more overseas bank branches there are, the easier it is for overseas investors to gain information, so the more equity they are prepared to invest overseas.

KEY POINTS

Investment portfolios show limited international diversification and a bias towards domestic securities, a home bias. International diversification has been increasing with declines in capital controls and may not be as limited as the data suggests. Asymmetric information seems one factor in explaining this home bias.

TABLE 20.5   Determinants of Cross-Border Equity Flows

Variable	Effect
Market capitilization in investing country	+
Market capitilization in recipient economy	+
Distance between two economies	−
Telephone call traffic between two economies	+
Sophistication of investing countries' financial markets	+
Number of bank branches of investing country in recipient economy	+
Absence of insider trading in recipient economy	+

Source: Portes and Rey, "The determinants of cross border equity flows," CEPR Discussion Paper No. 2225 (September 1999), forthcoming *Journal in International Economics.*

SUMMARY

In section 20.1, we outlined the enormous size of the foreign exchange markets, which have daily turnover approximately the same as the annual GDP of Italy. Capital, rather than current, account transactions motivate these flows.

In section 20.2, we introduced covered interest parity (CIP), which states that because of arbitrage the interest rate differential between two countries is equal to the difference between the forward and spot rate. The evidence supports CIP because it involves riskless transactions.

With uncovered interest parity (UIP), the investor does not use a forward contract to buy the currency. Instead, as we described in section 20.3, the investor estimates the future spot rate and then holds the currency in the hope of trading at that rate in the future. UIP implies that the interest rate differential between two countries equals the percentage difference between the expected spot rate in the future and the current spot rate.

In section 20.4, we explained why UIP implies that a currency appreciates when its interest rate rises and depreciates when other interest rates increase. In section 20.5, we saw that expectations play a crucial role in UIP and that the current exchange rate depends on the whole expected future path of interest rates in the two economies.

In section 20.6, we examined the empirical evidence on the success of UIP. While UIP has some empirical successes, it predicts a negative relationship between interest rate differentials and future exchange rate changes, whereas in practice the relationship is positive.

Allowing for risk aversion among investors helps the empirical performance of UIP, but we concluded in section 20.7 that macroeconomic data seem to have no role to play in forecasting short-run changes in exchange rates.

To explain both the short-run volatility of exchange rates and the high levels of exchange rate trades, economists have begun to analyze the microstructure of foreign exchange markets. We saw in section 20.8 that the evidence supports the theory that order flows drive exchange rates in the short run and that market transactions reveal information. This can lead to bandwagon effects and market momentum that may be very different from the forces that macroeconomic fundamentals generate.

In sections 20.9 and 20.10, we examined global capital flows in more detail. Global capital flows have risen substantially over the last decade but most investment continues to be financed domestically. Investment portfolios show a lack of international diversification, which means that national consumption is closely tied to GDP and national savings correlate strongly with national investment.

CONCEPTUAL QUESTIONS

1. (Section 20.1) What has happened to the yen–dollar or yen–euro rate over the last month? What factors help explain it?

2. (20.2) U.K. interest rates are 4%, U.S. interest rates are 3%, and the current exchange rate is $1.60:£1. What should be the 6 month forward rate? The one year ahead forward rate?

3. (20.3) If the chair of the U.S. Federal Reserve Board warns of an overheating economy, what will happen to the dollar? Why?

4. (20.3) Imagine that U.S. interest rates are 5% and Japanese interest rates are 0.5% and you are buying a house in New York. Should you take out a yen denominated mortgage?

5. (20.4) In response to a 1% increase in inflation, the central bank raises nominal interest rates by 1%. Use UIP *and* PPP to work out what should happen to the current spot rate. How would your answer differ if the central bank raised rates by 2%? Why?

6. (20.5) Imagine you are a central banker who feels that an exchange rate appreciation would reduce inflationary pressures, but you wish to avoid raising interest rates today. What can you say in public to make the currency rise? What difficulties might this strategy cause?

7. (20.5) Is exchange rate volatility an obvious sign of a poorly operating market?

8. (20.6) Considering Figure 20.10, in what period would holding dollar, rather than yen, assets have performed best?

9. (20.7) Examine the newspapers of recent days. What economic or noneconomic factors have they used to predict likely exchange rate changes?

10. (20.8) You are aware of all public macroeconomic information but note that many dealers are buying the dollar even though you think the dollar is overvalued. How would you respond? Why do you think order flows appear to predict future exchange rates?

11. (20.9) What differences are there between national and global financial markets that can account for Figures 20.18 and 20.19?

12. (20.10) How hard is it for you to find information about companies listed on foreign equity markets? Does this explain the home bias puzzle?

ANALYTICAL QUESTIONS

1. (Section 20.1) The spot euro/£ is 1.5 and the one year forward euro/£ exchange rate is 1.6 per £. What is the forward premium for £ sterling? If covered interest parity holds, what is the euro-sterling interest rate differential?

2. (20.3) What is the dollar rate of return on a $10,000 investment in Tokyo if the Japanese interest rate is 1% and the yen–dollar exchange rate moves from 100 to 110?

3. (20.3) Interest rates between the United States of Albion (U.S.A.) and the Republic of Oz are currently the same. However, you now think there is a 50% chance that the Oz dollar will depreciate by 30% over the next week. What has to happen to interest rates in Oz to keep a fixed exchange rate with the U.S.A.?

4. (20.4) This morning the exchange rate between the United States of Albion dollar and the Republic of Oz dollar was 1.50:1 and interest rates in both countries were 6%.

   (a) If the market thinks that later today the Republic of Oz will raise interest rates to 8%, what will happen to the exchange rate?

   (b) If instead interest rates in Oz are increased to only 7%, what will happen to the exchange rate?

   (c) What is the relationship between exchange rates and interest rates in your example? Does this contradict UIP?

5. (20.4) The exchange rate between the United States of Albion (U.S.A.) and the Republic of Oz is now 1:1 with inflation in both countries expected to be 2% and interest rates 4%.

    (a) What does PPP imply about the exchange rate in 20 years time?

    (b) If inflation in the U.S.A. increases to 3% how does your answer change?

    (c) What happens to the current exchange rate if U.S.A. interest rates rise to 5% along with inflation increasing to 3%?

6. (20.9) Total national income in three countries over a recent, and typical, 10 year period are shown below

Year	1	2	3	4	5	6	7	8	9	10
Country A	10	8	7	9	10	14	12	16	18	8
Country B	11	12	11	13	15	8	7	16	18	10
Country C	10	12	13	11	11	7	9	5	4	10

    (a) Is there scope for risk sharing between countries? Describe exactly how this might work.

    (b) With which country should country A look to share risk?

Currency Crises and Exchange Rate Systems

Overview

In this chapter we analyze the international financial system— in other words, the manner in which exchange rates fluctuate between countries and how capital account flows are regulated. We begin by examining currency crises—dramatic falls in the value of a currency. We outline a variety of models to explain such crises and consider their applicability to currency crashes in Argentina, Europe, and Southeast Asia. We examine the potential role of foreign exchange intervention by governments and the actions of the IMF in preventing such crises. A controversial factor in explaining currency crises is the role of capital account liberalization, and we review the evidence for and against capital controls. We finally consider the various choices governments can make over their exchange rate regime—from dollarization and single currencies to purely flexible exchange rates. We analyze the pros and cons of these alternative regimes and recent trends in their popularity and close with an analysis of the single European currency, the euro.

Key Concepts

Capital Account Liberalization	First- and Second-Generation Models	Law of Excluded Middle
Capital Account Controls	Fixed Exchange Rates	Moral Hazard
Currency Board	Flexible Exchange Rates	Optimal Currency Area (OCA)
Currency Crises	Floating Exchange Rate	Original Sin
Debt Intolerance	Foreign Exchange Intervention	Single Currencies
Dollarization	Impossible Trilogy	Sudden Stop

21.1 Currency Crises

The most dramatic form of exchange rate volatility is a currency crisis—when an exchange rate depreciates substantially in a short period. Such events push macroeconomics to the top of news summaries and onto the front pages of newspapers. They

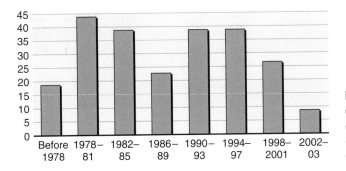

FIGURE 21.1 **Currency crises, 1978–2003.** Currency crises are a frequent occurrence. *Source:* Authors' calculations using IMF data.

can have huge political and commercial implications. In this section we will examine the frequency of currency crashes and outline theories to explain them.

A **currency crisis** must have two features: the exchange rate depreciation must be large relative to recent experience, and the nominal exchange rate depreciation must also affect the real exchange rate. In other words, the depreciation must not just reflect inflation and the operation of PPP. Even when we restrict our attention in this way, we still find that currency crashes are frequent. Figure 21.1 shows that between 1978 and 2003 nearly 250 currency crashes occurred.

Currency crises cause substantial economic upheaval and usually sharp falls in output. Table 21.1 shows GDP growth in a number of countries that have experienced currency crises. In each case, the currency crises produced large declines in GDP and sharp recessions either in the year of the crisis or immediately afterwards.

KEY POINT

Currency crises are large depreciations in exchange rates not driven by inflation differentials. Currency crises are a frequent occurrence, around 7–10 happening each year, and are often associated with substantial falls in GDP.

TABLE 21.1 **GDP Growth During Currency Crises**

Currency crises lead to dramatic declines in GDP.

	GDP Growth		
	Year Before Crisis	Year of Crisis	Year After
Argentina (2001)	−0.8	−4.4	−10.9
Indonesia (1997)	8	4.5	−13.1
South Korea (1997)	6.8	5	−6.7
Philippines (1997)	5.8	5.2	−0.6
Russia (1998)	1.4	−5.3	6.3
Thailand (1997)	5.9	−1.4	−10.5
Turkey (2001)	7.4	−7.5	7.8

Source: IMF, *International Financial Statistics* (March 2004).

21.2 First-Generation Models

Because currency crises tend to have enormous political, economic, and social implications, it is important to identify who is responsible for them. In so-called first generation models of currency crises, the answer is straightforward—the government is to blame for pursuing inconsistent domestic and external policies. When the crisis occurs, speculators and global capital markets are the main actors, and politicians blame them. But speculators are merely the messengers—and their message is that governments have to change their policy.

Consider the most straightforward first-generation model where a government announces a fixed exchange rate target but also pursues an expansionary fiscal policy.[1] To finance the fiscal deficit, the government uses the inflation tax (see Chapter 11) and prints money. However, such an expansionary monetary policy leads to low interest rates and capital outflows as investors seek higher returns overseas. In order to invest money overseas, investors sell the domestic currency leading to downward pressure on the exchange rate (see Chapter 20). In an effort to stop the exchange rate falling, the government will intervene and *buy* domestic currency and *sell* its reserves of foreign currency. This process is called foreign exchange intervention. In this scenario, the country is experiencing a large and continual fiscal deficit, high money supply growth, rapid inflation, and a fixed nominal exchange rate but an appreciating real exchange rate (because inflation is high). Further, government foreign exchange reserves are falling. This situation will continue as long as the government maintains its policy of fixing the exchange rate *and* simultaneously running a large fiscal deficit. If it dropped its commitment to a fixed exchange rate, it would no longer have to sell foreign exchange reserves to support the currency, and the exchange rate could depreciate. Alternatively, if it reduced its fiscal deficit, it would not need to increase the money supply, interest rates could be higher, less capital would flow out, and the exchange rate would not be under pressure. However, if the government does not change its policies, foreign exchange reserves will continue to fall—as shown in Figure 21.2.

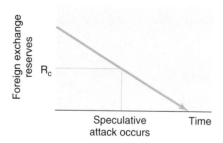

FIGURE 21.2 **First-generation models of currency crises.** Fiscal deficits cause foreign exchange reserves to fall and attack comes in advance of reserve depletion.

---

[1] This model is based on Krugman, "A Model of Balance of Payments Crises," *Journal of Money, Credit and Banking* (1979) vol. 11, pp. 311–325. Subsequent work has extended the relevance of the model, but the basic insights remain the same.

These circumstances cannot continue indefinitely—eventually the central bank will run out of foreign exchange reserves and the currency will depreciate sharply. However, the currency crash will occur *before* the central bank runs out of reserves. In particular, at a critical level of reserves (R_C in Figure 21.2), a speculative attack will occur, and the currency will drop. Why does this happen? Investors will not want to wait until the foreign exchange reserves of the central bank are zero. At this point everyone knows the currency will depreciate sharply, and anyone holding it will lose money. Therefore the investor will want to sell the domestic currency *before* reserves run out. When the central bank has high levels of foreign currency reserves, it can withstand the pressure of a speculative attack—investors selling the domestic currency. But when reserves reach the critical level, they are too low to offset the sell orders for the domestic currency. Investors know that in a few months reserves will be exhausted, and the currency will crash. At this point they sell the domestic currency in large amounts, and the government either wastes what little reserves it has left or immediately devalues the currency.

When all this occurs, the government will blame investors. They will argue that the government was committed to defending the exchange rate and that it still had several months of foreign exchange reserves left. However, according to first-generation models, this is beside the point. Domestic and external policy are so inconsistent that a sharp depreciation of the currency is inevitable. By simultaneously pursuing two inconsistent aims, the government has caused the currency crisis. These first-generation models cannot account for all currency crashes. However, they do explain the volatile exchanges of Latin America in the 1970s when governments tried to target the exchange rate to stabilize high inflation rates while still running large fiscal deficits.

> **KEY POINT**
>
> First-generation models explain currency crises as the inevitable consequence of governments running inconsistent monetary and fiscal policy. In order to control inflation, governments fix their exchange rate but find themselves having to print money in order to finance their fiscal deficit. When reserves reach a critical level, speculators will sell the currency and, in the absence of sufficient reserves or a change of fiscal policy, the government will have to devalue.

21.3 Second-Generation Models and the ERM Crisis

Although first-generation models can account for many features of Latin American crises in the 1970s and 1980s, they cannot shed any light on the currency crisis that hit the European Exchange Rate Mechanism (ERM) in 1992. The ERM was a system of fixed exchange rates among European countries. Each currency had a central exchange rate around which its value could vary within certain specified bands. Governments could either buy and sell foreign exchange reserves to keep exchange rates within these bands or change interest rates. If these policies did not work, the central parity (the midpoint of the bands) would have to be altered. In practice, the key country in the ERM was Germany, with countries effectively linking their currency to the deutschemark. For a country to fix its exchange rate against another country, PPP implies that both countries must have the same inflation rate. UIP implies that they should also share the same interest rates. Therefore ERM membership meant that countries had to adopt the same monetary policy as Germany. Given Germany's postwar record in achieving low and stable inflation, this was seen as one of the advantages of the ERM for participating countries.

KEY POINT

In a fixed exchange rate system, uncovered interest parity implies that a country has to adopt the same monetary policy as the country it fixes its exchange rate against.

In the early years of the ERM, realignments were common, but by the early 1990s, devaluations were increasingly rare, and governments wanted to avoid them; the ERM had become a stable system of fixed exchange rates. In September 1992, however, turmoil hit the European foreign exchange markets. Germany was experiencing rapid economic growth as a result of unification between East and West Germany. This strong growth was leading to inflationary pressures, and the Bundesbank (the German central bank) began raising interest rates. However, elsewhere in Europe economies were struggling with weak GDP growth. In order to maintain a fixed exchange rate countries had to follow German interest rates. Internally, however, they wanted to lower interest rates to fight off a recession. There was a conflict between the external and internal goals of monetary policy.

Events first developed on September 8 when Finland devalued its currency by 13%, and Sweden was forced to raise interest rates from 24% to 75%. By September 10, pressure had moved onto the Italian lira, which fell by around 7% (although it still remained within the ERM). However, on September 16 and 17, the system came under intense pressure. The pound sterling came under attack, and despite enormous sales of foreign exchange reserves by the Bank of England, and British interest rates increasing from 10% to 15%, the pound was eventually devalued by around 15%. British membership in the ERM was suspended. The Italian lira also came under renewed attack, and Italy also left the ERM with a similar size devaluation. Pressure continued. The Spanish peseta fell by around 5%, and Swedish and Irish official interest rates reached 500% and 300% respectively. Market focus then switched to the French franc, and France raised interest rates by 2.5%. However, the French managed to remain in the ERM, at the previous central exchange rate, and by the end of September, the crisis was abating. The three-week crisis had seen Italy and the United Kingdom leave the system, substantial devaluations of central rates for other countries, high interest rates, and huge depletions of central bank foreign exchange reserves.

What caused the crisis? Table 21.2 suggests that first-generation models cannot account for the currency crash. While countries had different experiences, there were no sharp differences between those that had to leave the ERM, or devalue, and those that remained. Further, although some countries had seen an increase in fiscal deficits, this was due to the fact that 1992 was a recession year for most countries and inflation re-

TABLE 21.2   European Inflation and Fiscal Deficits, 1990–1992

Before the ERM crash of 1992, there were no broad-based signs that European economies were running large fiscal deficits or had high inflation—this is not a first-generation crisis.

| | Fiscal Deficit (% GDP) | | | Inflation (%) | | |
	1990	1991	1992	1990	1991	1992
U.K.	1.5	2.8	6.5	8.0	4.7	3.5
Spain	4.3	4.5	4.1	6.5	6.4	6.4
Finland	5.4	1.1	5.5	5.8	5.6	4.1
Ireland	2.3	2.4	2.5	2.1	8.5	5.5
Sweden	−4.2	1.1	7.8	9.9	10.3	2.2
Germany	2.1	3.3	2.6	2.7	3.7	4.7
France	1.5	2.0	3.9	2.8	3.2	2.4
Italy	11.2	10.2	9.6	6.3	6.9	5.6

Source: IMF, *International Financial Statistics* (September 2000). Courtesy of IMF.

mained subdued. There were no substantive general signs of large and persistent fiscal deficits (with the exception of Italy).

To account for the ERM crisis, economists developed a new set of currency crisis models (called rather unimaginatively second-generation (SG) models). In SG models, a fixed exchange rate can survive indefinitely as long as the currency is not attacked. However, if the currency comes under selling pressure, the fixed exchange rate peg will go. SG models therefore possess "*self-fulfilling equilibria.*" If investors think the fixed exchange rate is stable, they will not attack, and the fixed exchange rate will survive. However, if they believe the exchange rate is vulnerable, they sell the currency and the exchange rate target will fail—investor beliefs are self-fulfilling. Such a model can explain the ERM crisis. There is no need to suggest that poor policies were in place before the currency crash. It can also explain why some countries with greater credibility (notably Germany and France) survived the crisis, while other countries (Italy, the United Kingdom) were forced to leave the ERM.

SG models are based on three key assumptions:

1. Governments want to maintain the fixed exchange rate because it yields benefits, such as lower and stable inflation.
2. Governments also perceive advantages in abandoning the fixed exchange rate. For example, they can loosen monetary policy and stimulate the domestic economy.
3. The perceived advantages to dropping the fixed exchange rate increase the more investors think that the exchange rate will depreciate.

In Figure 21.3 we have drawn the benefits from maintaining the fixed exchange rate as being constant regardless of investors' beliefs. However, the benefits from leaving

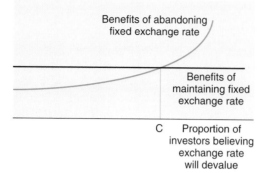

FIGURE 21.3 **Second-generation models of currency crises.** With second-generation models, the government no longer defends the exchange rate target when a large number of investors think a devaluation is imminent.

the system increase as investor confidence in the exchange rate target falls. Investors show their beliefs by buying or selling domestic currency. As more investors believe that the exchange rate is going to be devalued, interest rates have to increase to prevent capital outflow. The less confidence investors have in the fixed exchange rate, the greater the required increase in interest rates. However, the higher are interest rates, the greater the incentive for the government to abandon the pegged exchange rate by devaluing and choosing a looser monetary policy to avoid recession.

Below the point marked C in Figure 21.3, the benefits exceed the costs to the government of staying in the system, and it will defend the currency. However, if investor confidence in the fixed exchange rate deteriorates to a position above C, then the system is no longer stable. If investors start to sell the currency, the government will abandon the exchange rate peg because the costs of holding the line exceed the benefits. This model helps to make sense of the lament of ERM-country finance ministers that capital markets forced them to leave the system—without an attack and if investor confidence remains to the left of C, the government is perfectly happy to stay in the system. Only when this confidence deteriorates are governments no longer prepared to pay the price of membership in the fixed exchange rate system.

While SG models allow for self-fulfilling equilibria, fundamentals still play a role. Fundamentals have three relevant ranges. One range occurs where the fundamentals of the economy and policy are so strong that the fixed exchange rate is secure, no matter what investors believe. Another range occurs when a currency crash is inevitable because the fundamentals are so poor. Finally over an intermediate range, the self-fulfilling equilibria of SG models apply and a currency crisis depends on investor behavior.

KEY POINTS

Second-generation models suggest that currency crises are not inevitable but depend upon the beliefs of foreign exchange traders. If a sufficient number of investors believe a currency is overvalued, then the government will find it too costly to defend the exchange rate and a devaluation will occur. If only a few investors believe a currency is overvalued, it may be possible for the government to maintain a fixed exchange rate.

21.4   The Asian Crises—A Third Generation?

In 1997 the fast-growing economies of Southeast Asia experienced a currency crisis. The problems began in Thailand, but soon spread to Indonesia, Malaysia, South Korea, and the Philippines. Taiwan, Singapore, and Hong Kong also felt the pressure. During this period, the behavior of capital markets was so volatile that the Asian currency crises spilled over in a contagious manner to other emerging markets as far away as Russia, South Africa, and Brazil. These currency crises blended together aspects of both first- and second-generation models whilst also containing additional features—in particular the problems of a **sudden stop** in external financing and the way in which domestic financial systems are badly impacted by currency crises which, in turn, contributes to a sharp economic slowdown.

In the early 1990s, many Asian economies *liberalized* their capital accounts to allow for the free flow of capital in and out of the economy. After several decades of fast growth, and with seemingly robust fundamentals, these economies received large amounts of capital inflow. For instance, in 1996 the 5 largest Association of Southeast Asian Nations (ASEAN) economies had a capital account surplus of $55bn. But by 1998 confidence in these economies was reduced, and they now had a capital account *deficit* of $59bn. Instead of *receiving* an additional $55bn a year to fund investment, these economies had to *pay out* $59bn. External financing (that is, financing of these countries' high investment rates by foreign investors) came to a "sudden stop" and the shift from a large capital account surplus to a large deficit produced dramatic declines in exchange rates (a process explained in Chapter 19). As these Asian currencies fell, foreign investors became worried about the falling dollar value of their Asian investments and started to withdraw more funds. As a result of this investor flight, the Indonesian rupiah fell by more than 80%, the Thai baht by 50%, and the Korean won by 55%.

To prevent these collapsing currencies, Asian central banks sold their foreign exchange reserves (i.e., their holdings of dollars, yen, deutschemark) and bought their own currencies (selling well over $50bn of reserves); they also borrowed extensively from the IMF and other international institutions (over $100bn of loans were arranged) and they aggressively raised interest rates. Eventually the pressure on the currency subsided, but the large increase in interest rates and the dramatic outflow of capital from the banking system left economies in a severe recession (see Figure 21.4).

At first glance, first-generation models seem unlikely to explain the Asian currency crises. In 1996 Indonesia, Malaysia, the Philippines, and Thailand recorded fiscal surpluses and although South Korea had a deficit, it was only 0.1% of GDP. With few obvious fiscal problems and low inflation, the essential mechanism behind first-generation models seems inappropriate in this case. Second-generation models also seem unlikely as an explanation. All of these economies were benefiting from fast growth, stable inflation, and no unemployment problems. With governments committed to a fixed exchange rate and with no obvious clash between this external target and internal economic aims, the situation in Asia did not mimic that of the ERM and provide the conditions for self-fulfilling crises.

However, closer inspection of these countries suggests that both models may have some explanatory power after all. Although governments were running fiscal surpluses, it can be argued that, due to government guarantees to the financial system, government

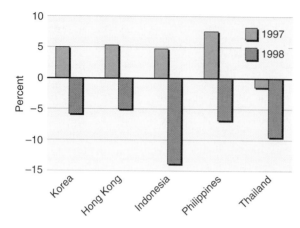

FIGURE 21.4   **Asian GDP growth, 1997–1998.** The Asian crisis saw dramatic falls in exchange rates, large increases in interest rates, and sharp recessions. *Source:* IMF, *International Financial Statistics.* Courtesy of IMF.

finances were deteriorating. In other words, first-generation models could explain the currency crisis in Asia. To see how, consider the following example. In 1997, U.S. corporate bonds yielded an interest rate of 7%, compared to 12.5% in Korea. The exchange rate was 900 Korean won to the dollar. If a Korean bank borrowed $1bn from the United States, it would pay $70 million in interest a year (7% of $1bn). If it then lent this amount to Korean firms but in domestic currency terms, it would loan 900bn won and receive interest of 112.5bn (12.5% of 900bn) which, at the prevailing exchange rate, equals $125 million. If the exchange rate doesn't change, then this represents a substantial profit ($55mn) for the bank. By encouraging its banking system to pursue this strategy of borrowing cheaply in dollars and lending in won domestically, Korea will find itself being able to offer plenty of credit to its corporate sector to fuel investment and hopefully GDP growth.

The risk in this strategy is that the exchange rate could fall. Uncovered interest parity (Chapter 20) says that because Korean interest rates are 5.5% higher than U.S. interest rates, we should expect the Korean won to depreciate over the next year by 5.5% to 950 won to the dollar. At the new exchange rate, the 900bn won loan repayment to the bank now amounts to approximately only $0.945bn. The bank therefore faces a $55mn shortfall—exactly equal to the surplus interest it has earned by lending in domestic currency. If the currency falls by more than 5.5%, then the repayment shortfall is greater than the profits on interest rates. With a 50% devaluation (which Korea experienced) the 900bn won is worth only $0.67bn. In this case the bank needs to find an additional $0.33bn to repay the loan. If the government is expected to bail out the banks in the case of a sharp devaluation of the won, then government liabilities are the level of government debt plus its commitments to the banking sector. In our example, when the fixed exchange rate holds, these liabilities to the banking system are $0bn. With a 5.5% devaluation, this additional liability is $55m, and with a 50% devaluation, it reaches $0.33bn. Therefore, although the actual fiscal deficit may seem small, the true extent of government's fiscal liabilities worsens sharply as the exchange rate falls. By allowing for this government commitment to the banking sector, we can explain the Asian currency crises through first-generation models. As the banking system borrows more funds from overseas, the liabilities of the government increase.

The role of the banking sector also helps explain the severity of currency crises. As the currency starts to depreciate, banks find themselves lacking funds to repay their foreign currency loans. As a result, they start calling in other loans they have made to domestic firms. To repay these loans, firms will have to sell off their assets, such as real estate. These sales will lead to a fall in real estate prices in general, which will lead other firms to find that the collateral they have offered to banks when they borrowed has now fallen below the value of their loans. This will further worsen the balance sheets of banks and lead the banks to call in more loans, producing further falls in real estate prices and a general vicious circle. The impact of this banking crisis will be even worse if banks were not very proficient at allocating funds and made large numbers of ill-advised loans. This combination of a currency crisis and a banking crisis (a so-called twin crisis) will have a dramatic impact on output, investment, and the banking system. One study finds that on average an emerging market currency crisis tends to lower output by 5.1%, but a twin crisis lowers output by 13.3%.

The fact that the health of the banking sector depends on the exchange rate because of foreign currency debt also opens up the possibility that second-generation models can explain the Asian crisis. If investors believe the exchange rate is fixed and will not devalue, then governments do not need to set high interest rates to attract funds. But if enough investors believe the exchange rate will devalue, then the currency will come under pressure. As the exchange rate starts to fall, this will create a deficit in the banks' balance sheets and they will experience a shortage of foreign currency when trying to repay their overseas debts. In order to encourage capital inflows to help finance this foreign currency shortfall, the government will seek to raise interest rates. But higher interest rates make corporate debts harder to service and lower real estate prices, further worsening the value of firms' collaterals and weakening the banking sector. Therefore the internal target of protecting the domestic banking system conflicts with the external target of achieving a fixed exchange rate. This is the essence of second-generation currency crises.

Support for this second-generation interpretation of the Asian currency crisis comes from surveys of investor confidence. Every year *Euromoney* surveys investors' rankings of the stability of different economies—the lower the number, the more stable and robust the economy is perceived to be. As Figure 21.5 shows, before 1997, there were few signs that investors were concerned about the economic fundamentals of the region. With no perceptions of problems before the crisis, this line of thought suggests that the crisis itself must have provoked the problems—that investor overreaction and panic led to the currency crash. Advocates of this view of the Asian crisis do not deny that policy mistakes were made nor that the fundamentals of the economy may have been weak. They criticize domestic banking regulation that did not monitor and prevent an excessive dependence on short-term borrowing in foreign currency to fund long-term real estate investments.

KEY POINT

The Asian currency crises of 1997 have aspects of both first- and second-generation models. In addition, they emphasize the key role of the financial sector and its exposure to exchange rate fluctuations and the danger of abrupt "sudden stops" in capital inflows.

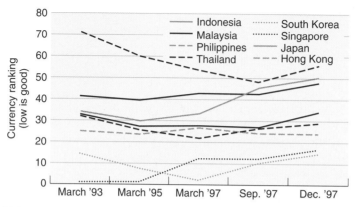

FIGURE 21.5 **Euromoney country risk ratings.** There was no evidence from credit rating agencies before the crash of an impending crisis. *Source:* Radelet and Sachs, "The East Asian Financial Crisis: Diagnosis, Remedies, Prospects," *Brookings Papers on Economic Activities*, 1:1998. http:www.hiid.harvard.edu/pub/other/asiacrisis.html

ORIGINAL SIN AND DEBT INTOLERANCE

At the heart of the twin crisis problem is the dependence of emerging markets on foreign currency denominated debt. If emerging markets could borrow in domestic currency terms, then the fall in the exchange rate would not create a hole in the balance sheets of the financial sector. However, financial markets are extremely reluctant to lend in the domestic currency of emerging markets due to a phenomena dubbed **original sin**. First-generation models tell us that countries with weak governments and poor institutions often repay debts by using the inflation tax—printing money. Foreign investors will therefore not wish to lend to such countries in domestic currency terms for fear of a devaluation. The phrase "original sin" reflects the fact that nearly all emerging markets, even those with good past performance as borrowers, are deemed vulnerable to the temptation to monetize their borrowing. As a result, as shown in Table 21.3, nearly all emerging market debt has to be denominated in foreign currency terms, usually the dollar. While an emerging market can always issue more of its own currency, it obviously cannot print U.S. dollars. Because emerging market debt is denominated in foreign currency terms, even quite low levels of borrowing (as a percentage of GDP) make a country vulnerable to exchange rate devaluations. As a result, emerging markets suffer from **debt intolerance**—they experience financial problems even though they borrow substantially less than richer OECD nations. Between 1970 and 2001, one in eight of emerging markets defaulted on debt even when debt was less than 40% of GDP and a further two out of five countries defaulted when debt was between 41 and 60% of GDP, moderate levels of borrowing compared to OECD nations. This fragility to external financing also makes these countries very vulnerable to "sudden stops" in capital inflows, for second-generation reasons. If investors are concerned that the financial system is too exposed to foreign currency borrowing, they withdraw their funds, precipitating a currency decline and a financial crisis. If investors feel that the level of borrowing is manageable, then the capital inflows continue and the fixed exchange rate holds.

TABLE 21.3 **Percentage of Foreign Currency Denominated Debt, 1999–2001**
Emerging markets have to borrow mainly in foreign currency terms.

U.K., U.S., Switzerland, Japan	8%
Euroland	9%
Other Developed Countries	72%
Developing Countries	93%
Latin America	100%
Middle East and Africa	90%
Asia and Pacific	94%
Eastern Europe	84%

Source: Eichengreen, Hausmann, and Panizzi, "Currency Mismatches, Debt Intolerance and Original Sin," CESifo Working Paper Series No. 563.

KEY POINT

Original sin refers to the fact that foreign investors prefer to lend to emerging markets in foreign currency, making the financial sectors of debtor nations very exposed to currency crashes. As a consequence, many emerging markets show debt intolerance—even relatively low levels of debt can prove unsustainable.

21.5 Foreign Exchange Rate Intervention and the IMF

When capital account outflows occur, investors sell the domestic currency and buy foreign currency, which puts downward pressure on the exchange rate. In order to avoid a depreciation, a government can raise interest rates in an effort to persuade investors to keep their money in the country. But as our discussion of second-generation models suggests, there may be limits to this policy, due to the weakness of the domestic economy or the banking system. Another option is for the government to instruct its central bank to engage in foreign exchange intervention, namely to buy the domestic currency being sold by selling the central bank's foreign currency reserves.

The central bank will sell foreign currency if it wants to stop its domestic currency falling but will buy foreign currency and sell domestic if it wants to stop the exchange rate rising. For instance, in 2004 central banks of Asia owned huge amounts of foreign currency reserves, more than $2.1trillion. Japan had $777bn of FX reserves, China $403bn, Taiwan $215bn, Korea $160bn, and Singapore $101bn. This came about because the United States was running very large current account deficits with this region, so that Asian exporters were receiving lots of dollars from U.S. consumers. If Chinese firms tried to sell these dollars to buy the Chinese currency, remnimbi, this would lead the dollar to fall and the remnimbi to rise. To stop this happening, the Chinese central bank intervened to buy the dollars and give remnimbi to firms. This stops the Chinese currency appreciating, although at the expense of increasing the Chinese money supply (because it has issued remnimbi).[2] Note that, as a result of this intervention, what is in effect happening is that Asian central banks are providing the credit (by expanding their own money supply) with which the United States can run a trade deficit with Asia. By continuing to accumulate dollar currency reserves, the Asian banks are continuing to provide the funding needed to finance the U.S. current account deficit. As Jacques Rueff, a French economist, put it in 1965: "If I had an agreement with my tailor that whatever money I pay him returns to me the very same day as a loan, I would have no objection at all to ordering more suits from him."

THE ROLE OF THE IMF

The only limit to this strategy of buying foreign currency is the inflationary pressures it may create through increasing the money supply. Aside from this constraint, the central bank can always issue its own currency. However the central bank cannot continuously intervene to stop its currency *falling*. To do this, it needs to be able to buy domestic currency and sell foreign currency. This can only continue as long as the central bank has foreign currency reserves to sell. If the central bank runs out of foreign exchange reserves, it will have to borrow foreign currency from other central banks or from the IMF (see Chapter 9 for an overview of the IMF and how it lends funds). For instance, in 1997 the IMF lent, or coordinated loans of $17.2bn to Thailand, $58.2bn to Indonesia, and $42.3bn to South Korea. In 1998 it loaned Brazil $41.5bn and Russia $22bn. The idea behind these IMF loans is to provide foreign currency reserves to help stop a falling exchange rate. If foreign investors believe that the IMF loan is enough to stabilize the exchange rate, then private sector capital may return once the fear of further devaluation is removed.

The IMF does not, however, automatically lend foreign currency to countries on request. If the IMF loan is to be used to buy a depreciating domestic currency, then the borrower country will be unable to repay the original loan if the currency continues to fall in value. Therefore, critical to the IMF making a loan is the belief that the underlying cause of the currency crisis is removed. From a first-generation model perspective, this will involve commitments by the country to improve its fiscal position by cutting expenditure and increasing revenue. From a second-generation model perspective, the very provision of the loan by the IMF may be enough to resolve the currency crisis especially if steps are also taken to improve the health of the financial system.

IMF lending to a country in a currency crisis is extremely controversial. Three key questions are:

1. Does IMF intervention work?
2. Is IMF intervention good for the economy?
3. Does IMF lending make emerging markets more volatile?

---

[2] To try and prevent central bank purchases of foreign currency from increasing the money supply, they can **sterilize** the intervention. This occurs when at the same time as buying foreign currency, the central bank sells bonds to mop up the extra domestic money supply it has issued.

DOES IT WORK?   The main aim of IMF intervention is to restore balance of payments equilibrium by reducing capital account outflows and so stabilize the exchange rate. The success of this policy will depend on many factors: One is improved policy. Are the policies the IMF suggests being successfully and enthusiastically implemented? Is there credibility that these policies will be maintained in the future? For instance, in 1997, when the IMF lent substantial funds to Korea, capital outflows continued because there was widespread doubt about the government's initial willingness to implement the desired IMF reforms.

Another key factor for the success of IMF lending is the size of the loan. Due to capital account liberalization (which is described further in the next section of this chapter) the amount of private sector capital flows has increased enormously. Therefore, for IMF loans to work, they have to involve ever larger amounts of money to counteract the large scale private sector outflows. These loans are now so large that some commentators doubt whether the IMF can respond to future currency crises unless it can boost its own capital reserves.

IS IMF INTERVENTION GOOD FOR THE ECONOMY?   At the heart of most IMF advice is the need to remove the imbalances in the economy that have led to a dependence on capital inflows. This normally leads to policy recommendations to reduce demand and the need to borrow and is accompanied by an improvement in fiscal balances and an increase in interest rates. Some observers suggest, however, that the policies recommended by the IMF actually worsen the economic situation and create a severe recession. These critics suggest that countries should pursue alternatives to IMF loans. The two obvious alternatives are to introduce capital account controls and stop investors withdrawing funds from the economy (as Malaysia did in 1997) or to simply default (as Russia did in 1998 and Argentina in 2001) as well as at the same time implementing more growth-orientated policies.

The difficulty in assessing whether IMF intervention helps the economy is in knowing what would have happened had the IMF not intervened. Figure 21.6a–c compares the performance of a range of emerging market economies. Both those who borrowed from the IMF between 1973 and 1999 and those who did not are included. All the figures are centered around the time of the crisis for each country. The impact of IMF conditions on these economies is clear—fiscal policy is much tighter and interest rates much higher. Both sets of economies show recoveries, but those in receipt of IMF loans recover somewhat less vigorously. These data are suggestive, but it is not enough for us to firmly conclude that IMF intervention is unhelpful. Perhaps countries that had to borrow from the IMF faced more severe crises than those who didn't borrow and this explains their worse GDP performance. Without a way to compare that happened with IMF intervention and what would have happened to the same economy with no intervention, this debate is hard to resolve.

DOES IMF LENDING MAKE EMERGING MARKETS MORE VOLATILE?   A common criticism of IMF involvement is the **moral hazard** it creates. Emerging markets are a riskier investment opportunity than the advanced nations. As such, investors should require a higher return. But if investors know that, in the event of a currency crisis, the IMF will

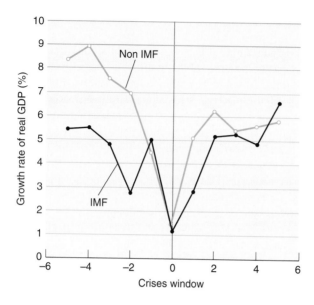

FIGURE 21.6a   **GDP growth compared.**

intervene and use funds to try and stop the currency falling, they face a reduced risk, which may encourage them to overinvest. The result will be too much lending and not enough focus on the quality of that lending. As Jeffrey Sachs once wrote "if central banks devote their resources to a defense of the exchange rate and if the IMF dedicates its funds to the defense of the central bank then lending to emerging markets is like shooting fish in a barrel."[3] Without the prospect of an IMF bailout, investors would

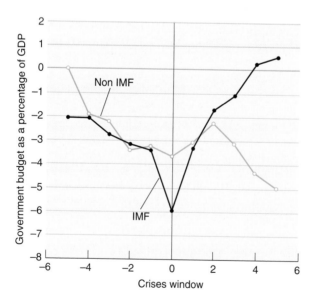

FIGURE 21.6b   **Fiscal deficits compared.**

[3] Sachs, *The Economist*, September 12, 1998.

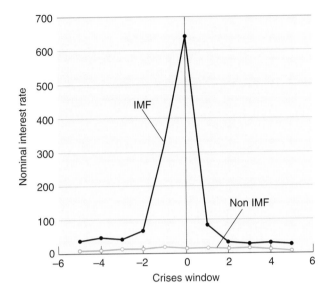

FIGURE 21.6c **Interest rates.** IMF intervention leads to tighter fiscal policy, higher interest rates, and slightly lower GDP growth. *Source:* Bordo and Schwartz, "Measuring Real Economic Effects of Bailouts: Historical Perspectives on How Countries in Financial Distress Have Fared with and without Bailouts," Working Paper 7701, http://www.nber.org/papers/w7701.

curb their lending, flows would be less volatile and, by implication, there would be fewer currency crises and less need for the IMF to provide huge funds to bail out investors.

The IMF is also accused of worsening the moral hazard problem in emerging markets by lending at very low interest rates to what are often very risky countries. Countries that borrow from the IMF pay roughly U.S. interest rates and, in some cases, even lower rates. However, one feature of IMF lending is its extremely low default rate. As of April 2003, only four countries were in arrears with the IMF—Iraq, Liberia, Somalia, and Sudan—and total arrears amounted to only 0.4% of total lending. Given the authority and importance of the IMF, not repaying them comes with a huge stigma. Countries will try to avoid defaulting on loans to the IMF because doing so would lead them to pay very high interest rates to borrow in future years, or even be locked out from foreign borrowing.

Many observers note that focusing only on outright arrears exaggerates the quality of IMF loans. Often the IMF will grant extensions to an existing loan if a country has difficulties in repaying (although, like the original loan, this extension once more comes with many conditions attached.) Between 1973 and 1997, the IMF was involved in 615 loan arrangements, and nearly 12 percent of these (73) were granted extensions. Table 21.4 shows that between 1947 and 1999, the IMF lent to 186 countries (column (1)). One hundred fifty-eight of these loans have been repaid (column (2)) and, on average, loans lasted for 8 years. However, as of 1999 there remained 93 unpaid loans (column (3)). Given that the average loan lasts for 8 years (column (6)), the most worrying unpaid loans are those issued before 1991, a total of 64 (column (3), last two rows). For 44 of these countries (column (4)), the amounts owed to the IMF in 1999 exceed what they originally borrowed; in other words, their arrears are mounting. Thirty-nine of these are countries who have never successfully repaid an IMF loan (column (5), last two rows). Therefore, although the IMF has a very low default rate, it is increasingly finding itself rolling over loans to countries whose economic situation remains poor.

TABLE 21.4   IMF Repayment Record

	Number of Countries (1)	Number Completed Debt Cycles (2)	"Incomplete" Debt Cycles			Average Duration of Cycles (years)	
				Countries with . . .			
			Total (3)	1999 Debt Exceeding Initial Borrowing (4)	No Completed Cycles (5)	Completed Cycles (6)	Incomplete Cycles (7)
All Countries	186	158	93	64	60	7.9	16.6
Industrial Countries	25	31	0	0	0	4.7	n.a.
Developing Countries	161	127	93	64	60	8.6	16.6
Africa	52	25	39	29	28	6.5	21.4
Asia	29	22	14	8	9	10.0	20.1
Europe	28	10	23	16	20	10.1	6.8
Middle East	14	14	2	2	0	9.1	8.5
Western Hemisphere	37	56	15	9	3	8.5	17.1
poor countries	79	29	52	42	38	6.4	20.5
not poor	82	98	39	22	21	8.3	14.9
Memorandum Items: excluding cycles initiated after 1991							
poor countries	79	29	44	34	32	6.4	23.3
not poor	82	93	20	10	7	8.6	22.2

Very few countries default outright on IMF loans but often loans are rolled over as debt increases. *Source: Jeanne and Zettelmeyer, "International Bailouts, Moral Hazard, and Conditionality," Economic Policy (Blackwell Publishers, 2001) vol. 16, pp. 407–432.*

KEY POINT

Central banks can try and stabilize their exchange rate through foreign exchange intervention. To defend a falling currency, the central bank needs to sell its foreign currency reserves. When these are depleted, the country can borrow from the IMF subject to satisfying certain conditions. These conditions are aimed at eliminating the source of a country's borrowing needs.

21.6   Capital Account Liberalization

During the late 1970s and early 1980s, the rich OECD nations removed **capital account controls**, allowing investment funds to flow in and out of their countries with few restrictions. During the 1990s, partly at the prompting of the IMF, this process of **capital account liberalization** also happened in numerous emerging markets—as shown in Figure 21.7. This policy became increasingly controversial as many of the countries that removed capital account controls, including Thailand, Korea, Indonesia, Brazil, and Argentina, experienced painful economic recessions in the wake of currency crises.

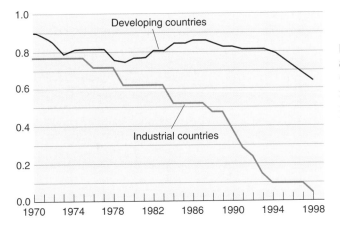

FIGURE 21.7 **Capital account restrictions, 1970–1999.** Capital account controls reduced over time especially in advanced nations. *Source:* Prasad, Rogoff, Wei, and Kose, "Effects of Financial Globalization on Developing Countries: Some Empirical Evidence," *International Monetary Fund* (March 17, 2003).

There are several arguments supporting capital account liberalization for emerging markets:

- *Financing investment and stimulating growth* According to the convergence growth models of Chapter 4, poor countries with low levels of capital should offer a high investment return. Therefore, capital account flows can help finance a high level of investment and rapid economic growth without depending on domestic savings.
- *Risk diversification* As we saw in Chapter 20, capital account flows also help share consumption risk, so that country-specific fluctuations in output do not need to affect consumption.
- *Improving government policy* Global capital flows also impose discipline on policymakers. If domestic and foreign investors can withdraw funds from a country that pursues poor policies, the government will be forced to adopt better economic policies (what Thomas Friedman calls the "golden straitjacket" in his book *The Lexus and the Olive Tree*).
- *Increasing efficiency of financial sector* Capital account liberalization is also claimed to lead to improvements in financial sector efficiency through TFP transfer. As foreign banks and financial firms enter along with foreign investment "best practice" techniques and strategies are adopted in the emerging market.

Despite these strong theoretical claims regarding the benefits of capital account liberalization, empirical evidence is much less conclusive. As Barry Eichengreen of the University of California, Berkeley, states "Capital account liberalization ... remains one of the most controversial and least understood policies of our day ... empirical analysis has failed to yield conclusive results."[4] This can readily be seen in Figure 21.8, which shows that there is no clear pattern between the degree of capital account openness, i.e., the lack of controls, and the growth of an economy. This suggests, at the very

[4] Eichengreen, "Capital Account Liberalization: What Do Cross-Country Studies Tell Us?" *World Bank Economic Review* (2001) vol. 15, no. 3, pp. 341–365.

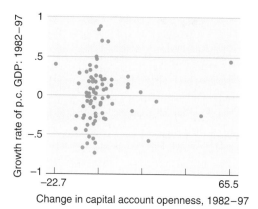

FIGURE 21.8   **Capital account liberalization and economic growth, 1982–1997.** There is no simple correlation between capital account liberalization and GDP growth. *Source:* Prasad, Rogoff, Wei, and Kose, "Effects of Financial Globalization on Developing Countries: Some Empirical Evidence," *International Monetary Fund* (March 17, 2003).

least, that capital account liberalization on its own is not sufficient to generate economic success.

Market imperfections can help explain why capital account liberalization does not boost growth. There may, for instance, be asymmetric information which leads foreign investors to lend too much money and into unprofitable sectors. If the domestic banking system is poorly regulated or lacking experience, then these funds will suffer further misallocation problems. Therefore capital account liberalization can lead to excessive risk taking and poorly allocated funds. Further, the volatility of these capital flows and the resulting economic fluctuations they cause may serve as a further restraint on investment and so slow growth. Many commentators of the 1997 Asian crisis argue that these problems were prevalent. Whether it be the measured tones of U.S. Federal Reserve Board Chairman Alan Greenspan ("In retrospect it is clear that more investment monies flowed into these [Asian] economies than could profitably be employed at reasonable risk.") or the more forthright comments of Malaysian Prime Minister Mahatir Mohammed (describing the global capital markets as "a jungle of ferocious beasts"), the behavior of global capital markets inspires increasing concern.

The severity and frequency of currency crises in emerging markets has dented the confidence of many of the proponents of capital account liberalization. While there is still belief in the advantages that it brings, there is much greater awareness of the problems that it produces. The growing consensus is that capital account liberalization should be pursued but not at too rapid a pace. In particular, countries should seek to develop a well regulated and sound domestic financial system before fully opening up their capital account.

KEY POINT

Capital account liberalization on its own may not benefit an economy, but needs to be sequenced appropriately with other policies if it is to boost long-term growth. In particular, a well regulated and experienced domestic banking system would appear to be critical to gain the maximum benefits.

21.7 | Exchange Rate Regimes

There are a range of exchange rate regimes available to countries, varying in the flexibility they allow for the exchange rate. With a **floating exchange rate**, the value of a country's currency can vary freely depending on the forces analyzed in Chapters 19 and 20. By contrast, with a **fixed exchange rate**, the government will either change interest rates or sell/buy foreign currency to maintain a fixed value for the currency, as described earlier in this chapter.

Throughout the nineteenth century (until 1914), and again for some time in the 1920s and 30s, a fixed exchange rate system (the Gold Standard) operated. Under this system, a country fixed its currency to be worth a certain amount of gold, which defined a system of fixed exchange rates between different currencies. Between 1945 and 1971, under the Bretton Woods system, only the dollar was pegged against gold, and all other currencies were pegged to the dollar. Since 1971, the world has experimented with flexible exchange rates and various reformulations of fixed exchange rate systems. In this section we will examine in detail how these various regimes operate and their relative advantages and disadvantages.

Table 21.5 lists the broad categories of exchange rate regimes that countries can adopt. Allowing the most variations in exchange rates are floating systems:

- *Pure float* The most flexible system is a pure free float. In this case, the exchange rate can rise and fall depending on fluctuations in supply and demand and the government does not need to adjust fiscal or monetary policy or intervene to try and achieve any particular value. The best current example of a pure float is the U.S. dollar.
- *Managed float* The next most flexible system is a managed float where although the government does not target a specific exchange rate, it does intervene by buying and selling foreign exchange to try and moderate fluctuations in the exchange rate. This best describes the recent behaviour of the Japanese yen.

TABLE 21.5 **Exchange Rate Regimes**
Countries can choose from a wide range of different exchange rate regimes.

Floating Regimes	Pure float
	Managed float
Intermediate regimes	Target zone
	Basket peg
	Crawling peg
	Adjustable peg
Fixed regimes	Truly fixed exchange rate
	Currency board
	Dollarization
	Single currency

Intermediate between floating and fixed exchange rates are a range of systems that try to fix the exchange rate but allow for changes over time:

- *Target zone* Target zone systems allow the exchange rate to fluctuate but only within certain prescribed bands, as was the case with the European Exchange Rate Mechanism and currently with the Danish krona against the euro.
- *Basket peg* More flexibility can also be provided if a country pegs its currency against a basket of currencies (as in Botswana and Kuwait) rather than just one.
- *Crawling peg* Another option for a country is to adopt a crawling peg (as currently used in Bolivia and Tunisia) where a fixed exchange rate is announced but so too is a profile over time that allows the exchange rate to change in a managed way.
- *Intermediate peg* The final possible intermediate arrangement is an adjustable peg where a fixed exchange rate is targeted but the system allows flexibility through periodic revaluations.

Finally there are the more rigid fixed exchange rate systems:

- *Truly fixed* A truly fixed exchange rate exists when the government commits to a specific exchange rate and there are no tolerance bands or preannounced option to revalue. An example of such a system was the CFA zone in sub-Saharan Africa, linked to the French franc.
- *Currency board* A currency board is a stronger version of a truly fixed exchange rate. Under a **currency board**, the central bank of a country is committed to exchanging its monetary liabilities at a fixed exchange rate. The monetary liabilities of a central bank are essentially the currency that it has issued. Therefore the central bank can only issue as much domestic currency as it has holdings of foreign currency, given the fixed exchange rate. For instance, the Hong Kong Monetary Authority (HKMA) operates a currency board based on an exchange rate of HK\$7.80 : US\$1. If the HKMA has U.S. dollar reserves of US\$80bn, it can issue domestic currency worth $7.80 \times \$80\text{bn} = \text{HK}\$624\text{bn}$. The domestic central bank can only expand the money supply by obtaining more foreign exchange. If instead its foreign exchange reserves fall, then so will the domestic money supply.
- *Dollarization* With a currency board, although a central bank has no choice over how much domestic currency to issue, it still does issue a currency. Under **dollarization**, a country voluntarily eliminates its own currency and adopts a foreign currency, such as the dollar or the euro. In effect, it closes down its central bank.
- *Single currency* Finally, two or more countries can come together and collectively adopt a **single currency**, e.g., they merge their central banks, as the participating countries of the euro have done.

THE IMPOSSIBLE TRILOGY

To understand the advantages and disadvantages of a fixed exchange rate, we begin with the **impossible trilogy**, which says that a government can choose at most *two* of the following *three* options:

1. Independent monetary policy—the ability to choose its own interest rates to achieve domestic targets
2. Fixed exchange rate
3. Capital account liberalization

In other words, if a country chooses a fixed exchange rate, it must either abandon an independent monetary policy or impose capital controls. Similarly, countries that liberalize their capital account have to either forego a fixed exchange rate or an independent monetary policy.

To understand the impossible trilogy, consider again the case of uncovered interest parity (see Chapter 20), which is based on an arbitrage relationship in which investors reallocate funds to the country that offers the highest expected return. This reallocation can only happen in the absence of capital controls. According to the impossible trilogy, a government that has liberalized its capital account cannot also operate both a fixed exchange rate and an independent monetary policy. This is because the key result of UIP was that interest rate differentials equal expected exchange rate depreciations. Under a fixed exchange rate, the expected devaluation is zero. Therefore UIP implies that interest rates should be the same between countries with fixed exchange rates—the countries cannot run independent monetary policies. If the fixed exchange rate regime allows for small fluctuations around a central rate, then interest rates can differ between countries in the expectation of small depreciations. Adding a risk premium to UIP allows for more interest rate differentials. However, even if interest rates do not have to be *identical*, there will be strong linkages. Countries that participate in a fixed exchange rate system will tend to raise interest rates together even if not by exactly the same amount.

With capital controls it is possible to have a fixed exchange rate *and* choose an independent monetary policy. Consider the case of a country with a fixed exchange rate that unilaterally lowers its interest rate. Without capital controls, investors would move funds out of the country to overseas where a higher return can be earned. This would put downward pressure on the currency and threaten the exchange rate target. If capital controls are in place, this outflow can be restricted and so pressures on the exchange rate can be avoided; with capital controls, the government can have an independent monetary policy *and* an exchange rate target. Without capital controls the impossible trilogy tells us that the cost of a fixed exchange rate is the inability to choose a monetary policy to suit the country's specific circumstances.

KEY POINT

Countries face a wide range of options when choosing an exchange rate regime. The impossible trilogy tells us that countries without capital controls effectively face a choice between a fixed exchange rate or an independent monetary policy.

ADVANTAGES OF FIXED EXCHANGE RATES

- *Providing a nominal anchor* According to the impossible trilogy, a country with no capital account controls and a fixed exchange rate has no choice over its monetary policy. In other words, the exchange rate is a nominal anchor that pins

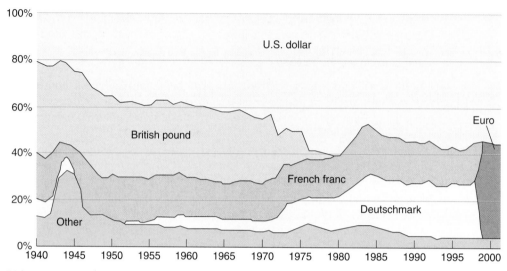

FIGURE 21.9 **Anchor currency choices, 1940–2001.** Countries choose the dollar and the euro as obvious pegs due to their low inflation. *Source:* Meissner and Oomes, "Why Do Countries Fix the Way They Fix?," IMF Working Paper forthcoming (2004).

down monetary policy. For countries with a poor or unreliable record in controlling inflation, this is a major advantage—for these nations giving up an independent monetary policy is an advantage. Figure 21.9 shows which countries are chosen most frequently as an anchor currency. Given their good inflation track record, it is not surprising that the dollar and the euro play a major role.

- *Encouraging trade and investment* It is widely believed that reducing exchange rate volatility boosts trade between countries and encourages FDI and investment, thereby aiding long-run GDP growth.
- *Avoiding speculative bubbles* Under floating, exchange rates show substantial swings that can lead to long-term and far reaching misalignments from their fundamentals.
- *Reducing risk premium* If countries can issue debt in their own currency, then investor fears of devaluation will lead to higher interest rates via a risk premium. A credible fixed exchange rate will remove the risk of devaluation and lower interest costs.

ADVANTAGES OF FLOATING EXCHANGE RATES

- *Independent monetary policy* By not adopting a fixed exchange rate, the impossible trilogy allows a country to have no capital controls and also to choose interest rates to achieve internal domestic targets rather than influence the exchange rate.
- *Automatic adjustment to trade shocks* Consider a country that experiences a fall in the price of its major export. With a fixed exchange rate, the only way the country can regain competitiveness is if prices, wages, and costs fall. This is a

painful and often protracted process, depending on the flexibility of labor markets. With a floating exchange rate, adjustment can occur almost instantaneously through a devaluation.

- *Seignorage and lender of last resort* With a currency board, single currency or dollarized economy, the central bank cannot act as a lender of last resort, that is, it cannot bail out the banking system by increasing the money supply. Therefore under a flexible exchange rate system, the central bank has greater ability to protect a fragile banking sector. The central bank is also free to choose how much seignorage to raise. In the case of a dollarized economy, the country earns no seignorage at all.

- *Avoid speculative attacks* As we have outlined in the first part of this chapter, fixed exchange rates are vulnerable to speculative attack. By not forcing governments to intervene to prop up a currency, floating exchange rates can avoid this problem.

EXCHANGE RATE ARRANGEMENTS

The choice of an exchange rate regime will vary from country to country depending on its circumstances. Table 21.6 documents exchange rate systems around the world. It shows that a wide range of different regimes are utilized in different countries, suggesting that no one single regime is appropriate for everybody. Further, the choice may change as a country's economy evolves.

TABLE 21.6 **Exchange Rate Regimes, 2003**

Regime	Number of Countries	Examples
No separate legal tender	41	Euro area, Ecuador, Panama, Eastern Caribbean Currency Union, CFA Franc Zone, Kiribati, Marshall Islands, Micronesia, Palau, San Marino, Timor-Leste
Currency board	7	Bosnia, Darussalam, Bulgaria, Hong Kong, Djibouti, Estonia and Lithuania
Other conventional fixed pegs	42	China, Malaysia, Saudi Arabia, Ukraine, Botswana, Bangladesh, Jordan, Barbados, Lesotho, Nepal, Syria, UAE, Zimbabwe, Namibia, Bhutan
Pegged exchange rates within horizontal bonds	5	Denmark, Cyprus, Egypt, Hungary, and Tonga
Crawling pegs	5	Bolivia, Costa Rica, Nicaragua, Solomon Islands, Tunisia
Crawling bands	5	Belarus, Honduras, Israel, Romania, Slovenia
Managed float	45	Indonesia, Iran, Czech Republic, Argentina, Ethiopia, Kenya, Vietnam, India, Nigeria, Russia, Singapore, Jamaica
Independently floating	37	Australia, U.S., U.K., Sweden, Brazil, Poland, South Africa, Sweden

Source: IMF Annual Report on Exchange Arrangements and Exchange Restrictions (2003).

Given our discussion of the advantages and disadvantages of fixed and flexible exchange rates, we can say that fixed exchange rates make more sense for a country the more it fulfils the following properties:

- poor reputation for controlling inflation, so it benefits from following another country's monetary policy
- significant levels of trade with a country whose exchange rate is being targeted, so there are substantial gains from lowering transaction costs
- similar macroeconomic shocks as the country whose exchange rate is being targeted, so little is lost from giving up an independent monetary policy
- relatively little involvement in global capital markets, so the exchange rate is not at risk from sudden stops
- flexible labor markets, so that in the face of export price shocks the country can regain competitiveness
- high levels of foreign exchange reserves, so in the case of selling pressure, the central bank can intervene to maintain the exchange rate peg.

As Table 21.6 suggests, smaller economies often meet these requirements—in particular they often are heavily linked through trade with other nations and their business cycle is also driven by developments in the larger nation. This explains why San Marino, Panama, Lesotho, and El Salvador have all dollarized and why Belgium, Netherlands, and Luxembourg were all enthusiastic participants in the euro. However, larger economies tend to be less exposed to trade and often have more independent business cycles so that flexible exchange rates are more desirable. The obvious reference cases here are the United States, the European Union, and Japan. While the member states of the EU have joined together in a single currency, the euro has a flexible exchange rate with no specific target against the dollar, yen, or any other currency.

THE LAW OF THE EXCLUDED MIDDLE

With increasing numbers of emerging markets adopting capital account liberalization, the logic of the impossible trilogy says that nations either have to adopt an independent monetary policy and float or adopt a fixed exchange rate. Further, the experience of many currency crises countries and the logic of second-generation models suggests that it is better to have a *very* fixed exchange rate system, such as a currency board or dollarization, rather than a more flexible target zone or fixed exchange rate system. The greater the political and institutional costs of leaving a fixed exchange rate system, the less likely are investors to believe that the currency will devalue and so the peg is more robust as it is less liable to second-generation crisis. This implies that the intermediate regimes described earlier are not a viable long-run choice—countries have to be based at either one of the extremes, a result known as the **Law of the Excluded Middle**. In line with the logic of the Law of the Excluded Middle, a number of countries have recently adopted extreme versions of fixed exchange rates—Ecuador and El Salvador have both dollarized, Estonia, Lithuania, Bulgaria, and Bosnia have all adopted currency boards, and 12 European countries joined together to launch the euro. Figure 21.10 also shows supportive evidence for the excluded middle—the proportion of countries with either floating rates or a hard peg have risen over time, especially during the 1990s. In the remaining sections of this chapter, we will investigate in more detail two of these more extreme fixed exchange rate systems—currency boards and single currencies.

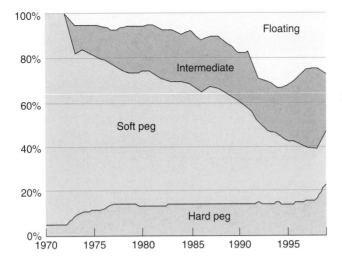

FIGURE 21.10 **Law of excluded middle.** Countries seem to be adopting more extreme versions of fixed exchange rates. *Source:* Rogoff, Husain, Mody, Brooks, and Oomes, "Evolution and Performance of Exchange Rate Regimes," IMF Working Paper 03/243 (December 2003).

KEY POINT

The appropriate exchange rate regime will vary depending on a country's circumstances and may even change over time. It will differ from country to country. A number of countries have adopted extreme versions of fixed exchange rates in recent years leading to discussion of the Law of Excluded Middle—the idea that countries either have to choose flexible exchange rates or extreme versions of fixed exchange rates.

21.8 Currency Boards and Crisis in Argentina

At the time of writing, there are 7 currency boards in operation—Bosnia and Herzegovina, Brunei Darussalam, Bulgaria, Hong Kong SAR, Djibouti, Estonia, and Lithuania. The currency board in Dijbouti has been in place for nearly 50 years and in Hong Kong since 1985. More recently, Argentina instigated a currency board in 1991 but was forced to exit in 2001.

As Figure 21.11 shows, currency boards have a good record in improving overall economic performance—inflation, inflation volatility, the fiscal deficit, and growth all improve under a currency board compared to alternative regimes. Under a currency board, countries cannot print money not backed by foreign currency reserves, so the central bank can no longer finance the government's fiscal deficit. As a result, a currency board without fiscal reform is unworkable—the pressure for the central bank to print money and abandon the currency board will become overwhelming. Therefore currency boards tend to be adopted as part of an overall package to reduce high inflation. Without broad-based reform, the adoption of a currency board alone will not produce the superior economic performance of Figure 21.11.

Argentina represents the most infamous recent example of a currency board. The country experienced inflation of 3177% in 1990 due to the need to create enough money for large and persistent fiscal deficits. In 1991, President Carlos Menem and his Finance Minister Domingo Cavallo introduced a currency board setting an exchange

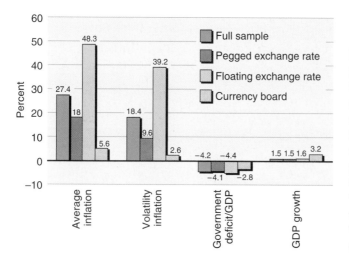

FIGURE 21.11 **Economic performance under currency boards.** Currency boards combined with fiscal reform produce substantial improvements in macroeconomic performance. *Source:* Ghosh, Gulde, and Wolf, "Currency Boards: The ultimate fix?" IMF Working Paper 98/8 (1998). Courtesy of IMF.

rate of 1 peso equals one dollar. The results were extremely impressive—by 1995 inflation had fallen to 4%, annual GDP growth was averaging 7.5% and the exchange rate remained unchanged between 1991 and 2001. However, in late 2001 Argentina dramatically abandoned its currency board in a manner that caused much tension between its government, the IMF, and international investors. What went wrong? Several things:

- *Real exchange rate appreciation* Although Argentinean inflation fell rapidly, for several years it remained higher than that in the United States, leading to a real exchange rate appreciation (because the nominal exchange rate was fixed) that contributed to an economic slowdown in the tradeable goods sector.
- *Labor market rigidities* With a fixed exchange rate, the only way to maintain competitiveness is through downward price and wage adjustments. However, wages in Argentina were not sufficiently flexible, which led to unemployment rates of around 18%.
- *Inappropriate monetary policy* The peso was linked to the dollar and so had to follow general trends in U.S. interest rates. However, the United States was enjoying its longest ever economic expansion while Argentina was in the midst of a recession and wanting lower interest rates. Further, the strength of the U.S. economy led to a strong dollar and so a strong peso. However, only 15% of Argentina's trade is with the United States—26% is with Brazil and 20% with the EU.
- *Recession* Inappropriate interest rates, inflexible wages, and a high real exchange rate produced a recession. This led to an increase in the fiscal deficit as well as causing investor concern over whether the government was prepared to raise interest rates to defend the currency while the economy was in recession.
- *Fiscal deficit* The fiscal deficit became increasingly large, and as political support for the government wavered, the chances of turning this around diminished causing growing concern amongst investors. The large deficit was not purely due to the recession but also reflected a failure of the government to pursue fiscal reform.

- *Foreign currency denominated debt* In order to keep interest costs low, the government issued dollar-denominated debts so that by 2001, 72% of its debt was dollar denominated. Government debt was not at particularly high levels (50% of GDP), although with negative GDP growth and high interest rates it was increasing. Moreover, with 72% of its debt dollar denominated, the government's fiscal sustainability was heavily dependent on the exchange rate.

In December 2001, with the economy shrinking by 4.5%, negative inflation, the government paying a 30% interest premium to compensate lenders for the risk of default, and unemployment at 18%, Argentina abandoned the currency board. The peso fell sharply—from 1 peso equals $1 to nearly 4 pesos to the dollar by May 2002. This dramatic fall in the peso caused a huge increase in the peso value of government and financial sector debts leading to widespread bankruptcies, disruption of the financial system, and debt default.

The experience of Argentina illustrates many of the themes of this chapter:

- *First-generation insights* Argentina attempted to maintain a fixed exchange rate while continually running fiscal deficits. Currency boards cannot work unless fiscal reform also occurs.
- *Second-generation insights* There was a growing conflict between the need to lower interest rates to get out of recession and the need to keep interest rates high to maintain the exchange rate.
- *Wrong regime choice* Argentina linked its currency with a country it does relatively little trade with and whose business cycle was out of step with its own.
- *Sudden stops* By the end of 2001, capital inflows into Argentina were grinding to a halt and domestic investors were withdrawing funds. Because of original sin, Argentina borrowed in dollars, and because of depreciation, suffered from debt intolerance even though debt was not at particularly high levels.

KEY POINTS

Currency boards require fiscal reform if they are to be successful at reducing inflation. Argentina's currency board collapsed due to a lack of fiscal reform and wage flexibility and the decision to link to the dollar.

21.9 The Euro

On January 1, 1999, 11 European nations permanently fixed their exchange rate against each other and launched the euro.[5] On January 1, 2002, the countries' legacy currencies, e.g., the deutschmark, the franc, the lira, were withdrawn and euro notes and coins became legal tender in all countries. The size of these countries and their

---

[5] The 11 countries were Austria, Belgium, Finland, France, Germany, Ireland, Italy, Luxembourg, Netherlands, Portugal, and Spain and were subsequently joined by Greece. At the time of writing Denmark, Sweden, and the United Kingdom are yet to join.

cooperation in launching a new currency is an unprecedented modern money experiment. Does it make sense for these countries to share one currency and one monetary policy?

The theory of **optimal currency areas (OCA)** argues that there are four criteria for adopting a common currency:

- *The degree of trade between countries who adopt a common currency* If countries trade heavily between each other, then a single currency significantly reduces transaction costs.
- *The extent to which different countries experience similar shocks* If countries experience the same shocks, then they will wish to set the same interest rates so they do not lose by having a common monetary policy.
- *The degree of labor market mobility in each region* If regions face different shocks but implement the same monetary policy, then if labor can move between regions, this will help stabilize the economy.
- *The amount of fiscal transfers between regions* If regions face different shocks, labor is immobile, and both regions face the same interest rates, then fiscal transfers between regions can maintain welfare standards.

HOW DOES THE EURO AREA MATCH UP AS AN OCA AND HOW DOES IT COMPARE TO THE U.S., WHOSE STATES ALL USE A SINGLE CURRENCY?

LEVELS OF EUROLAND TRADE   Figure 21.12 shows the percentage of intra-EU trade for each EU country. Clearly the countries are closely interlinked. On this criteria, the EU countries do seem to constitute an optimal currency area.

SIMILARITY OF SHOCKS   Figure 21.13 shows the extent to which each GDP in each EU country is correlated with the EU average. A strong correlation suggests that countries experience similar business cycles to the rest of the EU and so has no need to run a separate monetary policy.

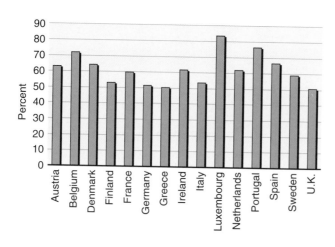

FIGURE 21.12   **Importance of EU trade for EU countries, 2002.** High levels of trade between EU countries make a single currency more feasible and attractive. *Source:* OECD (2004).

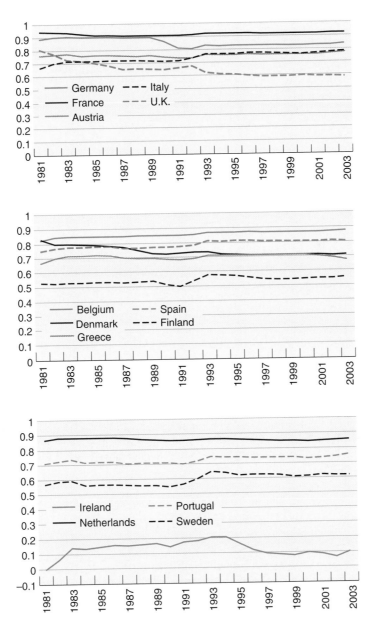

FIGURE 21.13   Correlation of GDP growth in EU countries. There is a core group of countries whose GDP is strongly correlated with EU GDP, e.g., France and Germany. Monetary union is more suitable for these regions. *Source:* Authors' calculations using IMF data.

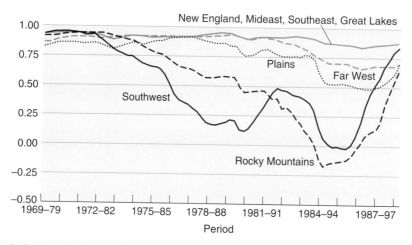

FIGURE 21.14   **Correlation of output amongst U.S. regions.** There is very little correlation across U.S. regions but still a single currency operates. *Source:* Mihov, "Monetary Policy Implementation and Transmission in the European Monetary Union," Insead, Paris mimeo (2000).

Figure 21.13 shows that the degree of similarity in GDP fluctuations varies across countries in the EU. A hard core of countries (France, Germany, Belgium, Netherlands) has a very strong correlation with EU average output growth. This suggests that these economies will find the transition to a single currency relatively easy. By way of comparison, Figure 21.14 shows the correlation coefficient between regions of the United States. Comparing Figures 21.13 and 21.14 suggests that the degree of business cycle synchronization is stong for Europe. However, there is also a group of European countries for whom the correlation coefficient is low, suggesting the need for the country specific setting of monetary policy.

LABOR MOBILITY   As we saw in Chapter 8, European labor markets tend to be much less fluid than those in the United States with regional migration three or four times higher in the United States.

FISCAL TRANSFERS   Another way of alleviating differences in economic performance among European countries would be through cross-country fiscal transfers. Such transfers are important in the United States, where the federal tax and expenditure system transfers income from the richer to the poorer states on both a temporary and permanent basis. By contrast, in the EU redistribution among economies is currently minimal.

Comparing the EU and the United States across these four categories suggests that the United States meets the criteria better. However, given that the United States has had a single currency for more than 100 years, this is perhaps not surprising. The four criteria of an OCA can be viewed not as a test that countries have to pass before they join but as a way of determining what needs to happen and develop if the system is to work. In other words, in response to establishing a single currency between European nations, we should expect to see an increase in intra-European trade, more labor mobility between regions, greater fiscal transfers, and a more common business cycle. It is noticeable that, since the launch of the euro, the participating countries have pushed European union further ahead in other areas and have also embarked on labor market reform. These developments are necessary for the participating countries to adapt to life in Euroland.

KEY POINT

A single currency is justified if countries constitute an optimal currency area. The more trade between nations and the more they share a common business cycle, the more they qualify as an optimal currency area. If countries do little trade or have different business cycles, then a single currency may work if labor is mobile and fiscal transfers between regions are substantial.

SUMMARY

In section 21.1, we defined a currency crisis as a large and sharp fall in the real exchange rate. We documented that 7–10 currency crises occur around the world each year.

In section 21.2, we outlined first-generation models of currency crisis, which explain currency crashes as being the governments' fault when they set inconsistent fiscal and monetary policy. Section 21.3 extended our analysis to include second-generation models where the currency crises depend on investor optimism/pessimism. In the case where there exists a conflict between the governments' internal and external goals, investors may begin to doubt the stability of an exchange rate and it will come under speculative attack.

In Section 21.4, we considered the 1997 Asian crisis and saw that it contained aspects of both first- and second-generation models. In addition, it showed the difficulties that occur when a country borrows heavily in foreign currency but is vulnerable to sudden stops of capital inflows. Section 21.5 outlined how central bank intervention works during a crisis. We also assessed the role and level of success of the IMF in preventing currency crises.

Section 21.6 considered the advantages of capital account liberalization. After much initial hope, most advocates are now more careful in their advice about the pace at which capital controls should be removed. A strong institutional setting and high quality regulation of the domestic banking system is critical for success.

Section 21.7 listed the various different alternative exchange rate regimes a country could choose and outlined the impossible trilogy, which states that countries can choose only two of the three options of independent monetary policy, a fixed exchange rate, or capital account liberalization. The Law of the Excluded Middle suggests that countries who liberalize their capital account have to either adopt a very rigid exchange rate or move to a floating rate. A number of countries have moved towards strongly fixed exchange rates offering some support for this "Law."

Section 21.8 examines the record of currency boards, and in particular, the experience of Argentina. We suggest that Argentina was too large and did too little trade with other nations in the area for a currency board to work painlessly. In 2001, after four years of recession, Argentina abandoned its peg due to inconsistencies between fiscal and monetary policy. Section 21.9 concludes by focusing on single currencies and the advent of the euro.

CONCEPTUAL QUESTIONS

1. (Section 21.1) Table 21.1 shows that currency crises lead to sharp falls in GDP growth. Why do you think this is?

2. (21.2) Use the insights of the first-generation model to consider the impact of the government refusing to publish its holdings of foreign currency reserves. Would this lower the risk of a currency crises? How would it affect the timing of a crisis?

3. (21.3) A government has poor opinion poll ratings in a recession but is attempting to maintain a fixed exchange rate. To defend the currency, it raises interest rates from 5% to 10%. How do you think the markets will respond?

4. (21.4, 21.9) If emerging markets were to completely abandon their own currency and dollarize, would this help them overcome their debt intolerance?

5. (21.5) How should IMF interventions differ in the cases of first- and second-generation currency crises?

6. (21.6) "Capital account liberalization is like a medicine that is usually beneficial but often produces horrific side effects. Such a medicine cannot be left unregulated." Discuss.

7. (21.6) National governments do not try to restrict the flow of finances between regions and sectors within a country. Why should they therefore use capital controls to restrict flows of finance between nations?

8. (21.7) China currently has a fixed exchange rate, capital controls, and independent monetary policy. Is this consistent with the impossible trilogy? How do you think these policies may change as China grows richer?

9. (21.8) In a pure currency board, the central bank can only print domestic currency up to the value of the foreign currency reserves it owns. What would be the impact if it was allowed to include in its assets not just foreign currency reserves but also the central bank holding of government debt?

10. (21.9) To what extent do you think the economic success of the United States is due to the fact it has a single currency? What lessons does this hold for the European Union?

ANALYTICAL QUESTIONS

1. (Secton 21.3) Interest rates between the United States of Albion (U.S.A.) and the Republic of Oz are currently equal. However, you now think there is a 50% chance that the Oz dollar will depreciate by 30% over the next week. What has to happen to interest rates in Oz to keep a fixed exchange rate with the U.S.A.?

2. (21.7) There is a fixed exchange rate system between the United States of Albion (U.S.A.) and the Republic of Oz and interest rates in the U.S.A. are always 2% higher than those in Oz due to a constant risk premium. Does UIP hold? What is the relationship between the monetary policy of the two economies?

3. (21.7) The Republic of Argent does 50% of its trade with Eurasia and 50% with Oceania. Over the last three years, the currency has risen from 1 to 1.1 and then to 1.3 against the Oceania dollar. However, against the Eurasian euro it has fallen from 1 to 1/1.1 to 1/1.3. What is the effective exchange rate? If the Republic wishes to fix its exchange rate, what exchange rate regime would you recommend?

4. (21.7/21.8) A country has GDP of 10bn pesos and its government has borrowed 1bn pesos of money domestically and $4bn in U.S. dollars. The exchange rate is $1 = 1 peso. Interest rates are 10% on peso denominated debt and 5% on dollar denominated debt.

    (a) What is the debt/GDP ratio?
    (b) How much are interest payments as a percentage of GDP?
    (c) According to UIP what should happen to the exchange rate?
    (d) If the exchange rate goes to $1 = 4 pesos, how do your answers to (a) and (b) change?

Active labor market spending Expenditure by the government aimed at increasing the probability of the unemployed being hired.

Adverse selection A problem of asymmetric information where one side of a transaction will find itself coming into contact with agents that make the transaction unprofitable and is unable to exclude them, e.g., when a bank fears that if it raises interest rates it will attract high risk borrowers who face a high probability of bankruptcy.

Aggregate demand curve The relationship between the overall price index and the level of total aggregate demand in the economy. Higher prices lead to lower demand.

Aggregate supply curve The relation between the overall price level and the aggregate level of output/supply firms wish to produce.

Appreciation An increase in the value of a currency in the market for foreign exchange. (Opposite of depreciation).

Arbitrage The process of making profit by buying goods where they are sold cheaply and selling them for a higher price. As a result of this process, prices between the two markets converge.

Asymmetric information A situation where economic agents have different information that cannot be revealed to each other.

Asymmetric shocks Shocks that affect different countries/regions/industries differently.

Automatic stabilizer The impact of policies that automatically tend to boost demand in a slump and reduce demand in a boom. For example, taxes on incomes tend to rise in a boom and fall in a slump; government spending on unemployment benefits has a similar impact.

Average propensity to consume (APC) The ratio of consumption to income (C/Y).

Balance sheet A record of the assets and liabilities of a company, an individual, or a nation.

Balance of payments Record of country's international transactions.

Balanced budget A situation where receipts equal expenditures.

Balassa-Samuelson effect The phenomenon where prices (especially of nontradables) are higher in richer, more productive countries.

Bank for International Settlements (BIS) An international organization that fosters cooperation among central banks and other agencies in pursuit of monetary and financial stability.

Bank run A situation where depositors withdraw funds from a bank for fear that it may go bankrupt and not honor its liabilities.

Bilateral exchange rates The rate that defines the terms at which two currencies can be exchanged.

Bond A financial instrument that promises to pay flows of money at specific intervals (sometimes called *fixed income securities*). Bonds are a form of debt issued by corporations and governments.

Borrowing constraint A restriction on the amount an agent can borrow. Individuals unable to borrow against the prospect of high future labor income may be constrained in their current consumption if current income is low.

Bubble Nonsustainable behavior of asset prices where values are bid up in a way that is linked to expectations of future capital gains not based on economic fundamentals.

Budget constraint The requirement that over the relevant horizon, the value of spending must equal the value of receipts.

Budget deficit A situation where receipts are less than expenditure.

Budget surplus A situation where receipts exceed expenditure.

Business cycle Medium-term aggregate fluctuations in output, incomes, and employment whereby the economy goes from expansion to recession over a period of normally less than ten years.

Business fixed investment Expenditure on equipment and structures that businesses use in production.

Capacity utilization A measure of the extent to which physical capital and employment are being fully utilized in production.

Capital stock The stock of physical equipment and structures used in production.

Capital account Record of a country's assets transactions with the rest of the world. Sales of a country's assets increase the capital account; purchases of overseas assets reduce the capital account.

Capital account liberalization The removal of controls restricting the flow of capital into and out of a country.

Capital accumulation Process whereby the stock of physical capital increases when gross investment exceeds depreciation.

Capital adequacy rules Rules that restrict the amount and type of funding structure that banks can have depending upon their assets.

Capital controls Restriction on the free movement of capital in and out of a country.

Capital gain The rise in the price of an asset.

Catch-up (see convergence). When rich countries grow more slowly than poor ones.

Central bank The institution that implements monetary policy, such as the Federal Reserve in the United States and the European Central Bank in Europe.

Chain weighting A method of calculating real GDP, which allows for the gradual evolution of prices rather than use of completely constant prices.

Closed economy   A country that neither borrows or invests overseas and does not trade goods and services with other countries.

Cobb-Douglas production function   A production function where output is given by $F(K,L) = AK^\beta L^{1-\beta}$, where K is capital, L is labor, and A and β are parameters. If capital and labor receive their marginal product, β is the share of capital income in total output and $1-\beta$ is the share of labor.

Commodity money   Money that has an intrinsic value even if it were to become unacceptable as a medium of exchange (e.g., gold, silver).

Comparative advantage   A situation where a country has a lower opportunity cost of producing a certain commodity. The industry in which a country has greatest productivity advantage (or smallest disadvantage) compared to other nations.

Competitiveness   Productivity in a country compared to other nations (often used with reference to high value added industries).

Conditional convergence   The process whereby countries that share a steady state show convergence to similar levels of GDP per capita.

Constant prices   The use of the same prices across several years when calculating real GDP in order to focus on output changes.

Constant returns to scale   A situation where the same percentage increase in all factors of production generates an equal percentage change in output.

Consumer price index (CPI)   A measure of the general level of prices that consumers have to pay for goods and services including consumption taxes.

Consumption   Goods and services bought and used by consumers.

Consumption function   The relationship between consumption and its determinants. The simplest consumption function has spending depending simply on current income.

Contractionary policy   Government actions that reduce demand in the economy and cause employment to fall, e.g., higher interest rates or taxes. (Opposite of expansionary policy.)

Convergence   Process whereby poor countries grow faster than rich ones.

Corruption   A form of rent seeking where agents demand extra-market payments for economic services or commodities.

Cost of capital   The overall amount of resources that has to be sacrificed to acquire the use of a unit of capital for one period. The cost reflects interest rates, depreciation and any rise or fall in the price of the capital.

Countercyclical   Tending to move in the opposite direction to aggregate output and employment over the business cycle. (Opposite of procyclical.)

Coupon   Regular (normally fixed) payment made to bond holders.

Covered interest parity   Prediction that the gap between two countries' interest rates should be the same as that between their current spot exchange rate and the current forward exchange rate.

Credit channel   Where monetary policy and the financial system affects GDP not through changes in interest rates and the price of credit but through the quantity of credit available.

Credit constraint   An inability to borrow against future income.

Credit crunch   Negative interrelationship between bank lending, property prices, and bank assets.

Crowding out   The tendency of extra government spending to cause reductions in private spending through inducing increases in interest rates.

Currency   Coins and paper money issued by the authorities of a country.

Currency board   An arrangement whereby a country can only issue domestic currency if the central bank owns matching quantities of specific foreign currency.

Currency crises   Sharp dramatic declines in the value of a currency (say, of more than 25%).

Current account   Record of trade between countries in goods and services including money earned from interest payments and dividends. A country that sells more (less) goods and services overseas than it purchases has a current account surplus (deficit).

Current prices   Use of current year prices when measuring the value of output in each year, which leads to measure of nominal GDP. Changes in nominal GDP reflect both output and price changes.

Debt intolerance   The inability of emerging market economies to successfully cope with even modest levels of indebtedness to foreign investors.

Debt sustainability   Whether current and future policy by governments, firms, or countries can maintain a stable debt to income ratio.

Deflation   Sustained falls in the general level of prices. (Opposite of inflation.)

Deflator   A price index that converts a nominal series to a real one.

Demand deposits   Bank deposits that are available on demand and that can be used to settle transactions, e.g., checking accounts.

Depreciation (1)   Wear and tear on physical capital that reduces its effective quantity over time.

Depreciation (2)   A fall in the value of a currency relative to other (foreign) currencies.

Depression   A protracted slump in output; an unusually severe and long-lasting recession.

Devaluation   A fall in the value of a currency relative to other foreign currencies.

Diminishing marginal product   A situation where increased use of a factor of production leads to ever smaller increases in output.

Discount rate   The interest rate set by the central bank when it provides loans to banks.

Discounting   Converting future income amounts into their present value, e.g., the amount of money today that when invested, yields the specified future amount.

Discretionary policy   Policy that is not fixed by preset rules but that can respond to different events in a flexible way.

Disinflation   A reduction in the rate of inflation.

Disposable income   Income available after deducting taxes.

Distortions   Factors that alter market outcomes away from the optimal invisible hand outcome.

Divergence   When poor countries do not catch up with rich ones through faster growth.

Dividend yield   Dividend payments on a share expressed as a percentage of the share price.

Dollarization   When a country gives up use of its own currency and switches to using foreign currency as legal tender, e.g., the dollar.

Effective exchange rate An index that expresses the average value of an exchange rate against several other currencies.

Efficient market hypothesis Prediction that equity prices reflect all available information about future share price and dividends.

Elasticity The responsiveness of one variable to another measured as the percent change in one variable caused by a one-percent change in another.

Employment protection legislation (EPL) Government regulations aimed at increasing the cost or speed with which firms can reduce employment by downsizing.

Employment rate The proportion of the labor force who are in employment.

Endogenous growth Models that offer an explanation for persistent long-run GDP growth even in equilibrium.

Endogenous variable A variable whose value is explained by the behavior of other variables in a model. (Opposite of an exogenous variable.)

Equilibrium A situation of balance between various forces, e.g., supply and demand in a market, such that there are no forces leading to change if the system is left undisturbed.

Equities (also shares or stocks) Paper asset reflecting part ownership of a company and its assets and a claim on the future stream of income it earns.

Equity premium puzzle The finding that returns on equities have in many countries far exceeded that on other assets even after allowing for the riskier nature of equity.

Equity risk premium The excess return that equities earn over safe assets that is required for investors to hold this riskier asset.

European Union (EU) An economic union (free trade of goods, services, labor and capital) and (limited) political union between a group of European countries. At the start of 2004, the countries of the European union were: Austria, Belgium, Denmark, Finland, France, Germany, Greece, Ireland, Italy, Luxembourg, Netherlands, Portugal, Spain, Sweden, United Kingdom. Ten new countries joined the EU in 2004.

***Ex ante* real interest rate** The nominal interest rate less expected inflation over a specific time horizon. Contrast this with the *ex post* real interest rate.

***Ex post* real interest rate** The interest rate minus actual, as opposed to expected, inflation.

Exchange rate The rate at which one currency exchanges for another on the foreign exchange market.

Exogenous variable A variable that is not explained by a model but whose value is taken as a given.

Expansionary policy Government policy that raises aggregate demand, and increases employment and incomes e.g., lower interest rates and taxes.

Exports Goods and services sold to other countries.

Externality When the behavior of an agent affects the return of others in a way that is not reflected in market prices.

Factor endowments The level of factors of production, e.g., land, capital, skills, and so forth, that a country possesses.

Factor intensity Extent to which a country or industry uses a particular factor of production.

Factor of production A resource used as an input into the productive process, e.g., capital or labor.

Factor price The price of one unit of a factor of production.

Factor price equalization Process whereby return paid to factors of production for producing output are equalized across countries as a result of trade in goods and services.

Factor share The share of total output paid out as income to a factor of production.

Federal Reserve (the Fed) The central bank of the United States.

Fiat money Money that is not valuable in itself but achieves its value by government legislation/fiat.

Financial intermediation The channeling of funds from savers to ultimate users of funds via financial institutions (e.g., banks, pension funds, mutual funds, unit trusts, insurance companies).

Fiscal deficit Government expenditure less government revenue.

Fiscal policy Government's policy relating to levels of spending and taxation.

Fisher effect The one-for-one link between the nominal interest rate and expected inflation.

Fisher equation The relation that makes the nominal interest rate the sum of the real interest rate and expected inflation.

Fixed exchange rate A rate of exchange for currencies that is set by the central bank and that is not allowed to vary in response to fluctuations in supply and demand.

Fixed income securities Assets that do not have any uncertainty about their future payoffs. Bonds rather than equity are normally considered fixed income securities.

Flexible prices Prices that move rapidly when supply or demand conditions alter to keep the market in equilibrium.

Floating (flexible) exchange rate A rate of exchange for currencies moving day by day to balance private sector flows of money across the foreign exchange market.

Flow A variable that is measured per unit of time and that only exists during that time period.

Foreign direct investment (FDI) Purchase of a substantial ownership in, or construction of, a factory/operation in a country by an overseas agent.

Foreign exchange intervention When a central bank intervenes to buy or sell its own currency by using its foreign currency reserves in order to influence the value of the exchange rate.

Foreign exchange reserves Holdings of foreign currency by a central bank.

Forward rate Price paid today for delivery of a currency at some future point.

Frisch-Slutsky paradigm View of business cycles as being triggered by random shocks that are propagated through mechanisms to influence the economy over time to create business cycles.

Fundamentals The real forces of supply and demand that determine the evolution of output, asset prices, and other real economic variables.

G7 Seven largest industrial nations (in order): United States, Japan, Germany, France, United Kingdom, Italy, Canada.

GDP *See* gross domestic product.

GDP deflator The ratio of nominal (or current price) GDP to real (or constant price) GDP. This is a measure of the level of prices for domestically produced output.

General Agreement on Trades and Tariffs (GATT) Precursor to the World Trade Organization, which arranged a sequence of trade negotiations leading to lower tariffs.

Globalization The unification of national markets for goods, services, capital, and labor into a single global market.

GNI Gross national income.

Gold standard A historical exchange rate system where countries defined their currency as worth a specified amount of gold and committed to buying and selling at that rate.

Golden Rule Investment criteria which maximizes consumption in the steady state.

Government purchases Goods and services bought by the government. Note that total government expenditure includes *both* government purchases and transfer payments (e.g., social security spending).

Gross domestic product (GDP) The total value of output produced in a country without any adjustment for the depreciation of capital. GDP also equals the sum of income earned domestically by both nationals and foreign citizens working in the country.

Gross domestic fixed capital formation (GDFCF) Total amount of output used within a period to augment the capital stock *including* repairs and maintenance.

Gross national income (GNI) The total income of all residents of a nation wherever they produce or earn this income. It includes income from abroad paid to national citizens owning factors used overseas.

Growth accounting Attempt to attribute observed growth in GDP to increases in various factors of production.

Hecksher-Ohlin model Prediction that countries export goods and services that require the intensive use of a factor of production that the country possesses in abundance.

Home bias The larger proportion of investor portfolios that are invested in domestic securities relative to what is needed for risk diversification.

Human capital Skills and knowledge possessed by individuals and society.

Human development index A broad measure of welfare constructed by the United Nations based around indicators of health, education, and GDP.

Hyperinflation Very high inflation rates (sometimes defined as over 50%) where the increase in inflation is rising over time.

Idiosyncratic risk Uncertainty or income variability that is specific to an individual consumer or firm.

Imports Goods and services bought from other countries.

Impossible trilogy The fact that a country can only choose two out of (a) an independent monetary policy, (b) a fixed exchange rate, and (c) no capital controls.

Imputed value The value of the services provided by ownership of an asset but not actually received as income in a market exchange, i.e., imputed rent of a house owner is the rent they would have paid on their accommodation if they did not own it.

Income effect The change in demand or supply for a good when income is different but the price of the good is held constant.

Indifference curves Set of points that show combinations of goods that yield the same level of enjoyment or welfare to the individual.

Infant industry An industry in its early stage of development which is often considered to need protection from more efficient and experienced foreign competitors.

Inflation A sustained increase in the overall level of prices.

Inflation targeting Central bank practice of changing interest rates to achieve a specified inflation target rather than an alternative exchange rate or money supply target.

Inflation tax Revenue raised by a government through printing money (equals inflation multiplied by stock of non-interest bearing money).

Information and communications technology Computer hardware and software and telephone equipment.

Infrastructure Part of the capital stock that is basic to the operation of an economy, e.g., roads, railways, and so forth.

Institutions The formal and informal organizations and practices that define the "rules of the game" or the ways in which economic agents interact.

Intangible assets Assets that have been accumulated over time but that do not have a physical manifestation, i.e., brand value.

Interest rate The return from lending money or the cost of borrowing money; the price of moving spending from one period to another.

Intermediate target Variable that a government tries to control/influence not because it is of direct policy interest but because it is closely linked with a variable that is.

Intermediation Process whereby financial markets and institutions pass the funds provided by savers to those who wish to invest.

International financial institutions (IFIs) The institutions such as the World Bank, the International Monetary Fund, the Bank for International Settlements, the OECD, and the WTO, which attempt to monitor and regulate the global economy.

International investment position (IIP) The accumulated stock of foreign net assets that a country owns.

International Monetary Fund (IMF) The IMF, founded in 1946, is an international organization of 183 member countries, established to promote international monetary cooperation, exchange stability, and orderly exchange arrangements; to foster economic growth and high levels of employment; and to provide temporary financial assistance to countries to help ease balance of payments adjustment.

Intertemporal budget constraint The constraint that makes the net present value of all future expenditures equal to the net present value of all future income.

Inventory investment The change in the stocks of finished and intermediate goods held by companies.

Investment Goods purchased by individuals, companies, or governments that increase their stock of physical or financial capital.

Invisible Hand Adam Smith's result that individuals pursuing their own self interest will be guided by market prices to an outcome that is efficient for society.

IS Curve Relation between interest rates and the level of demand within the economy.

Keynesian cross A component of the IS-LM model that shows the relationship between expenditure/income and planned expenditure.

Keynesian policies Use of fiscal and monetary policy to boost demand in a recession and reduce demand in an expansion.

Labor force Those in the population who either work or are seeking work.

Labor-force participation rate The proportion of the adult population in the labor force.

Labor productivity Output divided by employment (either persons or hours worked).

Labor supply curve Relationship between wages and hours of work supplied.

Laffer curve Relationship between tax rates and tax revenue in which revenue is maximized at tax rates below 100%.

Laissez-faire The free operation of markets without government intervention.

Law of excluded middle The hypothesis that only very flexible or very fixed exchange rate systems are viable and intermediate regimes are untenable.

Law of one price Notion that identical goods will sell for identical prices wherever they are sold.

Leverage Amount of borrowing (normally expressed as a proportion of income or revenue or total assets).

Life-cycle hypothesis A theory of consumption in which individuals plan a path of consumption over their lives that is smooth and that balances the present value of spending against the sum of current wealth and the future values of earnings.

Liquid Easily converted into a form that allows transactions to be completed at a predictable price.

Long-run supply curve The long-run link between output that is produced in an economy and the level of prices. Since sustained variations in capital, labor input, and technology are unlikely to be driven by changes in nominal magnitudes, the long-run supply curve is vertical.

LM curve Key part of the IS-LM model that summarizes the relationship between interest rates, money supply, and money demand.

M1, M2, M3 Different measures of the aggregate stock of money in the economy. Higher numbers encompass wider definitions of what counts as money and are therefore larger in value.

Marginal produce of capital (MPK) The extra output produced when the amount of capital used in production is increased by one unit holding fixed the labor force and technology.

Marginal product of labor (MPL) The extra output produced when the amount of labor used in production is increased by one unit holding fixed the capital stock and technology.

Marginal propensity to consume (MPC) The proportion of a rise in income that feeds through into higher consumption.

Market failure Where free operations of markets will not produce an efficient (or optimal) outcome. A failure of the invisible hand argument.

Mean reversion Process whereby a variable eventually returns to its long-run average.

Medium of exchange An item that is accepted as a means of payment for goods and services; one of the roles of money.

Menu costs The resources used in setting and changing prices.

Modigliani-Miller theorem Prediction whereby the financial structure of an institution's liabilities does not influence its value, i.e., firm's overall value does not depend on whether it is financed by bonds or equity.

Monetarism The theory that inflation results from changes in the money supply and that control of the money supply is a necessary and sufficient means to control inflation.

Monetary policy The central bank's decisions on the terms (usually short-term interest rates) at which it will lend money and buy securities to the private financial sector.

Monetary transmission mechanism The mechanisms by which changes in monetary policy affect the economy.

Money The stock of assets used for transactions.

Money illusion When individuals confuse nominal and relative prices.

Money multiplier The eventual increase in a measure of the money supply resulting from an increase in central bank (high powered) money.

Monopoly power Ability of an agent or firm to set market prices above costs.

Moral hazard The tendency of people to shirk or not try hard when their behavior is not monitored perfectly and where effort is costly.

Multinational enterprises (MNEs) Firms that both produce and sell their output across a range of countries. Also sometimes called transnational corporations (TNCs).

Multiplier Keynesian concept whereby the final impact on demand of an increase in expenditure is greater than the initial impact.

Nash equilibrium A situation where each agent is following an optimal strategy given the actions of other agents.

National income accounting The system used for measuring overall output and expenditure in a country and its constituent parts.

National income accounts identity Output can be used for either consumption, government expenditure, investment or net exports. $Y = C + I + G + X - M$

National saving A nation's income minus private and public consumption. The sum of government, corporate and household savings.

Natural rate of unemployment The rate of unemployment at which inflation can be steady and to which the economy will move when inflation is neither rising nor falling.

Net exports Exports minus imports.

Net foreign investment The net flow of funds being invested overseas, which equals domestic saving minus domestic investment.

Net investment Total investment expenditure less depreciation of the existing stock of capital.

Neutrality Result when nominal variables (money supply, prices, and so forth) cannot influence real variables (output, unemployment, and so forth).

Nominal Measured in current prices.

Nominal exchange rate The terms of exchange between a unit of one currency and a unit of another.

Nominal interest rate Interest rate paid/received without making allowance for fact that price of goods is changing.

Nontariff barriers Restrictions on trade other than tariffs such as quotas, health and safety standards, and so forth.

Open economy An economy in which people can freely engage in international trade in goods, services, and capital.

Open-market operations Purchase or sale of assets by the central bank in order to increase or decrease the money supply.

Opportunity cost Activities or revenue foregone through pursuing a course of action.

Optimal currency area Region over which it is optimal to have just one currency.

Organization for Economic Cooperation and Development (OECD) The OECD is a group of 30 member countries (Australia, Austria, Belgium, Canada, Czech Republic, Denmark, Finland, France, Germany, Greece, Hungary, Iceland, Ireland, Italy, Japan, Korea, Luxembourg, Mexico, Netherlands, New Zealand, Norway, Poland, Portugal, Slovak Republic, Spain, Sweden, Switzerland, Turkey, United Kingdom, United States) in an organization that provides governments a setting in which to discuss and develop economic and social policy.

Organization of Oil Producing and Exporting Countries (OPEC) A group of major oil producing countries who meet to discuss, and try to control, oil output and prices.

Original sin Refers to notion that all emerging markets are potentially high risk defaulters even if they have not previously defaulted. As a result, emerging markets have to borrow in foreign currency terms.

Output gap Difference between GDP and its trend level.

Overseas Development Assistance (ODA) Money given to poorer nations by rich countries to help boost their GDP.

Pareto efficiency Situation where it is impossible to make anyone better off without making someone worse off.

Participation rate Proportion of the population (sometimes non-institutional population) who wish to have a job.

Per capita Amount per person.

Perfect competition Where each agent/firm is small compared to the market place and has to accept prices as beyond its control.

Permanent income The level of income that someone can reasonably expect to be sustained into the future without running down their assets.

Permanent-income hypothesis The theory that consumption is proportional to the anticipated value of future average labor income (plus a share of current wealth) as opposed to the idea that current income is the prime determinant of spending.

Phillips curve The relationship between unemployment and inflation, claimed by A.W. Phillips to be negative.

Physical capital Stock of machines and buildings.

Poverty trap Situation where a country cannot grow because it is so poor it suffers from a low return on investment.

Precautionary saving Saving that reflects the impact of uncertainty about the future and is done as a form of insurance.

Present value The amount today that has the same value as an amount to be paid or received in the future having adjusted for the interest that could be earned (or must be paid) in the intervening period.

Price index Measure of the price of a basket of goods.

Primary balance Government tax revenue less expenditure *excluding* interest payments.

Private saving Disposable income less private consumption expenditure.

Procyclical Tending to move in a similar direction to aggregate output and employment.

Production function A relationship that describes how increases in factor inputs lead to an increase in output.

Productivity *See* labor productivity.

Profits Firm's revenue less costs.

Pro-poor growth GDP growth that reduces poverty or, more demandingly, GDP growth that reduces inequality.

Public good Commodity that it is impossible to exclude individuals from consuming, e.g., national defense.

Public saving Government receipts less spending on consumption and transfers. Same as fiscal surplus.

Purchasing-power parity (PPP) The theory that exchange rates will move so that the price of goods are the same in all countries so that a given amount of money buys the same amount in different countries.

q-theory of investment The theory that investment depends positively upon the ratio of the stock market value of a firm's assets to the cost of buying those assets. In equilibrium, this ratio should equal 1.

Quantity equation $MV = PY$ where M is the money supply, V the velocity of circulation, P prices, and Y output.

Quantity theory of money Theory that assumes that the velocity of money is predictable and that money is neutral for output so that increases in the money supply lead directly to inflation.

Random walk A variable with the property that the optimal forecast of its future value is its current value because it is impossible to predict whether the variable will rise or fall.

Rate of return Income and capital gains on an asset expressed as a percentage of its price.

Rational expectations A situation where forecast errors are unpredictable and agents' expectations on average equal outturns.

Real Measured in constant prices having allowed for inflation.

Real-business-cycle theory Theory that variations in total factor productivity cause business cycle fluctuations.

Real exchange rate The ratio of what a specified amount of money can buy in one country compared to what it can purchase elsewhere.

Real interest rate The cost of borrowing (or the return to saving) in real terms, i.e., after adjusting for inflation.

Real money balances The amount of money measured in terms of the quantity of goods it could buy; the nominal stock of money relative to an index of prices.

Real wages Wages divided by prices. A measure of what workers can purchase with their earnings and so a measure of the standard of living.

Recession A period of falling aggregate output in the economy. Often used to refer to the situation where output declines for two or more consecutive quarters.

Rent seeking Earning income in excess of the value of economic services offered.

Rental price of capital *See* user cost of capital.

Replacement rate Benefits (especially pensions or unemployment benefits) expressed as a percentage of average or previous earnings.

Research and Development (R & D) Resources spent on fostering invention or innovation.

Reserve requirement Rules governing minimum levels of reserves to be held with the central bank.

Residential investment Investment in new houses.

Ricardian equivalence Prediction that fiscal deficits or surpluses do not influence GDP.

Risk aversion When consumers prefer risk free assets even if the return on riskier assets is higher.

Risk premium Additional return required by investors if they are to invest in riskier assets.

Sacrifice ratio The (percentage) fall in output (or rise in unemployment) that is needed to reduce inflation by a full percentage point according to the Phillips curve.

Saving *See* national saving, private saving, and public saving.

Saving rate Savings expressed as a percentage of income or output.

Seasonal fluctuations Fluctuations in economic variables that repeat themselves but that complete their cycle within a year.

Seigniorage Revenue raised by central bank through printing money due to the difference between face value of money and costs of production.

Shock An exogenous and unpredictable change in an economic variable that generates changes in endogenous variables.

Shoeleather cost The cost of inflation from people holding fewer real money balances and having to incur more costs in financing transactions.

Single currencies When two or more countries agree to abandon their individual currencies and agree to share a new currency.

Small open economy An open economy that is small enough that its actions do not influence interest rates or other prices set in global markets.

Solow growth model Model of growth based around capital accumulation and diminishing marginal product of capital that culminates in a country reaching its steady state.

Solow residual The growth in total factor productivity, i.e., that part of a rise in output not explained by the increase in factor inputs.

Spillovers Events or actions in one industry or market that affect other industries as well.

Stabilization policy Government policy aimed at keeping output and employment on steady trend paths.

Stagflation A situation of falling output and high inflation.

Steady state A situation in which key variables are not changing. In the Solow growth model, this is where gross investment equals depreciation.

Sterilization Process whereby central bank intervenes in bond or money market to prevent its foreign exchange intervention from affecting the domestic money supply.

Sticky prices Prices that are slow to adjust when demand or supply conditions change.

Stock The outstanding amount of a variable at a point in time. Also used to denote a share issued by a firm and traded in the stock market.

Stock market The market in which corporate stocks (or equities) are bought and sold.

Stolper-Samuelson effect Result showing that a factor of production that is in relatively scarce supply sees a fall in its real income as a result of more trade.

Strategic Trade Policy Use of trade restrictions to achieve long-run advantages for high value added industries.

Substitution effect The change in demand or supply for a good due to a change in the relative price holding income constant.

Tariff A tax on imported goods.

Tax smoothing Attempts to avoid sharp swings in tax rates whilst still maintaining long run solvency.

Tax wedge Gap between price paid by consumers and received by producers because of taxes.

Taylor rule Relationship between interest rates and output gap and inflation.

Technical progress Improvements in knowledge that enable more output to be produced from given inputs.

Terms of trade Price of a country's exports divided by price of its imports.

Time inconsistency Problem where future plans are only optimal when announced but not when they have to be implemented.

Tobin's q The ratio of the market value of a company's existing capital to its replacement cost.

Total factor productivity Efficiency with which factors of production are utilized. Reflects a huge range of influences, both economic and sociocultural.

Trade liberalization Reduction or removal of trade tariffs and other barriers.

Transactions costs Costs incurred in trading assets or goods and services. Includes taxes and brokers' charges as well as transport costs, where relevant.

Transfer payments Payments from the government to people that that are not expenditure on goods and services, e.g., unemployment benefits; old age pensions.

Transitory income A current shock to income that people do not expect to persist into the future.

Trend growth Long-run average growth in GDP per capita.

Uncovered interest parity Prediction that interest rate differentials between countries will be exactly offset by future exchange rate depreciation.

Underground economy Economic activity not reported in official statistics due to tax evasion and illegal status.

Unemployment rate The percentage of those in the labor force who are not working.

Unit of account Units used to measure value of economic activity.

User cost of capital Cost of using a unit of capital during a period of time, including rental and depreciation charges and any capital gains.

Value-added The value of a firm's output minus the value of the intermediate goods and raw materials the firm purchased.

Velocity of circulation The ratio of aggregate nominal spending to the money supply, which reflects the average rate at which money changes hands.

Wage The amount paid for one unit of labor.

Wealth Assets less liabilities.

Wealth effect Influence of changes in value of wealth on consumption and investment decisions.

World Bank The World Bank uses its financial resources and staff to help developing countries achieve long-run sustainable growth and alleviate poverty.

World Trade Organization (WTO) The World Trade Organization deals with the rules of trade between nations. At its heart are the WTO agreements, negotiated and signed by the bulk of the world's trading nations and ratified in their parliaments.

Yield Discount rate that makes current bond price equal to the net present value of future income stream generated by the bond.

Yield curve Relationship showing how yields on bonds vary with the maturity of bonds.

Chapter 1 *Fig. 1.2:* International Financial Statistics 2003. *Fig. 1.4:* John Haltiwanger's homepage, www.bsos.umd.edu/econ/ haltiwanger *Fig. 1.5:* Statistics Netherlands. *Fig. 1.6:* BP Statistical Review of World Energy, June 2003.

Chapter 2 *Fig. 2.1:* Bureau of Economic Analysis. *Fig. 2.2:* World Bank Development Indicators. *Table 2.4:* Bureau of Economic Analysis. *Fig. 2.3:* Gollin, "Getting Income Shares Right," *Journal of Political Economy*, 110, 2 April 2002, pp. 458–474 UCP. *Fig. 2.4:* IMF International Financial Statistics 2002. *Fig. 2.5:* World Bank. *Fig. 2.6:* IMF World Economic Outlook 2003. *Fig. 2.7:* IMF World Economic Outlook April 2003. *Fig. 2.8:* IMF World Economic Outlook April 2003. *Fig. 2.9:* WEO Database April 2003, www.imf.org. *Fig. 2.10:* Enste and Schneider (1998) "Increasing Shadow Economies all over the World–Fiction or Reality?" IZA Discussion Paper 26. *Fig. 2.11:* Hamilton and Lutz, "Green National Accounts," World Bank Environment, Department Papers 39, July 1996. *Table 2.5:* Blanchflower, Oswald, and Warr "Well being over time in Britain and the USA," London School of Economics, mimeo. *Table 2.6:* T. Oswald "Happiness and Economic Performance," *Economic Journal*, 1997, Blackwells. *Fig. 2.12:* United Nations Human Development Index.

Chapter 3 *Fig. 3.1:* Baier, Dwyer, and Tamura, "How Important are capital and total factor productivity for economic growth?" Federal Reserve Bank of Atlanta Working Paper, April 2002. *Table 3.1:* Crafts and Toniolo, *Economic Growth in Europe since 1945*, Cambridge: Cambridge University Press, 1996 and Bassanini, Scarpetta, and Visco, "Knowledge, Technology and Economic Growth: Recent Evidence from OECD Countries' National Bank of Belgium," Working Paper No. 6, May 2000. *Fig. 3.3:* Michael Kremer, *Quarterly Journal of Economics*, 1993. *Table 3.2:* Peter Bernstein, *Against the Gods*, New York: John Wiley, 1996. *Table 3.3:* Angus Maddison, *Monitoring the World Economy 1820–1992*, OECD 1995 and Alan Heston, Robert Summers, and Bettina Aten, *Penn World Table Version 6.1*. *Table 3.4:* World Bank Poverty Trends and Voices of the Poor, www.worldbank.org *Fig. 3.5:* Adams, "Economic Growth, Inequality and Poverty," World Bank Discussion Paper, 2003. *Fig. 3.6:* World Bank. *Table 3.5:* Authors' Calculations. OECD and BLS www.bls.gov/fls/flsgdp/pdf *Table 3.7:* Angus Maddison, *Monitoring the World Economy 1820–1992*, OECD 1995. *Fig. 3.9:* Baier, Dwyer, and Tamura, "How important are capital and total factor productivity for economic growth?" Federal Reserve Bank of Atlanta Working Paper, April 2002. *Fig. 3.10:* Bureau of Labor Statistics. *Table 3.8:* Angus Maddison, *Monitoring the World Economy 1820–1992*, OECD 1995 and Economic Outlook 2003 OECD. *Table 3.9:* Angus Maddison, *Monitoring the World Economy 1820–1992*, OECD 1995 and Economic Outlook 2003 OECD. *Table 3.10:* Angus Maddison, *Monitoring the World Economy 1820–1992*, OECD 1995 and Economic Outlook 2003 OECD. *Fig. 3.11:* Baier, Dwyer, and Tamura, "How important are capital and total factor productivity for economic growth?" Federal Reserve Bank of Atlanta Working Paper April 2002. *Table 3.11:* Angus Maddison, *Monitoring the World Economy 1820–1992*, OECD 1995. *Fig 3.13c:* N.R.Crafts, "Globalisation and Growth in the Twentieth Century," IMF Working Paper 00/44. *Fig 3.14:* N.R.Crafts, "Globalisation and Growth in the Twentieth Century," IMF Working Paper 00/44.

Chapter 4 *Fig. 4.1a:* Summers and Heston dataset, Penn World Tables 5.5, http:/www.nber.org *Fig. 4.1b:* Summers and Heston, Penn World Table 5.5, http:/www.nber.org *Fig. 4.6:* Baro and Sala-I-Martin, *Economic Growth*, (New York: McGraw Hill, 1995). *Fig. 4.7:* Capital Stock data from Maddison, "Macroeconomics Accounts for European Countries," in van Ark and Crafts (eds) *Quantitative Aspects of Post-war European Economic Growth* (Cambridge: Cambridge University Press, 1996). *Table 4.1:* Crafts and Toniolo, "Postwar Growth an Overview," in Crafts and Toniolo (eds) *Economic Growth in Europe Since 1945*, (Cambridge: Cambridge University Press, 1996). *Fig. 4.9:* Crafts, "Productivity Growth Reconsidered," Economic Policy (1992) vol. 15, pp. 388–426 Blackwells. IFS Database 2003. *Fig. 4.12:* Maddison (1995) *Monitoring the World Economy, 1820–1992* Paris: OECD. Updated to 2002 by author using IMF data. *Fig. 4.14:* Summers and Heston, Penn World Table 6.1, http://www.nput.econ.nperr.edu *Fig. 4.15:* Author's own calculations based on Summers and Heston, Penn World Table 6.1 and World Economic Outlook, April 2003, www.imf.org *Table 4.2:* Author's calculation based on Summers and Heston, Penn World Table 6.1. *Table 4.3:* OECD National Accounts Volume II 1998. *Table 4.5:* Summers and Heston, Penn World Table 6.1, http://www.nput.econ.nperr.edu *Table 4.6:* Crafts, "East Asian Growth Before and After the crisis" IMF working paper 98/137, 1996. *Fig. 4.16:* Young, "Tyranny of Numbers: Confronting the Statistical Realities of the East Asian Growth Experience." *Quarterly Journal of Economics* (1985) vol. 110, pp. 641–680. *Fig. 4.17:* Young, "Tyranny of Numbers: Confronting the Statistical Realities of the East Asian Growth Experience," *Quarterly Journal of Economics* (1985) vol. 110, pp. 641–680. *Table 4.7:* International Financial Statistics, IMF. *Fig. 4.8:* IMF International Financial Statistics. *Fig. 4.9:* IMF International Financial Statistics. *Table 4.8:* Wang and Yao "Sources of Chinese Economic Growth 1952–99," World Bank Discussion Paper July 2001.

Chapter 5 *Fig. 5.2:* Barro and Lee (2002) International Data on Educational Attainment, Harvard University, CID Working Paper 42 and Penn World Tables 6.1. *Table 5.1:* Crafts, "Productivity Growth Reconsidered," *Economic Policy* (1991) vol. 15, pp. 387–426, Blackwells. *Table 5.2:* Barro and Lee (2002) International Data on Educational Attainment, Harvard University, CID Working Paper 42. *Fig. 5.5:* Mingat and Tan, "The Mechanics of Progress in Education," World Bank Discussion Paper 2015, Nov. 1998. *Table 5.3:* Fuller and Clarke. (1994). *How to Raise the Effectiveness of Secondary Schools? Universal and Locally Tailored Investment Strategies.* Education and Social Policy Discussion Paper Series No. 28. Washington, D.C.: The World Bank. *Fig. 5.6:* Hall and Jones, "Why do some countries produce so much more output per worker than others?" NBER working paper 6564. *The Quarterly Journal of Economics*, (1999) vol. 114, no. 1, pp 83–116. *Table 5.4:* Hall and Jones, "Why do some countries produce so much more output per worker than others?" NBER working paper 6564. *The Quarterly Journal of Economics*, (1999) vol. 114, no. 1, pp 83–116. *Fig. 5.7:* IMF World Economic Outlook April 2003.

Fig. 5.8: Xavier Sala-I-Martin and Arvind Subramanian, NBER working paper 9804.   *Table 5.5:* Transparency International.
Table 5.6: Transparency International.   *Fig. 5.9:* EBRD Bryan Whitford.   *Fig. 5.10:* King and Levine, *Quarterly Journal of Economics*, 1993.   *Fig. 5.12:* OECD.   *Fig. 5.13:* UN Human Development Report 2003, being processed.   *Fig. 5.14:* IMF World Economic Outlook Database, April 2003.   *Table 5.7:* UNCTAD World Investment Report 2002.   *Table 5.8:* *Information Technology & Productivity : Where are we now and where are we going?* Federal Reserve Bank of Atlanta, *Economic Review* 2002 Q3.   *Fig. 5.15:* "Cartoon" by Dan Wasserman, Copyright Tribune Media Services, Reprinted with permission.
Fig. 5.16: Arnal, Ok, and Torres, *Knowledge, Work Organisation and Economic Growth Without changes in workplace practices then high levels of ICT investment yield poor productivity growth*, OECD Labor Market and Social Policy Working Paper 50, 2001.   *Table 5.10:* Nick Crafts (2003) CEPR.

Chapter 6   *Fig. 6.5:* Penn World Table 6.1.   *Fig. 6.6:* Penn World Table 6.1.   *Fig. 6.7:* Penn World Table 6.1.   *Fig. 6.8:* Barro and Sala-i-Martin, Economic Growth, May 1991.   *Fig. 6.9:* Barro and Sala-i-Martin, Economic Growth, May 1991.
Table 6.1: Based on Sala-I-Martin, "I Just Ran Four Million Regressions," *American Economic Review*, 87 (2), May 1997, 178–83.   *Table 6.2:* Human Development Report 2003. Barro, Robert J. and Jong-Wha Lee, "International Data on Educational Attainment: Updates and Implications" (CID Working Paper no. 42), World Bank, http://www2.cid.harvard.edu/cid-data/barrolee/Appendix.xls   *Fig. 6.11:* Maddison (1995) *Monitoring the World Economy, 1820–1992* Paris: OECD and IMF WEO Database 2003.   *Table 6.3:* Alesina, Devleeschauwer, Easterly, Kurlat, and Wacziarg, "Fractionalisation," *Journal of Economic Growth*, 2003, 8, 155–94.   *Table 6.4, Table 6.5:* Bloom and Sachs, *Geography, Demography and Economic Growth in Africa*, Brookings Papers on Economic Activity.   *Fig. 6.12:* Daron Acemoglu, James A. Robinson, and Simon Johnson, "The Colonial Origins of Comparative Development: An Empirical Investigation," December 2001, *American Economic Review*, volume 91, pp. 1369–1401.   *Table 6.6:* Aggregate Governance Indicators 2002, World Bank, http://www.worldbank.org/wbi/governance/pdf/2002kkzcharts ppp.xls   *Table 6.7:* Alesina and Dollar, "Who gives foreign to whom and why? *Journal of Economic Growth* (2000) Vol. 5, 33–64.

Chapter 7   *Fig. 7.1:* OECD.   *Table 7.1:* OECD Employment outlook 2003.   *Table 7.2:* OECD Employment outlook September 2003.   *Fig. 7.8:* Nicolleti, Bassanini, Ernst, Jean, Santiago, and Swaim, "Product and Labor Markets Interactions in OECD Countries" Economic Department Working Papers 312.   *Fig. 7.11:* Nickell Stephen, "Labor Market Institutions and Unemployment in OECD Countries," CESIfo DICE Report, 2/2003 CHECK CESifo.   *Table 7.3:* OECD Assessing Performance and Policy, 1999.   *Fig. 7.14:* OECD Employment Outlook, 2003.   *Fig. 7.15:* Nickell (2003), "Labour Market Institutions and Unemployment in OECD Economies," DICE Report Summer 2003 CES-Ifo.   *Table 7.5:* OECD Employment Outlook, June 1999, p.55.   *Fig. 7.15a–f:* OECD Employment Outlook, June 1999.   *Table 7.6:* Nickell and Van Ours, *Economic Policy*, 2000, Blackwells.   *Fig. 7.16:* OECD Employment Outlook, September 2003.   *Table 7.7:* Autor, Katz, and Krueger, "Computing Inequality : Have computers changed the Labor Market?" NBER WP 5956.   *Fig. 7.17:* Jonathan Coppel, Jean-Christophe Dumont, and Ignazio Visco, Trends in Immigration and Economic Consequences," OECD Economics Department Working Papers No. 284.   *Fig. 7.18:* Jonathan Coppel, Jean-Christophe Dumont, and Ignazio Visco, Trends in Immigration and Economic Consequences," OECD Economics Department Working Papers No. 284.

Chapter 8   *Fig. 8.1:* WTO Annual Statistical Report 2002.   *Table 8.2:* International Trade Statistics, 2003, WTO-IMF.
Table 8.3: WTO Annual Statistical Report, 2003.   *Fig. 8.4:* G. D. A. MacDougall, "British and American Exports,"*The Economic Journal*, 1951, 61, 703–707 Blackwells.   *Fig. 8.5:* IMF International Financial Statistics.   *Fig. 8.6:* IMF International Financial Statistics.   *Table 8.5:* WTO Annual Statistical Report, 2003.   *Fig. 8.7:* US Census Bureau.   *Table 8.6:* Bowen, Leamer, Svelkauskas, "Multicountry, Multifactor Tests of the Factor Abundance Theory," *American Economic Review*, 1987, 77,791–809.   *Fig. 8.8:* Grimwade, *International Trade: New patterns of trade, production and investment*, Routledge, 1989.
Table 8.7: Mayda and Rodrik, "Why are some people (and countries) more protectionist than others?" Harvard University Kennedy School mimeo, 2002.   *Fig. 8.7:* US Bureau of Labor Statistics.   *Fig. 8.10:* Trefler, "International Factor Price Differences: Leontief Was Right!" 1993, *Journal of Political Economy*, 101, 961–87.

Chapter 9   *Fig. 9.1:* Wacziarg and Welch, "Trade Liberalization and Growth: New Evidence," NBER Working Paper 10152.
Fig. 9.2: O' Rourke and Williamson, "The Heckscher-Ohlin Model between 1400 and 2000," NBER Working Paper 7411 (November 1999).   *Fig. 9.3:* Maddison, *Monitoring the World Economy 1820–1992*, OECD 1995 and updated using WTO data.
Fig. 9.4: Yarbrough and Yarbrough, *The World Economy*, (Fort Worth: Dryden Press, 1997).   *Table 9.1:* Lindert and Williamson, "Does Globalisation Make the World More Unequal?" NBER Working Paper, WP8228, April 2001.   *Fig. 9.5:* Brown, Deardorff, and Stern, "CGE Modelling and Analysis of Mulitlateral and Regional Negotiating Options," in Robert M. Stern (ed.), *Issues and Options for US–Japan trade Policies* (Ann Arbor: University of Michigan Press, 2002).   *Table 9.2:* IMF discussion paper.   *Fig. 9.6:* Alan Heston, Robert Summers, and Bettina Aten, Penn WorldTable Version 6.1, Center for International Comparisons at the University of Pennsylvania (CICUP), October 2002. for GDP data and UN Statistics Division Online Database, www.unstats.un.org for tariff data   *Table 9.3:* Cyrus, Frankel, and Romer, "Trade and Growth in East Asian Countries: Cause and Effect?" Working Paper 5732 (1996).   *Fig. 9.7:* Wacziarg and Welch, "Trade Liberalization and Growth: New Evidence," NBER Working Paper 10152.   *Fig. 9.8:* Poverty in an Age of Globalization, World Bank October 2000.   *Fig. 9.9:* Paul de Grauwe and Filip Camerman, "How Big are the Big Multinational Companies?" University of Leuven, mimeo 2002.   *Fig. 9.10:* World Bank, 1994.   *Fig. 9.11:* World Bank Global Development Finance, 2001.   *Fig. 9.12:* Irwin, *Free Trade Under Fire*, (Princeton: Princeton University Press, 2002).   *Fig. 9.13:* IMF.   *Table 9.4:* Yarbrough and Yarbrough, *The World Economy*, (Fort Worth: Dryden Press, 1997).   *Fig. 9.14:* WTO World Maps.   *Fig. 9.15:* Authors' Calculations from WTO data.   *Table 9.5:* WTO Annual Report, 2003.   *Fig. 9.16:* WTO Annual Report, 2003.

Chapter 10   *Fig. 10.1:* OECD online database and IFS database, 2003.   *Fig. 10.2:* OECD online database and IFS database, 2003.   *Table 10.1:* Data are from Tanzi and Schuknecht, "The Growth of Government and the Reform of the State in Industrial Countries," IMF Working Paper 1995; updated with OECD.   *Table 10.2:* OECD.   *Table 10.3:* OECD.   *Fig. 10.4:* Miles, Myles and Preston, *The Economy of Public Spending* (Oxford: Oxford University Press, 2003.   *Fig. 10.5:* OECD.
Fig. 10.6: IFS database 2003.   *Fig. 10.7:* OECD.   *Fig. 10.12:* OECD online database and IFS database, 2003.   *Fig. 10.13:* Elmendorf and Mankiw, "Government Debt," in *The Handbook of Macroeconomics*, vol. 1c. North Holland (2000: OECD Economic Outlook).   *Table 10.3:* OECD Economic Outlook.   *Table 10.4:* OECD.   *Table 10.15:* OECD.   *Table 10.16:*

Laurence J. Kotlikoff and Willi Leibfritz, "An International Comparison of Generational Accounts," NBER Working Paper No. W6447, March 1998. *Fig. 10.17 and 10.18:* Laurence J. Kotlikoff and Willi Leibfritz, "An International Comparison of Generational Accounts," NBER Working Paper No. W6447, March 1998. *Fig. 10.19:* D, Leibfritz, W, Fore, D, and Wurzel, E., (1996), "Ageing Populations, Pension Systems and Government Budgets: Simulations for 20 OECD Countries," Economics Department Working Paper no 168, OECD, Paris. *Fig. 10.22:* OECD Online Database and IFS Database, 2003.

Chapter 11 *Fig. 11. Fig. 1.1:* B.R.Mitchell, *British Historical Statistics*, Cambridge University Press, 1988 and updated using Office of National Statistics data. *Fig. 11.2:* Authors' calculations from Figure 1. *Fig. 11.3:* www.nber.org Historical Data. *Fig. 11.4:* IMF International Financial Statistics, June 2003. *Fig. 11.5:* BP Statistical Review of World Energy, June 2003. *Fig. 11.6:* IMF International Financial Statistics, June 2003. *Figure 11.7:* IMF International Financial Statistics, June 2003. *Fig. 11.8:* Shiller *Why do people dislike inflation?* In *Reducing Inflation: Motivation and Strategy* (eds) C.D.Romer and D.H.Romer, University of Chicago Press 1997. *Table 11.1:* Shiller, "Why do people dislike inflation?" In Romer and Romer (eds.), *Reducing Inflation: Motivation and Strategy* (Chicago: University of Chicago Press, 1997). *Table 11.2:* Shiller, "Why do people dislike inflation?" In Romer and Romer (eds.), *Reducing Inflation: Motivation and Strategy* (Chicago: University of Chicago Press, 1997). *Fig. 11.9:* Barro, "Inflation and Economic Growth," NBER Discussion paper 5326, 1995. *Table 11.3:* Shiller, "Why do people dislike inflation?" In Romer and Romer (eds.), *Reducing Inflation: Motivation and Strategy* (Chicago: University of Chicago Press, 1997). *Table 11.4:* www.federalreserve.gov *Table 11.5:* www.ecb.int *Fig. 11.11:* IMF International Financial Statistics, June 2003. Calculated as change in monetary base divided by nominal GDP. *Table 11.7:* IMF International Financial Statistics, June 2003. *Fig. 11.12:* Author's calculations from data in Sargent, "The End of Four Big Inflations" in *Rational Expectations and Inflation*, New York, Harper and Rowe, 1986. *Fig. 11.13:* B.R.Mitchell, *British Historical Statistics*, Cambridge University Press, 1988. *Fig. 11.14:* IMF International Financial Statistics, June 2003. *Fig. 11.15:* IMF International Financial Statistics, June 2003. *Table 11.9:* George McCandless and Warren Weber, "Some Monetary Facts," *Federal Reserve Bank of Minneapolis Quarterly Review*, vol 19, no 3, 1995. Warren Weber, "Some Monetary Facts," *Federal Reserve Bank of Minneapolis Quarterly Review*, vol 19, no 3, 1995.

Chapter 12 *Fig. 12.1:* http://www.bls.gov/cex.htm *Table 12.2:* IMF International Financial Statistics, June 2003. *Table 12.3 and 12.4:* Consumer Expenditure Survey 2001, Bureau of Labor Statistics, www.bls.gov/cex.htm *Fig. 12.1a, b:* IMF International Financial Statistics, June 2003. *Fig. 12.2 and 12.3:* OECD. *Fig. 12.20:* Consumer Expenditure Survey, Bureau of Labor Statistics.

Chapter 13 *Fig. 13.1:* OECD. *Fig. 13.2:* OECD and IMF (for China). *Fig. 13.3:* OECD. *Table 13.2–13.5:* Corbett and Jenkinson, "How is Investment Financed?" The Manchester School, 1996, vol. LXV, pp, 69–94. *Fig. 13.8:* OECD (investment). *Table 13.6:* Rajan and Zingales, "What Do We Know About Capital Structure: Some Evidence From International Data," (1995) *Journal of Finance* (Blackwells). *Fig. 13.9:* Cooper, R., Haltiwanger, J., and Power, L. (1995) "Machine Replacement and the Business Cycle: Limps and Bumps," NBER Working Paper no 5620. *Fig. 13.10:* UNCTAD World Investment Report 2003. *Fig. 13.11a, b:* OECD calculations. Gordon K. and Tchilinguirian H. (1998) "Marginal Effective Tax rates on Physical, Human and R & D Capital," OECD Discussion Paper no 199. *Fig. 13.12:* Robert Hall, "The Stock Market and Capital Accumulation" NBER Working Paper 7180, June 1999. See also the later version of that paper with the same name that appeared in the *American Economic Review*, 2001, vol 91, p 1185–1202.

Chapter 14 *Fig. 14.1* and *14.2:* IMF. *Table 14.1:* Maddison, *Monitoring the World Economy 1820–1992*, OECD 1995. *Table 14.2:* NBER www.nber.org *Fig. 14.3:* IMF, International Financial Statistics, November 2003. *Table 14.3:* IMF staff calculations. *Fig. 14.4:* Economic Trends Annual Supplement, National Statistics Online, http://www. statistics.gov.uk/ statbase/tsdtimezone.asp?vlnk=etas *Table 14.4:* Author's calculations from date from Bureau of Economic Analysis, www.bea.doc.gov *Fig. 14.6:* From Data used in Basu and Taylor, "Business Cycles in International Historical Perspective," *Journal of Economic Perspectives*, 1999, pp. 45–68 and updated using The World Economic Outlook Database September 2003, OECD. *Figs. 14.7, 14.8* and *Table 14.5:* Clark, Leslie, and Symons: "The Cost of Recessions," *Economic Journal, 1994, 104, 10–37* Blackwells. *Fig. 14.9:* Alan Heston, Robert Summers, and Bettina Aten, Penn World Table Version 6.1, Center for International Comparisons at the University of Pennsylvania (CICUP), October 2002. http://datacentre2.chass.utoronto.ca/pwt/ *Table 14.6:* IMF International Financial Statistics, November 2003. *Figs. 14.15–14.17:* Hall, Walsh, and Yates. "How Do UK Companies Set Prices?" Bank of England Working Paper 67 1997. Reprinted with the permission of the Bank of England. *Table 14.7:* Canova and Nicolo, "On the Sources of Business Cycles in the G7," Universitat Pompeu Fabra mimeo.

Chapter 15 *Fig. 15.1* and *15.2:* Mervyn King, "Challenges for Monetary Policy: New and Old," paper presented at New Challenges for Monetary Policy conference. Jackson Hole, Wyoming 1999. *Fig. 15.10:* BIS Annual Report 2003. *Table 15.1:* BIS annual report 2003. *Fig. 15.11:* Clouse, Henderson, Orphanides, Small and Tinsley, "Monetary Policy When the Short Term Nominal Interest Rate Is Zero," *Topics in Macroeconomics*, vol 3 Issue 1, 2003. *Fig. 15.12:* Sterne, "The use of explicit targets for monetary policy: practical experience of 91 countries," *Bank of England Quarterly Bulletin* (August 1999) vol. 39, no.3. Reprinted with permission from the Bank of England. *Fig. 15.13:* Federal Reserve Board, *http://www.federalreserve.gov/releases/H6* *Fig. 15.14:* Economic Trends, UK Office for National Statistics, http://www.statistics.gov.uk/ *Fig. 15.19:* Monetary Policy committee, Bank of England, "The transmission mechanism of monetary policy," 1999. Reprinted with permission from the Bank of England. *Fig. 15.20:* Christiano, Eichenbaum, and Evans, "The effects of monetary policy shocks: evidence from the flow of funds" *Review of Economics and Statistics*, 1996. vol78, pp. 16–34. Copyright president and fellows of Harvard college and MIT. *Fig. 15.21:* Mihov, "Monetary policy implementation and transmission in the European Monetary Union," INSEAD mimeo, 2000. *Fig. 15.23:* BIS Annual Report 2003.

Chapter 16 *Fig. 16.1:* Mihov, "Monetary policy implementation and transmission in the European Monetary Union," INSEAD mimeo, 2000. *Fig. 16.7:* Reprinted from Haldane and Quah, *Journal of Monetary Economics*, 1999, vol. 44, pp.259–278. Copyright 1999 Elsevier Science. *Figs. 16.8* and *16.9:* The World Economic Outlook Database September 2003, OECD. *Fig. 16.10:* Reprinted from Haldane and Quah, *Journal of Monetary Economics*, 1999, vol. 44, pp.259–278. Copyright 1999 Elsevier Science. *Fig. 16.13:* Andersen, P and Wascher, W., "Sacrifice Ratios and the Conduct of Monetary Policy in Conditions of Low Inflation," BIS Working paper no 82, 1999.

Chapter 17 *Fig. 17.1: Financial Times*, February 2004. *Figs. 17.2–17.4:* Thomson Financial Datastream. *Fig. 17.5:* Robert Shiller. See Shiller "Market Volatility," (MIT Press, 1989), chapter 26, for details of the construction of the data. An Update of Data shown in Chapter 26 of Market Volatility, R. Shiller, MIT Press, 1989. *Fig. 17.6:* Jeremy Siegel, *Stocks for the Long Run*, (Second edition) McGraw Hill, 1999. *Figs. 17.10* and *17.11:* An Update of Data shown in Chapter 26 of *Market Volatility*, R. Shiller, MIT Press, 1989. *Table 17.1:* Dimson E., Marsh P., and Stauton M., *Triumph of the optimist 101 years of global investment*, Princeton University Press, 2002, Chapter 33. *Fig. 17.12:* Goetzmann W. and Jorion, P. (1999), " Global Stock Markets in the 20th Century," *The Journal of Finance*, vol 54, issue 3, June 1999. Blackwells. *Table 17.2:* Dimson E., Marsh P., and Stauton M., *Triumph of the optimist 101 years of global investment*, Princeton University Press, 2002. *Fig. 17.13:* Reproduced from chapter 5 of *Market Volatility* by Robert Shiller, MIT Press, 1989.

Chapter 18 *Table 18.1:* Bank for International Settlements (BIS). BIS Quarterly Review, December 2003. *Table 1: (A–D)* and *Table 16 (A–B).* http://www.bis.org/statistics/secstats.htm *Fig. 18.1:* Author's calculation with data from the BIS Quarterly Review, December 2003. *Table 12 (A–D)* and *Table 16 (A–B).* http://www.bis.org/statistics/secstats.htm *Fig. 18.5:* Thomson Financial Datastream. *Table 18.3: Financial Times*, February 2004. *Table 18.4:* Thomson Financial Datastream. *Table 18.5: Financial Times*, February 2004. *Table 18.6:* "World Economic Outlook, OECD, 2003. *Table 18.7:* Dimson E., Marsh P., and Stauton M., *Triumph of the optimist 101 years of global investment*, Princeton University Press, 2002. *Fig. 18.6:* Thomson Financial Datastream. *Figs. 18.7* and *18.8:* Jourion and Mishkin, "A Multicountry Comparison of Term Structure Forecasts at Long Horizons," *Journal of Financial Economics* (1991) vol. 29, no. 1, pp. 59–80. Reprinted with permission from Elsevier Science. *Figs. 18.9* and *18.10:* David Miles "Interest Rates from the 17th to the 21st Century," Merrill Lynch Report, June 1998. *Fig. 18.11:* Thomson Financial Datastream. *Table 18.8: Financial Times*, February 2004.

Chapter 19 *Fig. 19.1a:* ECB http://www.ecb.int/stats/eer/eer.shtml. *Fig. 19.1b:* Federal Reserve Board, http://www.federalreserve.gov/releases/h10/Weights/ *Figs. 19.2* and *19.3:* Ravn and Mazzenga, "Frictions in International Trade and Relative Price Movements," London Business School Working Paper, 1999. *Fig. 19.4:* Engel and Rogers, "How wide is the border?" *American Economic Review* Vol. 86, 5, 1112–1125. *Table 19.1:* Engel and Rogers, "Deviations from the law of one price : Sources and Welfare Costs," *Journal of International Economics*, 55, October 2001, 29–57. *Fig. 19.5:* Global Financial Data. *Fig. 19.6:* Lothian and Taylor, "Real Exchange Rate Behavior: The Recent Float from the perspective of the past two centuries," *Journal of Political Economy*, 104, 488–509, Updated by Mark Taylor. *Table 19.2:* The Hamburger Standard (based on Jan. 15, 2003 data). *The Economist. Fig. 19.7:* Alan Heston, Robert Summers, and Bettina Aten, Penn World Table Version 6.1, Center for International Comparisons at the University of Pennsylvania (CICUP), October 2002. *Fig. 19.8:* Authors' calculations from OECD data. *Table 19.3:* IMF International Financial Statistics, *9/2003. Fig. 19.9:* Lane and Milessi-Ferretti, "The External Wealth of Nations," CEPR Discussion Paper, 2000. *Table 19.4:* Lane and Milesi-Ferretti, "The external wealth of nations : measures of foreign assets and liabilities for industrial and developing countries," CEPR Discussion Paper 2231 1999. *Fig. 19.10:* IMF International Financial Statistics, September 2003 *Table 19.5:* IMF International Financial Statistics, 9/2003. *Fig. 19.15:* Mark Taylor.

Chapter 20 *Fig. 20.1:* Bank for International Settlements, "Central Bank Survey of Foreign Exchange and Derivatives Market Activity in April 1998" and "Triennial Central Bank Survey: Foreign Exchange and Derivatives Market Activity in 2001," March 2002. *Table 20.1:* Bank for International Settlements, "Triennial Central Bank Survey: Foreign Exchange and Derivatives Market Activity in 2001," March 2002. *Fig. 20.3:* IMF International Financial Statistics, September 2003. *Figure 20.10:* Federal Reserve Board, www.federalreserve.gov/releases *Fig. 20.11:* Authors' calculations using IMF data. *Table 20.2:* Cheung, Chinn, and Marsh, "How do UK-based foreign exchange dealers think their market operates?" NBER WP 7524 (2000). *Fig. 20.13:* Cheung, Chinn, and Marsh, "How do UK-based foreign exchange dealers think their market operates?" NBER WP 7524 (2000). *Table 20.3:* Cheung, Chinn, and Marsh, "How do UK-based foreign exchange dealers think their market operates?" NBER WP 7524 (2000). *Fig. 20.14:* Evans and Lyons, "Order flows and exchange rate dynamics," NBER Working Paper 7317. *Fig. 20.15:* IMF *Global Financial Stability Report*, 2003. *Fig. 20.16:* Obstfeld, "The Global Capital Market: Benefactor or Menace?" *Journal of Economic Perspectives*, 1999 and IMF International Financial Statistics, 2002. *Fig. 20.17:* "The Global Capital Market: Benefactor or Menace?" *Journal of Economic Perspectives*, 1999. *Fig. 20.18:* Authors' calculations from OECD *Economic Outlook* June 2000 and OECD database. *Fig. 20.19:* Hess and Van Wincoop, *Intranational Macroeconomics*, (Cambridge: Cambridge University Press, 2000)—Chapter 1, "Intranational versus International Savings-Investment Correlations." *Fig. 20.21:* Authors calculations using IMF *International Financial Statistics* September 2003. *Table 20.4:* Based on information kindly given by INTERSEC. *Table 20.5:* Portes and Rey, "The determinants of cross border equity flows," CEPR Discussion Paper No. 2225 (September 1999), forthcoming *Journal in International Economics.*

Chapter 21 *Fig. 21.1:* Authors' calculations using IMF data. *Tables 21.1* and *21.2:* IMF. *Fig. 21.4:* IMF. *Fig. 21.5:* Radelet and Sachs, "The East Asian Financial Crisis: Diagnosis, Remedies, Prospects," *Brookings Papers on Economic Activities*, 1:1998. *Table 21.3:* Eichengren, Hausemann, and Panizzi, "Currency Mismatches, Debt Intolerance and Original Sin," CESifo Working Paper Series No. 563. *Fig. 21.6:* Michael Bordo and Anna Schwartz, "Measuring Real Economic Effects of Bailouts: Historical Perspectives on How Countries in Financial Distress Have Fared with and without Bailouts," NBER working paper 7701. *Table 21.3:* Olivier Jeanne and Jeromin Zettelmeyer, "International Bailouts, Moral Hazard, and Conditionality," *Economic Policy* (Blackwell Publishers, 2001) vol. 16, pp. 407–432. *Figs. 21.7* and *21.8:* Prasad, Rogoff, Wei, and Kose, "Effects of Financial Globalizations on Developing Countries: Some Empirical Evidence," *International Monetary Fund* (March 17, 2003). *Fig. 21.9:* Meissner and Oomes, "Why Do Countries Fix the Way They Fix?" IMF Working Paper forthcoming (2004). *Table 21.6:* IMF Annual Report on Exchange Arrangements and Exchange Restrictions (2003). *Fig. 21.10:* Rogoff, Husain, Mody, Brooks, and Oomes, "Evolution and Performance of Exchange Rate Regimes," IMF Working Paper 03/243 (December 3003). *Table 21.11:* Ghosh, Gulde, and Wolf, "Currency Boards: The ultimate fix?" IMF Working Paper 98/8 (1998). *Fig. 21.12:* OECD, 2004. *Fig. 21.13:* Authors' calculations using IMF data. *Fig. 21.14:* Mihov, Economic Policy "Monetary Policy Implementation and Transmission in the European Monetary Union," CEPR (2002).

Note: n = footnotes or source notes, t = tabular information and f = illustrations.

Fastest Economic Growth Annual Growth in Real GDP, 1990–2003

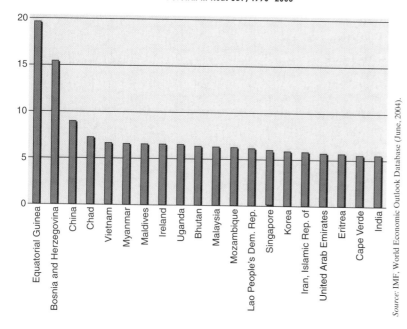

Source: IMF, World Economic Outlook Database (June, 2004).

Most Trade-Dependent Nations, 2001
Trade as Percent of GDP

Liberia	527.1
Aruba	126.2
Syria	105.8
Malaysia	89.5
Singapore	73.9
Belgium	70.4
Estonia	67.8
Swaziland	67.7
Slovakia	66.8
Tajikistan	63.2
Belarus	62.8
United Arab Emirates	62.6
Malta	62.4
Panama	61.9
Czech Republic	61.5
Ireland	61.3
Congo-Brazzaville	61
Lesotho	60.6
Bahrain	60.5
Gabon	59.7
Mozambique	58.3

Source: World Bank, World Development Indicators (2003).

Slowest Economic Growth Annual Growth in Real GDP, 1990–2003

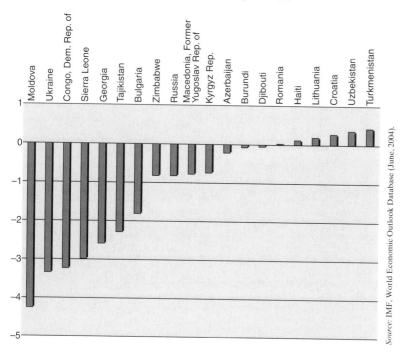

Source: IMF, World Economic Outlook Database (June, 2004).

Least Trade-Dependent Nations, 2001
Trade as Percent of GDP

Madagascar	2.5
Somalia	5.5
North Korea	7
Japan	8.4
Argentina	8.5
Bangladesh	8.8
Cuba	8.8
U.S.	9.3
Rwanda	10
Egypt	10.7
India	10.7
Brazil	11.3
Sudan	12.4
Central Africa	12.7
Burundi	12.9
Uganda	12.9
Guam	13.2
Peru	13.2
Tanzania	13.4
Uruguay	13.5
Burkina Faso	14.5

Source: World Bank, World Development Indicators (2003).

Leading Exporters in World Merchandise Trade, 2002 Percent of Total World Merchandise Export

Extra-EU15 exports	19.0	France	5.1	Italy	3.9	Korea, Republic of	2.5	Spain	1.8
U.S.	10.7	China	5.0	Netherlands	3.8	Mexico	2.5	Russian Federation	1.6
Germany	9.5	U.K.	4.3	Belgium	3.3	Taipei, Chinese	2.1	Malaysia	1.4
Japan	6.4	Canada	3.9	Hong Kong, China	3.1	Singapore	1.9		

Source: WTO International Trade Statistics, 2003